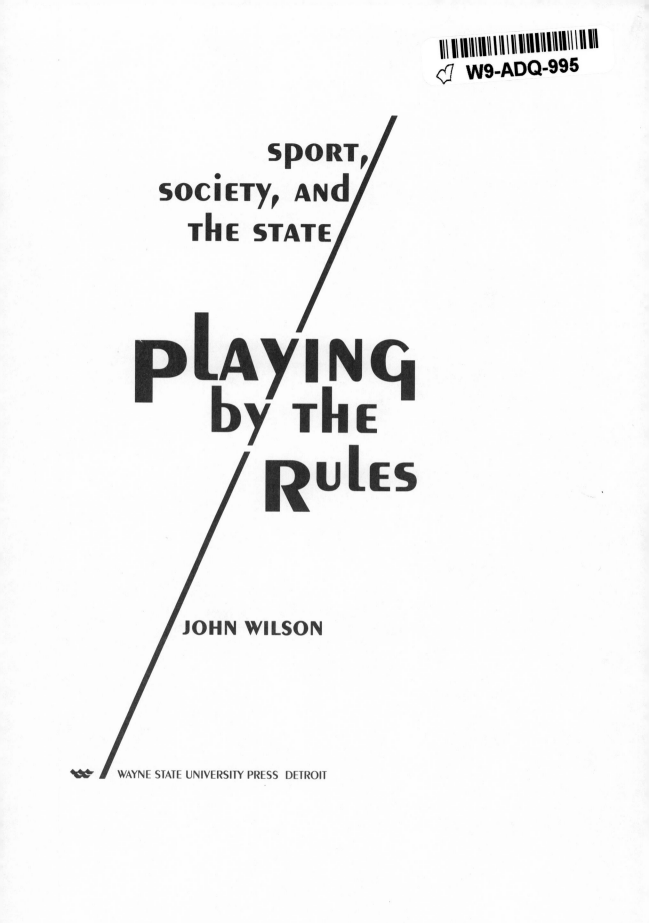

SPORT,
SOCIETY, AND
THE STATE

PLAYING
by THE
RULES

JOHN WILSON

WAYNE STATE UNIVERSITY PRESS DETROIT

LIBRARY OF CONGRESS CATALOGING-IN-PUBLICATION DATA

Wilson, John, 1942-
     Playing by the rules : sport, society, and the state / by
John Wilson.
         p.   cm.
     Includes bibliographical references (p.) and index.
     ISBN 0-8143-2107-0 (alk. paper)
     1. Sports—Social aspects—United States.   2. Sports
and state—United States.   I. Title.
   GV706.5.W55 1994
   306.4'83'0973—dc20   93-19671

DESIGNER: S.R. TENENBAUM

playing by the
|rules

CONTENTS

ABBREVIATIONS

AAU	Amateur Athletic Union
ABA	American Basketball Association
ABAUS	Amateur Basketball Association of the United States
ABL	American Basketball League
ACC	Atlantic Coast Conference
AFL	American Football League
AIAW	Association for Intercollegiate Athletics for Women
AOA	American Olympic Association
AOC	American Olympic Committee
ATP	Association of Tennis Professionals
BAA	Basketball Association of America
BOR	Bureau of Outdoor Recreation
CBA	Continental Basketball Association
CCC	Civilian Conservation Corps
CFA	College Football Association
ESPN	Entertainment and Sports Network
FCC	Federal Communications Commission
HBO	Home Box Office
IAAAA	Intercollegiate Association of Amateur Athletes of America
IAAF	International Amateur Athletic Federation
IBC	International Boxing Club
ILTF	International Lawn Tennis Federation
IMG	International Management Group
IOC	International Olympic Committee

ITF	International Tennis Federation
MLBPA	Major League Baseball Players' Association
MTC	Men's Tennis Council
NAAF	National Amateur Athletic Federation
NABB	National Association of Base Ball Players
NAIA	National Association of Intercollegiate Athletics
NBA	National Basketball Association
NBAPA	National Basketball Association Players' Association
NBL	National Basketball League
NCAA	National Collegiate Athletic Association
NFL	National Football League
NFLPA	National Football League Players' Association
NHL	National Hockey League
NHLPA	National Hockey League Players' Association
NLRA	National Labor Relations Act
NLRB	National Labor Relations Board
NRPA	National Recreation and Park Association
OPHR	Olympic Project for Human Rights
PL	Public Law
PRC	Player Relations Committee
PSAL	Public Schools Athletic League
UNLV	University of Nevada, Las Vegas
USFL	United States Football League
USGA	United States Golf Association
USLTA	United States Lawn Tennis Association
USOC	United States Olympic Committee
USTFF	United States Track and Field Federation
USWF	United States Wrestling Federation
WCT	World Championship Tennis
WHA	World Hockey Association
WPA	Works Progress Administration

PREFACE

In January 1992 the owner of the Seattle Mariners, a baseball franchise in the American League, received an offer of about $125 million to purchase the club. Jeff Smulyan had put the club up for sale the previous year. The Mariners had never made enough money to service the debt incurred in purchasing the club, and Smulyan's other business interests (chiefly broadcasting) had been badly hit by the economic recession.

The fact that the Mariners were changing hands was not, in itself, especially noteworthy. The American public had become accustomed to the trade in sport franchises. Indeed, Smulyan himself had owned the Mariners for only two years, having purchased them from George Argyros in 1989, for $76 million. Nor was it especially noteworthy that Smulyan stood to make a great deal of money on the deal. This, too, had become commonplace. What made the offer to purchase a news item was the identity of the potential buyer—the Baseball Club of Seattle. The innocuous title failed to conceal the fact that the group was headed by Hiroshi Yamauchi, president of Nintendo Company Limited, a Japanese manufacturer of computer games. Perhaps this in itself would not have sparked controversy had not baseball commissioner Fay Vincent declared that the sale would not be approved because of a rule barring foreign ownership of a major league baseball franchise. Was the commissioner not really interested in keeping the franchise in Seattle? Was baseball not ready to play a real "World Series"? Was the commissioner, perhaps, being racist in not wanting "offshore" interests in the game?

Such questions were likely to be asked, given the climate of "Japanese bashing" in which the offer to purchase the club had been made. Many Americans were apprehensive about Japanese expansionism as the result of the growing imbalance of trade between the two countries. However, the issues raised by Yamauchi's offer and its initial rejection were not particular to this time or place. Organized baseball had long frowned upon foreign ownership. Baseball franchises, it was thought, should be locally owned, because the relation between a baseball franchise and its community is broader, and deeper, than the relation other kinds of business enterprise have to their community. Local owners, it was argued, would be less likely to lose sight of how special the relationship was. The second reason given for denying foreign ownership was the belief that baseball is a uniquely American institution, not just a business but part of the nation's inheritance. It should not fall into the hands of foreigners. It mattered little to the owners that the manager of the local Nintendo plant had lived in Seattle for over a decade, while Smulyan, an Indianapolis businessman, had never set up residence in the city. It mattered little to the balking owners that other members of the Baseball Club of Seattle included a U.S. Senator (Slade Gorton).

Eventually, a compromise was reached. Organized baseball would authorize the sale to the Baseball Club of Seattle, on the condition that Yamauchi (who would contribute $75 million of the $125 million purchase price) agree to limit his power to decisions involving the team's sale or relocation and decisions involving dissolution of the partnership purchasing the team. By this time, however, the incident had served to remind everyone that modern sports are not only big business but big politics, too. Once the question of the purchase of the club had become embroiled in local community politics ("Keep the Mariners in Seattle") and once the purchase had been denied on the grounds of national interest ("foreign money" finding its way into the game), the whole affair had entered the domain of public policy, something about which the public at large—not just those immediately involved or just those interested in sport but all those interested in the public good—should be concerned. The episode was a reminder that sport, while it has its origins in the love of play and the desire to be entertained and diverted (which are very personal matters), is a social institution with important political, economic, and social consequences.

This book is about the process whereby sport has become a public policy domain, alongside other domains such as energy, health, transportation, and agriculture. It is my guiding thesis that policy domains are defined primarily by culture: "Domains are cultural constructs around which organizations and individuals orient their actions" (Burstein 1991, 328). There is nothing inherent in sport matters that would propel them onto the political stage, nor are there necessarily a set of organizational actors in American society who claim responsibility for such matters. Indeed, there is considerable opposition to the idea that sport matters comprise a public policy domain at all. Public policy deliberations in this area are thus characterized not only by substantive debates about the virtues of this or that policy (e.g., different ways to raise funds to support Olympic athletes) but also by more acrimonious arguments as to whether sport and politics should mix in the first place.

To the extent that they wish to make, or prevent, sport policy, people must influence how the state behaves. Policy is largely determined in legislative assemblies; but it is also shaped by civil servants and judges, whose job it is to execute and interpret legislation. The relation between state and society, insofar as it affects sport, is the focus of this book. Of course, the nature of that relationship is partly determined by broader, institutionalized understandings about sport in society; and these understandings cannot be ignored. The amount of pressure state actors feel to formulate a public policy with respect to sport is influenced by how interests in sport are distributed in society, but this distribution is not itself my focus.

In thinking about the phenomena with which this book deals, it might be useful to imagine society as being divided into three sectors, distinguished by their dominant principle of association. One sector is the state, which relies ultimately on coercion and is embodied in such organizations as legislative assemblies, political parties, courts, and regulatory agencies. Another sector is the market, where profitability is the guiding principle of association and the dominant actors are business corporations. The third is the voluntary sector, where the principle of association is mutuality and camaraderie and the dominant form of organization is the voluntary organization. Sport has its origins in this third sector, in the myriad informal and voluntary social groups that coalesce around a shared interest in leisure pursuits and passions. The more sport becomes institutionalized, the more it spills over into the other two sectors and different principles of association come into play. As Wuthnow points out, certain trade-offs among the three sectors are likely, because competition between the sectors is endemic: for example, a commercial leisure center might object to rival programs being offered by state-funded facilities (1991, 10). Cooperative arrangements between the sectors are also possible: for example, the state might ally with the voluntary sector (as in the management of the Olympic team) to achieve important social goals.

The broad direction of social change has been to shrink the voluntary sector as the state expands and the market reaches into more and more areas of social life (Wuthnow 1991, 16). The impact on sport has been not only to make a commodity of it but also to elevate it to the status of a public policy domain, to incorporate it, however indirectly, into the state sector. I shall show how far this incorporation has gone, why it has occurred, and what limits are placed on it by the market and by the voluntary sector. The marketplace has reshaped sport as an institution, for it has become a big business whose success or failure can have communitywide, and often nationwide, consequences. Sport policy has also been shaped by the conflict of different interests and outlooks found within civil society—differences of class, gender, and race. Finally, the state itself must not be overlooked. The creation of sport policy, by whom, and for what purpose is determined to some extent by how the state is organized to deal with this kind of issue and what kind of cultural expectations state actors have about it.

1

PLAYING
BY THE
RULES

Many people believe that sport and politics should not mix. But those who cry "Keep politics out of sports," usually mean "Keep the other person's politics out of sports." To insist on the purity of sports is to treat them as natural and unchangeable, and nothing could be further from the truth. Without rules to define access to decision making and authority—the stuff of politics—sports would not exist. A sport is defined, brought into being, by its rules. Sport is a method for administering play activity, a way to determine who should play and how they should play. Politics is also involved, because sport is play made public. An element of display, requiring a commonly understood code by which right conduct and superior performance can be judged and appreciated, is superimposed. This code does not emanate naturally from the activity itself but draws upon widespread assumptions about such things as the relationship between the body and social identity and the meaning of time and space. These assumptions, in turn, are political because they bear the imprint of class, gender, and racial hierarchies.

POLITICS AND THE STATE

Political activity is any practice whose object is power or dominion over others. Power has many centers. There is no set location

13

from which power emanates. All sport practices are "political" to the extent that they betray the use of power or the play of ideas about authority and subordination (Jo. Hargreaves 1986). Even the relationship between coach and athlete can be defined politically, because it implies ideas about discipline and respect for authority.

While the political element of even the most personal relationships is undeniable, such a decentralized view of power is not helpful in understanding the role of sport in modern societies. The view that virtually any activity has a political aspect reduces the concept of the political to vacuity, because it denies the institutionalization of the political in modern life, the growing separation of state and civil society. Although the private and public share interrelated histories, they are separate histories and one cannot be reduced to the other.

There is a real difference between the public and private spheres. For example, if adultery is considered a crime against society, rather than a personal transgression, that is not without significance. Nor is it insignificant if who gets to play on a softball team is considered a question of constitutional rights, rather than an expression of personal preference. It is also important to recognize that the public realm cannot be constructed simply as a composite of personal relations. Politics require rules and practices beyond the moral norms that obtain in private interpersonal relations. When the organization of play demands that decisions be made about teams, schedules, and discipline, it is necessary to settle upon rules to determine who should make those decisions and how they should be made.

Over the last two centuries, and with quickening pace, activities and organizations have evolved that are principally political. Admittedly, the boundaries around these activities are constantly shifting: social relationships become "politicized," and organizations become preoccupied with political objectives at the cost of economic goals. But this does not destroy the utility of drawing the distinction that while practically anything *can* be a political issue, not everything can be at once (Allison 1986, 18).

Modern societies thus distinguish between the state and civil society. Civil society denotes those areas of social life (the domestic sphere, economic activities, cultural affairs) that are organized by private and voluntary arrangements between individuals outside the direct control of the state. By the state is meant elected officials, political appointees, civil servants, the legal system, the police, and the military. Focusing on the state in the study of politics and society does not imply that power is located only there or even centered there or always dispensed from there; but it does mean that the relations of power tend to be concentrated there, albeit in often contradictory and conflicted ways (for different arms of the state often disagree). It assumes that the state today establishes the context in which relations of power—between capital and labor, men and women, blacks and whites—operate.

Modern states shape sports in many ways. They pr
many sport facilities, such as parks, marinas, and stadi;
(through licensure) and restrict (through taxation) pc
such as fishing and hunting; they provide subsidies a
the leisure industry (e.g., providing stadia rent-free, b
and furnish infrastructural support in the form of r
lakes; they create a suitable "business environment"
of leisure (e.g., land-use regulation); and they foster a ¡.
proach to sports management—administration by experts traineu ...
public schools of forestry and wildlife management and departments of
physical education who are expected to point the way to the more "effective" delivery of leisure services. The more active the state is in shaping sport opportunities, the more it encourages the view that sport is an
entitlement; that it is a right rather than an opportunity; that it is a form
of collective consumption containing certain indivisible benefits rather
than a commodity for private use; that equity in sport means removing
lack of financial resources as an impediment to its enjoyment.[1]

Most important of all, in an era of highly commercialized sport, is the
state's role in manipulating and enforcing property rights: "Property
rights actions are state activities that define and enforce property
rights, i.e. the rules that determine the conditions of ownership and
control of the means of production" (Campbell and Lindberg 1990,
635). The modern state shapes economic behavior principally by providing a legal-institutional structure in which economic activities can be
conducted. Examples of property rights actions include the establishment and enforcement of anti-trust, regulatory, labor, and contract law.

SPORT AND THE PUBLIC SPHERE

Having defined how terms like politics and the state will be
used in this book, it is time to define sport. Again, the scope is quite limited. The first limitation is imposed by conventional folk wisdom as to
the nature of sport. Until the middle of the nineteenth century, most
books on the topic of sport described only hunting, fishing, and shooting, "man's ritualized preying on other species" (Allison 1986, 5). Their
authors would have been well aware of the existence of vernacular or
commonplace pastimes, such as skittles and football; but such activities,
often accompanied by heavy drinking and "profligate" gambling, were
regarded as unrefined, too closely associated with the lower orders for
inclusion in a treatise on sporting life. Sport assumed a more precise
but, at the same time, more inclusive meaning in the 1840s, when Rugby
School "turned its form of football from a traditional, riotous, unofficial
game to one which was ordered and official and welcomed for

encouraging the virtues of discipline, obedience, teamwork and loyalty" (p. 9). Rugby's version of sport reflected the values of the growing middle class, the most important being a belief in the efficacy and goodness of bureaucratic organization, where authority was hierarchical and rules of membership and proper conduct were scrupulously enforced. This is the world of clubs, leagues, tournaments, and championships. Rugby's model included an appropriate subculture for each sport, a set of ideas and beliefs about the history and evolution of the game, self-consciously used to promote proper conduct and gain acceptance in the wider society. If it was a middle-class model, it was also masculine, reflecting patriarchal values of physical strength, explosive force, and aggression.

To write of the "growth of sports" is thus to write of a socially constructed circumscription of play by municipal authorities and federal governments, schools and colleges, churches and voluntary agencies, employers and unions. Folk wisdom reflects this view: sport is one kind of play, one of the things people do in their spare time. A second limitation on the activities covered in this book is imposed by the focus on the state. Any activity can be considered a sport, as long as the emphasis is on physical prowess and there is an element of competition combined with chance.[2] While many people immediately think of the most popular team games, such as baseball and football, when sport is mentioned, the sport pages of the newspapers will routinely cover automobile, motorcycle, horse, and dog racing, as well as hunting, fishing, skiing, sailing, softball, wrestling, boxing, and the like.[3] Seemingly, there is no end to the activities that might be considered sports. The answer to the question which activities this book should cover must be given on more pragmatic grounds.

Most sport activities are deeply embedded in the private sphere. They are exposed to the social control of the state (its laws, policies, and culture) very rarely. It is true that virtually all sporting events must conform to myriad local and state regulations; but these are incidental to their status as sporting events and have more to do with their status as spectacles at which a "show" is being produced by "workers," who are managed by promoters interested in making a profit. The same regulations would apply in the same manner to a rock concert, an American Legion convention or an antique show. For example, the state has not chosen to deliberate at length about the proper conduct of rodeos, about the rights of professional rodeo cowboys, about the proper location of rodeo championships or qualifying events, or about the consequences for immigration policy of allowing foreign cowboys to compete in American rodeos (the 1988 champion cowboy was an Australian). Only certain sports, at certain times, and in certain respects attract government attention. It is one of my purposes to account for this attention, but this also means limiting coverage to the sports that receive it.

The sociology of sport, once thought to be impoverished theoretically, now teems with ideas derived from the discipline's founding fathers. Most sociologists, taking their cue from Durkheim, believe that modern sport is the result of changes in social organization, principally the division of labor and the growth of cities. The study of the relationship between sport and politics must, however, draw heavily on the contributions of Weber and Marx: "Weber alone among the 'classical' sociologists . . . did not treat the state and politics as secondary phenomena subordinate to autonomous social forces" (Wrong 1984, 76), while Marx's observations on the extension of the commodity form, making private life a market force, are the most penetrating of all sociological commentaries on the consequences of the growth of capitalism and the emergence of bourgeois civil society.

Weber and Marx agreed that the emergence of capitalism was the most significant development of the modern era, although they accounted for this development in different ways and tended to characterize its essential features somewhat differently. For Weber, the rationalization of economic activity toward the pursuit of a calculable profit was the mainspring of capitalist development; the Marxist tradition employs a much narrower definition of capitalism, focusing on the sale of labor power by persons dispossessed of ownership of their means of production. For the Marxist, structure is imposed by the "logic" of the commodity form, by the social relations characteristic of all capitalist systems. Market forces, beneath their appeal to "choice" and "consumer sovereignty," dictate how and how often sport can be enjoyed. This is because the class struggle embraces free time. The bourgeoisie seeks to impose its own morality of consumption on those whose work and spending habits can have a serious impact on profit making. A sharp distinction is drawn between wage work and leisure, and leisure is seen as a preparation for work. While leisure is regarded as the quintessence of "freedom," it finds its best expression when accommodated to work and civic responsibilities. When leisure neither is "free" in this sense (e.g., people slavishly seek mere entertainment) nor equips people for work (e.g., gambling destroys commitment to the work ethic), it becomes a social problem. Marxists point out that while all this is doubtless true if the terms of the dominant discourse are accepted, underneath, it is possible to see that both leisure and work are social constructs. Work is not naturally the kind of routine and boring wage work for which recreation is needed; and the freedom much leisure provides is ephemeral and inconsequential. This separation of surface and deeper meaning is abetted by a market economy, where production is associated with compulsion and freedom is found only in consumption.[4]

Writing specifically about sport, Marxists argue that modern sport exemplifies the bourgeois separation of work and play, the transformation of play itself into a preparation for work or an object to be consumed as a diversion from work. The capitalization of sport means the separation of worker-player from the means of production and the transformation of the fan into the customer. Sport becomes a business.

From a Weberian perspective, sport represents the rationalization of play, the subsumption of play under the rules of formal rationality. Rationalization means principally, but not exclusively, bureaucratization. Sport becomes more organized, more closely regulated; physical prowess is scientifically cultured and precisely measured. Sport "becomes more specialized, bureaucratized, and oriented to the values of individual achievement expressed through the pursuit of 'the record' " (Gruneau 1988, 13). As sport is bureaucratized, it loses its attachment to specific substantive ends—its intrinsic gratification—and becomes important in its own right. Ironically, this then makes sport a deployable tool, available for use for a variety of different purposes, such as competition for educational resources, combating juvenile delinquency, enhancing military preparedness, boosting civic pride, and achieving diplomatic goals.

Implicit in both Marxian and Weberian theories is the idea that sport, so popularly associated with the notion of agency (of individual freedom, spontaneity, and impulsiveness) is highly structured, if not administered, behavior. Lest this picture conjure up images of a free time completely manipulated by hidden social forces, it should added that for the Marxist, a society where everything is for sale, where work and play have been separated, is also a society that gives room for resistance, an insurgency of everyday life. For the Weberian, a society where play has become formally rationalized is, from the standpoint of value rationality, substantively irrational and likely to encourage a return to ultimate values, an attempt to rediscover in sport those meanings and satisfactions that cannot be reduced to instrumentalism. Some sports are marginalized, some incorporated into more "respectable" ways of playing by the twin forces of rationalism and commodification. Other pursuits, however, resist incorporation, and still others spring up to take the place of those lost to "progress."

Finally, neither Marx nor Weber provided a satisfactory way of dealing with gender, for which theories of patriarchy must be invoked. One reading of Weber's sociology would suggest that with the advent of more rational societies, comes the breakdown of (nonrational) social ascription, which means more equality of opportunity in the area of sport for poor people, women, and other minority groups (Parsons 1971, 96). While sport has ceased to be quite the male preserve it once was, the modernization of sport has not dissolved the gender bias of sport practices and meanings. Most sports still subordinate women, and most women are still systematically prevented from participating in sports.

Feminist theory is necessary for this pattern to be interpretable. According to this theory, ideas of rationality are employed in the interests of hierarchy, control, and obedience. For example, women do not simply enjoy less leisure time than men in the modern world; their leisure is constructed by, and subordinated to, men's (rationalized) work, with its strict schedules and clear separation of home and factory. The rationalization of work has not obliterated gender differences in leisure but created new ones. Women *are* leisure, and help *provide* leisure, for men. Ideologies of formal rationality are meanwhile put to use to account for, and legitimate, the "soft," "expressive" leisure time pursuits of women, in contrast with the more "modern," strategic, complex and technically sophisticated leisure time pursuits of men.

MARKET AND STATE IN
CAPITALIST SOCIETIES

Capitalism is unique in having not one, but two, centers of authority, one built around the economic prerogatives of the business system, the other around the political prerogatives of the state. The realm of activities having to do with material life is removed from the reach of political authority: state officials do not exercise direct command over material resources. On the other hand, capitalists cannot freely operate as private governments; they cannot forcibly muster their work forces or compel people to sell to or buy from them.

Ordinarily, the state endorses the aims and objectives of the business community and seeks to create a framework of laws and administrative procedures to ensure that business can operate smoothly. Successive governments, whatever their political makeup, do this because they are dependent on the smooth running of business to provide the wherewithal to carry out their programs. The two realms are by no means always in harmony. The aims of capital are fragmented, individual, short-term, and competitive. The role of state officials, on the other hand, is to see the whole picture, seek the collective good, plan for the long term, and seek unity and harmony among citizens. These officials (often at the behest of capitalists themselves) restrain, adjudicate, and correct disruptive practices in the economy engendered by its necessarily competitive tendencies.

Theories of modern capitalism developed by followers of Marx and Weber anticipate that capitalist social relations will be extended into play. The structure and dynamics of play come to resemble those of any other capitalist activity. Having separated work time from leisure time, which is "time of one's own," capitalism has restricted the choices available during this time by destroying traditional forms of family and community life and their accompanying times and spaces. Time spent away from work becomes more and more dependent on the marketplace for gratification. All forms of entertainment and popular recreation are commodified. All are encouraged to think of sport as something that is produced in order to be consumed. A few become the producers of sport, while the rest learn to consume. As a consequence, the commodification of play—its transformation into professional sport—is as taken for granted today as the commodification of food. This is not to say that people cannot cook or play games for the fun of it. Market forces are incapable of penetrating all spheres of social life. The commodified form of play is nevertheless hegemonic. It is an inescapable presence, even for those who would resist it.

The extension of capitalist relations into play does not mean that sport is just like any other business and can be understood in purely economic terms. There are two reasons for this: (1) both owners and fans are reluctant to acknowledge the business side of sport and frequently allow non-utilitarian considerations to influence their buying and selling decisions; and (2) even the owners most anxious to extend capitalist relations further must use political means to do so, which means invoking non-economic values. For these two reasons, the study of sport means looking at the "givens" that most economists would choose to take for granted. The supply of, and demand for, National Football League season tickets; the distribution of earnings on the tennis circuit; the proportion of their scholarships colleges allocate to women athletes; the number of exhibition games shown on television; and funding for the national Olympic team—can all be accounted for in part by invoking traditional economic factors (preference schedules, labor inputs, revenues, competition, mobilized resources). But they cannot be accounted for adequately by these factors alone, because this would require making assumptions about things that in the world of sport, might well be untrue. Fans are willing to pay enormous sums of money to see sport contests; players cling very strongly to highly individualistic and competitive ideas about how the rewards assigned to them as a group should be allocated; males regard themselves as more deserving of sport opportunities than females; television networks sell not sports but entertainment; and city councilors hunger for the prestige associated with hosting athletic events. These are less economic, than sociocultural, factors; and they have considerable impact on the operation of economic factors in the world of sports.

Marx and Weber both assumed that political forces continuously impinge upon the operation of the economy. Rationalization affects sport and politics simultaneously. Sport must conform to both the logic of the market and an increasingly bureaucratized and extensive polity. These forces—the market and the state—combine (not always smoothly) to structure sport in preferred ways, to establish sport traditions selectively, and "to define the range of 'legitimate' practices and meanings associated with dominant sport practices" (Gruneau 1988, 22). It is the *relation* between political and economic forces that is of most theoretical interest. Neither should be treated as if they existed in isolation. A study of American sports from this perspective must take as its central theme the question. What are the effects on sport of the tension between capitalism as an economic system and democracy as a political system, and how has the evolution of sport heightened or eased that tension? During the twentieth century, the state has been obliged to absorb some leisure functions, while it has shunned many others. Why has this occurred? The reason must lie in the contradictory forces under which the state must operate in capitalist democracies.

LIBERTY VERSUS EQUALITY

Modern capitalist societies seek the twin goals of individual freedom and democratic decision making, of liberty and equality. Liberty can be realized, however, only at the expense of equality. George Simmel describes this contradiction:

> The need for freedom of the individual who feels himself restricted and deformed by historical society results in a self-contradiction once it is put into practice. For evidently, it can be put into practice permanently only if society exclusively consists of individuals who externally as well as internally are equally strong and equally privileged. Yet this condition exists nowhere. On the contrary, the power-giving and rank-determining forces of men are, in principle, unequal, both qualitatively and quantitatively. Therefore, complete freedom necessarily leads to the exploitation of this inequality by the more privileged, to the exploitation of the stupid by the clever, of the weak by the strong, of the timid by the grasping. (1950, 65)

The solution to the problem Simmel describes is to take away from individuals, by force if necessary, the possibility of exploiting their superiority over their weaker brethren. This goal of justice is the aim of democracy.

Historically, democracy stands for participation in decision-making. Historically, capitalism requires a state prepared to remove encumbrances to the market, especially the market for labor power. Thus, while one emphasizes equality, the other emphasizes liberty. So long as a society remains capitalist, the state must ensure the liberties (with respect to property) believed to facilitate capital accumulation, at least to some degree; but at the same time, in order for capitalist decisions to be acceptable to the citizenry at large, democratic desire must be taken into account. A society in which the egalitarian impulse predominates is typically called a "social democracy"; that in which the libertarian impulse predominates is typically called a "liberal democracy." The latter version of democracy has predominated in the United States. Western Europeans, on the other hand, are more inclined to consider liberty a serious threat to democracy because it generates inequalities of wealth and power that make formal political equalities such as those ensconced in the idea of "one man, one vote" meaningless. For social democrats, social and economic inequalities, a natural outgrowth of liberty, threaten the existence of the common interests in society upon which the democratic process depends.

In the United States, where the market system, or capitalism, is more powerful, democracy is "vowed to the cause of liberty" (Lindblom 1977, 163). The egalitarian tradition in democracy is subordinated to the libertarian. Furthermore, liberty is defined principally in terms of freedom to engage in trade, establish enterprises, move about, keep one's earnings and assets, and be secure "against arbitrary exactions" (p. 164). Egalitarianism is by no means stifled, but it is secondary to liberty. To a liberal democrat like Sartori, equality is a laudable principle, but only in the service of liberty or freedom of the individual: "The democrat is prepared to make a trade-off: more equality, or greater equality, for less freedom—but not at the too-great expense of freedom. It we take this last step, we move beyond liberal democracy, and also beyond social democracy, into an over-riding concern for material, economic equality" (1987, 344). Granting that some measure of equality is essential to preserve social cohesion and integration (people have to be treated *as if* they were equal in order for liberal democracy to work), Sartori seeks an equality that "suits diversity" rather than an equality that is simply another word for "sameness."

In a liberal-democratic regime, policy will be concerned chiefly with fostering individual initiative, removing political bondage, and avoiding coercive monopolies. Americans are sensitive to welfare, equality, and social cohesion; but these are secondary themes. In the history of the United States, the libertarian impulse is recognizable in the shift in the meaning of democracy away from equal participation and outcome toward the existence of certain formal political features, such as elections, the franchise, and agreed-upon rules of political discourse. It is also evident in the use of government to ensure "free" markets. The more muted egalitarian impulse is evident in welfare programs and schemes of redistribution developed since World War II, as well as government efforts to provide collective goods, such as roads, railways, parks, and the like; but throughout, the American impulse has been to think of equality in political, rather than economic, terms.

The relation between sport and state in the United States is precisely what would be expected in a liberal-democratic regime. By and large, sport entrepreneurs have favored policies that guarantee capital accumulation. Congressmen, civil servants and judges have also favored liberty over equality. In their eyes, the purpose of government, and the need of government itself, is to promote economic growth and opportunity. Businessmen lobbying for a tax reduction or arguing for exemption from government statutes do not appear before legislators as representatives of a special interest but as functionaries performing socially indispensable tasks whose welfare should be of paramount concern. The egalitarian impulse has not been completely stifled. Voters are quite capable of reasoning that justice is sometimes served by placing curbs on individual freedom (e.g., by closing a plant); that some "goods" (e.g., clean air) are in their nature collective and must be secured administratively; that some things (e.g., beaches) should not be regarded as private possessions but "belong to the nation"; and that some inequalities place insuperable burdens on people's abilities to enjoy basic human rights. Accordingly, in conjunction with, and in reaction to, the commercialization of sport, there has arisen the idea that sport is a "public trust," a collective good, subject to political, more than to economic, determination.

In any consideration of the politics of American sports, this tension between liberalism and egalitarianism must be taken seriously. Indeed, it underlies virtually every sport policy debate. One side will defend (or seek more) liberty while the other defends (or seeks more) equality. There is a *general* tendency for owners (and their political supporters) to favor policies to protect and enhance liberties, while players, excluded groups such as women, and fans (and their advocates) favor policies to protect and enhance equality. But the actual positions they adopt are always more subtle than this. The owners are quite capable of wanting simultaneously to capitalize their profits and socialize their losses—a socialism for the rich and free enterprise for the poor. The players are quite capable of seeking protection under collective bargaining laws while simultaneously asserting their right to independence when it comes to negotiating contracts.

SPORT ENTERS THE PUBLIC STAGE

Sports have always been political, in the most general sense of that term; but they have not always been influenced by the state. Before the end of the Civil War, there was little state to speak of; and it did not interact closely with the federal economy (Campbell and Lindberg 1990, 637). Furthermore, it was not until after the Civil War that professional sport leagues were established. A confluence of forces thus set the stage for a public debate over sport policy. For a long period, only the judicial branch of government had much to do with sport. Before 1950, Congress virtually ignored it. In the next thirty years, however, nearly three hundred pieces of legislation dealing with professional sports alone were introduced in Congress (Johnson 1979, 103). The reasons why are to be found partly within sport itself and partly in changes that occurred in the relation between the state and civil society.

Turning first to sport, it is obvious that the forces of commercialization and bureaucratization have made public what was once seen as an entirely private activity. Commercialization not only raises the stakes involved should disputes occur but places a premium on the ability to calculate risk and reward rationally. This requires that contracts be enforceable. Intensified business activity almost inevitably means more litigation and more frequent calls for state regulation. This general tendency helps explain why the blue laws protecting the Victorian Sabbath were upheld more vigorously against professional baseball than its amateur version (Riess 1980, 122). Commercialization also raises the potential social, as well as private, cost of doing business. This helps explain why the collapse of an amateur softball club goes unnoticed but the departure of a revenue-generating major league franchise triggers frantic reactions from city hall.

Bureaucratization also increases the likelihood that sports will end up on the political agenda. As sports erect elaborate and inclusive administrative structures to determine and enforce criteria of eligibility and rules of competition, they become ministates, and the players, coaches, managers, and even owners become citizens of them. In many cases, being denied eligibility is tantamount to total exclusion from the sport, perhaps from a livelihood. These ministates exercise considerable control over individual freedoms to use talent and explore opportunities. Sport organizations assume rights and responsibilities properly thought to reside in the state alone; thus, the stage is set for a clash between sport and the state.

Chapter 6 will deal with these private government issues. It will show that sport organizations are especially likely to attract state scrutiny when they appear to be unable to govern themselves. The first major congressional investigation of sports (baseball) occurred in 1951, precisely when the Mexican League was offering inducements to players to break their contracts with organized baseball, causing major league owners to crack down on their employees which, in turn, occasioned some highly-publicized lawsuits. Baseball no longer seemed capable of containing its own disagreements—to the detriment of individuals within the sport, whose bargaining freedom was threatened, and of the general public, whose faith in the integrity of the "national game" it was important to preserve. There is a parallel here with a professional body like the American Bar Association, which fended off close scrutiny from the state until increasing specialization and competition for jobs tempted lawyers to ignore its rule against advertising, at which point its

own internal policing mechanism proved inadequate and the Supreme
Court was called in to settle the dispute.

While some of the reasons for the increasing politicization of sport have to do with changes in sport itself, others have to do with more general changes in the relation between the state and civil society. Since World War II, the public has come to look upon the state for the protection of a wide array of entitlements. Many sport issues have been redefined in the process. Not just sport fans but the general public cares about where franchises are located, what kinds of stadia are built, whether homes games are to be shown on television, how much tickets will cost, and who pays for hosting the Olympic Games if these issues are framed in basic political terms, such as equality of access to public facilities and equitable and accountable use of public money. When political debate is filled with cries on behalf of the underprivileged, it should come as no surprise that the debate should cover what people have the right to enjoy. Sport becomes part of the politics of consumption. Sport will also be swept up in the fight for greater political freedom and distributive justice the more it becomes bureaucratically organized and commercially operated; for the reasonableness of hiring practices, dress codes, and health and safety regulations can be discussed in terms of constitutional guarantees. Sports can rapidly become political once defined in these terms. A relatively minor sport such as softball will find itself on the political agenda if it is the arena in which a sex discrimination case is to be fought.

Sports are especially likely to be swept up by political movements whose major concern is morality. Politics are by no means confined to the clash of economic interests. Issues such as welfare reform, reproductive rights, health care, race relations, and even defense expenditures are infused with ethical meaning, laden with ideas about appropriate behavior having little to do with economic interest and much more to do with status and honor. Status politics are especially likely to focus on what people should consume and how they should spend their leisure time. Thus, people will attack sport if they think it encourages vice and dissolution. For example, the opponents of boxing regard it as uncivilized and unseemly and are repelled by its association with gambling, illicit drugs, and extortion. Sports also lend themselves to appropriation and become part of a larger moral conflict, because they make moral claims themselves. Baseball likes to think of itself as "the American Game"—not just invented in America but also symbolizing "the American Way." People who own baseball franchises or play baseball for a living assume a moral responsibility those selling jai alai or soccer largely escape.

Moral crusades, during which civil society is subject to state control, have their counterpart in the economic sphere. In some periods of American history, the government has conspicuously kept its hands off the economy, while others are characterized by regulatory zeal.

Sometimes this zeal is directed at preserving competition, while at other times employment rights are to be protected. Sport is not immune from these fluctuations. Thus, although internal conflict might raise the call for more state regulation of sport, the government of the day must be disposed to provide it. If the government is interventionist, then sport issues will become politicized. If the tide is running for deregulation, the government will overlook sport's squabbles and let the marketplace decide the outcome.

Two of the major responsibilities of the state being national defense and the conduct of foreign policy, not even sport can remain untouched by the state's determination to meet these obligations. For this reason, a sport like table tennis can become the focus of political debate, despite its relative obscurity as measured by media coverage. A sport like soccer might attract political attention because of the number of foreign players being given visas permitting them to play, a violation, in the minds of some, of established immigration policies. Conversely, sports like hockey might complain that the Immigration and Naturalization Service is too slow in granting work permits to professional athletes; that in the case of sports, the usual bureaucratic delays render the permit useless because the season is over by the time it is granted; and that professional athletes should therefore be given special treatment. This, in turn, might lead American athletes to complain that foreign, "cheap" labor is being imported to drive down the wages of American workers. Indeed, in 1975, in response to pressure from the baseball players' union, the Department of Labor instituted minimum salary levels below which no aliens would be certified; all aliens would have to have a standard contract. The department sought assurances from baseball owners that they would continue their recruitment activities among American athletes (U.S. Congress, House, Select Committee on Professional Sports 1976, 213). Conversely, highly visible sports, like football and basketball, would figure hardly at all in these debates because they employ few foreign players.

The more intertwined state and civil society become, the more likely some kind of sport policy will emerge. State actors do not necessarily manipulate property rights deliberately to influence sport organization, although their actions may have that effect. Hence, it might be more accurate to speak in terms of state "action," rather than state policy, because the latter implies that the outcomes of state decision making are intended (Campbell and Lindberg 1990, 635). This would be true of many of the instances of political activity to be described in this book. However, many of the state actions to be described are a deliberate attempt to reach specific goals with respect to the role of sport in American society; and while it might be too much to speak of any particular administrations having a sport policy markedly different from its predecessor, there has emerged some consensus on how the state and market should combine to make sport available to the American public.

That the United States should have some kind of policy with respect to national defense, education, and health is hardly disputed today, but what of sport? Culturally, sport was until recently firmly rooted in the private sphere—serious but hardly important. Many politicians today continue to wonder whether sport is an appropriate subject for serious public debate. Senator Howard Metzenbaum was probably speaking for most congressmen when he said, during Senate Judiciary Committee hearings on a piece of sport legislation:

> I feel a bit troubled as I sit here today participating in the first of what may be a series of hearings concerning professional sports. And I note that the Commerce Committee is also spending a great deal of time on this issue. I just left the Budget Committee to come over here. The Nation faces serious problems with the deficit approaching $200 billion. We are in the middle of an arms race, the possible confrontation in the whole nuclear area. Unemployment has gone up, and the U.S. Senate is here debating sports franchises. Why? (U.S. Congress, Senate, Committee on the Judiciary 1986a, 31)

Although Congress has spent a number of hours debating sport issues and the occasional sport bill has been reported out of committee, the entire Congress has rarely troubled itself to enact a major piece of sport legislation. Elections are not won or lost on sport issues.

As if this were not enough, there are serious impediments in the United States political system to the articulation of any issue in public policy terms. The formation of American public policy occurs by means of shifting coalitions that are temporary and fragile. This is because the United States lacks a centralized bureaucratic structure and programmatic parliamentary parties. Capitalists largely distrust the state, and workers have failed to develop social-democratic programs. There is no labor-based party of consequence. Issues are therefore rarely debated strictly along party lines. Temporary coalitions form, only to divide on other issues. This "clientelist fragmentism" leads to piecemeal, inconsistent, and sporadic policy formation (Roth 1985, 224).

The combination of weak state and lack of programmatic parties (which could otherwise embrace a number of issues under a more general agenda of social reform) is near fatal for the prospects of a sport policy. No agency has emerged within Congress to speak with authority on this issue. Sports is not nested within any particular congressional committee. Sport has no equivalent of the civil servant in the Commerce Department who will fight for, or undermine, political appointments made by individual administrations. The sport lobby is thus unfocused because it has no clear target in government and is consigned to a permanent role as outsider in congressional deliberations.

How is it possible to speak of a sport policy in the United States at all? Sport, in its "appropriate" form, is undoubtedly a national value politicians feel they should preserve; and they feel this strongly enough to sacrifice other values they believe in (e.g., business competition) in order to do so. They often feel they must save the sport industry from itself in order to secure this valuable resource for the nation. Consequently, they are strongly motivated to act coherently and consistently with respect to sport. In face of the obstacles described earlier, responsibility has devolved over time to certain congressional committees (principally the Judiciary Committee). Their deliberations hint at the outlines of a sport policy. Their role has been partially obscured by the fact that as often as not, they have chosen not to act when invited to do so. But it must not be forgotten that when it comes to public policy in a mixed economy, *no* state action is as significant as *some* state action. It is an affirmation of the conviction that regulation should be left to the unfettered market. Indeed, it could be said that the chief goal of public policymakers is to decide upon the best blend of state and market. Which public goals are best met by the market mechanism and which need to be accomplished through planning and administration?

This study will show that Americans have been content to assume that the marketplace is the best measure of what is normal and acceptable. Normalcy is defined by the balance of supply and demand. Americans want their government to formulate policies with this definition of normalcy as the baseline. It is not always made clear in public discussion just how much this baseline reflects the interests of the more powerful actors in the market. As a result, policy formation takes place largely within understandings set down by these actors. The decision not to act is thus an expression of satisfaction with what the market itself will furnish. The attention of interested actors should be on maximizing gains within it.

There is a second reason why there is a more coherent sport policy in the United States than might at first appear. Sports have become big business. State policy designed to maintain and restore the necessary conditions of capital accumulation will inevitably affect them. This is but a specific instance of the more general principle that "there is no society more 'political' than the 'market society' " (M. Sklar 1988, 58). Professional sports might well be part of the free enterprise system, but their structure and function is much affected by the overall economic policy of the government. Not only does the state assume responsibility for the overall health of the economy and the environment, it also defends individual rights at work and in the marketplace. The state sets the ground rules for most economic transactions and directly regulates many industries. It provides the infrastructure of capital accumulation and manages the tempo of business activity. The more businesslike sport becomes, the more it is going to be affected by these state actions. Professional sports have also been part of the convergence of interest between big business and the state. As capitalist firms grow in size and strategic importance, they become more public than private, forcing the state and local governments to consider them more as partners than as private actors. Foreign diplomacy and "defense" spending are increasingly shaped by the interests of multinational corporations in stable and receptive regimes abroad, while at home, profits or losses of business corporations can mean life or death for their host communities. This applies as much to sport franchises as it does automobile companies.

This convergence of interest explains why, despite the fact that many businessmen are apprehensive about the expansion of government, they can be quite tolerant of government action when it serves their interest. Their support of the ideology of free enterprise does not prevent them from occasionally seeking help from the government when profits are endangered. The ideology of the free market does serve a purpose, however; for it allows businessmen to reject the idea of a quid pro quo for government assistance. The original favor from the government (e.g., tax abatements) is dictated by sound business logic; being required to return the favor would interfere with market rationality. Sport capitalists have learned these lessons well, lobbying for government protection when profits are threatened, appealing for more market freedoms when opportunities for gain arise.

There is a third reason to take the notion of an American sport policy seriously, despite the fact that legislative or executive action in this area has low priority. A relatively weak executive branch and a highly fragmented legislature means that many Americans look to the Constitution and the rule of law as the loci of fundamental sovereignty. In economic affairs, this has been true for a century. The tendency to rely on judicial action to regulate business on a case-by-case basis dates back to the last quarter of the nineteenth century, when the problem of dealing politically with the growth of capitalist enterprises was effectively given to the courts: "The legislature accommodated the conflicting demands of elite and popular interests for action by producing weak laws requiring clarifications which the court provided according to its laissez-faire principles" (Bright 1984, 147). If anything, it is now more widely believed than ever before that judicial power is, by and large, coterminous with state power. "The American proclivity to think of social problems in legal terms and to judicialize everything from wage claims to community conflicts and the allocation of airline routes makes it only natural to accord judges a major share in the making of social policy" (D. Horowitz 1977, 12).

Judges today not only make, but also execute, policy. To all intents and purposes, the National Basketball Association (NBA) operated under a "court order" between 1976 and 1984. In 1970, the NBA Players'

Association had filed suit against a proposed merger of the American Basketball Association (ABA) and the NBA. The NBA and ABA asked Congress to grant exemption from the antitrust laws to permit the merger. Congress refused. The players continued with their antitrust suit for five more years. Finally, in April 1976, the union reached a court-approved settlement that allowed the players to negotiate with employers more freely. Under this settlement, all activities relating to player restraints, movements, and freedoms were made subject to review by the federal court in New York. The federal court, through a special master appointed by both sides (Telford Taylor), protected the players against the monopolistic activities of club owners. Regulation in professional basketball was thus vested in the judicial branch of government, where it would reside until new collective bargaining structures could be put in place.

If it is true, in general, that "no courts anywhere have greater responsibility for making public policy than the courts in the United States" (D. Horowitz 1977, 3), this is likely to be all the truer in the case of sports. An ideology of individualism suffuses the world of sports. Problems and their solutions are defined in individualistic terms more amenable to legal, than to legislative, remedies. Sport capitalists, affirming this ideology, have strenuously resisted government regulation of sports, sheltering within the private sphere, where policy can be formulated by case law. Sport issues are, besides, often localized and private; they ferment within the world of schools, voluntary associations, the workplace, and private employment contracts. This is not to say that all sport policy is made in the courtroom. To examine the law as "state action" is not to assume that all state action occurs in legal texts. However, it does assume that legal decisions expose power and that when legislators and lobbyists do turn their attention to sport, they bargain in the shadow of the law.

The judicialization of policy formation is enormously consequential, for it has an effect on the kind of policy developed. Judges may focus on the circumstances of a particular case, rather than the larger social problem the case represents. The result is that issues are particularized, making it more difficult to see their general import and predict future developments. Judges tend to frame issues in terms of rights, rather than policy alternatives, and as a result, fail to appreciate the social realities within which these rights must operate. For example, a judge might decide that a student has a "property interest" in access to scholarship intercollegiate athletics based upon his formal status as a student, without taking into account the real context in which student and athlete statuses are differentiated today. Finally, judge-made law simultaneously encourages the somewhat romanticized image of sport as not really a business while at the same time making it easier for the party with the deeper pockets to win.

"IT'S ONLY A GAME": FORMAL AND SUBSTANTIVE RATIONALITY

Having said so much about politics and economics, it is time to reiterate that sports are not reducible to political or economic behavior. For this reason, the tension between egalitarianism and libertarianism, the conflicting pull of democracy and the market, is not the real issue in sport policy. Sport is the real issue. There is an irreducible core of meaning in the sport world. Play is irrepressibly spontaneous, providing intense emotional and aesthetic gratification. At play, human beings occupy a personal space, where spontaneity and disregard for convention are allowed free reign. In the grim world of politics, human beings struggle with each other to establish rules of domination and submission. The first is an essentially private world; the second is played out on a public stage. The first is emphemeral the second highly consequential. Play is not simply politics by another name. Sport policy cannot therefore be the same as transportation or agricultural policy. In the eyes of the general public, there is a difference between a sport franchise skipping town and a factory closing down; there is a difference between the professional athlete and a truck driver; there is a difference between men's and women's athletics; there is a difference between amateur and professional sports. The reason for these differences are the ideas and beliefs, values and convictions about sport that have developed over many years. These sociocultural phenomena have their own dynamic and resist being molded by political forces or chopped up by the market for resale.

Sports are admittedly amenable to commercial exploitation and political manipulation. It is not at all unusual for sport struggles to be reworked into political terms for use in the competition for office and influence. Bureaucrats and politicians believe they can gain or retain office or increase their influence by importing a sport conflict into the public arena and reproducing it as politics. In this case, political considerations will determine the meaning and practice of sport. In the process, the original dispute will have been changed; and its reimportation into the sport world will have many unintended consequences. Nevertheless, it would be the height of cynicism not to be believe the many protestations of legislators—and indeed, owners, players and fans—that sports are unique, that they should not be treated like "any other business," and that we "should keep politics out of sports." Their sincerely held beliefs reflect a more general culture of leisure, a culture teaching that humans at play are uninterested in dominion or pecuniary gain.

The history of sport policy depicts a struggle between two points of view regarding the true place and purpose of sports in the United

States. In one view, sport is regarded as properly subjected to the criteria of formal rationality, in which all sports and all athletes are treated as essentially alike—in which, indeed, all sport enterprises are treated as essentially like any other business enterprise. Exemplary of this position is the view that sports should be subject to the free play of market forces, that both the market for labor and the market for customers should be without restriction. In the other view, sport is considered to have its own inviolable, intrinsic values; sport is an end in itself and cannot be reduced, without loss, to the dictates of formal rationality. This would include not only the cry to keep politics out of sport but also the claim that sport is not just another business and that professional athletes are not just in it for the money.

Formal rationality, in the context of economic action, refers to the extent of quantitative calculation or accounting: "Expression in money terms yields the highest degree of formal rationality" (Weber 1978, 85). *Substantive rationality*, on the other hand, means "the application of certain criteria of ultimate ends, whether they be ethical, political, utilitarian, hedonistic, feudal, egalitarian, or whatever" (p. 202). The interplay of formal and substantive rationality in sport policy can make for complex and confusing actions. Many congressmen are inclined to measure baseball against the criteria of substantive rationality but insist on exposing football to the more universal demands of a formal rationality. Owners tend to espouse whichever view is expedient at the time. Thus, when they will benefit from a claim to uniqueness, they appeal to substantive rationality; when they will benefit from being treated like any other business, they appeal to formal rationality. Occasionally, they separate them and use them both simultaneously. They argue that the substantive rules of sports deserve immunity from state regulation while allowing that the formal side, the more businesslike side, does not. For example, they accept that collusion to fix the price of tickets is illegal, because this has to do with the more formal aspect of the sports business; but they are reluctant to agree that collusion in hiring players is illegal, claiming that this kind of restriction of competition is necessary for the preservation of the game. Likewise, the draft is a substantive rule, intrinsically legitimated and thus not subject to the employment regulations applicable to other businesses, while the owners are quite happy to apply trademark laws to their logos and team designs.

Over the course of its brief history, the sport business has relied very heavily on appeals to substantive rationality. For many years, owners astutely used their rich symbolic resources to shape sport policy. After World War II, the cultural capital of sport owners lost some of its value as their legitimacy came into question in a series of congressional investigations, themselves occasioned by the growing economic significance of the industry. For a while, owners attempted politics as usual and continued to draw on traditional symbolic resources. However, they turned increasingly to using alliances and coalitions to protect themselves, principally with the television networks and with sympathetic congressmen, to whom they could offer constituency benefits such as a major league franchise, much as might a defense contractor offering jobs and tax payments. This strategy of bargaining shored up the industry's declining symbolic resources but also exposed it to the criteria of formal rationality. By the 1980s, it had become very difficult for the industry to find protection from state regulation in its claim to special consideration.

In amateur sports, colleges have succeeded in preserving public support for the substantive rationality of amateurism, the value that dictates that sport should have no ulterior purpose, while at the same time restructuring the administration of those sports along formally rational lines, from the imposition of bureaucracies in athletic departments to the marketing of sport promotions. Far from being an obstacle to it, the rationalization of college sports has been made possible by people's faith in the substantive values of amateurism. Their support for college sports, albeit expressed through the box office, is the reaffirmation of an ideal. They "buy" the "administered" enthusiasm and "hustle," the genuineness and authenticity, of the college game without fully realizing the conflict between the two rationalities to which the game is now exposed. Policy debate in this area often involves attempts to reconcile these differences.

INDIVIDUALS, ORGANIZATIONS, INSTITUTIONS, AND SOCIETIES

A cursory glance at the politics of sport reveals a bewildering array of issues, debates, and actions taking place in widely scattered arenas. How should such a wide array of topics, from the legality of testing college athletes for drugs to the proper management of municipal stadia, be discussed? What is the relation between such different subjects, and which are more important? One solution to this problem is to distinguish the different sociological levels at which the relation between sport and the state is worked out. Problems in sociology differ according to their "unit," or the identity of the element selected for analysis. These units range from the micro level of individual actors, through the meso level of institutions, to the macro level of societies. For example, Wilbert Moore (1963), in his sociological analysis of time, treats sequentially the experience of time by the individual (or social actor), by the organization (or collectivity), and by "large-scale" systems such as communities and societies. Within the sociology of sport, the textbook by Loy, McPherson, and Kenyon orders the material into "logical units according to levels of sociological analysis" to move the reader "from micro- to macro-levels of concern" (1978, v). The authors deal with the status of athlete in the immediate group setting and move on to discuss sport organizations and thence to a discussion of the relation between sport as an institution and other institutions. From a sociological perspective, then, it is possible to see the struggle between liberty and equality taking place on each of four levels.

At the micro-level, the focus is on the individual or, more sociologically, on the identities and statuses people can possibly have and occupy in the sport world. How are these identities and statuses defined? This entails looking at the meaning of being an athlete (or a particular kind of athlete), a "fan" or spectator, an owner, a coach, or an official and at the array of statuses it is possible for people to occupy. At the next-highest level of generality, networks of social statuses, formal organizations, and the relations between them come into focus. In the field of sports, this would entail looking at amateur and professional sport organizations (e.g., clubs, colleges, and franchises) and confederations of organizations (e.g., associations, conferences, and leagues). What is the effect of the particular organization of social relationships in sport on those relationships? The next-highest level of generality is the institutional. Here, the discussion must deal with statuses and organizations as they cluster around, and focus upon, a particular societal function. Each of these clusters, such as those associated with the family, has its own norms, which apply to a particular category of relationships. Sport is one of a number of social institutions (along with, e.g., art and music) that motivate people to perform other roles by giving meaning and purpose to their lives. The issue here, then, is the relation of sport to other social institutions, such as education, the family, politics, and the economy. The most general level of all is the societal. At this level, policy has to do with the role of the society in relation to other societies. This includes the society's efforts to achieve integration and consensus, to distinguish itself from other societies and enter in exchange with those societies on favorable terms. In the case of sport, this would involve the "nationalization" of sports, the use of sports to achieve national integration, and the function of sport in intersocietal relations.

These levels are sociological abstractions: empirically, the struggle occurs at all levels simultaneously. Furthermore, the levels identify sociological, not social, problems. The participants in the struggle do not necessarily think of the issues in these terms. Nevertheless, the task of understanding the relation between sport and the state is greatly simplified if its evolution is considered at these levels separately. At the *individual* level, the struggle embraces issues of people's "rights" to some kind of leisure identity; their eligibility for sport participation and self-direction; how they are encouraged to understand the relation between their body and their social identity; how they are obliged to allocate their time between work and leisure; the appropriateness of the use to which they put their leisure time; their "welfare," safety and health in the leisure sphere; their rights as "professionals" to enter into contracts; and their rights as producers to manage their enterprises. The tendency in the United States has been to emphasize liberty over equality. Thus, distribution of leisure resources is phrased in terms of defending equality of leisure opportunity within the constraints of a predominantly free market for leisure goods and services. The equitable distribution of resources is put to the service of maximizing individual choice, of reproducing the leisure sphere as an opportunity for individual expression. Chapter 2 will deal with working hours legislation, leisure subsidies to rectify "leisure deficits," and the growth of the idea of an entitlement to leisure—eligibility for participation in sports in general and sex and race discrimination in particular. Chapter 3 sustains the focus on the individual actor by dealing with limits on individual freedom of contract and mobility within amateur and professional sports.

At the *organizational* level, the struggle concerns the legal, political, and economic status of the organizations that structure the sport experience. Issues embraced under this heading include the proper administrative treatment of amateur and professional sport enterprises (e.g., for tax purposes, for purposes of economic regulation) and the role of government in the internal operation of these enterprises (e.g., collective bargaining, drug testing). Individuals help constitute the organizational level; but rather than asking how individuals allocate their time, it is more appropriate to inquire how, given the collective goals of an organization, the tasks needed to reach those goals are allocated among individuals. Again, as would be expected, the state has rather consistently sought to maximize entrepreneurial freedoms in professional sports and has pursued a "hands-off" policy with regard to the organization of amateur sports. Equality ideals (e.g., the possibility of public ownership of sport enterprises) have taken second place, and the state has trodden very gingerly in the area of labor-management relations. Chapter 4 will deal with the treatment of the sport enterprise by the state. Chapter 5 will look at collective bargaining, and chapter 6 considers the status of sport organizations as private governments.

At the *institutional* level, politics concerns the role of sports in the community. What role, if any, should the state play in ensuring that sport be part of the community? Issues embraced under this heading include the nature of the relationship between sport enterprises and their community; the proper degree of public "access" to sports, both amateur (e.g., parks) and professional (e.g., television); and the contribution government can make to ensuring the fiscal health of sports. Again, the general tendency in sport policy has been to tolerate only indirect efforts to manage the relation between sport and the communities. At this institutional level, the debate over sport policy is most likely to touch on the "collective goods" provided by sport institutions and how an overemphasis on individual liberties can threaten them. Chapter 7 will discuss franchise location and movements; chapter 8 will deal with the question of state provision of parks, recreation spaces, and athletic facilities; and chapter 9 will deal with the mass media and sports.

At the *societal* level, the struggle becomes an international one as different societies seek, with more or less determination, to articulate social values and political ideals through sport competition. Issues embraced here include the proper role of the state in the Olympic effort, states' use of sports as tools of political mobilization, dissident groups' use of sports to change societal goals, and the significance of sports as political symbols of national identity. The tendency at this level, more than any other, is to see sports as a collective enterprise, whose mission is to achieve societal goals in competition with other nations. However, so powerful is the principle of liberty in the United States that this "public" purpose has been achieved largely indirectly, through quasi-private organizations. Chapter 10 will discuss the general usage of sports in political mobilization and integration, and chapter 11 will deal with the role of the United States in the international sporting order.

The fact that the individual level is dealt with first does not mean that it is most important. A complete sociological analysis requires inspection of social phenomena at all levels on the assumption that they operate simultaneously and that they are mutually influential. Just how sport enterprises are conceived and treated is a reflection of the role assigned to sport as an institution; where sports are assigned a social function, organizations that promote sport will be "protected." Just how "the sporting individual" is conceived will help shape the kind of organization that arises to administer that individual's play; where athletic achievement is associated with masculine identities, single-sex organizations are likely to appear. In the real world of political struggle, these levels are inevitably embraced within a single issue, often in ways only dimly recognized by those involved.

CHAPTER

2

CAN I PLAY?

It is widely believed that in sports, "natural" or "God-given" talents combine with determination and perseverance to produce success and acclaim. Even team sports have become gladiatorial combats between rival pitchers, quarterbacks, or centers. It is not for this reason, however, that this analysis of sport and the state begins at the individual level. When play is transformed into sport, the physical body is made social. Social identities are superimposed upon physical being. Sport, in giving value to certain physical attributes and accomplishments and denigrating others, affirms certain understandings of how body and mind are related, how the social and natural worlds are connected. The identity of the athlete is not, therefore, a natural outgrowth of physicality but a social construction.

When play is institutionalized (as sport), limits are imposed, licenses issued. When people define a sport, they decide for whom the sport role is most appropriate and fitting. Just as the law treats only "legal subjects" and refuses to recognize those who are not, so sports treat seriously only those who look, behave, and present themselves as athletes (Donnelly and Young 1988). The same could be said for the other identities that populate the sport world: managers, coaches, owners, umpires, and fans. Full citizenship is granted only to those who clearly qualify. Others are excluded or relegated to marginal status.

The subject of this chapter, then, is not why this or that person is a successful athlete but how athletic identities are formed. This is a more important question sociologically, for ideas about what an athlete is and can be play a major part in deciding who will succeed. I shall show that ideas about athletic potential draw on wider social understandings about the relation between mind and body and that ideologies of gender, race, and class are the most important influences. Sport absorbs ideas about the respective physical potential of men versus women, whites versus blacks, and middle-class versus working-class people. In so doing, sport serves to reaffirm these distinctions. However, my purpose here is not to consider all the sociological evidence concerning the effect of gender, race, and class on sport identities. This is a vast subject and has been the subject of a considerable amount of scholarly attention (Birrell 1988; Bourdieu 1978; Sage 1990). Only the effect of the interplay between the state and the market on the legitimation or delegitimation of these identities is of concern here.

The push and pull of market forces, the slow deliberations of courts of law, and the debates of elected officials all trade on taken-for-granted notions about sport identities. However, these do not go uncontested. Deprived groups protest their exclusion from the sport world or seek to redefine that world in ways more congenial to them. I shall document this struggle for recognition, which has become increasingly politicized and public. Nevertheless, for the most part, the struggle has not occupied the public arena. One reason is that those who have been excluded from the sport world entirely, permitted access on degrading terms, or seen their sports denigrated and stigmatized typically have little political clout. They are consumers, housewives, wage laborers, members of groups which suffer occupational discrimination. Their rebellion against leisure discipline is often personal and private. The struggle is also confined by the privileged position of sport in society, which has for many years been protected by the sentiment that "politics" should be kept out of sport. Collective action, direct-action protest, and legislative lobbying by subordinate groups to improve their access to power and resources in the sport world are frowned upon by the general public as inappropriate because "it is only play." Finally, the struggle remains largely hidden because of the assumptions people make about sports: "everybody knows" that fans are fickle, care only about winning and losing, and just like to be entertained; that athletes are egotistical, interested in making as much money as they can before they retire, and get paid for what is, in essence, mere play; that blacks have many qualities that make them excellent athletes–performers but, for that very reason, should not be taken seriously as political actors or be given positions of responsibility in sport organizations; and that women, at least as men prefer to see them, do not really belong in sport at all, so that those that do participate, particularly if they make political claims, should not be taken seriously.

GENDER

There are few social institutions more closely identified with masculine values than sport. The proper place of women in sport has always been circumscribed by societal attitudes toward women, filtered through ideas about health; beauty; femininity; and women's distinctive nature, physical capabilities, and wants. Women have never been entirely excluded from the sport world—Catherine Beecher included advice on exercise in her lectures on women's rights in the 1840s—but sport is largely a male preserve, and the terms of participation that women must accept if they do wish to participate were laid down by men.[1] More important, sport, far from being open to both sexes, is used to mark the differences between them. Sport is not so much a piece of territory women can invade and occupy as it is a code by which gender differences can be read and normalized.

While my principal purpose here is to examine how gender issues have affected, and been affected by, the state, some background on sports and gender is necessary. In no other area are deep-seated and taken-for-granted assumptions about the relation between sex and social opportunity so pervasive. They begin with the definition of leisure itself. So long as leisure is defined as the opposite of (paid) employment and so long as women are less likely than men to work outside the home, women cannot be said to have "earned" leisure. Men can enjoy their leisure as a right, but women cannot and are discouraged by men from thinking they can. What little leisure women enjoy is a "spillover" from their domestic work, such as knitting, evening classes in cookery, and voluntary work on behalf of the community, while men's leisure is compensatory, a refuge from work. Females' leisure is "low-activity," slotted into spaces or locations determined by the leisure, work, needs, and demands made by others (partners, dependent relatives, or children), much of it occurring simultaneously with work activities (e.g., watching television while ironing): "When the home is also a workplace it is much more difficult to switch off from other things which have to be done, to things which are chosen in their own right" (Deem 1986, 81). Women's leisure behavior is less influenced by their entering the world of work than it is by their relationship to men. Patriarchy makes an even bigger difference for those who have children: the man's leisure time entails getting away from the children; mothers' activities are mediated by, experienced through, or built around their children.

It is the impact of these deeper and more profound ideologies of sexuality—buttressed by a distribution of power and division of labor in the family, which are in turn supported by state policies on employment and child care—that explains why, long before the women's movement began to tackle the problem of gender inequalities in sport, the cooptation of sport by semiprofessional school and college programs and by professional leagues had framed the policy debate on sport opportunities in such a way that the exclusion of females was "natural." Sport is what men do. Sport has now become so naturally male that major policy decisions are simply framed within this assumption: "If a city were to devote twenty-five acres of prime downtown real estate and at least $85 million of public funds to a stadium in which only Anglo-Saxons could play, there would be howls of protest, but in the matter of sex, most of us take such favoritism for granted" (Kidd 1987, 256). This has prompted some feminists to argue that sport is "so thoroughly masculinized that it seems unlikely that it can be reclaimed to serve women's interests" (Bryson 1987, 350).

Leisure, in general, is gendered by the structure of family and work. Within this context, socialization into sport roles occurs. Through their privileged leisure experience, boys are taught to associate skillful performance with a sense of agency, of instrumentality (Connell 1990). Leisure activities of young women tend to be more home-centered than those of men. Females' underprivileged participation in play and games engenders lack of confidence, "lack of understanding of self in relation to environment, and lack of control over one's own physical destiny" (Bennett et al, 1987, 371). For women, the self is object; for men, the self is subject.

Sport constructs a masculinity that is competitive, confident, and space-occupying. Thus, a patriarchal society propagates the idea that certain sports are "feminine" and enhance "women's roles"; women who insist on participating in men's sports are either not really women or will experience severe role conflict in doing so. The issue is, furthermore, a private one, which must be dealt with individually and privately by the women involved. Women athletes, for example, must "come to terms" with the possibly masculinizing effects of sports participation, with the homophobia it often generates among both men and women, and take countermeasures to assert their essential femininity. Men are equally "en-gendered" by sport, all the more so in that the maleness of sport is much less frequently questioned than is its ethnicity, its nationality, or its class (Whitson 1990). Sport has therefore been one of the most powerful institutions reproducing a "compulsory heterosexuality." Women who enjoy and excel at sports are either masculine from the outset or have been made "mannish" by their participation (Lenskyj 1986, 57). Competition between men and women in sport is threatening to men not simply because they might experience defeat but because their ideas of femininity, and therefore their ideas of masculinity, are undermined.

Sexism in and through sport does not hurt men and women equally. Women athletes, it seems, are presented with an impossible choice: they can be the same as men, and then they will be equal; or they can be different from men, and then they will be women. Men are the norm, so women are different. For women to be treated as equals, they must be treated as men, because equality is premised on men. A woman treated as different from men cannot be treated as equal.

Politically, the issue for women is equality versus difference. Should they seek equality of opportunity in an institution established and defined by males or should they celebrate difference and define and govern their own sport? There is also the question of the means to be used. Should women have faith in modernity and assume that the universalism of the marketplace will erode gender disadvantages, or must they seek a more democratic sports world through political action? I shall show that while some women have asserted difference, the majority have sought equality of opportunity. I will also show that women have been largely excluded from the marketplace for sport opportunities and have been forced to seek an end to exclusion through political means. However, they have opted for a liberal politics of equality of opportunity, which has left the political structure of sports largely intact, in the hands of men.

Equality of Opportunity

During the 1960s, when equal opportunities for women in the sport world finally became one of the goals of the women's liberation movement, the issue was framed in terms that privileged men. How could women become more like men so that they could share in the rewards sports offered? Mainstream political organizations endorsed this type of discourse, which totally omitted the more profound and disturbing questions whether women *needed* to become more like men to achieve equality and whether sport could ever be a gender-neutral institution.[2]

Most men, and many women, have tended to "blame the victim" when accounting for the unequal treatment of men and women athletes. The language often adopted by the policymakers belies their stated intentions: phrases used to describe women and other underparticipant groups include "recreationally inert," "sports illiterate," and, more recently, "leisure-deficient." These phrases scarcely imply a sympathy with the member of the groups under discussion. Rather, they imply that the people so labeled fall short of the targets in some way and that

argets are more important than the people who make up their
bers (Talbot 1988, 33).

ne temptation for men, and many women, is to see sport as distort-
Women are trained to be weak, men to be strong. This accounts for
inferiority of women in sport. The political goal should be to eliminate irrational differences. The things that men have been, women
should be allowed to become. Eliminating distortions would permit all
people to realize their potential as individuals.

This way of thinking has dominated gender politics at all levels of amateur sports, ranging from Little League baseball to high school and college athletics. Before the 1960s, youth sport organizations were rarely
considered matters for political debate or government action. Their essentially private, and above all voluntary, nature distanced them from
talk of equal rights, despite the fact that many were sex-segregated. Even
then, amateur sports would not have become a political issue had they
not made extensive use of municipal facilities, for this helped render
them accountable to the public interest. Little League baseball was dou-
bly exposed, because it had been granted a charter from the federal government in 1964 in recognition of its important citizenship-building
role. To many parents, Little League was "as American as the hot dog
and apple pie" (L. Smith 1975, 63). Who could deny a girl the chance to
be a part of it?

The political confrontation over sex discrimination in youth sports
occurred in the (state) courts. Few avenues could be found for a direct
legislative assault on this problem, although some state legislatures did
change their laws as a result of some well-publicized court cases. The
sex segregation of Little League baseball was subjected to twenty-two
class-action suits between 1968 and 1975 (Kutner 1976, 893). Typical
was a case in Hoboken, New Jersey. Maria Pepe joined her local Little
League baseball team in 1972. The national headquarters revoked the
charter of the club because it had clearly violated the "boys only" policy
in place since the granting of the league's federal charter in 1964.
Maria's parents took her case to the Civil Rights Division of the State of
New Jersey and, in 1974, obtained a favorable ruling, the division's officer deciding that laws pertaining to places of public accommodation
were applicable to Little League. So long as the public at large was invited to watch Little League games and so long as Little League made use
of public facilities or received financial support from local governments, it would be subject to state and federal laws preventing discrimination (S. Jennings 1981, 84). Little League in New Jersey was
ordered to admit girls into full membership, and the order became an
extension of state law.

The key to victory in *Pepe* was the state's willingness to shift the status of Little League (and by implication similar organizations) from private to public and thus expose it to equal rights attack. The move was
highly controversial, and demonstrations were held to protest it. Many

of the fifty thousand people who signed the protest petition disapproved of boys and girls playing on the same team, but they also made it clear that they were unhappy with the "intrusion" of the state into what they considered their private life. They overlooked the fact that Little League had already "gone public" by seeking and obtaining a charter from the federal government.

In 1984, a case very similar to that in New Jersey occurred in Ypsilanti, Michigan, where Carolyn King had been barred from Little League play. This dispute spurred Martha Griffith, U.S. representative from Michigan, to propose legislation amending the charter of the Little League, providing for the admission of girls. Under threat of legislation, Little League became officially desegregated in that year. It soon after started a softball division, into which many of the girls seeking some form of organized sport drifted.[3]

In high schools, sports were also sex-segregated, at least until the 1970s. Most high school athletic associations prohibited mixed-sex teams or competition between boys' and girls' teams. Resources for girls' teams were usually inferior to those provided for boys. When these practices were challenged, the courts were generally inclined to invalidate policies that excluded participation by females on male sports teams or in male sports programs when no comparable athletic opportunities were available to females in a particular sport. Equal support to separate teams was, on the other hand, considered valid. During the 1970s, feminists tried to establish in judicial policy the principle that the segregation of athletic teams by sex violated the equal protection clause of the Fourteenth Amendment. They argued that equal opportunity to participate in school athletic programs was a right, because such programs are part of the basic benefits that schools provide for students: "It is unjust to deprive female students of any significant class of benefits that male students enjoy" (Warren 1983, 15). Their efforts to tie athletes' rights to students' rights failed, however; for judges uniformly held that playing sports was not a right but simply a privilege the school could bestow, using whatever criteria it chose.

The state's refusal to offer blanket endorsement of the right to participate does not mean that unequal opportunities in high school athletics have been sanctioned. Since 1985, most states have amended their statutes to permit girls to play on boys' teams. Furthermore, many judges, believing it unrealistic to suppose that boys and girls could always compete for places on the same team, have offered girls "protective" rulings. This is clearly shown in cases where a boy wanted to play on a girls' team because there was no boys' team in that sport. In these cases, judges seemed inclined to offer female athletes protection, even if this meant discriminating against a boy. In 1979, the Supreme Court sanctioned the Rhode Island Interscholastic League's exclusion of a boy from a girls' volleyball team on the grounds that this was necessary for the equal protection of the girls (Parkhouse and Lapin 1980, 53). In another case, a New Jersey court decided that while girls couldn't be barred from playing on boys' athletic teams, it was not illegal to bar a boy from girls' teams. School officials were thus justified in preventing a boy from playing on a girls' hockey team (it had no boys' hockey team) after the school's opponents complained. The court declared that "in order to constitutionally protect the institution of girl's interscholastic athletics from the negative effects of male participation, the law must recognize that the continued existence of women's athletics is itself a legitimate and important governmental interest which is worthy of protection" (Hetzel 1987, 286). The decision was upheld on appeal in 1987.

While many of the gender inequities found in high schools were replicated at the collegiate level, the political campaign to remove them assumed a different form. The reason was that many colleges and universities rely heavily on federal funding and are thus more vulnerable than high schools to pressure from the federal government to comply with national civil rights policy. The passage of Title IX of the Education Amendments of 1972, which barred sex bias in "any education program or activity receiving federal financial assistance," seemed to promise a bright future for women's athletics; for it seemed to invalidate inequities in spending on athletic programs at institutions receiving federal funds. Public policy, however, is only partly determined by legislation. It is also shaped by the work of the civil servants, whose job it is to put executive teeth into bills passed by Congress. Politics plays just as much a role in specifying the means of interpreting and enforcing legislation as it does in its original passage.

The precise meaning of Title IX was not determined for a considerable period of time. The National Collegiate Athletic Association (NCAA), fiercely opposed to the measure, lobbied against the idea that the state's civil liberties writ extended to athletic programs. The association described the amendment as an unwarranted intrusion into the affairs of a private body and claimed it was already catering to women to "the extent of their desire to participate." Alan Chapman, then president of the NCAA, called Title IX "arbitrary government in its most naked form" (Parkhouse and Lapin 1980, 26). A later NCAA letter, sent out to member institutions, complained of "interference and 'second guessing' in every aspect of university life, by Federal government personnel." Walter Byers, executive director, predicted that paying for women's sports would increase the burden on the men's football program to make money and encourage more cheating.

Much political wrangling occurred over the scope of Title IX. Did Title IX apply to particular programs directly receiving federal financial aid or did it cover whole institutions or school systems? And what was to be done about football, an all-male sport? In 1974, Texas senator John Tower introduced an amendment to Title IX that would have exempted revenue-producing sports from coverage. In its newsletter, the NCAA accused women of simply wanting to "live it up on big brother's credit

card" (Seha 1984, 136) and lobbied hard for the passage of the Tower
amendment. Despite its eventual deletion in conference committee, the
45

CAN I PLAY?
Tower amendment signaled the kind of opposition women faced in extending equal rights protection into sports. When the Office of Civil
Rights released a policy interpretation for Title IX specifically address-
ing the question of sports in 1979, Tower's more conservative views
had largely prevailed.

Not even the broadest interpretation of Title IX required that men
and women have identical sport programs. Rather, it expected equality
of opportunity in accommodation of interests and abilities, athletic
scholarships, and other benefits and opportunities (Wong and Ensor
1986, 361). Title IX preserved a considerable measure of sex discrimination in its distinction between "contact" and "noncontact" sports. It
was legal to prohibit mixed-sex teams or intersex team competition in
contact sports. Boxing, wrestling, rugby, and ice hockey—but most importantly, football and basketball—were defined as contact sports.

The confusion over the reach of Title IX led to a series of court cases.
The NCAA brought suit against Secretary of Health, Education, and Welfare Joseph Califano to prevent him from applying the statute to athletics almost as soon as Title IX was passed. The NCAA lost that case in
1978, the judge deciding that the NCAA lacked standing to sue, since it
was not injured by the regulations. For a brief period under the Carter
administration, the state pursued the broad interpretation of Title IX;
but after 1980, the Republican Justice Department adopted the most restricted of interpretations. The Supreme Court (itself more conservative) went along with this trend in a number of decisions of relevance
to women's sports. Its landmark ruling was contained in *Grove City College* v. *Bell* (1984).

A small, private institution affiliated with the Presbyterian Church,
Grove City College had refused to sign a letter assuring its compliance
with Title IX. In response, the Department of Education moved to enforce compliance by withdrawing student grants, even though all
agreed there was no evidence of discrimination. The college sued for
reinstatement. By the time the case wound its way to the Supreme
Court, the Reagan administration had so altered the original policy on
Title IX as to encourage a narrow, precedent- setting reading. The
Supreme Court agreed that student grants do trigger jurisdiction under Title IX but at the same time maintained that enforcement should
be program-specific—in this case to the financial aid office only: "The
Supreme Court . . . rejected the series of arguments . . . proposed in
earlier days when the Department of Education's policy was toward
more vigorous enforcement" (Carpenter 1985, 71).

The impact of the Grove City decision on the fight for equality of
opportunity for women in sports was immediate. Within weeks, the
Office of Civil Rights closed a number of cases it had already begun
work on. For example, it dropped its enforcement program against the

University of Maryland, because direct financial aid to athletes was in compliance with Title IX, even though many other aspects of the athletic program disadvantaged women (Carpenter 1985, 73). Within a year of *Grove City* v. *Bell*, the Office of Civil Rights had suspended sixty-four investigations, more than half involving college athletics. Progress toward more equality in the provision of opportunities came to a halt.[4]

Grove City v. *Bell* also had the effect, however, of mobilizing liberal sentiment in Congress against the Reagan administration's efforts to roll back the civil rights gains of the 1960s. While athletics were not the centerpiece of this political struggle, they were certainly implicated. In March 1988, Congress overrode a presidential veto and enacted the Civil Rights Restoration Act, thus reversing the 1984 Supreme Court decision limiting the reach of federal civil rights enforcement. Under the new law, all programs run by an institution must comply with civil rights statutes, even if federal aid is received by only part of the institution.

The Civil Rights Restoration Act helped revive the campaign for equal opportunity in athletics. When, in 1990, many colleges began to make cuts in their athletic programs as the result of budget deficits, the Office of Civil Rights of the Department of Education issued a memorandum warning that these cuts should be made equitably and not target women's athletics. More important, in 1992, federal officials upheld the complaint of two physical education professors at Brooklyn College that the college discriminated against women athletes in the provision of equipment and supplies, assignment of experienced coaches, practice facilities, scheduling, and sports publicity. While Brooklyn College was not considered important athletically, the decision in the case did seem to signal a new federal policy toward sex discrimination in college sports. Whether the same decision would have been made in the case of a "football power," where the argument would be made that football provided the revenues needed to support women's programs, remains to be seen.

Difference

The political campaign to achieve equality of opportunity for women in sports thus met with mixed success. Women did move the issue onto the political agenda and did win some important court cases. However, the costs of the campaign were high. At the high school level, the equal opportunity campaign had much the same effect as efforts to equalize rights in some other areas, such as divorce. A law is passed that in a formal way, ensures equality of treatment regardless of gender; but the historical and structural conditions creating differences in circumstance, ability, and general condition being deliberately ignored, the net effect is to recreate, and in some ways worsen, discrimination and inequities.

At the collegiate level, the "market realities" of college athletic funding seemed to condemn female athletes—or women who wanted to be athletes—to secondary status. Few college programs could survive without the revenues generated by men's football and basketball. Funding for women's sports was geared to "palpable demand," which would be lower for women than men; or funding would be split evenly, once football and basketball programs were removed. The results of an NCAA survey of 1991 expenditures on college athletic programs thus occasioned no surprise. It found twice as many men participating in college sports as women and men's programs receiving nearly five times the recruiting dollars and twice the scholarship money (*New York Times*, December 3, 1992).

The problem was that the liberals' attempts to rectify the distortions in sport administration nevertheless presumed a fixed set of personal identities that individuals brought to sport *and* a fixed set of institutional features that constitute sport as it "naturally" had to be. Both assumptions disadvantaged women, the first by handicapping women in the race for rewards, the second by helping ensure that the race could never be won. The political force of these assumptions was all the greater because they were rarely articulated.

Some feminists concluded that their goals are not served by seeking equality of opportunity in an antifeminist, basically flawed system, with its "dominance, star system, 'destruction' of one's opponent, maintenance of hierarchical power structures, a child-parent relationship between athletes and coaches, and authoritarianism in every aspect of the pursuit" (Bennett et al. 1987, 370). In this world, femininity means weak, violable, unathletic. This way of thinking seemed to suggest a different political strategy, one of seperation, rather than integration.

The difficulty with seeking equality of opportunity in a male-defined world had long been recognized by women athletes and administrators. Many of the women who, in the 1920s, supported the segregration of play (e.g., "play days") did so not because they accepted male stereotypes of female athletes but because they wanted no part of the male sports world: "The focus was to be on 'play for play's sake' rather than the stress and over-specialization associated with individual sporting accomplishments" (J. Hargreaves 1984, 60). Women physical educators were one of the few groups able to articulate a coherent argument against the growing professionalization and commercialization of the amateur sport world. Although they failed to prevent the professionalization of college athletic programs, they took pride in having stemmed "the rising tide of intercollegiate competition" in women's athletics (Jensen 1986, 154). Thus, while some physical educators wished to emphasize the rights that women (like men) deserved others wanted to emphasize the particular duties or services that women (unlike men) could offer society. Should women act primarily for their own advantage to secure a gender-neutral position, or should they act for the benefit of others to make a distinctive contribution to society? The drive to exclude women from competitive athletics was led by women interested in gaining control over women's play, who used conservative medical opinion to buttress their argument that women had something special to contribute to the world of sport, part of which included a redefinition of sport itself.[5]

Women's desire to be different led them to seek organizational autonomy. Of their many attempts to organize athletics for themselves, the most successful was the Commission on Intercollegiate Athletics for Women. Formed in 1966, it changed its name to the Association for Intercollegiate Athletics for Women (AIAW) four years later. The AIAW looked both backward and forward, invoking some of the ideals of the "play days" of the interwar period but in the context of a more militant and politically progressive form of separatism. It was intended to encourage the preparation of top women athletes without at the same time permitting the excesses of men's sports. No off-campus recruiting was allowed; no expenses to cover prospects' visits to campus could be paid; institutions could participate in different divisions, rather than following the NCAA practice of having to field squads in the same division in all sports; and students were included in its government (students served as voting members on each sport's governing board). The AIAW tried to recapture the kind of self-determination of student's athletics not seen since the collapse of the Intercollegiate Amateur Athletic Association in the 1920s.[6]

The AIAW was a remarkably successful social movement for women athletes. Many of its ideas about student–athletes' self-government, for instance, would be incorporated in the Amateur Sports Act of 1978 (Slatton 1982, 147). But it was also highly unstable, because it attempted to contain all of the contradictions of women seeking to distance themselves from men's semiprofessionalized athletics while at the same time sharing in some of the rewards they could provide. At its inception, the AIAW promised to run athletics differently, with a broader base of participation and a greater variety of sports. As it grew and began to score state legislative victories promising more rewards for women, it came under increasing pressure to imitate the NCAA. This is evident in its shifting policy on scholarships. It initially opposed granting scholarships to athletes at all. Under pressure from students, it permitted tuition-only scholarships in 1976. Finally, as a result of a lawsuit brought against the AIAW by a group of women athletes who felt that they should enjoy the same kind of scholarship opportunities as men, it began offering full athletic scholarships. Its leaders' ambivalence is also evident in their policy with respect to championships. Although the AIAW disparaged the elitism of the NCAA, its desire to compete with the NCAA in the staging of championships tended to drain money away from minor sports and from junior varsity teams (Carpenter 1985, 66).

Success for the AIAW thus meant that its rules and procedures came to resemble more and more those of the NCAA. There is further irony in the fact that the force that killed the AIAW was Title IX, an amendment for which most AIAW supporters fought hard. In requiring colleges to distribute athletic opportunities more equitably, this measure motivated the NCAA to strengthen its hold over women's athletics: "Male-dominated campuses were not prepared to subsidize athletic activities they did not control" (Chandler 1985, 14). While busy fighting Title IX in Congress and the courts, the NCAA was also preparing the ground for a takeover of women's sports in the event of a defeat. National championships for women's sports under NCAA auspices were being suggested by some member institutions as early as 1975. Its failure to have Title IX weakened in the enforcement regulations published in 1975 (which unequivocally included athletics) prompted the NCAA to proceed with a policy of co-optation; and at the 1980 convention, ten women's championships were established. The NCAA provided participating teams funds to cover their expenses and offered inducements to the television networks, promising them the men's championships if they also undertook to show some women's championships as well.

The AIAW sued the NCAA for violation of antitrust laws in its agreement with the television networks. The loss of this suit in 1983 effectively destroyed the AIAW and placed control of women's athletics firmly in the hands of the NCAA. Ironically, the U.S. district court in this case agreed that the NCAA would, as a result of its 1980 actions, monopolize college athletics; but it did not agree that this was the result of "the specific intent to develop a monopoly on the part of the NCAA" (Acosta and Carpenter 1985, 324).

If the proximate cause of the death of the AIAW was the loss of the lawsuit, the ultimate cause was the superior financial clout of the NCAA. Although the AIAW was unable to prove this in court, there can be little doubt that the power of the NCAA to offer its men's championships as bait for the networks to fund the less popular women's championships won the day. Besides, the women's sports had no professional leagues for whom they could operate as a farm system and no spectator following to speak of. Once Title IX had provided the goad and once women had themselves shown their eagerness to engage in nationwide competition, the writing was on the wall.[7]

Have Women Been Co-opted?

By the end of the 1980s, women had achieved much more equitable representation in college athletics than they had enjoyed less than twenty years before. Participation had grown from 16,000 women in 1966 to 158,000 in 1990 (Carpenter and Acosta 1991, 23). They had made little progress, however, in achieving much participation in the government of amateur sports. The average number of women involved in the administration of women's programs in 1990 was less than one per school (Acosta and Carpenter 1990). In 1972, women headed more than 90 percent of women's programs; by 1990, this proportion had fallen to 30 percent.[8]

These trends only served to buttress the arguments of the feminists who, emphasizing gender difference, rather than equality, saw the political issue as being not to improve women's chances of enjoying the same kind of leisure as men but to redefine what constitutes leisure (Talbot 1988, 34). More radical feminist demands remained on the table: move away from the conventional notion of leisure constructed around the separation between paid employment and "free" time; move away from the idea that athletes must treat each other as enemies to be intimidated and brutalized, when in reality they are coplayers without whom the rewards of playing could not be obtained; move away from the idea that the best sports are built upon physical strength, which, in the ideology of masculinity, men have and women lack.

Feminists continued to offer their critique of "malestream" sports. Sports, when defined as a form of combat where one asserts oneself against objects, objectified people, or standards—where one's goal is to vanquish enemies—must reproduce partriarchial values. They exclude and denigrate kinesthesis, pleasure in motion, cooperation, physical self-respect, self-possession, and sheer fun. Sports thus stand in the way of women's gaining a relation to their bodies wherein their bodies are their own; are acting, rather than being acted upon; are looking, rather than being looked at; are beings, rather than simply appearances (Theberge 1987).

This level of critique remained, however, far from the public discourse, where a backlash had already occured against even liberal affirmative action programs. More important, the radical feminist critique implicated sport in much more far-reaching ideas about sexuality; and these were unlikely to be changed by offering more scholarships to women college athletes. It would involve changing the image of sexuality as being captured by a man. It also means reconceptualizing power, as enabling another person, empowering another through your own actions, rather than controlling a person.

Does it really matter that the fastest women will never beat the fastest man? Absolute performance becomes irrelevant if sport is redefined to devalue the single-minded driving of the body to its limit and the elitism to which that leads and, instead, to valorize cooperation and nurturance through sport; if the goal is self-actualization through relationships and through community, rather than competitive achievement; if competition means not domination but joining with an opponent in a mutually supportive and rewarding experience. Thus conceived, the sport experience could encourage female bonding, women developing primary allegiances to each other. Far from being dominated in and through sport, by taking control of their own physicality in sport, women could actively resist their own subordination (Theberge 1987).

RACE

Like gender, race defines sport identities in the United States, just as sporting achievements are used to affirm racial stereotypes. Biological features and implied mental capabilities guide the allocation of sport resources and rewards. Like patriarchy, racial ideology plays on the idea of the "natural" inferiority of a group in the population to deprive that group of economic rewards and political power. There are differences between gender and race, however, in how they have molded sport identities. Most importantly for the purposes of this analysis of the relation between sport and the state, the legitimacy of a black sport identity has, from the very earliest years, been hedged by laws, court decisions, and executive actions. While deep-seated ideas about race have been as influential as deep-seated ideas about gender, the power of the state was invoked earlier—and has been used more extensively—to legitimate and enforce race ideas in the world of sport than gender ideas.

By the end of the nineteenth century, race had become the basis of a caste system the most crucial feature of which was a ban on sexual congress between white women and black men. The resulting caste system, much more than the gender order, was sanctioned by a variety of laws that made it virtually impossible for black athletes to compete with whites on an equal footing. These laws, however, at the same time, made possible the development of a parallel set of social institutions, including a variety of sports activities. Blacks were thus not entirely excluded from the sport world but largely segregated into a sphere of their own.

Unlike women, blacks were deemed fit for sports. Indeed, by the end of the nineteenth century, enough black athletes had distinguished themselves in competition against whites to pique the curiosity of social commentators. Ironically, the association they made between genes and group athletic achievement only served to legitimate racial discrimination in other areas.

> By acknowledging a physiological basis for black athletic superiority, whites in this country could more easily maintain the broad range of black character they found acceptable and had marked off so carefully. Acknowledgement of physical superiority did nothing to disrupt the feeling among a large segment of the white population that blacks were either docile or savage, faithful or tricky, pathetic or comical, childish or oversexed. (Wiggins 1989, 182)

The problem for blacks was not acceptance into the sport world but acceptance on terms that both demeaned them and reaffirmed racist ideologies. The more successful they became, the more competition they posed to white athletes, and the more anxious whites became to associate their success with biological "gifts" and to separate blacks' "physical" achievements from any "mental" contribution they might make. The competition between white and black athletes thus became a code for competing claims to mental versus physical superiority.

As John Dollard writes in *Caste and Class in a Southern Town*, a truly democratic society "guarantees equal opportunity to enjoy whatever goods and services society has to offer; there are no arbitrary limitations based on race and color" (1957, 62). These guarantees clearly did not apply to blacks before the 1960s. Since then, black athletes have largely broken down the caste barriers maintaining separate black and white sport worlds and have achieved a measure of equality of opportunity in the competition for athletic jobs. They have by no means rid white society of the need to associate racial characteristics with intellectual capabilities and moral worth. Consequently, few blacks are to be found in management or other positions of authority over whites.

As with gender, my purpose is not to provide a broad sociological picture of the impact of racial prejudice and discrimination on sport (for an overview, see Lapchick 1984). Rather, the focus is on how deep-seated and often taken-for-granted ideas about the relation between race and athleticism have been embodied in state actions (laws, court decisions, executive orders, policy pronouncements) and how the state apparatus has been used to both legitimate and delegitimate the association between race and sport.

One of the most important questions that needs to be answered is how far changes in the relation between race and sport have occurred because of the democratic guarantees Dollard describes. What role has pressure on the state to protect these guarantees played in desegregating sport? The breakdown of caste barriers in the marketplace occurs if the subordinate caste can exert enough pressure on the superior caste to convince it that maintaining the system is too costly. The subordinate caste has two kinds of pressure available to it. It may have "competitive" resources, such as special job skills; or it may have "pressure" resources. The latter would include boycotts, strikes, or public censure (Blalock 1970, 93). In short, blacks can either compete in the market place by offering desirable skills in short supply or exert pressure on the state, perhaps through public opinion, which in turn would pressure employers to open up employment opportunities to them. In a liberal-democratic regime, where political egalitarianism tends to be subordinated to market forces, competitive resources would appear to be more potent than those which rely on the power of the state.[9]

Pressure Resources

The caste system was imposed by political means. The National Association of Base Ball Players operated for nine years without race being an issue, but the Reconstruction era saw a gradual segregation of organized sport. The process could be said to have begun when the National Association banned racially mixed teams in 1867 and to have ended in 1898 when the Acme Colored Giants became the last all-black team to play in the predominantly white Iron and Coal League. Thereafter, sports would abide by the prevailing segregationist sentiment.

Three factors contributed to the racial segregation of sport. Each has a political dimension. First is the passage of Jim Crow laws designed to separate the social lives of blacks and whites. Sport did not cause the laws to be passed, but neither did it resist them. Second, few people at this time questioned the idea that sports were a private matter, free from the reach of the state. Sport promoters could thus shelter beneath the excuse that race relations were a political issue and should not be a concern of those who governed sports. Thus, baseball's owners, at their annual meetings, could justify their ban on mixed teams on the grounds that they must "keep out of the convention the discussion of any subject having a political bearing" (Tygiel 1983, 13). Racism could be sanctioned on the grounds of its being a private choice, at the same time that owners were seeking to benefit from the claim that sports, and baseball in particular, were "the national game."[10]

Third, racial segregation in sports received a boost from Progressive movement reformers, whose efforts to provide uplifting recreational facilities were more segregated than the streets from which they plucked their youth (Ruck 1987, 37). Not only were facilities segregated, but they were also grossly maldistributed: "In 1920, black children were permitted in only 3% of all American playgrounds and had few alternatives to the streets" (Riess 1989, 147). So often, the progressive efforts to civilize play meant expunging the disorderly and uncontrollable elements, which usually meant getting rid of its association with gambling, drinking, and spontaneous community celebration, which, in turn, tended to exclude the poorer groups in the population. The progressives thus targeted boxing for reform, even though it was one of the few sport opportunities open to blacks. Films of the Jack Johnson versus James Jeffries fight in 1910, which showed Johnson defeating a white boxer to become heavyweight champion, were banned on the grounds that they might stir racial hatred and violence (Sammons 1987, 59). It is worth pointing out here, however, that boxing has been one of the least segregated sports in America. Given the rather disorganized state of the sport, it has always been easy for white boxers to avoid bouts with black fighters, but they could not continue to do this if they aspired to a championship.

Over a fifth of the approximately 8,000 professional boxers in the 1930s were black, and there were five black world champions during this period, including Henry Armstrong and Joe Louis (Riess 1990).

The progressives not only gave tacit support to segregated leisure, but they also opposed the commercialization of college and professional sports and therefore helped perpetuate the myth that sports could and should be purely for fun or self-improvement. This made it more difficult for racial segregation to be fought politically; for, as Dollard points out, while *class* conflict centers around economic position and advantage, *caste* conflict centers around social (and ultimately sexual) contact (1957, 91). The latter is embedded in the private sphere, in patterns of social interaction outside the workplace, in the home and neighborhood. Despite its increasingly businesslike aspects, the sport world was still thought of as the kind of thing people choose to do in their spare time, the nonessential but nevertheless rewarding and fulfilling part of their life. This way of thinking about sport made caste considerations extremely important but also depoliticized the issue of race in sports.

Political pressure resources were employed on professional sports for the first time during the Great Depression. Socialists and communists (competing with each other for new members) seized upon the issue of segregation in baseball as a means of pointing out the racism fostered by capitalism. The Communist party, in particular, led the fight against segregation, with its open espousal of social equality and its elevation of blacks to positions of leadership within its own structure. Delegations to major league teams demanded tryouts for black players. Petition drives collected signatures to protest discrimination in the sport (Tygiel 1983, 37). The results were mixed. Blacks did join the Communist party in large numbers and attended the Party's interracial social events; but they remained skeptical of the motives of Communist party organizers. The Party did not dislodge loyalty to the "national pastime" in preference to loyalty to a broader international political movement.

After World War II, left-wing groups used baseball as a symbol of the hypocrisy of America's claim to be the defender of liberty in the atomic age. The war against Japan and Germany had been billed as a crusade against racism and for democracy, causes for which blacks conspicuously fought and died:

> The continuing absence of integration on most clubs inspired protests by fans, reporters, and political action groups in many cities. Pickets appeared sporadically at Yankee and Senator home games. 'HOW CAN WE GET GREATER DEMOCRACY ON THE YANKEES?' read a flier handed out in April by the Bronx County Labor Youth League. . . . Many league owners usually dismissed these demonstrations as the machinations of . . . "a committee of Commies." (Tygiel 1983, 291)

The city council of Boston threatened to deny the Red Sox and Braves permission to play Sunday ball if they continued to field all-white teams. In Los Angeles, blacks demanded that the National Football League's (NFL's) Los Angeles Rams not be allowed to play in the Los Angeles Coliseum unless they signed a black player. Partly as a result (but partly as a result of economic competition for playing talent from a rival league) the Rams broke the NFL color barrier by signing Kenny Washington.

Despite the obviously political nature of the race problem in baseball, when the color line was broken in 1946 and 1947 it was carefully staged as a nonpolitical event. Jackie Robinson was a model black. He was college-educated, an officer during the war, and a Methodist who neither smoked nor drank; and he had a "steady" girlfriend. He did not present himself as a political actor, and both blacks and whites sought to distance the desegregation of sports from politics. Branch Rickey, in a speech to middle-class blacks in New York in 1947, asked them not to make Robinson a symbol of social "ism" or schism, a triumph of race over race (Tygiel 1983, 162). Rickey persuaded Robinson to testify before the House Un-American Activities Committee against Paul Robeson's Paris speech declaring that blacks should not fight for the United States against the Soviets. Sport owners were not above using "their" blacks to promote an all-American image for baseball.

Brooklyn's example was soon followed by the Cleveland Indians (Larry Doby) and the St. Louis Browns (Henry Thompson and Willard Brown), all recruited from the Negro National League. Baseball's owners still refused to acknowledge any responsibility for dealing with racial discrimination in sport. As late as September 1953, six years after Robinson had joined the Brooklyn Dodgers, ten of the sixteen major league clubs remained all-white. The number would fall to six by 1954 (Tygiel 1983, 285). The *Brown v. Board of Education, Topeka* Supreme Court decision handed down that year actually made racial segregation in baseball in the South worse as southern clubs (e.g., those in the Southern Association) joined in resistance to the burgeoning Civil Rights movement. Ten years after Robinson's debut, there were still only eighteen blacks in professional baseball.

In football, the pattern was much the same. While only the Washington Redskins and the Detroit Lions were without at least one black player by 1952, it was not until 1961 that the Washington team hired its first black, a fact that some people use to explain the team's dismal performance during the 1950s. Stewart Udall had warned George Marshall, owner of the Redskins, to hire black players or face federal retribution. As secretary of the interior, Udall was able to intimidate Marshall because the Redskins' stadium was located at Anacosta Flats, part of the National Capital Parks system. By this time, Washington, a "southern city," had desegregated its schools, movie houses, theaters, playgrounds, swimming pools, bowling alleys, restaurants, hotels, and public transportation. Even the Washington Senators baseball team was desegregated. It ought to be noted, also, that by 1960, a majority of the city's population (65 percent) was black. Marshall was not so much a racist as generally conservative in his political opinions. He was vehemently opposed to the idea of a players' union and resisted proposals for a pension system for players. Many Washingtonians sided with Marshall, in the belief that Udall's insistence that the franchise hire blacks was a quota system discriminating against qualified whites. Others raised the cry "Keep politics out of sports," or argued more specifically that federal "interference" with professional sports in this manner smacked of communism (T. Smith 1987, 201). Nevertheless, Udall's declaration inspired members of the National Association for the Advancement of Colored People and the Congress of Racial Equality (CORE) to picket Marshall's home, the stadium, and Redskins' away games. Eventually, NFL Commissioner Rozelle intervened and persuaded Marshall to relent.

More direct political pressure on sports did not occur until 1967, when, under the influence of the Civil Rights movement, a part-time instructor in sociology at San Jose State College, Harry Edwards, organized a Rally Against Racism. One of his demands was that the college's opening football game not be played unless black and white athletes were treated equally. Edwards had calculated that "sports were the only arena of campus life where Blacks could exercise any political leverage" (1980, 161). He was successful in getting the opening game against the University of Texas, El Paso, cancelled. In the fall of that same year, he decided to broaden the protest to encompass the Olympic movement, with the Mexico games a year away, and formed the Olympic Project for Human Rights (OPHR). At a Black Youth Conference in Los Angeles in November 1967, he announced a campaign to persuade black athletes to boycott the Olympics. (Dick Gregory had made a similar suggestion at the time of the Tokyo games in 1964.) Edwards's plan drew support from CORE, the Student Non-Violent Coordinating Committee, Martin Luther King, and black athletes such as Bill Russell, Jackie Robinson, Jesse Owens, Rafer Johnson, and Roy Campanella. The OPHR organized a successful boycott of a track-and-field meet organized by the (segregated) New York Athletic Club, held in Madison Square Garden in February 1968. The club, rather than integrate, gave up holding the meets.

Martin Luther King's assassination in April 1968 and the riots that followed momentarily enhanced the political fortunes of the OPHR. Whites began to regard it as one of the few acceptable forms of nonviolent black protest. Furthermore, it was the only route both accessible to blacks and promising of an international protest platform, enabling the Civil Rights movement to portray black oppression as a violation of international human rights laws and principles. Against this, however, the movement had to fight the beliefs, held strongly by both blacks and whites, that politics had no place in sports, especially the Olympics.

As the Olympic games drew near, "it had become clear that commitment in the ranks was eroding" (Edwards 1980, 190); and the boycott effort collapsed. The raised fists of Tommie Smith and John Carlos on the victory podium in Mexico City was to be the "high water mark in the liberation efforts of Black youth during the 1960s" (p. 203), Edwards claims that he was fired from San Jose State because of his work for the OPHR (1984, 174). More equality of eduational opportunities for black athletes began to increase the number of blacks in college and to draw the sting of many of Edwards's criticisms.

There was little direct political pressure on the race issue in either professional or amateur sports after this time. The rapidly increasing proportion of black athletes at both levels seemed to have quieted the critics. Only the issue of blacks in management remained. After racist comments by Al Campanis, vice-president of the Los Angeles Dodgers, during a television interview in 1987, black activist Jesse Jackson threatened to use his political organization to mount pickets of games if the baseball commissioner did not institute an affirmative action program to increase the number of black executives. The commissioner agreed to set aside five hundred thousand dollars to support a program of education and recruitment for minorities into the coaching and managerial ranks. Jesse Jackson repeated his threats of an organized boycott in 1992, after the owner of the Cincinnati Reds baseball team, Marge Schott, made racist and anti-Semitic remarks in defending the underrepresentation of blacks on her administrative staff.

Competitive Resources

When the Civil Rights Act was passed in 1964, professional sport leagues, despite their history of race segregation, had become one of the most integrated of all American social institutions. The breakdown of caste barriers thus preceded the political mandate to do so. *Competitive resources* seem to have been more efficacious in the history of sport than pressure resources (Braddock 1989, 58). The more owners competed for playing talent, the greater the pressure to hire the best players, regardless of race.

Despite the existence of Jim Crow laws, the search for profit had constantly nibbled away at the caste barrier. Newspapers reported 436 interracial baseball games between 1900 and 1950, and there were undoubtedly many more that went unrecorded (Holway 1988, xii). Both white and black athletes had an economic interest in interracial competition. For whites, even major league baseball was a part-time job. Seeking to supplement their salaries, many white players formed barnstorming teams for winter play; and in many cases, their opponents were black. The finances of the black leagues were always more precarious than those of whites: only one black baseball club (the American

Giants, in Chicago) owned its own field (Riess 1989, 119). Independent black sporting enterprises (such as the Negro League and Negro American League in baseball) lacked capital and tended to rely heavily on funds generated by the numbers game and other gambling activities (Ruck 1987, 151). Many black "businessmen" (i.e., bookmakers) used sport to legitimate themselves and help build and solidify for themselves a political base in the community. They welcomed the opportunity to compete against white teams. Mutual economic need thus led athletes to cross the caste barrier informally. Independent black baseball teams played against all-white teams (in minor leagues), against white all-star teams (in the off-season) and against major league teams in exhibition games (until Commissioner Landis banned these practices in 1925).

In football, blacks played on several NFL teams during the 1920s, when the league was finding its feet and playing talent was in short supply: "Paul Robeson and Frederick Douglass 'Fritz' Pollard played for Akron, Fred 'Duke' Slater with the Chicago Cardinals, and Jay Mayo 'Inky' Williams with the Hammond Pros" (Smith 1987, 192). For its first thirty years, professional football had a "blue-collar" image, partly as a result of competition from the more elitist college football. It did not have as much symbolic weight as baseball, which was America's game. But professional football, less secure financially than baseball, suffered more severely during the Depression; and the black players were always the first to be cut. With the departure of Joe Willard from the Chicago Cardinals and Ray Kemp from the Pittsburg Pirates in 1933 the NFL was all-white until after the World War II. Good Black teams existed in many northern cities; but, just as in baseball, white team owners shunned this source of talent.

Throughout the 1930s, the black press (e.g., *Chicago Defender, Pittsburgh Courier*) was more vocal in its demands that blacks be admitted to football than to baseball. The part played by blacks in the formation of organized baseball was an indistinct memory for most sports enthusiasts, but blacks had only very recently helped the NFL get off the ground. However, the NFL owners paid little attention to the calls to preserve football's integrated status. They judged it bad business and worse public relations to be paying black men to do any kind of job when so many whites were unemployed (T. Smith 1988, 259).

Competitive pressures also undermined Jim Crow laws in basketball. Like baseball and football, basketball had its own black teams, although there was no black equivalent of the American Basketball League (ABL). The ABL was very fragile, however; and barnstorming (often in association with a dance) was an essential means of livelihood for both white and black teams. Contests between black teams like the Harlem Globetrotters and Renaissance Big Five and white teams like the Celtics were among the biggest basketball attractions of the 1920s and 1930s (Peterson 1990, 96). Black teams rarely toured the South and were always paid less than the white barnstorming teams they played against.

World War II drained sports of much its playing talent. The ranks of baseball were decimated, pointing up the illogic of ignoring the deep pool of black talent. The loss began first in colleges. A few black athletes had performed at white colleges prior to World War II; but otherwise, amateur sports were as segregated as the professional game: "Black colleges provided competition for hundreds of skilled performers known only to those in the black community" (Grundman 1986, 78). During and immediately following the war, however, more and more blacks were admitted to play on formerly all-white college teams.

In football, the effect of the military draft on NFL quality encouraged rival leagues to enter the industry. They announced their intention of hiring the best talent, regardless of race. The United States Football League and All-American Football Conference, both formed in 1944, announced that black players would be welcome. Only the All-American Football Conference actually played any games, and its Cleveland Browns franchise carried through on the desegregation promise by signing Marion Motley and Bill Willis in 1946. The NFL's rival collapsed in 1950, but not before it had forced the older league to more seriously consider hiring black talent.

Basketball underwent similar changes. The "Rens" actually entered a white league, the National Basketball League (NBL), in 1948, representing Dayton, Ohio. The league had by then already signed its first black players—William ("Pop") Gates to the Tri-City Black Hawks and William King to the Rochester Royals. The NBL merged with the Basketball Association of America in 1949 to form today's NBA; and further blacks were recruited, most notably Chuck Cooper, Earl Lloyd, and Nat Clifton.[11] The GI bill and the subsequent rush to colleges by young white men had by this time further reduced the pool of playing talent. Many of these white men secured good jobs and left the arduous job of athletic labor to those less fortunate.

The economic turmoil created by the player shortages of the 1940s soon passed, and the 1950s saw the ratio of supply and demand for talent stabilize in favor of the owners as they strengthened their monopoly in each of the major sports. Despite the political pressures being exerted by the Civil Rights movement on patterns of racial discrimination in the United States, owners did not resume their efforts to desegregate until the American Football League (AFL) came on the scene. Whereas in 1957, only 14 percent of NFL players were black by 1989 this figure had risen to 50 percent (Braddock 1989, 54; Lapchick 1986, 111). The reason was the formation of the AFL, hungry for talent. In its first year (1960), the AFL had twenty-nine black players on its total roster. The NFL was forced to follow suit and by 1962 had an average of six black players per roster, or 16.5 percent of the total (T. Smith 1987, 194). The effect of competitive resources is also evident in baseball. The hungrier, poorer clubs were the first to sign black players in any numbers. The clubs owned by wealthy individuals, like the Boston Red

Sox, the Detroit Tigers, the St. Louis Cardinals, the Philadelphia Phillies, the Chicago Cubs, and the New York Yankees, were among the last.

In professional basketball, the pressure of economic resources took a rather different form. In this five-man sport, individual players could make a much bigger difference to the fortunes of a club; and in the pretelevision era, profits depended heavily on ticket sales, which, in turn, were higher when the team was winning. The pursuit of black talent did not have to await interleague competition. Prominent teams like the Boston Celtics had all-black starting lineups by 1963. Interleague competition was not totally inconsequential, however. The NBA had to confront the American Basketball League in 1961–62 and, more damagingly, the American Basketball Association in 1967. Until its merger with the NBA in 1976, the ABA, in particular, provided a new labor market for black players, especially since it did not adhere to the NBA rule of waiting until a player's college class had graduated before making him eligible for the draft. The ABA was thus able to recruit black superstars such as Moses Malone, Julius Erving, George McGinnis, and George Ervin and to compete for black college seniors such as Artis Gilmore and David Thompson. The proportion of black players in professional basketball doubled during this period of interleague competition (Eitzen and Yetman 1979, 400).

By the end of the 1970s, the issue was no longer the underrepresentation of blacks in sport but their *over*representation, at least in the lower ranks. The number of blacks in uniform made their absence from the coaching ranks more obvious, and the question of racial discrimination in management positions became the issue of the 1980s. Here, competitive resources were to prove ineffective. In the case of players, skill and performance are relatively easily evaluated; and the development of skills (especially in sports like basketball) is difficult to confine to one group. Professional performance does not require interpersonal skills and is not highly dependent on the cooperation of others. Management, however, is thought to be an entirely different matter. Interpersonal skills and the trust and goodwill of subordinates are considered crucial. Here, blacks will be deficient in competitive resources because these take the form of cultural capital. Instead, they must rely upon pressure resources.

In 1982, the Employment Opportunities Subcommittee of the House Committee on Education and Labor held hearings on the underrepresentation of blacks in football management. While players and union representatives attended these hearings, the owners refused, pleading that their appearance would "be detrimental to the negotiating process" then under way with the unions for a new collective bargaining agreement (U.S. Congress, House Committee on Education and Labor 1982, 2). Gene Upshaw, representing the players, reminded the subcommittee that Commissioner Rozelle had abundant time to appear

were at stake.

The committee spent most of its time deliberating the findings of a study commissioned by the union revealing that between 1960 and 1979, when the players' roster averaged 25 percent black, of 261 assistant and 68 head coaches hired in the NFL, only 20 assistants and no head coaches were black. The study's author, JoMills Braddock, pointed out that even after education, central position assignment, professional accomplishments, and length of assistant coaching experience were taken into account, race continued to determine which former players were chosen to become head coaches in the National Football League. The NFL, in a written reply, traded on the Reagan administration's interpretation of equal employment laws, asserting that it was under no legal obligation to engage in an affirmative action program.

The league made a number of additional counterarguments to the union's charges of discrimination: (1) according to the chairman of the Equal Employment Opportunity Commission, statistical disparities by themselves could not be treated as proof of discriminatory hiring practices; (2) statistics could not be used to measure equitable representation, because each coaching position in the NFL was unique: "Coaching professional football players demands special qualifications which vary according to the specific requirements of each job" (U.S. Congress, House, Committee on Education and Labor 1982, 48); (3) few blacks applied for coaching positions because they could usually get better jobs outside of football; (4) the union's study ignored the "special interpersonal skills and abilities required for coaching" (p. 52); and (5) not all coaching positions were filled by former players. The league, in short, showed no sign of developing an affirmative action program.[12]

Achieving equality of opportunity in sports has required blacks to use both pressure and competitive resources, although there seems little doubt that the latter have been more effective in the long run. Competitive resources can be used to increase pressure resources, and vice versa. Thus, Harry Edwards's earliest protest movement targeted all forms of racism; but he chose to focus on athletics because he realized that competition for black playing talent among colleges gave black athletes leverage they lacked elsewhere. On the other hand, limited pressure resources can blunt the impact of competitive resources. For example, when the competition for black college athletes heated up after World War II, colleges in the South were slow to enter the market, for political reasons. In 1955, the governor of Georgia, Marvin Griffin, asked Georgia Tech to reject its Sugar Bowl bid because its opponent, the University of Pittsburgh, had a black player (Grundman 1986, 80). Conversely, when, in 1962, the Major League Baseball Players' Association demanded that clubs make greater efforts to integrate facilities in training camps (mainly situated in the South), they were able to make headway only because of pressure resources: elected officials in southern cities had begun to tie their political fortunes to hosting a major league training camp because of the tax revenues it would generate.

Where blacks lacked both competitive and pressure resources, caste barriers remained in place long after the passage of the Civil Rights Act and long after they had collapsed in many other areas of employment. Sports like tennis and golf were less vulnerable to either economic or political pressure from blacks. There was no pool of black talent from which competing promoters could draw, no shortage of white talent, and no rival leagues; and tennis and golf tournaments were considered private events, usually held in country club settings. Professional golf remained all-white until 1961, when the Professional Golf Association (PGA) removed a "whites only" clause from its bylaws and Charlie Sifford became the first black player to play in a PGA-sanctioned tournament. But the sport's privatism ensured that racial problems would persist into the 1990s. In 1990, the PGA was forced to acknowledge formally that many of the country clubs at which sanctioned tournaments were held did not admit blacks as members. After several corporate sponsors withdrew their advertising from televised events it passed a new rule prohibiting clubs from hosting PGA events unless they could provide evidence they were encouraging minority group membership. Five clubs chose to withdraw from the tour, rather than abide by the ruling.

In plotting political strategy with respect to sports, blacks have not suffered the same degree of schism as women. They do not concern themselves with equality versus difference. There is no black political voice to defend the idea of a black sport. There is not the same contradiction between black values and sport as there is between feminist values and sport. However, many blacks realize that there can be discrimination within sport that is just as injurious as that caused by total exclusion. The pursuit of a sport career can be a kind of ghetto, a dead end.

This issue became the center of political debate in the 1980s. Attention shifted from the causes and consequences of underrepresentation to the reasons for, and appropriateness of, overrepresentation. In the opinion of many, blacks had become mercenaries, hired by whites to entertain them. The black community became divided on the role of sports in achieving equality of opportunity for black youth. While many blacks see sports as a way into a college education and out of the ghetto, others condemn sports, as they are presently structured, as illusory progress. Leaders of opinion in the black community, such as Arthur Ashe, feel that there are a number of reasons why blacks should be wary of focusing too much on sports: sport institutions are dominated by whites, blacks being relegated to inevitably low-level, often temporary positions; the odds of achieving a career in professional sports being smaller than the odds of becoming a brain surgeon, black youth are being deluded by the mass media into have false role models; and the publicity given to black achievement in sports breeds complacency about lack of progress in other spheres. This kind of

reasoning, however speculative, shows just how politiciz
remains, because the argument is essentially about the d
power in sport and how this disadvantages blacks. It is ve
this context, to assess accurately, for public policy purpo
fect of encouraging blacks to pursue athletics in high s
lege, possibly at the expense of their academic work, in t
of a career in professional sports.[13]

The politics of race in professional sports has been muted since the
1960s, taking second place to questions of gender discrimination and to
larger issues of player-management relations. This has a lot to do with
the overall political climate, where the cause of affirmative action has
suffered during the shift to the right. It has also to do with characteristics peculiar to sport. Sporting achievement is still widely regarded as
meritocratic. People who would not be surprised at favoritism in offices or factories find it difficult to imagine that racism could be endemic where success and failure are so precisely measured and so
public. There is also the attitude of athletes themselves, each trained to
regard his own abilities as unique, and each encouraged to look out for
himself when negotiating a career. Finally, there is the publicity given
to multi-million-dollar contracts awarded to both black and white players. These contracts tend to obscure the fact that the three major team
sports have "taken on the appearance of a white man's game which employs well-paid gladiators" (Scully 1989, 171). This is especially marked
in baseball and football, where blacks make up only about 7 percent of
the crowd. The politics of race are not part of the "discourse" in sport.
This is only partly counterbalanced by the high visibility, glamor, and
media attractiveness of sports, which guarantee that racial remarks and
incidents will receive considerable attention if they do occur.

CLASS

Class barriers control access to sports, many of which require time and resources working-class people lack. Sport is also used
to "mark" class differences. Sports associated with the fee-paying
schools and country clubs require "taste" and "cultivation," which only
upper-class people have been able to acquire (Bourdieu 1978), while
"prole sports" such as Roller Derby, drag racing, and professional
wrestling, tend to emphasize brute force and danger (Eitzen and Sage
1986, 246).

As with gender and race, it is not my intention here to deal with all
aspects of the impact of class on sport identities. Class operates primarily in the workplace to determine "life chances." It does not inevitably
assume a political form. I shall examine how far class conflict over sport

opportunities has become a matter for state action. I shall deal first with the battle for free time, because time away from (paid) work is a major precondition for the enjoyment of sport opportunities, and there is evidence to indicate that people who work longer hours are less likely to attend sporting events.[14] The question to be answered is, How did political forces affect the battle between employers and employees for free time, and with what consequence for people's enjoyment of sport?

The section on the politics of free time will make two points. The first is that after an initial flurry of legislation to limit workers' hours (especially those of women and children), pressure on the state to guarantee more free time eased, and working hours were left to market forces to determine. The result has been that after an initial decline and a period of relative stability, a shift in the balance of power between employer and employee has caused working hours to begin to rise again. The recent rise has affected not only wage workers but many salaried employees, as well.

Why did the shorter working hours movement stall and what consequences did this have for class differences in leisure? To understand this, it is important to remember that class conflict is not absent simply because there appears to be consensus on public issues.[15] A consensus on the proper balance of work and leisure had already developed before World War II. This consensus guided the political debate over working hours. However, the agreement contained a class bias, because it was based on the assumptions that goods were more important than free time and that foregoing free time for more goods benefited all equally. In articulating the merits of capitalist expansionism, it negated freedom *from* the economy, which true leisure would require, and substituted freedom to consume, to satisfy what Marcuse called "repressive needs" (1964, 5). Class differences are reproduced not only in the distribution of material resources but in how issues are defined.

Reducing Working Hours

The long working hours of nineteenth-century factory workers and agricultural laborers meant that when sports first began to operate as money-making enterprises on a large scale, they had to rely largely on middle-class people for customers. Referring to the most popular sport of the 1890–1920 period, Cross notes that "working people lacked both the means and the time to participate equally in early baseball culture" (1990, 154). Well into the 1930s, professional baseball games were scheduled for times when most blue-collar employees were at work. Clubs did not really cater to the urban masses, who would produce lower revenues than middle-class males (Riess 1989, 70). Class differences persisted into the post–World War II period.

In 1954, the Baltimore Orioles conducted a survey of their attendance base and discovered that "nearly 42% came from white-collar professions against approximately 25% from blue-collar occupations" (J. Miller 1990, 16). Club officials concluded that the cost of attending the game was only part of the explanation for this class bias. The middle class also enjoyed more discretionary time. Later studies confirmed that attendance at professional team sports events was much more skewed toward the middle class than popular belief would suggest (Burdge 1969).

There was never any question, of course, that the class composition of baseball crowds would become a political issue. However, inequities in the distribution of free time did become a matter of public debate; and this, in turn, had some impact on opportunities to enjoy sports. The obligation of the state to protect workers from exploitation was not immediately recognized. The hours an employee worked were considered a private matter, to be settled between employer and employee. Matters changed once the trade unions and the Progressive movement, each with its own agenda, began to press for statutory limits on working hours to protect the weaker party in the employment contract. Together, they were able to get legislatures in about half the states (and, for some occupations, the federal government) to limit the working day to eight hours. The contribution of these political reforms to actual changes in work time should not be exaggerated, however. Hunnicutt's research has shown that the reduction in working hours that occurred between 1900 and 1930 actually outpaced state legislation (1988, 19). What legislation did achieve was to increase public and political support for organized labor's efforts in this area.

Although the eight-hour day had become standard by the 1920s—at least for unionized labor, firms with federal contracts, and occupations where safety issues were paramount—the movement for more free time halted at that point. Employers resisted the idea of a five-day week and nonunionized labor remained unprotected by state legislation. By 1928, a mere four hundred thousand wage earners were actually working a five-day week, more than two-fifths of these for Ford Motor Company alone (Roediger 1988, 142). The Depression did little to abet the movement for shorter hours. While there was some sentiment to "share the work," business leaders strenuously resisted this idea, as did Roosevelt (Hunnicutt 1988, 184). The National Industrial Recovery Act called for a self-imposed "code of competition" that covered maximum hours; but in practice, they were set at forty hours a week (Finegold and Skocpol 1984, 171). The Fair Labor Standards Act, passed in 1938, set maximum hours for workers engaged in interstate commerce at forty-four a week. However, few workers were covered by such legislation.

The data on working hours show that after a rise during World War II, a gradual but steady reduction occurred until 1960. The trend then leveled off, followed in the 1980s by a return to longer working hours (Kelly 1982, 122), as more people entered the paid labor force, more people worked overtime, and less time was taken off for sick leave and absences from work. These trends affected wage workers more than salaried personnel. However, the working hours of salaried employees also increased, as companies, faced with the need to tighten belts in more competitive times and unable to measure an employee's contribution to firm productivity exactly, used hours worked as a gauge of worker commitment and input (Schor 1991, 66); the inevitable result being a reluctance on the part of salaried employees to reduce their hours at the office.

One lesson to be learned from this history of the shorter-hours movement is that politics have played but a minimal role in distributing free time across social classes. Few attempts were made after the New Deal to structure work schedules by statute (Hunnicutt 1988, 311). This is not to say that the current balance of free time and work has no political meaning. On the contrary, it says a great deal about how Americans have been encouraged by economic elites and political leaders to think about the relationship between work, free time, and goods; for it implies that these represent choices, which people freely make.

The need of working people for more leisure time was rarely the main reason given for the passage of working-hours bills. Arguments for more free time were made principally on progressive grounds of safety, health, rest, and family life. Trade unions campaigned for shorter hours, but chiefly to raise the value of wages. Depression era arguments for shorter hours were framed in terms of work sharing. The idea was to "keep everybody employed by distributing the work; give everybody leisure by distributing leisure; make leisure desirable by making it usable" (Walker 1931, 153). Leisure was made part of an overall macroeconomic strategy, to help rebalance production against consumption. The effect of New Deal efforts to fight unemployment was not to establish the idea that working people were entitled to some free time. On the contrary, the New Deal "institutionalized a bias against free time in any form, leisure or unemployment" (Hunnicutt 1988, 309). Its programs were designed to get people back to productive work.

Ever since the Depression, it has been difficult for American workers to think of work reduction as a natural and desirable consequence of technological and organizational development. They have continued to regard leisure as a drain on the economy and have chosen to trade increased productivity for higher wages, rather than more free time. The state, in choosing policies intended to ensure "full employment," has abetted this tendency, progress being equated with economic growth. Unions have "jumped on the growth bandwagon" (Schor 1991, 78), refusing to press for shorter working hours out of fear that this would eventually lead to a reduction in wages (Hunnicutt 1988, 310).

The struggle for free time has thus been diverted to the struggle for more money to spend on goods to be used in that free time. Freedom is defined as the freedom to consume, for which work is necessary. The inequalities that are important are not differences in work time but differences in spending power. This is congruent with the ideology of social class in the United States, how people think about inequalities. Despite their egalitarianism, Americans at all levels accept the principle of a hierarchy of consumption. This is in keeping with their belief in the differential worth of occupations and the legitimacy of a hierarchy of income and wealth. Americans do not get upset over large inequalities in income and living standards, because they believe these inequalities have been produced by individual effort; and they do not regard these advantages as necessarily permanent for any one individual. Americans thus place liberty and equality into different compartments. So long as the economic system continues to expand so that even those who compare unfavorably with others can hope to better themselves, the demand for egalitarianism remains confined to the political sphere. In the economic sphere, liberty is exalted, the freedom to produce and consume. The consensus that productivity gains should be traded for spending money is consonant with this view.

American working-class organizations have done little to disturb this consensus. Instead, they have given priority to gaining more spending power and job security for their members. The struggle for more time to play has been subverted by the desire to obtain more purchasing power, greater liberties in the market. There is no meaning in the United States to the phrase "sport for all" outside of what this would mean in terms of the marketplace, that is, sport for all who can afford it. The class politics of sport has thus become refined into a marketplace issue.

Amateurs and Professionals

So far I have dealt with the *opportunity* of classes to participate in sport. Now I shall deal with the equally important struggle over the *meaning* of sport participation. Sport encodes class distinctions, objectifying cultural differences between different strata. The politics of sport must settle whose meanings sport will carry. In recent history, the most important issue with respect to the proper meaning of sport has been the validity of the distinction between amateur and professional. Amateurism was a middle-class movement tying sport identities to occupation and "character." Never particularly strong in the United States, it eventually crumbled; but its demise was not due to a desire to free sport identities from ascriptive ties and open up decision making. In other words, it was not brought about by a political movement to "free" sport for more popular control. Instead, the forces undermining amateurism were those of the marketplace. These forces offered individual liberties to compete and consume "amateur" sports, such as intercollegiate athletics and the Olympics. But these freedoms were often purchased at the expense of more democratic control over sport institutions, which remained under the control of elites (Sage 1990, 40).

The distinction between amateur and professional is a coded class distinction. Amateurism exalts the ideal of sport as an "avocation" and denigrates the play of a person who does it for pay. This makes it easier or more fitting for the rich than the poor to pursue the sports ideal. Reiger describes how, during the second half of the nineteenth century, hunting and fishing took on the attributes of sports by carefully distinguishing themselves from the kind of hunting and fishing carried on for a living. To be fully accepted as a sportsman, an individual "had to have a knowledge of the quarry and its habitat; a familiarity with the rods, guns, or dogs necessary for its pursuit; a skill to cast or shoot with precision, and coolness that often takes years to acquire; and most of all, a 'social sense of the do's and don'ts' involved" (1986, 26). Magazines written by and for hunters and fishermen applauded the "love of fair play" of the genuine sportsman, who, for instance, would refuse to take advantage of his prey by setting bait. This "irrational" conduct was explicitly set off from the more expedient behavior of the professional trapper and hunter. The vocation was carefully subordinated in this scheme to the avocation.

Well into the twentieth century, many sporting activities were forbidden to those deemed "professional."[16] An early English definition of amateurism is to be found in the declaration of the Metropolitan (later, Amateur) Rowing Association which, besides barring those who competed in rowing for a livelihood, also more sweepingly excluded any athlete who "is or ever has been by trade or employment for wages, a mechanic, artisan, or laborer or engaged in any menial duty."[17] The distinction was social, rather than economic: "The contradistinction to professional was gentleman" (Vamplew 1988, 183), the latter being the name given to amateurs in cricket. It also suggested that an "amateur" approach to sport, being "unserious," was the most appropriate, an attitude well suited to the public school ethos of stoical tolerance of suffering, keeping a stiff upper lip: "the game's the thing." This idea that how things are done is more important than what is done was appropriate for a leisured aristocracy (or would-be aristocracy) in a stable social order.

This distinction did not exclude nonamateurs from play, but it established a very clear hierarchy of types of engagement in sport. Professionals who did play in open competition were under the orders of their social superiors. Furthermore, it helped establish a prestige ranking of sports, so that even certain kinds of "amateurs" could appear less eligible. Thus, amateur softball would be less prestigious than amateur polo, because the latter requires more conspicuous waste to sustain than the former.

The distinction between amateur and professional must therefore be recognized for what it is, a means for the middle class to limit competition on the playing field from working-class athletes. The middle-class Victorians wanted to bestow upon sports some appearance of utility but were reluctant to accept the idea that seemed to follow from this view, that rewards would be distributed strictly according to merit. This would truly level the playing field. Accordingly, to the connotations of utility are added the connotations of status.

In the United States, amateur sports emerged after the Civil War as clubs were formed by communities, workplaces, churches, and schools to help organize people's play. It is tempting to see the roots of amateurism in the many baseball and cricket clubs that were a part of nearly every village and hamlet by this time and to see professionalism as a modern perversion of the earlier form. Thus, Betts writes that the "era from 1860 to 1890 was, in many ways, the age of the athletic club" (1974, 98). He believes that Saturday afternoon was assigned to ball playing by the time that professionalism entered the scene in the form of the Cincinnati Red Stockings tour of 1869. Freeman (1987, 118), likewise, traces the spread of amateur sports to colleges and schools, which, in turn, had learned their sporting culture from English elite educational institutions. But this is something of a middle-class rewrite of sports history. Baseball was never "pure" in the sense that players considered the means more important than the ends or disdained economic rewards. The idea of pure play seemed to grow in proportion to the strength of its opposite—play taken seriously enough to demand practice and discipline: "Only when professional baseball seemed to have reached a truly dominant position in the baseball world did the concept of pure sport and recreation receive formulation and attract champions" (Goldstein 1989, 122).

It is more accurate to see amateurism and professionalism as emerging simultaneously as the commercialization of sport and its democratization coincided. Commercialism increased the importance of winning and thus the temptation to hire professionals to do the job. On the other hand, professionals, because they were paid to win, could not be wholly trusted to "play fair." Commercialism increased the quality and expertise of the athlete; but professionals had also turned play into work, consumption into production. Commercialism allocated the choicest prizes to the best athletes, but professionalism tended to exclude the average player and transform him into a spectator. The increasingly strident calls to clarify and strengthen amateurism rules were usually justified in the name of making access to sports open to all, rather than to "journeymen" who would dominate the competition. Commercialism helped sports to become a mass consumption item but also threatened the distinctiveness of individual sports, their ability to function as a mark of status.

As in England, amateur sports were considered the pursuit of the gentleman; and as in England, voluntary organizations were formed to protect the ideal. The most prominent of these was the New York Athletic Club, patterned after the Amateur Athletic Club and London Athletic Club of England. It helped found the Amateur Athletic Union (AAU) in 1888. By 1889, the AAU "had gained control of amateur athletics," claiming jurisdiction over twenty-three sports (Flath 1964, 16). It was to stand for the amateur tradition in the United States for nearly one hundred years. It adhered doggedly to the ideal that sports should be pursued for their own sake, rather than for monetary gain or extrinsic reward, vigorously rejected the notion that sport should be harnessed to pedagogical goals or become subordinated to the demands of the academic curriculum, and clung to the voluntaristic principle by which participation in, and particularly the organizing and financing of, sport should be entirely voluntary and not-for-profit. Finally, it contained an implicit political message, all the more powerful in denying political motivation. The amateurists were "propelled by a vision of a genteel, harmonious world of sport, in which all classes and all ages and both sexes came together in healthful recreation under the governance of mainly middle and upper class men" (Goldstein 1989, 125).[18]

The distinction between professional and amateur proved to be less tenable in the United States than it had been in England. One reason was the greater permeability of social boundaries in the United States, which made all status markers less durable. In nineteenth-century England, with its more rigid class structure, boundaries between classes were crossed with the greatest difficulty: when soccer began to attract a working-class following, the public schools switched to rugby; when rugby began to attract a working-class following and the Rugby League was formed, the middle class created the amateur Rugby Union. In the United States, class sensitivities were not as keen, and there was less hostility to the idea of sharing a sport. Sports could transcend class boundaries.

Amateurism also had to struggle against the belief held by many Americans in freedom of opportunity. This legitimated all kinds of careerism, including the pursuit of professional advancement in entertainment and sports. And amateurism was not helped by the fact that Americans did not share the horror of making money exhibited by the elite groups in England from whom amateurist ideals sprang. Americans proved to be somewhat more tolerant of the professional athlete, who had made it to the top and should be paid what he deserved.

Perhaps the most important reason why amateurism did not play quite the same exclusionary role in the United States as in England is that youth sports were absorbed into schools and colleges on a scale unknown in Europe. Ironically, these schools and colleges were the original importers of the amateur ideal: only the elite attended college in the nineteenth century; and their education was modeled after the Oxbridge system, with its tradition of amateur sports. When the AAU began to claim jurisdiction over all amateur sports in the 1880s, the claim was immediately challenged by sport organizations already in place. The Ivy League colleges had already formed an Intercollegiate Amateur

Athletic Association in 1875, and there were a number of smaller athletic conferences also in existence when the AAU was formed. The AAU was able to offer only brief resistance to the counterclaims of athletic conferences, the latter soon securing control over the revenue-producing sport of football. By 1899, the AAU had also abandoned its claim to jurisdiction over soccer, baseball, and rowing.

The dual development within amateur sports of a club tradition and a college tradition meant that the line drawn between amateur and professional could not perform quite the same political function it had in England, especially as enrollment at secondary schools and colleges increased. The colleges assumed some of the responsibility for espousing the amateur ideal and, in many sports, were to become the dominant organizations. "The contradictory process of convincing utilitarian Americans to stress 'true amateurism' over personal gain was driven by the growth in commercial athletics and 'service station' universities on the one hand and pressure from athlete–reformers within an educational framework on the other" (Baxter and Lambert 1990, 412). But the colleges imposed upon amateurism their own particular interpretation, quite unlike that found in the club tradition in the United States or amateur sports in England. Under the cloak of furnishing wholesome, amateur sports within an educational setting, the colleges actually provided a quasi-professional sport for young adults. Indeed, Ronald Smith contends that college sports were never "purely amateur" (1988, 167). As early as the 1870s, college teams were competing against each other for both cash and noncash (but valuable) prizes, competing against professionals, charging money at the gate, providing food and board in return for play, subsidizing extra tutoring for athletes, spending heavily on recruitment and support of athletes, and hiring professional coaches. Yet because they tied sports to college attendance, they could use the expansion of higher education as a basis for the argument that their version of amateurism was more democratic and open than were the private, voluntary efforts of club sports. They could criticize the AAU for its snobbery and elitism, using their version of amateurism as a political tool against the version imported by the AAU from England. One did not have to join a club or be a gentleman to participate in sport. One merely had to be a student in good academic standing: "The myth of amateurism was adjusted to reflect the growth of the utilitarian 'service station' university that more directly serves social placement and training functions" (Baxter and Lambert 1990, 414).

All the while, college sports were becoming more commercialized. As more full-time coaches were hired, competition became ever more fierce, and recruiting and keeping athletes scholastically eligible became a full-time job. The net result of eligibility fights was to place tighter constraints on the athlete's role. The number of sports he could participate in was limited, as was the length of his playing career. Even his summer months were strictly supervised. For example, moves in the

1880s and 1890s to get rid of unfair competition from teams using graduate students meant limiting the number of years a college student could participate in intercollegiate athletics. Graduate students were effectively barred after 1905, as were freshmen, transfer ("tramp athletes"), and part-time students. Academic criteria ("the bona fide student") were used not to ensure that sport was played in the right spirit but to ensure fair competition between college athletic programs. By the 1920s, student athletes were not even free to quit "amateur" sports and turn professional, because of the collusion between the colleges and the professional leagues not to draft college players (R. Smith 1988, 211). The concept of the amateur came to have increasingly negative meanings (an amateur being someone who is not a professional) and thus simply a criterion of eligibility used to promote equality of competition among colleges. No longer was amateurism associated with participatory democracy, intrinsic gratification, and the sheer joy of play.

As the revenues accruing to college athletic programs rose and competition for athletes grew after World War II, it became even more difficult to defend the principle of amateurism. The author of a special report commissioned in the 1960s by the American Council on Education asked, "What else but a payment for services rendered is a grant-in-aid awarded [to a student–athlete] without reference to need?" (Hanford 1974, 25). To call these players "amateur," he complained, is simply to condone the use of hired labor from working-class backgrounds to masquerade as middle-class amateurs to make college sports programs more competitive. This report shifted the terms of the debate from the issue of whether a student-athlete was an amateur in the sense intended by the Olympic movement to the issue of whether the athletic dimension had overwhelmed and perverted the student dimension. In other words, the American Council on Education was less interested in what was happening to sports and who was eligible to participate in them than in what was happening to education and who was eligible to receive it.

The problem of controlling professionalism grew worse as the television networks began to appreciate the profits to be made from televising college sports. Television deepened the divide between the "big-time" colleges with programs attractive to networks and the "small-time" college athletic programs that no advertiser was interested in. In 1973, the colleges created a Division III, because there were those who thought it was important to maintain a truly amateur division, one in which the participants play for the sheer sport of it and not because they are being paid in the form of a scholarship. Again, however, the danger posed by television money was considered from the point of view of its threat to education, rather than its threat to sport. Television revenues would deflect student–athletes' attention away from the classroom.

By this time, the amateur ideal was rarely defended in its own right but simply as one means of maintaining a balance between academics and sports. The integrity of higher education, not the integrity of sports, had become the issue. This is clearly reflected in the congressional debates on college sports between 1960 and 1980. By the end of that period, many legislators seemed to have despaired of preserving the amateur ideal and attempted to shift student athletes more clearly into the ranks of the professional.[19]

Other legislators tackled the amateurism issue by concentrating on restoring some of the emphasis on college work in the athletic programs. In 1985, and again in 1986, Congressman James Howard (NJ) sponsored the College Athletic Education and Protection Act. The legislation would have required that 75 percent of student–athletes with athletic scholarships must graduate within five years. Failure to meet this goal would result in the removal of the tax deduction status for contributions to the athletic department. Howard explained:

> Colleges and universities must make a stronger commitment to educating their athletes. But these institutions have not sufficiently accepted this responsibility; therefore, pressure needs to be applied from outside sources. The federal government is one potential source of pressure.
>
> It is not hard to find a link between the federal government and intercollegiate athletics. Collegiate athletic departments are funded, in part, through the tax deductible contributions of individuals to alumni-type organizations. These contributions are tax deductible because they supposedly "advance education." It seems fairly obvious, then, that a school receiving a tax break for "advancing education" should advance education. (1987, 206)

In 1988, one senator (Bradley) and two congressmen (McMillen and Towns) introduced a bill (known as the Student-Right-To-Know and Campus Security Act) to compel colleges and universities to release graduation rates of all students, including athletes, broken down by race and sport. The National Collegiate Athletic Association (NCAA) condemned the bills as unwarranted governmental intrusion in college and university affairs. In 1990, the House Subcommittee on Post-Secondary Education consolidated several bills into one "right-to-know" measure that would require colleges to publish annually the graduation rates of athletes. Campuses would lose their eligibility for student federal aid if they did not comply. Proponents framed the bill in the context of "consumer protection" and sent the bill to the House Education and Labor Committee. The Student Right-To-Know Act was passed in 1990. Together with some house-cleaning measures instituted by the NCAA itself and pressure from a privately funded investigative commission (the Knight Commission), the Act promised to prevent future gross abuses of the academic programs of NCAA institutions by requiring stricter academic eligibility requirements. Expenditures were also cut or curtailed, but the purpose was less to return to a spirit of amateurism than to limit the excesses to which competition for championships and "media exposure" could lead.

The widespread skepticism about the meaning of the category "amateur" expressed in these congressional debates (in which congressmen seemed willing to concede that college athletes were, to all intents and purposes, paid for their services but were being exploited and deprived of their education in the process) no doubt derived some of its force from events occurring in international athletics, where the amateurism principle had been refined beyond all recognition. In 1974, the International Olympic Committee changed eligibility rules to permit lost-time income compensation for athletes. In 1982, the rules were changed again to permit athletes to contribute to, and eventually draw upon, "trust funds." In 1985, the rules were changed once more to permit each individual international sports federation to decide upon its own eligibility rules, most of which adopted more relaxed criteria.

By 1990, international sporting federations had acquired considerable power to redefine, or even abolish, the line between amateur and professional. On the one hand, this made it easier for defenders of the NCAA to claim legitimacy for the athletic scholarship as no violation of the amateurism principle. On the other hand, it further exposed the NCAA and its member institutions to the charge of simply acting as quasi-professional sports franchises on college campuses and thus perverting the goals of higher education. The net effect was to negate the once-powerful principle of amateurism as a class-linked measure of eligibility for sport participation. The colleges had indeed democratized sport participation and had indeed abolished the English-based distinction between the gentleman-amateur and the artisan-professional. But they had done so on their own terms. They had made sporting opportunities available to the sons, and eventually the daughters, of parents from all walks of life. These opportunities were available, however, only to those willing to attend college and only so long as they attended college. And they were available only to the best of athletes and only so long as those athletes continued to aspire to be among the best. The sports funded were also restricted to those "appropriate" for a college campus and those that would attract spectators. Ironically, the amateurism principle had been put to the service of defending a program of athletics professional in all but name, permitting participation only by elite athletes and relegating the rest of the student body to the status of spectators. It had furthermore concentrated athletic resources on college campuses, making them available not to the members of the community of all ages but to young adults who happened to be enrolled in colleges.

The line drawn between amateur and professional had not lost all its meaning by the 1990s. Some semblance remained of the association between amateurism and elite sports. More significant, amateurism symbolized the purity of play, enabling people to believe that it had not become totally subordinated to extrinsic considerations. While the existence of professionalism, whether explicit or disguised, was freely acknowleged, paying customers still wished to believe they were purchasing "pure play," hence the enormous popularity of college sports, inferior in quality to their explicitly professional counterparts. The distinction between amateur and professional had thus lost some of its old association with production relations; it no longer marked the difference between the artisan and the gentleman. But the distinction had not lost all meaning; for it had now become part of a package, "administered hustle," to distinguish one form of sport consumption from another, much as one brand might be distinguished from another. The most sacrosanct of the sumptuary norms of sport had thus lost much of its force.[20]

CONCLUSION

The exploits of modern athletes seem to epitomize contemporary individualism. The playing field vividly and dramatically reveals the truth that human beings are autonomous subjects, ultimately responsible for their own successes and failures. Even team games are framed as contests between individuals. The individual is thus not hard to find in the world of sport—all the more reason not to take this individuality for granted and to remember that modernity does not stifle individuality but nurtures it. How has the twentieth century helped form the modern athlete and to what degree has politics played a part?

Modern society has produced an athlete who is almost certainly male or expected to behave much like a male. Having been for many years almost certainly white (black athletes were invisible outside their community), he is now more likely than not to be black, especially if he plays for pay. If he is a professional athlete, he is likely to come from a working-class background (Riess 1991); but if he is a spectator, he is likely to be middle-class (Okner 1974, 345; Yergin 1986). All of this will depend to some extent on the sport in question, for there are differences in the demands of time and money that sports make on the athlete and spectator. Sports still function as a mark of status; it is no accident that American universities build squash courts, rather than indoor bowling alleys.

Over the course of the last forty years, while patterns of ownership and control have not significantly altered, sports have become slightly more female, less predominantly white, and less middle-class in terms of background and "style." The rules of eligibility have been stripped of some of their more irrational stipulations. What role, if any, has politics at any level played in this transformation? I have shown that many formerly taken-for-granted ideas about fitness for sport have been undermined during the last half-century. The level of correspondence between gender, race, and class categories on the one hand, and performance of the sport role on the other has declined. No doubt some of this decline has been due to political pressure to expand opportunities for sport participation to all. Eligibility should be based on desire and ability, rather than social position. However, I have also shown how weak has been the political pressure on the sport world to democratize participation.

There are two reasons for this weakness. The first reason is the politics of the domestic sphere. This remains a powerful influence on how sport identities are defined. Its effect on how gender is defined in sport is most marked. For women, the personal remains political; and no amount of formal rationalization at the institutional level, such as distributing college athletic scholarships regardless of gender, will alter how boys and girls are socialized to think of their bodies. The few advances women have made as the result of political action entailed considerable costs. The first was the collapse of an autonomous women's sport organization. Separate-but-equal is difficult to defend when the policy being pursued is equality of opportunity for all. The second was the price paid for using the leverage of educational policy. Women, in placing so much emphasis on Title IX, were at the same time subscribing to—placing their seal of approval on—an increasingly professional world of college athletics, thus losing any sense that women's sports were different from men's. Third, the path of litigation proved to be time-consuming and expensive, as well as fragmentary. It had the effect of individualizing each issue and confirming the view that sport problems were matters for private settlement between aggrieved parties.

The second reason for the weakness of political pressure is the countervailing power of the marketplace. Rationalization proceeds at a pace congenial to corporate profit making. Sport identities are becoming more universal and thus somewhat more egalitarian and democratic but remain within the limitations imposed by the needs of capital accumulation. The major driving force behind the breakdown of racial barriers in sport was not political pressure but competition for athletic labor among employers. Women athletes have not achieved the same level of "modernity" simply because a market does not exist for their services. The market does not create barriers to participation; but it does have the ability to raise or lower them, or redefine them. Thus, market forces have now created an overrepresentation of blacks in some sports, leading some white youths to conclude that they do not belong. This is a problem that does not seem to have a market solution, because it reflects the denial of opportunities for blacks in the occupational structure and their gravitation toward the few well-paying occupations in which they seem to be welcome.

Class plays only a limited role in defining sport identities and opportunities in the United States, with the clear exception of the opportunity to own or manage sport enterprises. The fight for free time was concluded in the 1940s; and workers have subsequently settled for higher pay, rather than less work, if productivity permits. It might be said that the market was more powerful than the state in deciding this issue as workers expressed their preference for more goods over free time by the choices they made at the bargaining table. The nineteenth-century barriers between amateur and professional have largely broken down. This has rarely surfaced as a political issue, because sport authorities have fought successfully to contain the debate within the private sphere. To the extent that amateurism has lost some of its ability to mark status differences, this has been due as much to the pressure of market forces (principally on colleges and the Olympic movement) as to a desire to democratize participation. There has, however, been one reason for the erosion of the amateur–professional distinction that is political. Since the 1950s, the United States has become increasingly anxious about its ability to compete in the international sporting order against state-subsidized amateurs from other countries. Although the commercialization of international athletics has also contributed to the disappearance of amateurism, the role of foreign policy cannot be ignored. This subject will be taken up in chapter 11.

CHAPTER 3

FROM
PEONS TO
PROFESSIONALS

The politics of sport begin with a definition of citizenship. Who is entitled to sport? Sport politics maps the social terrain on which play shall take place. It establishes rules defining proper performance of the sport role and punishes deviation from it. As I have shown, much of this mapping and policing takes place informally, in the private sphere: it is "natural" that men are more interested in sports than women; it is "obvious" that whites make better coaches than blacks; it goes without saying that amateurs are more "genuine" than professionals. At this level, the institutionalization of play is so subtle that people find it difficult to accept the view that the sport role has to be learned. But learn it they must, for the values and norms associated with sport are as important as the technical skills necessary to play. Learning the sport role means accepting the conventional wisdom about who belongs in sport and how they should behave, who should give the orders and what happens to people who disobey. Those who do not qualify for inclusion must learn what disbars them and how to regard those lucky enough to be admitted.

Chapter 2 described how popular assumptions about physical achievement combined with social norms as to the relative status of different categories of people to describe the ideal sport citizen. This individual is no stranger to privilege: the white gentleman represents the ideal in this, as in so many other spheres of life. In this chapter, the focus of attention is on the politics of sport organizations. Here, the issue of eligibility is more tangible. It is a question not of whether one is permitted to think of oneself as interested in, knowledgeable about, or proficient at sport but whether one is qualified to perform a specific function within sport organizations. The politics here are the politics of allocation. If chapter 2 described who is available to play, chapter 3 will describe where, when, and for whom they can play. How and by what criteria are specific sport positions defined? By what processes are those positions allocated?

It is inevitable that a study of sport, politics, and society will eventually turn to the question of the allocation of positions in organizations. Sport means regulation, control, selection. Eligibility to play is one means of guaranteeing an even match between individuals and teams. It is also one way of maintaining discipline once individuals are admitted, for eligibility can always be withdrawn. In amateur sports, eligibility has to do with the line drawn between amateur and professional, which is essentially a matter of status. In professional sports, eligibility is usually a more contractual matter: sport performance is undertaken for pay, and a contract is implied in which performance is expected in return for rewards. There are reciprocal obligations involved. Athletes undertake to provide their labor power in return for a financial consideration.

The question to be addressed in this chapter concerns the status of the individual athlete in sport organizations and, in particular, conflict over the individual athlete's freedom to participate, to choose for whom he or she should play (or work). As in the previous chapter, the scope of the analysis is quite limited. The social construction of athletic statuses and athletes' rights and responsibilities within sport organizations is commonly considered a private matter. Occasionally, however, these matters become the subject of intense policy debate, as private conflicts over the status of the athlete spill over onto the public stage. I shall explain why and describe some of the consequences.

ELIGIBILITY

Rules of eligibility are the gateway to sport opportunities. They are typically devised to equalize competition—hence weight classes in boxing, gender and age proscriptions in many sports, and performance minima in sports like golf and tennis. As such, they can be considered an integral part of the game; they help make the game exciting and meaningful. But rules of eligibility can also serve other purposes. Most strikingly, they can be used to minimize transaction costs for would-be employers. Limiting the size of the pool of new talent by an eligibility rule (e.g., by declaring people under a certain age to be ineligible) lowers the cost of competition for that new talent. Such rules can also be used to limit competition for athletic talent between two competing industries by allocating players among them by some artificial criterion. In either case, issues of public policy are raised. In the first, individuals are denied the opportunity to pursue their livelihood; and in the second, "firms" are colluding to depress the price they pay for their "work force."

All four major team sports in the United States have rules of eligibility; and in each case, these rules have become the subject of political action. Because it has largely internalized its method of nurturing talent in the minor league (and farm) system, baseball has the least restrictive eligibility rules. Baseball declares that a player becomes eligible for the draft only after his senior year in high school, after junior or senior year in college, or after his twenty-first birthday. When professional football began, it lacked a minor league system from which to draw talent. The obvious source of recruits was the ranks of college players. To prevent interteam competition for rookies, the National Football League was quick to declare underclassmen off-limits to recruiters. The colleges welcomed this 1926 agreement for their own reasons. When Alonzo Stagg declared professional football a "menace," he clothed his criticism in a defense of the ideals of amateurism; but few missed the point that he also regarded professional football as strong competition for college football, particularly when it came to players. Whenever the no-tampering rule became a subject of political debate—which it did with increasing frequency in the 1980s—NFL Commissioner Rozelle liked to remind congressmen that the rule was instigated at the behest of the colleges (U.S. Congress, Senate Committee on the Judiciary 1983, 130). George Halas, one of the founders of the NFL, was later to explain that professional football copied its ideas about player eligibility and the reserve system from the NCAA (U.S. Congress, House Committee on the Judiciary 1957, 2715).

Under the no-tampering rule, NFL club owners agreed not to "raid" colleges for underclassmen, at least not until their eligibility as defined by the NCAA had expired. No mention was made of the athletes' actually graduating. Athletes were thus confined to amateur status until the NCAA and the professional leagues declared them fit to turn professional. The owners argued that a no-tampering rule was necessary to protect the academic integrity of college athletics; but the rule was oriented more toward the notion of eligibility to play than to graduation, and ulterior purposes were being served by the rule. The refusal to admit players who had not used up their eligibility or whose classes had not yet graduated gave the owners ample time to amass information on new talent. And it conveniently eliminated competition between professional and college teams for playing talent.

The Decline of the No-Tampering Rule

The NCAA lobby in Congress was for many years powerful enough to sustain a high level of concern about "raiding" by the professional leagues. The colleges were safe as long as there was only one league in a sport and that league could police its members to make sure they obeyed the no-tampering rule. However, during interleague rivalry, competition for star players heated up. The upstart league would be especially desirous of adding star players to its roster in order to acquire instant credibility.[1] One of the most famous cases involved a University of Georgia player, Herschel Walker, who became the focus of controversy when he signed with the United States Football League (USFL) franchise, the New Jersey Generals. The United States Football League was founded in 1983 as a rival to the established National Football League. The USFL struggled from the outset and was desperate to sign a big name. Walker had won the Heisman Trophy in his junior year at Georgia and had already broken numerous NCAA records. He decided to forego his senior year and turn professional. With some irony, the USFL justified signing Walker on the grounds that to honor the no-tampering rule would be a violation of antitrust law. Interleague competition thus caused a professional league to pay ostentatious obeisance to the very legislation owners usually sought to ignore.

The signing of Walker was highly controversial, because it threatened to reduce even further the low graduation rates of college athletes, who would now be tempted to consider the professional option *throughout* their college careers, rather than after they had graduated. The NFL defended delaying eligibility on the grounds of protecting the students' academic interests, as did the college coaches. Both, of course, also benefited from the arrangement whereby college coaches did need not to worry about having their best players poached. Owners did not have to worry about other owners stealing a march on them by snatching sophomores and juniors out of college. Even the USFL owners would have preferred a no-tampering rule, and Walker's signing was actually a violation of an agreement among owners in the new league to respect the NFL rule. This prompted Bob Boris, a former punter at the University of Arizona (who sought, unsuccessfully, to play in the USFL before his class graduated), to sue the USFL, charging that its no-tampering rule was a violation of the Sherman Act. In 1984, the U.S. District Court agreed (Staudohar 1986, 80).

By this time, the raiding of college ranks had generated so much anxiety within college circles that Senator Arlen Spector was prompted to sponsor a bill that would have provided antitrust immunity to any professional sport league entering into an agreement designed to encourage college students to complete their undergraduate education before becoming professional athletes. As Spector noted, "There is substantial public interest in promoting policies which encourage student athletes to finish college and obtain an education" (U.S. Congress, Senate, Committee on the Judiciary 1983b, 122). His policy preference was thus to make it easier for the student-athlete's amateur status to be protected. Opponents of the bill saw it as a dangerous infringement on the rights of student-athletes to make choices about their careers. Ed Garvey, executive director of the National Football League Players' Association, reiterated his opposition to any legislation that would immunize professional sports from antitrust law. It was his opinion that the student-athlete was not an amateur at all, but a professional: "I think it is time that we just admitted the fact that he is a professional, but others who have their own interests at stake define him as an amateur" (p. 31).

Spector's effort to shore up the no-tampering rule was triggered by the Walker case; but in truth, the most serious problem at this time lay in basketball. While owners of professional football clubs were dubious about wisdom of signing underclassmen on grounds that they were not "ready," owners of professional basketball franchises had no such doubts. In any given year, there were several underclassmen they were anxious to sign. The NBA had modeled its eligibility requirements on those of football, and the no-tampering rule went unchallenged until 1971. Once again, interleague rivalry was a catalyst for change. The dispute had begun in the American Basketball Association, a rival league to the NBA and one in which enforcement of the eligibity rule was lax. Spencer Haywood had signed with the Denver Rockets of the ABA less than four years after his high school class had graduated. He later signed a contract with the NBA franchise in Seattle, the Supersonics, and the NBA commissioner voided the contract on the grounds that it violated the NBA rule against signing underclassmen. The court ruled that the NBA did not provide "procedural safeguards" for an individual to contest his exclusion under the rule and decided in favor of Haywood. While not a direct invalidation of the no-tampering rule, the NBA altered it to permit the signing of underclassmen where "hardship" could be proven. Establishing hardship proved to be easy for the college basketball players attractive to the professional leagues, most of whom came from impoverished backgrounds. Eventually, the hardship provision was dropped, and the no-tampering rule effectively abolished.

Football's no-tampering rule would eventually share the fate of basketball's. It began to crumble in 1986, when the NCAA ruled Ohio State wide receiver Chris Carter and University of Pittsburgh running back Charles Gladman ineligible to continue playing college football. As underclassmen, neither met the NFL eligibility requirements; but the owners relented and held a special supplemental draft for the two in the summer of 1987. In 1988, running back Craig Heyward, a junior at the University of Pittsburgh, intentionally ended his eligibility by hiring an agent, in violation of NCAA rules. He threatened to sue the league if he was not cleared for inclusion in the draft. Heyward's lawyers argued that football players deserved the same freedom as basketball players, plumbers, and sportswriters to enter their chosen profession. The league relented, and a "special entry draft" became standard in the league. In 1990, the NFL, after a period of having to tolerate underclassmen because it did not want to test its policy in court, officially announced that college underclassmen would be admitted to the draft to be held each spring. Those applying would irrevocably lose their college eligibility. In 1992, thirty-four college juniors left school early to join the spring draft.

In gradually relaxing the no-tampering rule and permitting more freedom of movement out of college into the professional ranks, the owners were not only bowing to pressure in favor of giving more freedom of choice of employment but also tacitly acknowledging the professionalization of college athletics. It is the latter, as much as any broader shifts in political opinion with respect to the eligibility rule, that accounts for the collapse of the no-tampering rule. By the 1970s, the anomaly of the "amateur" college athlete had become so glaring that serious consideration was given to treating the scholarship athlete as a hired worker. This made some sense. Scholarships were awarded for a period of one year. Injury might mean that a scholarship was not renewed. On at least one occasion, state laws providing compensation for employees who suffer personal injuries as a result of accidents arising out of, or in the course of, employment were applied to student-athletes. In *Rensing* v. *Indiana State University* (1982), the State Court of Appeals decided that Rensing, rendered a quadriplegic in spring football practice, was an employee. The Indiana Supreme Court reversed on the grounds that Rensing was not actually paid to play and could not be discharged (Atkinson 1984). The justices declared that "an athlete receiving financial aid is still first and foremost a student" (Rafferty 1983, 101). Scholarships that take the form, if only in part, of tuition payments could not be seen as wages. Furthermore, those student-athletes who took part-time jobs could only claim compensation for injuries received while working at those jobs.

In many ways, the lower court's ruling was the more realistic of the two in the Rensing case. At least, the lower court faced up to the fact that most of the "jobs" athletes were given (e.g., irrigating playing fields) were given them only because they were athletes. In return for playing, the student-athlete got a sinecure. Nor was the state supreme court's argument that tuition payments are not wages convincing. There can be no question that scholarships to athletes are a form of compensation. Admittedly, the award may not be adjusted during the award period because of declining ability or injury, but those reasons are valid for not *renewing* a scholarship. In addition, a scholarship can be taken away if the recipient is declared ineligible for athletic competition, engages in fraud or serious misconduct, or withdraws from sport for personal reasons (Shulman 1985, 714).

Legal interpretations of the status of the student-athlete, then, had moved the college athlete much closer to the ranks of the professional and thus closer to being free to move out of the "amateur" ranks into the "professional." In both football and basketball, the claim that college sports were different (a claim based on substantive rationality) had been largely discredited by the increasing commercialism of the college game, replaced by an understanding that there was little real difference between the two forms (an acknowledgment of formal rationality). The two forms thus merged into a single market, and rules to prevent individuals from participating equally in that market became anachronistic.[2]

A further reason for the decline of the no-tampering rule—but one that also gained impetus from the fact that college and professional sports were becoming formally alike—was the advent of player's agents. While over 90 percent of professional athletes in team sports now use an agent, this practice was almost unknown before the late 1960s. Free agency and, above all, rivalry between leagues for college playing talent increased the incentive to search out professional prospects aggressively, especially among underclassmen. It is now believed that the widespread use of agents to find underclass talent began during the war between the ABA and NBA (Crandall 1981, 826). Alarmed at these developments, the NCAA adopted the position that in the event a college student signed a contract with a professional sport team *or* a sport agent, he would forfeit his amateur status, scholarship benefits, and college eligibility. Under challenge, the NCAA's attempt to limit student's access to agents was upheld in court, the judge agreeing that the revocation of a student's amateur status for signing a contract was "rationally related to the goal of preserving amateurism in intercollegiate athletics" (ibid.).

The NCAA's power over students did not extend to their agents, however, who initially scoffed at the organization's efforts to restrict their contacts with prospective clients. Thus, in 1979, players' agent Mike Trope declared: "The rules are ridiculous and they're not being followed by anybody. . . . Why should I honor the NCAA rules when I'm not even bound by them? And I don't intend to honor them, not ever, unless Congress says all the rules of the NCAA are the laws of the United States and you can go to prison for ten years if you break them"(Sullivan 1984, 55). Trope was not a member of the Association of Representatives of Professional Athletes, founded the year before to encourage more ethical conduct by agents. His attitude indicated that such voluntary efforts at self-regulation would have little impact.

Public Regulation of Players' Agents

Some states became so concerned with the threat agents posed to the integrity of college athletics that they decided to regulate them by statute. The California Athletes Agents Act of 1981 added a new section to the state's labor code providing that "no person shall engage in or carry on the occupation of an athletic agency without first registering with the Labor Commissioner," to whom he would have to provide proof of "good moral character." By 1989, nineteen other states had enacted legislation to regulate the activities of sport agents (Shropshire 1990, 43). But the licensing procedure was considered largely ineffective because of poor screening. In any case, lawyers (who made up the bulk of players' agents) were exempted from regulation. Much of this legislation seemed to be geared to protecting the college game more than the individual athlete: "Many state legislators support what many consider to be outdated concepts of amateurism and the college athlete" (p. 32). For example, the Texas and Oklahoma laws simply gave statutory powers to the existing NCAA rules, declaring a student ineligible as soon as he or she agreed to be represented by an agent. Legislators ignored the fact that there was nothing inherently unethical about an athlete's retaining an agent while still participating in college sports. Indeed, it might be beneficial to his studies. Furthermore, the NCAA rule has no counterpart elsewhere: it does not apply to drama students (who might be similarly endangered), only to football players. The principal purpose of the statutes was to protect the college game from being raided by agents waving attractive contracts.

The owners of professional sports teams have displayed little interest in regulating agents. The players' unions, on the other hand, have been more sympathetic, not because they wish to preserve the no-tampering rule but because they believe that many players, not just rookies, are being victimized by unscrupulous agents charging exorbitant fees and mismanaging a player's financial affairs. Agents representing several players might be guilty of a conflict of interest if more than one client was seeking employment with the same club. Some union officials regard agents as parasites, especially those who charge a percentage of the player's salary as commission. They point out that any such percentage is likely to be excessive if it is based on the full amount earned by the player (including the minimum salary collectively bargained for by the union), rather than simply on the amount by which the player's salary exceeds the minimum, because every NFL player should be paid the collectively bargained-for minimum, whether he has an agent or not.

When the players first began to consider certification of agents, precedent existed, for Actors' Equity had been regulating agents for over fifty years (and many of those offering their services as player's agents were also agents for actors). In a collective bargaining agreement signed in 1982, the National Football League Players' Association agreed to "certify" agents and to help formalize a fee schedule for agents. Ironically, this arrangement did not cover agents negotiating on behalf of rookies, the very players most in need of protection. It was finally extended to them in 1989. In 1986, the National Baseball Players' Association and the National Basketball Association Players' Association set up their own certification procedures, both of which covered rookies.

The force of union certification depends on the strength of the union at the time, since members are required to deal only with certified agents. When unions weaken, as they did in the late 1980s, the certification program loses force. In 1985, the Sports Lawyers' Association, anxious to limit competition for business, lobbied unsuccessfully for a Federal Professional Sports Agency bill, which would have centralized the regulation of athletes' agents and created a uniform body of rules governing the activities of agents under the jurisdiction of the U.S. Secretary of Commerce.

Sports agents, who function as a conduit between amateur and professional ranks, have a vested interest in seeing the no-tampering rule abolished. However, they do not wish to see the boundary between college and professional sports knocked down altogether; for that would diminish the need for their services—hence the support by the sport lawyers for some regulation of the activities of sport agents. They showed little sympathy for two agents who in 1988 were indicted on charges that included racketeering, mail fraud, and conspiracy to commit extortion in connection with the signing of forty-four student-athletes to professional contracts before their college eligibility had expired. The indictment alleged that the agents, Norby Walters and Lloyd Bloom, offered players clothing, concert and airline tickets, automobiles, cash, interest-free loans, hotel accommodations, insurance policies, and other inducements in exchange for the athletes' signatures on contracts. Postdating of contracts would make it appear they had been signed after the players had completed their last year of eligibility. In return, the agents received the exclusive rights to represent the players when they turned professional. Some of those who tried to back out of the contracts were threatened with bodily harm. The indictment also charged that the agents (and the players) had defrauded the athletes' schools, because the schools had awarded scholarships to athletes who had been rendered ineligible to receive money by signing the contracts. Although it is an NCAA regulation, not federal law, that prohibits signing with an agent while eligibility remains, the government charged agents and students with defrauding the colleges in accepting financial aid while knowingly ineligible. One Ohio State athlete, Chris Carter (who later signed with the Philadelphia Eagles), was charged with mail fraud and obstruction of justice (concealing payments). The other forty-three athletes were not prosecuted, in exchange for their making restitution to the schools and performing up to 250 hours of community service. Carter was the first college athlete to be charged with criminal fraud as a result of accepting improper payments while playing as a college athlete. In 1989, a federal jury found Bloom and Walters guilty of five counts of racketeering and fraud.

The public focussed its indignation in the Bloom and Walters case on the greed and duplicity of the accused, while the student-athletes were portrayed as victims. But the agents were merely competing in what had already become a thriving market place for athletic talent, offering the kind of inducements it would take to complete successfully, while the student-athletes were not the innocent victims portrayed by the media but realistic appraisors of the balance of opportunities facing them as athletes first and students second. Both parties operated on a more realistic assessment of the relation between college and professional sports than judges, juries, legislators or college administrators wished to acknowledge. Market forces had caused the line between amateur and professional to become highly permeable. Subscription to substantive values of amateurism was not strong enough to preserve the distinction between college and professional sports, especially in light of the vulnerability of both college and professional sports to antitrust action (which made all efforts to control the flow of talent suspect) and in light of widespread sentiments in favor of giving youth from disadvantaged backgrounds a chance at a career "in the pros."

Eligibility in Individual Sports

In the case of sports where athletes usually compete as individuals, like tennis and golf, eligibility issues are slightly different, because athletes present themselves as independent contractors, rather than employees, and authority within these sports is less centralized. Although these sports have developed (albeit weak) commissioner systems, they do not form leagues and therefore do not face the problem of owners competing for players or athletes jumping from team to team in midseason. Although there is competition among tournament entrepreneurs for star talent, it more resembles the competition of dance halls for bands than basketball teams for the "franchise player." No long-term commitment to the entrepreneur is implied.

Eligiblity standards are nevertheless important, for each sport needs to limit the right to compete to ensure even competition and predictable scheduling. These rules can strike an individual player as an unjust exclusion from a means of earning a livelihood. Thus, in *Deesen v. Professional Golfers Association of America* (1966), the expulsion of a player from the PGA because of poor scores was upheld. It was found to be reasonable to restrict the number of golfers on the tour, since only a limited number of golfers could play an eighteen-hole golf course under tournament conditions during the daylight hours of a single day. In *Heldman v. United States Lawn Tennis Association* (1973), the USLTA's threatened blacklisting of players in a rival circuit was upheld as legal on the grounds that eligibility rules were necessary to ensure uniformity with respect to play, to maintain ethical standards, and to schedule tournaments. The courts have also acknowledged the right of the United States Automobile Club (which sanctions the Indianapolis 500) to exclude drivers who had participated in the rival National Association of Stock Car Drivers events, a right defended on the grounds of safety.

Safety is one reason given for eligibility rules in boxing. Licensing of boxers is also justified as necessary to assure an even match for paying customers. The problem with these rules is that while they might contribute to even competition, they also, in practice grant, contractual powers to tournament directors, sponsors, and promoters. The power to license can be exploited for purposes of controlling the supply of talent, thus driving down wages and driving up prices charged to those who "consume" the competitions. Thus, by the use of licensing rules, boxing promoters have been able to limit the earnings of boxers while simultaneously raising ticket prices and the rights fees they charge television. Exorbitant prices must be paid to managers and agents to secure the services of the more attractive fighters.

During the boom years for boxing after World War II, the manipulation of licensing laws attracted considerable public attention and led, in 1951, to senators Warren Magnuson and Harry Cain's introducing into Congress resolutions calling for an investigation of the International Boxing Club (IBC), the leading boxing agency of the time. The actual issue was the case of a light heavyweight, Harry Matthews, whose manager complained that the IBC was depriving him of a chance at big-time fights. This, in turn, led to a Department of Justice investigation of potential violation of antitrust laws by the IBC. In March 1952, a federal grand jury recommended that the government file an antitrust suit to end restraint of trade in the promotional broadcasting of championship matches. The Supreme Court was eventually (1955) to decide that the IBC had indeed violated the law. But although the courts broke the power of the IBC, little changed with respect to the practice of licensing boxers. State licensing agencies were suspected of lax supervision at best and corruption at worst. Powerful promoters and managers remained free to manipulate the licensing provision to obtain and secure control over their boxers.

THE DRAFT

A dispersal draft of eligible amateurs exists in all the major team sports. Restrictions on the drafting of players as rookies have tended to attract less political attention than the no-tampering rule. Providing teams in a league with draft choices in inverse order of their finish the season before appeals to people's sense of equity and their desire for balanced competition. The draft is nevertheless a severe restriction on the freedom of players to choose their employer. Industrywide restrictions such as this do not exist in areas of the labor market other than sport, although, of course, many large firms engage in such practices within their own "internal" labor market.

The NFL introduced the reverse-order draft in 1936. Last-place-finishing teams from the season before were awarded first pick of rookie talent. The NBA adopted this rule at its founding in 1949 (later modifying it to require the bottom-placed teams to enter a lottery for first draft choice to prevent a team from deliberately playing poorly in order to secure first pick the next season). Baseball did not introduce a reverse-order draft until 1965. James Miller believes that the timing is not accidental. American League attendances had been declining for some years, and this was thought to be due to the dominance of the Yankees. Organized baseball's response was a draft similar to that existing in football, designed to overcome the problem of rich teams' exploiting their farm systems (J. Miller 1990, 91). This was a tacit admission that the reserve system did not itself equalize talent, because trades were permitted at the owners' discretion, including trades out of a minor league team, so that a rich team could get richer by selling its minor league talent. Baseball is unusual in that it does not limit the number of rounds in the draft and does not permit a franchise to "trade" its draft pick to another club (although it does allow the minor league clubs to participate in the draft after the majors have exhausted their rights). Unlike the football and basketball drafts, the baseball draft is held in private.

While players and their agents seek more freedom with respect to eligibility, the principle of the reverse-order draft has not been vigorously opposed by the players. They seem to accept the argument that parity in a league requires that weaker teams get first pick of new talent and that rookies cannot, therefore, have complete freedom of choice when it comes to selling their labor power. In fact, outside of a collective bargaining agreement that sanctions it, the reverse-order draft is of dubious legality. Yazoo Smith established this in 1978, when he won a court case against the Washington Redskins. Smith alleged that the draft denied him bargaining power. The U.S. District Court agreed that the draft procedures under which Smith entered the NFL in 1968 were illegal. However, the court also noted that as a result of pressure from the players' association, subsequent changes in the draft reducing the number of selection rounds had diminished the owners' antitrust liability. Rather than seek to overturn the draft, then, the players have whittled away at the number of selection rounds and the length of time a rookie can be held to his first contract. Thus, the NFL's 1982 collective bargaining agreement stipulated that players need not play for the team that drafted them but could sit out the year and become a free agent for the following season, the same freedom accorded basketball players. A 1993 court-imposed agreement between players and owners saw the number of draft rounds reduced from twelve to seven rounds. Under their agreement, baseball players are tied to their drafting team for six years, the number of draft rounds being unlimited. In the National Hockey League, the amateur draft currently has twelve rounds, and players do not enjoy even restricted free agency until they reach the age of twenty-four or have at least five years of professional experience (Staudohar 1986, 135). When hockey players mounted an unsuccessful strike in 1991, they demanded a shorter first contract period and a limit on the number of draft rounds to six.

THE EMPLOYMENT CONTRACT

In the early days of many team sports, barnstorming was the norm. Autonomously contracting, each team sold itself (the product) and bought factors of production (players) on the kind of open market in which "faceless buyers and sellers . . . meet . . . for an instant to exchange standardized goods at equilibrium prices" (Williamson 1986, 112). Many sports, such as golf, tennis, and boxing, continue to use this method of operation today, although constraints on contracts between athletes and tournament promoters have become more frequent, and the practice of tying a boxer to a particular promoter has a long history.[3]

Eventually, this mode of contracting for athletic labor was replaced by a system that by imposing severe limitations on the freedom of players to move from team to team and some limits on the freedom of owners to enter the labor market for new players, "internalized" the transaction between employer and employee. The reason given for internalizing this transaction was the peculiar structure of the team sports industry, but it also served the purpose of creating a "master-servant" relation between owner and player. It was to become one of the most controversial of all of the features of professional sports, the topic of many court hearings and congressional committee deliberations.

Many argue that an open market for athletic labor cannot be permitted and that the employment relation must be internalized for a sport to survive at all. Unlike normal businesses, sports teams have little interest in improving the quality of their product in relation to competitor firms. This is because their product—exciting competition between two evenly balanced teams—is collectively or jointly created. Under these circumstances, no single owner can fully recoup the money he spends on improving his team because those improvements will be shared by the owners who buy no new talent at all. Indeed, it makes sense to let other owners assume this burden. Each owner knows that there is a distribution of winning percentages among the teams in a league that would maximize joint profits; but because transaction costs are so high, such joint profit maximization is discouraged. One solution to this problem is to place constraints on player mobility, artificially balance the playing strength in the league, and thus (in the jargon of the economist) internalize the external diseconomies associated with maintaining league balance (Daly and Moore 1981).

Others argue that while sport events are indeed joint products and while some balance of competitive strength is indeed desirable, there is no reason why the players should be asked to assume the major burden of achieving this balance. They look upon restraints on player mobility as more the outgrowth of the difference in power between the wealthy capitalists who own sports and the working athletes who must sell their highly perishable talents to them in order to survive. These critics believe that the owners have misled the public into thinking that the "rotating" of players and player disloyalty is the cause of competitive imbalance, all the while reserving to themselves equal, if not greater, powers of mobility.

The employment contract in professional sports supports each of these arguments in some respects. Even players believe that redistribution of playing talent is necessary for competitive balance; but this redistribution can be achieved in many ways, only one of which is to place restrictions solely on the player's freedom to move. I shall describe the evolution of the employment contract not to account for employment relations in all their detail but to document the role of the state in structuring this relationship. To what extent have questions of national policy intruded into the private sphere of professional athletics?

Over the brief span of modern sports history, the employment contract has undergone four periods of development. The first period is characterized by a craftlike relation between owner-promoter and athlete, in which the player retains control over his skills and "revolving" from team to team is widely tolerated. The second period sees the capitalization of sport and the standardization of managerial discipline over the athlete. The third period brings about the total absorption of the professional athlete, and he becomes raw material for sport firms vertically integrated through such devices as the farm system (or colleges functioning as farm teams). The fourth period sees collective bargaining provide a framework within which the athlete recovers some of the craftlike independence he enjoyed in the nineteenth century.

From Craft to Occupation

The kind of standardized player contract seen in professional team sports today had its origins in baseball. As early as 1866, it was well known that many so-called amateur clubs paid their better players either salaries or shares of gate receipts on "benefit days," despite an NABB ban on such payments. At the same time, clubs began to divide into "members," who were exempt from dues payments because of their playing skill, and that class of associates "who do the paying part of the business" (Goldstein 1989, 95). The differentiation of capital and labor in baseball had thus begun.

Fully professional teams emerged in the 1866–76 period. Players were now treated not as craftsmen with full-membership voting rights in the club but as "completely mobile, unfettered individuals free to contract with any club independently of familial, geographical, or fraternal considerations" (Goldstein 1989, 136). On the field, self-discipline was replaced by managed discipline; and in the clubhouse, a three-level hierarchy formed, consisting of wealthy club backers, managers, and players. Players were now prized for their "quietness" and "steadiness," and contracts were aimed principally at enforcing discipline on and off the field. Baseball statistics were developed the better to measure each player's productivity (p. 144). "Owners" established profitable connections with railroads and other transportation companies and fostered civic boosterism in order to increase ticket sales. Their capital thus became less mobile and their interests more distinct, from the player's, who benefited from easy mobility. In short, the baseball club became capitalized; and the employment relation became more hierarchical and exploitative. The sport had created (or absorbed) a two-class structure, breaking down the old craft organization that had prevailed before the Civil War. It is with this nexus of social relationships that baseball entered its years of major expansion and commercial establishment in the 1900–1921 period. It is this nexus within which the employment relation acquires meaning.

The Negative Covenant

The contract between the owner and the professional athlete has two aspects. One is a requirement for the performance of certain services, the other is a "negative covenant," an undertaking by the player not to play for another team during the term of the contract. The problem with the first aspect is the difficulty of measuring and ensuring adequate performance, a difficulty particularly acute for any outside parties that might be called in to settle the dispute. This, and the courts' reluctance to enforce contracts that seem to require involuntary servitude, has meant that the emphasis in sport contract law has shifted to the second aspect, the negative covenant. The courts are more comfortable with contracts forbidding a player under contract from playing for another team, because they require no measure of performance and do not raise the expectation that the courts would be called in every time a player was suspected of slacking off. Of course, the negative covenant does not by itself force the player to work hard—or indeed work at all (and players have been known to "sit out" a year)—but the assumption is that "independent economic forces" can be relied on to motivate the player (Weistart and Lowell 1979, 340). (That is, no other club will hire him for fear of litigation, he must eat, and his talents are highly perishable, so he continues playing for his present club.)

It is important to distinguish these two aspects of contracts because therein lies a power differential. It is in the players' interests to have the labor market operate as freely as possible. A completely "commercial" approach to labor contracting would work to their advantage; that is, each player is treated as an independent businessman, offering an "intermediate" product to the producer of the final product, the game. Services performed would thus quite closely resemble inanimate goods provided. The players would have some justification for taking this approach, considering the very short careers most of them have and the very high turnover rate of athletes in a sports organization. (That is, *in practice* they are quite like the raw material of a factory; and they are treated as highly replaceable.) In other words, they would benefit from having the first aspect of the contract emphasized and money damages used to compel contract performance. This would help keep the labor market open. To ensure this, they would have to establish the policy position that players are fungible, easily replaceable.

The owners, on the other hand, benefit from a policy position that regards each player as unique, because "finding that the athlete has unique skills establishes that it is unlikely that the club could secure a replacement who would perform in precisely the same manner as the player who has defected" (Weistart and Lowell 1979, 360). Unique skills mean that the damage caused by the player's defection cannot be precisely measured, which means that money damages cannot be used to compensate the aggrieved party. Unique skills mean that the emphasis in contract law shifts from the first to the second aspect, from a positive inducement to perform to a negative inducement not to perform for another team. The negative covenant is thus of crucial importance in the process of internalizing labor contracting.

It might seem self-evident that contracting for athletic performance is costly, given the nature of the activity. However, ideology must be separated from fact. Baseball mythology paints a picture of the relation between athlete and team to evoke ideas of communal loyalty and fraternalism. Fans have never been particularly receptive to the idea that professional baseball players are universally interchangeable: "Rather than face the complete industrialization of the game, a development for which there was little emotional support, it was far easier to participate in a fictive process of hometown identification" (Goldstein 1989, 117). Owners fostered a double standard on behalf of the fans:

without stigma, they could enter the market to buy the talent needed to win championships; but the players were "disloyal" if they entered the market in search of the highest salary.

During the early years of professional baseball, the question of whether or not players were unique was by no means settled. Indeed, the trend was away from uniqueness, since the more wealthy club members created a class of interchangeable, journeymen players, exempt from dues paying but without voting rights in the club. Such players were regarded as temporary, and "revolving" was widely accepted (Goldstein 1989, 97). The goal here was to break down the "craft" independence of the player. This view was reflected in several early cases (1891–1902), when courts rejected the argument that any given player was unique (Weistart and Lowell 1979, 362). By the early 1900s, however, the owners' capital investments and profits were such that they no longer had an interest in highly mobile players but sought to fix them as firmly to one enterprise as was their own capital. They fought the idea that players were interchangeable in an attempt to control the market for labor, especially during periods of interleague competition.

The court case that signaled this change of direction was *Philadelphia Base Ball Club* v. *Lajoie* (1902). Napoleon Lajoie had skipped his contract with the Philadelphia National League team to play with the new American League club in the same town. The National League club wanted him back and, in the process, was anxious to have the court believe that the services of the players like Lajoie were so unusual, so incalculable, that compensible money damages could not be assessed and the negative covenant was therefore warranted. The lower court, reflecting the older wisdom, accepted the defendant's argument that he was not so unusual that the National League club would have difficulty replacing him; declared the contract lacking in mutuality and thus unenforceable because of the negative covenant and the reserve clause; and found for Lajoie. The appeals court, reflecting the more modern view, reversed, on the grounds that Lajoie was "a bright particular star," and that his high salary excused the one-sidedness of the contract. The appellate court declared: "The defendant is an expert baseball player in any position. . . . He has a great reputation as a second baseman; . . . his place would be hard to fill with as good a player; . . . his withdrawal from the team would weaken it, as would the withdrawal of any good player, and would probably make a difference in the size of the audience attending the game" (Weistart and Lowell 1979, 337). A number of judgments beneficial to the owners were embedded in this ruling: Lajoie is an "expert" (and thus rare); he has "a great reputation" (impossible to measure); and his withdrawal from the team would "weaken it" (the departing player is an *integral*, but immeasurable, part of some larger whole).

Two of these judgments in particular—the assumed uniqueness of the player and his functioning as a member of a team—would prove to be powerful weapons in the hands of the owners. How was a player's uniqueness decided? Typically, the courts would hear from witnesses who had closely observed the athlete's performance. Needless to say, the evidence given by witnesses for the owner would differ from the evidence given by witnesses for the player. In partial acknowledgement of this difficulty, the courts would also gauge uniqueness by the relative level of the athlete's salary and the amount of salary increases he had received. These were obviously very crude measures. Besides, they seemed to measure imputed excellence as much as uniqueness. The player was thus shackled by his level of performance. The better he played, the more unusual were his imputed talents; the more unusual his talents, the more difficult it would be to measure the damages incurred by his loss; the more difficult this calculation, the more reasonable the negative covenant seemed.

More important, the courts became more and more likely to assume that *any* professional athlete must have unique skills, otherwise he would not have the job at all. All players were thus to be regarded as unique! In *Winnepeg Rugby Football Club* v. *Freeman and Locklear* (1955) an Ohio court granted a preliminary injunction on behalf of the rugby club to prevent the Cleveland Browns from signing Freeman and Locklear, who had earlier signed with Winnepeg, despite the fact that the Browns' coach, Paul Brown, testified that the players were merely good, not extraordinary, players: "The court ruled that a standard of special skill and ability must have some relation to the class and character of play" (Berry and Wong 1986, 74). In 1961, the court in *Central New York Basketball* v. *Barnett* declared that "professional players in the major baseball, football, and basketball leagues have unusual talents and skills or they would not be so employed" (Weistart and Lowell 1979, 363). The Lajoie court had set about deciding whether Lajoie was "readily replaceable in the existing labor market" (p. 362); the Barnett court simply assumed that if Barnett was a professional basketball player, he must be irreplaceable, despite Barnett's own protestations that he possessed no "exceptional skill and ability." The Barnett court also used the salary increases Barnett had earned to demonstrate his uniqueness, thus putting Barnett in an awkward position: the better he bargained, the more likely was his inequitable contract to be legitimated by the court. And by tacitly including all professional athletes in the category of "unique," the courts coveniently glossed over the fact that the negative covenant did not forbid the player from taking another job but simply from taking another job with a competing sports franchise.

The interpretation of contract law thus evolved in a direction highly favorable to the owners because it legitimated the negative covenant aspect of contracts: "Modern courts now routinely enforce negative covenants in professional sports contracts" (Weistart and Lowell 1979, 342). The standard player contract in the major sports leagues today contains a clause in which the player agrees that his services are unique and not compensible in terms of money.

Uniqueness was not the only grounds for justifying the negative covenant. Another reason the court gave for sanctioning Napoleon Lajoie's contract was that he had become an indispensible member of a team: "He has become thoroughly familiar with the action and methods of the other players on the club, and his own work is peculiarly meritorious as an integral part of the team work which is so essential" (Berry and Wong 1986, 71). *Lajoie* set precedent in this area, too. Thus, in *Long Island Association Football Club* v. *Manrodt* (1940), the court declared, "Once a team is organized and the football season begins, it may be extremely difficult to find adequate replacements for players about whom play has been planned" (Weistart and Lowell 1979, 337). The courts conveniently overlooked the fact that a lively market existed for players' contracts in most teams sports. Owners, while occasionally expressing apprehension about how new players would "fit in" or about the "gap" left by departing players, did not allow these apprehensions to stand in the way of a market over which they exercised complete control.

The owners could not rest assured that restrictive covenants in player contracts would be seen as legitimate until another condition of labor contracting had been satisfied. Classical contract law held that only an employer who could show that the loss of the employee would render harm to the employer's enterprise not reparable in money damages could prevail over an employee. The actual loss was less important in this context that the difficulty of calculating its magnitude. This, too, proved to be a controversial issue. Players maintained that teams would survive quite well without them and that no problem was created by calculating the loss. But they did not prevail, and the courts came to accept the owners' view that the loss they suffered when a player resigned was incalculable.

How was loss defined? The courts made no effort to try to measure loss, accepting the owners' judgment of its difficulty. Since *Lajoie*, the courts have generally imputed this damage on the basis of the athlete's "star" quality. Only in *Boston Professional Hockey Association* v. *Cheevers* (1972) did the court actually make an attempt to gauge the impact of the departure of two of the Bruins' players for the rival World Hockey Association. Ironically, the court concluded that no damage had been done. Public policy states otherwise, however, and assumes that transactions are costly because so little is known about the consequences of a breach of contract. "Because so many individuals and such diverse external factors influence the financial success of a team, the effect of the loss of any one player, even the best player, is thought to be wholly speculative" (Weistart and Lowell 1979, 338). This uncertainty, which might actually be used as grounds to argue that one player is as good as another, is used to argue the reverse—that the damage created by the loss of a player, being incalculable, is something the state should ensure the employer against.

The negative covenant in players' contracts would not have been so significant had it not been coupled with the reserve clause. In the early days of baseball, teams competed vigorously for players, many of whom changed teams frequently, even in midseason. Owners bid fiercely for players and frequently depleted each other's teams of better players during the season. In 1879, they entered into a secret agreement not to bid for players on the "reserve" list of other clubs. Each club had exclusive property rights to five players (about 50 percent of their roster at this time), a figure increased to eleven in 1883 and fourteen in 1887 (and currently standing at forty). The peace was disturbed in 1881, when the American Association was formed, for it created more competition for players from owners who had not been part of the original secret agreement. The first National Agreement—the 1882 accord between the National League, the American Association, and various minor leagues—stifled open bidding for players by imposing harsh penalties on a club operating without a reserve restriction.

The reserve clause stated that if a player refused to sign for the next playing season, the club could unilaterally renew the contract for one year under the same terms and conditions. The reserve clause explains why sport contracts evolved in a direction different from the entertainment contracts in which they originated. In entertainment contracts (e.g., music hall stars), specific performances could not be stipulated, given the creative nature of the work, and negative covenants were enforced; but the terms of the contract were for a specific period of time and breaches of contract would typically occur during that time. In many sport cases, however, the breach would occur after the original signing period had elapsed; but the club would hold the player to the contract by invoking the reserve clause, which, in effect, made contracts perpetual. Inequities were thus created by enforcing the negative covenant in the context of the reserve clause.

Contract Law

At first, the reserve clause created problems for the owners because it seemed to violate public laws. Nineteenth-century law required that contracts be mutually agreed. A contract could be declared void if it lacked mutuality, that is, either "allocated grossly uneven rights and privileges between the parties" (Weistart and Lowell 1979, 374) or did not provide both parties with the same remedies if the contract were broken. Common law principle prohibited "unreasonable" labor contracts (e.g., those that bound the employee for a long period or "perpetual servitude"); and the reserve clause seemed to place the professional athlete squarely in that position.

Equity issues did not long trouble the owners, however, in large part because of changes in contract law that saw the requirement of strict mutuality fade into the less stringent understanding that "sufficient exchange of consideration" is provided in an employment relation simply by requirement of notice (Weistart and Lowell 1979, 377). Thus, the *Lajoie* court did not see any lack of mutuality in Lajoie's contract, which contained the standard reserve clause: after all, the fact that Lajoie could be terminated on ten day's notice while having no termination rights of his own was "part of a consideration for the large salary paid to the defendant" (Berry and Wong 1986, 72). The law was moving steadily in the direction of a theory of contracts in which each party was assumed to be acting voluntarily in pursuit of his own self-interest. If Lajoie did not like the exchange with which he was presented, he could seek work elsewhere—as long as it was outside of baseball. The players, locked into an essentially inequitable relationship, thus saw the safeguards of contract law stripped from them. Not until the 1930s did the courts acknowledge, once again, that there might be inequities in labor contracts that they should help rectify.

Antitrust Law

Contract law thus provided players with little protection against the reserve clause. There was another weapon available to them, however, that would eventually prove much more destructive. It is noticeable that during the 1890–1914 period, when many contract disputes were being litigated, judges were much more likely to see players' contracts as "overly repressive—too much the product of a league and its clubs," during periods of interleague competition (Berry and Wong 1986, 90). Not only did more players jump teams when different leagues were competing for their services, but the courts would be more lenient with players who jumped from one league to another. The reason is that they were seeking to enforce laws intended to promote business competition between economic enterprises. The employment contract in professional athletics could be read as anticompetitive if leagues, rather than teams, were competing with each other. After all, the power of the reserve clause rested in an agreement *among the owners* not to "tamper" with each others' reserved players.

From the earliest days of professional teams sports, then, the reserve clause was seen as vulnerable on antitrust grounds. Even during periods of league monopoly, the courts tended to read contract language more narrowly than perhaps they would have done otherwise (and thereby favored the players), precisely because to do otherwise would raise "serious antitrust problems" (Weistart and Lowell 1979, 286). They were so anxious to do so that, ignoring much evidence to the contrary, they chose to interpret the reserve clause as meaning that the player was bound for one more term contract, rather than to a perpetual rollover of a succession of contracts.

The shadow of antitrust law is evident in a number of early legal decisions. In *Metropolitan Exhibition Company* v. *Ewing* (1890), a New York State Supreme Court denied an injunction by Metropolitan (New York Giants) to stop Ewing from jumping to the Players' League, because the terms of his contract were indefinite. The club was no more successful in enjoining John Ward from making the same move and for the same reasons: Ward's contract with the Giants was "indefinite and uncertain" (Lowenfish and Lupien 1980, 42). During the period of conflict with the Federal League, the American League lost its case against Hal Chase (1914), when the New York Supreme Court, while agreeing that Chase could not be replaced easily, struck down the negative covenant this would otherwise have warranted on the grounds of an "absolute lack of mutuality" created by the reserve clause in the National Agreement that the Chicago club had signed (Berry and Wong 1986, 94). Chicago White Sox's Hal Chase, the foremost first baseman of the era, had signed a contract with the Buffalo Federals in 1914; and the White Sox filed an injunction to bar the move. The injunction was denied on the grounds that organized baseball was "in contravention of common law" by its invasion of "the right of labor as a property right." The lot of the baseball player at this time was described as "a species of quasi-peonage" (Seymour 1971, 210). The Chase court went so far as to describe a sports league as "an illegal combination."

Although the Chase defeat was a setback for the owners, they did not strike out the reserve clause. They simply blacklisted troublesome players (Krasnow and Levy 1963, 754), a task much more easily accomplished once they had vanquished the rival Federal League. Thereafter, the negotiation of a player's contract was "more ritualistic than substantive, an exchange of gestures between player and owner" that concealed from the public the absolute power of the owners (Seymour 1971, 354).[4] Nevertheless, the owners had to walk a narrow line. If they squashed rival leagues too obviously, charges of monopoly power would be drawn; if they permitted league rivalry, players were more likely to win their contract disputes in court. The owners made some attempt to limit their more flagrantly monopolistic practices: the national commission instituted rules against hoarding or "farming" of players in minor league teams to prevent other owners from getting at them, rules that might have tempered the control of the owners over the players; but the commission lacked the power to police these rules (Seymour 1971, 187).[5]

Although contract disputes (such as those of Ty Cobb) often made the headlines, the reserve clause was not considered a cause for public concern. Most fans saw the reserve clause as necessary to keep players from gravitating to clubs able and willing to pay more, while at the same time approving the trading in which the owners could indulge because they were anxious to have winning teams. There does not appear to have been much public sentiment that professional athletes were exploited by this device, despite the economic wisdom that the very existence of the reserve is itself a confession that some clubs are underpaying their players: "Other things being equal, if all clubs were paying the players what they were worth, the reserve clause would not be needed to hold the men" (Seymour 1971, 174). Most players, too, seemed to accept the need for some kind of restraint on player mobility, although they did complain about their lack of freedom and their exclusion from the money that changed hands when they were bought and sold. In 1925, a sympathetic Fiorello La Guardia, then U.S. representative from New York, proposed a 90 percent federal tax on the sale of player contracts involving over five thousand dollars unless the player himself received the sales price (Gregory 1956, 192).

The Reserve System in Decline

The reserve system in professional sports did not become a subject of serious political debate until after World War II. One reason might have been the renewed commitment to ideals of democracy and individual freedom fired by the war against totalitarianism and by the advent of the Cold War. Returning servicemen "came with reformist notions about discipline, salaries, pensions, and job security" (Voigt 1983, 55). The first sign of a change involved a returning serviceman who, under the terms of the Veterans Act, should have been given his old job back with the Seattle Rainiers, a minor league baseball club in the Pacific Coast League. The player, Al Niemic, was told by the management that he was "too old" to contribute and was released by the club in 1946. An appeal to the Seattle draft board resulted in a court case. The judge in the case, Lloyd Back, found for Niemic and in so doing described the modern baseball player as "a chattel" (Lowenfish and Lupien 1980, 135).

The case of *Gardella* v. *Chandler* (1949) was another signal of a change in judicial attitude toward the reserve clause. The lawyer whom Danny Gardella consulted, Frederic Johnson, an expert on "baseball law," had only recently discovered that organized baseball had never argued that the reserve clause was legally binding on players, referring to it, instead, as an "honorary obligation" (Lowenfish and Lupien 1980, 161). Gardella had been forbidden by Commissioner Chandler to play in organized baseball after spending the winter playing in the Mexican League. Johnson believed that his client had a particularly strong case, because, although offered a contract with the New York Giants, he had never actually signed with club and was not, therefore, a player who could be reserved. Gardella sued for the right to play. In February 1949, an appellate court found that Gardella's case was strong enough to warrant a trial, Judge Jerome Frank commenting, "If the players be regarded as quasi-peons, it is of no moment that they are well paid; only the totalitarian minded will believe that high pay excuses virtual slavery" (Krasnow and Levy 1963, 756). Judge Learned Hand, concurring, saw a clear possibility of violation of antitrust laws in any contract "which unreasonably forbids anyone to practice his calling" (Lowenfish and Lupien 1980, 164). With the trial set for November 1949, Commissioner Chandler announced in June an immediate amnesty for all Mexican League veterans. Gardella, unable to afford a long court fight, settled out of court in October, during the World Series.

In the aftermath of the Gardella fight, Congressmen Syd Herlong and Wilbur Mills introduced a bill that would have exempted the reserve clause from antitrust liability, thus setting in motion a succession of legislative efforts to grapple with this problem. From this moment, the reserve clause was never very far from the political agenda. The owners doggedly fought efforts to weaken the reserve system legislatively. Ford Frick, commissioner of baseball, was sent before Congress to protect the owners' immunity from antitrust laws.[6] Removing this immunity, he argued, "would seriously injure professional baseball with no offsetting benefit to the public" (U.S. Congress, House, Committee on the Judiciary 1957, 91). He defended the reserve clause as essential for public confidence in the game:

> Industry does not have the problem of public confidence in the loyalty of employees to employers. The public buys Lucky Strikes without concern as to whether the employees of American Tobacco Co. are doing their best for that company or are trying to get jobs with Liggett and Myers or Reynolds Tobacco Co. But the public demands that each baseball player have full loyalty to and extend his best efforts for his club. How can public confidence in player loyalty and will to win be maintained if the player, while playing for one club, may seek a job with another, or may be pressed with offers from several other clubs, against some of which he is playing? (p. 297).

Frick did not dwell on the fact that owners were not expected to be "loyal" to their players and traded them freely for financial gain, dispensing with players at their peak in order to cash in on their maximum value. Nor did he acknowledge the uncomfortable fact that the fans seemed to have no objection at all to the idea of buying a pennant by signing "franchise" players.

Organized baseball also used the expense of maintaining the minor league system as a reason for the reserve clause. Between 1945 and 1950 the New York Yankees spent over four million dollars on player development, and they doubled their spending on minor league operations over the next five years. It was not untypical for a club to spend more than a third of its total budget on its farm system (J. Miller 1990, 45). Commissioner Kuhn was to testify in 1972 that "the average expense by major league clubs to develop players is $1.5 million a piece per club," which was the reason, he argued, why baseball needed greater control over player movement than other sports (U.S. Congress, House, Committee on the Judiciary 1972, 185). Baseball's critics were quite familiar with these arguments. They drew different conclusions with respect to the link between the reserve system and the farm system. They pointed out that the National Hockey League also supported a minor league system without the exemption from antitrust prosecution enjoyed by baseball. They also reminded congressmen that baseball had imposed a uniform (and very low) pay scale for the minor leagues, which the players could neither challenge before the court as a violation of antitrust laws nor bargain about, because they had no union. Minor league players received no notice of termination; they could be assigned to a different club without option; if they incurred an incapacitating injury, they received no pay; they were entitled to no pension or moving expenses when traded and were without recourse to arbitration in the case of salary disputes. Baseball's critics also noted that when college baseball began to improve in the 1960s and provide a new source of talent for organized baseball, the owners instituted the college draft in order to control competition for these rookies also, thus imposing a reserve system upon players whose training had cost them nothing.

Not many critics of the reserve system were to be found in Congress. Emmanuel Celler, who introduced a 1957 bill to eliminate baseball's exemption, was a lonely voice. A representative from New York, Celler was irked by the departure of the Dodgers from Brooklyn to Los Angeles. He was openly skeptical, in light of the secrecy surrounding this move, of Commissioner Frick's idea that "public sentiment" would be sufficient to keep baseball within the bounds of decent employment practices. His colleague Kenneth Keating, also from New York, while angered by the departure of the Dodgers, expressed more sympathy for the owners' point of view. Keating saw himself as protecting baseball from future adverse court rulings: "If we do not go into at least baseball, the next time a baseball case gets into the Supreme Court, the Court may knock down some of the very practices which have made the sport the great sport it is today" (U.S. Congress, House, Committee on the Judiciary 1957, 30).

Keating need not have worried; for baseball, in particular, seemed to lead a politically charmed life. The reserve system was safe as long as baseball's immunity from antitrust prosecution survived. Congressmen such as Ed Herlong of Florida could not bring themselves to question the Supreme Court ruling despite the modern realities of baseball. "The baseball game," he argued, "is a product which is produced on that particular field" and cannot therefore be considered interstate commerce (U.S. Congress, House, Committee on the Judiciary 1957, 71). More generally, however, there appeared to be strong congressional opposition to state intervention in private commerce. In particular, there was little sympathy for the regulation of wages. Players, congressmen argued, are not *forced* to be third basemen. Other congressmen resisted the idea of using antitrust laws to settle management-labor disputes, rather than using them to protect the welfare of the consumer, the fan. They accepted, in other words, that the reserve system was a "private," game-related issue and not, like ticket prices or the sale of television rights, a question of monopolizing markets.

When it was founded in the 1920s, the National Football League instituted its own version of the reserve clause. Under its two-year option clause, a team had the option of renewing a player's services for the two years following the expiration of a contract. With two one-year contracts and the two option years, an owner could control the entire playing career of the average player. Football's reserve system was to suffer much more damage from political attack during the postwar period, largely due to the owners' failure to establish an identity between football and baseball. The seeds of defeat were cast by the decision in *Radovich* v. *National Football League* (1957). The NFL had argued that it could blacklist William Radovich (for having jumped to the All-American Conference and then wanting to rejoin the NFL) because it was exempt from the antitrust laws, just like baseball. The Supreme Court disagreed with the NFL and declared for Radovich. The justices, acknowledging the illogic of treating football and baseball so differently, chided Congress for allowing this anomaly to persist and recommended legislation to eliminate it.

Congressmen were not quite ready to take this step. While some were willing to treat football as first-and-foremost a business (with some slightly unusual aspects because it involved sport), most Congressmen clearly saw football as first-and-foremost a sport, with insignificant business aspects. Predictably, NFL commissioner Bert Bell favored the latter view. He painted a picture of football as an avocation. He justified low salaries and the reserve clause on the grounds that such conditions were acceptable in an industry where the playing career was so brief. The typical player, he argued, was simply playing "while establishing himself in a business or profession" (U.S. Congress, House, Committee on the Judiciary 1957, 2539). George Halas was even more upbeat. He imagined his players going on to be "doctors, lawyers, or dentists, or . . . executives"; football was "not their livelihood" (p. 2712). Athletes, at this time, were indeed seen as part-time workers and many did take different jobs in the off-season. Many people shared Halas's view that a career in athletics, while short, was a stepping-stone to something greater. There was some truth to these views. Riess finds that professional football players active in the 1930s and 1950s were "extremely successful" after their playing days were over. (1991, 240). Almost all wound up in some kind of white-collar job, with half becoming professionals, executives, or owners of large companies. However, these subsequent careers were less the result of having played professional football than of having earned a degree while playing college football. A contrast with base-ball makes the point. Unlike football players, baseball players during this period came mainly from working-class backgrounds and did not attend college. Riess reports that 66 percent of players active between 1940 and 1960 ended up in low white-collar jobs (p. 90). Halas's argument that restrictions on player mobility should be tolerated because a playing career is a stepping-stone to something greater, is undermined by these data. Congressmen were persuaded by it, however, for they leaned toward the rosier view of a career in athletics and were unsympathetic to claims of exploitation. They tended to exaggerate how many athletes made it to the "big time," how long they stayed there, and the success they enjoyed once they retired (U.S. Congress, House, Committee on the Judiciary 1957, 1798).

The pace of legislative action on the reserve clause picked up toward the end of the 1950s and into the 1960s. Emmanuel Celler was in the forefront of efforts in the House, while Senator Estus Kefauver was an active sponsor of sports bills in the Senate. Both were liberals, and it can only be speculated what impact the Civil Rights movement had on their efforts to alleviate the peonage under which professional athletes of the time still served. In every year between 1957 and 1975, with the exception of 1968 (an election year of considerable social turmoil), at least one bill was introduced into Congress aimed either wholly or in part at ending, buttressing, or seriously modifying the reserve system.

Evidently, the system had its defenders. Some congressmen wanted legislation to protect all player controls from antitrust action. Other congressmen spoke up for the players and sought to limit the restrictions. The majority position seemed to be that there are simultaneously "commercial" and "sport" aspects in the professional sport leagues. Some practices are there because the game could not exist without them; others are there because they help increase profits. The latter should by all means be subject to commerce laws; the former should be exempt.

The only bill actually to make it out of committee (the Senate Judiciary Committee), in 1961, reflected this compromise position. It would have removed baseball's immunity (and denied it to other sports) but protected the draft and the reserve system, on the ground that neither was part of the commercial aspect of the game. In the end, congressmen could not resolve among themselves where to draw this fine line. Not surprisingly, the owners wanted to think of all player relations issues as "sport" and not "commerce"; the players refused to accept that their conditions of work and terms of payment were not part of the business of sports. The status quo thus prevailed, at least in the halls of Congress.

The rivalry between the National Football League and the American Football League, which lasted from 1960 until 1966, no doubt helped the owners' case and weakened that of the players. It was hard to convince congressmen of the peonage of the players when rival leagues were bidding for their services. By the time the merger occurred and the monopoly in football was restored, the players' unions had become a presence on the political scene, and congressmen could begin to shelter behind the argument that they had no part to play in established management-labor relations. Perhaps this is why football's reserve system managed to survive the merger between the National Football League and the American Football League in 1966, which Congress had to approve.

The new era of players' associations did, nevertheless, bring about a major change in the politics of the reserve system; for the players were able to exert considerable pressure on the owners to bargain over the terms of the reserve system and then complain to Congress, through the National Labor Relations Board and directly at committee hearings, over any failure to bargain in good faith. They were also able to provide individual players with support in their legal challenges to the reserve system. A major test came in a suit brought by Curtis Flood against major league baseball in 1970, alleging that the restrictions on his movement as a player were a violation of the Sherman Act. Flood not only had union backing, but his case was also made part of the fight for civil rights for blacks. At the end of the 1969 season, Flood had been traded from St. Louis to Philadelphia. Flood, after twelve years with the Cardinals, did not want to play in Philadelphia, a city perceived to be hostile to black people. The black power movement had asserted itself in the 1960s: "While Flood was not politically active, he was sympathetic to the goals of the activists" (Lowenfish and Lupien 1980, 208). Flood managed to persuade the players' association to pay the legal fees for a court challenge to the reserve system and to hire as his lawyer Arthur Goldberg, a former Supreme Court justice. At the first trial, in 1970, Judge Irving Cooper decided that "the preponderance of credible proof does not favor elimination of the reserve clause" and declared for Commissioner Kuhn. The Supreme Court affirmed in 1972. However, in delivering their opinion, the majority of justices also declared, "We are convinced that the reserve clause can be fashioned so as to find acceptance by player and club" (U.S. Congress, Senate, Committee on the Judiciary 1972, 55). Unfortunately, they did not spell out how this could be done.[7]

The *Flood* v. *Kuhn* Supreme Court decision epitomized the awkward relationship of the legislative and judicial branches at this time. The Supreme Court, in denying Flood's appeal of a lower court decision against him, felt compelled to honor the precedent set in 1922. However, the lower court reminded the public that "in the face of and seemingly in response to a series of judicial decisions which uniquely and emphatically pose the question to Congress of whether there should be regulation in antitrust terms or otherwise" for baseball, Congress had stubbornly refused to take action (U.S. Congress, Senate, Committee on the Judiciary 1972, 51). The majority of the justices on the Supreme Court seemed to believe that because Congress had failed to act on immunity, it therefore approved of it. The dissenting justices argued quite the contrary, that Congress had steadfastly refused to *extend* the immunity (even when this refusal took the form of inaction) and therefore clearly disapproved of it. The 1922 decision had effectively isolated baseball players from congressional action. It was therefore up to the courts to remedy the problem.

The players were not helped by congressional inaction. They were driven to use litigation, which was not only expensive and time-consuming but also tended to individualize the issue. Moreover, when a player sought help with litigation, he lost some control over the case. Scully believes that Flood's case was lost because his personal interests were subverted by the union (1989, 31). Flood's attorneys failed to establish that their client had been hurt financially by the reserve clause, nor did they show that Flood's activities had been unfairly restricted. They staked too much on the claim that Flood—and all baseball players—were condemned to slavery or involuntary servitude when a claim of unreasonable control might have been more acceptable: "In return for shouldering the trial costs, Flood allowed the Players' Association to wage a broadened attack on the reserve clause rather than pursue personal damages for Flood" (ibid.).

Chided by the justices for their indecision, members of the Senate Judiciary Committee had to acknowledge that more than fifty sports bills had been introduced into Congress between 1953 and 1972, covering the spectrum from blanket immunity for all sports to removal of the baseball exemption and that although many of these bills spoke both directly and indirectly to reserve issues, congressional action had been taken only with respect to league mergers and approval of joint venture negotiations with television networks. No legislation had been passed speaking directly to the reserve system. In fact, most bills would have exempted the reserve system from antitrust liability (U.S. Congress, House, Select Committee on Professional Sports 1977, 40). Of course, inaction by governments is policy of a kind. The owners could therefore draw comfort from the failure of Congress to act. But Congress had hinted at its wishes by refusing blanket exemption to all sports, and the courts were routinely finding for the owners but writing into their opinions their sentiments in favor of the players. The net result was to frighten the baseball owners into making some concessions to the players, the most significant of which was an agreement by the baseball owners in 1974 to take salary disputes to binding arbitration, an agreement that was to be of very great consequence for the subsequent fate of the reserve system in that sport.

Football had survived the political maneuvering over the merger between the NFL and the AFL in 1966 with its option clause intact. However, the competition between the leagues had caused the NFL to make some changes in its reserve system that would prove to be its Achilles' heel. The NFL owners had long conspired not to raid each other's players. The AFL created a shortage of playing talent, and NFL owners began to look at each other's rosters with increasing interest. In 1963, the Baltimore Colts' owner Carol Rosenbloom violated the agreement among the owners by signing R. C. Owens away from the San Francisco Forty-Niners. The collapse of the option clause seemed imminent; and to avoid this, the owners instituted what came to be called "the Rozelle Rule." It mandated compensation (money, future draft picks, players) to be paid to the teams "losing" a player to another team, thereby increasing the price of players and stifling competition for them. In effect, the Rozelle Rule denied players the opportunity to sell their services to other teams. To sign a player who had played out his option was risky, because it was uncertain what penalty would be imposed on the purchasing club by the commissioner. The option clause had thereby become much more restrictive, making it nearly indistinguishable from the reserve clause in baseball. Indeed, between institution of the Rozelle Rule in 1963 and the Mackey decision in 1976, only four players played out their options and signed with other clubs (Staudohar 1986, 78).

Commissioner Rozelle defended his rule. He argued before Congress that unrestricted competition for players would be detrimental to the game not only because it threatened bankruptcy for the owners but because it would sap the morale of the players. Escalating salaries threatened "a complete deterioration of interest and morale on the playing field"; players receiving huge sums in bonuses and salaries "would lose the vital interest that has made the game great, lose their interest on the playing field" (U.S. Congress, House, Committee on the Judiciary 1966, 52)—a consequence Rozelle obviously did not choose to trace either to himself, having enjoyed regular large increments to his salary, or to his capitalist employers, all of them successful and highly paid businessmen. The implication was that the ordinary player could not handle such large sums of money.

The Rozelle Rule proved to be an embarrassment to the NFL, because it made more explicit the inequitable control of the owners over the players. As is typical, the issue was fought out in the courts and involved a well-known player:

> [Joe] Kapp was a quarterback for the Minnesota Vikings, and when his contract expired, the club invoked its option clause for the 1969 season. Kapp then agreed to play for the New England Patriots in 1970, but did not sign a standard player contract with the Patriots. When he refused to sign such a contract for the following year, he was not allowed to play. His lawsuit sought damages from the NFL for terminating his playing career. Although the federal court rejected Kapp's claim that the Rozelle Rule was an illegal conspiracy to restrain trade and monopolize football in violation of the antitrust laws, it did find that the NFL's enforcement of the

rule was too severe and caused undue hardship on the players. (Staudohar 1986, 78)

Kapp received no damages and retired from football.

A second court challenge to the Rozelle Rule was made in 1976, when John Mackey, tight end for the Baltimore Colts and president of the National Football League Players' Association (NFLPA), alleged that the rule violated the Sherman Act. The judge in the federal District Court in Minneapolis decided that "the Rozelle Rule constitutes a *per se* violation of anti-trust laws, . . . clearly contrary to public policy" (Harris 1986, 221). Football players whose contracts had expired seemed poised to recover the freedom they had enjoyed before 1963. It was not to be, however; for the collective bargaining agreement signed that same year restored to the commissioner some limited rights to assign compensation payments for signing free agents.

The Mackey case was not entirely wasted, for it sparked hearings in Congress to consider a number of bills focusing specifically on the player contract. These bills clearly showed the influence of the Civil Rights movement on thinking about player-management relations in sports. The House Judiciary Committee hearings were entitled "Rights of Professional Athletes" and the discussion focused on expanding the players' economic freedom of choice. The legislation would have prohibited anticompetitive practices by professional leagues by banning the draft, the Rozelle Rule, and the like. The hearings were enlivened by the appearance of Emmanuel Celler, past chairman of the committee and now a lawyer in private practice. He appeared in the company of union spokesmen to castigate "the monopolistic practices of football barons" (U.S. Congress, House, Committee on the Judiciary 1977, 7). Committee members grumbled about the piecemeal nature of sports legislation, decried the obstinacy of the owners, and expressed some sympathy for the players but reported no bills to the full House.

By the mid-1970s, efforts of the baseball owners to fend off reforms in the reserve system earlier in the decade by agreeing to arbitration in the case of unresolvable disputes between management and player had begun to backfire.[8] It began in 1974 with a seemingly innocuous dispute between "Catfish" Hunter, a pitcher for the Oakland Athletics, and his employer, Charles Finley. Hunter's hundred-thousand-dollar annual contract had stipulated that half his salary must be paid as deferred income. Finley discovered that unlike regular salary, the fifty-thousand-dollar deferred annuity he was obliged to pay Hunter's insurance company was not a tax-deductible item. Only when Hunter actually received the payments would Finley be able to claim the deduction. He renounced the contract, demanding that Hunter take full payment immediately. Hunter refused and asked for arbitration. The arbitration panel decided in favor of Hunter (who promptly signed with the Yankees). The panel's decision was upheld by a California Supreme Court:

Although the Hunter case seemed a freakish accident, it handed players an opportunity to outflank the reserve clause. The astute Miller [executive director of the MLBPA] had already spotted an opening. On the tail of the Hunter case, he filed a grievance procedure against the option clause in player contracts. Miller sought to know the entire meaning of the one-year option-to-renew clause in most player contracts. Did it amount to a perpetual "roll-over" contract, binding a player to a club as long as the owner wanted him? Or, did it limit owners to one year's option on a man's service? (Voigt 1983, 213)

Miller's opportunity came when Andy Messersmith (Los Angeles Dodgers) and Dave McNally (Montreal Expos) played out the 1975 season without signing new contracts and appealed to the Major League Baseball Players' Association (MLBPA) for an arbitration hearing on their status. In December 1975, arbitrator Peter Seitz ruled that the players were free agents, since the reserve clause bound a player to his team for only one year after the expiration of his contract. The decision meant that every baseball player with a one-year contract could become a free agent simply by refusing to sign and play out the 1976 season. The owners had always assumed that the arbitration procedure had no jurisdiction over the reserve system (MacPhail 1989, 102) and promptly fired Seitz. The players' association brought suit against them for violation of the Sherman Act. In *Kansas City Royals* v. *MLBPA* (1977), the Eighth U.S. Circuit Court of Appeals affirmed the arbitration decision, observing that "although professional baseball was exempt from the antitrust laws, the business of professional baseball affected interstate commerce and was therefore subject to other federal laws including national labor laws." The Seitz decision, once upheld in court, signaled a major reform of the reserve clause. Indeed, there are some who believe that had Miller not acceded to a six-year reserve period in the 1976 collective bargaining agreement, the reserve clause would have disappeared altogether soon thereafter.

The owners' undertaking to abide by the decisions of a third party added to the baseball players' sense of injustice when those decisions were ignored or overturned and strengthened their political case against the reserve system. The players decided that they simply could not depend on private remedy to achieve greater freedom within sport. Meanwhile, after a fifty-one-day strike in 1974, the football players had been unable to reach a collective bargaining agreement with the owners and the structure of labor-management relations erected earlier in the decade collapsed. The players were once again left to face the owners as individuals. In professional basketball, interleague rivalry—which the players were seeking to prolong and the owners trying to stop—had also occasioned a flurry of litigation, while the World Hockey Association had started a bidding war for hockey players.

In the face of such instability and uncertainty, Congress took a major step in identifying professional sports as an important public policy domain. The House of Representatives appointed a Select Committee on Professional Sports. Its mandate was to review all aspects of professional sports, but there is little doubt that its main target was the reserve system. The committee confronted the problem that back in 1951, Congress had ducked the task of dealing with the status of the reserve clause, passing the buck to the courts. The courts, for their part, had interpreted this action as *inaction* and assumed that at least as far as baseball was concerned, no change from the 1922 decision was desired and no rationalization of sport policy across all sports was intended. Despite the fact that 1976 was a busy election year for congressmen, the committee's deliberations were to last for seventeen days.

Thrust into the public spotlight, the owners stoutly defended the reserve system and sought legislative approval of it. Called to testify by the Select Committee, NFL Commissioner Rozelle offered the standard defense of the reserve system, that its primary purpose was to prevent the best players "flowing primarily to the top teams" (U.S. Congress, House, Select Committee on Professional Sports 1976, 113). Kuhn used the same argument to defend the reserve system in baseball, hoping that the congressmen knew little enough of baseball history to remember that "pennant monopoly is the norm in major league baseball; those brief periods when a different champion is crowned each year are exceptional" (Voigt 1983, 24).

The commissioners' arguments were rebutted by the liberal economists and union leaders who testified, among whom there was a consensus that the reserve system did little to equalize competition. Studies had revealed that even with the reserve system in place, franchises in lucrative markets tended to buy up the best players and win most of the championships: "Small city teams have had little, if any, chance of surviving in professional sports. . . . High drawing potential areas get more than their share of championships" (Quirk and el-Hodiri 1974, 51). Ironically, the chief reason for this imbalance was that the reserve system was not restrictive enough. Players were indeed traded, if the owners could reach mutual agreement. Player contracts and future draft selections were highly marketable commodities. The richer teams could thus buy the contracts of, or secure in the draft, the best players. All the reserve system did was allot "to teams the difference between the value to fans of player skills and costs of producing such skills, whereas in a competitive market the players received the sum" (Canes 1974, 102). In short, the reserve system did nothing to equalize competition and everything to exploit the players.

The owners' defenders in Congress had three counterarguments available. Even the liberal economists had to admit that franchise owners were not profit maximizers. Wealthy clubs situated among large populations would bid for superior players and offer them higher

salaries, in apparent disregard of the effect this might have on profits.
More interested in playing success than financial success, they continued bidding for players long past the point when the addition of another star player would add to revenues—although the player might add to the numbers in the win column or to the glamor of the team and its owner. Neither a free market nor the rather weak reserve system could forestall this form of aggrandizement.

A second counterargument available to the owners was that after the introduction of liberalized free agency in the early 1970s, there had indeed been a tendency for free agents to gravitate toward larger cities. The inference could be drawn that prior to this time, the reserve system was functioning to equalize the distribution of playing talent (Daly and Moore 1981, 93). Another argument available was that the reserve system, while it treated player contracts and draft choices as marketable, did not completely commodify them. Player-for-cash deals were very uncommon in baseball throughout the postwar period, by tacit agreement among the owners enforced by the commissioner. This was intended to add muscle to the reserve system by eliminating costly cash bidding for players. A hungry owner always had to have players or draft choices to offer, a system resembling barter more than buying and selling.

At the Select Committee hearings, Commissioner Kuhn, as usual, tried to deflect the investigation from baseball, which, he argued, was not broken and therefore did not need fixing. He pointed with pride to the arbitration system, but was careful not to mention that the owners had fired the arbitrator, Peter Seitz, who had declared Messersmith and McNally free agents precisely because he had nullified the reserve system. He defended the existing reserve system by reminding committee members that the players had agreed to a modified version in the collective bargaining agreement signed that year (1976), that the courts had recognized the need for some kind of reserve system, and that past congressional investigations had acknowledged its legitimacy. He repeated his arguments that the reserve system was essential for parity in the league and that the system was a necessary prop for the minor leagues, because owners would be reluctant to invest in farm teams if players could simply move at will. He urged the committee not to change baseball's status legislatively, fearing that this would occasion endless litigation. If consistency were needed, he urged, extend immunity to other sports, rather than remove baseball's.

Kuhn's was a *bravura* performance; for, as he related in his autobiography, 1976 was a kind of watershed in the history of baseball:

> Through the long domination by the clubs before 1976 the game had been run as something approaching a public trust, laying aside the kind of cheapskate practices that had contributed to the Black Sox Scandal of 1919 . . . For all their faults, the clubs had

shown a sense of responsibility for the long term welfare of the game and the fans. . . . Free agency threatened that sense. Players' agents and the Players' Association were concerned only with the financial welfare of the players. (Kuhn 1987, 364)

The reserve system was thus linked by Kuhn to the ability of baseball to serve the public interest. Making it easier for players to move had led to "shoddy, halfhearted efforts on the field, lack of respect for managers, indifference to fans, increasing player days on the disabled list and abuse of drugs" (p. 171). Before the Seitz decision, there was order; after, "chaos." Kuhn's annual "State of the Game Message" thereafter "carried a doomsday song that blamed greedy players for driving owners to bankruptcy" (Voigt 1983, 311). Arbitration was undoubtedly a victory for the players, but Kuhn's picture is overdrawn. Between 1973 and 1989, fewer than one thousand cases were filed for arbitration out of a group of eight thousand eligible players; and of those cases, only 8 percent were actually arbitrated (Scully 1989, 161).[9]

Despite the length of the Select Committee's deliberations, it made no specific legislative proposals; and its recommendation that a successor committee be appointed fell on deaf ears. The owners, who had steadfastly lobbied against statutory action, could consider this a victory. It is surprising how badly the reserve system's critics were beaten. The climate of opinion seemed to have shifted between the 1950s and the 1970s toward an acceptance of individual rights and freedoms over against the organized power of business and toward support for the idea that the state should play a role in securing the entitlement of individuals to freedom of movement in the labor market. The social movements of the 1960s also seemed to signal renewed support for ideals of participatory democracy and the rights of subordinate groups to participate in making decisions affecting their lives. Congress and the general public seemed to be ready to see professional athletes less as peons and more as professionals. Even the Justice Department had changed its mind since the 1950s, testifying not only that the reserve system in football and basketball violated the Sherman Act but also that the immunity provided baseball should be abolished by statute (U.S. Congress, House, Select Committee on Professional Sports 1976, 292). The players' associations were much stronger than they had been in the 1950s and were able to testify persuasively about the owners' many abuses under the reserve system. Tellingly, they could remind congressmen how much Congress had granted to the leagues by previous statutory action: it had sanctioned joint negotiation of television packages, and it had approved the merger of the NFL and the AFL. They could point out that the net result of these changes was to permit the sharing of revenues among football owners. This meant that it did not matter whether an owner's team won or lost, he would still earn the same amount of money. Indeed, he had a positive disincentive to pay high salaries to attract good players. The result, in football at least, was a virtual absence of competition for "free agents," a stifling of the market as effective as the tightest reserve system or the most draconian Rozelle Rule.

Despite these advantages, the players were unsuccessful in their effort to persuade the Select Committee to initiate legislative action against the reserve system. The reasons are varied. One was parliamentary. Not all congressmen by any means agreed that a Select Committee on Professional Sports was a useful expenditure of congressmen's time. Other congressmen were prepared to have Congress consider making law in the area of sport but did not believe that a Select Committee was the appropriate body in which to do so. The powerful chairmen of the House and Senate Judiciary Committees were jealous of their role as de facto oversight committees for sport policy. The very strength of the players, especially the recognition they had gained for their unions, was also a weakness as far as the reserve system was concerned. The courts, as in *Mackey* v. *National Football League* (1976), were quite willing to declare restrictions on player mobility a violation of the Sherman Act but forestalled this political strategy by declaring at the same time that the reserve system was now part of an established management-player relationship and should be worked out in the process of collective bargaining. Congressmen were not inclined to second-guess the courts and were more than anxious to incorporate the whole question of the reserve system into the collective bargaining process.

The Courts Set Policy

A third reason why no legislation came out of the committee is that the path of litigation, although tremendously expensive and time-consuming for the individual players involved, was slowly modifying the harshness of the reserve system. In *Robertson* v. *National Basketball Association* (1975), the court held that the draft and the reserve system of the NBA were analogous to price-fixing devices condemned by antitrust laws. In a series of cases beginning with *Philadelphia World Hockey Club* v. *Philadelphia Hockey Club* (1972), the National Hockey League (NHL) was found in violation of antitrust laws, because its reserve clause was perpetual and had not been agreed upon in collective bargaining.[10]

Similar trends were evident in baseball. Despite the fact that Curt Flood lost his case on appeal in 1972, the court's opinion clearly indicated that change in favor of the players was overdue. In football, the Kapp case found the Rozelle Rule to be an unreasonable restraint of trade. Despite the fact that Kapp lost, and then lost again on appeal (1978), the pretrial ruling in the initial case, which held that the Rozelle

Rule violated the antitrust laws, was a significant legal precedent and no doubt influenced the ruling in favor of Mackey in 1976.[11]

In basketball, free agency had been won largely through aggressive collective bargaining, coupled with litigation. The landmark case had been *Oscar Robertson* v. *National Basketball Association* (1975). Robertson, a guard for the Milwaukee Bucks, had sued on behalf of other players to prevent the merger of the NBA and ABA.[12] The court determined that the reserve clause was a per se violation of the Sherman Act but determined in a collective bargaining agreement reached that same year that within four years, "a right of first refusal system was [to be] established under which a player whose contract had expired who receives an offer from another team can be retained by his original team if that team matches the offer" (Staudohar 1986, 106). A subsequent agreement, reached in 1989 after the players' union threatened to decertify itself (an action that could have voided the college draft and pulled the league into antitrust court battles), stipulated that players with seven years in the league who had completed at least two contracts should be given the chance to negotiate with any team without being limited by the right of first refusal by their previous teams. It was further agreed that the required length of service would be reduced to four years in the 1989–90 season, to reach three years by the expiration of the agreement in 1994.[13]

In the case of football, *Mackey* v. *National Football League* seemed to have dealt a death blow to the Rozelle Rule and opened the way to more freedom of movement. However, the NFL owners refused to bid for free agents. Although over two thousand players became free agents between 1977 and 1988, only two were traded to another team. In 1987, after an unsuccessful strike and failure to reach a collective bargaining agreement, the NFL Players' Association once more took the owners to court on antitrust charges. Partly in response to this litigation, the NFL Management Council unilaterally began an experiment with a new kind of free agency. Under this system ("Plan B"), designed to satisfy U.S. District Court judge David Doty, presiding over the antitrust suit filed by the players' union, each team could protect 37 players, including stars whose contracts had expired. Any loss of these players to another team would entitle the team to compensation under the old system—the Rozelle Rule. The rest of the players, including those already under contract, would be free to sign with another team.[14] At the time of the inauguration of this new system, in early spring of 1989, 619 players, mostly young and relatively unknown but also including a few better-known but perhaps overpaid players were free to move; and 229 did so. In 1990, the first year of the plan's operation, there were 491 Plan B players, 184 of whom moved to another team, the rest returning to fight for jobs on their original teams.[15] Eight NFL players, doggedly pursuing their rights to free agency, were successful in having Plan B struck down in 1992, when a jury declared that the plan had a harmful effect on competition for professional football players' services and had injured them financially. In the absence of any labor-management agreement, the ruling effectively established free agency in professional football.

Plan B was resisted by the players, a group of whom, led by Freeman McNeil, sued the NFL, claiming that the plan violated antitrust laws. McNeil won his case in 1992, and a new era of free agency for football players began. Because the players' union had decertified itself after the 1987 strike, the exact terms of the new system had to be worked out between a committee of the owners and the plaintiffs' lawyers in the McNeil case. Under the agreement, set to run for seven seasons beginning in 1993, players with five years' experience were free to offer their services on the open market provided their contracts had expired. The owners also agreed to make a $195 million payment to settle all outstanding litigation by players who sought free agency. In return, the players had to agree to a cap on each team's player salaries if player costs reached 67 percent of designated league gross revenues. They also agreed that each team could exempt one "franchise" player from free agency for the duration of his career. The agreement broke an impasse in negotiations between owners and players over free agency that had existed since 1987, but the players' gains were limited in view of the proposed cap on salaries and the waiting period for free agency—few players survived five seasons in the NFL.

In baseball, rapidly escalating salaries were a sign that restrictions on player movement had eased. Between 1951 and 1975 average baseball player salaries rose from $13,300 to $46,000, or 5.3 percent per year, about the same rate as the rise in revenues. Between 1979 and 1984, after more relaxed free agency rules were introduced, player salaries rose an average of 25 percent per year, compared with increases of 15 percent in club revenues (Scully 1989, 152). The percentage of total costs devoted to player salaries rose from 17 percent in 1974 to 37 percent in 1983 (p. 123). The rate of exploitation thus declined proportionally to the freedom of players to move. Calculations of how much of their contribution to the economic success of a franchise the players received showed that 1968 players received between 9 percent and 12 percent, 1974 players received 40 percent, and 1976 players received 55 percent (Medoff 1975; Raimondo 1983; Scully 1974).

Baseball owners displayed some reluctance to accept the implications of a freer market for baseball labor. Evidence began to accumulate that they were taking steps to restrict player movement once again. Under baseball's collective bargaining agreement, players whose contracts had expired and who had at least six years of major league experience were entitled to free agency. The agreement stipulated quite clearly that the clubs could not act "in concert" in their dealings with free agents. Despite this ban, the owners virtually ceased bidding for free agents after the 1981 strike and stepped up their efforts in the 1985 and 1986 seasons, when only five of sixty-two free agents signed with new teams. The players' association filed a grievance on behalf of this group. In 1987, arbitrator Thomas Roberts (who was dismissed by the owners in the middle of hearing the case, only to be reinstated by another arbitrator) found the owners guilty of collusion. He later awarded $10.5 million to be distributed among the 135 players eligible for arbitration at the end of the 1985 season. Later, in 1988 and 1990, arbitrators would make similar rulings on behalf of the players victimized at the end of the 1986 and 1987 seasons.[16]

Dealing with free agency issues by various forms of private arrangements (e.g., collective bargaining, arbitration) helped remove the issue from the public policy agenda. By the end of the 1980s, the reserve clause issue had moved to the congressional back burner. It did not disappear altogether but became a tangential part of a new debate over franchise location and movement. The owners argued for the reserve system in order to be able to meet communities' needs for sport. Without the stability provided by the reserve system, cities could not depend on their franchises' remaining economically viable and were likely to lose them. Without the evenness of competition that the reserve system guaranteed, the distribution of playing strength across cities could not be assured. Players argued that granting immunities to sport leagues in order to make it easier for those leagues to meet community needs would only make the reserve system more onerous. Hearings held on bills to immunize sports from antitrust liability in franchise location hearings saw Ed Garvey arguing: "In reality, with the sharing of revenues, it is not practical to discuss how player mobility will work in the National Football League. It simply will not work" (U.S. Congress, House, Committee on the Judiciary 1984, 36). By and large, however, congressmen did not connect the status of the reserve system to the larger policy question of how franchise location and movement should be determined; and as congressional attention became preoccupied with the latter issue, the rights of the players to greater freedom of movement faded from the congressional agenda. Mobility issues would continue, however, to figure prominently in labor-management negotiations (as in the NHL strike of 1992) and in numerous court cases.

CONCLUSION

The subject of this chapter has been the evolution of a system that includes the "reserve clause," the "option clause," and the "draft." Ironically, there has been something of a convergence in professional sports: team sports have seen their system of controls weakened, and individual players enjoy more freedom of movement within the labor market; the individual sports, faced with many more tournaments and players, have been forced to a set of limits on the freedom to participate that resemble those found in team sports.

In their attempts to reform the reserve system, athletes initially relied heavily on the courts. They were obliged to accept the definition of the problem as being one of individual contracts, to be settled between individual player and management. If the dispute could not be settled, litigation was the player's only recourse short of leaving the sport or jumping to a rival league. After World War II, the legislative branch became more active in the debate over restrictions on player mobility. The emerging players' unions helped focus attention on this issue and highlighted the inconsistencies in how individual workers were treated both between sport and other industries and within the sport industry itself, between baseball on the one hand and the team sports unprotected by the 1922 decision on the other. However, the players' associations have rarely situated their attack on the reserve system in the context of a fight for a more democratic organization of professional sports. Like other American unions, only more so, they have adopted the role of defending the rights of individual workers to negotiate fair and equitable contracts with their employers. They have placed individual freedom well ahead of collective equality; they have interpreted rights chiefly in terms of the right to strike the best bargain, rather than the right to make major policy decisions within the industry. Thus, their attack on the "peonage" of the reserve system has been intended to achieve equality of opportunity and freedom of movement; the players' skills are their property. The owners have consistently argued that restrictions on employment freedom are necessary to equalize competition. They therefore adopt the position that equality should be achieved by limiting the use of inputs (i.e., players), rather than outputs (i.e., revenues). Of course, it would be quite possible to imagine parity being achieved by, for example, more equal sharing of gate receipts; but owners are "generally opposed" to this idea (Markham and Teplitz 1981, 22).

Despite their frequent and often loud criticisms of the reserve system and notwithstanding several efforts to remedy its defects or abolish it altogether, Congress has at no time mounted a serious attack on the problem. Indeed, it might be said that the net effect of what statutory action it has taken (to be discussed later) has been to strengthen the system. For example, approving the joint negotiation of television rights and mergers between leagues enhances the ability of the football owners to operate their cartel without simultaneously strengthening the players' hand to resist the owners' control. Most congressmen seem to accept the argument that some rules of eligibility and some rules for the distribution of talent other than those of the marketplace are necessary to preserve the integrity of the game. The courts have largely validated this view, on condition that such rules be "reasonable," observe constitutional rules of due process, and respect basic individual rights. They have preferred to frame the issue of restrictions on player mobility in terms of the state's responsibility to ensure economic competitiveness, targeting the leagues with the weapon of antitrust law. This frame has tended to divert attention away from the state's responsibility to ensure workplace freedoms enjoyed by workers in most other industries.

4

Natural
Monopolies

Much of the politics of sport, as I have shown, have to do with how the sport role is defined so as to marginalize certain groups in the population. The politics of sport also sees arguments of economic necessity being used to limit the liberty of individual athletes to exploit their talents. In the next three chapters, the actor is no longer the unit of analysis. Instead, attention focuses on the organizational level. What is the nature of sport organizations? How are they treated by the state? How is their structure—and their relation to each other—shaped by the political and social environment in which they operate?

It is a commonplace that modern sports are big business. Even "amateur" sports such as college football generate enormous revenues and cost vast amounts of money. A modern NFL franchise is a business corporation in every sense of the word, with a payroll of ten to twenty million dollars a year. If it changes hands, a price in the region of eighty to a hundred million dollars is likely to be asked. Yet the public has been slow to acknowledge that sports is "just a business," reluctant to admit that sport enterprises should be judged by the same criteria as "real" businesses. This reluctance extends to the Supreme Court justices and powerful congressmen who have helped form sport policy in the United States. Sports owners encourage this view by denying that they are motivated chiefly by the pursuit of profit.

This appeal to values limits how formally rational the sports industry can become. The "blind" imperatives of the market do not totally govern the way leagues and franchises operate. The sports industry demands special consideration from the state by virtue of the values it espouses and defends, much as the farming lobby demands legislation to protect not only the supply of cheap food but also a "way of life." The sport business is thus shaped by state action designed to ensure both the efficiency of markets and the preservation of national values. However, the idea that sports are part of the national heritage and should be preserved even at the expense of commercial profit has not been enough to override the economic imperatives of the modern sport business. Rather, as I shall show, national values have been *harnessed* to economic goals in order to ensure that sport enterprises are viable. Sport businessmen have invoked these noncommercial values to create a state policy toward sport that better protects their investments.

Most capitalists expect the state to protect individual property rights and, in principle, favor a free market. However, they would benefit from being in monopoly positions in their particular markets, which would enable them to set their own prices for raw materials and products. The next best thing to monopoly is collective pricing. American history is replete with examples of groups of capitalists who have persuaded state officials to "facilitate the development of a collective governance regime in place of the more market-based system" in the interest of price stability and industry survival (Campbell and Lindberg 1990, 639). Thus, while the state has generally sought to maximize individual liberties, lowering barriers to entry into an industry and expanding the number of options from which customers can choose, it has also on occasion sanctioned "collusive competition" among enterprises when the public good has seemed to demand it (Davenport 1969). A sport league would appear to just such an occasion.

When owners of sport franchises call for special consideration by virtue of the unique status of sports as an industry, their arguments fall on receptive ears. This is not merely because many state officials share the substantive values of the sport world and believe strongly that it should be preserved from the ravages of the marketplace. It is also because they believe that many private governance regimes (in which prices are administered, rather than settled by the market) serve public purposes. In the case of sport leagues, these arguments are especially persuasive. Among the multitude of business enterprises, there is not one, other than a sport team, that is incapable of providing its product, generating revenue, or adding value to any good or service by itself. Only sport teams, regardless of how much talent, capital, and management skill they have at their disposal, are incapable of producing anything of independent value by themselves. Absent other restrictions, every other type of enterprise would prefer to be the only firm in its product market, that is, positioned to exact monopoly profits. A single sport team cannot do this. Club owners must accept that the whole is more than the sum of the parts. Before there can be any divisional championship race, any Super Bowl or World Series winner, every game played between any two league members must be endorsed—and the results recognized and accepted—by every club.

This argument has considerable force when applied to the product market for sports. Sport leagues must arrange schedules, appoint officials, determine rules of play, and the like in order for competition to be regular and attractive; and to do so, they must determine which teams are in the league and which are not. A league can also justly claim the right to be concerned with the economic health of all its members and thereby avoid ruinous competition between them for customers or television rights. Much the same argument can be applied to the "factor" market. Owners claim the right to control the flow of *factors of production* (chiefly players) on the grounds that this is necessary to produce "the game": it contributes to evenness of competition. For example, the player draft and subsequent restrictions on player mobility are necessary in order to ensure that the richer teams do not buy up all the best players and upset the competitive balance. In this sense, a league is a "natural monopoly." Its organization is the result not of a conspiracy to drive out competitors but a natural outgrowth of the enterprise. Leagues are not temporary coalitions of otherwise independent businesses but "joint enterprises" producing a single product.

There is much to be said for these arguments; but if their economic logic were indisputable, there would be nothing for this chapter to record. In fact, it is no easy matter to decide which forms of collaboration between club owners are necessary for the league to exist as a coordinated activity and which forms of collaboration exist simply to limit competition among owners and enhance their profits. This explains why the legal status of professional sports leagues has been the subject of almost continuous political debate since they originated in the 1880s. The debate is complicated by the fact that the law does not prohibit all kinds of collusion between businesses, simply those considered "unreasonable restraints of trade." The debate about natural monopolies in sport thus contains two arguments: (1) which agreements between owners are part of the game itself and which are ancillary business agreements subject to regulation by public law? and; (2) which ancillary business agreements are reasonable—those that help stabilize the market and improve the quality of the product—and which are unreasonable—whose sole purpose is to drive down the cost of inputs and drive up the price of outputs? As I shall show, while social scientists can provide some of the answers to these questions, the debate is ultimately political because the "data" that must be used to analyze the problem are based on interpretation and inference, which in turn are influenced by economic interest and political beliefs. For example, the law requires that businesses must share the risk of loss in order to be considered "joint ventures." To some, this criterion clearly places a sports league in violation of the law because club owners do not pool either their profits or their losses. To others, this criterion clearly places sports leagues within the law because all club owners are hurt financially by a league's declining revenues, to such a degree that they might have the right to "rescue" a failing franchise should its mismanagement threaten the welfare of all.

The problem of defining the property rights of individual franchise holders is the subject of this chapter. In the name of the public interest in sport and using the argument of natural monopoly, the owners have sought government backing for an arrangement that permits considerable collusion among them while at the same time preserving their individual right to benefit from their property and dispose of it at will. They have been largely successful, because state officials accept their public interest argument. Less consistently, the state has agreed that most forms of collusion between sport firms are reasonable. The thrust of public policy in this area has been to rely on the market to provide sport entertainment, albeit one structured in a unique way to meet the special needs of club owners. The government, in other words, sanctions collusive competition because sports leagues are believed to need it in order to survive as business enterprises. Many people in government—congressmen, judges—realize that they are providing an institutional basis for power in the industry by their actions. They tacitly acknowledge that "the state's ability to define and enforce property rights determines social relations, and therefore, the balance of power" between club owners, players, fans, and the general public (Campbell and Lindberg 1990, 636). Market regulation—in this case permitting more collusion than usual—takes power away from the players and gives it to the owners; it weakens the bargaining position of municipalities and strengthens that of leagues; and it creates a seller's market for the rights to broadcast sports events.

My analysis of the political debate over the status of sport franchises assumes that the owners are primarily interested in establishing the broadest possible immunity from antitrust prosecution. These interests are not guided simply by the desire to maximum profits. For a sport league, the ability to "collude" is the foundation for private government powers. As later chapters will show, leagues need monopoly power to control each other, as much as to control players and customers. Consistent with these interests, the owners have always maintained that their leagues are joint ventures, not monopolies. They have fought to keep this question off the congressional agenda and, where obliged, have presented this argument in court. Their fortunes have been mixed, and I shall show why.

Antitrust policy in the United States typically targets major business corporations and trade associations in markets considered important for economic growth and consumer welfare (e.g., telecommunications). Sport is neither particularly big business, nor normally considered a strategically important part of the economy. A number of factors have affected the degree to which sport has been influenced by state antitrust policy. At the level of the individual firm, growth in size and a shift away from an individual, entrepreneurial form of ownership toward a more bureaucratic form has exposed sport enterprises to state regulations designed to ensure free markets. At the level of relations between firms, rising affluence, especially after World War II, increased demand for leisure opportunities and created room for rival firms to enter the sport market with the expectation of making a profit. Rivalry between leagues increased the odds of antitrust issues being raised. Economic growth in the sports industry also reshaped the "organizational field" in which club owners operated. In the postwar period, television became a major purchaser of sports entertainment. After a period of contracting with television networks on a one-to-one basis, each club negotiating its own deal, the leagues eventually moved to a system of jointly negotiated contracts, where the league commissioner represented all clubs in the league in negotiations with the networks. Television revenues rose dramatically as a result of this restructuring, but there was also a less desirable consequence: the leagues became more vulnerable to the charge of monopoly, especially since they agreed to share the television revenues equally. The same thing happened later, when individual sports like boxing, tennis, and golf restructured themselves to improve their bargaining position with respect to the television networks: they, too, became more vulnerable to antitrust action.

The impact of television on the sport industry was not all one-way, however, for in some other respects television helped insulate sport leagues from charges of monopoly. At the same time that owners were being encouraged to negotiate jointly with television networks, the telecommunications industry as a whole was helping differentiate the market in which they operated. No longer were particular sports associated with particular seasonal markets (and therefore with a monopoly over them). All manner of televised sports could be watched, as over the air and cable transmissions multiplied. Furthermore, sports programs now competed with other programs for "ratings." In the context of such intense competition for the entertainment dollar, charges of monopoly became harder to sustain. I shall have to take note of this countertrend, if only because it seems that the immediate future of the relation between television and sport lies in the direction of a more open market, which means old antitrust issues will fade away.

While these changes in firm size and market concentration have played the major role in determining the impact of government regulatory policy on sport, the fact that government policy itself has changed should not be ignored. A policy of vigorous trust-busting before World War I was followed by a more "laissez-faire" approach until the Great Depression. During the New Deal, many quasi-monopolistic practices were tolerated in the interests of economic recovery, and the same means were used to achieve war goals until 1945. During the Eisenhower administration, free-market policies became popular once more, providing a congenial climate for several congressional investigations of monopolistic practices in sports. The more liberal Kennedy and Johnson administrations also favored more free-market policies; but the goal changed, away from securing more efficient business enterprises toward protecting the consumer and the "little guy." Under the Reagan administration, policy shifted again. The values of the free market were vigorously reasserted; but they were connected to the goal of organizational efficiency, and broader goals of protecting consumers or the public good were repudiated. To oversimplify, the question asked by policymakers during the liberal administrations of the 1960s and 1970s was, Does the practice benefit society as a whole? During the more conservative administrations that followed, the question was, Does the practice benefit the company, in the sense of making it more efficient? While the economic changes I shall describe have played a major part in increasing the exposure of sport organizations to antitrust action, the changes in state policy have at times accelerated, and at times decelerated, this trend.

TRUSTS AND LEAGUES

Sports leagues pose acute problems with respect to economic policy because of their hybrid status. They are single firms yet do not seek to relate to each other through the medium of the market. However, it is by no means unusual for economic enterprises in the United States to restrict competition among themselves, seek state approval to do so, and secure state authorization for any discipline they might exercise over those who balk at the restrictions. Railroad operators were among the first to advocate expanded state action to regulate and stabilize competition in the free market. By the end of the nineteenth century, American business had become "increasingly desirous of a more active state, capable not only of distributing resources and promoting enterprise, but also of regulating the economy and repressing the chal-

lenge of labor" (Bright 1984, 145). Legislators responded with a number of items of legislation (e.g., the Sherman Act, the Federal Trade
Commission Act, the Clayton Act) whose purpose was to permit
reasonable combinations and restraints of trade, the "indirect government regulation of a corporate-administered market" (M. Sklar
1988, 324).

Antitrust policy did not, therefore, prohibit all collusion between
capitalists. Only practices resulting in artificially high prices were
frowned upon; and even high prices were better than chaos and instability in the marketplace (Leuchtenberg 1958, 190). Much more important than the fact of cooperation between independent capitalists was
the degree of control the public felt they exercised over them. The real
issue to many people was not whether there should be regulation but
whether it should be public or private (Hofstadter 1965, 234). Here,
moral and political judgments were as important as economic. What
was the appropriate balance of private freedom and public accountability for combinations and trusts? At what point did the price and employment stability combinations provided, paid in terms of the
concentration of power in the hands of a few, become too high? If the
state permitted combinations and trusts, what could it expect of them
in return?

This is the backdrop against which sport leagues were formed. Organizers had to acknowledge the popular sentiment that business ventures with the appearance of monopoly should be targets of political
scrutiny, especially if the results of the monopoly were to drive up
prices or if the cartel seemed to provide undemocratic powers. But
they could also trade on the favorable attitude toward those combinations whose public morality and public regard were accepted by the
general population. They could not ignore the fact that trust-busting
served politically symbolic functions: consumers protected by their
government; fair competition preserved; small, independent, family-
owned businesses defended; deceptive advertising and business practices weeded out; and abuses of economic power forestalled. But they
also knew that the symbolism of trust-busting would be less persuasive
in the case of professional sports if the public could be convinced that
sport was not simply one business among many, subject to the same economic imperatives and abuses, but a unique case entitled to exceptional
privileges.

Finding their niche in the emerging economic order also meant establishing a more precise understanding of what a sport league was in
commercial terms, defining customers' expectations and organizing
their industry to meet them. Owners soon discovered that they were in
the business of selling competition, not simply entertainment; for crowds
would not show for "meaningless" contests. They discovered that fans
were interested in championships, not simply unconnected games.
These market imperatives made a difference to how the industry could

structure itself. Owners learned to their cost that baseball fans would not attend games unless they believed that the contest was fair and above board, and this meant that the teams had to be independently owned. Turnover of franchises in the National League led the owners to experiment with syndicated baseball. The wealthier owners had developed the habit of assisting their weaker brethren in order to keep the league alive. In 1901, they formalized this arrangement and formed a syndicate to run the league. This proved to be highly unpopular among the fans, because, without formal independence, the outcomes of games were highly suspect. Fan interest shifted to the rival American League, and the National League owners terminated the experiment after one year. The market, it seemed, would not tolerate an arrangement that would have absolved professional sports of all future threats from antitrust litigation.[1]

Neither the Sherman nor the Clayton Acts were intended to outlaw every type of agreement or restraint upon competition. Their purpose was to declare illegal those which "unreasonably" restrained trade and competition. This "Rule of Reason" was later to prove very useful for sport franchise owners. They could claim that virtually any practice challenged was ancillary to a more central purpose, that of putting on a competitive game. Their unique status requiring cooperation in order to compete, seemed to be precisely the kind of situation the rule of reason was designed to deal with. They could appeal to it in defense of the practice of blacklisting players convicted (or simply suspected) of gambling, on the grounds that such a rule was a reasonable means of protecting the integrity of the game. They could also appeal to it when justifying licensing and registration procedures.

FROM FAMILY FIRM TO
CORPORATE DIVISION

The formative years of sport after the Civil War saw a free-wheeling mixture of entrepreneurialism and voluntarism. Volunteers, keen to set up teams and leagues, were eager to attract sponsors to provide them with capital resources and stability; promoters, hunting for lucrative investments, saw in sport an exciting new field in which to make money. Commercial sport enterprises (chiefly baseball at this time) were small-scale and highly competitive. Teams and leagues came and went almost overnight.

The growth of major urban centers in the 1890–1920 period helped baseball attract bigger crowds. Clubs like the Chicago White Sox, Chicago Cubs, and New York Giants began to make six-figure profits annually, a substantial amount in those days. Crowds of seventy thousand flocked to Yankee Stadium to watch Babe Ruth play. A new image of the sports club began to emerge, that of a business enterprise, whose owner had to meet a payroll by putting people in the seats. Yet, with the exception I will note below, this era did not see much antitrust action against sports leagues. The reason lies partly in myth and partly in fact. Club owners assiduously cultivated an image of being small business-men, constantly on the edge of economic disaster. Indeed, most clubs were very modest operations: "Besides the owner a club might have a treasurer, a road secretary, a business manager, responsible for con-cessions and sale of advertising, and a team manager" rounded off by more casually employed groundskeepers, ushers, ticket-takers and scouts (Seymour 1971, 21). Club owners also enjoyed the halo effect of college sports, which were if anything more popular at this time and a respected institution among the middle class. They cultivated this asso-ciation with the purity of amateurism, being careful not to compete with the college game in scheduling or recruiting, the better to disguise their interest in profits. In this they were abetted by congressmen and judges reluctant to acknowledge the businesslike aspects of sport even as it was rapidly commercializing, a reluctance signalled in the 1922 Supreme Court decision likening major league baseball games to Chau-tauqua lectures and declaring that the sport was not "commerce" in the sense intended by the Sherman Act.

Added to this mythological aspect, in reality a sports enterprise at this time, even an entire league, was nothing like the kind of business corporation against which antitrust laws were aimed, in scale, profits, or public significance. The emergence of sports clubs capable of mak-ing consistent profits was a novelty, but it did not make the leagues they comprised targets of trust-busting sentiment on those grounds alone. Sports other than baseball were even less likely targets. The National Football League, founded in 1920 to capitalize on the postwar "hysteria" for college football (Betts 1974, 255), grew to twenty-six teams by 1926, but shrivelled to eight by 1932. A professional football game in the early 1930s was a very modest affair: a Sunday home game of the Chicago Bears was likely to be outdrawn by an exhibition of pool by Willie Moscone the night before (Polsky 1969, 19). The National Hockey League was even more fragile. Founded in 1917, it had lost nine of its original fifteen teams by 1942. Basketball was highly localized through-out most of the interwar period, an attempt to expand nationally lasting only five years (the American Basketball League between 1926 and 1931). Most of the better basketball teams barnstormed for a living much like a traveling circus or dance band. None of this activity was likely to attract the attention of trust busters.

The one exception was that of baseball in the period leading up to World War I and here the reason was not the economic impact of league collusion on the product market (e.g., ticket prices) so much as the constraints on player mobility already described in chapter 3. For two reasons these constraints were more likely to trigger antitrust action. For many people, the players were the game: they paid for opportunity to see players play and the fortunes of players on and off the field were their primary interest. Trades and movement of players were the subject of intense fan concern. The second reason why constraints on player mobility would have more readily inspired antitrust action is that competition for players—and players' eagerness to be competed for—was the most important source of internal strife in the sports industry, a struggle in which antitrust law was a ready and effective weapon. Sport leagues, particularly baseball, absorbed some of the bad odor emanating from "combinations," less because they drove up ticket prices and more because they combined to exploit players. As I have shown in chapter 3, the players were not slow to level charges of monopoly in their fight against the reserve system; and they were successful enough to convince the general public that the typical club owner was "a grasping skinflint with a public-be-damned attitude" (Voigt 1970, 107). The owners felt vulnerable to the charge of monopoly and exploitation brought by the players. They avoided testing the reserve system in court after 1902 for this reason. Instead, they colluded not to compete for contract jumpers and thus deflected antitrust attention, at least until after World War II.

As the sport industry grew, so did its vulnerability to antitrust law. The asset value of individual firms, or franchises, grew from four-figure sums before World War I to multi-million-dollar investments after World War II. Family ownership was replaced by corporate ownership, making it more difficult to defend the notion that sport was a vocation rather than a business. These changes were fueled by the boom in attendance at professional sports events immediately following the defeat of Japan. Before 1946, a combined major league baseball attendance in excess of ten million would have been considered marvelous, "but in 1946, 18.5 million fans jammed the parks" (Voigt 1970, 293). Between 1940 and 1955, every club in the National League except the Cubs and the Giants changed hands. A different group of owners, "wealthy plutocrats," moved in (Voigt 1983, 87). Knowing little about baseball, they appointed general managers to run their operations. The Yankees' manager Casey Stengel remarked on this change: "The post of general manager is a latter day origination. . . . Not until the rich men got into the game as a hobby . . . was the post created" (quoted p.89). The "hustling new promoter" did not scruple to uproot traditional franchises and transplant them to more promising sites and exploit tax loopholes in order to protect income from other business ventures (Voigt 1970, 274). Later, business corporations, for whom ownership of a sport franchise might be a profitable adjunct to their other lines of operation, bought into sport, especially when national television exposure became possible. Breweries were very active in this market, as were communications companies. As the nature of the club changed, so did its relation to the state, and particularly to antitrust laws. No longer could owners so convincingly present themselves as small and relatively powerless businessmen whose primary interest was in "the good of the game" (Flint and Eitzen 1987).

INTERLEAGUE RIVALRY

An expanding market not only changes the structure of individual enterprises, it also attracts new entrepreneurs to the industry. Would-be team owners, denied access to the established leagues, band together to form a rival. This is a serious threat to existing owners because it devalues their assets and sows confusion in the minds of the fans, who desire a single championship. Interleague rivalry frequently causes political conflict because each league tries to legitimate its position or discredit its opponent's. The present structure of organized baseball, with its division between American and National Leagues, commemorates one of the most famous interleague rivalries. The National Football League has been challenged by American Football Leagues in 1926–27, 1936–37, 1940–41 and, most seriously of all, 1960–66. An American Football Conference sought to supplant the NFL in 1946–50. The short-lived United States Football League (1983–86) is therefore only the latest in a long line of challengers. The National Hockey League had to fight off the World Hockey Association between 1974 and 1979; and the National Basketball Association suffered so much from competition from the American Basketball Association between 1967 and 1976 that it was forced to negotiate a merger.

Interleague rivalry weakens the warring owners. It is worth noting that the earliest baseball players' union, the Players' Protective Association, thrived during the brief war between the National League and the American League (1900–1903), and that a second attempt at unionism was made during the war between the National Commission and the Federal League (1913–15). Interleague competition not only makes the owners more vulnerable to unionism but also provokes them to attack each other. Often, they resort to antitrust law to achieve victory. Practices, such as "reserving" or "blacklisting" players to prevent them from jumping to another league, suddenly become reprehensible when they hurt not the players but would-be owners.

There is some irony in the fact that the 1922 Supreme Court decision immunizing baseball from antitrust action for so long was itself the outcome of rivalry between leagues. Organized baseball had been challenged by a number of rivals since the signing of the National

Agreement in 1903, including the Pacific Coast League (1904), the Tri-State League (1905–07), and the California State League (1907–09). Entrepreneurs had not forgotten that the American League had once been an "outlaw" and that the National Agreement represented a major victory for the upstart league. In 1913, the monopoly of the National and American Leagues was threatened once again, by the new Federal League, which began operations with six clubs. Within two years the new league had grown to eight clubs, most of them located in eastern and midwestern cities with established National or American League franchises and most of them reasonably well financed. A bidding war for players ensued: 221 players jumped from organized baseball to the Federal League, including 81 major-leaguers (Murdock 1982, 111). Organized baseball was obliged to raise salaries and liberalize the standard player contract in order to compete. However, it continued to ask for (and usually received) injunctions prohibiting contracted players from jumping to the Federal League. As a result, the Federal League filed suit in 1915 in the United States District Court for Northern Illinois (Judge Kennesaw Mountain Landis presiding), charging the sixteen National League club presidents with forming a conspiracy in restraint of trade in violation of the federal antitrust statutes. The case eventually wound up in the Supreme Court, where, in 1922, the justices upheld a lower court decision declaring that baseball was not "trade or commerce in the commonly-accepted use of those words."[2] Baseball was fortunate in having a good friend of the game as chief justice of the Supreme Court: former president William Taft was half-brother of Charles Taft, former owner of the Chicago Cubs.

This decision goes a long way toward explaining why baseball was never again to face the threat of a competitor league. Owners of professional football clubs, however, have not been so fortunate, because baseball's immunity has not been extended to other sports. Aspiring team owners have thus been granted a powerful weapon with which to break down the barriers to entry into the industry. This weapon was rarely used between the wars because the market for professional football was quite limited. But the sport's popularity rose rapidly in the 1960s, and the NFL's monopoly of markets began to irk those anxious to capitalize on the public's appetite for the game. Between 1960 and 1981, the NFL was to be subject to more than fifty antitrust suits (Rosenbaum 1987, 758). Many of these cases were brought by players or players' associations using the antitrust weapon in labor wars, where the monopoly status of the league was incidental to the main purpose of the struggle, but many others were a frontal assault on the NFL's stranglehold on the market for professional football. Among the litigants was the most serious of the NFL's rivals during the postwar period, the American Football League. In its very first season (1960), it brought suit against the NFL, charging it with monopolizing the market for football by assigning exclusive franchises to particular territories and by controlling the sale of television and radio rights. At this time, football had not evolved into a truly national sport, nor had television revenues become as significant as they would later. Judge Roszel Thompson dismissed the case, arguing that the NFL had in no way monopolized or intended to monopolize professional football competition *in the relevant market area for that product*, which is the United States.[3]

APPROVING MERGERS

One of the most important functions of the Antitrust Division of the Department of Justice and of the Federal Trade Commission is to approve mergers and acquisitions, because the takeover of one company by another or the decision by one or more companies to join forces often creates the appearance of an effort to monpolize a market. When the AFL owners decided it was time to petition for peace in their war with the NFL and seek a merger, they reversed their position with respect to the status of professional leagues. Now they were concerned to get Congress to approve the merger and lobbied hard for immunity from the Sherman Act for the combined league. Their lobbying efforts paid off. After terms of the merger had been agreed, the Senate duly passed a bill (S3817), on September 26, 1966, exempting the agreement from antitrust action. The House did not act quite so swiftly. The chief obstacle there was Emmanuel Celler's Judiciary Committee, the body responsible for considering S3817 (and twenty-five similar bills introduced into the House). Celler had long been an opponent of granting antitrust exemption to sports. His committee held rancorous hearings on the merger bills but did not conclude them or reconvene on the proposed legislation. Celler objected to "buying a pig in a poke" (U.S. Congress, House, Committee on the Judiciary 1966, 261).

The owners realized that the House Judiciary Committee was a serious obstacle in the path to the merger. They persuaded Senator Everett Dirksen to add an amendment or rider to a House-passed anti-inflation tax bill.[4] The Senate, it must be remembered, had already approved the merger's exemption. The owners had persuaded enough senators that interleague competition for players was driving many franchises to bankruptcy. The Senate Judiciary Committee, in reporting S3817, spoke of the danger, absent a merger, "that some of the less favorably situated franchises in both existing leagues face dissolution or transfer to other cities" (U.S. Congress, House, Committee on the Judiciary 1966, 5). Dirksen referred to his rider as "almost a bailout procedure," so desperate was football's condition. Russell Long, of Louisiana, hoping to attract a new franchise to New Orleans, complained that the House was dragging its feet on a measure the Senate had repeatedly approved. The Senate Judiciary Committee's report on S3817 had also been quite blunt about the quid pro quo implied: "One of the results of the merger will be the bringing of professional football teams to new cities. In addition to the two new teams added this year—Miami and Atlanta—the merger calls for two additional franchises in 1968 and two more franchises later" (ibid.). With these kinds of sentiments prevailing in the Senate, it was no surprise when the amendments to the tax bill were agreed to after brief discussion, with no dissension. The House-Senate conferees also approved the amendments.

In the House debate on the final bill, Celler vigorously opposed the amendments. "Why the haste?" he asked. "We do not know what this joint agreement is. It is not set forth in the pages of the report. It is not set forth in the statute itself. I pray that the House will not accept anything of this character" (U.S. Congress, House, Committee on Ways and Means 1966, 1437). Celler argued that the extent of the immunity granted football was not specified in the amendments, that Congress should not be in the business of rescuing owners from each other, and that the merger would weaken the bargaining power of players, especially rookies. Celler was painfully aware that he had been tricked by a parliamentary stratagem: "There may be some rejoicing in some quarters that an end run was made around me by adding this provision as a rider to this investment credit bill" (ibid.). His opponents in the House included not only Hale Boggs (like Long in the Senate, hoping for an expansion franchise in New Orleans) but also congressmen like Peter Rodino, who had grown tired of Celler's stonewalling on the antitrust issue.

Supporters of the amendment used two somewhat contradictory arguments. The first was that sport was unique, that the "independent" firms could not actually operate independently, that each had a vested interest in the health and vigor of the others. The second was that sport was not all that unusual. Few businesses, it was argued, were genuinely competitive in the costs and prices of what they buy and sell. Businesses, often with the help of the government (e.g., the Federal Trade Commission), frequently seek to "rationalize" competition, especially at the level of prices. The House approved the Dirksen rider; and the bill became law on October 21, 1966, signaling the greatest legislative victory professional football was to achieve.[5]

The merger and its congressional approval achieved its purpose, and no serious challengers to the monopoly of the NFL appeared for more than a decade. However, team owners used their monopoly position to keep a tight lid on expansion, proceeding at a much slower pace than they had promised when lobbying for the merger. In the face of rapidly rising television revenues, the almost inevitable result was emergence of the World Football League (1974–75) and the United States Football League (1983–86). The former did not choose to fight the NFL on antitrust grounds and soon collapsed, but the latter was more persistent and eventually decided that it had to fight the NFL in the courts, as well as at the ticket office. The USFL had initially tried to avoid competing with the NFL, by playing its games in the spring. However, poor attendance and low television ratings prompted the USFL to think of going head-to-head with the NFL in the fall. At the same time, the new league brought suit against the NFL in 1986. The jury found that the NFL was indeed guilty of monopolistic practices; but it awarded only one dollar damages, tripled to three dollars under United States law. The jury clearly regarded the NFL as a monopoly but considered it "natural." Although the judge would later require the NFL to pay the USFL $5.5 million in attorney's fees and $62,000 in other court costs, the decision effectively restored the status quo in professional football, permitting the owners to continue to monopolize their product market. The decision in this case neatly captures the anomalous status of all sport leagues without grant of baseball's immunity. They appear so vulnerable to the charge of monopoly but judges and juries have great difficulty thinking of them as a "predacious conspiracy."

Five years after the football owners secured congressional approval for their merger, another request for merger approval came before Congress, this time from the basketball owners. The bill to permit the merger between the NBA and ABA, submitted to the Senate (S2373) and House (H10185) in 1971, was actually an amendment to the amendments sanctioning the football merger in 1966. The Senate bill had twenty-five cosponsors, the House bill forty-five. In addition, some congressmen seized this opportunity to introduce yet more bills to exempt all professional team sports from antitrust laws. However, the politics of the merger between the ABA and NBA were to prove even more complicated than those of football. In the end, the basketball owners were denied the statutory authorization won by the football owners.

There are a number of reasons why the basketball merger did not proceed in the same manner as football. One difference was television. While owners, especially those in the ABA, pleaded imminent bankruptcy caused by competition for players, their opponents could with equal conviction argue that rising television revenues, if appropriately shared, could pay for these higher salaries. The most important reason, however, had to do with the players' associations. When the football leagues merged, the players' associations were too weak to mount significant opposition. By the time the merger initiative occurred in basketball, the players were well organized. Each league had its own union, and the question arose whether the owners needed approval from both unions in order to establish a common draft. The players opposed the merger idea, anticipating that their bargaining leverage would suffer if they were faced once more with a single management committee. The unions lobbied Congress not to follow the precedent set by football and, in the person of Oscar Robertson, brought suit against the NBA to block the merger, using antitrust law to do so. In May 1970, the court issued a preliminary injunction prohibiting the merger. The owners had promised to ease restrictions on player movement in return for Congress's sanctioning the merger. The reserve system would be reduced to one option year, with compensation paid to the selling team if a player was traded, an arrangement identical to the Rozelle Rule in football. The players had rejected this offer. They also vigorously objected to the legislation approving the merger: "We are pleading that Congress not throw its weight on the side of the owners" (U.S. Congress, Senate, Committee on the Judiciary 1972, 244).

The players, who saw the resort to Congress as an attempt by the owners to protect themselves from future lawsuits, wanted "the ability to continue to litigate" (U.S. Congress, Senate, Committee on the Judiciary 1972, 246). They wanted, above all, two leagues that would compete for players' services. Larry Fleisher, counsel for the National Basketball Association Players' Association (NBAPA), described what life was like for the professional basketball player before the ABA came along. The minimum salary had been $6,000; 50 percent of the veterans earned less than $20,000 a year; the median salary was $27,000; and the pension fund contributed $2,400 a year to retired players, half of the fund being provided by the players themselves. By 1971, the minimum had risen to $16,500; only 10 percent of veterans were earning less than $20,000; the median salary had risen to $43,000; and the pension fund, now fully funded by the owners, paid $7,200 a year (p. 231). Fleisher's testimony was forceful and aggressive. It was unfortunate for him that the American Basketball Association Players' Association (ABAPA) did not speak with such a united or persuasive voice, due in part to the greater variation in the financial solvency of ABA franchises (some players could look forward to the merger more than others) and the weaker organization of the union. There was considerable debate in both House and Senate hearings as to the true position of the ABAPA on the merger. Nevertheless, the voice of players could not be ignored to the same degree as had that of the football players.

Basketball owners seeking to merge faced more opposition than football owners for another reason. The antimerger forces in Congress had regrouped since their football defeat. Many were convinced that the football merger had been "railroaded through Congress." They had also gained a powerful ally in Samuel Ervin, chairman of the Senate Judiciary Committee, who declared from the outset that this merger would get more careful attention than the last: "The common draft and the option clause which result from the merger are issues concerning the economic enslavement of professional basketball players, and are too important for such ephemeral treatment as was accorded the football merger" (U.S. Congress, Senate, Committee on the Judiciary 1972, 14). Ervin was a staunch champion of individual rights and associated the owners' monopoly power with the denial of freedom of contract for athletes:

> S2373 proposes to rob every man in America who possesses skill in basketball of the right to sell his skill to the highest bidder on a free market and negotiate a contract with anybody who desires to purchase his athletic skill. . . . It is clear to me that the only reason for the institution of the common draft and the passage of this bill is the pocketbook of the owners (p. 15)

Ervin referred to the existing practice of trading players as "selling souls." He actually sponsored a bill (S2616) in 1971 explicitly applying the Sherman Act to professional sports. The basketball owners were not helped at all by the Washington Senators' departure for Texas during the middle of the Senate hearings, prompting Ervin to threaten that "as a result of what happened here with respect to the Washington Senators Congress might have to give serious consideration to the question of passing a bill without delay which would put baseball under the antitrust laws" (p. 226). There was, in any case, little hope of basketball's achieving baseball's immunity. A federal district court had declared in 1956 (*Washington Professional Basketball Corporation* v. *National Basketball Association*) that basketball was trade or commerce among several states within the meaning of the Sherman Act.

Political positions on the merger issue reflected preestablished ideas about the legitimacy of the reserve system in either league. Politicians who, like Ervin, believed that the draft and reserve system were clear violations of antitrust laws were, for that reason, especially fearful of the consequences of a merger. Those who, like Roman Hruska, sided with the leagues on the necessity of the draft and the reserve system, could not see how the merger in itself would make things worse. Positions were also affected by how convinced each congressmen was of the argument that basketball was on the verge of bankruptcy. Hruska was quite sure that the basketball industry was on its last legs. He likened the need for merger approval to the need for the regulation of freight carriers, who had been driving each other into bankruptcy and thereby threatening the American public with inadequate carriage services before the government stepped in to regulate the industry. Ervin could not accept this parallel:

> I will say the distinction between the Interstate Commerce Act and this proposal is just about 1,000 times wider than the Pacific Ocean. When the railroads needed restraint, they established the Interstate Commerce Commission to regulate the ones that needed restraints, the railroads. But here the ones that need restraints against uneconomic bidding for players are the club owners. There is no proposal here to put any restraints on the club

people who have athletic skills. It would be like the regulation of the railroads if they regulate the people, the shippers, instead of the railroads. (U.S. Congress, Senate, Committee on the Judiciary 1972, 134)

Congress never did legislate the merger. The NBA backed away from seeking legislative sanction when it became apparent that it would be approved only if a number of provisions unacceptable to the NBA were attached to the merger authorization. In return for approving the merger, the U.S. Senate Antitrust Subcommittee declared that the reserve clause could not be part of the merger agreement. The subcommittee prepared a bill outlawing the reserve clause and replacing it with an option clause, meaning that a player could switch to another team a year after ending his contract without his original team's retaining his rights. This was enough to dissuade the already-reluctant NBA (Pluto 1990, 424).

The merger was eventually authorized by the Robertson court; and in June 1976, the NBA and ABA consolidated into a twenty-two-team league. Of the remaining ABA teams (several had folded), New York, Denver, Indiana, and Virginia were admitted to the NBA, while St. Louis and Kentucky were bought off by payments from the first group. The amalgamation was never referred to as a merger but as an "expansion" of the NBA, signaling the relative weakness of the ABA, which had never secured a television contract for the broadcast of regular season play. As part of the agreement, the court was to monitor league practices for the following decade, using the services of a "special master" whose rulings could be appealed in the courts. Julius Erving, a star in both leagues, remembers that "the ABA players felt as if we were sold down the river by the merger" (Pluto 1990, 434).

Interleague rivalries and league mergers become so heavily politicized because they exposed the element of business competition in professional sports. The owners have a strong, vested interest in limiting the number of firms competing in the industry, because this increases the value of their assets. Interleague rivalry and league mergers highlight this side of professional sports. Congressional critics were shocked by the practice of charging "indemnity fees" against new franchises. These fees were determined in what seemed to be an arbitrary fashion. Benjamin Sisk, chairman of the 1976 House Select Committee on Professional Sports, bridled at the notion of having to pay to enter the league at all: "Is that the justification for the price, just because you can get it?" (U.S. Congress, House, Select Committee on Professional Sports 1976, 425). Economist Roger Noll reminded the Select Committee that the judgment of whether or not a monopolistic practice was excessive should be based on whether or not it had market value. Given the price charged to enter the league and the capital appreciation shown by league franchises, the leagues were clearly a monopoly. Baseball clubs bought for three or four million dollars in the 1950s were selling for over ten million dollars in the 1970s. The average rate of capital gains was 6.5 percent per annum (Scully 1989, 143). In the absence of interleague competition, a franchise became a monopoly right granted by Congress. Noll alluded to the case of the New York Nets having to pay "indemnity" to the New York Knicks when the ABA and NBA merged, on grounds that the Nets (who actually played 40 miles away from the usually sold-out Knicks) were "encroaching" on the Knicks territory (U.S. Congress, House, Select Committee on Professional Sports 1976, 141).

By the 1970s, then, few state actors—congressmen, judges, civil servants—could claim to be unaware that professional sports were, to all intents and purposes, a strictly commercial enterprise. Not only had the pattern of ownership changed, but all four major team sports had undergone rapid expansion, transforming them into significant economic enterprises with considerable asset value. These changes, in turn, triggered more intense competition within the industry and compensating strategies on the part of owners to restrict it. These changes were sufficient to impell state action by themselves, but there were additional reasons why the state would become embroiled in the operation of sports enterprises. One has to do with changes occuring not in the structure of the enterprise itself but in the relation of enterprises to each other.

THE "ORGANIZATIONAL FIELD"

The student of sport enterprises does not need reminding that "all organizations have relationships with other organizations" (Hall 1991, 216). Other organizations (i.e., other franchises in the league) are a precondition for the existence of a professional sport team. But each franchise (and the league it has helped form) has relationships with many other organizations too, from which it obtains raw materials and to which it sells its product. In other words, the enterprise is situated within an organizational field, "made up of key suppliers, resource and produce consumers, regulatory agencies, and other organizations that produce similar services or products" (Dimaggio and Powell 1983, 148). In the case of professional sports, after World War II, this organizational field began to change and, with it, the relationship of each franchise to the others in the league. The result was the emergence of a new kind of joint venture, in which franchises became much more interdependent and, in becoming more interdependent, became more vulnerable to state regulatory action aimed at protecting the free market

New Joint Ventures

Until the 1960s, sport franchises were largely autonomous economic enterprises, in the sense that the financial health of each depended on its gate receipts, concession income, and the sale of local media (radio) rights. Each franchise operated in an environment where the retail outlet for its product was independent. With the advent of joint negotiations over television revenues, particularly where these were coupled with revenue-sharing agreements, the organizational field changed and franchises became more interdependent. With more interdependence came more "collusion" and the taint of monopoly.

With baseball sheltering under its 1922 immunity, professional football was the first to feel the effects of the change in the organizational field. An opening salvo was fired by the Justice Department, in a 1953 suit against the NFL, in which the court decided that the NFL could not enter into the joint sale of radio and television rights: "The court reasoned that radio and television were clearly involved with interstate commerce, and therefore professional football was an interstate business subject to the antitrust laws" (Freedman 1987, 35). The Supreme Court affirmed this interpretation in *Radovich* v. *National Football League* (1957), arguing that football could not be immunized from the Sherman Act, on account of its "volume of business." Revenue-sharing agreements were more popular and more strongly enforced in football than in baseball.[6]

Television was also responsible for restructuring sports featuring competitions between individuals. Exploiting the new medium of television, the International Boxing Club (IBC) secured monopoly control over the market for championship-level boxers in the early 1950s: it received 81 percent of all revenues from title contests held between 1949 and 1953 (U.S. Congress, Senate Committee on the Judiciary 1961, 60). In 1951, the Justice Department charged that beginning in 1949, the IBC had "combined and conspired to restrain trade and to monopolize interstate trade and foreign commerce through the promotion, exhibition, broadcasting, telecasting and motion picture production and distribution of professional championship boxing contests in the United States" (Sammons 1988, 160). In 1954, U.S. District Court Judge Gregory Noonan dismissed the government's case, citing *Federal Baseball* (1922) and *Toolson* (1951), arguing that no valid basis could be found to distinguish baseball and boxing. This decision was reversed on appeal, the Supreme Court ruling in 1955 that boxing did fall within the scope of the Sherman Act, allowing the case to go forward. In the subsequent trial, the district court found (1957) that beginning in 1949 and continuing thereafter, the IBC had monopolized trade and commerce in the promotion of world championship boxing contests and ordered the disbandment of the organization. On appeal to the Supreme Court (1959), the verdict was upheld, a verdict that in the opinion of some commentators, only served to drive the monopolistic practices underground into the arms of organized crime (U.S. Congress, Senate, Committee on the Judiciary 1961, 898).

The lure of television concentrated power within the boxing industry and subsequently attracted the attention of the Justice Department. But the scrutiny boxing has received is exceptional for a sport not organized into leagues and probably has as much to do with its moral stigma as with its marketing practices. In other sports, like tennis and golf, individual players compete with each other on a circuit of tournaments; and without firms to conspire with each other, there would appear to be little room for the kind of monopolistic behavior witnessed in the team sports. Such sports are not entirely without their cartel-like features (the number of tournaments is limited, and only "qualified" or "eligible" players can participate in them); but these have rarely been judged monopolistic.[7]

Other practices have attracted attention, however, especially when they appear to limit the supply of players. When an individual sport restructures itself along the lines of a team sport in order to have greater television appeal, it can run afoul of the same antitrust laws that govern football and baseball. Thus, in *Drysdale* v. *Florida Team Tennis* (1976), Team Tennis's draft system requiring that a chosen player negotiate only with a designated franchise was found to be a violation of the Sherman Act.

Antitrust issues are also raised by another creature of television, the sport management firm, such as the International Management Group (IMG), Proserv, and Advantage International. These firms handle the business and legal affairs of hundreds of professional athletes from a number of sports. They also arrange merchandising and promotional deals for their clients. They have bureaucratized the role of the player's agent. Just as important (and more troubling from a public policy point of view), they also manage and package the events in which their athletes compete. They organize tournaments, contract with their own clients to appear in them (rather than in tournaments organized by others), and frequently sell a televised version of the tournament to the television networks or cable companies, using their own television production team. An IMG subsidiary, Trans World International, is the world's largest independent source and distributor of televised sport programming.

The issue here is whether economic competition between players and between tournaments competing for the services of those players is fostered or inhibited by this degree of vertical integration. By the end of the 1970s, boom years for televised tennis, many players came to believe that these management groups were beginning to dominate the sport. The Men's Tennis Council (MTC) charged that the management groups were leveraging their control over the supply of players to obtain control over tournaments and television appearances. The council passed a conflict-of-interest rule, prohibiting companies from representing players while concurrently promoting, managing, or broadcasting tournaments. International Management Group and Proserv promptly sued, alleging that the regulation was an agreement in restraint of trade in violation of the Sherman Act. The court, in *Volvo North America v. Men's International Professional Tennis Council* (1987), rejected the argument on the grounds that the council could not conspire with itself. In any case, the court decided, the conflict-of-interest rule was a reasonable measure to preserve the integrity of the sport.

The Men's Tennis Council countersued, charging IMG, Proserv and the sponsor with whom they mainly dealt, Volvo, of monopolistic practices in violation of the Sherman Act. Unlike the suit against the MTC, which seemed to target the actions of a body representing the sport as a whole, its counter-suit, *Men's International Professional Tennis Council v. Volvo, North America* (1988), required the court to evaluate the actions of two corporations acting to maximize profits. The likelihood of a finding of monopoly was thus greater. In its decision, the court exonerated the management firms on the grounds that their domination of the player market had not resulted from conspiracy but from the quest for efficiency. Strangely, the court did not address a central issue in the case—that the management groups had unfairly used their power in one market (that for labor) to destroy competition in another (that for tournaments). Such use of power, known as a vertical tie (since the supply of one product is tied to another) is an antitrust violation and is frequently struck down under the *per se* doctrine. But *Volvo* did not deal directly with this situation, since the claims in that case also involved the actions of the large corporate sponsor, Volvo. An implication of the court's reading of the case, however, is that the dominance of management groups in both markets is simply a by-product of their greater efficiency and competitiveness in both and represents no violation of public policy. This ruling was consonant with the change of antitrust interpretation described earlier, in which vertical restraints were given greater latitude than horizontal ties.

Despite these developments in golf and tennis, prompted largely by the lure of television money and shifting both sports in the direction of the kind of closely coordinated and regulated industries that might attract the attention of the state, it would appear that so long as the focus of each sport remains on the individual player, it will be treated very differently from a sport comprised of teams and leagues. Much more than in team sports, the public buys the individual in golf and tennis. Tournaments do not appeal to fan loyalty in the manner of baseball franchises; they are simply exchangeable venues for individual competition. This carries through to the conflict over property rights, which tends similarly to be conducted on the individual level, rather than by unions, as is the case with team sports.[8]

The rise of the television industry also changed the organizational field for college sports, and with much the same result. Until recently, nonprofit organizations were considered beyond the scope of the Sherman Act, and the state refused to consider antitrust charges against them. Amateur sport organizations like the NCAA were accordingly immune from charges of monopoly. For example, in *Jones* v. *National Collegiate Athletic Association* (1975), the court rejected an antitrust challenge by an athlete negatively affected by eligibility rules. The court reasoned that these rules were designed to promote amateurism: the resulting restraints on trade were incidental to this legitimate goal.

The NCAA did indeed begin as a reform organization. Its original objective was "the regulation and supervision of college athletics throughout the United States in order that the athletic activities of the colleges and universities of the United States may be maintained on an ethical plane in keeping with the dignity and high purpose of education." According to the current NCAA Manual, the association exists to promote "amateur student-athletics," catering to those for whom "sport is an avocation." The NCAA was intended to be an advisory body, and responsibility for the conduct of athletics was clearly lodged with member institutions. After World War II, however, the organization began to deviate from its passive role "and undertook a program designed to force member institutions to conform to the policies of the Association under threat of expulsion from membership, if found in non-compliance with these policies" (Sage 1982, 132).

By this time, there was little doubt in the minds of some legal scholars and economists that the NCAA functioned as a cartel if considered from a strictly economic point of view, because it

> (a) sets the maximum price that can be paid for intercollegiate athletes; (b) regulates the quantity of athletes that can be purchased in a given time period; (c) regulates the duration and intensity of usage of those athletes; (d) on occasion fixes the price at which sports outputs can be sold; (e) purports to control the property rights to activities such as the televising of intercollegiate football; (f) periodically informs cartel members about transactions, costs, market conditions, and sales techniques; (g) occasionally pools and distributes portions of the cartel's profits; and (h) polices the behavior of its members and levies penalties against those members of the cartel who are deemed to be in violation of cartel rules and regulations. (Koch 1983, 361)

The actual purpose and function of the NCAA had indeed shifted over the years, away from that of a reform organization intended to

protect amateurism and provide safe playing conditions for college athletes and toward a production and marketing organization intended to
maximize its own revenues and those of its members; that is, its regulations over the input side of athletics had been supplemented, and perhaps overwhelmed, by its regulation of the output side, thus placing it
more squarely within the reach and intent of antitrust laws. A special
Committee on Recruiting reported to the association in 1956 that
schools were spending huge sums of money recruiting athletes and
proposed limits on spending so that all schools "would lower their
costs" (Lawrence 1987, 57). Significantly, school officials become more
concerned about recruiting excesses whenever there is significant evidence of competitive imbalance between colleges. As Koch notes, the
"Sanity Code" was passed shortly after World War II, when returning
veterans presented a tempting pool of potential student-athletes and recruiting got out of hand:

> The effect of these and other "reforms" has nearly always been to
> suppress and equalize competition. Indeed, there is little evi-
> dence that in the long-run the NCAA is truly interested in reforms
> that have the effect of enhancing academic standards. The NCAA
> and its members have seldom supported academic initiatives that
> would result in competitive imbalances or reduce the profitabil-
> ity of intercollegiate athletics. (1985, 16).

The NCAA continues to police the recruitment of athletes, albeit with
a grossly inadequate force; but the intent of that control is to limit competition for athletes among colleges and thus hold down athletes
"wages." The association has also taken care to erect barriers to entry, especially into the lucrative Division IA, by imposing rules of institutional
eligibility such as stadium size and average attendance prohibitive for all
but the largest programs. Of greatest significance is the right to negotiate an agreement with the television networks on behalf of member institutions. By the 1980s, the idea of the NCAA's being "non-profit" had
lost all credence. The case of *Board of Regents, University of Oklahoma* v.
National Collegiate Athletic Association (1982) marked a new direction for
the courts. The justices argued that if a nonprofit entity entered the marketplace and conducted activities that in any other context, would be
those of a business for profit, the Sherman Act would apply.

As was the case with professional sports, the exposure of amateur
sport organizations to antitrust prosecution came about as a result of
their closer relationship to television. The NCAA originally set up a television committee to keep the medium at arms length. Its function was
to manage the televising of games, enforcing a strict blackout rule to
prevent televised and live games from competing. The power of this
committee is indicated by how effectively it dealt with a challenge from

the University of Pennsylvania, which refused to abide by the new regulation and was promptly declared "a member not in good standing." The university appealed to the Federal Department of Justice to investigate the NCAA for violation of the antitrust laws. Ironically, the Justice Department was already embroiled in an antitrust case against the NFL owners for colluding to negotiate the league's television contract and begged off the case (Lawrence 1987, 79). The University of Pennsylvania decided the next year that membership of the NCAA was essential to its athletic survival and abandoned its stand.[9]

Television revenues thus provided an early base of power for the NCAA, but they were also responsible for one of its greatest defeats. As television revenues increased, member institutions began to fight over how they should be distributed among them. The smaller colleges lobbied for wide distribution, football powers lobbied for a share commensurate with their input. The restructuring of the NCAA into different "divisions" did not satisfy the football powers, who formed the College Football Association (CFA) in 1977, with sixty-one schools participating. In July 1980, the CFA board of directors presented a plan to representatives of NBC and ABC for a television contract involving only its member institution; and the next year, the CFA tentatively approved a four-year contract that would have paid each member one million dollars over two years. The NCAA immediately threatened sanctions against member institutions who signed this contract, and on behalf of the CFA, three of its members (Georgia, Oklahoma, and Texas) filed for injunctive relief, at the same time filing suit against the NCAA, charging that its control of television violated antitrust laws. Injunctive relief was granted, but the CFA was unable to consummate the agreement with NBC.

The dispute continued, as the district court found the threat of future NCAA sanctions to be a major factor in the decision of many CFA members to reject the NBC contract. The district court eventually decided that:

> like all other cartels, NCAA members have sought and achieved a price for their product which is, in most instances, artificially high. . . .The cartel has established a uniform price for the products of each of the members producers, with no regard for the differing quality of these products or of the consumer demand for these various products. (Rowe 1985, 382)

On appeal, in June 1984, the Supreme Court upheld the lower court ruling, affirming that the right to televise college football games rested with individual institutions. It terminated the NCAA's control over football television contracts, finding it monopolistic. The immediate results were that smaller colleges lost revenues; gate receipts fell because more games were being televised; and since more games were being marketed, advertising rates also declined (p. 378). In the long term, the decision weakened the cartel-like power of the NCAA.

It is not without interest that two associate justices dissented from this majority opinion, one of whom, Byron White, a former football letterman, saw the NCAA's television contract as "eminently reasonable" on the grounds that it "fosters the goal of amateurism by spreading revenues among various schools and reducing the financial incentives toward professionalism" (Rowe 1985, 384). The dissenters thus hearkened back to earlier days of the NCAA, when it was more explicitly oriented to, and capable of realizing, the equitable distribution of resources in the interest of supporting all student athletes. In fact, the NCAA had long abandoned this posture, except in rhetoric. While its agreements with the television networks were justified on the grounds of maintaining competitive balance and while revenues were distributed among participating teams, it had never been able to pass legislation that would have stipulated how those revenues should be spent in order to maximize student participation.

Congress was forced to adopt a reactive stance to these events. For example, in 1984, hearings to discuss the implications of the Supreme Court decision in *Board of Regents, University of Oklahoma* v. *National Collegiate Athletic Association* were held in both House and Senate. Many congressmen lamented the decision on the grounds that it would further commercialize college sports. The decision set the precedent that a major extracurricular activity program for higher education established a property right that was to be regarded as a consumer product similar to those produced for profit alone. The president of the University of Georgia, Fred Davidson, reminded the House Committee on Energy and Commerce that "the University of Georgia receives no state support for its athletic programs" and must rely on the efforts of the Athletic Association to retire its long-term capital debt, which could only be achieved by the profitable sale of television rights (U.S. Congress, House, Committee on Energy and Commerce, 1984a, 86). Both the courts and Davidson neglected to point out that the value of the game depended on its association with the college and its ethos of amateurism. Davidson spoke as if the Athletic Association owned the product when, of course, the University of Georgia enabled the association to have a product to sell at all.

There can be little doubt that the NCAA has functioned as a cartel. It pools the rights of its member colleges and universities (who are natural competitors) to sell telecasting rights to selected games and tournaments to a national television network. As part of the pooled contracts, the networks agree to honor certain territorial restrictions benefiting the NCAA and its member institutions (e.g., the blackout rule). Indeed, there are some legal scholars who, while reluctant to see the professional leagues as guilty of trust law violations, have no such hesitation when it comes to the NCAA. They look upon the NCAA as quite clearly a "trade association" and not a league. Its member institutions, which are "clearly economic competitors," could survive and be productive without the NCAA: "The 187 College football teams are not inherent coproducers of an indivisible season of related games; instead, the college game' is a collection of isolated contests produced by this large group of essentially barnstorming teams that play when, where, and with whom their respective coaches and athletic directors independently arrange" (Roberts 1984, 245). Conferences, such as the Big Ten or the Atlantic Coast Conference (ACC), come somewhat closer to the status of a league.

The NCAA is not a very efficient cartel, as even its most severe critics would admit. It has been remarkably inefficient in regulating the flow of "inputs." There are a number of reasons for this. It is very difficult to oversee nearly nine hundred member "firms." These firms are by no means alike and have quite dissimilar interests, depending on the size of their student body. The cartel is also weakened by the presence of too many "points of initiative" (places where inputs can be bought and sold) for the cartel to regulate them all: "The times and locations where rules violations might take place are virtually infinite in number" (Koch 1983, 363).

The NCAA's problems with the state are somewhat different from those of the professional leagues. Whereas the public wish has been to see a separation between professional clubs, the impetus in college sports has been to provide more structure in order to approximate a league and provide a seasonal championship. This, coupled with the "packaging" encouraged by television companies, creates the need for more cartel-like practices, which in turn politicizes what was once an exclusively private arrangement.

New Markets

The coming of television changed the organizational field in which sport franchises operated, presenting them with an oligopoly of buyers for their product and giving them a powerful incentive to collaborate more closely but, simultaneously, exposing them to political attack. Another change in the organizational field, also related to television, had the opposite effect. This change concerned the market in which sport franchises operate. The state's policy with respect to business competition is to encourage a free and open market. But how is the market defined? The narrower the definition of the market, the more likely it is that any combinatorial practice will be seen as anticompetitive. Because markets can change as the result of demographic and technological trends, it is possible for a firm to find itself moving from a narrowly defined, to a broadly defined, market. The result is that its liability to state scrutiny under antitrust laws diminishes.

In economic terms, sport is not a narrowly defined product; nor is its market clearly defined. Pesticides, by contrast, have fairly specific identities and a rather narrowly defined potential market. It is not that difficult to decide when monopolistic practices exist in the production and sale of pesticides. There are few alternatives and few alternative uses. The politics of sport trust-busting is by no means as clear. One question is the meaning of sport itself. Is the product the actual game, the season, or the "sport"? Or is it simply "entertainment"? The answer to these questions makes a difference to the definition of the market affected by questionable practices. When a particular practice of football club owners is in dispute, is the market all fans at any given game, all NFL fans in New York, all NFL fans, all football fans, all sports fans, or all consumers willing to pay money for three hours of entertainment?

The definition of the sport market is determined by broad changes in working hours, spending habits, consumer preference, ownership of television sets and automobiles, participation rates in various leisure activities, changing life-style preferences, and the like. Whenever these factors change, competing forms of entertainment arise; and new markets are discovered or existing markets change their structure (e.g., become national or international). When this happens, the role of a "firm" in an "industry" is likely to be reinterpreted. For example, in the early 1950s, baseball began to suffer serious competition from professional football and basketball, not so much for customers as for players. As the supply of recruits diminished, major league owners entered into costly bidding wars, which, in turn, led them to treat more seriously the reserve system preventing players from moving from one team to another. This, in turn, generated discontent among players, which eventually found its way to Congress.

During the interwar period, the product market for a particular sport was comprised only of the sport, played in a designated geographical area, in which existing franchises were already located. Markets were local, specific to a place. Markets also had a different time structure. Each sport had its own season; indeed, it helped define the season. After the war, markets became national; and seasons began to overlap. The more seasons overlapped, the more precarious that sport's role in the sports industry became. By 1959, Hockey's Stanley Cup playoffs competed with baseball's April opening; and football's preseason exhibition games challenged baseball in the fall. The culprit was television, which helped change the length of the seasons. With longer seasons, different sports began to overlap and compete with each other, as well as with the quasi-professional collegiate ranks. Television also helped popularize games like tennis and golf and to extend their seasons across those traditionally "reserved" for one of the major team sports. By the 1980s, viewers choosing to spend September afternoons in front of their television sets could select from the last few games of regular season baseball, the first games of the new NFL season and the college football season, the U.S. Open tennis championships, a golf tournament, automobile racing, and professional wrestling. This meant that a sport league's ability to attract fan loyalty might come at the expense of other sport leagues' offerings or, as in the case of professional wrestling, at the expense of all other entertainment. This changed the definition of the product market. A football franchise no longer competed just with other football franchises. Together with all other football franchises, it competed with all other sports.

The net result of these changes in the market was to diminish a specific league's susceptibility to antitrust law. Overlapping seasons broaden the definition of the product market to all sports (or, indeed, all entertainment) and thus weakens a league's ability to monopolize that market. The broader the market in which a league competes, the more compelling the view that it is simply a joint venture, rather than a monopoly. It is easier to think of major league baseball or the National Football League as simply one "firm" in the entertainment industry when they routinely negotiate with television networks as single entities, where "ratings" of different programs across a broad spectrum of entertainment are possible.

ANTITRUST POLICY

The state's antitrust policy has not been consistent during this century, favoring now a free market, now regulation. All businesses, including sport, have felt the force of these changes in policy. While "combines" were aggressively hunted down before World War I, antimonopoly feeling abated immediately after: all five federal laws passed between 1915 and 1930 affecting antitrust laws granted exemptions to specific industries (Levine 1988, 41). During this period, the Supreme Court was "the most ardent champion of purely liberal values," frequently limiting or turning back legislative efforts to regulate trade (Wolfe 1977, 57). It is therefore not surprising that the 1922 Supreme Court decision exempting baseball from liability under the Sherman Act received no serious challenge in the interwar years. The New Deal is miscast as the origin of the welfare state. It would be more accurate to say that it gave rise to the "franchise state," in which public power was delegated to a number of essentially private agencies. This approach was quite compatible with the corporate structure of sports leagues at the time.

After War II, the Supreme Court had to acknowledge that the vast bulk of trade and commerce in the United States was now national in scope. It therefore reassessed its criteria for classifying interstate commerce activities. The first sign for sport owners that judicial policy had altered came in 1946 when Judge Lloyd Black ruled in favor of the returning veteran Al Niemic, who had been denied his old job back by the Seattle Rainiers of the Pacific Coast League. Black warned professional baseball that recent decisions of the Supreme Court indicated a shift in the interpretation of antitrust laws, referring to interstate commerce affirmations of the insurance and news-gathering business. In *Gardella* v. *Chandler* (1949), a court of appeals reasoned that the interstate commerce clause had changed since *Federal Baseball* and that baseball's interstate activities through radio and television had increased to the point that the antitrust immunity should be lifted (McAnderson 1968, 84). In this case, Judge Jerome Frank, ruling that Gardella's case was strong enough to go to trial, likened organized baseball to the American Medical Association, which had by this time been defined as engaged in interstate commerce.

Although a victory in the courtroom was aborted by the swift reinstatement of Gardella, it came close enough to encourage critics to mount a new challenge to organized baseball's monopoly; and by 1951 baseball was under attack in eight separate antitrust suits. The owners hurried to shore up their defenses legislatively. Three bills were introduced into the House and one into the Senate intended to give baseball complete immunity. In 1951, the Anti-trust Subcommittee of the House Committee on the Judiciary held hearings on these bills. Chairman Emanuel Celler declared, "If baseball is illegal, then we must prosecute the owners or change the law" (Lowenfish and Lupien 1980, 174). Celler was a formidable foe for baseball interests. Together with Senator Kefauver, he had successfully expanded the scope of the Clayton Act in 1950 by adding amendments to it, making it easier for courts to convict on the basis of dominant market position and lessened the need for specific proof of abuse.

The Anti-trust Committee reached no agreement on legislation that would have granted blanket immunity to baseball in return for some oversight or regulatory commission, although it did pressure the owners into expanding the league. It returned the task of policy formation to the courts. The committee's reasoning at this juncture was that professional sports leagues were indeed unique in certain respects, enough so to induce it to ask just which practices were essential to the survival of the league and which were simply there to enhance profit. However, the responsibility of differentiating "the unreasonable features of baseball's rules and regulations from those which are reasonable and necessary" was assigned to the courts (U.S. Congress, House, Select Committee on Professional Sports 1977, 39). Baseball's lawyers were to capitalize cleverly on this game of volleyball between Congress and the courts, "suggesting to each body that the other had the proper authority" (Lowenfish and Lupien 1980, 181).

The judicial analysis Celler's committee had anticipated duly followed, but the result was to throw the ball back to the legislature. Four important cases in the mid-1950s set the tone for judicial policy with respect to professional sports. One case firmly restated the Supreme Court's commitment to the principle of stare decisis. In *Toolson* v. *New York Yankees* (1953), the court majority tacitly admitted that there might be "evils in this field" but refused to overturn the 1922 *Federal Baseball* decision. Baseball's immunity was thus preserved. Three other cases just as firmly refused to grant this immunity to other, similar, enterprises. In *United States* v. *Shubert* (1955) the court refused to agree with the argument made by theatrical producers that they, like baseball owners, should be immune from antitrust action, because their business was so similar. In *United States* v. *International Boxing Club* (1955), boxing promoters were found guilty of violating the Sherman Act despite their efforts to hide behind baseball's immunity. In *Radovich* v. *National Football League* (1957), the Supreme Court, despite referring back to *Toolson*, made it quite clear that it regarded professional football as interstate commerce and thus subject to antitrust litigation. The sum total of these rulings was, of course, to render even more glaring the anomalous position of baseball, a fact that the courts recognized in urging Congress to resolve this issue legislatively.

These various rulings reflected a more vigorous state policy with respect to business monopolies but did little to fill the vacuum that existed in the setting of sport policy. The courts simply repeated that the baseball anomaly ought to be eliminated but that legislative action must do the job. In *Radovich* v. *National Football League* (1957), the Supreme Court looked across at baseball and, acknowledging the inconsistency, argued that "the orderly way to eliminate error or discrimination, if any there be, is by legislation and not by court decision" (Freedman 1987, 55). The *Flood* v. *Kuhn* (1972) court, clearly in sympathy with the player they were deciding against, explicitly indicated that the remedy lay with Congress and not the courts.

Judges understandably have an abiding commitment to the principle of stare decisis, even if it perpetuates practices that seem anachronistic. The Flood court referred ambivalently to the 1922 decision as being "with us now for half a century." But in their various rulings, the justices have also made it clear that the legality of professional sports should be settled in the halls of Congress and not in the privacy of judges' chambers, as if in recognition that, by delegating the formation of sport policy to the courts, congressmen were effectively giving power to the existing owners and diminishing the power of players, would-be owners, fans, and municipalities.

The owners cleverly exploited this situation by drawing a parallel between their private interests and the interests of the public at large, reinforcing the view that the status quo was in the national interest. They had two lines of defense. Knowing that trust-busting serves important political purposes for congressmen, they played up the "mom and pop" nature of their firms, emphasized their entrepreneurial flair and courage, and pointed out the risks of doing business in the world of sports. A second line of defense had to deal with the fact that the sport fan was reluctant to see sport as just another business, subject to the same economic imperatives and abuses. Correspondingly, the sport fan was less disposed to accept the owners' need to defend their economic "integrity" by securing congressional favors as legitimate. The owners' strategy for dealing with this was to justify special treatment on the grounds of the historical mandate the leagues had been given, a public trust. George Halas put the owners and Congressmen on the same side of the fence, both having fiduciary responsibilities toward the public. Congressmen, he explained,

> represent the large majority of people who believe in our way of life—and that is where we are on the same side of the table; you are here to protect the public; and we are under obligation to protect the public—and would not support any veiled efforts to institute government sponsored, financed and controlled athletic programs in our college and professional sports with the European style of regimented and disciplined mass calisthenics. (U.S. Congress, House, Committee on the Judiciary 1957, 2710).[10]

The court's refusal in *Radovich* (1957) to make state policy toward the different team sports consistent prompted Congress to take this issue up once more. In 1957, fifteen days of hearings were conducted by the Antitrust Subcommittee of the House Committee on the Judiciary. The explicit purpose of these hearings was to consider a number of bills to make the treatment of professional sports *uniform* with respect to the antitrust laws. HR5307 and HR5319 would have included baseball with all other sports; HR5383 would have exempted all professional sport enterprises from antitrust suits; HR6876, HR6877, HR8023 and HR8124 exempted certain agreements (e.g., playing rules) from antitrust liability but otherwise sought to make all sports equally vulnerable.

Deliberation on these bills was bedeviled by the difficulty of deciding where to draw the line between the business aspect of a sport and what was intrinsic to it as simply a game. Not surprisingly, the contending parties could not agree where this line should be drawn. While even owners could agree that ticket and hot dog prices were part of the business side of a franchise and clearly subject to antitrust laws, they would not acknowledge that the draft was a business matter; for they regarded it as intrinsic to equalizing competition in the game. Baseball Commissioner Ford Frick reminded the committee that "Baseball is a sport—a game. It must have rules as to how it shall be played and who shall play it. The reserve clause is one of the rules dealing with the question as to who is eligible to play" (U.S. Congress, House, Committee on the Judiciary 1957, 297). The 1950s ended with baseball's immunity intact.

During the 1960s, antitrust activity in the sports arena focused largely on the issue of labor-management relations. This did not reflect any major change in overall antitrust policy so much as a concerted drive on the part of the players and their unions to weaken the position of the owners, a subject to be discussed in the next chapter. A change in antitrust policy did occur in the 1970s, however; and it would in time make an impact on sport policy. For many years the provision of services was less liable to antitrust prosecution than the manufacture and sale of goods. For this reason, the professions, which were not considered a "productive" activity, were not targeted for antitrust action. The similarity between this attitude and the attitude toward baseball in the 1922 decision is striking. The government rarely questioned the monopoly status of either institution. Thus, despite declaring that exemptions from antitrust laws should not be lightly proffered, the Anti-trust Division of the Justice Department refused to make a specific recommendation about baseball's immunity, nor would the Federal Trade Commission. In *Goldfarb* v. *Virginia State Bar Association* (1975), however, the Supreme Court ruled that "professions" constitute "trade or commerce" in which monopolistic practices could exist. "This landmark decision . . . opened the way for a variety of anti-trust investigations into the medical and legal professions by the Justice Department and the Federal Trade Commission, and for actions brought by individuals against the professional associations on anti-trust grounds" (Powell 1985, 285). Prodded by consumer activists, government agencies became more vigilant with respect to antitrust violations. This climate made it much easier for players and others to charge the providers of sport entertainment with antitrust violations. It was during this period, for example, that Senator Ervin was conducting his attack on the basketball merger.

In the 1980s, the political pendulum swung once more in favor of the owners. Throughout the 1960s and 1970s, the owners' efforts to limit the mobility of players were the chief focus of antitrust attention. Under the Reagan administration, the Sherman Act was put to different use. Legal scholars and judges began to argue that the Sherman Act was designed above all to maximize consumer welfare and prevent product market dislocation (Roberts, 1986a). It had been improperly applied to restrictions on player mobility in the 1960s and 1970s because the courts then had a broader public policy objective in mind—equity and fairness in employment practices—an objective neither the Sherman Act nor the Clayton Act had ever been designed to achieve. The Reagan administration and its appointees pursued a much narrower definition of the purposes of antitrust legislation. Antitrust policy was to be

concerned only with allocative and productive efficiency and their relation to net economic welfare. Broader political and social goals were
deemphasized. Sympathies thus shifted from the players to the consumers. Antitrust policy should not be concerned with "factors," that is,
with the extent to which league practices affected employment conditions of workers. How power was distributed was not relevant to antitrust law. Now the emphasis was less "populist," less on protecting "the
little man" and more on making sure that markets worked efficiently in
order to drive economic expansion. Hence, the return to the old idea of
competitiveness, but with fewer connotations of equity and fairness. Antimonopoly became more a tool of fiscal and commercial policy and less
a weapon in the struggle to redistribute power.[11]

How ironic that the owners, who for many years had resisted state
regulation on the grounds that theirs was a peculiar industry, not governed by the normal "laws" of economic behavior, would now benefit
from a very conservative judicial approach to monopoly, which took
the view that the antitrust laws should be narrowly defined as intended
to achieve an efficient market to maximize consumer benefits—a view
that if applied directly to sport, tended to gloss over the very features
that made it unlike other businesses. It overlooked sport leagues' monopoly over the opportunity to pursue a career in athletics; leagues'
need for public legitimacy; and the fact that a sport league has obligations beyond maximizing profits, that its enormous private power
brings commensurate public responsibilities. In other words, it exaggerated the distinction between the private and public worlds and argued, erroneously, that the activities of the sport league were
unequivocally private (Heidt 1985).

CONCLUSION

The question whether a sport league or college athletic association violates the law or seriously contravenes public policy goals
simply by its method of operation is important in its own right. The public cares that private entities should respect the law. The laws in question, those designed to protect against business monopoly, are intended
to ensure efficiency in the marketplace. But there is much more to the
issue of monopoly in sports than economic efficiency. From the start,
antitrust laws were aimed as much at private concentrations of power
as they were market inefficiencies. These twin goals have not always
been equally emphasized (much depending on swings of political sentiment), but they are present in public policy debate, nevertheless.

A sport league or an athletic association is, by necessity, a form of "collusive competition," by its very nature a threat to the twin goals of eco-

nomic efficiency and the dispersal of powers. The state has been given the mandate to control private entities that exploit market advantage and concentrated power; and as they have grown, both professional and amateur sport associations have felt the force of this mandate. But history shows that "the same policy could not be used to maintain a diffusion of economic power and promote efficiency—the goals were clearly in conflict" (Eisner 1991, 117); and in this conflict the latter goal has been most often the victor. In applying antitrust law to sports, the state has been more interested in efficiency than in justice, more interested in protecting liberties than in dispersing power. This is important because while antitrust issues can be conceived narrowly as a problem of the marketplace (an economic problem), the structure of an industry is also, inevitably, a political problem, because legitimated economic concentration bestows unequal political powers—of management over workers, of producers over consumers, of private goals over public needs. Thus, many of the other issues I cover, from the freedom of players to move to the public's right to watch the Superbowl on "free" television, are affected by the determination of a league's standing before antitrust law. It is the pivot around which almost all other debates turn.

Congress has never determined in law the exact status of a sport league. Is it a joint venture or an aggregate of firms? Are the players all working for the same enterprise, or are they working for twenty-eight different employers? These questions had proved impossible to answer. A sports league *does* defy definite placement into either category. One thing is certain, that the public wants the "firms" in the league to be independent and competitive. The fans require an obvious separation of the clubs in order to maintain their faith in the integrity of the game. This is the reason given for prohibiting joint ownership in baseball and football and its uneasy tolerance in basketball and hockey (where, for a time during the 1950s, the Norris family owned the Chicago Blackhawks and Detroit Redwings, as well as having effective control over the New York Rangers by virtue of its ownership of Madison Square Garden).

Given these uncertainties, it is understandable that much of the responsibility for making sport policy has fallen to the congressional judiciary committees. These committees have become the sport committees in Congress. Significantly, the hearings conducted in 1981 to consider a bill (HR3287, the Sports Anti-trust Reform Act) to eliminate baseball's exemption from the antitrust laws and a bill (HR823, the Sports Franchise Relocation Act) designed to protect communities from the departure of franchises by setting up an arbitration board to review movements, were called "oversight hearings," implying a continuing role for the House Judiciary Committee. Chairman Rodino, in his opening statement, announced "These hearings take up a task that was left unfinished by the House Select Committee on Professional Sports in 1976" (U.S. Congress, House, Committee on the Judiciary 1984, 1). Luckily for baseball, the judiciary committees simply lacked the time and single-mindedness of the Select Committee and were quite unable to follow its lead.

Despite all the attention Congress has paid to the issue of antitrust laws in relation to sports, the law in this area remains, with few exceptions, essentially the same as was delineated by the Supreme Court in the *Toolson* and *Radovich* cases. Congress has not been persuaded to put baseball on an equal footing with other team sports, nor has it seen fit to expose sports more explicitly to antitrust liabilities. Indeed, on several occasions, when professional sport activities have raised serious conflict with the antitrust laws, Congress has stepped in to remove the statutory obstacles. Thus, in 1961, when a federal court struck down the NFL's decision to pool television rights of individual teams, Congress immediately responded by providing *all* professional team sports with the right to do the same despite the antitrust laws. Again, when litigation threatened the proposed merger of the American Football League and National Football League, Congress stepped in and approved it. Thus, in the 1960s at least, Congress, rather than restricting in any way the immunity baseball enjoyed, moved the nonimmune sports to an antitrust status closer to baseball's. Furthermore, in most instances when a committee reported a bill favorably, and in most cases where one of the houses of Congress voted approval of a sport bill, the result further immunized sports.

It seems that Congress has simply thrown up its hands with respect to the task of reaching some final determination of the status of sport franchises and leagues. Thus Congressman Joseph Fisher (Virginia) complained of the difficulty of legislating in the area of professional sports, because they "are not really in the free enterprise system for various reasons, nor are they in the public utility classification either" (U.S. Congress, House, Select Committee on Professional Sports 1976, 580). Almost exactly the same words were chosen by Senator Slade Gorton (Washington) ten years later. Professional sport leagues, in his opinion, "are *sui generis*, unique organizations which fall somewhere between a wholly private enterprise existing in a fully competitive market, and a public utility" (U.S. Congress, Senate, Committee on Commerce, Science, and Transportation 1985, 4). Such statements elide, of course, the leagues' essentially political nature. Market forces have consistently driven them into embrace of the state. Owners have sought to use the state to legitimate the definition of most benefit to them, but this definition has seldom been that favored by the players.

CHAPTER 5

MANAGEMENT
AND
LABOR

In professional sports, the property rights and reach of authority of the owners has been under constant political challenge from those who would question the peculiar status that franchises and leagues have secured before the law. In the previous chapter, the owners were seen defending their right to act in concert while at the same time treating their franchises as autonomous enterprises from which they could reap exclusive benefits. They were not always successful in this fight, but they won many victories. While many of the old customs and practices had to be abandoned, they at no time were forced to relinquish the position that sport enterprises are a peculiar business, subject to their own unique needs and deserving of particular respect from the state. The collusion necessary to sustain sport team leagues makes them "natural monopolies."

The owners thus preserved more or less intact their special relationship to each other. They survived the challenge from would-be owners and from those who sought to subject the sport industry to the same kind of state regulation and oversight as more conventional businesses. They did not win this battle without suffering casualties, however, the chief of which was the patriarchal principle by which players had been managed in the past, when players were "boys" and their employers assumed the role of father figures, especially in baseball, where

155

the nurturance period was prolonged. Management ideology emphasized the mutuality of interests of the two parties and the uniqueness of each players' contractual relationship. Although the reserve clause was always a bone of contention between management and players, discontent tended to focus on particulars, on the frustrations imposed by this or that contract. Well into the 1970s, most players accepted the need for restrictions on player mobility such as the reserve clause and the player draft (M. Miller 1991, 271). In public, at least, most players seemed to agree that the owners needed to protect their investments and that they themselves had less of a stake in the good of the game. The owners were permitted to assume the role of guardians of the game and individual malcontents were assigned the role of selfish troublemakers. Players were expected to be "hungry" on the playing field but humble in the negotiating room. As Curt Flood discovered, "Only a narrow margin separates the Hungry Ball Player from the Ingrate" (1971, 51).

All this began to change in the 1970s, when players' associations finally achieved the support, organizational solidity, and direction needed to present the case for the players as a whole to management who, of course, had been engaged in "collective action" since the inception of professional team sports. The players' associations would bring about dramatic changes in the world of sports, principally in the measure of control that management was able to exercise over individual players and, in turn, the percentage of gross revenues devoted to the players' salaries. They would achieve this by a combination of tactics, not always carefully planned, using conventional collective bargaining, litigation, strike action, political lobbying and good public relations.

The players had come a long way. Once baseball's "craftwork" period immediately after the Civil War was forgotten, the idea of trade unions in sports had become almost unthinkable. Not only the owners and the general public but the players themselves proved unreceptive to the idea that they were merely workers pitted against greedy capitalists, that sport was just a business, that playing baseball was just another job. Players also shared the public's ambivalence about the value of trade unions in a land of individual opportunity. Yet by the 1970s, the ranks of the professional athlete had become one of the most heavily unionized in the whole work force, at a time when membership of trade unions was declining steadily. I shall document the rise of players' associations, paying special attention to how it has been conditioned by, and in turn helped change, the relation between sport and the state.

The publicity surrounding the players' associations in the 1980s obscures the fact that collective action was slow to form among professional athletes. Sociological theory can help account for this. Unionism has less appeal to those who occupy jobs that are structurally ambiguous, being tied neither to the capital function nor unmistakably to labor.

Professional athletes have always preferred to see themselves as independent craftsmen or, more lately, as independent practitioners, true "professionals." Unionism is also slow to take hold where each worker's services are highly specific, difficult to replace. For many years, athletes exhibited their ambivalence about the nature of their services, all too aware of their replaceability, but anxious, at the same time, to demonstrate their indispensibility.

A craft union (made up of workers in the same occupation but not tied to the same firm or even industry) would have been one answer to this problem; but the conditions of work and the relations of power in the four major team sports, not to mention individual sports, were so different that movement among them (or, because of the reserve rule, within them) was unthinkable. An industrial union (consisting of the permanent work force in a specific business establishment) would have been another solution had it not been for the belief in the specificity of each player's services, the difficulty of separating worker from job. The form of unionism that slowly developed was modeled on actors' unions, with the added complication, however, of having to deal with devices such as the amateur draft and reserve rule.

Players' efforts to form a trade union to protect their interests faltered during the years when government protection for unionism from capitalist power was weak. The collective power of the professional athlete would never match that of the miner, steelworker, longshoreman, or automobile assemblyman. Workers in these industries were able to organize unions and mobilize them for strike action long before the New Deal era. Professional athletes had to wait somewhat longer, until administrative law was in place to offer more protection for striking workers against retaliatory management. Once the apparatus for legal unionism was in place, however, professional athletes used it to restructure their relationship to each other and to management. They were not able to do this all at once. Their advances and retreats were closely related to the shifting balance of power within the sport industry as first owners and then players gained strength. They were also related to changes in the rules and regulations with which Congress and the courts sought justice and order in management-labor relations.

BASEBALL

Trade unions in sports have a much longer history than many people realize. A National Brotherhood of Professional Baseball Players was organized as early as 1886, its purpose being to end the reserve system. The courts during this period refused to prohibit what the owners called "contract jumping," on grounds that the typical contract lacked mutuality and definiteness; but the owners had circumvented this by conspiring not to raid each other's teams. The brotherhood was a response to the owners' collective action.

These early efforts at unionism took place in a climate of economic depression and considerable extralegal violence against striking workers and union members in general (M. Sklar 1988, 20). It is hardly surprising, then, that the owners refused to recognize the brotherhood. Denied a position of equality in the existing league, the players set up their own Players' League in 1889. Ironically, this league allowed for the compulsory transfer of players to other teams in the league to equalize teams' playing strength. It collapsed within two years, for want of operating capital. This defeat was "devastating to the self-esteem of the players" (Lowenfish and Lupien 1980, 50) because the league stood for their claim to be independent practitioners of their craft, rather than simply wage workers. It expressed their claim to be able to conduct their own business affairs, to be part of capital, rather than labor. It would take nearly one hundred years before this sentiment was expressed so forcefully again.

The National League baseball players tried again in 1899, with a Protective Association of Professional Baseball Players. This organization resembled more closely the new kind of occupational grouping that was to lead, in other spheres, to professional unions, such as the American Medical Association and the American Bar Association. It sought to capitalize on the challenge being mounted to the National League by the rival American League; but it could not prevent its own members from jumping to the American League and collapsed after three years when a merger became imminent. It chose not to affiliate with the American Federation of Labor for fear of antagonizing the owners and was able to wrest only minor concessions from them, in return for which it was forced to tolerate owners' blacklisting players who had jumped to the American League and wished to return.

The Fraternity of Professional Baseball Players followed in 1912. The fraternity was recognized by the National Commission, in part because organized baseball was then at war with the Federal League and in part because the fraternity grudgingly accepted the reserve clause as "a necessary evil" (Seymour 1971, 237). Membership grew to 1,215 in four years. The fraternity's accomplishments were minor (e.g., owners would henceforth supply uniforms). The rise in salaries during this period was the result of interleague rivalry, rather than unionism. The promanagement *Sporting News* called the fraternity's president, David Fultz, "an outlaw and a baseball anarchist" (p. 228). With the demise of the Federal League in 1915, the fraternity lost most of its leverage against organized baseball, and the union began to falter. It collapsed in 1917 after calling an unsuccessful strike; and by 1918, it had disbanded (Gregory 1956, 190).

It was unfortunate for the players that the fraternity had mobilized only toward the *end* of a spurt of union growth. Union membership had increased by 300 percent between 1897 and 1904; but after this date, a concerted employers' offensive managed to arrest the growth, and membership remained almost constant through the entry of the United States into World War I (Gordon, Edwards and Reich 1982, 153). The years following the war were even less conducive to labor organization. The "American Plan," a campaign by business to break the unions, was successful enough to eliminate virtually all the gains made by labor during World War I: "Union recognition and collective bargaining, which were under the protection of the state administration, had become things of the past by the mid 1920s" (Levine 1988, 37). The judiciary—the arm of government assigned the principal role of regulating management-labor relations during this period—sought to preserve individual liberty and the concomitant right of workers to contract with employers on any terms they wished and made it "extremely difficult for government to redress injustices generated in the workplace" (K. Sklar 1988, 131).

If the climate was unhealthy for unions, it was invigorating for owners. Sport franchises emerged during the growth period of modern corporations. The more progressive and vocal of corporate leaders, represented by the National Civic Federation, declared that management and labor should be united in a common commitment to production, efficiency, and competitive excellence. Sport owners could appeal to this ideal to legitimate their relationship to each other and then turn around and appeal to old-fashioned but still respectable principles of individualism and laissez-faire when defending their employment practices. In this, they were simply reflecting the economic ethos of the day. The Progressive movement had persuaded many businessmen that it was in their interest to smooth off the sharper edges of industrialism, but progressive ideals did not include support for trade unionism. Collaboration between owners in the interest of economic growth and social stability was quite justified; but collaboration between workers, especially workers organized into unions, was another matter. Baseball's owners were thus able to argue that matters of salary, the reserve clause, and just about anything else pertaining to control of the players were none of the players' business—that the players must operate independently, while the owners should, in the interest of the league's stability, operate collectively.

Union organizers faced not only a general climate of hostility toward organized labor but particular problems of recruitment among athletes. Each "firm" was small, even if the league as a whole were considered the relevant organizing unit; the firm was not manufacturing staple goods or providing essential services but was, instead, providing entertainment; players knew that their careers would be brief and did not find the idea of disrupting them with industrial action attractive; players were transferred frequently from firm to firm, making worker solidarity hard to achieve; their work was highly seasonal, almost part-time; there were wide differences of status and earnings among players, making it difficult for them to recognize common interests; and athletes were, by worldview and conviction, highly individualistic and keen to think of themselves as businessmen, rather than blue-collar workers or "farm boys." Union organizers also had to confront a hostile public, who believed that athletes were, if anything, overpaid for what they did. Besides, athletes were "paid to play." They should be pleased to get any money at all and had little stake in the game, compared to the owners. In any case, the owners were too poor—or their franchises too insecure—to pay higher salaries. Shifting players from club to club was good for the player and made clubs more efficient, and the reserve system was necessary to maintain equity.

It did not help the cause of unionism that baseball, especially during the 1920s and 1930s, worked hard to foster a heavily agrarian ideology. Ballplayers, especially the stars, were portrayed as "farm boys." Many did return to work their farm during the off-season. Likewise, "the best fans were former farm people, 'people who are really worth-while' "(Crepeau 1980, 56). Country boys, unlike their city and college cousins, did not get "uppity" or "vindictive" and did not waste their money on fast cars and women or fancy hotels.

The players' reluctance to think of themselves as members of the proletariat was not simply a matter of naive pride. It is quite legitimate for a professional athlete to ask, Do I help produce a game—an event—or am I the product? Am I a worker employed to produce something, or am I an independent producer who markets himself? Neither owners nor unions particularly encouraged the latter view. Ironically, in their early efforts to control players, owners frequently argued that one-sided contracts were necessary because each player was irreplaceable, thus adding substance to the idea that each player was unique. This view was upheld in the case of *Philadelphia Baseball Club v. Lajoie* (1902), in which the court declared that Napoleon Lajoie "may not be the sun in the baseball firmament, but he is certainly a bright particular star" (Berry, Gould, and Staudohar 1986, 26). It was a common complaint among players that they *were* the game, especially the stars. Who would come to watch an owner own? The eventual result of this ambiguity was a bi-furcated system of remuneration. Players would share a minimum wage and other benefits; but they would negotiate often-complex contracts, first individually and subsequently, with the help of agents.

As if all this were not enough, union organizers had to deal with the problem that major league baseball players were not poorly paid, so long as they were employed. Before World War I, their average annual salary was about $3,000, when average earnings in the labor force were $525 a year (Seymour 1971, 173). Much publicity was given to the earnings of star players: Ty Cobb was paid $11,300 in 1912; Babe Ruth earned $80,000 a year in 1930 and 1931 (about $665,000 in 1988 dollars). Furthermore, salaries rose steadily between the wars. In terms of purchasing power, 1950 players were paid twice as much as 1929 players (Gregory 1956, 95). During the Depression, major league salaries fell less than did earnings in all industries; and they recovered faster than earnings in general.

Labor organizers had one powerful argument in their favor, however; and that was the growing disproportion in rewards reaped by owners and players in an increasingly prosperous industry. The "just" salary of a professional athlete was, after all, difficult to measure by comparison with similar occupations, because the work was so unusual. Nor was it very easy to tie salaries to individual productivity, especially in football. Issues of equity thus tended to pivot around the respective contributions of, and rewards for, the owners versus the players. Throughout this period the *relative* position of players worsened, as is shown in the declining proportion of clubs' outlays going to player salaries, falling from 50 percent in 1890, to 35 percent in 1929 and 22 percent in 1950 (Seymour 1971, 174). Gross receipts in baseball rose eightyfold between 1883 and 1950, while salaries increased only sevenfold (Davenport 1969, 17). Life in the minor leagues was also a different story. The salaries of minor leaguers in 1950 had less purchasing power than in 1929 (Gregory 1956, 98). In 1950, the median salary in the majors was $10,500; Triple A salaries averaged $4,250, at a time when the overall median salary for all employed workers was $3,024 (Gregory 1956, 101).

The economic conditions were not, then, altogether unpropitious for organized labor in sports. Between the wars, Ray Cannon, a Milwaukee lawyer and baseball enthusiast, twice tried to organize a union: once following the Black Sox scandal (he had tried to get the banished players reinstated), when he organised the National Baseball Players' Association, and again in the 1930s. Neither of these efforts got off the ground; but labor shortages caused by World War II shifted the balance of power from capital to labor, creating a more favorable climate for players' associations.

There was a rash of strikes in manufacturing industries immediately following the war: there were more man-days idle due to work stoppages in 1946 than ever before or since. The considerable prounion sentiment among American workers made itself felt within professional sports. In 1946, Boston attorney Robert Murphy formed the American Baseball Guild. Murphy got the endorsement of the AFL and CIO but no recognition from the owners. The National Labor Relations Board (NLRB) refused Murphy's request to determine whether the guild should represent the players in collective bargaining, because no interstate commerce was involved, so he decided on a local strategy and, exploiting discontent among the Pittsburgh Pirates players, petitioned the Labor Relations Board of Pennsylvania for certification. An election was duly held among the players, and Murphy lost by a vote of fifteen to thirteen. The closeness of the vote startled the owners into conceding a "Diamond G.I. Bill of Rights," granting players more meal money; a minimum salary for major leaguers of $5,000; $25 weekly "Murphy Money" for spring training expenses; a guaranteed World Series pool of at least $250,000; and a pension to five-year men, 80 percent of it funded by radio and television money.

Murphy's failure indicates how unpopular the idea of unionism among professional athletes was at this time. A 1946 Gallup poll revealed overwhelming public opposition to unionization of ball players (Seymour 1971, 169). In any event, the labor agitation of the immediate postwar years was followed almost immediately by the passage of antiunion labor legislation, most notably the Taft–Hartley Act in 1947. This was the beginning of managed capitalism, born of a tendency to see Big Capital and Big Labor as produced by the same social forces and capable of working in harmony for the benefit of all. The right to withdraw labor collectively was firmly established, but it fell far short of the idea that a job was a "property right" that workers owned. Indeed, workers were seen as being as much in need of protection from union leaders as from bosses; their individual rights must not be restricted by majority rule. Congress limited the power of the union to picket, mount sympathy strikes, and prevent scab labor: "Business and many union leaders accused anyone who opposed cooperative collective bargaining policies of having a communist orientation" (Gordon, Edwards, and Reich 1982, 185).

To forestall further union efforts and to fight off the threat of the "outlaw" Mexican League, the owners set up and financed the Association of Professional Baseball Players of America in 1947. This company union was intended chiefly to oversee the pension fund jointly financed by players and owners. The association was funded by occasional receipts from the all-star games, membership dues, and "small contributions from the Commissioner's office" (Gregory 1956, 117). This arrangement was in line with the general trend of unionism at this time, which stressed the "social contract" between workers and management and the responsibility of workers to maintain productivity in return for "welfare" programs from the owners. As Gregory points out, the pension fund was set up specifically to prevent unionization (p. 194).

By 1953, the political climate had become more conservative and management more aggressive in the labor wars. Baseball owners proposed to abolish the pension system it had agreed to six years before. In response, the players' representatives met in Atlanta and hired J. Norman Lewis to represent their cause. Lewis was the former law partner of Leo Bundy, for many years counsel, treasurer and vice president of the New York Giants; and he had himself been legal counsel for the New York Yankees for twenty-six years. He helped charter the Major League Baseball Players' Association in 1954. The owners resented the intrusion of this "third party" into baseball. The *Sporting News* predicted that "the informal give-and-take attitude" would be replaced by "cold legalistic bargaining" (Gregory 1956, 201).

Lewis did not disappoint. He threatened legal action over the pension plan, and the owners promptly dropped their proposal to abandon it. In 1955, Lewis announced that he had negotiated an increase in the minimum salary, from five thousand to six thousand dollars. Lewis was not hired as a union official, however. His job was to represent the players before management. Besides, he devoted only a small proportion of his time to the work. In addition, in 1957 he took on the job of representing the NHL players. A players' "union" at this time was little but a "conduit for information" (McCormick 1982, 1150). The players were clearly ambivalent about unionism. Robert Feller, the MLBPA's first president, declared in 1956 that "You cannot carry collective bargaining into baseball"; and in 1963, his successor, Robert Friend, expressed his opinion that "a union, in the fullest sense of the word, simply would not fit the situation of baseball" (Berry, Gould, and Staudohar 1986, 52). The players spurned several offers to be represented by real unions (Gregory 1956, 204).

In 1957, the Supreme Court ruled on behalf of a football player, William Radovich, who had been blacklisted for refusing to play for the team to which he had been assigned. The case inevitably became a focus of congressional hearings on professional team sports then being conducted by House Judiciary Committee chairman, Emanuel Celler. At these hearings, Lewis spoke in favor of a "reasonable" reserve clause, stressing that the precise meaning of *reasonable* must be decided in the courts. Ironically, the three players he brought along to testify with him confessed to having "no complaints" about the reserve system. Stan Musial, testifying independently, declared, "I don't think the reserve clause needs to be changed in any way" (U.S. Congress, House, Committee on the Judiciary 1957, 1306). Curiously, at the very same hearings, Robert Feller, still president of the Major League Baseball Players' Association, proved to be much more combative, pointing out that the pension plan the owners were boasting of had been won by the players only after a long and bitter struggle (p. 1311). He had some demands he would like to see negotiated in collective bargaining, including a reserve clause restricted to five years, no restrictions on winter league or exhibition play, a maximum of three years before a minor league player who has not been drafted is declared a free agent, a guaranteed pension plan, expansion of the league, an elected commissioner, an arbitration system for salary disputes, collective bargaining, and a higher minimum salary. Feller, it seems, was much more in tune with what could be achieved by the players than his lawyer–advocate Lewis. While most of his demands were to remain on the bargaining table throughout the next twenty years, many of them would eventually be met by the reluctant owners.

The players voted to dismiss Lewis in 1959 and sought a more aggressive successor. They chose Judge Robert Cannon. Despite being the son of the Raymond Cannon who had tried to form a players' union in the 1920s, Cannon "catered to the owners throughout a tenure that lasted until 1966" and was clearly oblivious of, or had no intention of using, the Taft–Hartley labor laws (Voigt 1983, 207). His real ambition was to succeed Ford Frick as commissioner (Lowenfish and Lupien 1980, 191). He even received a stipend from the commissioner's office. He seemed unable to appreciate that the level of player discontent was rising rapidly. They had to watch most of the new money from television go into the pockets of the owners. They had to tolerate an increase in the number of games, from 154 to 162, and more travel as a result of expansion in 1962. He did not see that the players had begun to make the transition from heroes and idols (largely symbolic roles that cast them as passive objects, the creations of others) into professional entertainers, a role that endowed them with more autonomy, creativity, and power.

In 1966, Marvin Miller, a labor economist for the United Steel Workers Union, was appointed to the new position of executive director of the MLBPA. Miller had served on the National War Labor Board in World War II, where he was assigned to train labor mediators and "learned the importance of studying both sides in a labor dispute" (Voigt 1983, 208). Miller also worked for a time as a member of the federal conciliation service. Yet Miller "had an iron belief in the principles of unionism" (Lowenfish and Lupien 1980, 197). Miller's initial encounters with the commissioner and league presidents of baseball "convinced him that they were owners' men—hence, his enemies" (Voigt 1983, 210). Despite Commissioner Kuhn's claims concerning his own impartiality, there could be little disputing Miller's view. Kuhn disingenuously described how he would often attend the meetings of management's Player Relations Committee, even during strikes, "usually as an information gathering exercise" (1987, 157).

Unlike his predecessor and his opponents, Miller was knowledgeable in labor law. He invoked the check-off law, forcing owners to become dues collectors for his union. More important, he cleverly maneuvered the owners into recognizing the players association as a legitimate bargaining agent. Miller's predecessors had been paid partly out of funds provided by the owners. Miller recognized immediately that this was a violation of the Taft–Hartley Act prohibiting payment of money by an employer to an employee's organization. When, in an effort to block Miller's election the owners invoked this law as justification for not paying him, Miller knew that he had secured an important victory: "I realized much more clearly than they did that by citing Taft–Hartley, the owners had inadvertently acknowledged that baseball was an *industry* operating in interstate commerce . . . and that the Players Association was a *labor organization*" (M. Miller 1991, 68).

Miller soon enlisted the support of the vast majority of major league baseball players (Voigt 1983, 210). He negotiated his first collective bargaining contract in 1966, arranging for an increase in owners' contributions to the pension plan. A more complete agreement, "the first ever negotiated in any sport," was reached in 1968, significant most of all because it placed restrictions on the power of owners to change rules unilaterally and established the rule that players' individual contracts could not violate the terms of an existing basic agreement (M. Miller 1991, 97). The agreement also instituted the first formal grievance procedure.

One of the union's most important victories was actually a legal defeat. Miller, after some hesitation, had encouraged Curt Flood to bring an antitrust suit against baseball's reserve clause. This suit, filed in 1969, provided a backdrop to the bargaining that resulted the next year in the Second Basic Agreement signed between the players' association and the owners. The agreement recognized the association as the "sole and exclusive collective bargaining agent for all Major League Players" and, among other things, raised the minimum salary to twelve thousand dollars.

As it turned out, the most significant achievement of the 1970 agreement was getting the owners to agree that player grievances should be settled outside the commissioner's office, by a permanent, impartial, arbitrator. The role of the arbitrator was to interpret ambiguous language in the game's governing documents: the collective bargaining agreement, the uniform player contract, and league rules. The agreement to arbitrate grievances did not at first seem all that important when set beside pension benefits and minimum wages. But it was to rank "very near the top in terms of importance to players" of all the gains made during the 1970s, because it would eventually be extended to the reserve clause (Dworkin 1981, 71). In the next round of negotiations, arbitration was extended to salaries, but not without a struggle. Before the start of the 1972 season, the major league players went out on strike, the first industrywide stoppage in baseball history. The immediate issue was the owners' unwillingness to add what the players regarded as a fair cost-of-living increase in their pension and medical benefits during a time of high inflation. The strike lasted thirteen days and led to the loss of eighty-six games. It achieved an increase in the pension fund from surpluses in the fund's securities, a suggestion made by Miller before the strike began (Lowenfish and Lupien 1980, 216). The basic agreement negotiated in 1973 raised the minimum salary once more but, more importantly, earned players the right to salary arbitration.

Baseball's arbitration system—first agreed to in the 1968 collective bargaining agreement and reaffirmed in subsequent agreements in 1970 (when the commissioner was replaced with a neutral third party), 1973 (when salary arbitration was introduced), 1976, 1980, and 1985 agreements—is the most extensive in all the major team sports. That in football does not include salary arbitration, although arbitration over the interpretation of contract terms can have salary implications for a player. In a review of baseball grievances arbitrated between 1970 and

1984, five cases concerned the reserve system (e.g., special covenants included in players' contracts that would have contravened collectively bargained rules); five were complaints by players that they had not been granted free agency when it was due; two concerned interpretations of salary agreements (e.g., the timing of bonuses); ten concerned termination and termination pay issues; nine were disputes over the payment of expenses; seven were disciplinary; six had to do with the grievance procedure itself; two involved the distribution of World Series or League Championship pools; and two were "miscellaneous" (Wong 1986a). Players' grievances that go to arbitration usually involve a conflict between collective and individual interests. This can be seen in the case of special clauses in individually negotiated contracts: "Although players and clubs can enter into special covenants that afford the player actual or potential additional benefits, those special covenants and the benefits therein must be consistent with the terms of the collective bargaining agreement" (Wong 1986b, 473).

A lockout by the owners in the spring of 1976 lasted for seventeen days of spring training. Owners were trying to recoup the pension benefits previously ceded to the players. The union, on the other hand, was buoyed by the decision of arbitrator Peter Seitz, in 1975, that two pitchers, Andy Messersmith and Dave McNally, were free agents because they had played out their "option years" (i.e., one year without a contract). The Seitz decision was a delayed victory for the union, which had bargained for neutral arbitration in 1970. It is unlikely that at the time, union officials anticipated how significant this concession would prove to be. The owners certainly did not believe that the reserve clause was subject to arbitration when they signed the 1970 agreement, and they continued to assert this position after Seitz made his decision. This was eventually settled in court.

The Messersmith and McNally affair (dubbed "the emancipation proclamation of baseball" in Wong 1986b, 467) underlined one of the most important functions of the unions in the 1970s, especially in baseball, where a system of arbitration had been agreed to. The union had come to play a role in helping players settle disputes over the interpretation and application of contracts, providing legal advice, money and moral support against a more powerful adversary. This proved to be its most functional role, in an industry sector where there is less emphasis on collective, than on individual, action. The union had to see itself as clearing the way for greater labor market freedom for players to negotiate individual contracts, without presuming to have a role in their actual negotiation.

While many believed that Miller would take advantage of the Seitz decision to push for complete free agency as a means of settling the dispute, the agreement he signed stipulated that a team could still reserve a player for six years of major league service, a proposal made by the owners at the beginning of the lockout. Miller later explained that he "did not believe that free-agency rights after one year were in the best interests of the players—that a large supply of free agents every year would hold salaries down" (M. Miller 1992, 255). Miller might also have suspected that players would show less solidarity behind the cause of free agency than they had behind that of better pension benefits.

Throughout the second half of the 1970s, management take-aways and union give-backs were common as the national economic recession increased unemployment and shifted public sympathy toward business. Union membership dropped from 30 percent of the work force in 1963 to 20 percent in 1983 (Raskin 1986, 30); public opinion polls showed approval of unions declining steadily between 1965 and 1981 (Lipset 1986, 101). In 1980, the owners tried to impose tighter controls over free agency by requiring that the buying team compensate the selling team when free agents were traded, a version of the Rozell Rule in football. The players' association did not back down, however; and the result was the 1981 strike. Both sides prepared well in advance, the union accumulating a strike fund and the owners taking out insurance with Lloyds. Miller believes that owners were "intent on provoking a strike" (M. Miller 1991, 290).

The strike lasted fifty days and canceled 713 games. The warring parties eventually agreed to the idea of compensation for signing "premier free agents" from a pool of players (not necessarily players of the selling team), an arrangement Miller considered much less of a restraint on free agency. The players refused to consider an end to salary arbitration and also turned back the owner's demand for a pay scale for players with less than six years' major league service (Berry, Gould, and Staudohar 1986, 73).

The strike was notable for its involvement of the executive branch of government. The NLRB upheld the players' claim that management had not bargained in good faith, failing to provide financial data to prove the necessity for free agent compensation (K. Jennings 1990, 52). With both sides obdurate, Secretary of Labor Raymond Donovan flew to New York and talked with the bargaining teams, exhorting them to settle the dispute as soon as possible, indicating that the Reagan administration was taking an interest in the conflict above the level of the Federal Mediation and Conciliation Service. At Donovan's suggestion, the talks were moved to Washington for five days to permit him to join the federal mediator in the talks. The press wondered why Donovan had chosen to spend so much time on baseball at a time when coal operators, air traffic controllers, and postal employees were approaching possible strike action. To Miller, the reason was simple: "The cities with major league franchises were complaining bitterly about lost revenues" (M. Miller 1991, 311).

The reason why the players preferred to strike rather than concede the salary arbitration agreement is that it had worked very well for them. Between 1974 and 1984, there was an average of 19 cases a year.

Of these, 104 decisions were made in favor of the club, and 86, in favor of the player, under the system where the arbitrator must choose one or the other of the "bids." Average salaries had risen from $40,839 to $329,408 (J. Miller 1990, 266). In view of this fact, it is surprising that only half of all eligible players file. The reality is that players gain a tremendous amount from even the threat of arbitration. For example, while the "winning" players in 1984 averaged increases of 160 percent, the "losers" nevertheless received 46 percent pay increases; in 1985, the figures were 174 percent and 39 percent. Players thus used the threat of arbitration to intimidate the owners, filing salary claims and using these claims to leverage higher salaries. Seventy-two percent of the filing players actually settle before the final stage of arbitration is reached (Dworkin 1986). The amount players demand also tends to rise under the arbitration. In 1974, the spread between owner's and player's bids was 20 percent of average salary; by 1985, it had risen to 40 percent, $163,000 (Dworkin 1986, 66).

The system worked so well for the players—and salaries escalated so sharply—that the owners began to take measures to limit competition for playing talent by subterfuge. Lee MacPhail, past president of the American League, preferred to believe that the owners "finally, gradually, invoked some self-discipline" (1989, 228). In fact, they broke the law. During the 1985 and 1986 seasons, they secretly conspired not to bid for free agents: at the end of the 1985 season, only two of sixty-two free agents were picked up by another team. The collusion is reported to have cost the players between twenty and thirty million dollars in 1985 and between fifty and sixty million dollars in 1986 in lost salaries. Arbitrators' rulings in 1987 and 1988 found the owners guilty of violating the basic agreement by conspiring among themselves to fix the price they would pay for baseball talent.

Proof of the collusion soured labor-management relations in baseball, and both sides began preparing for difficult bargaining in 1989-90 at the end of the basic agreement then in force. The MLBPA began using licensing fees from the sale of baseball cards to amass a strike fund. To match the seventy million dollars the players would have accrued by the time talks began, the owners set aside a hundred-million-dollar strike fund. They also dismissed the law firm handling their labor matters (Wilkie, Farr, and Gallagher), which did not specialize in labor law, and hired a firm (Morgan, Lewis, and Bockius) with a better record of fighting unions. The owners had already outlined a new "pay for performance" idea in which players with less than six years service would be paid according to a statistical scale heavily weighted toward games played. In exchange, a set amount of revenue would be designated for players, and salary arbitration would be eliminated.

The structure and culture of labor-management relations in baseball had clearly changed since the 1960s. Against tremendous odds, Miller had inaugurated a new era in management-labor relations. Not least of these achievements was getting the owners to take collective bargaining seriously and set up a Player Relations Committee to handle it, headed by an experienced industrial relations man, the first being John Gaherin. On the other hand, Miller was very controversial. It is ironic that when they created the new salaried position of executive director in 1966, the players' first choice for the job was the "company man" Cannon: "Cannon continually reminded the players that they were the luckiest men alive to be paid to play ball, even saying, without a trace of irony, that baseball had the 'finest relationship between players and management in the history of the sport' " (M. Miller 1991, 7). The players were fortunate that once elected, Cannon began to demand conditions of employment that the player representatives found completely unacceptable; and the decision was made to "start the election process all over" (p. 34).

Lee MacPhail, then assistant to Commissioner Eckert, regretted that Cannon had not got the job, recalling later, "we were remiss in not researching Miller's background more carefully and possibly in not trying to divert the players from Miller before his election was ratified" (1989, 10). Commissioner Kuhn would later recall that Miller's "left of center views" made it difficult for him to deal with "highly establishmentarian" baseball people. Kuhn implied that his own, centrist, position was more reasonable than Miller's, which by contrast had "left a legacy of hatred and bitterness between clubs and players that would destructively sour labor relations in baseball for years to come" (Kuhn 1987, 362). In Kuhn's view, there were those who represented "the interests of baseball" and those who were "in it for themselves." He and most owners were in the first group, and Miller was clearly in the second. Miller, Kuhn complained, could play the press while he and the owners were "rightfully hobbled by . . . policies requiring more attention to accuracy and less stirring up of public controversy" (p. 79). During the bitter 1981 baseball strike (which he insisted on calling "Miller's strike") Kuhn, while claiming to represent the interests of all of baseball, simultaneously expressed his frustration at not being able to intervene more effectively in the dispute to push management's point of view: "I did not have the power to direct the activities of a federally protected labor union. Had it been otherwise, there would have been no strike. No sensible person would have permitted the Players' Association to strike over the compensation issue" (p. 353).[1] It is understandable that Kuhn should have a jaundiced view of this strike. It led to calls for his resignation from nine of the owners, and he was convinced that this laid the seeds for his eventual dismissal. However, his view of Miller and his activities was by no means untypical of management and its representatives. The president of the American League, Lee MacPhail, complained that Miller, whom he described as "a traditional labor zealot," was "never that concerned with the relationship between clubs and players" (1989, 175). Like Kuhn, MacPhail associated the players' political activities with special interests, while those of management were associated with the public interest: "Management is the only side that must always be concerned for the game itself" (ibid.).

A more objective view is that Miller used his considerable skills as a negotiator to defeat owners, who, for many years after Miller became executive director, could not reconcile themselves to the fact of collective bargaining, in large part because of the exemption granted baseball from antitrust suits. The owners, accustomed to, and comforted by, this exemption, would refer to it as a justification for the way they ran baseball. Miller recognized the owners' strength against a frontal assault on antitrust grounds and did not directly attack the reserve system. Indeed, in the basic agreement ratified in 1976, Miller showed a spirit of compromise by negotiating a limited free agency only months after Arbitrator Seitz's rejection of the system of contract "rollover." Miller, faced with the antitrust immunity of baseball and sensing that this could not be as powerful a weapon for him as it might be in football or basketball, chose to develop a clear collective bargaining strategy and thus was able to develop a much stronger union than was found in other team sports (McCormick 1982, 1150). Miller was also astute in recognizing that professional athletes might be difficult to organize and that, in negotiating with the owners, he should emphasize concerns all players shared, such as pension benefits, scheduling of games, health and life insurance, and salary arbitration. Ironically, it was the decline in importance of pension benefits (as more and more players secured lucrative long-term contracts) that weakened the union after Miller retired in 1982.

Miller was succeeded by Ken Moffett in 1982, a former federal mediator who proved to be much too conciliatory for the players, who fired him after one year, to be replaced by the MLBPA's general counsel, Donald Fehr. The 1980s saw a counter-offensive by the owners, most notably the collusion not to bid on free agents that lasted from 1985 until 1988. The basic agreement signed in 1985 also was a victory for the owners. Eligibility for salary arbitration was increased from two years of service to three; and for the first time, the union agreed to accept less than one-third of the national television and radio revenues for the pension plan.

With their collusion exposed, the owners prepared for the 1990 round of bargaining by arguing that salaries should be limited to a certain percentage of the total revenues. The players refused to accept such a "partnership" without commensurate participation in decision making that could affect the size of the revenues being divided. They pressed their claim for a reduction in the number of years before a player became eligible for salary arbitration from three to two. The result was a lockout during spring training for 1990. The agreement ending the lockout was a compromise, mandating that players with at least two years in the major leagues could qualify for arbitration if they had a minimum of eighty-six days of major league service the previous year and their total major league service ranked in the top 17 percent of eligible players in that group.

While this agreement was described by the combative Miller, looking on from the sidelines, as a sign of weakness on the part of the union, 1992 nevertheless saw major baseball players enjoying a minimum salary of one hundred thousand dollars and 273 (out of a total of 650) earning more than a million dollars a year. Two players (Bobby Bonilla and Danny Tartabull) were paid more in 1992 than the total payroll ($9.5 million) of all the major league clubs combined in 1966, when Marvin Miller took office. While some of this increase reflected inflation and the larger television revenues accruing to the sport, the major portion has been a direct result of the power of the players' association and the skill of its executive director for most of those years. In no other team sport was the union to be quite so effective.

FOOTBALL

The less tradition-bound and less well-protected sport of football experienced a somewhat different union history. At first, it appeared that the football players' union would enjoy greater success than the baseball players'; but history has demonstrated otherwise. The National Football League Players' Association was founded in 1956. (The American Football League Players Association would follow in 1963.) Early negotiations between management and players were sporadic. The NLRB had refused in 1946 to take jurisdiction over baseball labor disputes, on the grounds that baseball did not involve interstate commerce and that given the court rulings of the time, there seemed little hope that the state would adopt a different policy toward football. In addition, the ruling patriarchy in the NFL could trace its roots to the league's founding in the 1920s. These owners had difficulty seeing their sport as an industry needing modern labor-management structures. George Halas was one of the founding owners. In congressional hearings conducted in 1957, Halas, while asserting his support for a players' association, objected to idea of a pension fund and even more strenuously to the idea of collective bargaining (U.S. Congress, House, Committee on the Judiciary 1957, 2701). The owners refused to allow the players to be represented before them by anyone other than Commissioner Bert Bell.

The players did not see the matter in quite the same light. Emboldened by the *Radovich v. National Football League* decision in 1957, they threatened the owners with a $4.2-million antitrust suit, managing by this means to get the owners to agree to a five-thousand-dollar minimum salary, fifty dollars for each exhibition game played, and a clause that continued a player's salary and provided medical and hospital care in the event of injury. A pension plan followed in 1959. Compared to later achievements, these gains were relatively minor; but the bargaining power of the unions was weakened during the 1950s by the lack of television revenues. Congressional hearings at that time rarely made reference to television money in connection with labor relations. Competition for players could be portrayed by management as much more destabilizing where no television revenue sharing of any kind was even feasible.

The attorney for the NFLPA, Creighton Miller, was not keen on bargaining by threat of litigation. Just what constituted "reasonable" employment terms, he argued, would lead to endless litigation if left to the courts to decide, litigation that the owners were much better equipped to win than the players. He nevertheless expressed his frustration at management's refusal to deal fairly with the players' representatives, threatening at the time to have "recourse to the National Labor Relations Board" and file unfair labor practice charges against management (U.S. Congress, House, Committee on the Judicary 1957, 2631). Even the sympathetic Celler was shocked by this combative talk, which, he said, was "straining it pretty far" (p. 2654). Ironically, Commissioner Bert Bell, under persistent questioning by Celler, dramatically announced his "official" recognition of the NFLPA during these very hearings. However, the owners subsequently brought him to heel and he refused to sign an actual recognition agreement, citing as grounds that the players sought to include as issues for bargaining such non-negotiable items as minimum salaries. George Halas's was perhaps more typical of the attitude of owners at this time: he refused to meet with union representatives, let alone negotiate with them.

When the NFLPA formally registered with the NLRB in 1968, it became the first professional athletes' union to do so. The players looked well placed to fight the power of the owners through statutorily protected collective bargaining methods. For example, the players' association could appeal to the National Labor Relations Board if the owners did not bargain in good faith; it could press charges of unfair labor practices if the owners threatened retaliation against union representatives; and it could mount a legal strike. But the registration had occurred during the rivalry between the NFL and AFL and perhaps exaggerated the power of the players at the time. The players vigorously fought the merger of the two football leagues. Quite correctly, they calculated that a single league would drive down wages. In 1966 and 1967, the last year of AFL–NFL competition, players were receiving 60 percent of gross revenues. Once the merger took place, this proportion fell steadily, finally leveling off in 1972 when a new television contract was negotiated. By this time the proportion of gross going to players was 28 percent (U.S. Congress, House, Committee on the Judiciary 1984, 39). When Congress approved the merger, the players followed suit by merging their unions; but the owners seized this opportunity to deny recognition to the "new" union. The NFLPA was forced to undergo the arduous process of seeking certification from the NLRB once again. The owners were clearly still very reluctant to work within a regular collective bargaining framework and eager to exploit any means to keep the players divided.

In 1971, Edward Garvey became executive director of the NFLPA, succeeding Daniel Shulman, who had taken over from Creighton Miller in 1968: "Under his leadership, the union became more aggressive at the bargaining table and in the courtroom" (Staudohar 1986, 63). Garvey was much more willing to consider strike action than his predecessors, although the players had boycotted training camp in 1968 and 1970. He seized the opportunity of the formation of the World Football League to organize a strike against the NFL in 1974. It collapsed rather ignominiously after forty-four days due to erosion of player solidarity and lack of public support. The strike so soured management–player relations that Garvey was unable to negotiate another basic agreement for three years, and the union shifted the conflict to the courts. There it gave its support to a suit brought by the tight end for the Baltimore Colts, John Mackey, against the Rozelle Rule on the grounds that it violated the Sherman Act. Mackey happened to be president of the NFLPA at the time.

The federal court sided with the union in this case; and the basic agreement signed one year later, in 1977, relaxed the terms of the Rozelle Rule sufficient to promise professional football players much more freedom to negotiate contracts. Such was not to be, however, for the agreement simply served to push the owners back to their old practices of blacklisting. After five years, even though 510 players had become free agents, only 23 had received offers from other teams, and only 6 of these had switched (Scott, Cong, and Somppi 1983). The most notorious case was that of Chicago Bears' Walter Payton, arguably the best running back of his day, who was sought by no other owner when his contract with the Bears expired.

Garvey declared that the conspicuous lack of trading for free agents was clear evidence that the owners were not abiding by the 1977 agreement. Their ability and willingness to collude in this way was made possible by the practice of sharing television revenues, which robbed individual owners of the incentive to build winning teams by hiring new talent. Yet Garvey did not believe that the union could get Congress to legislate changes in the reserve system or alter owners' attitudes toward free agency. He therefore sought equity in terms of income share by demanding 55 percent of the gross revenues from television as part of the negotiations for the next basic agreement. There is some reason to believe that this demand had been inspired by an agreement negotiated in 1980 by the Screen Actors' Guild with the television and movie industry after a lengthy strike, granting the guild 4.5 percent of gross income from pay television and videocassettes (Berry, Gould, and Staudohar 1986, 132).

Considerable criticism was leveled at Garvey for the 55 percent demand. Owners dismissed the claim on the grounds that it would give the players the status of owners. Others refused to believe Garvey's assertion that football teams had no financial stake in winning because of revenue sharing and therefore do not compete for players. They cited economic studies indicating that "the difference between winning and losing one game in a 16-game NFL season is $169,500" (Scott, Cong, and Somppi 1983, 262). Garvey`s critics wondered whether Garvey himself was all that interested in more free agency. The abolition of the reserve system, after all, would give more power to individual players and their agents and strip power from the unions. Free agency would also tend to increase differences in salaries among players (Raimondo 1983). Unions were developing considerable interest in the activities of players' agents at this time, expressing some interest in their regulation. Individual negotiations, especially those involving multiyear contracts and deferred compensation, would tend to undermine collective goals such as pensions.

The slow pace of negotiations on the 55 percent share, rumors concerning the possible formation of the USFL, and a successful baseball strike in 1981 emboldened the union to strike again in 1982. This strike lasted for fifty-seven days but could not be considered a success for the players. The agreement ending it was identical to that offered by the owners before the strike began. It did not grant the 55 percent share. In addition, the union's president, first vice president and second vice president were either cut or traded by the end of the season: "Within a year, a total of twenty union officials and players' representatives had been cut or traded. Of the seven men on the union's negotiating committee, only two would still have jobs a year after they set their first picket line" (Harris 1986, 184).

The players struck again in 1987, the chief issue being free agency. In the decade since the introduction of the Rozelle Rule, only one player had changed teams. The strike ended after twenty-four days, during which teams played with "scab" players and about a quarter of the players originally on strike crossed picket lines to resume work. When the striking players reported back to work, the union filed an antitrust suit against the league, challenging, among other things, the college draft and the restraints on free agency. The suit would eventually be settled in 1990, when the Supreme Court let stand a 1989 federal appeals court decision that the players could not sue for antitrust while a labor "relationship" remained in effect. The union also filed

charges with the NLRB of bad-faith bargaining on the part of the owners: the owners had begun assembling replacement teams before the
strike was declared and management had threatened players to get
them to cross picket lines and management refused to even negotiate
the major issue of free agency.

In December 1987, the NLRB issued a complaint against the owners
(a complaint is the equivalent of an indictment in the area of labor
law), ordering them to pay between twenty-one and twenty-five million dollars in wages and bonuses to players who had been barred
from playing on Sunday and Monday following the strike's end. The
board found that the owners had stipulated that "non-roster replacement players" (i.e., scabs) could be signed to play in a Sunday game
with as little as twenty-four hours notice, while players returning from
the strike were obliged to report three days in advance of a game in order to be eligible. The owners professed concern for players' safety,
but the board saw this as illegal coercion in violation of the National
Labor Relations Act. By the end of the 1980s, any semblance of orderly
collective bargaining between management and labor in professional
football had disappeared.

There is no more convincing evidence of the weakness of the union
movement in professional football than the manner in which the failure to negotiate a basic agreement in 1987 was finally overcome in
1993. As noted earlier, when the 1987 strike failed, the NFLPA sued (in
the name of Marvin Powell) over the right of the first-refusal system,
which permitted teams to refuse a player's contract terms and offer a
new deal at a predetermined minimum salary. The suit also attacked
the compensation system that required a club signing a free agent to
compensate the player's old team with draft choices. The loss of this
suit on the grounds that the NFL was immune from this kind of antitrust charge while a collective-bargaining structure existed (the "labor exemption") prompted the players to disband their union; the
union decertified itself. While the Powell case was in court, the NFL
imposed its Plan B system. A suit filed to protest the introduction of
Plan B (by Freeman McNeil, on behalf of a number of players) proved
more successful than the Powell suit. The way was open for more liberal employment practices in the NFL. But by this time, the union no
longer existed, and the question of how to deal with restrictions on
player mobility in the absence of a collective bargaining framework
was left up to the courts. The judge in the McNeil case (David Doty)
threatened to impose his own settlement on the dispute if the owners
and the players could not come up with one of their own and, under
this ultimatum, an agreement was reached. But it was an agreement
between the owners' management committee and the lawyers hired
by McNeil and his fellow plaintiffs to protest Plan B, not between the
owners and the union, which no longer existed. The agreement was
far-reaching and highly significant, for it provided genuine free agency

in the NFL for the first time, albeit for players with a minumum of five-years' experience, in a league where the average playing career is less than four seasons.

The effective unionization of professional football players had proven extraordinarily difficult. Marvin Miller was convinced that professional football players were less militant than professional baseball players because minor league working conditions were inferior to the college campus training grounds for the NFL (K. Jennings 1990, 67). But there were political reasons for the relative weakness of the NFLPA. The football owners obtained Congressional approval to negotiate television revenues jointly and, in the process, established a system whereby these revenues would be shared equally among participating franchises. While basketball, baseball, and hockey franchises sell fewer than half their seats as season tickets (the sale of the rest depending on performance on the field), and rely heavily on local and regional radio and television contracts, football presents an entirely different case. Unlike the other three sports, almost every seat to every game is sold each season; and the teams receive equal shares of the money the networks pay the league for broadcast rights. The NFLPA compiled statistics for 1983-86 showing that the top seven teams in the league had an average of 9.6 wins, paid an average base salary of $156,000, and received average gross revenues of $27.4 million. The bottom seven teams averaged only 6.1 wins and paid $142,800 average salary but grossed $27 million in revenues each (Ross 1989, 678).

Even if some NFL teams prove more successful than others, there are few ways they can significantly increase their revenues. Because other sports allow individual clubs to negotiate with local media for rights to broadcast games, each club is affected differently by a work-stoppage; football owners are all affected the same. Football is, in this sense, more concentrated (i.e., more closely approximates an oligopoly or single firm); and concentration is recognized as a source of strength for capital against labor (Wallace, Griffin, and Rubin 1989, 203).

Union power seems to have been greatest in the case of basketball, then baseball and hockey, then football. Sociological wisdom suggests that this results from variations in the supply of labor. Where labor is scarce, unions have more power. While the labor pool for baseball players is certainly larger than any other major team sport (because it includes high school, junior college, college, postcollege, and even foreign players), there is no significant difference between the size of the pool of basketball and football players. However, sheer numbers might be less important in this case than the perception that an individual basketball player can make a much bigger difference to the profitability of a franchise than an individual football player. Competition for players is thus more intense among basketball owners than among football owners, and this gives more power to the players and the union representing them.

Professional basketball players established a system of representation in 1954 when they set up the National Basketball Association Players' Association and hired, on a part-time basis, a lawyer to advise them on legal problems and an insurance agent to give them financial planning assistance. Each team elected representatives to the association; and from these representatives, two were chosen to sit on the owners' executive committee. They had no voting rights, however; and the House Judiciary Committee correctly judged this form of representation, which had been tried in baseball, to be "of little consequence" (Gregory 1956, 205). Although owners "recognized" the union in 1957, it was largely moribund until 1962, when Lawrence Fleisher became counsel. Even so, owners in the NBA did not allow players to have any collective legal representation before 1967.

The first collective bargaining agreement was signed by NBA owners anxious to stem the flow of players to the ABA, which began in 1967. During this period of interleague wars, the union did not push a collective bargaining strategy vigorously. Under later questioning before the Senate Judiciary Committee, Larry Fleisher, general counsel of the NBAPA, could recall no "particular reason" why his union had not filed with the NLRB by that time (U.S. Congress, Senate, Committee on the Judiciary 1972, 278). He did not choose to mention that players were doing quite well as long as the two leagues were competing for their services. The players had been ambivalent about the utility of a union under these conditions of healthy competition. Consequently, it was not hard for congressmen hostile to unionism to find star players to support their position. Roman Hruska, Republican representative from Nebraska, was able to get ABA player Rick Barry to agree that professional athletes, not being workers, need no union:

> HRUSKA: The Players' Association is pretty much like a union, isn't it?
>
> BARRY: Well, ours isn't very strong but we are trying to make it better, but it is very similar, yes.
>
> HRUSKA: It has some of the principles of a union?
>
> BARRY: Definitely.
>
> HRUSKA: It is not a labor union; you fellows don't work; you play. That is why they call you players?
>
> BARRY: That is exactly right.
>
> HRUSKA: You like the game well enough and are paid well enough to play?
>
> BARRY: If you like it enough it is play. (p. 153)

Barry was present to testify on behalf of the ABA-NBA merger, which the unions opposed, and confessed to being a "happy slave." To be fair to Barry, who had played in both leagues, he later wrote to the chairman of the committee, Samuel Ervin, amending this part of his testimony. "I am firmly convinced," he wrote, "that the passage of merger legislation without eliminating the reserve, option, or any other type of clause that restricts a player's freedom of movement would be extremely harmful" (p. 308).

The owners eventually traded a willingness to enter into collective bargaining for the players' agreement to the merger of the NBA and the ABA, which took place in 1976. An equally important result of the owners' desire to merge was that after many years of refusing to discuss the reserve clause with the players, they now agreed to include it in the issues that could be negotiated at the bargaining table. However, the parties could not agree about what to do in the event that their differences proved irreconcilable; and once more recourse was made to the courts. In the settlement of a suit brought by Oscar Robertson against the NBA in 1970 to block the merger on antitrust grounds, the court, while it rejected Robertson's suit, did "retain jurisdiction to enforce the terms of the settlement by giving enforcement power to a special master, whose decisions were subject to review by the court. Thus the judiciary became involved in what is normally carried out by the parties themselves through the grievance procedure and arbitration" (Staudohar 1986, 106). Not surprisingly, this arrangement spawned frequent litigation. The most notorious case was that of the trade of Marvin Webster from Seattle to New York in 1979, a trade for which Commissioner Lawrence O'Brien ruled that Seattle should be compensated one player and $450,000. The special master, Telford Taylor, affirmed the award, whereupon the union appealed on the grounds that it would have a chilling effect on the market. The U.S. District Court and, in turn, the court of appeals, invalidated the award. Taylor was obliged to reverse his earlier judgment: "Although the special masters function like arbitrators, their decisions are not necessarily final or binding because the federal courts retain jurisdiction to review decisions. What are really matters of contract interpretation rather than law have been dragged into the courts where they do not belong" (p. 108).

For this reason, perhaps, the NBAPA is quick to draw the weapon of antitrust law against the owners when talks bog down. In 1987, after nine fruitless collective bargaining sessions aimed at replacing the labor agreement expiring that year, nine players filed a class-action suit on behalf of all players, targeting the college draft, the "right of first refusal," and the salary cap as restrictive practices in violation of the Sherman Act. As noted in chapter 3, this suit was settled out of court, the "right of first refusal" clause being waived for players with seven or more years in the league, a term to be reduced to three years by 1994.

A players' association was formed in hockey in 1957, forty years after the founding of the National Hockey League. The formation of the association had been provoked by the signing of a television contract in 1956, from which the players received no additional revenues. The association hired Norman Lewis, lawyer for the baseball players. He filed a suit and got more money for player pensions, but the union ceased to function shortly thereafter and did not revive until the appointment of R. Alan Eagleson as executive director. In 1967, the NHL signed an agreement recognizing the union; but it could achieve no collective bargaining agreement until 1975, when a five-year pact set up, among other things, the outside arbitration of grievances (including salary arbitration for players in the option year). Although the players were substantially underpaid when the National Hockey League Players' Association (NHLPA) was formed, the union has been weakened by the financial instability of the NHL compared to the other three major team sports. The refusal of NBC to renew its contract with the NHL in 1975 because of poor ratings was a major blow to the league and its players.

In 1991, Eagleson was replaced as executive director by Bob Goodenow, who proved to be much more combative than his predecessor. When the basic agreement signed in 1986 expired in 1991, he did not hurry to negotiate another. Hockey players had begun to look across at the rapidly escalating salaries in baseball and wonder whether fewer restrictions on free agency might have the same effect for them. Annual pay in hockey at this time ($254,000) averaged less than one-third that in baseball and half that in football. Goodenow articulated a series of demands, including increased bonus payments for playoff participation, but chiefly aimed at easing restrictions on player mobility by modifying the compensation rule then in force.[2] When negotiations stalled, Goodenow waited until the approach of the Stanley Cup playoffs in the spring to begin threatening to strike. Hockey players make most of their wages in the six-month regular season and are paid only bonus money for playoff participation. Owners look to make extra profits during this period.

When owners refused to give way on the compensation issue, pleading losses of nine million dollars on the season, and countered with a demand for a share of revenues from trading cards, the players voted 560 to 4 to strike, their first such action in the sport's history. The strike lasted eleven days. It ended with what all sides agreed was only a provisional agreement (until 1993), the most definitive part of which was the owners' acknowledgement that players have the exclusive rights to their likeness and are thus entitled to all revenues from trading cards. The agreement did increase pension and insurance benefits and raised

the minimum salary to one hundred thousand dollars; but no significant changes were made in the free agent system.

Tennis

The union movement reached tennis by the 1970s, when
control of the game by the International Lawn Tennis Federation (ILTF)
was being challenged by Lamar Hunt's World Championship Tennis
(WCT). Hunt had signed up so many of the leading players that he was
able to demand more money from major championships, most of which
had been declared "open" by 1968. In an attempt to wrest control of the
game back from WCT, the ILTF barred WCT players from the official circuit. The result was the formation of the Association of Tennis Professionals (ATP), in 1972. The Women's Tennis Association followed in
1973. The ATP organized a boycott of Wimbledon in 1973 in support of
Yugoslavia's Nikki Pilic, who had been suspended by his country's tennis federation over his failure to play in a Davis Cup tie. The association
was concerned not only about low pay and restricted access to the official circuit but also about the rise of World Team Tennis, which
seemed to threaten the players' independence.

After 1973, men's tennis was run by the Men's Tennis Council. The
MTC was an uneasy alliance of representatives from the ATP, the International Tennis Federation (ITF), and tournament directors. The ITF's
role as the corporate voice of the national tennis associations was primarily to oversee the rules of play and promote tennis worldwide, both
amateur and professional. However, it was also on the Men's Tennis
Council to maintain some control over professional tennis. The tournament directors were on the council to secure a steady—and possibly
increasing—supply of entertainment events from which they (and the
players) could make money. While the ATP had flexed its muscles in
1973, it had subsequently been caught in the middle as the ITF warred
with tournament promoters. The ITF controlled the grand slam events
and the world team championships for the Davis Cup and Federation
Cup and, beginning in 1988, the Olympics. The ITF was also responsible for innumerable minor tournaments, supported by national associations, which guaranteed a supply of talent for the major tournaments.
The tournament directors, however, controlled the bread-and-butter
grand prix circuit: their job was to sell tickets and attract media coverage and sponsors. They competed intensely for the top players.

By the late 1980s, the ATP was beginning to chafe at the grueling
schedule players were forced to maintain in order to remain eligible to
compete for the biggest prizes: the 1988 grand prix circuit consisted of
seventy-nine tournaments, and each ATP player was expected to par-

ticipate in at least fourteen. In 1988 the ATP announced that it would inaugurate its own tour, starting in 1990. The players proposed that an ATP tour board should promote and regulate the sport. It would be made up of player representatives, tournament representatives, and one independent member. The new tour would have a shorter, well-defined season, culminating in a masters-style championship (similar to that in golf) at the end of the season. It would also establish three levels of competition, with two lower levels confined to lower-ranked players, in order to distribute playing time and lessen demands on top players. The ITF was left with the Davis Cup and the grand slam events, complete with a new grand slam cup event at the end of the year.

The players thus gained more control over playing opportunities than they had under the old system, but their independence brought fresh problems. The ATP failed to secure an "umbrella" sponsor (i.e., one for the tour as a whole) and, with some irony, hired the International Management Group (IMG) to do so. Shortly thereafter, the IMG brought in IBM to give the new tour the financial backing and credibility it sought; but in reaching this goal, the ATP had to relinquish some control to the IMG; in return for a commitment of $56.1 million over three years, the ATP gave the IMG the right to sell sponsorship rights, as well as domestic and international television packages. The agreement obligated certain designated "marquee players" to eight of eleven single-week events during a year.

COLLECTIVE BARGAINING OR ANTITRUST?

During the 1970s, when the structure of labor–management relations in professional team sports assumed their modern form, the most crucial strategic issue with which not only labor and management but also government officials had to deal was that of the framework within which player and owner should relate to each other. Was theirs a relationship governed by established laws of collective bargaining or a relationship governed by laws of individual contract? Were the athletes independent businessmen or wage workers? Were the franchises a cartel or competing firms?

The owners had been very reluctant to engage in collective bargaining. However, they soon began to appreciate that it could afford them some protection from antitrust litigation. The players, on the other hand, while anxious to set up a collective bargaining apparatus, also wanted to preserve room for the antitrust weapon. The players' argument was strengthened by the close links between the labor and product markets in the sport industry. The activity of a franchise in the labor market is very closely related (or so it is thought) to the quality of the product the franchise has to sell. The players could claim that controlling the labor market was tantamount to controlling the product market.

Very much involved in this strategic maneuvering was the question of the "location" of the reserve clause. What was its status in law? While some continued to argue that the reserve clause was a restraint of trade, others believed that however much this might have been true in the past, employment practices had now changed so much that not the Sherman Act but another federal statute, the National Labor Relations Act, must be taken into account. Baseball owners in *Flood* v. *Kuhn (1972)* had argued that the draft and reserve clause were really NLRB matters. The court rejected this argument, finding that the antitrust issues involved in the case were outside the "special competence" of the NLRB and that the federal court should appropriately decide the case. Likewise, the football owners sought to have the reserve system recognized as a matter of collective bargaining. In 1975 they charged the NFLPA with refusing to bargaining over the Rozelle Rule. Once again, however, the state sided with the players, the NLRB agreeing that the union could refuse to bargain over the reserve clause.

This strategic maneuvering required quick footwork and a clear head. Garvey gave his version of this struggle to a congressional committee:

> The National Football League has been unwilling to bargain in good faith with this union. Yet, three weeks after being found guilty of sweeping illegal conduct in the 1974 negotiations, spokesmen for management turned to this committee and suggested that the answer to all problems in professional sports is in the arena of collective bargaining. In 1970, when the owners refused to recognize the union, we were forced to go to the National Labor Relations Board to ask for certification as a union. The owners urged the NLRB to turn down our requests and stay clear of professional sports. It was their argument then that any government interference in sports could mean the ruination of the game as we know it. Six years later, because they now have a theory that the union can exempt them from anti-trust attack by agreeing to procedures that restrict player movement, owners now are the "champions of collective bargaining" in the hopes that they can achieve immunity from the public policy of this country designed to promote competition. (U.S. Congress, House, Select Committee on Professional Sports 1976, 220)

Garvey was referring here to the labor exemption. United States labor policy seeks to promote collective bargaining to resolve important employer and employee conflicts. By and large, corporations and unions have been left to establish the specific agreements on virtually all issues. Because many agreements between labor and management also serve to restrain competition within the omnibus language of the

Sherman Act, a judicially created device, the so-called "labor exemption," has been fashioned. The labor exemption attempts to accommodate inherent conflicts between national labor and antitrust policy and to protect labor–management agreements over issues of central importance to labor from antitrust exemption. The precise nature of the exemption has been largely left to the courts to determine. Sports have been caught at the intersection of these two conflicting national policies. Antitrust policy would appear to frown upon any agreement that restricts trade; labor policy seeks to protect the right of management and labor to devise working arrangements in collaboration. Labor law and antitrust law are therefore frequently in conflict in sports and resolving this conflict has meant that the labor exemption is frequently invoked.

The Clayton Act and the later Norris–LaGuardia Act (1932) amended the Sherman Act to exempt a company from antitrust charges if the practice or activity in question was part of a collective bargaining agreement. The intent of the amendment was to provide protection for labor unions; they could not be charged with combination or conspiracy to restrain trade. No longer could management accuse them of violating antitrust laws. The policy justification for the exemption was that in the NLRB, Congress established a mechanism by which disputes between employers and union-represented employees could be resolved exclusively in collective bargaining under ground rules established by labor law and without government interference in the substance of negotiation. In light of the intent of these statutes, the courts have bent over backward to protect union activity from the onslaught of the antitrust laws. They have adhered firmly to the line that most of the issues in question should be settled by collective bargaining, not by legislation, adjudication, or case law. This position is consonant with the "liberal state" interpretation of laws regulating economic behavior and industrial relations. The state must assume some responsibility for regulating the process of collective bargaining, but its outcome is a private matter. This posture implies that the outcome is the result not of government action but of the relative bargaining skills and determination of the parties negotiating, parties assumed to be more or less equal.

The labor exemption was thus devised to protect organized labor. In sports, however, the weapon has been turned around and used by capital against labor; for the owners invoke the labor exemption when defending management practices of which the unions disapprove: "The defense is raised not for the purpose of seeking immunity for a union-imposed restriction but rather to immunize an employer-devised restraint which may or may not have been approved by the union" (Freedman 1987, 52). The owners maintain that virtually all player practices are immune from antitrust attack, because they are contained in collective bargaining agreements with respective players associations, thus qualifying them for the nonstatutory labor exemption to the antitrust laws. Thus, in *Wood* v. *National Basketball Association* (1984), the court rejected Leon Wood's claim that the college draft and the salary cap rules contained in the collective bargaining agreement of 1983 violated the Sherman Act, because the players' association had agreed to both the draft and the salary cap in that settlement. In *McCourt* v. *California Sports Incorporated* (1978), McCourt challenged the validity of the NHL's "equalization provision," hockey's version of the Rozelle Rule, offering compensation to the selling club. McCourt argued that the provision inhibited trading and therefore violated the antitrust laws. The court rejected his argument, declaring that the provision was exempt because it had been agreed upon as the result of bona fide collective bargaining.

The owners would like to see this line of argument pushed even further. For example, it implies that whenever a union-management collective bargaining *relationship* exists, what is exempt from antitrust review is not merely specific agreements reached through the bargaining but any *subject* of the bargaining. This would mean that even when a collective bargaining agreement expires or collapses (as it did for the NBA and NFL in 1988), the labor exemption continues, because owners still recognize the unions and the unions are still certified to represent players (Tagliabue 1987). The suit filed by the NFLPA at the conclusion of the 1987 strike, *Powell* v. *National Football League* (1988), was rejected on precisely these grounds, the court determining that the labor exemption continued to shield the player restraint system at least until the impasse in bargaining had ended. In *Bridgeman* v. *National Basketball Association* (1987), the court seemed to go even further, holding that the player restraint system would be exempt from antitrust scrutiny so long as the owners left the system unchanged and the owners reasonably believed that the practice or "a close variant of it would be incorporated in the next collective bargaining agreement" (McCormick 1989, 511).

Players' associations faced with this kind of offensive can mount a number of counterattacks. They can threaten to decertify, thus ending the relationship. They can also argue that the entry draft *cannot* be considered part of a collective bargaining agreement because it concerns future employees (i.e., college students). They can claim that the draft is not a mandatory part of collective bargaining but is incorporated into collective bargaining simply due to the weakness of the players' associations. In any case, they can argue that bona fide bargaining over the draft has never actually occurred (McCormick and McKinnon 1984, 400). Most important of all, they can seek to have the reserve clause declared illegal and therefore an inappropriate subject for collective bargaining. During the 1970s, Larry Fleisher, then general counsel to the NBAPA, doggedly fought the owners' argument that the draft and the reserve system were not monopolistic because they had been agreed upon in collective bargaining. Besides pointing out that he could not have bargained about "illegal subjects," he reminded the House Select Committee that the owners had always refused to discuss these issues in the past, claiming them as managerial prerogatives (U.S. Congress, House, Select Committee on Professional Sports 1976, 650). More important, he argued that collective bargaining in sports could never be "equal" until the reserve system had been eliminated.

The players' associations have not, then, chosen simply to shelter beneath the labor exemption (however much the state seems willing to grant them this protection), because the price they must pay—the legitimation of the reserve clause—is too high. Players' associations have treated the removal of the reserve system as a precondition for collective bargaining, not as something to be bargained about. Antitrust laws thus became a weapon in the conduct of collective bargaining. Owners, on the other hand, argue that without immunity from antitrust litigation, collective bargaining cannot function. For example, without the franchise stability that the reserve system provides, the owners cannot function jointly.

There is another reason why the players have been reluctant to stake all on a collective bargaining framework. The right to exercise individual bargaining power without restraint, claimed by such litigants as Flood, is explicitly denied to employees with a bargaining representative validly recognized under the National Labor Relations Act (NLRA). Also, under labor law, the reserve clause and common draft raise the issue not of group boycott but of the scope of the duty to bargain. The issue is no longer whether Congress should exempt professional sports from antitrust laws but whether unions should get special help from Congress in bargaining with their employers. The NLRA expressly forbids individual bargaining because it seeks to strengthen the hands of the union, making it more difficult for employers to divide and conquer and more difficult for the more selfish of the skilled employees to opt out of agreements. Because of the disadvantage to the more talented workers, unions realize they have to keep salary differences to a minimum. This does not foreclose all possibility of leaving certain issues to be resolved by individual negotiation, but this possibility itself should be decided by collective bargaining. The combination of individual negotiations in the context of collectively bargaining "basic agreements" (envisioned in the original NLRA) is exactly what professional athletes have fought to achieve. A wholehearted embrace of the collective bargaining strategy under NLRB rules would upset this arrangement.

The owners believe that the players would like to have their cake and eat it, too. They complain that unions cannot both litigate on antitrust issues and collectively bargain about those same issues. If collective bargaining covers, for example, the reserve clause, then the NLRA cannot permit players at the same time to accuse owners of collusion under the antitrust laws. Owners must surely "collude" in order to bargain jointly. For example, had Curt Flood won his case, the courts would have been in the position of permitting an individual player to sue his employer merely because that employer had been part of a joint negotiation with the players' association. By the time the players' associations had secured recognition, the owners were already using this argument to counter congressional efforts to remove their immunity from antitrust litigation. The owners found many congressmen to agree that the antitrust laws were intended to prohibit collusion in the *product* market, not the labor market, unless, of course, the unions *conspired with management* to affect product markets. This position had a credible pedigree in antitrust policy. The "proper" reason for invoking the antitrust laws when it came to deliberating economic policy and considering the rightness of economic arrangements was that these arrangements threatened the "general public interest," that interest being defined principally in terms of consumption. What was the impact on the fans? That economic arrangements might have detrimental effects on the producers in an industry was not thought to be of relevant concern to antitrust law.

Both sides thus sought to duck in and out of the respective shelters provided by the competing labor relations and antitrust statutes. Victories won in courts would be matched by defeats lost in collective bargaining. Demands rejected at the bargaining table could be won back in the courts. Thus, *Mackey* v. *National Football League* (1976) seemed to open the door to free agency had the players continued to pressure the owners in the courts. But the football union, instead, threw its strength into collective bargaining. A new collective bargaining agreement was signed in 1977. Owners agreed to recognize the union as "an agency shop where you have to pay dues even if you don't join" (Harris 1986, 257). The owners also agreed to pay $13.65 million in damages as a result of the Mackey case to be distributed (based on seniority) among 3,200 active and former players. In return for this settlement, the players agreed to tolerate the Rozelle Rule, thus completely abandoning the free agency it seemed to have won in court. The union traded away the rirights won in the courtroom for a return to collective bargaining. The ccompenstation penalties exacted on teams that traded players remained severe, even after a 1982 agreement had liberalized free agency somewhat.

Bringing the State In

As labor–management relations in professional sports have evolved more formally, the state has become much more involved. The private laws of sport have become increasingly subject to public regulation, because a framework of collective bargaining has been erected, chiefly as a result of pressure from players' associations. Other changes (of the kind described in chapter 4) making it much more obvious that sport franchises were business ventures and that sport markets were national in scope made it easier for players to invoke state powers to protect their interests against the superordinate power of the owners, chiefly by invoking laws designed to protect workers' right to organize enacted during the New Deal.

At first, federal officials were extremely reluctant to think of professional athletes as equivalent to factory workers. When in 1946 the American Baseball Guild filed charges of unfair labor practices with the NLRB in connection with a threatened strike by the Pittsburgh Pirates, the board refused to hold hearings on the grounds that baseball was not interstate commerce. The board refused to order an election to determine representation, for the same reason (Hoffman 1969, 244). The board used the same argument to rejected a 1959 petition from the Teamsters Union calling for an election covering the grounds crew and maintenance employees at the Pittsburgh Pirates' field. During the 1950s, it also declined jurisdiction over horse racing, on the grounds that the sport is regulated by individual states (notwithstanding the interstate movement of employees in the industry).

By the 1960s, the climate of opinion had begun to change. Support for the union movement among the players was growing, despite harassment from owners.[3] The NLRB was prodded into action in 1968 by a California Supreme Court ruling in a case involving picketing action against the Oakland Athletics for hiring nonunion musicians. The Court granted the NLRB jurisdiction over this dispute despite the fact that a baseball franchise was involved. A further sign of change was the board's assertion of jurisdiction over efforts to organize employees in the Nevada gambling industry, citing the prevalence of interstate gambling. The court added that the "entertainment industry" was becoming increasingly national, rather than local, in character (Hoffman 1969). In 1969, in a ruling concerning baseball umpires, the NLRB finally reversed its 1946 refusal to become involved in baseball labor issues. This landmark NLRB case concerned efforts by American League umpires to form a union. The board asserted jurisdiction over this dispute, on four grounds: (1) that the method of arbitration (using the commissioner) neither was neutral nor had been mutually agreed to; (2) that baseball was just like any other industry and was not specifically exempted by congressional action from the NLRA; (3) that baseball was clearly interstate commerce; and (4) that umpires are not "supervisors," as the owners had maintained (U.S. Congress, House, Select Commmittee on Professional Sports 1977, 460). One dissenting board member did come to the defense of baseball, pointing out that when the NLRA was passed in 1935, baseball had been granted a "unique and favored status" and that therefore Congress could not have had any intention of including the labor relations of professional baseball within the reach of the board's jurisdiction.

The players' associations sought to capitalize on the shift in position on the part of the NLRB during the 1960s, for which they were in part responsible. In 1971, the NFLPA filed charges that the owners had unlawfully refused to sign a collective bargaining agreement made between them. The NLRB backed the players in this instance; but the parties negotiated a new contract, and the charges were withdrawn. In that same year, the NFLPA filed charges that the owners had illegally refused to bargain over synthetic turf and over fines imposed on players found guilty of fighting. The NLRB backed the players on the turf issue in a 1972 decision. It initially backed the owners on the fines issue until a court appeal by the players forced it to reverse its position.

One of the union's most conspicuous victories occured in 1976, when administrative law judge Charles Schneider declared that the NFL Management Council had engaged in unfair labor practices against the NFLPA in 1974. The case arose out of the inability of parties to reach agreement on a new contract to replace the one in effect between 1971 and 1974. The players went on strike in July 1974, ending their walkout in August 1974. The union charged that during the strike players' representatives had been traded or waived because of their work for the union, owners had demanded the return of their signing bonuses, clubs had spied on union meetings, nonplaying union organizers had been denied access to training camps, fines had been threatened against players who did not report, and data necessary for bargaining (e.g., average wages, injury rates) had been withheld. Schneider found that three NFL teams had indeed engaged in unfair labor practices and demanded "they cease and desist therefrom" (U. S. Congress, House, Select Committee on Professional Sports 1977, 517). In 1991, a National Labor Relations Board judge ruled that the owners discriminated against players who supported the 1987 strike by making the players, for no valid reason, wait one game (worked by "replacement players") before returning to work, and stipulating that the owners owed an average of thirteen thousand dollars to the eleven hundred present and former NFL players affected.

These NLRB actions explain union officials' enthusiasm for administrative law as a solution to the labor–management conflict in professional sports. Executive Director Ed Garvey was of the opinion that in football, at least,

> recourse to the NLRB has been invaluable to the players' association. First, certification forced the owners to recognize the NFLPA for collective bargaining purposes; we were the first organization of professional athletes to seek certification; secondly, the filing of an unfair labor practice charge was the primary factor in forcing owners to sign the collective bargaining agreement. (U. S. Congress, House, Committee on Education and Labor 1972, 15).

On the other hand, the players remain skeptical about the practical benefits of throwing themselves entirely on the protection of the NLRB.

The chief problem is the delay in the determination of cases. Charges of unfair labor practices can take as long as three or four years to reach settlement. In an industry where playing careers average 4.5 years, this is a major disincentive to filing grievances. In the 1976 settlement, for example, discharged football players won the right to reinstatement two years after having been dismissed, by which time several of them had retired. Players are painfully aware that the machinery of government is unlikely to work expeditiously enough for them to benefit from union-won protection.

Conclusion

What accounts for the growth of union power in sport during the 1960s and 1970s? This was, after all, an anomalous trend: between 1945 and 1980, the proportion of unionized workers in the nonagricultural labor force steadily declined, from 35.5 percent to 24.7 percent (Cornfield 1986, 1113). One explanation must lie in events outside the sport industry entirely. The 1960s saw a series of legislative, executive, and administrative initiatives aimed at improving civil rights in the workplace. These included Title VII of the 1964 Civil Rights Act, providing remedy for discrimination in private sector organizations and various executive orders banning discrimination in public employment. Together, these civil rights mandates recognised new membership-based rights to fair treatment, thus producing a basis for criticism of organizational governance by employees and the general public. They opened private organizations to an unprecedented level of public scrutiny. In a "more rights-conscious environment for organizations," the treatment of professional athletes as "serfs" by management assumed greater significance (Edelman 1990, 1408). The new regulations did not speak directly to unionism; but they did provide legitimacy to organizations principally concerned with protecting individual liberties in the workplace, and it was not difficult to present the athlete's job as being close to servitude. The unions targeted oppression, rather than exploitation, and lack of freedom, rather than poverty, and thus grew quickly in the new legal environment.

Players' associations formed by professional athletes resemble quite closely white-collar professional associations (e.g., teachers' associations) and even more closely professional societies formed by actors, musicians, journalists, screenwriters, and the like. The individualization of services makes it impossible to limit recruiting in any serious way, while the high rewards offered to the most successful attract a horde of marginal competitors. In each case, the latter tendency has led to attempts to establish a minimum wage in order to prevent marginal competitors from disorganizing the occupation. This resemblance to professional associations helps explain the relative success of players' associations at a time when union membership in general was declining. Their success might also be due to the fact that they have largely avoided the stigma of traditional unions. The American public sees large units (both capital and labor) more negatively than smaller ones. Americans' mistrust of unions is attributable to their size; they tend to look more favorably upon individual unionized workers and smaller unions.

The timing of the union surge in sport also has something to do with the business cycle, for it is known that unionism increases during upturns in the economy, because then workers can better afford to pay dues and employers are least likely to retaliate. The late 1960s and the 1970s were boom years for sport owners. However, the source of this money is more important than its amount. Much of it came from television. With its new television contracts, the sport business was restructured, becoming, in many respects, vertically integrated with—or at least tied to—the mass media in more essential ways. Games were integrated into program schedules; leagues were tied to networks and cable companies. The owners had inadvertently increased the "positional power" of professional athletes by increasing their ability to disrupt industries downstream in the production process (Perrone 1984). The tie to television also indirectly increased the capital investment of the owners, for it brought into play the much more capital-intensive mass communications industry: the greater management's investment in capital, the more anxious it is to ensure that capital is continuously used, and the greater the threat imposed by work stoppages.

Ironically, the very failure of the state to resolve the anomalous position of the sport leagues vis-à-vis the antitrust laws enabled players' associations to use those laws as a weapon. Indeed, the unions could be said to owe their very existence to the government's failure to act. Policy outcomes do not always hinge on what the government does; they as often depend on what a government refrains from doing. Unlike most Western European countries, "the adversarial employment relationship in the United States relies almost exclusively on the right to unionize to balance authority between management and labor" (Cornfield 1986, 1112). Professional athletes struggled for many years to harness the powers of the state to shape the employment relationship by passing laws or winning legal suits brought against the reserve system or under contract law. They found the state very reluctant to interfere in this private sphere. Not until the 1970s did the courts seriously consider the proposition that restrictions on player mobility were subject to federal antitrust laws (Berry and Wong 1986, ix). Up to that time, what went on between player and manager was their own business, subject to the legal protections of a law of contracts

that assumed that either party could terminate the relationship if
dissatisfied.

To obtain improvements in working conditions, players were obliged to adopt the strategy of collective bargaining. The state could thus be said to have structured this strategy of reform. The role of the state in the emergence of sports unionism does not stop there, however; for the players did not rely on collective bargaining alone but coupled it with a continuing attack on the owners for violation of antitrust laws. Eventually, the labor exemption would foreclose this strategy; but by that time, the unions had become a significant presence and had made major gains. The importance of each of these prongs was demonstrated by the voluntary decertification of the NFLPA after the 1987 strike, so that the players could sue the owners without being forestalled by the labor exemption charge. The players were thus expressing their belief that reliance on collective bargaining alone would not achieve their free agency objectives.

Over the years, practically all portions of the employment relationship in professional team sports have been collectivized with the help of the courts and the NLRB. In return, the state has imposed a range of obligations on the unions representing players, for example, the fair representation of all workers in a bargaining unit. At the same time, the owners have been obliged to collectivize, too, in the form of some kind of management council or player relations committee. A different kind of "joint employment" has thus emerged. The union movement, with the help of the NLRB, has recreated solidarity among the owners but on terms different from those found before unionization.

Unions may represent attempts to offset, as far as possible, either the imbalance in market power in the bargaining procedure between worker and employer or the subordinate control position of the worker in relation to the performance of his task in the division of labor. The latter is a more obviously and directly political struggle, in that it attempts to gain a measure of control over the government of industry. American trade unions have overwhelmingly adopted the more economistic strategy, seeking to improve the market capacity of their members by limiting the supply of labor, quite unconnected to the broader political objectives of socialism and cooperativism.

The development of players' associations could have been more politically charged had they adopted a more assertive role, but this was never likely. American workers tend to think of their unions in instrumental terms as opposed to thinking of them as agents of social change. They value them for improvements in wages and benefits. Their unions are expected to enter politics, if at all, only to promote collective bargaining. Not only have players' associations avoided this kind of role, they have not even sought a voice in strategic decision making over investments in their industry, "plant" location, and the like. Only when these issues threaten to solidify the power of the owners (e.g., if the state grants to the owners the right to control franchise movements) do union leaders become involved.

The players' associations have thus encapsulated economic conflict and separated it from the larger political issues of who controls sports. This is true even though the professional athlete closely resembles the craftworker when it comes to the relations of production, for he necessarily retains a considerable amount of work knowledge that management cannot completely rationalize and thus alienate. The economic conflict is chiefly over who should get the biggest slice of the income pie; as long as the pie is growing in size, the conflict can be largely avoided by wage concessions owners can provide to workers in return for productivity agreements and no-strike clauses. This makes the players' association as interested as the owners in maintaining a high level of production and in the general prosperity of the industry. This sort of solution is not available in relation to control, since what one party gains the other must lose.

6

PRIVATE
GOVERNMENTS

This chapter examines how the government of sport organizations has been affected by the state. Most people are of the opinion that what they do in their leisure time is their own affair. This zeal for privacy extends to the kinds of clubs and associations they form to organize their leisure pursuits. How these clubs are run—their governance—is not a proper matter for public scrutiny. Those who disagree with the way a club is run can always leave and join another. But the matter is not quite so simple, as I shall show. Clubs and associations can become so powerful that they begin to threaten individual freedoms granted people in society at large. Even aside from threats to constitutional rights, the loss of a job or the opportunity to continue one's education "may be more hurtful than a term in jail" (Selznick 1969, 38); and serious public policy issues are raised if these deprivations are made arbitrarily and with no recourse to a third party. The question is then raised as to what right such an organization has to restrict these freedoms under the cloak of privacy. Conversely, a club or association might grant more freedom (license) to its members than would be permitted publicly (e.g., to use physical force), on the grounds that "it is part of the game." These are not only intrinsically political issues (having to do with the distribution of power between individuals and organizations) but also involve the state to the extent that groups or individuals seek its help to extend, or restrict, liberties in the name of sports. In short, the state shapes economic and social behavior not only by allocating the flow and direction of important resources but also by "its capacity to ratify or undermine new governance regimes" (Campbell and Lindberg 1990, 640).

WHY PRIVATE GOVERNMENTS FORM

Government is an agreed-upon means of making rules and settling disputes over those rules. Adjudication in modern democracies is typically an activity of public authorities, their sanctions imposed by the compulsory powers of the state. In practice, however, there is an immense amount of adjudication in the private sector, in tribunals embedded in various institutions. Parallel to public government is, therefore, private government. Private government is a principle of organization within human associations, in which powers similar to those of the state are assumed (including the right to command labor and property) but contending groups are recognized and constitutionally provided for and grievance procedures and due process rules are instituted:

> The concept of private government contains three ideas. The first of these asserts that private groups are "governmental" insofar as they act for, or fulfill the responsibilities of, the official or public government. The second holds that autonomous groups in modern society often have very considerable social effects; therefore they should assume corresponding "public" responsibilities. Finally, it may be argued that some private groups exercise distinctively governmental functions, on their own account and apart from any connection with public government, and therefore should be subject to the rules of just governance. (Selznick 1969, 260)

Private government is a matter of degree; it varies according to the complexity and formality of rules about rule making. More government means more rules about more rulings. In other words, private government has two dimensions: *rules about rules* and the scope of the rules. An example of *rules about rules* is a system of arbitration about employment contract disputes, which is more government than a set of rules specifying what employment contracts should be, which in turn is more government than autonomous or "spot" contracting. Another example of rules about rules is an organization with a deliberative council, which is more government than an organization governed simply by a steering committee but less government than an organization in which members are represented by parties in the council. An example of the *scope of the rule* is that the more constituent members sacrifice autonomy, the more private government an organization has. By this criterion, an organization has more private government if it requires constituent units not to compete with each other in certain respects, if it forbids its members from joining another organization, or if its scope is extensive. This last is well illustrated in the case of the power of high school athletic associations over their student members. Thus, in *Wellsand v. Valparaiso Community Schools* (1971), the court upheld the right of the state high school athletic association to declare ineligible a high school athlete because he was married, on the grounds that if married students were in the locker room, the discussion would inevitably center around their sexual experiences and that this would encourage sexual experimentation and teenage marriages. The high school athletic association thus assumed responsibility not only for the student's athletic welfare but also for his sexual maturation.

Why should one association have more private government than another? Private government varies by the degree to which the relations within the association are governed by market principles. The more the principle of the market governs the association's activities, the less private government there will be. Selznick explains the incidence of private government in human associations by reference to their position on a continuum running from contract to kinship (1969, 270). Neither purely contractual nor purely kinship based associations require private government: the first is too fleeting and limited, making governance structures too costly and inefficient; the second stresses personal ties and satisfactions, which make the impersonality and universality of governance structures inappropriate. If contract becomes status (if, e.g., a customer becomes a "regular customer" or if a fellow worker becomes a fellow trade unionist), "participation thickens" and the concept of membership is appropriate. This carries with it the right to some kind of tenure and also a certain kind of authority and a concomitant system of objective rules. Thus, in a private association, "a member is said to be bound to the discliplinary rules of his association because he has consented to them, as evidenced by the fact that he accepted membership in the group" (Weistart and Lowell 1979, 263). Conversely, private government weakens as status is replaced by contract—as relations between members cease to be based on their common status and are based on voluntary, contractual agreements. The evolution of private government and its subsequent strengthening or weakening thus has to do with the group's own problem-solving strategies, which, in turn, are explained by the basis of the relationship between constituent members.

Private and Public Governmen

It is not enough to explain private government solely in terms of the kind of relationship members have to each other. Private government implies its opposite, public government. Private government is chosen as an organizational principle by human associations whenever public government is unsuitable or illegitimate: "If it appears alarming that certain functions of private economic organizations have become very much like those of public agencies it must also be realized that such functioning is in many instances the alternative to an increased exercise of 'governmental' authority" (Wirtz 1952, 471).

Private government is thus not only an alternative to no government at all; it is also an alternative to public government. Many of the associations that people form are private in the sense that they are thought to be based on free contract and choice. A private association—a particular club, church, or business organization—is the kind that if you become dissatisfied with it you can go elsewhere; and "this threat of exit or competition supplies all the regulation needed" (Macaulay 1986, 486). Private government is distinguished from public government in that the goals of public governments are unrestricted and withdrawal by constituent members is not possible. Following from the constitutional guarantee of freedom to associate and common law precedent that membership in private associations is a privilege bestowed, rather than a right to be protected, the courts have been reluctant to become involved in the affairs of private associations and will intervene only when there is a violation of the association's rules, where other illegality exists, or when an action is taken by the association in bad faith.

Private government is considered legitimated if the alternative, public government, is undesirable. It would thus seem safe to predict that private government will arise as a principle of ordering social relationships whenever those relationships are considered beyond public scrutiny. Unfortunately, the situation is not quite so simple, because the line between public and private is not clear and agreed upon. What is private and what is public is a political matter. For example, the practice of law is "private" and regulated by a private body (the American Bar Association), because that is the way lawyers like it. Because it is private, constitutional guarantees do not always apply: a debarred lawyer, although prevented from practicing his livelihood, is not considered to have been constitutionally injured (deprived of life, liberty, or happiness), because membership of the bar is not a right but a privilege. In short, one dimension of private government is its usurpation of public powers (e.g., to confiscate property); and an organization's ability to exercise this control depends on how convincingly it can claim to be private, which depends on its political power.

Macaulay suggests that the state will leave a private association alone when (1) members have easy exit and available options, (2) insider knowledge would be necessary to settle a dispute, (3) members are strongly committed to the goals of the organization and would resent state control as the greater of two evils, and (4) the state subscribes to a public policy position of freedom and autonomy in that sphere (e.g., the arts) (1986, 446–454). Conversely, the state would be more likely to involve itself when the association controls the extent to which important services are available to the public.

Professional and amateur sports would clearly fit Macaulay's description of activities that a liberal-democratic state would leave alone: they do not present an "urgent case for judicial intervention" (Weistart and Lowell 1979, 262). Sports satisfy the first condition in that relations in professional sports are contractual, with the implied right of all parties involved not to agree to contracts they regard as injurious, and amateur sports include an explicit "exit" option available to all concerned. Sports satisfy the second condition in that their satisfactory performance requires a degree of "impacted" knowledge that no third party could be said to possess; disputes can only be resolved by the parties closest to the case. Amateur sports quite clearly meet the third condition in that they signal a commitment to goals of autonomy, self-expression, and intrinsic gratification that would be perverted by too close and formal supervision from remote administrative agencies. Sports satisfy the fourth condition in that sport is consigned to the private sphere in American political culture, along with religion, domestic life, and artistic expression, and sport resources (playing fields, stadia, equipment, coaching skills) are not regarded as important public goods in the same category as housing, health care, or roads and bridges.

For all of these reasons, it makes sense to anticipate relatively little state intervention in the governance of sports associations of any kind. Indeed, they have been customarily given considerable autonomy: "Non-compulsive, non-proprietary ventures have never commanded a high degree of judicial or political concern" (Weistart 1984, 168). State and federal courts have traditionally refused to rule on the fairness of the Amateur Athletic Union rules or the consequences of their enforcement, because of the AAU's status as a private voluntary association (Shuck 1979, 57). However, it is the purpose of this chapter to show that the private governance of sport associations has frequently been a subject of political controversy. The reason is that it is by no means clear that sport associations should be left to govern themselves, because it is by no means clear that they meet the criteria outlined by Macaulay.

The first problem has to do with the assumption that sport associations rest on voluntary commitments—either of a formal, contractual kind (as in professional sports) or of the more diffuse, informal kind (as in most amateur sports clubs). If professional sport leagues were simply part of the entertainment business and if nonprofessional sport organizations were democratically run and "exit" really were an option to "voice," then no state intervention would be called for. But sport leagues and athletic associations are not merely in the entertainment business, and they do not necessarily afford their members easy exit.

The status basis of sport relationships is easily demonstrated. Professional sport leagues can suspend players who gamble on the outcome of games. They have this right because players who gamble cast doubt on their willingness to play their best in every game, and therefore on their willingness to live up to the terms of their employment contract; they cast doubt on the authenticity of results, impugn the reputation of the product, and thus threaten attendance and revenues; they cast a stigma over the league as a whole, threaten the "integrity" of the game, and degrade its status; and they fail to live up to their responsibilities as public figures and models of behavior to younger people. Owners who suspend gambling players are doing more than disciplining workers; they are performing a public service.

It is equally easy to support the argument that sport associations are not as voluntary—nor exit as much of an option—as is often supposed. While it is true that the state is unlikely to concern itself with how an association is run "if affected parties are allowed to participate fully in the affairs of the regulating entity" (Weistart 1984, 169), it is not a settled matter at all that these conditions prevail in sport organizations, many of which exercise monopoly powers over the right to participate in a given sport. I shall show that athletes have little "voice" in the running of sport organizations and that "exit" is not a viable option. The realities of the exit option in sports is important; for the state *will* concern itself with how democratically an association is run and how respectful of individual rights an association is, *if membership is something less than voluntary.* Where members have little actual say in the running of the association and little choice but to belong, because of the penalties of exclusion, then the association has assumed the responsibility of operating in as "constitutional" a manner as does the state.[1]

A second criterion for lack of state intervention in private governance is that the sport association does not control important public services. The problem here is with deciding what is an important public service. Most would agree that public utilities fall into the category of providing such a service, but what about taxi cab companies? Like a utility, a sport association can find itself saddled with responsibilities once it begins to assume the role of government service.[2]

Sports are, to some extent, a law unto themselves. Mark McCormack, president of the sports management firm IMG, has said:

> The place where Arnold Palmer makes his living, the professional golf tour, is in many ways like a small nation that moves its capital from one town to another. . . . The tour has its own citizens, merchants, politicians, law enforcers and visitors, just like a country or private community. . . . the politicians are the tournament committeemen, the law enforcers are the PGA officials. (Aris 1990, 14).

Sports have their own "private law" to which all who participate in them are subject as long as they choose to participate. In this, sports are like other institutions in the private sphere. For example, religions practice private law (e.g., dietary regulations, tithing, child-rearing practices) with which the state ostensibly has nothing to do. Similarly, private corporations often have their own private law (e.g., dress codes, drug regulations). These private laws occasionally impinge upon people and oblige them to break public laws, or else they violate the individual's rights under public law. Either reactively or proactively, the state might be forced to intervene.

Such intervention is more likely today than it was in the past. Throughout most of the nineteenth century, it was taken pretty much for granted that private activity (sport would have been unquestioningly so regarded) should be free of government restraint, subject only to the boundaries set by the law of property, contract, tort, crimes, and similar legal categories. Private associations of all kinds were touted as a valuable counterbalance to government and to each other. Nor was there much fear that they would be undemocratic. Being essentially voluntary associations, the threat of exit would be enough to constrain leaders to temper authoritarianism. The government thus adopted a hands-off posture, on the understanding that private institutions were basically good for society and should be left to run themselves except under the most dire circumstances.

By the end of the century, however, the relation between public and private had begun to change. A great number of professional associations were forming; and there was a rush to pass occupational licensing laws for plumbers, barbers, lawyers, pharmacists, midwives, nurses, and the like. Competition for "turf" placed a premium on getting the state to "franchise" control over some of that turf, so that others could not occupy it. Thus arose the idea of "nonpublic administrative action undertaken by private voluntary associations, wielding considerable power in the name of public policy" (Friedman 1985, 441). The way was clear for a sport league to operate in much the same way as the American Bar Association or the Chicago Board of Trade, as long as it could make a credible claim to serve the public trust.

The rise of the welfare state during the Great Depression also made scrutiny of private government more likely. Although private enterprise was still sacrosanct, public regulation was to be used as an adjunct to help it reach its goals. At the same time, private associations, most notably business corporations, began to grow in size and economic strength, assuming what, to many people, seemed to be public functions, thus further blurring the line between the private and the public.[3]

Sport associations found that they could profit from this shift in the boundary between public and private, setting up their own internal governance structures, protecting the interests of their members by serving a public purpose. Sport associations came to resemble a "franchise" granted by the state. An essentially public power was granted to an essentially private agency. At first, this assumption of public powers was tacit and frequently challenged. Neither in professional nor in amateur sports did any association have the monopoly power necessary to claim franchise status. But the pre-World War I period saw the establishment of the National Commission in baseball (1903) and the NCAA in college sports (1906), both of which would eventually form the foundation for private governments. The idea of the franchise was even more explicitly contained in the formation, during this period, of state athletic commissions, essentially private bodies given public powers. Thus, as early as 1913, the state court of New York was approving the state athletic commission's power to ban a boxer, Robert Fitzsimmons in "the best interests of the game." Fitzsimmons, in the opinion of the commission, had become too old to fight and had to be protected from himself. The courts thus set a precedent for "state action" in the case of sports (Sammons 1988, 66).

The idea that private organizations could function as franchises of the state found its most far-reaching expression in the National Industrial Recovery Act (1933), which, while eventually declared unconstitutional by the Supreme Court, survived as the principle of delegated power. This principle was gradually extended: "movies were rated, food evaluated, commercials tested, young Christian and Jewish men exercised, amateur athletics 'protected', morals and decency scrutinized, parades organized, libraries kept up, professional standards maintained, and historical landmarks preserved—all by private agencies wielding public powers" (Wolfe 1977, 144). Franchises were granted in areas that, although in reality heavily politicized, were popularly considered nonpolitical. They became the watchdogs of the national conscience in their respective areas. In return for acting in a "mature" and "responsible" manner and on condition that they conduct their internal affairs with circumspection and some consideration for constitutional rights, they were granted a mandate to provide services on a monopolistic basis—collective goods for the purposes of private profit.

This brief history of the relation between the public and the private shows that the relationship is highly unstable, the social membrane separating them by no means impermeable. Public norms may be applied in private tribunals and enforced by private sanction; conversely, public tribunals, officials, and sanctions may be used to enforce private norms. The actions of private governments thus take place against a backdrop of public government. For example, players and owners in professional team sports "bargain in the shadow of the law"; the courts confer on the parties a "bargaining endowment," a set of "counters" to be used in bargaining (Galanter 1986, 213). These can be "cashed in" whenever one of the parties feels threatened with severe loss or extinction. Thus, players can hold the sword of antitrust suits dangling over the owners, while owners can always threaten to invoke contract law to keep "free agents" in line.[4]

The relationship between private and public government is by no means as formal and insistent as that between a corporation and its franchises; and in this sense, the franchise metaphor is misleading. Sport enterprises remain very much private. The metaphor simply suggests that sport administration be treated as a delegated public function. The concept of "private government" assumes that sports are essentially private but acknowledges that they enforce governmentlike powers, which are effective only in so far as they have the tacit backing of the state.

COLLEGE SPORTS: STUDENTS LOSE CONTROL

The principle of private government evolved fairly quickly in college sports, as student-athletes were forced to relinquish control, first to the faculty, and then to full-time professional administrators and coaches. The erection of an elaborate government apparatus (rule committees, athletic conferences) provoked some resistance, as students began to complain that they were being denied constitutional rights. At first, these cries went unheeded, because athletic conferences were able to justify their government powers on the basis of their protection of the student–athlete's status. Eventually, however, as the barrier of privacy surrounding educational institutions was lowered and the student–athlete's status began to fall into disrepute, the private government powers of bodies like the NCAA were more seriously challenged.

It is not widely known that control over college sports in the United States was originally vested in the students themselves. Athletics belonged to "the college." That part of university life centered around residential halls, where students tried to "protect themselves from the harsh and seemingly arbitrary authority of their faculty" (H. Horowitz 1987, 111). Athletics were an important source of social integration in the years before students were co-opted by "student government" and before the advent of coeducational campuses, when dating became a more important source of prestige than athletic prowess.

Since there was no financial support forthcoming from college funds for sports, "students soon learned that under certain conditions funds could be secured from gate receipts and from enthusiastic alumni" to pay expenses (Staples 1943, 16). Beginning in 1874 at Harvard (Princeton, Rutgers, and Michigan followed in 1876), student athletic associations were formed "to provide financial assistance to relieve athletes of the entire expense of their support and to give moral support for college athletics" (R. Smith 1988, 119). These associations, in bringing together interested students, faculty, and alumni and in exerting considerable pressure on the student body to "get behind" the school's teams, laid the groundwork for the autonomous athletic committees that were to follow.

The first organization to attempt to coordinate college sports, the Intercollegiate Association of Amateur Athletes of America (IAAAA), had been formed by students in 1876 and continued to be self-governing until its demise in 1929. While control remained in the hands of the students in associations such as these, the gap between college and other amateur sports was not very wide. Later conferences (such as the Big Ten and the Southern Intercollegiate Athletic Conference) effected the "transfer of athletic governance from students to alumni to college faculty and administrators" (Hardy and Berryman 1982, 17). The students running the IAAAA opposed these moves, because they regarded athletics as their own creation and their own responsibility to conduct as they saw fit (R. Smith 1983, 376). But they were powerless in the face of the growing popularity of football as a spectator sport.

Students themselves had to accept some of the blame for these trends. They quickly learned that support for their athletics was more generous for winning, than for losing, teams; and the next logical step of hiring "tramp" athletes and instituting rigorous training regimens run by full-time coaches, all to secure a winning season, was easily taken. The attitude of most faculty toward these activities appears to have been not opposition but toleration, with the result that alumni "achieved dominion by default" (Savage 1929, 24). The dean of college coaches, Walter Camp, "regarded with great satisfaction the growth of football not merely as a game, but as a spectacle . . . the bustle of the crowds, the cheering, the excitement of the spectators" (Ryan 1929, 72).

As late as 1900, there was still strong sentiment among faculty at elite colleges that students ought to manage their own sports (R. Smith 1988,

that date. Faculty had long sought to limit their growth, but the power to determine the structure of athletics passed not to them but to athletic committees over which faculty had very little control.[5] Most faculty were relieved to assign this extracurricular activity to a specialized committee. Alumni, on the other hand, were a growing influence over higher education and welcomed the opportunity to continue to guide university policy and practice: "alumni support of athletics, particularly financial, often meant alumni governance" (p. 132). Students lost all control over athletics, while that of the faculty was seriously eroded.

A very important stage in the emergence of private government in college sports was the evolution of the coach as a distinct occupation. The professionalization of coaching was a direct result of the freedom and competitiveness of the educational marketplace. Any individual, group or level of government could found a college; and any college that wanted to raise intercollegiate athletics to a level of excellence was free to do so with a commitment of time, effort, and financial backing. The emergence of the professional coach had a most damaging effect on the power of the students to regulate their own playing time and paved the way for total control over the student athlete by the college administration—where he lived, what he ate, how much he earned.[6]

Although coaches at this time were ostensibly educators, varsity athletic experience constituted the core of their professional identity. Nearly all high school and college coaches were ex–college athletes. The professional journals and associations that appeared in the 1920s focused their attention on varsity games. With their energies absorbed by interscholastic competition, rather than physical education, coaches found it expedient to justify their occupational roles in terms of their opportunities to develop character; but they developed managerial, rather than pedagogical, skills.[7]

The formation of the NCAA between 1906 and 1910 cemented in place an evolved structure of control over athletics, which, under the mandate of boards of trustees, sympathetic or indifferent faculty, cooperative physical educators, enthusiastic alumni, and professional coaches "eroded student freedom to control their own game" (R. Smith 1988, 211). The structure provided by the NCAA, ostensibly designed to preserve amateurism, merely increased the emphasis on intercollegiate rivalry and winning. Athletics became too precious to be left in the hands of students. This view became more popular as boards of trustees changed their composition to take on businessmen and financiers, who were more interested in budgets and the institutional images that would improve them than in learning and academics. The assimilation of athletics into the administrative echelon "left students with fewer rights, less freedom, and a lack of control over their own athletic lives" (ibid.).

Throughout the first half of the twentieth century, educators and reformers would make sporadic efforts to restore control, if not to the students, then at least to the faculty. For example, the famous 1929

Carnegie Report, in deliberating whether control of college sports should rest with students, alumni, faculty, administration, or trustees, recommended that it was time to return control to the students (Hanford 1974, 111). Subsequent reports and recommendations were not so sanguine about student control, perhaps because the financial stakes had become so high.

THE NATIONAL COLLEGIATE ATHLETIC ASSOCIATION AS GOVERNMENT

The NCAA has undergone a transition from a purely advisory voluntary association to a quasi firm with prohibitive regulatory powers. Founded in 1906, the NCAA began as a voluntary association designed to help protect college athletes from injury by clarifying the rules regarding rough play. It also took a stand against paying athletes to attend and play at colleges. By 1952, the NCAA had ceased to be an advisory voluntary association and become a regulatory body with enforcement powers.

The most rapid period of development of government in the NCAA was the decade following World War II. A rise in the number of football bowl games as cities competed for the revenues; increasing revenues from television networks; the development of air transportation, making possible national scheduling and recruiting; a desire to regain closer control over collegiate sports in order to prevent games being fixed; and the introduction of scholarships for athletes—all increased the temptation of individual athletes, coaches, and their institutions to violate the amateurism rule or opportunistically negotiate their own deals with those anxious to further commercialize college sports.

The result of these changes was that hierarchy replaced market as an ordering regime in the NCAA. A weak Constitutional Compliance Committee was replaced by a Committee on Infractions in 1951 that had much more police power than its predecessor. Indeed, complaints that the committee fused the roles of prosecutor and judge led to amendments in 1973, after which it functioned solely as a tribunal, and a separate staff handled investigations, with the NCAA Council acting as an appellate tribunal. Hierarchy is also evident in the fact that more restrictions were placed on scheduling (e.g., conferences, limits on number of games, postseason play) and recruiting. The NCAA refused to permit a free market for postseason play, sanctioning football bowl games or selecting those teams qualified to compete in the basketball tournament.

The development of private government in the NCAA would not have been so controversial had there been more agreement on the exact nature of the NCAA's role in intercollegiate athletics. What justified the expansion of government powers? While its original mission statement had included protection of the student–athlete's amateur status, many had come to believe that the true purpose of the NCAA was to regulate economic competition between colleges. From this perspective, the rules on recruiting and funding were necessary not to protect amateurism but to limit the amount of "free riding" in intercollegiate athletics. When it came to scheduling, it could be assumed that each college desired to win all its games and therefore would rationally schedule fixtures with much weaker teams. However, spectators required competitiveness. This collective good no individual college could rationally pursue: no athletic director would voluntarily schedule a stronger opponent (pay more for each victory) unless he was sure that all other teams would do the same. As far as recruiting was concerned, the more precise the rules governing recruiting without any real means of enforcing them, the stronger the incentive to "ride free." It was in the interest of each individual college not to invest heavily in enforcing NCAA recruiting rules on its coaches, once they were in place, because it could not be sure others were doing likewise. The restrictions on recruiting and funding, in the context of an expanding live and television audience for college sports, took on the appearance of the kind of structure a business conglomerate might erect. Charges that the NCAA engaged in monopolistic behavior were heard more frequently after 1950. In this climate, it became more acceptable to question the rules by which the NCAA governed itself.

For most of this century, college sports, although frequently scandal-ridden, were considered off-limits to public law. The courts usually refrained from intervening in disputes between the NCAA and its member institutions or individual athletes, on the grounds that the association was private in nature and the dispute "internal." They were more inclined to liken the NCAA to a medical or fraternal association (Shropshire 1988, 18), that is, an organization with some admittedly economic or commercial aspects but in which the protection of status (amateurism) and performance of a public trust (education) were still paramount responsibilities, for whose execution a measure of private government was warranted. For example, the courts held that athletic departments have the right to terminate grants-in-aid made to athletes who chose, for academic reasons, to discontinue practice and play. The student is considered to have entered into a private contract, to "play for pay" (Stotlar 1985, 129). Eligibility determinations, for the most part, were deemed by the courts to be the prerogative of the enterprise in the regulation of its own affairs.

Only when the NCAA clearly assumed the role of public government did its governance become a matter of political debate. The Fourteenth

Amendment prohibits a state from depriving an individual of life, liberty, or property without due process of law. Due process would typically involve being given adequate notice of hearings, being judged impartially, and keeping and granting access to records. In the nineteenth century, such rights were shed at the gates of private institutions like the NCAA. During the course of the twentieth century, however, the due process concept had gradually stretched to cover much more territory than originally intended, spilling over from the courtroom into institutional and administrative behavior in general, including many private bodies.

Due process constitutional protections apply to private governments only where "state action" is involved. In *Arlosoroff* v. *National Collegiate Athletic Association* (1984), the Fourth U.S. District Court of Appeals presented two conditions, either of which had to be present for a private enterprise to be made accountable under the U.S. Constitution. The first was that the activity had to involve a traditional public function; the second was that the state, through its involvement with the enterprise, had to have caused or procured the action complained of. For example, it might be argued that if a sport organization used a stadium paid for by the taxpayer, then state action was implied in its conduct.

This question of whether or not an organization was public or private would prove to be very important in the dispute over the governmental powers of the NCAA. An aggrieved athlete would first have to prove that action by a sport association constituted state action before he could establish that an association's disciplinary measures deprive him of life or liberty without due process. If athletic associations are considered to be at least in part public, then they become subject to "open meeting" or "sunshine" laws, requiring that their records be open to public inspection. The NCAA has consistently maintained that it is not subject to these laws and that without some guarantee of privacy, its investigative powers would be impaired.

Over the course of its history, the NCAA has become increasingly vulnerable to the "state action" criterion. In 1948 the NCAA assumed regulatory powers for the first time. Its new "Principles for the Conduct of Intercollegiate Athletics" (colloquially called the Sanity Code) denied aid for athletic ability alone, limited the amounts that could be paid in need-based scholarships (no room-and-board expenses allowed), restricted the disbursement of support to the office of financial aid, and (most important of all) provided for the expulsion of violating schools on the basis of a two-thirds vote of the convention. Violators were to be answerable to a new Compliance Committee.

The chief advocates of these reforms were the smaller schools, anxious to control expenses by regulating competition for players. They also urged that the administrative staff of the NCAA be expanded and that a full-time director be appointed to ensure good government. The larger schools feared that the association would restrict their ability to generate revenues.[8] By the time the reforms were finally approved, in 1952, the NCAA had been granted the right to discipline member institutions for violations of rules, marking "the complete transformation of the NCAA from a loose confederation designed for mutual support and dissemination of rules into a powerful control agent capable of inflicting serious financial losses on member schools caught in violation of its rules" (Stern 1979, 247). Its powers in this regard were boosted with the advent of television, although heavy reliance on income from this source was to prove its Achilles heel.

The ultimate weapon in the hands of the NCAA was the suspension or even expulsion of a member institution. This weapon became even more powerful as television networks began to show more interest in broadcasting college sports. At first, television threatened to weaken the authority of the NCAA as individual colleges entered into contracts with networks and sponsors. Not only did this create inequalities of revenues, it also attracted people away from live attendance at other college games in the region. The NCAA became convinced that television would seriously diminish live attendance, that the colleges were, in a sense, giving their product away or selling it very cheaply. The fact that only a few of the major football powers were of interest to the television networks or corporate sponsors permitted the NCAA Convention to outvote them and impose a moratorium on live telecasting of college football in 1951: "Hindsight reveals that this resolution gave the NCAA more power to limit competition between the producers in the intercollegiate athletic industry than it had ever before enjoyed" (Lawrence 1987, 77).

As college sports became more commercialized and the strain of trying to reconcile the roles of student and athlete increased, so private government became more elaborate. The multiplying rules and regulations were always justified as serving the interests of the student, but many critics began to wonder whether the NCAA's mode of governance was really serving this purpose or restricting competition between member institutions. Was the NCAA pursuing private ventures under the cloak of defending the public interest in a well-rounded education? Were its private government powers being used to negate, rather than further, collective ideals? For example, in 1959, the NCAA Convention decided that in order to protect high school "prospects" from being pestered by college recruiters, each would be required to sign a "letter of intent" to attend his chosen school by a given date in the spring. The new regulation served another purpose, however, which was to make the recruiters' jobs easier by abbreviating the recruiting period and ultimately reducing competition between them for rookies. Lawrence reports that even while this new rule was being passed, "most of the representatives wondered why a superior high school athlete would want to commit himself when any school would enroll him at any time"(1987, 63). Critics would not have been so concerned had the

NCAA's deliberative body been more democratic, but the student–athlete has no voice in how the NCAA is run.[9]

Ironically, the case that focused public attention most sharply upon the private government powers of the NCAA involved not a player but a coach. In 1978, the House Oversight and Investigations Subcommittee held ten days of hearings following four months of investigation into the regulatory practices of the NCAA. Over seventy congressmen signed a letter requesting that the hearings be held. The NCAA's sanctions against the University of Denver and the University of Minnesota were a catalyst for these hearings, but their chief purpose was to discuss the case of Jerry Tarkanian. In 1977, after a four-year investigation, the NCAA had ordered the University of Nevada, Las Vegas, to suspend its basketball coach for two years for having committed thirty-eight rules violations. A severe punishment by NCAA standards, it was no doubt motivated by Tarkanian's association with earlier recruiting scandals at California State University at Long Beach. At the University of Nevada, Tarkanian was charged with offering financial incentives to recruits, providing current students with advance copies of examinations, and arranging to have a grade altered. Officials of the NCAA also accused Tarkanian of interfering with their investigation by discouraging his players from cooperating and encouraging them to lie. The University of Nevada complied with the NCAA directive, whereupon Tarkanian sued in a Nevada court, requesting an injunction to prevent the suspension. The court granted the injunction, and the university appealed the decision to the Nevada Supreme Court.

Responding to widespread public interest in the Tarkanian case, the Oversight and Investigations Subcommittee examined thousands of documents, interviewed hundreds of individuals and deliberated dozens of potential findings and recommendations. The first signature on the petition calling for an investigation of the NCAA was that of James Santini, representative from Nevada and well-known college sport enthusiast, who, it was no secret, had long harbored resentment over the NCAA's disciplinary action against the University of Nevada. The university's president, Donald Baepler, defended his basketball coach, expressing his skepticism about the NCAA charges. However, Baepler knew that if he did not agree to suspend his coach, the basketball program's probationary period would be extended or applied to all the college's sports. Nor could he ignore the fact that a special faculty senate committee had concluded that there was substance to the NCAA's charges. It found that some irregularities in recruiting, testing, and management of athletes did occur involving unprofessional and unethical conduct of coaches and boosters. It was especially critical of "an overexuberant Boosters' Club," the "win at any cost attitude of the two head coaches," and an uncooperative administration (U.S. Congress, House, Committee on Interstate and Foreign Commerce 1978a, 849).

The purpose of President Baepler's testimony was not so much to vindicate Tarkanian or the University of Nevada as to argue that the NCAA's procedures for dealing with possible infractions of its regulations routinely denied due process:

> At the hearings before the infractions committee, the university was surprised to note that the NCAA staff presented no empirical evidence whatsoever against the university. The NCAA staff presented no affidavits or depositions but, rather, in every instance, the staff relied upon hearsay to make its case. In every instance, the staff would present to the infractions committee their recollections of conversations held with various informants based on memoranda they had prepared at some point in time after conducting the interview. . . . No opportunity was presented for cross-examining or interviewing those sources who apparently gave conflicting information to the NCAA and to the university.

A subsequent unsuccessful appeal to the NCAA Council was, in President's Baepler's opinion, "a charade, since such limited time was allowed the university to present its case" (U.S. Congress, House, Committee on Interstate and Foreign Commerce 1978a, 810).

From the outset, Tarkanian had denied the charges against him and accused the NCAA of singling him out for punishment. In an unusual move, he went to court to secure an injunction against the execution of the NCAA suspension, which the court agreed to issue. The stage was thus set for the more overt politicization of the conflict. The most important issue before the House Subcommittee was the arrogation of power by a "private" organization like the NCAA, an issue broader than sport. The chairman, John Moss, confessed to being neither interested nor active in sports, but he nevertheless saw important public policy issues in the case:

> The question is whether or not there is in fact, by this private organization, and I want to emphasize that this is a private organization that has taken the power—we can say the membership is voluntary, but whoever is so naive as to believe that is indeed one of the most naive individuals I have seen. It is not voluntary. It is a fact of life, it is essential that you belong. It has the power to destroy careers of men who have sports as their sole occupation, and to totally frustrate the ambitions of younger men, and it can do it without the basic fabric of protection that we have been accustomed to regard as our right. (U.S. Congress, House, Committee on Interstate and Foreign Commerce 1978a, 870)

Referring to the requirement that the college and not the NCAA declare a student ineligible, Moss stated, "To me it is completely repugnant that you should have an organization that can order a finding against an individual and direct someone else to assume the responsibility for making the finding" (p. 1344). Chairman Moss's hostility toward the NCAA was not appeased by the attitude of Walter Byers, executive director of the NCAA, toward the investigation. Byers "refused to have the Committee dictate what a private voluntary association of education institutions must do" (Shuck 1979, 57). He initially refused to provide materials for the committee, on grounds that confidentiality would be violated. He urged member institutions not to cooperate and asked that they write their congressmen to protest the investigation; only a subpoena secured his compliance (U.S. Congress, House, Committee on Interstate and Foreign Commerce 1978a, 2).

Some congressmen defended the NCAA's government powers. One was Norman Lent, representative from New York. In a minority report, Lent and two other committee members pointed out that of the seventy-four member institutions subject to investigation since 1972, only nine had been heard from in the congressional hearings. They complained that inordinate attention had been paid to the Nevada case and sought to rebut the charge that the NCAA held a monopoly over college athletics by pointing to the 1976 partial breakaway of the College Football Association (U.S. Congress, House, Committee on Interstate and Foreign Commerce 1978a, 75). At follow-up hearings in 1979, Lent expressed his astonishment that the subcommittee had spent so long on this subject. Indeed, in 1978, it spent more time on college athletics than any other issue, including oversight of the federal regulatory agencies "and such vital questions as cancer-causing chemicals in foods and decontrol of crude oil in gasoline products" (U.S. Congress, House, Committee on Interstate and Foreign Commerce 1979b, 2).

At the conclusion of its first set of hearings, in March and April of 1978, the subcommittee sent to the president of the NCAA a list of fifty recommendations that had emerged at one time or another from the testimony given, asking that the NCAA Council consider them before the time of the second set of meetings scheduled for the fall of 1978. These recommendations covered investigative procedures, the hearing process, sanctions, appeals, and various miscellaneous areas (e.g., a statute-of-limitations proposal). At the second set of hearings, the president of the NCAA, J. Neils Thompson, defended his organization, pointing out that eleven of the suggestions were already implemented, six were under review, and twenty-three had in the past been deliberated by the NCAA convention and considered unworkable. There is no doubt, however, that the subcommittee's investigation prompted the NCAA to make some reforms in its governance procedures. For example, new provisions were made to allow student–athletes to have legal representation before the NCAA which their university would be permitted to pay for.

The NCAA refused to concede that its governance procedures needed radical reform. Ironically, the NCAA defended some of its questionable practices on the grounds that being only a voluntary association, it lacked the powers of government. It was precisely because it lacked governmentlike powers such as the ability to issue subpoenas that its investigative practices had the appearance of unconstitutionality.

The chairman of the NCAA Infractions Committee, University of Texas law professor Charles Wright, could see no violation of due process in the organization's proceedings and attributed much of the controversy to sour grapes:

> If I represented an institution or a coach facing charges before the NCAA, I would make many of the criticisms of the enforcement procedure that the Subcommittee has been hearing these many months. I would do so particularly if my client was guilty, and if I were trying to get it off nevertheless, rather than make a real effort, as so many institutions that have appeared before us have done, to find out what had been wrong with the athletic program and correct its mistakes. I would insist on the right to be present and to tape record all interviews by the NCAA staff, knowing that this would inhibit many young athletes and they would not tell of violations of which they had knowledge. . . . I would be insisting that witnesses be live and subject to cross-examination, knowing that if there were such a requirement, many witnesses would refuse to appear and meritorious charges would have to be dismissed. (U.S. Congress, House, Committee on Interstate and Foreign Commerce 1978a, 1297)

At the conclusion of its hearings, the House Subcommittee on Oversight and Investigations issued a report. Believing that federal intervention into intercollegiate athletics was not the best course of action, the report was intended to stimulate self-reform on the part of the NCAA. It contained eighteen specific proposals for change. At the January 1979 convention of the NCAA, six of the eighteen proposals were adopted, and two others were partially implemented.[10] The subcommittee held further hearings in 1979 to receive a report from the NCAA at which these reforms were outlined, to the apparent satisfaction of its members.

Tarkanian's case eventually reached the Nevada Supreme Court in June 1984, by which time the NCAA had been added as a defendant. The court ruled that the NCAA had indeed violated his constitutional right to due process under the law by ordering the University of Nevada to suspend him. The court argued that in punishing Tarkanian, the NCAA had acted in concert with the University of Nevada, which is a state entity. The court was highly critical of the NCAA's investigative procedures, for example, the reliance on unrecorded interviews and the recollections of interviewers. The NCAA appealed the decision; and in 1988, the U.S. Supreme Court agreed to hear the case.

The Court elected not to consider the question of whether Tarkanian had been granted due process. Instead, it agreed to focus on whether the NCAA acted as a governmental body when it regulated college sports. In short, the judges agreed to adjudicate the private government powers of the NCAA.

The U.S. Supreme Court, in December 1988, reversed the Nevada Supreme Court's decision by a five-to-four margin, ruling that the NCAA was not a state actor and therefore could not have violated the coach's constitutional rights. The court thus rejected Tarkanian's claim that the NCAA was merely an agent for the University of Nevada (a public institution). It also rejected the claim that the NCAA directly disciplined the coach. The action of suspension, the court ruled, was taken by the University of Nevada, which, if it did not like to take this action, had the option of withdrawing from the association. The court, therefore, also rejected Tarkanian's claim that the NCAA, in effectively monopolizing college athletic opportunities, left the university with no choice but to comply with its demands. In short, the court concluded that the university conducted its athletic program under the color of the policies adopted by the NCAA, rather than that those policies were developed and enforced under color of Nevada law. The court thus chose to see the NCAA and the University of Nevada as operating independently, while the minority opinion chose to see them as acting "jointly." The case was finally settled in February 1990, when Tarkanian consented to pay $21,000 in legal fees incurred by the NCAA and, more importantly, agreed that a Nevada court could lift its injunction preventing the NCAA from suspending him. The agreement technically allowed the NCAA to proceed with its action against the university for violations of NCAA rules for which Tarkanian had been held responsible. One month later, Tarkanian's team won the NCAA men's basketball championship.

The 1988 Supreme Court ruling was something of a surprise. While the NCAA had maintained all along that it was a private association entitled to set its own rules and enforce its own discipline, this position had become increasingly untenable. Beginning in the 1960s, educational establishments became much more liable to public regulation. Demographic changes expanded enrollments, increased strains on schools, and focused attention and money on younger people. Civil rights movements drew attention to denial of constitutional rights to students, workers, prisoners, hospital patients, and the like. There was more widespread acceptance of the theory of normative pluralism, according to which all affected interests in an organization could and should participate in the decision making of the administrative agency that regulates their lives. In 1969, the Supreme Court, in a landmark case, upheld high school students' right to wear black armbands in school on grounds of rights to free speech. In 1975, the Supreme Court overturned the suspension of a student because he had been denied

due process. Students' rights were dramatically enhanced in the 1970s,
and the schools and colleges were less convincing in their claim to be
private institutions not liable to constitutional sanctions.

Several lower court decisions in the 1970s seemed to signal that the
judiciary now considered the NCAA responsible for protecting constitutional rights (e.g., *Buckton v. NCAA* [1973], *Howard University* v. *NCAA*
[1975], *Parish* v. *NCAA* [1973], *Regents of University of Minnesota* v. *NCAA*
[1976], *Associated Students, Incorporated* v. *NCAA* [1974]). Many believed
that the case of *Parish* v. *NCAA* (1975), where the court ruled against the
NCAA on the grounds that it was a "state actor," would provide a precedent for *Tarkanian* v. *NCAA*. The *Parish* court declared that "in light of
the national . . . scope of collegiate athletics and the traditional government concern with education, . . . were NCAA to disappear tomorrow,
the government would soon step in to fill the void" (Kolback 1985, 221).
The court further argued that the NCAA and the state were so "entan-
gled" that their actions could not be distinguished. About 50 percent of
member institutions, it pointed out, were state-funded; and to this extent, the NCAA was subsidized by the state. The fact that many colleges
were funded by tax dollars and that all were engaged in providing education was usually sufficient for the courts to consider the activities of
colleges examples of state action: "In those cases that have challenged
NCAA action, the finding of state action has been consistenly upheld"
(Gaona 1981, 1086). The chief reason was that colleges had proven that
they had an indispensible interest in participating in intercollegiate athletics: "Once the university has a property interest in athletic revenue,
any proceeding depriving the university of those revenues must adhere to constitutional due process requirements" (p. 1095).

Others believed that *Arlosoroff* v. *NCAA* (1984) would set the precedent; for in this case, the courts had determined that the NCAA could
limit the eligibility of a player (in this case because he was too old) because the rule was a matter of private conduct, not state action. Public
subsidies were not sufficient to warrant a determination of state action
and the regulation of intercollegiate athletics was "not a function traditionally exclusively reserved for the state" (Kolback 1985, 222). The
Tarkanian courts had to decide, in effect, between the *Parish* decision
and the *Arlosoroff* decision. In the end, a shift in legal thinking favored
the *Arlosoroff* judgment. Beginning in the early 1980s, the Supreme
Court had begun to narrow its definition of state action and state actors.
The federal district courts had accordingly altered their perspective on
the NCAA. Virtually all federal court decisions between 1983 and 1988
had found that actions by the NCAA did not constitute state action (Lederman 1988, A32). The 1988 Tarkanian decision was consistent with
this trend.

The NCAA thus won ratification for its policies and disciplinary procedures and shored up its defenses against legal attacks based on the
U.S. Constitution. While suits based on antitrust laws, contract law, and

the law of private association would remain available as weapons in the fight over the private government powers of amateur sport organizations, these weapons were not powerful enough to satisfy the state assemblymen upset at the treatment "their" college had received. In 1991, Illinois became the fourth state to require due process in NCAA investigations, claiming that existing NCAA practices did not allow the accused to face their accusers or get copies of evidence against them.[11] In 1990 and again in 1991, bills were introduced into the House of Representatives that would require due process of the NCAA on the grounds that it was a state actor. The NCAA responded by setting up its own committee of inquiry. In 1992, this committee recommended new guidelines for conducting investigations. The committee's main recommendation was that an independent hearing officer should determine the facts of the case if the NCAA and accused could not agree on the violations and penalties. The committee also recommended that enforcement hearings be open to the public.

There can be little doubt that much of the concern over the private government powers of the NCAA in the 1978–90 period was politically motivated. Both in the 1970s and in the 1990s, the NCAA's harshest critics—those expressing the most alarm at the NCAA's private government—were politicians from states where leading institutions of higher education had suffered from the NCAA's use of its disciplinary powers. Local politics were being played out on the national stage. State assemblymen and U.S. congressmen leaped to the defense of their embattled institutions, whose athletic programs stood to lose millions of dollars by virtue of the actions of the NCAA. The state bills and congressional hearings did not represent any major rethinking of the principles and practices of private governments. It is noteworthy that these same congressmen showed little concern over the use of private government powers when it had little impact on their alma mater's ability to compete for revenues. For example, while the NCAA was heavily criticized for its disciplinary rules pertaining to recruiting and player management, it was given a virtual free hand when it came to investigating and controlling drug abuse among college athletes, as I shall show.

Private government extends to any actions considered dangerous to the health and safety of participants or that provide an unfair advantage to a player or team. Drug use clearly falls within this mandate. Some drugs are of concern because they give their users a competitive edge; others arouse concern because, by endangering the health and safety of the players, they tarnish the image of the game. While often grouped together as policy issues, they actually represent very different private government problems.

In 1973, the NCAA adopted bylaws prohibiting the use of performance-enhancing drugs in preparation for championship games and required the executive committee to authorize methods for testing competitors in those events. This attempt to handle the drug problem failed, because the rules governed only championship games; and, in any case, the NCAA did not follow up on the tests that were performed. In 1986, the NCAA approved a new drug-testing program. The focal point of the program was a consent provision requiring student–athletes to sign an annual statement agreeing to be tested in the event of postseason play for chemicals the NCAA prohibits. Over three thousand substances were banned. A range of penalties were imposed on those testing positive, from a ban on play for the rest of the season to (for repeat offenders) loss of eligibility. The restriction of this program to postseason play made it all but ineffective. Athletes, knowing when testing would occur, could simply abstain from use in advance. These loopholes made congressmen angry. Much symbolic weight was attached to the steroid problem among college athletes. Senator Joseph Biden complained that "using drugs to improve athletic performance undermines our most basic notions of honesty, discipline and hard work as a means of achieving" (U.S. Congress, Senate, Committee on the Judiciary 1990, 2). The Anti–Drug Abuse Act of 1988 prohibited the distribution of anabolic steroids for any use in humans other than for medical treatment. In 1990, the NCAA adopted yet another drug-testing program, continuing the testing program in postseason play; but adding a year-round test for performance-enhancing substances by football players, whose use of steroids had received extensive media coverage.

The right of private governments to require, on penalty of dismissal, that their members submit to a screening device such as urine test, is by no means settled as public policy. The Constitution does not shield a person from private conduct by a private institution, regardless of how discriminatory or wrongful the conduct, because participation is considered to be voluntary. In the matter of drug testing (as in so many others), the applicability of constitutional guarantees therefore depends on whether the association is defined as private—in other words, on whether "state action" is involved.

Through a welter of often-conflicting signals from lower courts, the Supreme Court has sided with the view that a body like the NCAA is not a state actor (*National Collegiate Athletic Association* v. *Jerry Tarkanian*, 1988). This decision bars attacks on the NCAA's drug-testing program based on violations of due process and equal protection clauses of the federal constitution. In 1988, a U.S. district court judge dismissed a claim by Elizabeth O'Halloran, a runner at the University of Washington, that the drug-testing rule violated her constitutional rights. The court decided that some surrender of privacy was to be expected in the context of college athletics. The right to privacy was outweighed by the interests of the University of Washington and the NCAA in ensuring fair competition and reducing the abuse of drugs. This repeated similar rulings, in a federal court in Louisiana and in a state court in Florida, declaring that no "state action" is involved in NCAA testing (Monaghan 1988). Cases brought under state constitutions are not thus barred, however; and the NCAA cannot afford to ignore the possibility of suits at this level (McBride 1989). For example, its list of banned sustances (which, ironically, does not include alcohol) is impossibly vague; and its restriction of testing to athletes, particularly football players, seems to violate the equal protection clause, especially at schools priding themselves on not treating students and athletes differently. This would seem to suggest that student–athletes who believe that their privacy has been invaded by drug testing or feel injured on other legal grounds ought to prevail if they charge their individual institutions with violations (if they attend a public school), rather than the NCAA, which is better protected by not being deemed a state actor. However, a 1989 decision by the Massachusetts Supreme Court upholding the constitutionality of Northeastern University's mandatory drug-testing plan for athletes would seem to belie this.

THE COMMISSIONER SYSTEM

Selznick's theory of private government predicts that this principle of organization will be slow to develop where social relationships are contractually based, where social order is maintained by the marketplace. On this basis alone, professional team sports should exhibit only weak private governments. There is another reason to assume that private government will be weak in this case: professional sport leagues will not turn to private government, because "the club owners and their athlete–employees do not have the singular community of interests which typifies most associations" (Weistart and Lowell 1979, 262). The owners' interest in making a profit and the players' interest in job security and high wages frequently place them at odds. Given this basic antagonism, not the law of private association but labor law and contract law would seem to be most appropriate tools for dealing with disputes in this area.

There is much to be said for these arguments, because they underline the economic realities of relationships within sport leagues; but they are both misleading, because neither pays enough attention to the public role both owners and players are expected to play. Neither owner nor player is an "autonomous contractor." Neither is free to conduct his bargaining in private or to consult only his own self-interest, because neither the public nor elected officials wish to regard him as a purely economic actor. In professional sport, employer and employee are related to the other, not simply on contract terms, but on terms of common status, and they must erect some governance structure to order their relationship so as to preserve this status.

The governance of professional team sports is popularly referred to as "the commissioner system," a term whose origin lies in baseball. From the signing of the National Agreement in 1903, organized baseball (i.e., the National League, American League, and minor leagues) was ruled by a National Commission, a troika consisting of the two league presidents and a third person. The commission was dominated by Ban Johnson, the pugnacious president of the American League; but he had limited control over the National League owners. In 1921, internal squabbling led to a new agreement providing for a single commissioner with the broadest investigative powers, not least of which was "the power to take punitive action, including fining or blacklisting, against Leagues, clubs, officers or players found guilty of . . . detrimental conduct" (Seymour 1971, 322). There was no doubt, given the structure of baseball at the time, that players would be subservient; but owners also agreed to be "bound by the decisions of the Commissioner and the discipline imposed by him" and, most important for the principle of private government, waived the right to recourse to the courts in the event of disagreements.

While it is often supposed that the commissioner system was an outgrowth of the Chicago "Black Sox" scandal, the collapse of the troika method preceded, if not the playing of the 1919 World Series, at least the public charges that the series had been fixed. However, the crisis was certainly exploited by foes of Johnson to undermine his power within the National Commission. And the new commissioner, Judge Landis, used the scandal to establish his own power and become the first "tsar" of sport.

Although Landis had a deep affection for baseball and looked upon the players more as heroes than as employees, he brought to baseball "a disdain for law and due process" (Tygiel 1983, 31). Furthermore, his "spare frame housed a narrow, arbitrary, and vindictive nature" (Seymour 1971, 368). He banned for life the seven Chicago White Sox players accused of throwing the 1919 World Series, despite the fact that the players were acquitted in court of all charges of fraud, thus "completely ignoring the players' civil liberties" (N. Sullivan 1987, 8), and included, for good measure, two other players who were not even indicted but who, Landis became convinced, had known about the fix in advance and failed to warn the authorities (Seymour 1971, 338).

A pattern was thus laid down that lasted well into the final quarter of the century. In the absence of appropriate public laws, baseball law would have to prevail. Thus, Landis was moved to severity by the absence of any criminal statutes by which to punish the offending players.[12] Landis used the acquittal of the accused players and the absence of applicable public law to argue that his private powers were even more necessary.

Landis later banned players accused of crimes (e.g., auto theft), even though they had been acquitted (Spink 1974, 89); and he permanently blacklisted others for negotiating with "outlaw" leagues that had not signed the National Agreement. Within three years of taking office, Landis had placed fifty-three players on the ineligible list for disciplinary reasons (Seymour 1971, 388). Landis was only slightly less severe with owners, although the consequences of his actions were always less damaging for them. He forced owners to relinquish holdings in horse-racing and casino enterprises. In 1943, Landis permanently suspended William Cox, owner of the Philadelphia Phillies, for betting on Phillies games. In the mid-1930s, after a Detroit Tigers victory over the Yankees, Tigers owner Walter Briggs invited all twenty-five Detroit players to visit his New York tailor to be measured for expensive suits, thus provoking the wrath of Commissioner Landis, who ordered Briggs to let the men buy their own clothes. Landis insisted that such gifts gave rich clubs an advantage (Gregory 1956, 111).

Seymour argues that Landis's tenure as commissioner "refutes the cliche that in America laws, not men, govern the land" (1971, 368); but this is not strictly true. Landis was merely enforcing what he understood to be the private law of baseball, a law he believed in with as much fervor as he did public law. It so happens that baseball law at this time favored the owners and oppressed the workers. Landis was not particularly troubled by this, even if he was aware of it. Landis came into the office with the reputation of a trust-buster; and this image served him in good stead when exercising control over the owners, because his opponents would find it hard to accuse him of keeping owners in line simply to strengthen baseball's monopoly power. Landis also had another reputation, however, as the foe of the working man. He had been one of several prominent figures sent a parcel bomb in 1919, allegedly by anarchists, because they considered him such an enemy of organized labor (Leuchtenberg 1958, 72).

In creating a commissioner to rule over them, the owners established the first "industrial doctor" in America (Seymour 1971, 323). Soon after Landis's appointment, the movie industry hired Harding's postmaster general, Will Hays, to be "the Judge Landis of the movies" (Leuchtenberg 1958, 169). The motive appeared to be the same, both industries seeking to head off closer state regulation over their private government. The sport industry was plagued with gambling, the movie industry accused of purveying obscenity. In both cases, the private government they erected was to prove troublesome and unstable.[13]

As in the case of the NCAA, the erection of a private government apparatus in professional sports, by instituting a hierarchy of social relationships, weakens the sense of community among owners, players, and fans. Baseball lost its innocence and some of its populist appeal with the establishment of the commissioner system. Landis misread popular sentiment with respect to the White Sox players, most of whom were sympathized with (as shown in the jurors' verdict and the celebrations following their acquittal). The target of public anger and blame was the gamblers who fixed the games, many of whom were supposed to be of "ethnic" origin. Under Landis's strict control, baseball was to take on more and more the antidemocratic values associated with the organization of industrial firms, where democracy and democratic rights were surrendered at the factory gates.

The courts backed up the new commissioner, holding that owners and players could be asked to waive rights of appeal as long as the decisions of the commissioner were not arbitrary, fraudulent, or prejudicial. In a 1930 case, Phil Bell, then owner of the St. Louis Browns, brought suit against Commissioner Landis because Landis had declared a player (Fred Bennett) a "free agent." Bennett was being kept by Bell in one of his farm teams. The court ruled in Landis's favor: "The various agreements and rules, constituting a complete code for, or charter and by-laws of, Organized Baseball in America disclose a clear intent upon the part of parties to endow the Commissioner with all the attributes of a benevolent but absolute despot and all the disciplinary powers of the proverbial *pater familias*" (Spink 1974, 169).

Landis died in 1944, by which time the owners had decided that the commissioner system was too oppressive, at least for them. They set about diluting the powers of the commissioner. In future, it would take only three-quarters—rather than all—owners to approve or dismiss a commissioner, thus guaranteeing that any future incumbent would be more compliant than Landis. They also removed the clause in the National Agreement of 1921 by which each owner waived his right of recourse to the courts (they reinstated it in 1964). The chosen successor, Albert ("Happy") Chandler, was little more than a mouthpiece for the owners. He lasted until 1951. His successor was Ford Frick: "Had the entire country been searched, owners could hardly have picked a more reliable front man" (Voigt 1983, 94). Nevertheless, while he lacked Landis's authority, Frick could sanction owners. He forced Fred Saigh, owner of the St. Louis Cardinals, who in 1952 had been sentenced to fifteen months in jail for tax evasion, to sell the club, which was bought by Anheuser-Busch. For the most part, however, Frick "seldom bucked the owners or supported the players" (p. 95). Frick's successor, General William Eckert, lasted for three years, 1965-68. He was a "bumbler" and a "figurehead" (p. 309). Lee MacPhail, then American League president, describes how Eckert knew so little of baseball that "he had me in his office with him for ready consultation on telephone calls"(1989, 98). Eckert was instructed by the owners to "stay out of the decision making" (ibid.). Bowie Kuhn was able to recapture some of Landis's power, perhaps because baseball was becoming increasingly national, and the need for the owners to act in concert had increased. In 1974, Kuhn suspended George Steinbrenner for two years because of his plea of guilty to a charge of making illegal campaign contributions.[14]

Compared to the often fractious baseball owners, the football owners were "refreshingly collegial" (Klatell and Marcus 1988, 135). With

one or two exceptions, they were much less prone to internal squabbling and readier to cede to their commissioner considerable authority, especially in the business aspects of the sport. The NFL's bylaws
declared the commissioner's rulings as binding, without further appeal, leading one member of a House investigation committee in 1957
to declare these bylaws "contrary to public policy" (U.S. Congress,
House, Committee on the Judiciary 1957, 2652).

The power of private government in professional team sports did
not become an object of serious public attention until the late 1950s.
Although the structure of private government was never the focus of
congressional attention, several hearings on antitrust and labor-management problems in professional team sports touched on this issue.
Some congressmen wondered why professional team sports could not
be run more democratically. Why could the commissioners in team
sports not be elected by owners and players' representatives? The
owners and their appointed representatives did not see democracy as
a viable option. Baseball Commissioner Frick chose to liken baseball to
a university, where the students do not elect the president. Football
Commissioner Bell saw his position as analogous to senior management in a corporation; that the "players should have a voice in the selection of the commissioner of football" was unthinkable (U.S.
Congress, House, Committee on the Judiciary 1957, 2732). When players' unions became more assertive, they would constantly complain
about the power of the commissioner. The NFLPA's Garvey reminded
a later congressional committee that "the commissioner under the
constitution and bylaws may fine any player up to $5,000, may bar him
from the league for conduct detrimental to football, he is apparently to
settle any dispute between any player and owner and his decision is
conclusive, binding, and unappealable" (idem, Committee on Education and Labor 1972, 15).

The claim to have the right and power to protect the "integrity of the
game" has been the commissioner's most potent weapon. In this context, it is worth noting that the NFL forbids corporate ownership of
franchises. This helps to preserve a public "sportsman" image for the
owner (and to prevent franchises from being used as a promotional
device for some other business); but it also makes it easier for the commissioner to monitor the finances of the owners. Without this rule,
Commissioner Rozelle explained, it would be "impossible for us to control ownership in our league" (Demak 1991, 15). The three other major
team sports do not have a rule forbidding corporate ownership, but
the role of the commissioner in protecting the sport's "good name"
nevertheless looms large. When baseball agreed to outside arbitration,
it forced the players' association to agree to reserve to the commissioner jurisdiction over those disputes affecting "baseball's integrity or
public confidence in the game" (Kuhn 1987, 141). The obligation to de-

fend the integrity of the game is a blunt weapon, much given to abuse,
because the phrase is susceptible to multiple interpretations. In 1966,
ABA basketball star Connie Hawkins was prevented from joining the
NBA by Commissioner Walter Kennedy on grounds of his alleged involvement in a college basketball gambling fix in 1961. Hawkins filed
suit again the NBA, claiming that he had been denied due process because Kennedy had made no specific charges against him or identified
his accusers. The commissioner, concerned above all with the image
of the NBA in its rivalry with the ABA, could not substantiate his
charge; and in an out-of-court settlement, Hawkins was admitted to the
league.

The owners typically make reference to the peculiar economic structure of professional leagues to justify the commissioner system. Kuhn
caused a stir in 1976 when he nullified the sale by the Oakland Athletics of three players (Vida Blue, Rollie Fingers, and Joe Rudi), charging
that the trades would have weakened the team competitively and that
the owner, Charles Finley, was selling the players simply to raise cash:
"If we run this business like any other businesses are run, then we
would have trouble with public acceptance. We have to do things that
are different because it is a sports business" (U.S. Congress, House, Select Committee on Professional Sports 1976, 50). Finley sued the commissioner on this occasion, charging that his rights to due process and
equal protection had been violated. Kuhn successfully argued that
since major league baseball was a wholly private organization and the
commissioner a private individual, the nullification of the trades could
not constitute "state action" and therefore was not subject to the constitutional guarantees: "*Finley* is a case illustrating great judicial defer-
ence to a sports commissioner's attempts to protect the best interests of
the game" (Pachman 1990, 1425). Of the appeals court's final decision in
his favor in 1978, Kuhn writes, "Nothing so strengthened my hand during my sixteen years as Commissioner as this decision" (1987, 182).
When Commissioner Bartlett Giamatti was forced to defend his suspension of Cincinnati Reds manager Pete Rose in 1990, he cited the Finley decision to argue against court intervention in the dispute.

One year after the Finley affair, Kuhn was once again called upon to
discipline an owner, Ted Turner of the Atlanta Braves. Turner's legal
appeal against his fine was firmly rejected by the court in *Atlanta Baseball Club v. Kuhn* (1977).

> The Commissioner has general authority, without rules or direc-
> tives, to punish both clubs and/or personnel for any act or con-
> duct which, in his judgement, is "not in the best interest of
> baseball" within the meaning of the Major League Agreement.
> What conduct is "not in the best interest of baseball" is, of course,
> a question which addresses itself to the Commissioner, not this
> court. (Pachman 1990, 1424)

roth was too obviously a hired hand. (He is widely suspected of having coordinated the collusion among the owners not to bid on free agents that lasted from 1985 until 1988 [Zimbalist 1992, 109]). He strengthened the business side of the commissioner's job but, by so doing, undermined the fiduciary side of the Commissioner's office—the side that justified the police powers of his predecessors.

The balance was restored somewhat when Ueberroth resigned in 1988, to be replaced by the former president of the National League and former president of Yale, A. Bartlett Giamatti. His background in the humanities, and his highly publicized love of the game and distate for some of its less attractive commercial aspects restored to the office of the Commissioner some of the legitimacy bestowed by Landis. He was relatively well-prepared by this background to deal with the first crisis he faced, which involved a clear challenge to the integrity of the game. Under Ueberroth's jurisdiction, rumours had begun to circulate that Cincinnati Reds manager Pete Rose had been betting heavily on baseball games, including those of his own team. Rose denied the allegations, and Giamatti instituted an investigation. Rose, faced with the prospect of a lifetime ban from the sport, asked for, and received, a restraining order barring Giamatti from holding a hearing regarding the betting charges. A lower court judge (Norbert Nadel) granted the order, having decided that the commissioner had prejudged Rose.

Despite the judge's ruling, few believed that Rose would prevail against the commissioner. Due process binds government, not private associations; and the general consensus seemed to be that the commissioner had broad and legitimate enough authority to prevail. The courts had generally declined to intervene in the affairs of a private organization unless a person's contractual rights had been flagrantly violated by a private proceeding. Most judicial decisions "recognize that commissioners are restrained by the requirement of due process," such as being given "meaningful notice" and being given a fair hearing (Pachman 1990, 1430). In a settlement announced on August 24, 1989, Rose was banned from baseball for life for "conduct not in the best interest of baseball"—the fourteenth player, coach or team owner to be suspended for gambling-related offenses in the history of baseball. The settlement did not require an admission of guilt from Rose; but he did undertake not to "challenge, appeal or otherwise contest the decision of, or the procedure employed by, the Commissioner" (Chass 1989). Rose was later convicted for tax-evasion, having hidden the income from sales of trading cards and memorabilia. The Commissioner system had thus withstood its most severe challenge in the postwar era.[15]

Giamatti died of a heart attack shortly after the resolution of the Rose dispute and was succeeded by the deputy commissioner, Francis ("Fay") Vincent. An old friend of Giamatti, Vincent shared his view of the value of the sport of baseball to American society and his distaste for some of its more commercial aspects. Under his leadership, the

Like all commissioners, Kuhn claimed to be a neutral and impartial administrator, thus legitimating his authority. Kuhn portrayed himself as sometimes supporting players, sometimes the owners, depending on what seemed to him to be "right for baseball." Of course, he was hired, paid, and fired by the owners; and when it came to the crunch, this dependence showed. Explaining his actions during a particularly acrimonious stage of collective bargaining between the union and the owners' Player Relations Committee (PRC), he writes:

> While it was not the commissioner's job to formulate the PRC proposals, I could assure that they bargained in good faith, a fact that was fully understood, if sometimes resented, by individual PRC members. Keep in mind that as a practical matter the PRC chairman, the league presidents and the league lawyers were at all times closely allied with me and I with them. (Kuhn 1987, 336)

In the crisis that rocked baseball over the Messersmith and McNally dispute, however, Kuhn was among the first to recommend that arbitrator Peter Seitz be fired for his "barely concealed, antimanagement bias" (p. 157). Curt Flood described Kuhn as "straight Establishment, a grinder of the owners' ax" (1971, 169).

By the end of the 1960s, it had become clear that much of the power of the commissioner lay in his ability to negotiate lucrative deals with the television networks. Congressional approval of joint negotiations with the networks in 1961 was crucial to cementing the power of the commissioner. This, more than any other single factor, was responsible for the length of ""Pete" Rozelle's tenure as NFL commissioner, which ended in 1989. Kuhn was somewhat less successful in this regard, although he had fewer cards to play with, because baseball had never accepted the principle of equal sharing of television revenues. Kuhn's eventual dismissal was, in all probability, pushed most vigorously by those closely tied to media interests (e.g., the Chicago Cubs), owners of superstations (e.g., Ted Turner, owner of the Atlanta Braves), and those anxious to get local media rights (e.g. George Steinbrenner, owner of the New York Yankees), all of whom resented Kuhn's efforts to centralize revenues (now chiefly from television) to the point of proposing the kind of revenue sharing used by football (Klatell and Marcus 1988).

Kuhn's successor, Peter Ueberroth, was more skillful at negotiating television rights packages. When he came into office in 1984, twenty-one of the twenty-eight baseball franchises were losing money. Four years later, there were none. National television revenues had doubled, and licensing income increased sixteen times. He was not particularly liked, but was nevertheless admired and valued by the owners. Ueberroth's strengths were also his weaknesses. He had no prior connection to baseball, evinced no particular love of the game, and made little effort to legitimate his position in terms of the "good of the game." Ueber-

administration of major league basebell seemed well able to restore the sense of community Giamatti believed baseball must have in order to survive, and which the commissioner must assume is there in order to have any authority—if the commissioner is to have any authority at all it must derive from the consent of owners, players and fans alike. Such was not to be the case, however, for within three years Vincent had been forced to resign by the owners, angered at a number of Vincent's actions, not least of which was a proposed reorganization of the National League. The reorganization would have moved the Chicago Cubs into the Western Division and meant that its away games would be played in the early hours of the morning, Chicago time; an important consideration for the Cubs, who were owned by a television station. The Cubs sued to block the move; and they also organized baseball's other owners to pressure Vincent to resign, which he did, in September 1992. To many commentators, the executive committee of owners that assumed the governance of major league baseball after Vincent's departure resembled nothing so much as a board of directors of a corporation. Contract had replaced status; market had replaced hierarchy; business had replaced sport; and, community having been destroyed, private government had lost much of its legitimacy.

The Pete Rose case demonstrates that private government is most likely to become a public issue when an association appears to be incapable of enforcing its own procedures. Over sixty years before, rivalry between American League president "Ban" Johnson and Baseball Commissioner Landis led, in 1924, to a call for the federal regulation of baseball, sparked by widespread reports of attempts to bribe players involved in the World Series that year. Johnson, in a move to undermine Landis's authority, called for a federal investigation of the bribery allegations. Representative Sol Bloom (New York), former chairman of the House Foreign Affairs Committee, declared that the federal government had as much right to regulate baseball as it did the interstate operation of railroads and introduced a bill that would have set up a commission to regulate the sport. The bill never made it out of committee (Spink 1974, 121). Owners need to be aware that, if they do not keep their own house in order, the prospect of public scrutiny increases.[16]

SPORTS AND VIOLENCE

Failing to enforce private law often has public consequences. Public law will be invoked where private law is inadequate. When private governments can no longer maintain their own law and order or when their definition of law and order offers more license than public law will tolerate, then the state steps in. Contact sports must deal with the issue of violence and how it should be defined and regulated. Each sport's law will define excessive force and punish those who use it. Traditionally, this regulation has been a private matter, intrinsic to the sport itself. More recently, however, private governments have not been left alone in this matter, and public law has been invoked. I will show why.

There are two sets of governance issues involved in the debate over violence in sport. The first is the growing sense on the part of the players that their contract entitles them to protection of life and liberty versus the traditional notion that participation in contact sports, particularly if it is for pay, implies consent to the risk of injury. The latter implies a more total commitment to the athletic role and to the notion that sport knowledge is specialized and concentrated: the athlete should do as he is told or get out. The former reflects a revolution of rising entitlements. It assumes that players are complete human beings, for whom athletics is only part of their life, who have as much knowledge about fitness and playing conditions as management. The second set of issues has to do with the license that private governments must exercise (because the state lacks the expertise and resources to govern directly even if it wished to) versus the state's desire that public law-and-order norms be upheld, especially by institutions, such as sport, that are given a public mandate to uphold social values. The question is, Should the task of defining excessive force be decided by the same governing body that decides the length of the game? Should the commissioner, an official with no public powers, be responsibility for punishing those found guilty of assault?

The state has traditionally been inclined to accept the argument that private governments are entitled to keep their own law and order. Rules exist in all sports to protect players from physical harm, and commissioners and referees have broad discretion in meting out penalties to offenders. The reasons for this were suggested at the beginning of this chapter. Both the nature of the product and the relationship between member and association requires some kind of policing apparatus. Thus, the courts accept arguments put forward by leagues and associations that outsiders simply know too little about sports to adjudicate grievances properly. For example, injuries caused by "reckless disregard" would normally constitute grounds for tort action; but which actions engaged in by a football player would be considered reckless? Malicious, or intentional, injury also constitutes grounds for action; but how is the intent to injure distinguished from a "solid hit" or an effective body check? In the heat of competition, might not a player commit "violent" acts that are neither planned nor reckless? Add to this the fact that autonomy from outside supervision is itself a sport value. Many players subscribe to the view that the game is, and should be, self-contained, with its own morality and code of ethics. Players refrain from initiating lawsuits out of love of the game, reluctant to sully its image. Furthermore, they believe that any breakdown in law and order is, for this reason, best dealt with by vigilante justice: retribution on the playing field is sufficient. This is not only more swift and effective but more in keeping with the masculine image of the game. Both management and players believe that once outsiders get involved in deciding permissable amounts of force, the game becomes tamer and is less appealing to fans.

The relationship that the athlete is expected to have to the association of which he is a part is a second reason why law and order is policed internally. Where players have few alternative opportunities to pursue their athletic career, more elaborate adjudication procedures tend to develop because the consequences of exclusion are severe. Public law is too crude a weapon to deal with grievances where the stakes are so high and knowledge so specialized. Jurors are reluctant to stigmatize a player with a conviction or jail term for assault, especially if they believe the act in question is endemic to the sport. Private governments thus emerge where commitment to the association is total. Athletes, especially those who are paid to play, are expected to make a total commitment. The public assumes that there is consent implied in the decision to participate in a contact sport; and where the player is paid to perform, he is expected to consent to greater risks. Thus, while criminal prosecution of violence is rare at the professional level, it is more common at the amateur level. Between 1960 and 1980, close to one hundred convictions for criminal assault were secured at the amateur level, none at the professional level (DiNicola and Mendeloff 1983, 863). The first U.S. criminal prosecution involving assault at the professional level (resulting from David Forbes's attack on Henry Boucha in a Boston versus Minnesota ice hockey game in 1975) ended in a hung jury. The first U.S. athlete to be jailed for a playing offense was Minnesota North Stars right winger Dino Ciccanelli, sentenced to one day in jail and a one thousand-dollar fine by a Toronto provincial judge in 1988 after having assaulted a Toronto Maple Leafs player.

These were rare instances. State prosecutors no doubt felt they had enough real crime to handle without taking their time prosecuting athletes. However, the revolution of rising entitlements during the 1970s emboldened players whose grievances had been ignored or rejected by private government to invoke state powers. As the rewards for playing professional sports increased, so did the penalties of injury. The informal methods by which sports like hockey had controlled the level of violence between players began to break down; and the fact remained that even if private government did decide in an aggrieved player's favor, it could not provide compensation for loss of earnings or expenses incurred in their recovery. By invoking state powers, players could be paid for their injuries and the pain and suffering accompanying them. In the first case of tort liability in professional sports, Dale

Hackbart of the Denver Broncos suffered a fractured neck as the result of a blow from Charles Clark during a game in 1973 with the Cincinnati Bengals. The ball had been blown dead before the blow was administered but no foul was called. A lower court ruled that Hackbart assumed the risk of receiving such blows when he consented to play football and found Clark innocent of any wrongdoing. The Tenth Circuit Court of Appeals reversed this decision on the grounds that Clark had acted in an unsportsmanlike and unexpected fashion and awarded damages to Hackbart.

Such cases did not seriously erode the power of private government, however negligently it might be applied, because each case would have to be brought separately, and necessarily vague terms like *excessive force* would have to be defined in each case. However, there is an important difference between regulating violence by public and private means. Resort to the state gives the injured player the opportunity to hold the batterer's employer or athletic association to account, thus generalizing the offence from an individual act to a systemic feature of the organization. This is the significance of blows to the head inflicted on Rudy Tomjanovich of the Houston Rockets by Kermit Washington of the Los Angeles Lakers. Tomjanovich suffered multiple fractures to the face and skull; and he sued not Washington but his employer, California Sports Incorporated. The trial court awarded Tomjanovich three million dollars in damages. The Lakers appealed, but the issue was eventually settled out of court for an undisclosed sum. The significance of this verdict was that players could now maintain that adjudication procedures in professional sports (which so often gave the aggrieved player little choice but to accept violence as routine) could now be seen as biased in favor of the owners and therefore not democratic, because they ignored the fact that players were expected to be "aggressive" as part of the contract and were made the scapegoat when a seemingly arbitrary line was crossed.

Ice hockey and football have always attracted public scrutiny on account of the level of violence in the game. In 1980, Representative Ronald Mottl introduced a sports violence bill that sought to make it a federal crime to use excessive physical force in sport. The Justice Department opposed the bill on grounds that its terms were too vague. Mottl tried again in 1981 with a sports violence arbitration bill that would have required each major league to establish an arbitration board empowered to impose fines on a club and players for unnecessary conduct occurring during the course of a game. This effort to establish a "Sports Court" also failed to make it out of committee. Public efforts to beef up private law, therefore, had to rely on the courts.

If, in the case of team sports, the problem with the regulation of violence is that there has been too much private government standing in the way of efforts to regulate the sport publicly, in the case of boxing, the problem is that there has been too little government. Part of the reason for the criminalization of boxing at the turn of the century was the "violence" and "brutality" of the sport. When states began to relegitimate the sport in the 1910–20 period, they did so under the supervision of weak and corrupt state athletic commissions that did little to control the use of excessive force in the sport.

The civil rights era marked something of a change in the political regulation of boxing, however; for it gave support to those seeking to intervene in private government to protect boxers from exploitation and physical danger on the grounds that the promoters and managers were engaging in unfair labor practices. Typical was a bill introduced in 1985, the federal boxer protection act. This would have established in the Department of Labor a Federal Boxing Commission to prescribe and enforce fair labor standards. Another bill introduced in that year would have established a Congressional Advisory Commission on Amateur Boxing. There was also a bill to ban boxing altogether. During hearings on the federal boxer protection act, it was revealed that since 1901 an estimated 449 boxers had died as a result of injuries sustained in the ring, 181 since 1960 (U.S. Congress, House, Committee on Energy and Commerce 1985b, 241, 304). Committee member Henry Gonzales (Texas), speaking for the bill to ban professional boxing, did not consider it a sport at all but "an industry that capitalizes on the brutal display of the crude force of one boxer over another" (p. 306). A spokesman for the American Medical Association, George Lundberg, advocated a total ban on boxing, pointing to the "strong evidence of chronic brain damage in a very high percentage of long-time boxers" (p. 326).

The federal boxer protection act would have permitted boxing but provided a quasi-federal corporation (consisting of five commissioners appointed by the secretary of labor) to provide a registry of fighters and a uniform ranking system, as well as establishing uniform standards for health, safety, equipment, contracts and pensions. The states, which licensed boxers and sanctioned events, would be expected to come under the sanctioning authority voluntarily. The bill's sponsors were attempting to "federalize" the sport of boxing and, in so doing, make it more publicly accountable. They pointed out that the boxing industry was altogether lacking labor standards and that given the enormous variation from state to state and the competition between states for fights and fighters, it was all too easy to evade what few state regulations there were. Many state licensing boards were moribund or powerless for lack of funds; other states lacked licensing boards or had simply assigned the task to the secretary of labor or the insurance commissioner. The bill's sponsors proposed to have the industry itself pay for this regulation, drawing a parallel with baseball and football. Here, the issue seemed to be not an overbearing private government (as in the case of the NCAA or the professional sport team leagues) but an inadequate and corrupt private government that had failed to protect the rights of both athletes and fans.

In the end, the method of adjudication of disputes over excessive force in sports would appear to rest on the degree of voluntarism implied in the participation. Where private government offers little chance of "exit," membership becomes a surrogate form of citizenship. Citizenship implies duties, but it also guarantees rights. With respect to the private powers of sport associations, a public policy seems to have emerged in which certain limitations are placed on the association's authority to adjudicate law-and-order issues. Sport associations are normally left alone to define and punish excessive force up to a point, which is defined by the idea of "implied consent." This idea hinges on the assumption that sport participation is voluntary and that the individual is cognizant of the risks involved. The state adopts the role of the guardian of the contract implied by this agreement. Sports are left to use their discretion to develop rules to protect their athletes and keep them from physical harm. It is against these rules that the athlete must calculate his risk of injury. It is a public, not a private, matter if this implied contract is violated—if injuries caused by a violation of a sport's own safety rules go unpunished. It is especially likely to be considered a public issue if the athlete has little choice but to belong to the association and submit to its government. A second set of limits is defined by the notion of "sportsmanlike conduct." This appeals to the autonomous values mentioned earlier. A sport government that tolerates unsportsmanlike conduct is like a school association that denies free speech. By its own action, it is contradicting the mandate on which private government was established in the first place. Thus, physical force can be considered excessive if it violates the normative rules of the sport or is intended to gain an unfair advantage.

CONTROLLING DRUG ABUSE

Both safety and sportsmanship rules are constitutive; they help define what the sport is. Within the boundary they describe, private government reigns supreme. If the action seems to step outside this boundary, public law is more likely to be invoked. The question of the control of drug abuse illustrates this principle, as well as does that of the control of excessive force. Two issues of private government are involved. The first has to do with the government of performance-enhancing drugs. Some athletes use drugs to enhance performance and thus gain an unfair advantage. Here the issue is whether private government efforts to eliminate their use violates public law. The second has to do with the regulation of "recreational" drugs, such as cocaine. This is not a purely private matter, for the laws involved are criminal statutes. Furthermore, professional athletes are expected to maintain a clean image and, especially, to set an example for younger people. Their recreational habits off the field are thus subject to special scrutiny. They are also held more accountable to the paying customer, who expects full value for his money and is suspicious of subpar performance. The issue here is whether private government (which usually lacks the civil rights guarantees of public government) should be used to enforce public law.

Until the 1980s, drug use among athletes was not a public issue at all, although it was widely known that professional athletes used performance-enhancing drugs like steroids and recreational drugs like alcohol and marijuana. During the Reagan administration, however, the boundaries around private governments were breached in the war on drugs as workplace drug tests became an increasingly popular weapon in the fight, justified by concerns for safety and productivity. In 1986, the Reagan administration asked all federal agencies to test employees in "sensitive" jobs. By 1988, half the Fortune 500 companies had testing programs. Civil libertarians took the issue to court, complaining that the Fourth Amendment's prohibition on unreasonable searches was becoming a casualty in the war on drugs. They were most concerned about random testing, which seemed more likely to intrude on the privacy of innocent employees. Union lawyers argued that the testing procedure was demeaning (in many cases, workers had to urinate while an attendant watched) and charged that the tests were frequently inaccurate.

Private government issues were at stake in this debate. What rights did the worker surrender when he agreed to join an organization? Sport organizations were to face the same problems because of the moral expectations imposed on athletes and the concern to keep competition "clean." The professional leagues were slow to respond to the political call for more rigorous drug controls, because owners could not trust each other to discipline their own players unless assured that all others would do likewise. Eventually, the commissioners were obliged to invoke their mandate to maintain the integrity of the game in order to discipline drug-using players. The police powers of the commissioners were strengthened by several Supreme Court decisions indicating that the justices did not think that "particularized" suspicion was always necessary to warrant a search. In 1980, Baseball Commissioner Kuhn suspended Texas Rangers pitcher Ferguson Jenkins after he was arrested for possession of drugs but before his trial had taken place. (Jenkins was reinstated following an arbitrator's ruling made as a result of a grievance filed by the players' association.) NFL Commissioner Rozelle imposed his first suspensions in 1983.

Although performance-enhancing drugs were widely used during this period, most of the internal policing was directed at recreational drug use. The use of marijuana, cocaine, and other hard drugs made the leagues most vulnerable to attack from without and were the biggest threat to the organizations' private government powers. In 1988, a district court judge in Cedar Rapids, Iowa, ruled that the Continental Basketball Association (CBA) was justified in banning Lewis Lloyd because of the former Houston Rocket player's past drug use. Lloyd had been banned from the NBA after he tested positive for cocaine in 1987. Lloyd had applied for readmission to the NBA but was meanwhile seeking to sharpen his skills with the Cedar Rapids Bullets of the CBA. Lloyd sued the CBA after its commissioner had refused to allow him to play in the league, charging violation of the antitrust laws. The judge, in dismissing the suit, traced a connection between drug-using athletes and the image of a league, arguing that image was very important for the CBA, which did not want to seem to be an "outlaw" league.

Athletes argued that it was the government's job, not a private organization's, to enforce the law against the use of recreational drugs. In baseball, the union routinely filed appeals to arbitrators against Commissioner Kuhn for disciplining athletes convicted of drug possession. The union appealed against Kuhn's suspension of Jenkins in 1980, and the arbitrator ruled against him. Kuhn complained that the "drug problem" in baseball was due in part to escalating salaries but chiefly to obstructive tactics by players' associations (1987, 306). The baseball arbitrator usually sought some kind of compromise in drug-testing cases, upholding Kuhn's decision but reducing the sentence.[17]

The players oppose random testing for three reasons: (1) that it is the state's job to enforce the law against the use of illegal drugs and that any action by private governments is vigilante justice; (2) that drug testing is unreliable and can lead to a player being falsely, and publicly, accused; and (3) drug testing is likely to be used to discipline and weed out players (U.S. Congress, Senate, Committee on the Judiciary 1990, 214). For these reasons, the MLBPA rejected any kind of drug-testing program, prompting then-commissioner Ueberroth to impose a program unilaterally. The program, on complaint from the players, was struck down by an arbitrator because it had not been negotiated (Rose and Girard 1988). In football, drug testing for "reasonable cause" began in 1982; but commissioner Rozelle ordered mandatory testing in preseason training camp to begin in 1987. At the insistence of the NFLPA, testing was announced in advance. The NBA includes drug testing in its collective bargaining agreement, which authorizes the NBA to test players without notice but only on a reasonable-cause basis. Testing of NBA players is allowed only if it is ordered by the league's independent investigator, who determines whether the evidence before him constitutes "probable cause" that the player is using drugs. A player who tests positive is disqualified for a minimum of two years.

While a relationship of collective bargaining exists between players and owners, players are fairly safe from a unilateral imposition of drug-testing schemes. If the agreement breaks down, one-party rule returns, the players are more exposed, and private government issues resurface. In 1987, the collective agreement between players and management in football broke down in the aftermath of the strike. In 1989, Commissioner Rozelle suspended thirteen NFL players as a result of positive tests in preseason camps. Two efforts by the NFLPA to obtain injunctive relief prohibiting those suspensions were rejected by federal courts. Emboldened by this and feeling the force of public opinion, the new NFL commissioner, Paul Tagliabue, unilaterally announced in 1990 that all NFL players would be subject to year-round unscheduled testing for steroids (U.S. Congress, House, Committee on the Judiciary 1990, 6).

CONCLUSION

Private government powers are more secure when an organization can claim a particular right, based on special knowledge, to administer some aspect of human behavior. In the matter of drug abuse, private government powers with respect to performance-enhancing drugs are much less controversial than those aimed at controlling recreational drugs. Drugs like steroids threaten the essence of the game—much like the use of a piece of equipment that gives an unfair edge—and therefore clearly falls within the province of private government.

The overall trend reflected in this analysis of private governments in sports has been toward limitations on their powers. Amateur and professional athletes have secured more protection from the control of sport authorities over their opportunities to play and gained more democratic rights to participate in the decision making that goes on in those governments. In Selznick's terms, sport administration still rests heavily on "status," rather than "contract"; but there has been a decline in substantive rationality, as sports lose some of their aura of being a special preserve to be trusted to take care of themselves and their own, and a rise in formal rationality, where universal principles are applied to sport organizations regardless of their mission and mandate. Nowhere is the trend toward more formal rationality more striking than in the area of torts. For many years, sports have been all but immunized from personal damages suits because they are considered voluntary, private, activities. But tort actions are more likely as sports become less personal and more businesslike. As status is replaced by contract, the legitimacy of private government declines. Thus, an organization like Little League baseball, run on patriarchal principles on a voluntary basis and firmly part of the private sphere, finds itself facing an increasing number of lawsuits in which coaches and officials are defendants in personal damages cases. Coaches and officials are sued by parents when their children are injured in the course of play; and insurance premiums for coaches, officials, and leagues become prohibitively expensive as damage payments reach six figures.

The decline of private government powers has not been the result of deliberate state policy, nor has the state agreed to set up the supervisory bodies so often proposed as substitutes for private government. There is little reason to suppose that in a liberal democratic society, state control of private governments would extend much beyond a rather remote and largely reactive supervision of constitutional guarantees. Indeed, in the case of professional sports, private government has been legitimated and strengthened by the rise of players' associations, which function as a "loyal opposition" and serve to justify a laissez-faire attitude on the part of state officials.

7

BIG

LEAGUE

CITIES

Many historians believe that team sports have their origin in rivalry between neighboring communities. Disputes over property, often violent, gradually became displaced onto more ritual forms of competition, including sports we now recognise as wrestling and football. In the late Middle Ages, sport contests, usually held during annual festivals and holidays, would have involved almost the entire community. Later, in the eighteenth century, these competitions became more structured; and clubs were formed to organize the community's involvement in the contest. With the advent of clubs, more people became spectators, and fewer participated. Since the traditions and practices of sport clubs varied considerably from one locality to another, they would naturally become associated with place. To play for or follow a club was to represent a place. Conversely, to watch a club compete was to watch a community perform. The confederations of clubs that later developed to rationalize playing rules and arrange schedules did not destroy but, instead, exploited this localism (Elias and Dunning 1986, 38).

The tie between club and community is thus an important aspect of sport, especially where team games are concerned, when the symbolic connection between community and club is more easily made. Sport clubs derive meaning from their attachment to place, while places acquire a more distinct identity when represented by a sport club. American baseball "was built on a geographical and psychological sense of lo-calism" (Goldstein 1989, 101). Baseball has preserved a rule that says franchises should be locally owned. Industrialization and urbanization weakened the attachment to place to some extent. Factory life separated work and residence. Some sport clubs became associated with the workplace, rather than the residential community. Other clubs were formed by members of the same occupation and became detached from location altogether (Gelber 1984). With the expansion of higher educa-tion to meet the needs of industry, many sport clubs became affiliated with schools and colleges. Some colleges were cosmopolitan and sought to transcend the boundaries of the local community by forging the alle-giance of a "subway alumni." The growth of commercialized sports also weakened the bond to place because entrepreneurs moved teams from place to place in search of profit. Much later, television was to create its own global village, packaging some clubs as "America's team."

Yet the tie between sport and community has not only survived these changes but has in some ways been strengthened by them. Industrial-ism did not totally divide occupational and residential communities. In-deed, in many cases, it helped form new communities (e.g., "steel towns"), in which work and residence were bonded to form a distinct identity that a sport team could then express. It is true that much ama-teur sport became absorbed into schools and colleges, but only a few of these institutions were truly cosmopolitan. Most had strong ties to place and, indeed, assumed some of the burden of representing the lo-cal community and articulating its values. Finally, while commercialism did transform sport clubs into moveable assets, entrepreneurs were not slow to realize that the commodity they were selling was not merely diversion but attachment; that their best customers were not casual browsers but fans; and that this kind of relationship was forged most ef-fectively by trading on, rather than destroying, the link between club and community. Owners could capitalize on the more wholesome as-pects of the tie to community, from which they benefited financially, while at the same time retaining the right of all owners of capital to move when more profitable opportunities arose elsewhere.

The mass market for professional sports did not, therefore, destroy the link of club and community but placed it on a new footing. The re-lation between place and club was commodified, something to be bought and sold. A club could "sell itself" as part of a city, while the city could purchase or lease the glamor associated with a major league fran-chise. Since a sport franchise is quite literally ownership of an area or "spot" in the marketplace—a grant of territorial rights—it can be mutu-ally beneficial for club and community. Franchising bestows power on the club where the supply is scarce; and playing host to a franchise where the supply is limited places a city among the elite. This is espe-cially valuable when professional team sports are signs of modernity. The Cincinnati Red Stockings were formed after the Civil War "with the express purpose of advertising the progressive character" of the city (Riess 1989, 35). The White Sox were regarded as symbols of Chicago's rise to national significance.

Sport policy debates in the 1980s were dominated by the issue of franchise location and franchise movement. While the movement of franchises was nothing new, it began to occur with much greater frequency after World War II. Johnson (1983) records sixty-eight franchise movements between 1950 and 1982, thirty-seven of them since 1970. By the end of that period, movement of franchises had become such a controversial issue that the term *free agency* no longer referred to freedom of movement for players but freedom of movement for owners, a shift in meaning most appropriate for the Reagan years. Encouraged and abetted by eager municipalities, owners challenged the traditional authority of leagues to control franchise location. An era of uncontrolled movements did not occur, however, chiefly because the leagues and the rejected cities sought relief on Capitol Hill.

How and why did the problem of the location of sport franchises enter the public policy domain in the 1980s? The relation between a municipality and a sport franchise is much like that between a city and any major firm, an exchange of subsidies and tax benefits in return for jobs and tax revenues. Local politics is clearly important in forging this relationship, because city officials might well see their political fortunes as depending on securing and retaining a major league franchise. Why did this politics not remain local? The answer lies in three interrelated trends: (1) sports went national, (2) cities became "growth machines," and (3) collective league authority weakened. After World War II, all the major team sports became national in coverage and scope (ice hockey lagged behind in the United States). Having a franchise in each major city became increasingly important for a sport league, especially with the advent of television. Economic survival depended on being able to adjust to population trends and changing markets. Then, cities themselves changed, especially after World War II. They became "growth machines," hungry for new development, new enterprises to increase their tax revenues. Competition between "entrepreneurial" city managers became the norm. Finally, for a number of reasons unrelated to the franchise location issue, the collective authority of the league over individual owners, mediated through the commissioner, weakened during the 1970-80 period; and this opened the door for opportunism on the part of franchise owners wishing to move to greener pastures. The issue of the controlling authority of a league was something Congress and the courts had long debated. Franchise movements merely represented this issue in a new form. This chapter will review each of these trends in turn and then describe the policy debate to which they led.

The major team sports spread across the country, following population movements that accelerated after World War II. Of course, baseball, in particular, was already well established in American folklore as "the national game"; but in reality, it was still very much a regional sport, largely confined to the upper Midwest and the East Coast. There were no teams in the South or West. The migration of two major New York baseball franchises to the West Coast in the 1950s, and the inclusion of a Los Angeles franchise in the American Football League begun after World War II, were dramatic reminders that the sport industry was becoming national in scope. As chapter 4 has shown, by the mid-1950s, policymakers had become skeptical of any claim that the major team sports were essentially local, not engaged in interstate commerce.

The appeal to localism (made most often by baseball) was, in any case, specious. Sport leagues have a strong vested interest in being considered "national." It adds to their credibility with customers and today is a prerequisite for national network television contracts.[1] In this context, it is important to note that modern owners have a keen sense of theirs being a national market. Although they often justify their move from one city to another by referring to lack of fan support, this is rarely the sole, or even the most important, reason. More often, the team owner thinks he can meet an unfulfilled need in the national market for the game by moving. He is perhaps moving from a city where there is more than one team to a city where he can exercise a monopoly or from a weak, to a strong, television market. He enjoys being wooed by city fathers in distant locations.

The economic boom in sports, which made franchises so attractive, hurt cities in another way. By the 1960s, most of the larger cities were playing host to several different major league sports, each of which competed for the citizen's entertainment dollar. From the point of view of revenue enhancement, this growth was healthy for a city, but it also posed problems when individual franchises came calling for subsidies. When the Chicago White Sox began making noises about moving out of seventy-year-old Comiskey Park, Chicago city officials and the Illinois State Legislature quickly moved to offer the club an inducement to stay, in the form of a new stadium across the road. The problem with this deal was that Chicagoans were equally proud to play host to four other major league franchises—the NFL's Bears, the NBA's Bulls, and the NHL's Blackhawks—and these, too, now began threatening to leave if they were not given treatment as generous as that provided to the White Sox (Pelissero, Henschen, and Sidlow 1991, 117).

CITIES BECOME GROWTH MACHINES

The public debate over franchise movement was fueled in large part by intense competition among American cities to play host to major sporting events. The reason for this competition is not hard to find. City officials believe that hosting a sport franchise bestows "major league" status on their city, generates revenues and jobs, and boosts civic pride. Municipal competition for franchises amounts to a form of collective speculation, in which corporate actors (in this case, municipalities) compete to attract other forms of capitalist development or actively defend a local economy against devaluation: "A curious reversal in nineteenth century capitalism has taken place in which multilocal organizations [e.g., sport leagues] benefit from the competition among entrepreneurial governments each seeking to entice economic growth by providing the most favorable political climate" (Mollenkopf 1983, 220).

This form of speculation became much more common after World War II, when cities began selling themselves as opportunities for self-realization and the social spaces of distraction and display became as vital to urban centers as spaces for working and living. Above all, cities had to appear as innovative, exciting, creative, and safe places to live. Post-Keynesian theories of growth, stressing state-backed, debt-financed consumption, made it easier for city officials to justify spending public money to attract industry. Cities became entrepreneur—venture capitalists—capable of making wrong choices and losing out to their competition just like companies in the private sector.[2]

In this climate, hosting sport events became very attractive. A sporting event offered a rare promise of community consensus and the opportunity for officials to demonstrate "leadership." Not all sports were equally well adapted for this purpose. Those that honored individual accomplishments, such as tennis, golf, track, and swimming, did not attract the attention of cities unless they could be turned into truly mass spectator events in which the city itself was the stadium, as in a marathon or an automobile race; but there were plenty of opportunities for cities to participate in the marketplace for other kinds of sport.

One other market opportunity was college sports. Cities could compete to host the NCAA Men's Basketball Championships or, best of all, a postseason "bowl game." College football had never developed a national championship format, and bowl games had emerged (beginning in the 1930s) as a way for the higher-ranked teams in the nation to meet at the end of the season. Bowl game organizations, ostensibly charities, competed with each other for the opportunity to host the best two teams, the best "match-up." Depending on how well bowl organizers competed for teams, their host cities stood to lose or gain millions of dollars in fan expenditures. Naturally, these host cities took a keen interest in the bidding war. In order to attract the right teams, the bowl organization and its host city would offer financial incentives, each wanting to be the "super bowl of college football."[3]

The number of bowl games increased steadily during the 1960s and 1970s as more and more cities sought this path to civic glory. The city of Phoenix was one winner in this competition. In 1970, it first requested permission to host the Fiesta Bowl and was turned down by the NCAA Extra Events Committee, which was beginning to worry about the proliferation of bowls. To further its chances, the organizing committee did not scruple to use the influence of U.S. Attorney General John Mitchell, a resident of Arizona. Mitchell let it be known that he believed the NCAA to be in violation of antitrust laws by denying the bid. The bowl was certified the next year.[4]

Municipal competition for baseball's spring training camps goes back to the early 1900s (Seymour 1971, 131). For years, Florida has served as the spring home of eighteen of twenty-six major league franchises, seven others being located in Arizona. After World War II, many Northerners migrated South to live, and states like Florida experienced boom years. New communities were formed almost overnight. Many became convinced that the six week's worth of activity and publicity provided by a training camp might be worth spending public monies to secure. New communities aspiring to growth and seeking to establish an identity for themselves, many of them already relying heavily on tourist dollars—must now offer the kind of deal that Charlotte County, Florida, did to the Texas Rangers: in return for a ten-year lease the county would acquire an eighty-two-acre plot of land, and build a five-thousand seat stadium and a state-of-the-art training complex, which the team would lease at nominal cost. The county would maintain and operate the facility. The small town of Port St. Lucie, on the east Florida coast, lured the New York Mets from St. Petersburg by building a training complex for the franchise, complete with a diamond (one of six) to the exact specifications of Shea Stadium. A farm team for the Mets uses the stadium when practice season is over. The clubhouse features a doctor's office, a twenty-seat conference room, an audiovisual room, a full kitchen, a spacious sauna, and a sunken whirlpool.

While college bowl games, spring training camps, and annual events like the U.S. Open Tennis Championships are attractive prizes for a city to land, a major league franchise is the most eagerly sought after. Professional sport teams are ideal for putting a city "on the map." The pursuit of a major league franchise is "nearly impossible for any [city] official to resist" (Johnson 1982, 218).[5] Today, this pursuit will entail the use of huge public subsidies as bait. For example, in 1972, the City of Arlington, Texas, agreed to pay Washington Senators owner Robert Short $7.5 million in return for ten years of local media rights if he would bring his baseball team to Texas and rename it the Rangers. This, together with stadium and infrastructural improvements, came to $28.5 million, which, with interest on a ten-year bond issue, brought the city's investment in the Texas Rangers to $44.3 million. The maximum revenues the city could ever have derived were $22 million. In the end, Arlington sold the facility to the Rangers, who assumed the low-interest bond payments (Rosentraub 1988). Already home to an NFL franchise, the Louisiana Superdome Authority in New Orleans became desperately anxious to attract a baseball team. It offered organized baseball the Superdome rent-free up to the first 1.2 million spectators in any given year, admitting that no franchise could afford the sum that would have to be charged to break even on the running costs of the building (U.S. Congress, House, Select Committee on Professional Sports 1976, 496). Superdome officials described the building as a "capital investment in the tourism and convention industry." To attract the St. Louis Cardinals, the city of Phoenix offered the NFL franchise $17 million in ticket and concession incentives, and a guarantee to build sixty glass-enclosed skyboxes, a diamond-vision scoreboard, two thousand more seats as part of a six-story office building in the stadium, and a $5 million practice and training facility. The Cardinals moved in 1987. To lure the Raiders away from Oakland, the Los Angeles Coliseum provided the Raiders with, among other things, a $6.5 million loan, deferred rents, and full rights to $8.25 million a year from rentals of luxury box seats built at city expense. The "loan" was actually a gift, because repayment was deferred and took the form of a commission on future ticket sales so low as to fail to cover the interest on the loan.

Faced with this kind of competition, cities already hosting major league franchises were forced to defend themselves. Although New York City officials were unable to prevent the move of the Dodgers and Giants to California or the NFL's Giants and Jets to nearby New Jersey, they were determined not to lose the Mets or the Yankees, especially the latter. In the 1970s and 1980s, major corporations began leaving the city in great numbers because of the high cost of living and fear of crime. The city government began making increasingly attractive offers to corporations to induce them to stay.[6] Thus, when Yankees owner George Steinbrenner began making noises about leaving the city, the city council was quick to urge upon him a new thirty-year lease and, as an inducement, undertook to build a new thirty-two-hundred space parking garage and a new railroad station and to install twenty-four luxury boxes in Yankee stadium, the cost of which Steinbrenner could pay back over a twelve-year period.

New York thus joined the long list of cities blackmailed by sport franchise owners into increasing their stadium subsidies. In 1971, the Minnesota Vikings threatened to move to Phoenix, sparking a long legislative battle that culminated in 1979 with the State of Minnesota's agreeing to build them a new stadium (completed in 1984). When the Philadelphia Eagles threatened to leave their city, city officials agreed to add fifty luxury boxes to Veteran's Stadium and defer the six-hundred-thousand-dollar annual rent for an undisclosed number of years. It also undertook to improve practice facilities, aid promotions, and provide free game security. In return, the club signed a lease extended to the year 2011. The city of St. Louis reacted to talk of the baseball Cardinals' leaving in 1986 with a promise to build a new hundred-million-dollar stadium. In 1988, the Chicago White Sox, which had been playing baseball in Chicago since 1901, threatened to move to St. Petersburg in response to an offer from the governor of Florida of a new domed stadium (having already made efforts to move out to the suburb of Addison). The governor of Illinois had to counter-offer with a revised lease on a new stadium that would save the club over sixty million over ten years (Scully 1989, 144). Perhaps the most extreme measures were those taken by Pittsburgh in 1986, when the city sold twenty-million-dollars' worth of bonds to keep the Pittsburgh Pirates from leaving town. The money was lent to a consortium of nine corporations and four wealthy individuals, who had bought the financially troubled baseball franchise. The city thus became mort-gagee not only of the facilities used by the club but of the club itself. Overall, these maneuvers shifted the funding of sports infrastructure from the private to the public sphere. By 1988, 80 percent of all facili-ties used by major league sport teams were publicly owned (Riess 1989, 239).

The bidding war for franchises tended to pit newer, prodevelop-ment cities against older, more democratically run communities. Cities in the South, Southwest, and West, such as Atlanta, Houston, Dallas, San Antonio, Phoenix, Los Angeles, Miami, and San Diego were espe-cially well adapted to more open competition because they had weaker public sectors, fewer calls for public accountability, an unorga-nized working class, and a far stronger military influence. Their goal was to encourage growth, rather than regulate it. They were not dis-turbed by the fact, commonly acknowledged, that the sports business mainly benefited developers, financiers, and realtors, rather than the average citizen, who could only be expected to enjoy its benefits as they "trickled down." In contrast, the older cities were dominated by local Democratic party officials, labor unions, and urban planners, who were reluctant to spend public money on building new stadia, es-pecially at the expense of housing. Without their support, private de-velopment was virtually impossible. Typically, inner-city land would be owned by many different people, who would hike the price if news of redevelopment leaked out. Without aggressive use of government requisition powers, private development in the center of the older cities was impossible. Walter O'Malley, for example, had made some ef-forts to keep the Dodgers in Brooklyn, being prepared to purchase land and construct a new stadium; but he needed the cooperation of the city government—not to build him a stadium but to condemn pri-vate land, compensate original owners, and then sell the property to the Dodgers (N. Sullivan 1987, 57). The city, reluctant to undertake this effort, did offer to build a multipurpose sport center of which the Dodgers would be a principal tenant; but O'Malley declined the offer.

The "liberal" New Yorkers balked at using eminent domain powers to acquire land necessary to build the stadium that would keep the Dodgers, while the more politically conservative, prodevelopment Los Angeles, staunchly opposed to using land for public housing, readily agreed to build a stadium instead. The prodevelopment *Los Angeles Times* urged its readers to support the stadium initiative:

> Do you, a citizen voter, want Los Angeles to be a great city, with common interests and the civic unity which gives great cities character, or are you content to let it continue its degeneration into a geographical bundle of self-centered sections each fighting with the others for the lion's share of the revenues and improvements that belong to all? (quoted in N. Sullivan 1987, 159)

During the referendum on the bond issue necessary to finance the stadium, city fathers promised that the new stadium would serve "the little people." Ironically, a Los Angeles County superior court judge declared the city's contract with the Dodgers (approved in the public referendum) invalid, on grounds that public funds could not be used to benefit the Dodgers, a private corporation. The decision was overturned by the state's supreme court on grounds that the financial windfall that would accrue to the Dodgers was "incidental."

Older cities were thus poorly equipped to compete with the eager newcomers in the Sunbelt. This is well illustrated in the case of Baltimore, a old city with a long-established sport tradition. In March 1983, Baltimore Colts owner Robert Irsay, unhappy with poor attendances at his team's home games and openly searching for more appreciative customers, found himself in the enviable position of being courted by three different cities. In order to keep the NFL franchise in Baltimore, the city was prepared to spend $7.5 million on stadium improvements; give Irsay a ten-year loan of $15 million; subsidize his payments on that loan to the tune of $500,000 a year; grant him $4.4 million in cash and $2.2 million in industrial revenue bonds; and guarantee the sale of at least forty-three thousand tickets per game for the duration of the lease. When Irsay complained that Baltimore's blue law prohibiting games from beginning before 2:00 P.M. was hurting the franchise by preventing it from being the East Coast game on Sunday afternoon television, the law was changed. Donald Schaefer, Mayor of Baltimore, explained to Congress:

> We got it changed. We got the cooperation with the community, we got cooperation with the churches, we got the cooperation of the Governor, we got the cooperation of the legislature, the city council, everyone. And I personally said to the communities: This is necessary. He [Irsay] wants it changed. It was changed for him. For him. (U.S. Congress, House, Committee on Energy and Commerce 1985a, 37)

Schaefer had every right to be bitter because he had staked his own political fortunes on keeping the franchise in Balitmore. Working with the governor of Maryland and successive presidents to funnel money into Baltimore's urban renewal, he had "helped Baltimore rediscover a sense of urban identity" (J. Miller 1990, 199). Professional sports played an important part in his strategy. Schaefer's problem was that Phoenix was meanwhile offering Irsay a $15 million loan at 8 percent interest with no payment of the principal for ten years, free stadium rent for up to twenty years, and an agreement to underwrite the Colts in any year that gate receipts dropped below $7 million. Indianapolis, the only one of the three with a brand-new luxury-box-equipped stadium, was offering a ten-year, $12.5 million loan at 8 percent interest; a $2.5 million line of credit; a brand-new $4 million training facility; the first $500,000 of luxury-box income for the first twelve years; half the suite income thereafter; exclusive rights to sell programs and novelties; and a guarantee of $7 million in ticket income for the first twelve years (Harris 1986, 605).

Irsay sold himself to the highest bidder, and Baltimore was left with the Orioles as sole tenants of Memorial Stadium. Even then, the city could not rest. The city government came under pressure again when a more aggressive owner, Edward Bennet Williams, began to threaten to move the Orioles if stadium improvements were not made. Several Florida cities made attractive offers to him. In 1989, Schaefer, now governor of Maryland, got the Maryland State Assembly to approve the construction of a new two-hundred-million-dollar stadium in downtown Baltimore for the exclusive use of the Orioles. The stadium opened in 1992.

City officials felt manipulated and demeaned by sport franchise owners. The Oakland City Council engaged in long and often acrimonious negotiations with Al Davis (owner of the NFL's Raiders) over the Oakland Coliseum lease. Faced with the alternative of losing the Raiders, city officials felt they had little choice but to continue to meet Davis's escalating demands. When, in February 1980, the city finally made its last move, a young attorney from the Oakland firm of Crosby, Heafy, Roach, and May attempted to deliver the Coliseum's formal written offer. The document was some twenty-pages long and the attorney took it to the Raiders' office. Al LoCasale [Davis's attorney] refused to accept the twenty pages and told the attorney to taken them away with him. Instead, the attorney left the document on the counter. At that point, according to Al Davis, LoCasale grabbed the document and came over to the counter, demanding that the young attorney take it back. When LoCasale chased him into the parking lot and he still refused to take it back, Al Davis's principal assistant flung the lease offer on the asphalt and left it there (Harris 1986, 425). Oakland's foe was not really Davis but the city of Los Angeles, which was trying to get him to move south. Davis's power derived from the competition between the cities bidding for the economic bounty his franchise was expected to provide.[7]

As if competition between cities were not enough, rivalry also sprang up between cities and suburbs. Politically independent suburbs discovered that they could function as more than "bedroom communities": they could attract offices and shopping malls, too, and thus increase their revenues. Why not also prospect for sport franchises?

While city-center populations were growing, an attractive downtown ballpark was as important to a franchise as a television contract would be today: it could mean the difference between profit and loss.[8] But the central city concentration of population and employment peaked as early as 1919 in New York and a number of other cities. By the time of the economic boom that followed the declaration of peace in 1945, the trickle of jobs and people from the inner cities to the suburbs had become a flood. As whites left the city centers, blacks moved in (Mollenkopf 1983, 23). The type of people attending the game also changed. Baseball parks ceased to be largely a male preserve (an often rowdy clientele) and began to attract more affluent family groups. These new customers demanded safer and more comfortable amenities. Cities unable to provide them risked having their sport franchises lured away by communities near enough to keep the loyal fan but far away enough to offer new stadia, plentiful parking, and a safer environment. The deal struck by the Dallas Cowboys with the city of Irving, Texas, is typical of this kind of arrangement and "influenced the standards of rewards and control in the superstadium for years to come" (Harris 1986, 31). In return for their short trip from downtown Dallas, the Cowboys were given complete management control of the new stadium even though its construction had been financed through the sale of government-backed thirty-five-year bonds. The contract for the construction of the stadium was awarded to J. W. Bateson Company, owned by the Murchison brothers, one of whom, Clint, also owned the Cowboys. The contract to sell concessions at the stadium went to the Cebe Corporation, a subsidiary of the Cowboys, while the exclusive right to sell liquor at the stadium went to the Cowboys Stadium Club. The insurance contract was purchased from another Murchison company. By offering similar inducements, Anaheim stole the Rams from Los Angeles; Pontiac, the Lions from Detroit; Rutherford, the Giants and Jets from New York; and Orchard Park, the Bills from Buffalo.

City officials especially resented being bid up in the competition for franchises, because they believed that much of the value of a sport franchise was bestowed by the city itself. Each franchise was quasi-public property. The mayor of Kansas City, Richard Berkley, elaborated on the contract implied in the relation between a city and a franchise, seeking to make the point that a sport team was not just any other business the city was anxious to keep:

Professional sport leagues are a unique form of business. On one level, they sell entertainment, but they also sell civic identity, emotion and community involvement. The name *Kansas City* Chiefs says it all. The Chiefs belong to the fans and the community of Kansas City. We support the team. We share the glory of their victories. We share the bitterness of their defeats. It is because we, the citizens of Kansas City, share so much with our team that we have been willing and will continue to be willing to make the public investments in stadia and other projects to provide the teams with the facilities which are necessary to operate. (U.S. Congress, Senate, Committee on the Judiciary 1983a, 161)[9]

Not only were the owners holding cities hostage, but they were hypocritically ignoring the very claims to public trust that they found convenient to make on other occasions. City officials were aware of the fact that the supply of franchises was in part a result of state actions in the past, actions undertaken to protect the game in the national interest. The structure of the market for franchises had been created in something like a partnership between state and industry. Ending the bidding war would require a revision of the terms of that partnership. City officials and their representatives thus turned to Congress for help.

COLLECTIVE AUTHORITY
BEGINS TO CRUMBLE

The whole question of the right of a club owner to move his franchise in search of higher profits would have been moot had the governance structure of professional sports remained intact during this period. No matter how rapidly sports expanded, and no matter how intensely cities competed to host major league clubs, the supply and location of franchises would not have become a matter of political debate had the owners abided by the agreements they had forged earlier to control the supply of franchises and allocate them by mutual agreement. But in the boom years of professional sports in the 1970s, the owners became greedy and their solidarity began to crumble. A desire to exploit opportunities in other markets led enough of them to ignore, or challenge, league rules restricting the right of owners to relocate at will. Even this would not have been enough to spark Congressional debate had it not been for the fact that much of the owners' ability to govern themselves rested on prior agreements with Congress itself. Congress and the courts had legitimated the rules determining the conditions of ownership in the sports business. But now the owners, or at least some of them, wished to rewrite these rules without Congressional approval, or ignore the rules when their interests would be served by doing so.

The issue of franchise location strikes at the very heart of a league's authority to maintain itself as an economic enterprise. The essence of a league—amateur or professional—is its ability to decide which teams are qualified to play and the manner of their participation. The "product" that professional sports sell is entertainment, created by competing teams of relatively evenly matched aggregates of athletes, the purpose being to determine a champion for each season. To manufacture this product certain rules designed to ensure competitive equality and stable schedules are necessary. One of the most important of these rules is that each team in the league is assigned an *exclusive franchise* to conduct league contests within some specific geographical area. In baseball, the National League established the exclusive area of each club as the city limits of the franchise's location plus ten miles in all directions. The American League set a boundary of one hundred miles. The NFL's area is the city plus a seventy-five-mile radius. The NHL sets its franchise area at fifty miles, while the NBA has no space restriction.

The rights of the franchisee are protected by rules governing the sale and transfer of franchises, the creation of new franchises, and the movement of franchises between geographical areas. In a very important respect, each franchise is constituted by these rules and would have little foundation (and less profitability) without them. For this reason, most leagues have rules prohibiting the location of a franchise in a city that already has a league team unless that team gives its permission. A team wishing to relocate must gain the approval of the other teams. New franchises must pay "entrance fees." The price for one of the new baseball franchises, only 40 percent of which, beginning in 1993, can be financed, is ninety-five million dollars, under league rules. Even teams moving with permission might have to pay an "indemnity fee" to the team upon whose territory they encroach.

The property rights of baseball owners were sanctioned by the 1922 Supreme Court decision granting immunity to baseball from antitrust prosecution. This is important, because the "state's presence as an actor in the initial selection of a new governance regime lends a certain legitimacy and, therefore, stability to it" (Campbell and Lindberg 1990, 642). The justices' decision, absent any congressional contradiction, bestowed a collective authority on the baseball owners to regulate entry into the industry and to carve up the market for customers between them. All owners had to agree to a move before it could take place. The same "governance mechanism" for defining and regulating the market was adopted by football, hockey, and basketball owners, albeit without specific state sanction.

In the interwar years, the collective authority of the owners to regulate franchise placement was rarely questioned. There were no franchise additions in baseball between 1922 and 1953, and no serious rival leagues appeared. The more fragile football, hockey, and basketball leagues, far from seeking to limit entries, devoted most of their energies to stabilizing those they had. Signs of change began to appear in 1951, during an investigation of baseball conducted by the House Judiciary Committee. Although the chief focus of the investigation was the reserve clause, baseball's monopoly position inevitably came up for discussion. Seeking to appear less like monopolies, both baseball leagues changed their decision rule for franchise relocation from consensus to a three-quarters majority. Subsequently, the Boston Braves moved to Milwaukee in 1953, the St. Louis Browns moved to Baltimore (Orioles) in the same year, and the Philadelphia Athletics became a Kansas City franchise in 1954. A further set of House Judiciary Committee hearings, sparked by the departure of the Giants and Dodgers for California in 1957, gave tacit approval to the new rule on approving franchise movements.

In 1965, organized baseball approved the move of the Braves once more, from Milwaukee to Atlanta, to take advantage of a low-rent public stadium and a bigger television market. The rules on franchise movement again came under public scrutiny. Wisconsin senator William Proxmire tried to prevent the move by ending baseball's antitrust exemption (in the professional sports antitrust act) or, failing that, by getting baseball to share television revenues so that larger markets (like Atlanta) would not be able to lure franchises away from smaller markets (like Milwaukee) (U.S. Congress, Senate, Committee on Commerce 1965a). In 1966, when it was clear Proxmire's legislative efforts would be fruitless, the city of Milwaukee brought suit against the league, arguing that *approval* of the move violated the Sherman Act. The court had to remind the plaintiffs that baseball was immune from antitrust prosecution. More significantly, perhaps, the move caused one of the owners to "break ranks" and challenge league authority. Kansas City Athletics owner, Charles Finley, threatened to sue the league because he had been hoping to occupy Atlanta himself. He was assuaged with a move to a new stadium in Oakland.

While baseball was by no means politically invulnerable on the franchise location issue (many congressmen were angry that baseball had not sustained a franchise in the nation's capital), its rules of ownership seemed to be more secure than those of other sports not specifically included in the 1922 Supreme Court decision. While debating these issues, congressmen were quite likely to call for more accountability from football and basketball with respect to franchise location, threatening antitrust action for failure to comply while simultaneously defending the exemption granted baseball and allowing baseball owners more autonomy from government oversight (U.S. Congress, Senate, Committee on the Judiciary 1983a, 335).[10]

Rebellious owners in the football and basketball leagues could thus anticipate more state support for their rights of ownership than could owners of baseball franchises. This is clearly demonstrated in the case of the Oakland Raiders' move to Los Angeles. The dispute between the NFL and the Oakland Raiders was in many ways a symbolic fight for authority between an individual owner, Al Davis, and the representative of collective authority, Commissioner Rozelle; but it was much more than this. After all, fights between egotistical owners and stubborn commissioners were common in baseball: Davis had his counterpart in Charles Finley. But the governance regime in football was less securely mandated. It was much more likely in football than in baseball that a conflict of this intensity would occur, and that the outcome would be a victory for the owner.[11] The details of the case are worth examining for the light they throw on the politics of franchise location.

Ironically, the seeds of the dispute were cast by a decision to *approve* the move of the Los Angeles Rams to a new stadium in nearby Anaheim. The Los Angeles Coliseum, bereft of a tenant, inquired of the NFL whether an expansion club might soon be available. Not receiving a satisfactory reply, the coliseum sued the NFL in order to obtain a declaration that the NFL's rule requiring unanimous consent before a team could be placed in another club's home territory was an unlawful restraint of trade by the terms of the Sherman Act. The suit was dismissed as premature, since no team had as yet committed itself to move to Los Angeles. Sensing trouble, the NFL changed its movement approval rule to require a three-quarters, rather than a unanimous, vote in favor.

Soon thereafter, Al Davis, the Oakland Raiders' managing general partner, commenced negotiations with the Los Angeles Coliseum Commission. In 1966, the Raiders and the Oakland-Alameda Coliseum Commission had entered into a license agreement calling for the Raiders to play their home games in the Oakland Coliseum for five years. The Raiders were granted options to renew the agreement for as many as five additional five-year periods. The Raiders proved to be a highly successful franchise. At the end of the third extension, the Raiders decided against another renewal clause because they were no longer satisfied with the facilities. Negotiations were held with the Oakland Coliseum Commission, but an alternative accord could not be arranged. On December 31, 1979, the licensing agreement formally expired. Subsequent proposals were to no avail; and on February 4, 1980, negotiations irreparably broke down.

In March 1980, Davis and the Los Angeles Coliseum signed an agreement for the relocation of the Raiders in Los Angeles. Following the announcement of his intentions at an NFL owners' meeting, the owners voted twenty-two-to-zero to deny Davis permission to move, with five abstaining. Upon learning of Davis's determination to consummate the move, the league (in *Philadelphia Eagles v. Oakland Raiders*) charged Davis with breach of contract and requested that he be restrained from moving. In a countermove, the Los Angeles Coliseum Commission, joined by the Raiders, renewed its suit against the NFL. The Coliseum Commission contended that any opposition to the Raiders' move would be anticompetitive. For the Coliseum Commission, the relocation rule interfered in the competition among stadiums to obtain football clubs as tenants. The NFL had created a cartel among stadiums of which it was an unwilling member. The NFL counterargued that it was a single economic entity with a unitary product and therefore could not enter into a conspiracy to commit antitrust violations.

The Raiders and the Coliseum Commission initially argued the case on substantive grounds. No economic harm had been done to the league by the Raiders' move to Los Angeles, because, in approving the move of the Los Angeles Rams twenty-five miles to Anaheim by a unanimous vote, the owners had created space for a new franchise to enter without injuring them. The owners denied that the Rams had relocated. They had simply moved to a newer stadium within the same metropolitan area. The outcome of the case, however, would not depend on substantive, but on technical, arguments. What was the nature of the market in which the National Football League operated, and what was the legal status of the league itself in this market?

The first trial, in 1981, resulted in a hung jury. In a second trial, after the court concluded as a matter of law that the league was not a "single entity" but, rather, was made up of twenty-eight separate business units exercising independent business judgments in significant areas of individual concern, the jury returned a verdict in favor of the plaintiffs on their antitrust claims and the court issued a permanent injunction against the NFL for any interference with the Raiders' transfer.[12]

An appeals court subsequently rejected the NFL's argument that it was a "single entity," on the grounds that each franchise retained control over entrepreneurial issues. Each team, said the court, was separately owned and had complete control over ticket prices, marketing strategy, and personnel recruitment. Some revenues are shared, but not all. Finally, the court concluded, the vote concerning franchise location reflected the individual interests of existing franchise owners, not necessarily the common good. The justices expanded on this last point: the rule requiring three-quarters approval of a move was too restrictive, and the criteria used to determine the appropriateness of the move, too vague. They intimated that restrictions on franchise movement could be justified on a "rule of reason" basis if the criteria were "objective" and if the majority were a simple one.

The chief reason that the NFL lost the case was its failure to persuade the court that it was a single entity, rather than a cartel comprised of independent firms. The question of the relation between the franchise and the community was very much germane to this deliberation. The determination was made on the basis of a definition of the market in which professional football operated. The NFL took the position that the product market in which it competed was the entire entertainment market, throughout the United States. For this reason, the NFL had long prohibited cross ownership of sport franchises: owners were not permitted to own franchises in other sports, because it might involve a conflict of interest on the part of the individual owner. The implication was that football competed with basketball, baseball, hockey, soccer, and the like. This was consistent with the NFL's position that it was a joint venture competing for the entertainment dollar with other sports. The Raiders argued that the market in question was for NFL football in Southern California (the coliseum argued that it was for stadia offering their facilities to NFL teams in the United States). The court seemed to accept the Raiders' definition of the market, whereas in the *Seals* case the court had used a much wider definition of the market, perhaps because the court saw hockey as much more exchangeable than football; that is, the court could imagine that hockey as a whole must compete with other sports and other entertainment possibilities. The court in the Raiders case had difficulty thinking of football as exchangeable; it was itself an industry, and the franchises were firms competing within it. The NFL could not therefore be a "single entity," as it claimed. It did not help the NFL case that the rival USFL was active at the time the decision was handed down, for this inspired the court to exaggerate the independence each franchise owner enjoyed. The owner could at any time (the court declared) leave the NFL and "play" in the USFL.

The loss in the Raiders' case was a major blow to the collective authority of all the professional sport leagues. Simultaneous developments in basketball indicated a broad shift in state policy toward franchise location rules. In 1984, the Clippers franchise of the National Basketball Association announced its intention of moving from San Diego to Los Angeles. The other NBA owners permitted the move but sued for a declaration that they were entitled to twenty-five million dollar compensation from the Clippers for the difference in value between the San Diego franchise and a second (more valuable) Los Angeles franchise. A district court granted summary judgment for the Clippers, dismissing the league's complaint. While the Ninth Circuit Court reversed this judgment and seemed to vindicate the NBA, federal district court judge Leland Nelson reconfirmed the district court's ruling and found for the Clippers in 1986. The case was eventually settled out of court. In return for being allowed by the NBA to remain in Los Angeles, the Clippers sacrificed their share of the entry-fee revenues from the NBA's 1988 expansion, about three million dollars (Noll 1991, 34). In both football and basketball, then, the freedom of movement of the individual owner was increased in relation to the collective authority of the rest.[13]

THE DEBATE IN CONGRESS

The parties to the franchise location debate aligned themselves with respect to how the property rights of the individual owners were to be defined. Some owners, city officials, and state actors (and most owners) wanted to strengthen the governance mechanism controlling franchise movement, making it more difficult for individual owners to relocate at will and for cities to lure them. Some owners, city officials, and state actors (and most players) thought that the rights of individual owners should be strengthened, permitting greater freedom of movement for individual owners and opening up the market for more cities to enter. Another group wanted to shift property rights from the private to the public domain and subject professional team sports to more state regulation, making the relocation decision more publicly accountable.

These positions did not reflect any coherent political vision, nor did they represent party platforms. The politics of franchise location were inevitably parochial. They resembled the kind of pork-barrel politics in which congressmen fight with each other (but occasionally conspire) to land defense contracts for businesses in their district. Legislative action of any kind was most likely to be initiated by congressmen whose districts had a direct vested interest in the issue. Congressional alliances were ad hoc and fragile.

Returning Power to the Leagues

The task facing congressmen interested in shoring up the leagues' governance regime was to sanction the leagues' own relocation rules without violating other state policies, such as those intended to protect market freedoms. For example, one of the earliest congressional bills, introduced in 1980 (the major league sports community protection act), would have defined sport leagues as "de facto single economic entities," thereby insulating relocation rules from antitrust challenge. This bill would have allowed community interests to override individual owners' desire to move but would have permitted the league to approve relocation.

The early policy of the NFL owners was to trade on congressional concern about franchise location to get the same antitrust immunity for football as that enjoyed by baseball. To get their point across, they retained the services of nine lobbying firms and contributed to the campaign chests of senators thought to be sympathetic to their position on the trust laws (Harris 1986, 539). They discovered that the many congressmen, state politicians and municipal authorities already hosting NFL franchises drew great comfort from the league rules on franchise stability. This presented the commissioner with a weapon he could use, because he could always threaten to relax these rules and create chaos.

With the defeat in the Raiders' case, however, the NFL went on the defensive. It was no longer so confident of its control over individual owners. The commissioner had to be much more circumspect about imposing his authority, lest he run afoul of antitrust law once more. To curry favor with Congress, he revised the league's procedures for approving franchise moves, so as to make them appear more "reasonable" and less monopolistic. In December 1984, he announced that henceforth, owners wishing to relocate had to file data with the commissioner's office justifying the move on economic grounds. These data would include comparisons of the franchise's home revenues with league averages, ticket sales projections, information on the new site, and an estimation of the effects of the move on other teams' travel expenses. Also called for were a copy of the existing lease, audited financial statements for the preceding four years, a financial analysis of the new lease, and a projection of the profits and losses for the next three years in the new location.

To buttress his authority, Commissioner Rozelle supported legislative initiatives such as the 1985 bill (the sports community protection and stability act), which offered immunity to the league in return for the assurance that *some* kind of objective standards would be used to determine franchise moves, the precise standards being left to the owners to determine. The bill, sponsored by Senator Dennis DeConcini, proposed to leave the task of running sports to "the business men and women" who make their living from it. DeConcini's views were typical of those sympathetic to the league's position. He did not favor a "government solution" to the problem, least of all one that involved "government regulating sports." On the other hand, he was not comfortable with the idea of sports teams gravitating toward "big metropolitan markets where owners might reap financial bonanzas"; to prevent it, he was willing to allow revenue sharing, which would require immunity from antitrust laws (U.S. Congress, Senate, Committee on the Judiciary 1986a, 34).

DeConcini was a senator from Arizona, a sparsely settled state, which, if it was ever to attract an NFL franchise (which it eventually did in 1987, when the St. Louis Cardinals moved to Phoenix), would rely very much on shared television revenues, as did franchises like the Green Bay Packers. It is not without significance that the DeConcini bill would have *required* the NFL to expand in exchange for its immunity, while another bill sponsored by Senator Eagleton (Missouri), contained no such requirement. Eagleton was more worried about the *flight* of teams (e.g., St. Louis Cardinals, Kansas City Kings) than about attracting new teams. In the DeConcini bill, the NFL saw a way of preserving its status as a private enterprise while at the same time securing some protection from the laws that would typically apply to other businesses. In short, the legislation would have moved the league closer to the status of a joint venture.

The politicians most active in trying to shore up relocation rules during the 1980s were from California, Missouri, and Maryland—homes of the Raiders, Cardinals, and Colts, respectively. Eagleton (Missouri), Mathias (Maryland), Sarbanes (Maryland), Stark (California), Mikulski (Maryland), Specter (Pennsylvania, worried about the Eagles), and Edwards (California) figured prominently. Mikulski, testifying on behalf of her professional sports franchise community protection act proudly proclaimed, "Mine is a Baltimore bill" (U.S. Congress, House, Committee on Energy and Commerce 1985a, 231). Mikulski's robust defense of Baltimore's interest conveniently overlooked the fact that both the Colts and the Orioles had been "stolen" from other cities—Dallas and St. Louis, respectively. Senator Rudy Boschwitz (Minnesota) "made it no secret" that his interest in the legislation was motivated by fear that the Minnesota Twins would depart for Tampa (U.S. Congress, Senate, Committee on Commerce, Science, and Transportation 1984, 19). In the absence of any governing principles, the tug of a constituency's interests could occasion bewildering changes of position. Charles Mathias (Maryland) originally opposed those 1983 bills containing a retroactive clause (aimed at restoring the Raiders to Oakland after they had left for Los Angeles) on grounds of unconstitutionality. By the time the professional sports team community protection act of 1984 (which also contained a retroactive clause) came to be considered, Mathias had changed his mind: "Times have changed. The situation has worsened. The Colts have left Baltimore. And right now just a little bit of retroactivity would suit me just fine" (p. 23).

Commissioner Rozelle cleverly used the competition between cities to play on the fears of congressmen and legitimate league power. He explained that the league had stopped expanding because franchise movements had made life too unpredictable. Franchise location had become a zero-sum game: if one city won, another was bound to lose. This argument was calculated to strike fear into the hearts of congressmen with unstable franchises in their area. They would become even more anxious if the league seemed to be losing its control over individual owners. For example, Senator Russell Long (Louisiana) had reason to be worried about the future of the New Orleans Saints, a losing team throughout the 1970s, especially as they were the principal tenant in a heavily indebted Superdome.

> LONG: Now, if people there want to protect their own interest, they would want you to be in a position that you could act in their behalf to keep the faith rather than be without any right to do justice as far as the league is concerned.

> ROZELLE: Yes, sir. (U.S. Congress, Senate, Committee on Commerce, Science, and Transportation 1984, 90).

Rozelle left conservatives like Long with an unsavory alternative: erect a federal regulatory body to govern the movement of franchises or give the league itself more power to do so.

Even the Reagan administration, ardent supporter of free enterprise, concluded that municipal competition for sport franchises was getting out of hand and spoke in favor of strengthening the authority of the commissioner. Charles Rule, spokesman for the Justice Department, testified that "a league's franchise relocation rule should be deemed per se lawful, unless it adversely affects competition with other leagues or is merely a subterfuge to disguise some other egregious anticompetitive conduct" (U.S. Congress, Senate, Committee on the Judiciary 1986a, 390). This represented a change of policy since the hearings before the House Select Committee on Professional Sports in 1976, when Justice Department officials declared that team transfer issues were a purely private affair and had nothing to do with the antitrust laws.

Creating a Free Market for Franchises

Congressmen representing districts without franchises were more likely to *oppose* restrictions on movements and to favor giving more liberties to individual owners. In the early 1980s, Senator Frank Lautenberg (New Jersey) spoke out against restrictions because they would prevent the movement of the New York Jets to the Meadowlands. When placed in the position of supplicant, congressmen found the owners' collective authority irksome and unfathomable. In 1977, when rumors were rife that the Giants would leave San Francisco, Senator Russell Long called Commissioner Kuhn, urging that the franchise be assigned to New Orleans, promising that he "could help baseball in Washington" (Kuhn 1987, 249).[14]

The players, through their union representatives, also opposed strenghtening the commissioner's powers. The football players' association opposed "community protection" bills as "private special legislation for the sole benefit of the sports entrepreneurs" (U.S. Congress, Senate, Committee on the Judiciary 1986a, 85). The unions had always been vigilant in opposing any attempt by owners to have their league declared a joint venture, for this would prevent a player from ever being able to resort to the courts to prohibit the league from imposing restrictions on player movements (U.S. Congress, Senate, Committee on the Judiciary 1983, 89). If the league were truly a joint venture, they asked, why did the franchises seem to be unable to amass and provide financial data for Congress to peruse? The unions saw, perhaps more clearly than Congress itself, that "community protection" legislation would not have been needed in the first place had Congress not tacitly approved the antitrust exemption. No scarcity of franchises would mean less competition for them.

Government Regulation

While some politicians wished to strengthen the hand of the league over individual owners and others wished to empower the owners in relation to the league, a third group sought a solution in closer public regulation of franchise movements. The idea was to strengthen the collective authority of the league statutorily in return for more public accountability. In 1980, Senator Warren Magnuson introduced a bill (S3183) that became the prototype for the restrictive variety of franchise relocation legislation. Under his bill, a team would be prohibited from relocating unless it gave the locality one year's advance notice and showed that (1) any party to a stadium lease agreement had materially failed to comply with the provisions in the lease, (2) the stadium in which the team played was inadequate and stadium authorities evidenced no intent to remedy the inadequacies, or (3) the teams had incurred a continuous loss of income for the three preceding years.

The first bill aimed at more public accountability to be reported out of a congressional committee was Slade Gorton's professional sports team community protection act of 1984. Gorton, a Republican Senator from Washington who had been involved as a lawyer in the dispute over the move of the Seattle Pilots to Milwaukee, felt that Congress needed to get involved in the location issue because the market for franchises was "so heavily tilted in favor of team owners," rather than cities. This, he reasoned, was "in large measure attributable to a series of congressional manipulations of the free market" (Gorton 1985, 2). His and other franchise movement bills introduced in the Ninety-Fourth Congress died.

A very similar bill, the professional sports community protection act of 1985, was introduced by Senator Eagleton into the next Congress and also made it out of the Senate Commerce Committee. The bill offered the National Football League the immunity it sought with respect to control over franchise relocations but, in return, asked the NFL to draft procedures for ruling on a proposed move and establish criteria by which a decision on the move should be made. The bill even went so far as to suggest what some of these criteria should be, such as "the adequacy of such member club's existing stadium or arena in relation to other stadiums or arenas within such league" and "the extent to which fan support for such member club has been demonstrated by attendance, ticket sales, and other factors." And it specified that the league's decision to deny relocation should be subject to judicial review by a federal district court. Eagleton's bill also included what might be considered a "due process" clause, no doubt inspired by the midnight departure of the Colts from Baltimore to Indianapolis. It specified that before applying the relocation rule in a particular case, the league had to conduct proceedings at which "interested parties" would be afforded an opportunity to present oral or written testimony. The NFL at first supported the Eagleton bill but quickly withdrew when it was amended and reported out of committee. As amended, the bill did not give the NFL the retroactivity clause it needed to force the Raiders and Colts to return to their original cities (Wong 1985, 68).

The professional sports team community protection act, introduced by Slade Gorton, also in 1985, would have gone even further in state control of franchise movements. It prohibited team movements in any sport unless the move was found to be "necessary and appropriate" by both its league and an ad hoc, three-person arbitration board. Both the league and the board would have to consider nine criteria listed in the bill, similar to those found in Eagleton's. If the board found the relocation to be necessary and appropriate, it would then consider whether any offer that would retain the team had a value greater than, or equal to the proposed relocation; if it did, the board would disapprove the relocation. This "regulatory" approach would have entirely circumvented the antitrust laws. Not surprisingly, the NFL did not see this as the most appropriate solution to its problems. Rozelle spoke scathingly of the Gorton bill: "We view the regulatory and arbitration board provisions of S.287 as further emasculating professional sports leagues in their efforts to deal responsibly with team location issues, and we view the governmentally forced expansion provisions of that bill as unwarranted in economic, legal, practical and policy terms" (U.S. Congress, Senate, Committee on Commerce, Science, and Transportation 1985, 76). The league's critics refused to accept Rozelle's argument that regulation would deny private property rights, pointing out that in joining the league, each franchise owner *voluntarily* surrendered his right to move except with the consent of other owners in the league. Rozelle and the owners were not persuaded. They could not see their interests being served by any bill that left them as exposed to antitrust litigation as before.

Congressmen pushing more public accountability by the industry received little support from Reagan's Justice Department. Spokesman Charles Rule did not favor the idea of an arbitration board, "a new and unique regulatory regime":

> Professional sports have become so popular precisely because the entrepreneurs who own teams have been able to rescind the market forces. Indeed, professional team sports in this country represent a triumph of capitalism. We would be unwise to ignore the importance of private economic decision making in that success. But, the quasi-regulatory regimes that these bills would create would do

just that. Moreover, they would provide a dangerous precedent for further, even more harmful, federal regulation of professional sports. (U.S. Congress, Senate, Committee on the Judiciary 1986a, 395)

Since the Raiders' decision, the department had obviously had a change of mind. Al Davis had forcefully reminded politicians that the NFL's "internal affairs" were very much in the public domain. Rule assured senators that his department "would not, therefore, oppose an anti-trust exemption for league decisions to block franchise relocations"; thus, despite a stated policy of "maximum reliance on the marketplace," Rule believed that "because of the uniqueness of professional sports and their place in American life, the cost of leaving the solution to the courts may be prohibitive and makes a limited immunity appropriate" (p. 392).

TRADING SELF-REGULATION FOR EXPANSION

The ad hoc character of franchise location legislation, the manner in which it seemed to speak only to the interests of a particular geographical constituency, combined with general congressional antipathy to interference in capital markets, was enough to beat back the flurry of legislative efforts to cement the ties between communities and franchises that occurred in the 1980s. According to Johnson, Congress had already "decided not to intervene in non-sports industries to resolve the plant shut-down and relocation issue. Neither the 95th nor the 96th Congress chose to adopt the National Employment Priorities Act, which was designed to respond to the economic and social impacts of plant closings and relocations" (1983, 524). It was unlikely that the same congressmen could make a stronger case for a sport franchise than they could an automobile assembly plant. Most of the sponsors of the various bills were also, as Johnson points out, disingenuously identifying the "public good" with the existing distribution of franchises, thereby guaranteeing opposition from those who desired their redistribution (p. 525).

Toward the end of the 1980s, a policy position began to emerge in which some compromise seemed possible between those insisting that the sport industry be left to mind its own business and those insisting that sport owners have a public responsibility to their communities. Congressmen, searching for a quid pro quo for granting the leagues immunity from antitrust suits occasioned by franchise movement restrictions, suggested expansion, arguing that since the owners had expanded only when threatened by a rival league or by a lawsuit, if Congress were to immunize them from such lawsuits, the nation should get something in return. Many recalled what had transpired after the Dodgers and Giants left New York. An angry Mayor Wagner formed a study group to consider the prospect of setting up a new Continental League, to be managed by Branch Rickey. The scheme had powerful backers, particularly in the states eager to have a major league baseball team. Senate Antitrust Committee hearings in 1959 considered the question of expansion and its chairman Estus Kefauver spoke in favor of the new league. His staff drafted a bill to permit a third league to compete on an equal footing with the two older circuits. The debate continued into the 1960 session, but Kefauver's 1960 bill was defeated in committee because "the major leagues were able to mobilize senators with baseball in their states into a near solid front" to oppose it (J. Miller 1990, 83).

The possibility of "trading" expansion for state protection was thus part of public policy debate as early as the 1950s. Sport owners were initially rather slow to appreciate the implications of this trade. Commissioner Kuhn later described the migration of the Dodgers and Giants as "a blunder by the National League," declaring that baseball should have expanded to the West Coast with brand new teams (1987, 22). Several baseball owners were later to express regret at having permitted the Dodgers' move because it both deprived New York of a franchise and tarnished the image of baseball as a public service. Baseball's expansion of 1961 (Houston Astros, New York Mets, Los Angeles Angels, Minnesota Twins) was intended to palliate congressmen angered by the Dodgers' move and to deflect support for the new Continental League (p. 94).

Fear of losing an antitrust suit also prodded the American League to expand to Seattle in 1976, where baseball fans were still angry over the departure of the Pilots to Milwaukee. Other congressmen also remembered that expansion deals were implicit in a number of previous concessions granted by Congress to the sport leagues. The addition of the Dallas Cowboys and Minnesota Vikings was tied to the 1960s Sports Broadcasting Act granting the leagues the right to negotiate jointly with the television networks. The New Orleans Saints and Atlanta Falcons were added in return for the 1966 legislation approving the merger of the NFL and the AFL. The Tampa Bay Buccaneers and Seattle Seahawks were admitted to the league after the NFL had succeeded in persuading Congress to forego additional statutory limitations on the league's ability to black out games in home areas.

The more percipient politicians were well aware of the fact that the evils of municipal competition were induced by a scarcity of franchises and that this scarcity was itself the creation of Congress. Tennessee senator Albert Gore, Jr., testifying at the hearings to consider the professional sports community protection act of 1985, complained that

> Memphis has been trying to get a team for a long time. This is what originally provoked my interest in this issue. The closer I looked

into it, the more I saw what I believe to be the injustice of the current situation, . . . because you have got an artificial scarcity, legally sanctioned by Congress, giving enormous power and enormous revenues to a limited number of people. (U.S. Congress, Senate, Committee on the Judiciary 1986a, 239)

When the 1985 legislative battle ended in stalemate, Rozelle secured backing from "five or six senators" for what he saw as a compromise bill, which would have granted the league the right to control movements by a three-quarters vote in return for the criteria earlier specified. It would also have approved revenue sharing of television money. In return, the NFL undertook to expand by two franchises. Movement on this legislation was blocked by Senator Gore, who threatened a filibuster. Gore was keen to land a franchise for Memphis and believed that the expansion should be by six, rather than two, franchises.

It was extremely irksome for congressmen that owners were able to use the very power that the state had bestowed in order to extract private concessions from local governments. To twist the knife in the wound, Commissioner Rozelle was particularly fond of dangling the prospect of expansion as bait to obtain support in Congress only for his position. He could, of course, "offer" expansion back to Congress only because Congress itself had granted the league the right to restrict the entry of new franchises in the first place. It was not lost on congressmen that established leagues were more likely to expand if presented with a rival.

The idea that expansion could be bought from the leagues in return for congressional protection from the laws of the market became increasingly popular during the 1980s. In 1987, Colorado senator Timothy Worth organized the Senate Task Force on Expansion of Major League Baseball, a coalition of legislators from Arizona, Florida, Louisiana, Indiana, Tennessee, Ohio, and New Jersey. The task force acted as a kind of ginger group within Congress to agitate for the expansion of all the sport leagues. Commissioner Ueberroth, meeting with the task force in December of that year, could only promise the congressmen that baseball would "actively consider" expansion. In 1988, the task force threatened to remove baseball's antitrust exemption unless a timetable for expansion were established. That same year, the Major League Baseball Players' Association commissioned a study to investigate the feasibility of expanding the number of baseball franchises. Executive Director Don Fehr accused club owners of making franchises artificially scarce. Many more cities, he claimed, could support franchises than presently had them. Members of the task force met again with the new commissioner, A. Bartlett Giamatti, in the summer of 1989; but he would only promise expansion some time in the 1990s. In 1991, the National League finally announced that it would add two more franchises, in Denver and Miami, by 1993. That same year the NFL owners announced that they, too, would add two franchises by 1993. The NHL added one new franchise in 1991 (San Jose) and planned two more for 1992 (Ottawa, Tampa).

EMINENT DOMAIN: SEIZING WHAT IS THEIRS

For cities faced with the dire prospect of losing their major league franchise, these protracted congressional debates were no remedy. For more immediate relief, they invoked their power of eminent domain. This power had traditionally been applied to land or other real property, and it remains unclear whether public authorities have the Constitutional right to sequester intangible property like a sport franchise. Oakland adopted this strategy in the final stages of the fight to keep the Raiders from moving to Los Angeles. In 1983, the California Supreme Court declared that intangible property *could* be acquired by eminent domain, pointing out that taking intangible property was authorized by state law. Oakland's case was dismissed, however, on the grounds that the city's attempted use of its eminent domain authority was arbitrary, capricious, and a gross abuse of discretion. Al Davis's lawyer (Joseph Alioto) took pains to point out to the court that Commissioner Rozelle, in having submitted an affidavit saying that as long as Oakland promptly resold the franchise to another private owner, the city's condemnation would be acceptable to the league, seemed to be acting in conspiracy against Davis. Oakland's case was not helped by the NFL rule prohibiting cities from owning NFL franchises. Davis's lawyers used this rule to show that the NFL itself clearly did not see a football franchise as a public entity for public use. The verdict in the eminent domain case was hailed by Davis's lawyer as a victory not only for the Raiders, but for the American Dream and free enterprise. Later, the city of Baltimore likewise instituted legal action against the departing Colts to condemn the franchise under its power of eminent domain, but with no more success than was enjoyed by Oakland. The city and the Colts eventually settled all legal action between them, with no significant financial loss to the team's owner.

CONCLUSION

Having begun as purely private ventures, sport franchises have gradually assumed many of the characteristics of public institutions. Many people believe that their owners should not be completely free to dispose of them as they choose. This constraint would, of course, not be directed, but mediated through the league, upon whom public responsibilities can be easily imposed.

This overlay of private and public is quite familiar to congressmen from their dealings with the telecommunications industry. There, too, the boundaries between private and public have become obscure. The Federal Communications Act provides that station frequencies be assigned for three-year periods, to be reallocated at the end of the period "in the public interest." However, a system that assigns the right to use a frequency for a limited period, subject to an open, public interest assignment, impairs the incentive of the holder of the frequency to maximize its long-run value by making investments whose pay-out period exceeds three years. To compensate for this, both industry and government treat the station license as a vested property right; licenses are almost always renewed, and they are freely bought and sold. In the case of radio stations, what was once public now seems to be private; in the case of sport franchises, what was once private is now public. In both cases, however, it is tacitly understood that certain economic benefits have been bestowed by the state, in return for which the private capitalist is expected to assume some public responsibility and to be motivated by considerations loftier than private greed.

The sport policy deliberations of the postwar decades largely focused on this issue. In light of the public welfare consequences of franchise location, should the state move the boundary between public and private? Should the state modify the governance mechanism by which the market for sport franchises was regulated? Should government play a more active role in regulating the relationship between individual owners and their league?

Largely missing from this debate was the question whose welfare was most affected by the location of franchises and the competition for them among municipalities. In other words, class politics hardly figured in these debates at all. They are of significance, then, as much for what was not on the agenda as for what was on it. This silence was a reminder that the "essential contradiction of advanced capitalism remains that between the social production and private appropriation of wealth" (Klare 1979, 126). The real issue with sport franchises is how local elites are able to get public sanction and subsidy for the private accumulation of wealth.

Local capitalists stand to gain much from a city's successful pursuit of a sport franchise. While they claim that the economic benefits will be widely distributed, these "trickle down" arguments should be treated with caution. Publicly funded stadia remove property from the city's tax rolls, resulting in millions of dollars of lost revenues that might otherwise go to help the city's working- class citizens.[15]

While economic impact figures are always an important part of the debate over franchise location, the inequities caused by the competition for major league franchises tend to be glossed over. Rarely does political debate include a careful estimate of how tax monies spent to generate the anticipated benefits would be distributed among the taxpayers. Revenue from stadium rentals is rarely sufficient to meet the full costs (including debt servicing) of the operation of sport stadiums—particularly for newer facilities (which are very expensive to build) and especially if property taxes foregone are considered an opportunity cost. More important, the immediate impact of the sport subsidy is to transfer income from the local government treasury to the teams using the facility. If local taxes are not raised to finance the subsidy, the real cost of the subsidy to the city lies in the diversion of funds from such services as education, health, police, and fire protection.

Playing host to a sport franchise can therefore have a negative impact on the relation between taxation and services. Subsequent to stadium construction and the installation of teams in Irving and Arlington, those two cities experienced the largest increases in sales and property taxes of any comparable Texas cities. Several other Texas cities saw their services increase with their tax payments, but the rate of increase was larger than for either Irving or Arlington. Both Arlington and Irving increased their indebtedness more than comparable cities (Rosentraub 1988).[16]

Even aside from the class consequences of how tax monies are raised and spent, there are typically inequities in the public subsidy of sport franchises arising from the fact that working-class people are much less likely to be in a position to take advantage of this opportunity to consume. Since buying a ticket to attend a sporting event is a discretionary purchase, it is reasonable to assume that these events will be attended mainly by middle-class people, especially where the market is such that season ticket purchases are necessary: "There is probably a regressive impact on the distribution of income in the community from the benefit side of the stadium subsidy as well as from the cost side" (Okner 1974, 345). The presence of a franchise in a city that has in all probability subsidized the facilities being used merely serves to redistribute the entertainment dollar. Indeed, if a city renovates an old stadium or builds a new facility in order to keep a franchise, it will probably see some negative impact on personal income and retail sales: "A possible explanation of this result is that stadium subsidies could bias local development toward the kind of low wage, seasonal jobs (like ushering and food service work) which are directly associated with sports attendance, at the expense of other sectors with higher wages and more stable employment (manufacturing, for example)" (Baade and Dye 1988, 42).

Why, if "public funding of sports stadiums has proved to be a major error in government policy" (J. Miller 1990, 310), do cities continue to compete for major league franchises? The reason is that franchise location and movement is not a purely economic issue. The benefits thought to accrue to a city from hosting a franchise are less tangible, but sooner or later they will be invoked in defense of a city's spending tax dollars to attract or retain one. Baade and Dye describe the typical sequence of events during debates on public funding for sports franchises:

> At the first level, there is disagreement on the meaty, earthy matters relating to direct municipal revenue projections on stadium income statements. If these projections fail to support stadium plans, the discussion usually ascends to a second stage, where the stadium advocates recruit indirect benefits or multiplier effects in boosting their stadium proposals. Failure here generally ignites a third booster-phase, in which the city economy is said to be propelled upward by the ability of stadiums and their big-league sports franchises to attract other businesses to their environs. Failure to convince skeptics at this level produces deep space debate on the stadiums' intangible benefits. In deep space, any weight can be assigned to these benefits, and stadium advocates have assigned a weight sufficient to support their case on "rational" grounds. (1988, 38)

Like so many other principally symbolic, emotion-laden issues in politics, the debate over the role of public authorities in professional sports reaches the point where rational debate is no longer possible, where to be against the franchise is to be against progress, pride in one's community, and economic development—in short, against being American. Thus, a judge in approving the City of Pittsburgh's decision to commit general revenues to pay obligations incurred in building a stadium for the Pirates declared:

> There is a need today to provide the public with facilities for recreation, sports and enjoyment of outdoor athletic competition. Even passive participation as an onlooker in competitive sports stimulates a desire for physical exercise. In any event it takes the spectator into the open air and provides him with exuberant escape from the cares of the day and arms him with recharged energy to meet his responsibilities as a citizen. And this helps to build up a healthy community. (Mitnick 1984, 985)

Toward the end of the 1980s, successive Republic administrations had managed to discredit many of the Keynesian principles justifying public expenditures and built a more favorable climate for the privatization of formerly public ventures. Referenda seeking approval for public funding for sport stadia failed in Cleveland, San Francisco, and Miami; and Oakland's citizens forced their city council to rescind an inducement to get the Raiders to return. Private–public arrangements became more common. For example, when Miami citizens turned down proposals to finance a new stadium for the Miami Dolphins, owner Joe Robbie worked out an arrangement with Dade County. When Joe

Robbie Stadium opened in 1987, the county had provided public funding for the stadium through a tax-free industrial development bonds issue, infrastructure support, and land provision. The bonds were structured to be repaid privately through the sale of ten-year leases on skyboxes and club seats. In order to get this kind of financing, however, Robbie not only sold leases to exclusive and high-priced boxes (minimum of twenty-nine thousand dollars a year) but also reserved ten thousand of the best seats in the stadium to "club" members (who are also guaranteed a parking space), at a minimum of six hundred dollars a season. In other words, privately financed sport facilities become the preserve of the rich, country clubs for team sports. The city had "granted" its name (receiving precious little in return) and, besides, had sanctioned the maldistribution of opportunities to watch professional football. As the 1980s ended, similar arrangements were being negotiated in Phoenix, Chicago, Tampa, and Atlanta. This is one solution; but it does not deal with the issue of equity posed by public–private partnerships, whether explicit, as in the Miami case, or implicit, as in most others. Public money is still being spent, although it will benefit only a few.

CHAPTER 8

Sport

and

Citizenship

Previous chapters have shown that sport organizations (and their mutual relations) are shaped by two sets of forces, often pulling in opposite directions: one that would privatize them in the interest of individual freedom and one pushing for more equality of access to sport opportunities, which would give sport organizations a more public role and expose their internal governance to public scrutiny and accountability. While at the individual level, the tension between liberty and equality creates conflict over identity claims and criteria of eligibility, at the organizational level, the issue causing most political contention is whether sport entities are private or public, governed by the market or the state? Or can they survive as part of a third sector, civil society, that is independent of both?

At this level of analysis, sport organizations are properly considered corporate actors within a larger political and economic framework. The appropriate line of investigation is to ask what powers these actors have in relation to each other and in relation to others in society. Rarely does the question of the role of sport as a whole within that larger framework become the subject of debate. Only occasionally do participants in the debate refer to the role of sport in general or raise the question of how the organization of sport serves to meet national goals or help realize societal values. In short, the institutionalization of sport (that there should be sport in some form and that it is functional for society) is largely taken for granted, as is the part played by the state in this process of institutionalization. Sociologically, however, these processes cannot be taken for granted. Popular understandings of the "contribution" of sport to society and, more specifically, to the national purpose are social constructions. They emerge in the interplay of ideas about play and games and about national identity and mission, in which the simple rules and practices of common pastimes come to assume the status of "national heritage," to be protected and guaranteed by the state, and in which national identity can come to be defined partly in terms of a sporting tradition. To study this process, it is necessary to transcend the organizational level of analysis and consider society as a whole.

STATE AND NATION

Sports encode national identities. They are an "inscriptive space" in which ideas about nationhood can be recorded (Brown 1991, 49). Through sports, Americans construct a coherent vision of what it means to be truly American. Thus, baseball, the "national game," is believed by its fans to "mirror the *condition of freedom* for Americans that Americans ever guard and aspire to" (Giamatti 1989, 83). Similarly, political culture is athleticized by the use of sport metaphors: presidents become "quarterbacks," cabinets become "teams," elections become "races." In this process of mutual influence, both sport and politics are transformed. National politics, viewed through the lens of the agonistic paradigm of sport, appears more contested, more populist, than it really is. Sport, when linked selectively to national traits like individual freedom and choice, seem less commercial, less hierarchical, than it really is. The symbolic relation between sport and national identity is hermetic, each defining the other: "America *means* baseball because baseball *means* America" (Brown 1991, 67). The use of sport to define national identity, while it is found in many cultures, is especially pronounced in the United States, where sport has been more explicitly oriented to the goal of assimilation, the absorption of immigrants into the mainstream, in contrast to Europe, where the primary goal of sport has been to absorb the working class into the public sphere.

There is much that could be said about the contribution of sport to national identity and how sport cultures are shaped by national history and collective memory. Because it is regarded as "the national game" by most Americans, baseball would figure prominently in the story they tell of their past. To its supporters, baseball "exhibits almost perfectly the myths of the white Anglo–Saxon population that settled the towns, prairies, and southlands of America" (Novak 1976, 61). It is "a kind of contract theory in ritual form, a set of atomic individuals who assent to patterns of limited cooperation in their mutual interest" (p. 59). Seeing America through the lens of sport offers assurance that those who have power deserve it and those who do not have had their fair chance. For its part, baseball zealously guards its status as part of the national heritage, being slow to change its playing rules and careful to burnish its pastoral, ageless image as "the summer game." But a consideration of the larger issues of sport's contribution to national identity and nationalism would divert attention from my focus, which is the relation between sport and the state. State and nation are not the same. The nation is much broader than the state and embraces culture, language, ethnicity, and a sense of place. Some of these broader issues will be taken up in chapter 10, when the contribution of sport to national assimilation will be discussed.

Separating nation and state conceptually by no means implies they are unrelated. In many ways, the claim to be a nation is the claim to be entitled to a state. The legitimacy of a state depends on how convincingly national identity claims can be made. Conversely, the claim to nationhood is more successful where there is a viable state. The state demarcates boundaries and fosters internal integration and homogenization (e.g., through rules of citizenship). The state uses nationalism to help legitimate its policies and practices ("in the national interest"). Nationalists use the state to legitimate "folk" ideas (e.g., immigration restrictions). State policy in any domain, then, will be shaped in part by questions of national identity. However, these are by no means the only reasons why sport policy takes the form it does; and they must be put in the context of other ideas—about sport itself and about the proper role of the state in civil society.

A Right to Sport?

Sports can be used in multiple ways to enhance a person's sense of belong to a nation. Where nationality is legitimated by a state, however, the ties are made more specific: they become claims of citizenship. Citizenship provides a person with rights and imposes obligations— by virtue of birth or residence in a territory; it is the link between nation and state: "The development of modern citizenship has corresponded to the development of a system of nation–states within a capitalist economic system" (Turner 1986, 139). It is a much more concrete and specific tie between individual and community than is expressed in the idea of nationality.

At first glance, it might not be self-evident that sport and citizenship have much to do with each other. Citizenship means having the right to vote (and the obligation to pay taxes), the right to a jury trial (and the obligation to serve on juries). These civil and political ties do not exhaust all forms of modern citizenship, however; for they have been supplemented in the twentieth century by social rights and obligations. These would include the right to health care and decent housing, which, in many modern nation–states, would now be considered "entitlements" due any citizen, regardless of ability to pay. The question arises, If a citizen has the right to a decent house to live in, does he also have the right to open space in which to play?

The expansion of citizenship rights to include a more extensive range of welfare benefits has been highly controversial and has proceeded much further in some countries than others. "Welfarism" is politically unpopular in the United States, but the idea is far advanced in some European democracies. In a few, it now includes the right to leisure. When the socialist Francois Mitterand was elected president of France in 1981, he created a Ministry of Free Time as a complement to, and not a substitute for, a Ministry of Culture. Existing junior ministries of tourism, youth, and sports were soon absorbed into the new ministry. The first minister of free time spoke unambiguously of leisure as a citizenship right of the French people. His staff worked hard to increase leisure opportunities, especially for population groups previously slighted. The work week was reduced by decree to thirty-nine hours in 1982, and a fifth week of annual paid leave was extended to all workers in 1983 (Hantrais 1989).

The attitude toward social rights is very different in the United States. In setting state policy, Americans desire to maximize their freedom of choice and individual liberties at the expense, if need be, of the equal distribution of opportunities and experiences. They are nevertheless intolerant of distributions of opportunities so grossly unequal that they threaten political freedoms. Consequently, they expect their government to intervene in the workings of the market to afford them some measure of protection if glaring inequities arise.

Public sentiment with respect to the "right" to sport participation fits in with this ideology. Where capitalism and democracy must coexist, an ideology of leisure based on notions of individual freedom, choice, and responsibility fights with an ideology where leisure is a source of social liberation (Coalter, Long, and Duffield 1988, 23). Few Americans subscribe to the latter view. The idea of leisure as a component of citizenship (essentially a moral, not a utilitarian, idea) receives little support. Americans see leisure as an area of the sovereignty of the individual and believe that freedom of choice is soonest achieved by leaving the distribution of opportunities to the marketplace. If the federated structure of government were not enough, this ideology would alone render centralized planning of leisure a contradiction in terms. The result is "reluctant collectivism." For those who can afford it, leisure is privately provided; for those who cannot, a minimum level is provided publicly. Consequently, the public provision of sport opportunities is highly decentralized (so that "government" resembles, as closely as possible, popular will); sport is administered through "the local state" (municipalities, townships, public colleges and high schools); and sport is operated on the basis of a market model (in which resources are distributed according to palpable demand, rather than principles of equity).

At the federal level, successive administrations, with varying degrees of determination, have indicated their concern for the public's access to sport by trying to compensate for inequities in sport opportunities, providing facilities at low cost, and "collective goods" that private capital finds unprofitable to market and "repairing" damage to the natural and social environment caused by the unfettered operation of the market. There are some citizenship aspects to public recreation. It is "an attempt to administer justice in the sense of making some opportunities available to those least able to provide for themselves" (Kelly 1982, 380). Americans also expect the state to protect sport in much the same manner as it protects religion, helping sanction the institution in principle without endorsing or being part of any particular manifestation of it. President Eisenhower once said, "Our government makes no sense unless it is founded in a deeply felt religious faith—and I don't care what it is" (Herberg 1960, 84). It would be no exaggeration at all to say that many Americans could say as much for sport and therefore expect there to be a close relation between sport and the state without, however, "establishing" sport as a state function.

The role of the state as cheerleader for sports is, however, a far cry from the French model. The voluntary sector has been very important in the administration and funding of sports in the United States; and although that sector is dominated by the business class, it has fought to preserve sport as an essentially private, voluntaristic endeavor. This remains largely true, despite the fact that much amateur sport in the United States has been absorbed into tax-supported schools and colleges. Indeed, more than most other advanced capitalist societies, the United States has assigned to educational institutions the task of organizing play. The state is therefore present, but at one remove; and this more distant relation creates room for the commercialization of amateur sport, as the market, rather than the state, invades civil society, which can work against any notion of a right to sport opportunities. It also means that while amateur sport in the United States has its origins in the British sporting tradition, there are some distinguishing traits. The public school ethos, with its emphasis on teamwork, self-effacement, and intrinsic rewards, which in England socialized a new bourgeoisie into "national service" values, has been largely absent except, perhaps, for the Ivy League colleges and some pockets of amateur sports. Instead, the emphasis is more individualistic and instrumental: winning is very important, losing is personally degrading, and extrinsic rewards are primary.

I shall describe a set of state actions committed in a general way to the protection of opportunities for sport participation but stopping far short of a "sport for all policy." At the most general level, state officials express their support for sport as an essential ingredient of Americanism. However, public initiatives to furnish sport opportunities are highly localized, fragmentary, and always secondary to other more "important" concerns. In only three brief periods of American history has there been a concerted political effort to tackle the problem of the unequal distribution of sport facilities. The progressives, the New Dealers and the liberal democrats of the Johnson's Great Society all sought to push sport policy in the direction of greater egalitarianism. In each case, however, market forces and their political backers reasserted themselves.

An apparent exception to this pattern would appear to be interscholastic athletics. Through high school and intercollegiate athletics, most of which is publicly funded, the state would appear to have been heavily and directly involved in the provision of sport opportunities. Compared with capitalist democracies in Western Europe, this is certainly true. I shall show, however, that the encapsulation of amateur sports by schools and colleges has not resulted in a democratic sport policy in which membership of a community is an entitlement to sport opportunities. Rather, interscholastic sports have developed in the direction of a market model, in which a few, elite athletes perform for the benefit of paying customers. Opportunities for sport participation are rationed on the basis of academic eligibility: playing sports implies a "deal" in which athletic labor is exchanged for free tuition. The state has done little to disturb this arrangement.

Sport, the State, and National Identity

It is difficult for American politicians (usually male) to appear indifferent to sports. An interest in sports is considered to be a mark of true Americanism, a natural product of the American people's activism and desire to excel. When a sportswriter polled congressmen in 1910, he "found that all but two had played baseball, the exceptions being a blind man and a cripple" (Voigt 1970, 83). As the nation's symbolic leaders, presidents must show their respect for sports. Theodore Roosevelt had no problems in this respect, for he was an active sportsman himself and helped prod the colleges into forming the NCAA in order to make football safer and protect the amateur ideal. President Taft, whose brother owned a major baseball franchise, regularly attended professional baseball games, beginning the annual custom of attending the opening day game. Franklin Roosevelt was in the habit of "clowning with League officials and politicians, posing for photographers, and usually tossing the first pitch wildly into a scrambling crowd of players" (Rable 1989, 367). Kennedy's media advisers used his fondness for touch football to evoke images of youth and vigor. He was not the first

president to use sports electorally, however, because Harding had, under the instruction of his election manager, downplayed his interest in golf (considered too elitist to get votes) and developed an interest in baseball. Richard Nixon synthesized the symbolism of political leadership and sport leadership most zealously, using sport images and sport lessons to elaborate on his political agenda for the nation while at the same time seeking to associate himself with success in the sporting arena by calling in plays during NFL games and by visiting winning teams in their locker room. Ford's public image as a stumbler was brightened by his having been a letterman in college football. Carter evinced only a little more interest in sport than had Johnson, but he did symbolize the Puritan ethos of his administration by public displays of masochistic jogging. Reagan's presidency routinely mixed fact and fiction, and the sports world was not omitted. He had been a radio sport commentator in his younger days, and one of his most famous film acting parts portrayed Knute Rockne. Like John Wayne, he seemed to become the character he played: "Bush's media-created image as an outdoor sportsman, and his pointed use of locker-room language first as vice-presidential and then as presidential candidate, revealed his own or his strategists' awareness of the power of sporting rhetoric with voters" (Oriard 1991, 325).

So powerful is the appeal of sports as an American icon that even patently unathletic presidents must respect it. The intellectual Woodrow Wilson was a baseball enthusiast, attended four games during his first year in office, and declared his conviction that "athletics is indispensable to the normal life of young men" (Ryan 1929, 56). Coolidge also wished to appear warm toward sport, although his knowledge was clearly deficient. The story is told that an Illinois senator introduced George Halas and Red Grange to President Coolidge with the words, "These gentlemen are with the Chicago Bears." "How interesting," Coolidge is said to have replied, "I've always enjoyed animal acts" (D. Anderson 1985, 28).

Politically, sport is useful for symbolic purposes, especially in creating a sense of the "imagined community" of Americans and symbolizing the triumph of liberty over repression. In the nation's confrontation with the totalitarianism of fascism and communism in the 1930s, words like *play, leisure time,* and *recreation* seemed to evoke all things distinctively American, in contrast to the subordination of the individual to the mass in totalitarian regimes. Leisure meant "the broadening of horizons, the worth of the common man, the freedom to choose what one will do, the warmth of new friendships, the humility of spirit that comes with understanding people better, the development of personality, the satisfaction of learning new ways of expression" (Staples 1943, 72).

It is because sport is such a potent integrative symbol that congressmen combine romanticism and rationalism in their attitude toward it.

They shift easily from seeing sport as the quintessence of private, voluntaristic behavior to seeing it as vital to the national purpose, a trust as sacred as the Constitution itself or a national monument. Thus, Congressman Patrick Hillings (California), said:

> Baseball is essential to American youth. There is no question but what the young people get health, sportsmanship, and moral fitness as a result of playing and watching the game and idolizing some of the players who have become the heroes of young Americans. Professional baseball is a high goal to which the youth of our country can always aspire. (U.S. Congress, House, Committee on the Judiciary 1957, 1797)

Owners of sport teams welcome these political embraces. George Trautman, then president of the National Association of Professional Baseball Leagues (the minors), testified before the House Judiciary committee in 1951:

> Baseball is a game which is a precious possession of the American people. One which belongs no more to those of us in the professional field than to the millions of loyal fans, young and old. We in baseball must and do accept the obligation to jealously guard the game, its spirit, its mighty contribution to succeeding generations of our youth, as clean recreation, as a teacher of fair play, and as an example of fair, yet earnest competition. (Krasnow and Levy 1963, 750)

For many years, major league baseball touted the minor league system as a "public service" provided to small towns, much as a utility company might promote its role in rural electrification. The farm system seemed to be an ideal way for the public good to be furthered by maximizing the interests of private capital.

The myth of public service concealed a deeper reality. A closer look at the farm system reveals exactly how this private–public partnership worked and how the interests of private capital were paramount. A "farm system" of minor league teams had begun to develop by the 1930s, using Branch Rickey's example. At one point in the 1930s, the St. Louis Browns owned the entire Nebraska State League (J. Miller 1990, 111). By 1952, major league clubs owned 175 out of 319 minor league clubs (Seymour 1971, 400). The owners burnished their image by drawing attention to the money they were spending on the farm system, but it was a rational form of vertical integration for them while often being a bad bargain for host communities. The major league team typically paid the salaries of the players, managers, and coaches; but the city usually had to pay for the grounds crew, upkeep of the park, insurance, and even dues to the league. Most of the city's expenditures had to be covered by money raised from concessions and ticket sales, and these were often insufficient. The city therefore ended up partially subsidizing the farm team; and where this was not forthcoming, the franchise was likely to move to a more hospitable community.

If further evidence were needed that the major league owners were not interested in minor league teams for anything other than profit, it was provided by television. After World War II, major league club owners succumbed to the lure of television contracts—first local, then national. As a result, attendance at minor league baseball games plummeted. In 1948, there were 58 minor leagues; by 1975, there were only 20 (U.S. Congress, House, Select Committee on Professional Sports 1977, 55). Between 1953 and 1956, 94 minor league clubs folded. At the same time, major league clubs began to sell off their wholly owned subsidiaries. In 1951, the majors owned 207 minor league clubs; by the beginning of the 1957 season, they owned 38 (J. Miller 1990, 53).

The public service claim must therefore be taken with a pinch of salt, at least as far as the minors were concerned. In 1946, the Sioux Falls baseball team had ceased to operate independently and had become a farm team of the Chicago Cubs. During hearings before the House Judiciary Committee, minor league baseball player Ross Horning described what had happened to it under the "protection" of the major leagues:

> By obtaining this agreement [the owners] lost complete and effective control of their club. They had to pay half the manager's salary, all of the players' salaries, pay the rent on the ballpark, pay for the lights, bats and uniforms, provide the entire cost of the transportation, pay all of the meals and hotel expenses when the team was on the road, risk the entire profit and loss of the operation while, at the same time, they did not have control of the most essential factor of success and the heart of the operation, the ball players on the field. (U.S. Congress, House, Committee on the Judiciary 1957, 2471).

The enterprise was unable to function under these conditions and collapsed in 1954. This was not the consequence of television, so often cited as the immediate cause of the decline of the minor leagues, for television had not by that time reached Sioux Falls. The reason for the collapse of the farm system was that it worked well when only a few clubs were vertically integrated. But "baseball soon discovered that most of the advantages of large farm systems vanished when everyone had one and 'bonus wars' broke out" (J. Miller 1990, 11).

While baseball owners continued to declare their commitment to the welfare of small-town America well into the 1970s, in light of what they had allowed to happen during the preceding twenty years, their claims had a hollow ring. While minor league baseball did enjoy a revival in the 1980s, it had little to do with organized baseball's sense of national purpose. The minor leagues' mixture of profit and patriotism (where, however, private gain always wins out over public service) explains why the love affair between sports and the state has not been formalized in marriage. There is little desire on the part of congressmen to elevate sport to the status of an entitlement. Most Americans probably believe that hosting a sport franchise is part of what it means to be a community (and in this sense, the franchise does take on public significance); but they stop short of treating it as equivalent to a school. They hope that the community will support a franchise and thus demonstrate how "American" they are, but the market will determine whether or not they do. Thus, while many American politicians express their devotion to sports, they do so in much the same way that they express their support for religion in a society that has no established church; they lead by example and exhortation, rarely by executive action. They have been content, otherwise, to leave the market and private, voluntary efforts to meet the sport needs of their constituents.

The Playground Movement

In only three periods has there been a concerted political campaign to secure justice, rather than liberty, in the provision of sport opportunities. The first occurred between 1906 and 1917, when the number of American cities with managed recreation programs rose from 41 to 504. The impetus was the Playground movement, whose leaders "abhorred the unsupervised, unstructured play that arose from the spontaneous impulses of children" (Rader 1989, 132). The impact of the Playground movement on municipal politics was relatively short-lived, however; and it generally failed to extend its management of spare-time activities to working-class children living in the slums or children living in rural areas. Many were uncertain about the legality of using funds or facilities for the purpose of providing sport facilities. While some of the larger cities, such as New York, Chicago, and Boston, had funded municipal parks previous to this date (public playgrounds were in operation in eleven cities prior to 1900 [Steiner 1933, 14]) they were of dubious legality. Some courts decided that the city government could not be sued for injuries incurred in the use of playground equipment, because it fell into the same category with, for example, fire-fighting equipment, which was essential for carrying out the authority's mission. Other courts decided that damage claims were allowable because playgrounds were "enterprises not essential to good government" (Truxall 1929, 90).

In the absence of a more general political movement in favor of sport for all, public schools played a vital role in bringing sport opportunities to more children. They were to provide the model for later, more broad-based programs. Thus, the earliest laws sanctioning publicly

funded recreation programs were those permitting the use of school
buildings and grounds for this purpose. Once enabling legislation was
in place, however, and as a result of more progressive approaches to local government, facilities for community play outside the school playground became much more widely available. In 1907, there were 307
citydwellers for every one acre of city park; by 1930, this figure had
fallen to 184 (Steiner 1933, 25). Seymour believes that public recreation
was boosted by the experience of the military during World War I,
when it proved to be an important morale booster: in the 1920s, government officials and influential community leaders "marshalled the
resources of some 600 war camp communities" to try to ensure that the
wartime gains were preserved (1990, 68).

By 1927, twenty-one states had passed enabling legislation, taking
over from the schools much of the responsibility for organizing sports
leagues (Truxall 1929, 21). There were also qualitative changes. Parks
were provided with a greater range of equipment, less of the type designed for "improvement" (e.g., parallel bars) and more of the type to facilitate fun (e.g., swings, slides). More space was devoted to playing and
watching team sports. Park administrators, more and more of whom
had received specialized training, assumed responsibility for organizing sporting schedules and planning special events. A sense of the government's responsibility to distribute leisure opportunities more
equitably seems to have been established.

On the other hand, few of these initiatives were undertaken in response to widespread popular demand. Indeed, citizens were no more
anxious to pay for recreational facilities than they were for water,
sewer, or garbage collection. Nor was a public–private partnership popular. Various bills to get developers to include small parks in their developments failed (Truxall 1929, 22, 36). The federal government
played little part in these initiatives. Steiner writing at the end of the
1920s, could discern "no strong movement in the direction of federal
promotion of recreation beyond the present efforts on the part of the
federal administrative authorities to develop better facilities for the
recreational use of land under their control" (1933, 172).

The New Deal

The Depression caused a great deal of rethinking in public
policy circles about the role of the state in civil society. At first, the down-
turn in the economy produced a decline in local appropriations for the
administration of public recreation services. Many private companies
scaled back their industrial recreation programs, leaving the cities to
pick up the slack. The claim that recreation programs contributed to
character development, prevented delinquency, and promoted good

citizenship had persuaded city officials to fund recreational programs. (Such efforts were rare in rural areas.) Suddenly, the 1929 crash made these programs seem a luxury. On the other hand, the demand for "free" recreational facilities increased as incomes declined and unemployment rose. More importantly, recreation became part of the "public works" effort mounted by the government in order to provide employment. Hiring the unemployed to work on construction and service projects would not only improve leisure resources but could also be put to political use:

> Recent events have focused the country's attention on the tremendous possibilities of using leisure time for the strengthening of the democratic state. Freedom, choice, individual uniqueness, and recognition of human values are essential virtues of a genuine democracy. They can be fostered and developed by leisure-time activities. But these, in turn, can no longer be adequately facilitated by individuals alone. Public agencies must come to their assistance in planning leisure. (Cline 1939, 2)

The Works Progress Administration (WPA) set up a Recreation Division designed to train the unemployed (especially those formerly employed in white-collar jobs) as community leaders of leisure-time activities. Thus, not only would the government provide jobs for middle-class people, it would also help those still unemployed use their enforced leisure constructively. By 1937, approximately forty-four states had 46,000 employees at work on recreation activities funded and planned by the Recreation Division (p. 28). All told, the WPA helped build 3,600 baseball fields and 8,800 softball fields as well as 6,000 athletic fields (Seymour 1990, 70).[1]

A second New Deal activity to help public recreation was the Civilian Conservation Corps (CCC). Much CCC work focused on federally owned land: "Since the establishment of the first national park more than 60 years ago, probably no other period saw such an advance in the development of outlying areas for recreational use as was brought about during the years 1934 and 1935" (Steiner 1937, 61). Providing work of this kind was especially attractive because it did not compete with private enterprise for business. The CCC completed over twenty thousand different projects related to recreation, including parks, pools, beaches, golf courses, stadia, trails, hostels, and camps.

All told, the New Deal agencies spent about $750 million on athletic facilities and "probably had a greater positive impact on sport participation for the average urbanite than anything else in American history" (Riess 1989, 143): "It was during this period that local communities developed park and recreation commissions and charged them with the responsibility of providing diversionary recreation opportunities. . . . Organized recreation took a mass approach, and for many, sports became synonymous with recreation" (Sessoms 1984, 17).

The New Deal had much less effect on state and federal government,
however, leaving nothing to match the new agencies for dealing with
unemployment or with labor–management relations. New Deal re-
formism left the state leisure services highly fragmented and decen-
tralised. A U.S. government report issued in 1937 found that
"approximately 35 units scattered throughout 12 departments of the
federal government are engaged in promoting 60 or 70 separate programs affecting the citizen's use of leisure" (Cline 1939, 111).

The Great Society

Policies oriented more toward egalitarianism than liberty
regained popularity in the 1960s. The political shift to the left that began in the early 1960s made people more aware of the uneven distribution of public leisure opportunities. Existing sport facilities were
criticized for their tilt toward the middle-class. Why should the working-class taxpayer help fund low-cost public camping, swimming, or hiking facilities, only for them to be chiefly used by middle- and
upper-income groups? In order to get a better sense of the balance between demand and supply, the Outdoor Recreation Coordination Act of
1963 mandated periodic surveys of recreational behavior and attitudes. National Recreation Surveys were carried out in 1968, 1972,
1977, and 1982. The act also set up the Outdoor Recreation Resources
Review Commission, which led directly to the organization of the Bureau of Outdoor Recreation (BOR) in the Department of the Interior. In
1968, environmental pressure groups were influential enough to force
through the Land and Water Conservation Fund Act, the Wild and
Scenic Rivers Act, and the National Trail System Act. These measures
were in conformity with a number of policy guidelines, namely that the
protection of unique assets (e.g. the Grand Canyon) is a public good, the
private provision of many recreational opportunities is unpredictable
and weighted in favor of the affluent, the state has a responsibility to
guarantee a minimum level of recreational opportunities for all people,
and private development is frequently inefficient and damaging to the
environment.

"Clientalist fragmentation" continued to be a problem for state-
administered sport opportunities, however, as noted in the Presidential Commission on Americans Outdoors, which listed no "less than 70
federal agencies now providing some recreational service to some constituents." It continued: "A convincing argument may be made for the
consolidation of a number of federal agencies, each having similar or
competitive functions, under the aegis of one umbrella bureau of administration. Such a procedure might do much to eliminate bureaucratic infighting, financial waste, programmatic inefficiency, and
redundancy" (Shivers 1986, 56). The writer proposed a Federal Recrea-

tion Service Administration, located in the Department of Housing and Urban Development.

The chief obstacle facing those trying to formulate a coherent, democratic sport policy was that the American creed exalts property rights as the foundation of all others. The freedom to work, to control one's own productive activities, is more important than the freedom to play. Sport is always secondary to other "more important" issues. This by no means implies that government policy leaves sport untouched. Many social problems have consequences for leisure; and government programs to tackle unemployment, inadequate child-care facilities, poor housing, inadequate health care, infrequent public transportation, a polluted environment, and racial and gender discrimination all have some bearing on how people spend their leisure time. But in all these cases, social engineering a better sport world is not the primary object of social policy.[2]

Partly for this reason, sport has no coherent lobby in Congress. One of the few organizations to focus on leisure issues in Washington has been the National Recreation and Park Association (NRPA), which primarily emphasizes building up public recreation under government auspices. The NRPA was formed in 1966, consolidating five organizations (and excluding the American Association for Health, Physical Education, and Recreation) into one organized lobby. There can be no doubting the professional expertise that members of the NRPA bring to leisure policy deliberations, but the organization lacks clout. This is partly the result of having no clear political target at which to aim, but it is also the result of lack of legitimacy in Congress. Few congressmen respect the credentials of a professional recreator. Most see professional recreators as elitists seeking to impose their own rather narrow views of how people should spend their leisure time on a population whose real leisure wants are very different.

The only area having to do with sport that Federal and state officials have paid attention to is outdoor recreation. While little of this has to do with the more glamorous of the professional and amateur sports, actions by state officials can have quite an impact on pastimes such as fishing, hunting, boating, and rock climbing. The difference here is that outdoor recreation policy is really about the control and use of land or (more broadly conceived) the use of natural resources, many of them publicly owned. The state cannot absolve itself of responsibility in this area. What best serves the public interest: preservation, recreation, or development? The degree to which legislation mandates access and use, as opposed to protection and preservation, has been the subject of long-standing debate. Much of this debate takes place *within* federal and state bureaucracies, with different agencies defending different policies. In these areas, the state has been forced to make choices that have a bearing on sport opportunities because land-use regulation is a responsibility that it cannot easily avoid. Even inaction has practical consequences. Outside of this limited area, however, explicit sport policy has been only minimally developed.

At the local level, community recreation is varied and diverse. It ranges from extensive and expensive programs in larger cities like Chicago, to the single ballparks of small towns, where much of the upkeep is based on volunteer labor (Kelly 1982, 388). Recreation needs have become part of the long-range land-use planning of most public authorities, as are the varied needs of special populations within the community. However, public leisure facilities tend to be the first to suffer when tax revenues decline; and they are subject to attack from private interests when they offer competition.

When it comes to the incorporation of sport into the state, then, the United States lies at the less-developed end of the spectrum of Western democracies. The state accepts no official responsibility for sports. Currently, the highest-ranking government official with any responsibility at all toward sports is the under secretary of state for security assistance, science, and technology. The public administration of sports is thus grossly underdeveloped compared to nations like Canada (which has a Ministry of Fitness and Amateur Sport), France (which has a Ministry of Culture), the United Kingdom (which has a Ministry of Culture with responsibility for sport) and the Federal Republic of Germany, where the amateur German Sports Federation, under the aegis of the Ministry of the Interior, receives a share of the profits gained from the national lottery.

Only during the brief periods of social democratic government described above has the United States developed more egalitarian sport policies. When the mood of the country began to shift back to the political Right in the 1970s and 1980s, the collectivist approach to leisure of the 1960s was discredited. Ronald Reagan's Secretary of the Interior, James Watt, reversed the policies of his predecessors in the interest of privatizing recreational facilities and reducing the amount of land owned or controlled by the federal government (Shivers 1986, 58). Policies were formulated on the assumption that recreational provision should follow demand, a system in which the consumption figures for existing facilities are used to set budgets. By favoring the market model, the Reagan administration made it very difficult to use leisure for the purposes of challenging the status quo. Where leisure is to be marketed, it is responsive to effective demand in the form of money, it must satisfy the more affluent and more educated. The only method the consumer has of communicating dissatisfaction is through a refusal to "purchase." The market model is, in other words, inherently nonegalitarian. It assumes a distinction between producers and consumers of leisure, between the few, professional, middlemen and the many, amateur, consumers.

The laissez-faire attitude of government toward sport, especially at the federal level, might lead to the conclusion that sport is not part of the state apparatus at all. This would be a false conclusion, because educational institutions, the majority of which are funded and managed publicly, have taken over much of the social responsibility for providing sport opportunities. To a degree unknown in other capitalist democracies, Americans turn to their schools and colleges for their sports. Not only does this reserve many sport opportunities to those who stay in school and attend college, it has also had a powerful effect on the kind of sport experience they have.

The pattern, peculiar to the United States, of supporting athletics chiefly through schools and colleges was firmly in place by the 1920s; and little has changed since. The essential features are rationalized and functionally differentiated departments of athletics, professional coaches, alumni support and booster clubs, and students recruited on the basis of their athletic ability and financially supported through athletic scholarships. In accepting sports onto their campus and into their curriculum, schools and colleges tacitly accepted the responsibility of defending a particular version of those sports. The amateur ideal ceased to be purely private affair but become part of the public domain, to be taught along with literacy, numeracy, and citizenship. But this responsibility proved to be as difficult to meet as the pedagogical goals, perhaps because it was never clearly acknowledged.

The contrast with other capitalist democracies is startling, especially at the college level. In countries like the Federal Democratic Republic of Germany, "universities devote themselves to education (including physical education and the scientific study of sports), while private clubs provide both participant and spectator sports. . . . The intense interest in sport has been institutionalized in the private club rather than in the public university" (Guttman 1982, 77). There is some irony in the fact that the voluntary, community-based support for sports in the United States (a nation that prides itself on its voluntarism and distaste for government bureaucracy) should be so weak in comparison to Western Europe. Most Americans abandon serious participation in sports after graduation from high school, while Europeans will continue to play well into adulthood if they have been socialized into the sport role in their youth.

Schools as Social Centers

Much more than their European counterparts, American high schools are governed locally, on a township, county, or school district basis. The supreme authority at the grassroots level is the school board. School boards are typically filled electorally, and elections are won not by those interested in scholarship or the intellect but by "practical men" who can meet a payroll. The business background of many board members (and the fact that they are answerable to the voters) means that they tend to favor material symbols of education, that their constituents can plainly see and readily comprehend, such as buildings. Most board members being male, their enthusiasm for athletic prowess and competition comes as no surprise.

American high schools are important symbols of community pride and achievement, as well as of "spirit" and solidarity. They are expected not only to produce well-adjusted, socialized individuals but also to integrate the community. Politically, the school serves as a "total institution," attempting to influence all aspects of its pupils' lives (Violas 1978, 12). As the least controversial and most accessible aspect of schooling, sports are ideally suited to transcend a community's racial, economic, and social differences.

Many of these ideas about the functions of public schooling can be traced back to John Dewey, who believed that schools should be not simply educational, but also social, centers. By replacing the streets, saloons, and dance halls as centers of recreation, they could improve the quality of urban living. Dewey believed that education should be defined, and effected, wholistically, the school being thoroughly integrated into the surrounding social community and itself operating as a focus of community life. His contemporary, the sociologist Edward Ross, described the expansion of school activities as an "economical system of police" and placed it under his more general heading of social control (Spring 1972, 75). The activities of the public school gradually supplanted the social training role of other institutions, such as the family and the church.

This more general, political mission was especially important in the larger cities, populated by recent immigrants whose religion was suspect and who had no "American" family tradition, whose children were daily exposed to the temptations of saloons and dance halls and the "hot, busy, bare streets or alleys" (Spring 1972, 63). There the civilizing mission of the schools was taken very seriously. In 1903, New York City took the lead in organizing a Public Schools Athletic League to conduct athletic contests between New York's schools. By 1910, most New York City schools were keeping their playgrounds open under supervision after school hours and during the summer: "The schools offered organized games, folk dancing, theatricals and showers during the summer months" (p. 73). The community use of public schools as social centers was given great impetus during World War I through the efforts of the Council of National Defense to make the school the headquarters for the promotion of local war work (Steiner 1933, 140). The effort did not slacken after the war. Spring claims that during the 1920s, "extracurricular activities developed into an educational cult" (1972, 112). Schools were given responsibility not only for turning out efficient workers and citizens but also people who would use their leisure time wisely and efficiently.

The idea of the school as social center remains a very powerful theme in American life. Many Americans continue to believe that the high school is ideally suited to integrate community life, "a kind of department store of constructive activities" (Kirschner 1986, 46). During the 1920s, however, the ideal underwent some subtle but important changes that would alter the face of sports in schools. As schooling became more professionalized and bureaucratized, the input of ordinary people in the local community declined. Extracurricular activities (the newspapers, student governments, clubs, and athletics) now formed the bottom rung of an educational system becoming increasingly structured along the lines of a business corporation (Spring 1972, 22). Sports likewise became increasingly hierarchical, as power shifted from the students themselves to hired professionals. Looking back on the use of schools as public recreation centers during the 1920s, Steiner reported, "The recent trend has been in the direction of official control" (1933, 141). As a consequence, amateur sports were gradually transformed into a bureaucratically organized and professionally managed source of entertainment for the community—as little the creation of that community as the local radio station.

The same trends have been evident at the collegiate level. Compared to their European counterparts, American colleges lack a clear "charter" or sense of how they might go about achieving their objectives, opening the way for "a variety of notions concerning the appropriate purpose of these social institutions" (Chu 1989, 42). The Morrill Act of 1862 had provided enormous funds for the more practically oriented college, and others learned to their cost that they could not ignore the call for a curriculum to fill the needs of the emerging business class. Massive land-grant colleges were constructed to meet the agricultural, mechanical and business needs of the taxpayer: "The university . . . soon began to conceive of itself not merely as an agency for training students to think hard and clearly, but as a place where, without fundamental education, people can acquire the elementary techniques of business, banking, accounting, transportation, salesmanship, journalism, and, in effect, all the vocations practiced in the modern industrial state" (Savage 1929, x). The political decision to carry great masses of young people through college with minimal regard for their intellectual fitness and often aided by reduction of fees called for institutions much broader than the European model. Community service was embraced and justified as a legitimate function of higher education (Chu 1989, 17). By operating as a "service station" in a highly competitive environment, a college could appeal to as many constituencies as possible. Diversification into the athletic marketplace, given the growing popularity of sports, was an appealing strategy for developing resources. Colleges competed for students "in much the same way in which railroads competed for passengers, [and] the attraction of athletic distinction [was] added to the other reasons for choosing a particular college" (Savage 1929, xvii). This practice became more insidious as improvements in transportation and communications made it easier for colleges to "invade" each other's "territory." Inevitably, college competition became national in scope, and sport was not slow to follow. The first Associated Press poll to declare national champions took place in 1936, making it that much easier to spot the more attractive colleges.

That sports enhanced the image of a college and cemented alumni loyalty were not the only reasons they were absorbed onto campus. Sports could also serve pedagogical purposes. To do so, however, they had to be modified. The modern form of scholastic sports is a result of the push of two contradictory sets of forces. On the one hand was the pressure to develop elite teams of athletes who could successfully represent the school in competition with other schools and whose glory would reflect on the school as a whole. On the other hand was the pressure to retain some of the educational mission that had been the pretext for the incorporation of athletics into the school in the first place. Here, within the educational system itself, are the two forces of liberty and equality at odds: freedom to pursue and exploit athletic excellence—if need be, at the expense of the mass of the population who would thus be relegated to the status of spectator–versus equality of access and experience not only for students but for those not enrolled in school at all, possibly at the expense of athletes who would otherwise attain elite status. Athletics became part of the growing up of most Americans; but, incorporated into the schools, it was far removed from the egalitarian play of the street and field.

The price paid for the college's freedom to exploit athletics is evident in the changes sport underwent as it became absorbed into the school. Because athletics now had to have an intellectually justifiable rationale, they were promoted as avenues of maturation and therefore as in need of structured supervision. Eventually, they would come to be seen as educational in themselves. Because they now had to serve exterior purposes, they had to be organized hierarchically, with executive leaders and "worker" athletes, the latter with little control over the sport. Whereas the earliest intercollegiate contests had been entirely managed by students themselves, the increasing dependence on fundraising gave alumni a foot in the door; and with the faculty inattentive, they "achieved dominion by default" (Savage 1929, 24).

Organized athletics in college were justified on two grounds. Team play would help bring intense individualism and competitiveness under control; and everyone could be taught his or her own job for the good of the total social organism. Americans must, said Theodore Roosevelt, "develop a system under which each individual citizen shall be trained so as to be effective individually as an economic unit, and fit to be organized with his fellows so that they can work efficiently together" (Spring 1972, 13). By 1907, when this statement was made, "meeting the needs of individuals" meant training in the ability to work with others. The apostle of scientific management, Frederick Winslow Taylor, "a tennis champion and golf devotee," was said to have learned through sport "the value of the minute analysis of motions, the importance of methodical selection and training, the worth of time study and of standards based on rigorously exact observation" (Betts 1984, 162). Taylor inveighed against the elective system in schools, asserting that the typical student had "but the vaguest idea of the nature of the subjects which lie before him" (1906, 579). Most significantly, Taylor ridiculed the idea that a student could "lift himself up by his bootstraps." He preached the virtues of cooperation, as in the "cooperation of the various parts of a watch"; football was ideally suited to teach young people how to work together for a common goal for the football player "does just what some one else tells him to do, and does it at the same time and in the manner in which he is told, and one or two lapses from training rules are sufficient cause for expulsion from the team" (p. 581). In short, the new attitude toward the relation between the individual and society, together with the new corporate structure for public education made athletics, suitably rationalized, an attractive component of modern educational methods. Sports provided competition under close supervision, motivation for intense individual effort, responsibility within the context of teamwork, and a source of community cohesion derived from rooting for the school team.

Physical Education: The Trojan Horse

Opposition to the manner in which high schools and colleges were exploiting sports came from the growing body of specialists in physical education. Under the influence of its Swedish and German founders, the Physical Education movement initially stressed gymnastics for purposes of improved health and hygiene. The Civil War had revealed shockingly poor health among the nation's fighting-age men and this had been (falsely) attributed to lack of proper exercise. In addition, the Morrill Act had mandated that colleges offer military training, which was usually interpreted as drill. Physical education was not then and is not today confined to academe (the Young Men's Christian Association [YMCA] and its women's counterpart were early exponents); but the idea that play was something to be learned and that properly supervised exercise could be of general benefit to the individual (and society) gained widespread acceptance only when it became part of the educational experience of the American child, and this had to await the changes in the educational system that opened the way for "extracurricular activities." Thus, although California required courses in physical education in public schools as early as 1866, most states did not embrace this idea until after 1900 when the schools themselves were ready to receive it and put it into practice.

Physical education seemed to offer a healthy counterbalance to the hedonism and irrationalism of competitive sports. Many believed that its admission to the school curriculum would help restrain some of sports' excesses. Under its influence, intercollegiate athletics would move closer to the educational mission of the university if more resources were provided for these activities (thus immunizing student–athletes from reliance on boosters); and through intramurals, more students would become involved, even if some of them were simply training to enter the varsity teams.

The source of tension between interscholastic sports and physical education was control. While physical educators complained most loudly about the "excesses" of interscholastic competition (such as the preoccupation with winning), they worried most about who should control play in the formative stages of a child's life. They were concerned about control not only because of the alleged health benefits of properly conceived and supervised play but also because they attached to physical education a mission of moral uplift. It is no coincidence that the passage of state laws making physical education compulsory was persuasively advocated by the Women's Christian Temperance Union, a very powerful influence on the National Education Association at that time (Freeman 1987, 102). Indeed, much of the credit for whatever success the physical educators enjoyed must be given to women. They played a major role in legitimating the claim that properly managed exercise could yield benefits for the individual, especially when combined with instruction in hygiene and diet.

The movement of physical educators to secure control of athletics was immeasurably aided by the popularity of John Dewey's teaching on the concept of "the whole child," demanding the treatment of both the mind and the body of the child as a unity. Dewey made respectable the incorporation of physical education as a requirement in the curriculum. This, more than the rather narrow health objective, seemed to promise physical educators the achievement of their goal. Concern over abuses and serious injuries from improperly supervised play also aided their case. Equally helpful was the tendency, after 1900, for the high schools to imitate the colleges in organizing interscholastic competition: "Competitive high school sports were gaining considerable impetus from publicized athletic contests between colleges, especially from those contests waged in football" (Rudy 1965, 115). Commentators began to notice the development in high schools of a highly organized "student life" modeled on that of the colleges, "finding expression in the formation of all sorts of clubs, leagues, societies, fraternities, organizations, and publications. . . . Athletic associations and teams played games with rival high schools, calling forth 'unbounded enthusiasm' " (p. 7). Given the obvious abuses at the college level, the spread of this practice to adolescents seemed to make an even stronger case for the physical educators' role.

Physical educators did not intend to eliminate interscholastic sports. Their goal was to position physical education as their foundation. Improvement in health and hygiene were obvious advantages of physical education, but there was much more to be gained. It could prepare more people for participation and thus obviate the complaint that interscholastic sports were elitist; train spectators in the appreciation of the finer points of the game and thus weaken the argument against the "passivity" of the spectator role; and educate the student-athlete in discipline, sportsmanship, cooperation, endurance, and poise. Physical education was thus touted as a prerequisite for sporting achievement and a necessary, if not sufficient, condition for the achievement of the character-building benefits sport was supposed to yield. It was also presented as more accessible to the average individual and more completely integrated into the rest of the student's life.

The physical educator's nemesis was American football: its physical demands relegated most students to the role of spectator or cheerleader and truncated the career of the player:

> By their thirtieth birthday the great majority of graduates feel more at home in their seats at football spectacles than they would in suits upon any field. In Great Britain this is not the case. English Rugby, soccer, . . . once mastered, are not infrequently played almost until middle age. The interest of Americans changes early from the active to the passive. (Savage 1929, 193)

Another writer argued that the preoccupation of America's youth with "the Big Game" was the reason why other countries were so much more successful in international sporting competition: "We talk athletics, but there is too much 'grand stand' and too little actual participation in games. . . . We are not an athletic nation as compared with Germany, where, for instance, the annual *Turn* festivals at Frankfurt produce 20,000 active athletes on the field and there is no grand stand" (Ryan 1929, 21). A survey conducted in the late 1920s revealed that schools emphasized football, basketball, track-and-field, and baseball to the virtual exclusion of all other sports. Sports with "carry-over value" (i.e., those that could be continued into adult life) were "notably overshadowed" by those, notably football, with no such value (p. 50). When polled, school administrators said the the worst problem of interscholastic competition was that so few students benefited from the expenditure (p. 130).

The end of World War I seemed to hold bright promise for the physical education profession. The war had heightened public interest in health questions and physical fitness training, as had the Civil War before it. By 1920, twenty-seven state legislatures had enacted legislation making physical education and health care courses compulsory in public schools (Rudy 1965, 119). But there were counterforces at work that would, in the long run, weaken the Physical Education movement in the schools. The 1920s, the "Jazz Age," was a time of increased fascination with the competitive, expressive, even spectacular side of sports. Critics complained that "we permit our interscholastic contests to become the avenue of escape for all the neurotic jazz hysteria of the entire community, of the sensational newspapers, of commercial clubs and boosters' clubs, of the town sports and gamblers, of the hangers on of pool-rooms and smoke shops" (quoted in Ryan 1929, xxxix).

Physical education seemed dour and prosaic compared with the spectacle of interscholastic competition, at least with respect to men's sports; and it tended to be swamped by its more attractive cousin: "By the time sports merged with physical training and hygeine into a broader program of physical education, such programs consisted almost entirely of sports instruction" (Seymour 1990, 76). Indeed, even before World War I, the more realistic were having to admit that "students showed considerably more zest when taking part in athletics than they did in gymnastics" (Staples 1943, 23), although this was more true of men than women. Try as they might, they could not gain control of the sports and games that students had organized for themselves and in which alumni showed such inordinate interests—quite the reverse; for they were to discover that sports and games had "moved irresistibly into programs of physical education, to the point of replacing the traditional activities" (Freeman 1987, 104).

There were four reasons for this. First and most generally, the American public was by no means ready for the professionalization of physical education and derided the idea that matters such as health, hygiene, housework, play, and even education in general should be given over to "experts." Second, gymnastics was supplanted because competitive games were considered more "natural" and, equally important, more American. A contemporary writer described gymnastics as "artificial exercises that arose in response to a group of ideas wholly foreign to the traits, characteristics, and needs of American boys and girls" (quoted in Ryan 1929, 55). Third, despite the physical educators' claim that only their values could justify interscholastic sports, football, basketball, and baseball had already established their legitimacy on the campus by appealing to their own independent values, such as character building, sportsmanship, and loyalty to school. The attachment of interscholastic sport to this value system could not be severed even by its most determined critics. Fourth, physical educators found that ironically, their place in the academic world was questioned by teachers and faculty precisely because they were so close to the sport world. Theirs was guilt by association. Their foothold in the academy had always been precarious. They had been dismissed as unscholarly by academics on the one hand and as irrelevant by both the coaches and administrators of interscholastic athletics on the other. Even the Amateur Athletic Union gave little recognition to the physical education profession (Lehr 1985, 259). It might be said that athletics, having ridden into college on the back of physical education, eventually consumed it. State universities began developing physical education departments in the late 1880s. By 1921, 86 percent of 231 colleges surveyed had established physical education departments. By that time, however, 82 percent of the staff of these departments were also engaged in interscholastic athletic coaching. By 1929, of 177 directors of departments of physical education surveyed, only 23 had majored in physical education as undergraduates (Chu 1979, 74). This transition is accredited to the "business-minded" boards of trustees, who, feeling the need to rationalize athletics in the educational structure, decided that this could be best accomplished "through unification with an already somewhat accepted department of the university" (ibid.). Physical education simply lacked the political clout or professional legitimacy to avoid being co-opted in this manner.

Their failure to wrest control of sports created conflicts among physical educators, between the more practically oriented professionals and the more scholarly oriented researchers and teachers. Many physical educators were ambivalent about their added responsibility for intercollegiate athletics, needing to make their own claim to academic respectability. Perhaps because of this, they were to prove incapable of controlling its growth. Ironically, the NCAA lobbied hard to have athletic staff granted faculty status: "By 1921, 187 institutions answering a survey from the American Physical Education Association pointed out that their chairmen of athletics and physical education did, indeed, enjoy a seat on the faculty" (Hardy and Berryman 1982, 23). This was important for the sport fraternity, because it meant that intercollegiate athletics would become a regular line item in the school's budget. However, faculty status for athletic directors and coaches seems to have neither integrated them into the liberal arts college nor reoriented athletic departments toward educational principles. A study of high schools in the late 1920s revealed that "although interscholastic sports may be considered part of the school's general program of physical education, they nevertheless form an independent part, and often dominate, rather than yield to other phases of the general program" (Brammell 1933, 104).

School authorities cared more about sports than physical education: all but one of the states in the union in 1928 had interscholastic athletic associations, but only seventeen had departments of physical education

(Savage 1929, 54). Throughout states like Indiana, high school basketball teams became sources of entertainment; and appropriate facilities had to be built. Many school campuses possessed gymnasia out of all proportion to their enrollment. A 1932 survey of 327 secondary schools uncovered instances of local boosters contributing the expenses of building large, independent gymnasiums: "In some cases, at least, holding companies were organized in towns where gymnasiums were to be built" (Brammell 1933, 86). The idea was to have prominent citizens advance money for the construction costs, which would be later reimbursed through the sale of tickets. As Brammell dryly notes, "certain evils are a natural consequence when the athletic plant in a school must be procured from gate receipts" (1933, 87). The same survey found that interscholastic athletics were largely independent of, and often dominated, other phases of the physical education system. Few schools during the late 1920s and 1930s achieved much of a balance between their physical education, intramurals, health-and-hygiene instruction, and interscholastic sports. Coaches were rarely trained in physical education, athletic facilities were not designed for mass participation, and interscholastic contests were confined to a few sports with no recognized carryover value into adult years.[3]

The Silent Faculty

One potential ally of the physical education profession was the teaching faculty: "American faculty were a major source of opposition to the formal incorporation of athletics into the structure of American higher education" (Chu 1989, 58). The earliest opposition came from faculty who were imbued with English ideals of amateurism.[4] The voice of the teacher was muted, however, because the faculty were so weak politically. Indeed, at the secondary school level, they had yet to gain recognition as a profession. To make matters worse, the appropriation, by bureaucratic administrative structures, of formal powers over the practice of teaching developed in conjunction with the movement of women into high school teaching. This marginalized faculty opinion on interscholastic athletics to an even greater extent. At the college level, also, faculty gradually lost power over full-time administrators and trustees.

College faculty at least had the prestige and resources to make the role of sports on the college campus a quasi-public issue. In the late 1920s, a report by the Carnegie Foundation documented widespread abuses of the amateur ideal, particularly in recruiting and funding, and "received considerable publicity" (Lawrence 1987, 27); but it was issued on the same day as the stockmarket crash and rapidly lost any impact it might have had. Despite its prestige in educational circles, the Carnegie

Foundation could bring only moral persuasion to bear upon the NCAA and its member institutions; and the Depression that soon followed only intensified the competition for financial support that had been a major cause of the abuses detected by the foundation. Subsequent major studies, in 1952 and 1974, by the American Council on Education concluded that "the system [was] designed to serve the survival needs of big-time schools and not the educational needs of the players" (Chu 1989, 140). In the wake of both, ambitious reforms were proposed, focusing chiefly on arresting the trend toward professionalism in college athletic programs and recoupling the athletic and academic roles.[5]

Athletic departments assumed more and more the characteristics of independent economic enterprises beyond the control of the faculty, with the student–athletes functioning as poorly paid employees divorced from the academic community of which they were ostensibly a part, the rest of the students serving to fill the bleachers and populate the cheerleading squads.[6] The athletic programs were generating more revenues and using those revenues to build up their own administrative apparatus. While some revenues were distributed to "minor" sports; few reached the intramural level; even fewer were allocated to the general fund of the university; and of course, none were distributed to the community at large.

By the 1980s, few would have seriously considered justifying educational expenditures on college athletics in terms of health and general educational benefits, although some did justify expenditures (and protest proposed cuts) on the grounds that athletics provided youth from impoverished backgrounds the education that was their right (and which richer youth could buy). By this time, however, public debate had shifted away from how sport could revert to its its public mission and toward the damage that sport as entertainment was doing to education. The right to a good education, not the right to sport, became the issue, with education as the victim and sport as the culprit.

In the process, the NCAA assumed some of the burden of upholding educational, as well as sport, standards. The NCAA had been given the public job of protecting the educational mission of colleges. This is evident in an exchange between Congressman Carl Perkins and the executive director of the NCAA, Richard Schultz during hearings before the House Education Committee.

PERKINS: How is the NCAA going about trying to see that the athlete, the individual athlete or the individual student, is, in fact, getting a sound education? What is the NCAA doing about seeing that the attrition rate or the dropout rate among these students is reduced significantly?

SCHULTZ: First of all, I think that it needs to be remembered that the primary function of the NCAA is to govern intercollegiate athletics. I think the NCAA has been drawn into the educational side of it, which really should not be their basic responsibility because of a perceived need. (U.S. Congress, House, Committee on Education and Labor 1989, 67)

Perkins replied that the NCAA could not divorce itself from the "educational side."

Perkins and Schultz were debating the merits of the Student-Right-to-Know Act, introduced by Senator Bill Bradley, together with representatives Tom McMillen and Edolphus Towns. The bill would have mandated that all schools receiving federal financial assistance report to the secretary of education the graduation rates for students receiving athletics scholarships, categorized by sport, race, and gender. A General Accounting Office report prepared for a Senate committee concluded that the rate of graduation for men's basketball and football division I programs was much lower than that for the general student body (U.S. Congress, Senate, Committee on Labor and Human Resources 1989). Bradley's bill would also require that an athlete's letter of intent to attend a college acknowledge that the athlete had reviewed the report and discussed it with a high school counselor or principal. Bradley had been unsuccessful in persuading the NCAA to release its own figures (it would later do so), and higher education authorities opposed both bills on the grounds that they were unwarranted federal intrusion into academic affairs.

In fact, the proposed legislation represented only a minimal "intrusion" into college athletic life. It amounted to cleaning up athletics by letting the market decide, giving the student–consumer more information to drive out of business inferior "products," that is, colleges that failed to graduate their students. Indeed, the bill was presented as a consumers' bill, a labeling measure. Student–athletes were treated as consumers of higher education: "As such they are entitled to relevant and basic information in order to make informed choices about which college to attend" (U.S. Congress, Senate, Committee on Labor and Human Resources 1989, 6). When it eventually passed, in 1990, the Student-Right-To-Know Act left power firmly in the hands of the major actors in the market, the "big-time" athletic programs, relegating individuals to the status of consumers whose only power lay in exercising choice among existing options.

Those debating the Student-Right-To-Know Act were aware that as they talked, yet another quasi-public investigatory commission on college athletics had been formed. The Knight Foundation Commission was appointed in 1989 and included as members U.S. Secretary of Education, Lamar Alexander and representative Tom McMillen (Democrat, Maryland) a former college and professional basketball player and a vocal critic of the NCAA. The Commission issued its report, "Keeping Faith with the Student–Athlete" in 1991. The report made over thirty recommendations designed to restore integrity to, and public confidence in, college athletics. The recommendations aimed at restoring control over college athletics to college presidents (both within their own institutions and within the NCAA). They were further intended to protect the "academic integrity" of college athletics by raising the educational qualifications for athletic eligibility. A third group of recommendations were aimed at limiting escalating costs and imposing some controls over the rewards being offered athletic programs by television networks and cable companies (e.g., dividing the one billion dollars from television basketball contracts more evenly among member institutions).

The report attached a great deal of importance to the role of the college president in effecting the needed reforms. While this was no doubt due in part to the fact that a majority of members were either present or former college presidents themselves, it also reflected the view that the colleges needed to put their own houses in order and that more public intervention was not the best way to tackle the problem: the college president was described in the report as the "linchpin of the reform movement." Shifting power back to the president and away from the athletic director, the coach, and the boosters clubs would restore some of the spirit of amateurism that the commission sought to preserve.[7] The presidents needed also to play a more active role in the NCAA convention, through the presidents commission.

Some reforms were enacted in the 1991 NCAA Convention, in anticipation of the commission's report and in the shadow of bills presented to Congress aimed at forcing colleges to reform. Scholarship limits were lowered, athletic dorms phased out, seasons shortened, and coaching staffs cut. Further reforms were enacted in the 1992 convention, several of them explicitly tied to the commission's recommendations. Educational qualifications were raised, coaches' outside income would now be subject to presidential approval, and punishments for rules violators increased.

The overall thrust of these reforms was to slow the commercialization of college athletics—not so much to reform athletics as to limit the harm the pursuit of athletic goals might to do a student's educational progress. Neither the Knight Foundation Commission nor critics within the NCAA wished to pursue a strategy of reform that would have required more government action, preferring to leave the task in the hands of college presidents. Much, therefore, depended on individual presidents' having the strength of will to contradict powerful athletic administrators and influential trustees. Critics were not quite so sanguine about the chances of presidentially guided reform, given the enormous sums of money individual institutions could derive from athletic competition and the power exercised by boards of trustees, many of them strong supporters of college athletic programs.

The commission's report did not put a stop to bills being introduced into Congress, most of them designed to use state power (e.g., the threat of antitrust action) to effect needed reforms. But these bills were simply stronger versions of those introduced in earlier sessions, designed to protect the educational mission of schools and colleges from the ravages of big-time athletics. Rarely did a legislator articulate the view that educational institutions had the responsibility to provide—and students the right to claim—sport opportunities for all.

CONCLUSION

Historically, sport organizations have been defined as private, voluntary associations, sheltered from public scrutiny. But the boundary between the private and the public is constantly shifting. Privatized in the eighteenth and nineteenth century, leisure has become more public in the twentieth century. The expansion of leisure time and discretionary income has triggered "a more or less unwitting re-evaluation of the appropriate division between the private and public sectors" (Meisel 1978, 194). The public costs of tourism, attendance at professional sports, hunting and fishing, dirtbike racing, and boating escalate as the number of people with the incomes to pursue these pastimes increases. Water, soil, and air all deteriorate in quality, threatening the very amenities that initially fueled people's interest. In this "tragedy of the commons," the boundary between private and public moves if the clamor to prevent further private abuse leads to stricter public regulation. How far the boundary moves depends on how much the more politically powerful groups desire, and are able to mobilize the resources of the state. Thus, the affluent and influential boating population secures Coast Guard protection for themselves (all in the public interest), a solicitude the state does not show to motocross racers.

The absorption of much of the administration of amateur sports into educational institutions has been highly consequential for the notion that people have a right to sport participation. To some extent, sports have benefited from the link forged early in this century between sport and health and between sport and a healthy mind, or character. The first meant that sport would be associated with the right to health care, an important part of the justification for physical education. It was not too far from this position to the claim that all have a right to supervised recreation. Sport also benefited from the idea that education (also a recognized social right) included properly supervised play. Public policy designed to improve the nation's health and education thus also promised to improve its sport opportunities. I have shown, however, that forces have been at work to counter these arguments. High school athletics and college sports have come to resemble entertainment, provided by the few to the many. It is difficult to make a case for entertainment as a social right. State actors have mobilized periodically to try to restore some of the original features of interscholastic sports in order to recapture some of their public benefits, but with little success. In becoming part of American education, sports have been forced to accommodate and change. They have become commercialized and professionalized; they have become hierarchically organized, coach dominated, and largely undemocratic; they have become elitist and highly specialized, segmented from the rest of life.

There have always been groups anxious to oppose these trends, retain democratic control over games, orient games to the development of the whole person, and make games available to all as a form of active, informal enjoyment. Many of these groups exist on high school and college campuses. The NCAA itself has sought to place some restrictions on professionalism. But a thick rule book absent vigorous and certain enforcement has simply not been enough to slow the pace of the differentiation of athletics from academics. College athletics are, for the most part, semiprofessional enclaves within the campus, dispensing sport opportunities to the general student body on a charitable basis when funds permit.

For the most part, public government, despite its involvement in the academic component of education, has chosen to treat the NCAA and state high school athletic associations as private organizations entitled to regulate their own affairs. Only when abuses become the subject of mass media attention does Congress pay heed. Even then, the issue is not so much what has happened to sport as what sport is doing to the educational mission of the school. Thus, low graduation rates of athletes trouble politicians because they suggest a pattern of exploitation of defenseless young men and women in the interest of athletic competition and a violation of the public trust invested in institutions of higher education, both public and private, not because they represent the perversion of some sport ideal.

Some sort of recognition of sport as a right has therefore developed in the United States, although it is often buried within, or subordinated to, other concerns considered more important. The impact of the state has been decentralized and indirect, through schools and colleges, federal agencies set up to manage public lands or administer parks, and local governments and quasi-public voluntary agencies. Nevertheless, the idea that Americans are entitled to sporting opportunities is clearly present amid the conflicting directives, inadequate funding, reactive legislation, and rhetorical flourishes. At no point has this idea been allowed to threaten the command of the private economy over the provision of leisure services: the public is always subordinate to the private. At no point has the idea of a leisure expertise or leisure professionalism gained public credence or political clout, but the idea is now more a part of political debate than it was even during the Progressive Era. Its enemies are much the same: commercial entertainments, economic development and the consequent destruction of leisure resources, exploitative and distorting educational programs, self-interested professional sport owners. Its political credibility, in an era of general entitlement to the privileges of social citizenship, is, however, much stronger.

CHAPTER 9

SPORT

IN THE

WIRED CITY

The modern sports community is as much electronic as it is geographical. The Dallas Cowboys and the Atlanta Braves both claim to be "America's team" because they are watched simultaneously by people living on either coast with the help of satellite telecommunications technology. The NBA can claim to represent "America's game" because it saturates the airwaves with hundreds of games a season, its better players being as familiar as news anchors and soap opera stars. Television is even the foundation for the global expansion of sport: the World League of American Football was largely a creature of the mass media, having been floated on the basis of a forty-eight million-dollar contract with ABC and USA Network, trading heavily on European fascination with American television programming and cultural exports, and aiming at a large share of the growing number of satellite television networks in the new united Europe. Televised games are also the life blood of college sports: one of the most feared of all NCAA sanctions is to be prohibited television exposure.

The most influential media of mass culture—originally newspapers, then radio, and today television—have always devoted much of their attention to sport. Sport events are relatively easy to cover and inexpensive to produce and admirably meet the media's need for the dramatic and sensational. They also deliver better than any other kind of programming an audience of the more affluent male members of the population. Most Americans' exposure to sport is through a mass medium. The meaning and significance of sport, as well as its distribution and mode of operation, are therefore affected by social forces that bear upon it indirectly through the mass media. As they change, so will the public's access to sport.

Television has proved to be a mixed blessing for professional and amateur sports, for two principal reasons. First, when television networks and cable companies come bidding for the right to exclusive transmission of sports events, they provide a powerful incentive for sport owners to band together more firmly in order to bargain from a position of strength. This increases their vulnerability to antitrust prosecution. Second, televised sport can grow from being a useful adjunct to, and promoter of, the live game to being a competitor with it. Television restructured the market for sporting events, with important consequences for public welfare in this area. This chapter will deal with the political problems raised by the relation between television and sport. What role, if any, should the state play in ensuring public access to sport through television broadcasts?

Mass media such as television are largely under the control of telecommunications conglomerates for whom the media are a means of selling advertising for the purposes of profit. In the television business, the final commodity is not the program but the viewer, who is purchased from the station at a certain price per head by the advertiser. The program itself plays an intermediary role in the commodity circuit; it is the bait that the station uses to hook the viewer. This essential fact structures the relation between television and sport.

The telecommunications industry is regulated by a variety of government agencies, the chief of which is the Federal Communications Commission (FCC), specifically charged with the task of overseeing the electronic media. The FCC has the authority to license stations, suggest broadcasting regulations to Congress, and prosecute stations and networks for alleged violations of existing laws. The warrant for government regulation is found in the acknowledged public ownership of the airwaves and public concern that private interests not abuse them. A broadcast license, by the terms and intent of the Radio Act of 1927 and the Communications Act of 1934, is a public trust. Private industry has largely succeeded in keeping the role of the FCC to a minimum. It has achieved this by carefully cultivating a public image as the donor of "free" services and, of course, by using the media it owns to convey favorable images and censor opposing views.

After a brief initial period of hesitation (during which the major networks dismissed sports as lower-class pursuits), the television industry realized the tremendous potential of sport programming as a tool for attracting advertising revenues. The fragmented, episodic nature of sport, with its recapitulation of basic situations of tension from week to week, was ideally suited to the logic of advertising, the "commercial break" that repeats the same basic message. Of course, sport would have to undergo some modification to be suitable for broadcasting: its duration would have to be more predictable, there would have to be breaks in the action to allow for advertisements, and the pace would have to be quickened. The more action and drama, the better, as far as television was concerned. The first sports to be televised on a regular basis were wrestling (which had assumed its current highly dramatized form by the end of the 1940s) and roller derby (which was essentially an invention of television). Eventually, television would come to determine the length of "the season" and the schedule, the duration of games, and how they were played.

Television helped nationalize the major team sports after World War II. The baseball diffusion of the 1950s—the Braves to Milwaukee, the Athletics to Kansas City, the Dodgers to Los Angeles and the Giants to San Francisco—while in part spurred by deteriorating stadiums in older eastern cities, was also encouraged by the expanding television market. Television also restructured the sport industry. For example, it helped concentrate the production of baseball in the hands of a few owners, those who owned major league rather than minor league, franchises. Before 1951, when the riches to be gained from television were unappreciated, organized baseball protected minor league club owners by prohibiting major league television broadcasts to minor league markets. When the possibilities of gain from television became more obvious, the owners rescinded the rule, and many minor league owners were driven out of business. Television even affects how the leagues govern themselves. As commissioners acquired the power to negotiate increasingly lucrative television contracts, power shifted from individual owners into the commissioners' hands. Indeed, the role of the commissioner in the major sports is now defined largely in terms of his ability to negotiate with the networks. This is most evident in the case of the NFL, where Commissioner Rozelle solidified his power on the basis of his ability to intimidate network executives in bargaining sessions. While president of the National Hockey League, John Ziegler was frequently criticized for his failure to negotiate a network contract: the proportion of NHL revenues coming from (unpredictable) ticket sales is around 65 percent, highest of all the major team sports. Baseball is rather different; for a long tradition of negotiating broadcast rights locally means that as the value of network contracts has grown, many of the owners see the commissioner as "at best a competitor for those revenues, and at worst an impediment to receiving them at all" (Klatell and Marcus 1988, 116). In amateur sports, the authority of the NCAA over member institutions was enhanced by its ability to regulate access to the television screen.

By the 1980s, the relation between sports and the mass media, especially television, had become so close that it is doubtful whether either could survive without the other.[1] The sport leagues were relying increasingly on television for revenues, and the networks themselves looked to sports as the largest single advertising revenue producer: in 1986, 20 percent of all network advertising revenues came from sport advertising (Klatell and Marcus 1988, 26). In 1989, CBS purchased the right to broadcast the baseball World Series, the play-offs, and a dozen regular season games through 1993, for $1.1 billion and paid $1 billion dollars for the seven-year right to broadcast the NCAA basketball tournament (more than twice the price of its previous contract), having already promised the International Olympic Committee $243 million for the 1992 Winter Olympic Games in Albertville, France, and $300 million for the 1994 Winter Olympics in Norway. In that same year, NBC purchased the rights to broadcast four years of NBA basketball for $600 million, and committed $401 million for the 1992 Summer Olympics.

SPORTS ENTER THE PUBLIC DOMAIN

The telecommunications industry and the sport industry both occupy an ambiguous position with respect to government policy, each possessing both public and private aspects. The airwaves are in the public domain and cannot be privately owned. They belong to the people, and their use is granted only under license. The extent to which the American public has the "right" to hear or see a sports event is therefore both a communications issue and a sport issue. For example, in 1939, the World Series was carried on radio by the Mutual Network, the highest bidder for the broadcast rights. Unfortunately, the reach of the network was quite limited; and the sporting press was inundated with letters protesting the arrangement: "The most common complaint was that the workingman of America had been sold down the river to the highest bidder" (Crepeau 1980, 30). In 1978, the House Interstate Commerce Committee became concerned about the televising of the forthcoming Moscow Olympic Games. Congressmen were worried that NBC, the rights holder, would be manipulated by the Soviets. "Are you sure," asked one committee member, "that if NBC News is approached . . . with a 'good idea' for a program from the Soviet Union, and elects to turn down that telecast, there will not be any second guessing of that decision?" (U.S. Congress, House, Committee on Interstate and Foreign Commerce 1978c, 84). Would the Soviets, the committee members wanted to know, allow NBC to show any protests that might occur at the games? In the first case, the resolution of a problem arising in the world of sport arouses concerns about the proper use of the airwaves; in the second case, efforts to deal with a problem arising in the world of telecommunications threatens to deprive the public of access to a sporting event.

NEWS OR ENTERTAINMENT?

While the relation between sports and the mass media today is symbiotic, it is nevertheless a contractual relationship in which conflicts of interest and competition are endemic. The media appreciate the value of sports to sell advertising slots and newspapers, just as the sport industry appreciates the free publicity to be derived from coverage of their games. But the media would like to get the sport material for as little as possible, while the sport industry would like to maintain a proprietary interest in what it produces for public consumption. Each turns to the state to defend its interests.

So long as mass culture was disseminated chiefly by mass circulation newspapers, the question of the mass media rights to sporting events was unlikely to be an issue. News of a sporting event would arrive after the event had concluded and could in no way match the experience of witnessing it in person: nothing grows stale faster than a sport competition. With the advent of radio, simultaneous descriptions of sporting events became possible; and these could much more readily substitute for the real thing. The control of the mass mediation of sports thus became a political issue.

The right of a sport franchise to control the (radio) broadcast of its games was not effectively established in court rulings until 1934 and 1938, when it was finally decided that the "news, reports, descriptions or accounts" of games belonged to the individual clubs. The games were not news events but private entertainments, staged by their owners. News of the game could be broadcast, but only after the final whistle. The earliest deals arranging simultaneous broadcasts were negotiated locally, and teams typically split the money equally. They were not considered serious competitors with live attendance. However, after World War II, both television and sport became national in scope; and television presented itself as a much more attractive substitute for the live game.

JOINT NEGOTIATIONS CAUSE
POLITICAL PROBLEMS

The original agreements between sport clubs and television were individually negotiated and were limited to the club's catchment area. The owners soon realized, however, that more money was to be made by negotiating as a group and offering exclusive broadcasting rights for their sport to the highest bidder. Unfortunately, joint negotiations, especially when coupled with an agreement to share the revenues among the member teams equally, made it much easier for critics to make a charge of monopoly. It is worth noting that one of the rare occasions on which the state actually *initiated* action against professional team sports for any reason had to do with the question of joint negotiations with the networks. In 1952, NFL commissioner Bert Bell had obtained from the owners the right to negotiate on their behalf a single contract with competing television networks. A suit brought by the Justice Department (*United States* v. *National Football League* [1953]) saw the court decide that the NFL could not enter into the joint sale of radio and television rights: "The court reasoned that radio and television were clearly involved with interstate commerce, and therefore professional football was an interstate business subject to the antitrust laws" (Freedman 1987, 35). As a consequence of this decision, it became the practice until 1960 for owners to negotiate agreements independently.

As more and more people bought television sets, football's owners became convinced not only that a league package would distribute revenues more evenly but that higher fees could be negotiated if the networks were faced with only one seller. The Justice Department warned the NFL in the spring of 1960 that any such package would violate antitrust laws, and the older league hesitated. However, the NFL by this time had a new and hungrier rival in the American Football League (AFL), which decided to go ahead and sign a package plan offered by ABC (a network weak in other programming and anxious to land a contract with a football league), providing approximately $185,000 to each team, funds crucial to the survival of many of its franchises. In 1961, the NFL followed suit, negotiating a league package television broadcast with CBS, a two-year agreement calling for annual payments of about $300,000 per team. While the Justice Department had ignored the AFL-ABC agreement, it could not turn a blind eye to that between the NFL and CBS. Subsequently, the court invalidated the contract on the grounds that member clubs had eliminated competition among themselves in the sale of television rights to their games and had thereby broken antitrust laws. The NFL was forced to revert to the policy of individually negotiated contracts.

Anxious to exploit the opportunity television afforded to compete with the AFL and without a major network agreement, the NFL turned to Congress for relief. Representative Emanuel Celler and the House Judiciary Committee had been concerned since 1957 with a sports bill, containing legislation designed to exempt professional sports from antitrust laws. Celler's bill received prompt and favorable attention from the Antitrust Subcommittee of the House Judiciary Committee on its introduction in August 1961 and reached the floor of the House one month later. The bill sought to have Congress recognize the special need for controlled business competition in professional football. It affirmed the need to negotiate television contracts jointly on the grounds of equalizing competition on the playing field. The Senate passed its version of the House bill on September 21, 1961; and the result was the Sports Broadcasting Act of 1961.

It is unlikely that Congress would have made the concessions granted in the Sports Broadcasting Act had not the NFL and AFL coexisted at the time. Their rivalry made it easier for each to be regarded as a "joint venture" for whom joint negotiating was perfectly appropriate. Twenty years later, interleague rivalry was to have a different effect on the relationship between sports and television. When the United States Football League (USFL) came along to challenge the NFL, the result was a major court suit precisely over the older league's grasp on the broadcasting of football. The NFL and the AFL had merged, and Commissioner Rozelle had negotiated a series of highly lucrative television contracts under the authority of the Sports Broadcasting Act. Television revenues had become crucial to the survival of several NFL franchises. Access to television had become a significant barrier to entry for aspiring new leagues. When the USFL sued the NFL twenty years later, the bone of contention was not so much the NFL's monopolization of the football industry as its monopolization of the airwaves. The USFL charged that the NFL was making it impossible to secure a contract with the major television networks. It accused the NFL of violating a commitment it had made to Congress when lobbying for passage of the 1961 Sports Broadcasting Act. During hearings on that bill, Commissioner Rozelle had testified that "there is no intention on our part of using more than one network if this legislation is passed," implying that rival leagues would be free to negotiate their own deal (U.S. Congress, Senate, Committee on the Judiciary 1986a, 173–74). In 1966, when Congress amended the Sports Broadcasting Act to exempt the merger of the AFL and NFL, the NFL had a pooled agreement with CBS, the AFL, with NBC. The merger retained these agreements, the result being that the combined league now had a relationship with both the major networks. In 1969, the NFL further solidified its grip on network television when it signed its Monday Night Football agreement with ABC. Congress thus permitted the NFL to establish itself in a monopoly position with respect to all major networks, despite its expressed intention to the contrary. It was not lost on USFL owners that each NFL owner's revenues from television had risen from $1.5 million in 1970 to $15 million in 1985.

The Sports Broadcasting Act was passed on the understanding that it would not limit the public's access to televised football. The implication was that competition between the networks for the right to broadcast football would guarantee this. By the time Commissioner Rozelle had reached his agreement with all three networks simultaneously, this understanding seemed to have been violated. At hearings to consider the antitrust implications of NFL agreements with cable companies, Senator Arlen Specter reminded Commissioner Rozelle of his undertaking, implying that the new contract with cable television was a further violation of it. Rozelle, with NFL counsel and future commissioner Paul

Tagliabue at his side, referred back to his 1961 testimony, pointing out that he had also said, "Perhaps in 20 years from now the television picture will change. The single network may no longer be desirable, and it may become much better for the public and the league to use more than one network" (U.S. Congress, Senate, Committee on the Judiciary 1987, 28). Specter was left to rue the day he had not insisted the undertaking be included in the act itself.

When the USFL began playing in the Spring of 1983 it was carried by both ABC, and the Entertainment and Sports Network (ESPN): "In fact, it was widely regarded as a 'television league' from its inception because the television contracts were signed before some teams had names, coaches, players, or playing fields" (Klatell and Marcus 1988, 89). When the USFL decided to move to a Fall playing schedule, ABC declined to join in the head-to-head competition with the NFL. The USFL promptly sued the NFL, contending an "involuntary conspiracy" between the three major networks and the NFL. The jury in *United States Football League* v. *National Football League* actually agreed that the NFL had acquired an unlawful monopoly. However, it also found that the USFL had not been damaged by this exclusion, that its economic woes had been occasioned by mismanagement. Nominal damages of one dollar were awarded, and the NFL survived unscathed.

Baseball largely escaped these political threats because of the antitrust immunity granted in 1922 and also because, since the beginning of a formalized relationship between radio and baseball in the 1930s, fees for *local or regional* rights had been a major source of revenue for baseball teams. Successive commissioners held back from pursuing the kind of national agreement struck by football, despite the fact that baseball could have formed these relationships without having to look over its shoulder at the Justice Department. They simply lacked the power to bring recalcitrant owners into line. Thus, in contrast to the NFL, nearly half the 1987 income of baseball from the electronic media was derived from non-network television. The result was wide disparities in television income. The 1987 local rights income of the New York Yankees was $17.5 million; that for the Seattle Mariners, $2.2 million (Bellamy 1988, 77).

While the more powerful or fortunate owners benefited from this arrangement, baseball owners as a whole recognized that their joint contracts with the networks were less lucrative than they would be if they could guarantee to those networks exclusive rights. By the time Peter Ueberroth became baseball commissioner, *USFL* v. *NFL* had been decided, seeming to give the go-ahead for joint negotiations. The single greatest contribution Peter Ueberroth made as commissioner of baseball was to negotiate a national rights agreement with CBS for $1.6 billion to be paid over a three-year (1990–93) period. This represented less a growing tolerance for monopoly in baseball, however, than did growing competition within the television industry. Joint negotiations with the major networks became more politically tolerable as those networks found themselves in increasing competition with cable companies, as I shall show.

BLACKOUTS: PUBLIC ACCESS DENIED

Television's money created severe problems for the sport leagues because it tended to concentrate power within the leagues in the hands of the commissioner and, by encouraging joint negotiations, to expose the leagues to unwanted antitrust liability. Market forces created—or recreated—political problems for the leagues, both internal and external. Television also created problems because it was a competitor for the live game. This proved to be irksome to the owners; but it also became an issue of public policy, because it raised the question of the public's right to see the programming of their choice and their right of access to sporting events.

In return for passing the Sports Broadcasting Act of 1961, Congress expected sport owners to be more sensitive to the viewing needs of the public. One of the most irritating examples of the owners' callousness had always been the blackout rule prohibiting the live telecasting of sports events within the territory from which that event might draw spectators unless it was sold out. Some blackout stipulations also prohibited the telecasting of a game back into a team's "territory" even when that team was playing away. As early as 1951, congressmen were complaining that boxing contests, confined to closed-circuit television broadcasts, were violating "a right that should not be denied the tax-paying public of America" (Sammons 1988, 158). But television decimated attendance at boxing matches, and other sport promoters and owners became wary about giving sports too much television exposure. Baseball's minor leagues were especially worried about the telecasting of major league games and twice took their case to Congress (1953 and 1957), urging that blackout rights be granted. One of the conditions the NFL imposed on each of its owners was that when they negotiated an agreement with a television network for permission to broadcast their games, they had to prohibit the network from televising home games within a range of 75 to 120 miles of the stadium. A challenge to the blackout rule was included in the 1953 Justice Department suit described earlier. In deciding that case, the federal district court determined that prohibiting the local telecast of the home team's game was a "reasonable" restraint of trade and therefore lawful. However, it struck down the part of the rule requiring an owner to black out *all* NFL games in his territory when his team was playing at home. Under this court-imposed arrangement, not only were owners forbidden to negotiate jointly, they were also expected to tolerate the telecasting of rival games when their team was playing at home.

All this was changed by the Sports Broadcasting Act. It exempted from the antitrust laws any agreement among professional hockey, basketball, baseball, or football clubs whereby the league of such clubs sells all or part of the television rights of its member clubs. In short, it allowed the sale of a "package" of television rights. The act did not explicitly authorize blackouts because, by convention, each owner had the power to sell or not sell his games to television. What it did was to permit leaguewide contracts for the sale of television rights without taking away the existing blackout power, because it was only by having a leaguewide contract that equal access to television for all teams, rich or poor, first-place or last-place, could be ensured. It is worth noting that the Department of Justice opposed granting this exemption on grounds that, in authorizing joint negotiations, it clearly violated the terms of the Sherman Act. The Sports Broadcasting Act was seized upon by the NFL as authorizing existing blackout practices not only of home games but also of outside games broadcast into home territory.

In 1966, the NFL removed the ban on the broadcasting of outside games (i.e., games not involving the "home" team). It was generally recognized that this change in policy was prompted by competition from the rival American Football League, which televised AFL games in the "home territory" of NFL clubs on the same days and at the same times as NFL games were being played. Those without tickets for NFL games were thus strongly encouraged to watch AFL games (U.S. Congress, House, Committee on Interstate and Foreign Commerce 1973a, 14). The partial lifting of blackouts did little to quiet those fans who resented not being able to watch their team on television. When the game was sold out, they could neither get a ticket nor watch on television. Fans argued that absent a ticket, televised games were the only way they could get a return on the tax dollars they had contributed to building the stadiums in which most NFL teams played. A letter read out before the Senate Commerce Committee's Subcommittee on Communications expressed this point of view:

> I am employed in Cincinnati and I pay a city payroll tax which actually makes me a Cincinnati taxpayer, so I along with thousands of others help pay off the deficit on the stadium. This is the Bengals' fifth season and I and my family, we all dearly love the Bengals, have never been able to see even one game together, due to the fact we cannot get tickets. (U.S. Congress, Senate, Committee on Commerce 1972, 13)

Bills to end the blackout practice were introduced into the House in 1969, 1970, 1971, and 1972. The 1971 Superbowl Game, played in

Miami, had aroused great discontent because it was blacked out over a wide area of South Florida despite being sold out. Seventy-five thousand Floridians signed a petition protesting the blackout. The 1972 Superbowl in New Orleans was also blacked out: a protest petition drew thirty-thousand signatures. During Senate hearings in 1972 to consider further bills aimed at prohibiting blackouts, the sponsor of one of the bills, Robert Griffin (Michigan), accused the NFL of wanting it both ways: "On the one hand they want antitrust protection to increase television revenues through package contracts, while on the other hand they want antitrust protection in order to protect gate revenues from too much television" (U.S. Congress, Senate, Committee on Commerce 1972, 10). Other congressmen argued that with television in the public domain, football had been granted the right to use television in a certain manner, had made tremendous profits under the protection of that right, and should now be asked to offer something in exchange, in the form of taking the risk of televising home games. The Department of Justice, pointing to sellout crowds at football games and the fivefold increase in television revenues since 1961, joined the fight against the blackout. Even the president signaled his willingness to sign a bill prohibiting it.

The Federal Communications Commission (FCC) and the major networks also supported the prohibition. The role of the FCC in this debate throws an interesting light on sport policy in the United States. The chairman of the FCC testified on behalf of the antiblackout bill while at the same time declaring that his agency had nothing to do with sport as such. The FCC did, however, have a responsibility to see that the Communications Act of 1934 (of which the 1961 legislation was an amendment) was adhered to by the networks. The FCC would have preferred a "hands off" role in this case but was persuaded to side with the networks in opposing the practice of blacking out games in the public interest.

The NFL, NHL, NBA, ABA, and organized baseball all supported the blackout rule and sought to have the 1961 legislation stand. Commissioner Rozelle presented figures purporting to show lower attendances at televised games and predicted that "no-shows" would increase, thus reducing the concession and parking spending on which many municipalities depended. He also pointed to the decline of boxing as an example of what could happen to a sport overexposed on television (U.S. Congress, Senate, Committee on Commerce 1972, 57). Rozelle was circumspect enough, however, to announce that the upcoming Superbowl, scheduled for January 1973 in Los Angeles, would be televised "in the nature of an experiment" if all tickets were sold ten days prior to the event. This was a concession. It was not enough to forestall any blackout legislation but perhaps accounts for the fact that the bill eventually passed, Public Law (PL)93-107 (1973), was considerably weaker than the previous bills, all of which had taken issue with the antitrust exemption granted in the 1961 legislation. The 1973 act simply prohibited local blackouts of all network games sold out seventy-two hours in advance for a trial period of three years. The bill also instructed the FCC to conduct annual studies of the effects of the legislation on live attendances.

One reason why the owners were unable to prevent the bill from being passed was the robust health of the industry. The 1961 amendments had been justified on the grounds that football, in particular, was financially insecure: the jointly negotiated television package would save the league. A report made available to Congress in 1973 showed that between 1958 and 1972, regular season attendance at NFL games had increased 250 percent; the number of franchises from twelve to twenty-six; the number of games played a season, from twelve to fourteen; and average attendance, from 41,700 to 57,300. Television revenues had risen from $332,000 (NFL) and $212,000 (AFL) per team to $1,670,000 per team. In 1972, 81 percent of the NFL games played had been sold out (U.S. Congress, House, Committee on Interstate and Foreign Commerce 1973).

PL 93-107 expired in December 1975. In that year, hearings were conducted in both houses of Congress to consider extending the legislation for another three years. The FCC had by that time conducted three of the impact assessments called for in the bill. A spokesman for the FCC declared, "Our studies . . . have not revealed that the antiblackout law has had any adverse effect on organized sports" (U.S. Congress, Senate, Committee on Commerce 1975, 6). Although a House bill (HR 9566) introduced during this session called for making PL 93-107 permanent, the FCC did not consider the data adequate at this time to evaluate the impact of the prohibition accurately and called for a simple extension for a further three years, which the Senate version of the bill adopted. Over the strenuous objections of the owners, the Senate Commerce Committee approved the extension; but the bill died in conference.

After such a close call, the owners decided to continue the limited blackout rule on a "voluntary" basis and Commissioner Rozelle, in a letter to the Senate Commerce Committee, agreed to lift the television blackout of sold-out home games. In 1979, bills were once more introduced into the House to prohibit all blacking out of games. The owners once more complained that such legislation would increase the number of "no-shows" and eventually decrease the number of ticket buyers. They managed to imply that it was un-American to prohibit blackouts. Hugh Culverhouse, owner of the Tampa Bay Buccaneers, stressed the importance of having people actually attend the game:

> I had dinner the other evening in Switzerland with the Soviet Ambassador. . . . He was questioning me in a rather detailed manner about our sport. If it's the one thing that I think worries them most

is that throughout our sports programs . . . we bring about a lot of community and national unity by people having something to belong to, to be a part of, cheer together, have a prayer together . . . and sing the national anthem on Sundays. (U.S. Congress, House, Committee on Interstate and Foreign Commerce 1979, 61)

The owners need not have feared. Congress lacked the will to formalize legislatively the "voluntary" agreement under which the NFL was working, and the bills were not reported out of committee.

Surprisingly, the antitrust laws, a trusty weapon in the fight to control sports leagues, were rarely invoked in the debates over blackout agreements. The owners persuaded Congress that the decision to blackout was made by the individual club and that therefore antitrust laws did not apply. Congress thus chose to ignore leaguewide rulings, especially powerful in the NFL, that individual owners integrate blackout agreements into their contracts with the media and equally to ignore the fact that the agreements with the major networks were jointly negotiated, not individually struck. One reason for this rather narrow interpretation might well have been that blackouts were discussed in terms of the ownership of the event, and the right of a sport franchise to control broadcast of its games had been clearly established in case law by the 1950s. In the Copyright Act (1976), Congress, at the urging of the professional sport leagues, extended federal copyright protection to live sport broadcasts, rejecting the broadcasters' contention that they were co-producers of sporting events. On the legitimated assumption that the individual clubs were the copyright holders, the league commissioners could thus present themselves as "middlemen" before Congress, undertaking to persuade each of their individual owners to be as generous as possible with air time for their games. Congressmen and the fans they represented were placed in the position of supplicants.

CABLE TELEVISION: SPORTS REPRIVATIZED

Although the owners could use their established right to copyright the telecasting of their games to shelter themselves from antitrust attack and place their critics at a disadvantage, they also found that this ability to negotiate individually could be an Achilles' heel. The problem was cable television. Its development presented sports club owners with a dilemma. Each might exploit cable as a potential new revenue source, but they were also mindful of the extent to which they benefited from the networks' monopoly over sport broadcasting. This monopoly could be used by the networks to charge advertisers higher fees, which, in turn, enabled the networks to pay the leagues more for the right to broadcast their games. The emergence of cable in the 1970s multiplied the number of places where holders to the rights to sporting events could peddle their wares. Cable companies sought to lure individual franchises into striking local deals, but the danger was that such deals would not only cheapen the product on a national basis but also create an imbalance in the league.

Cable television was not foreseen in the 1961 Sports Broadcasting Act by either the sport owners or the major networks. It was welcomed by the major networks at first because it brought television to communities otherwise unable to receive signals and added viewing opportunities in those communities where the number of broadcast stations was small. The growth of cable posed two problems for both the networks and the sport owners: (1) cable systems competed with the broadcast stations and thus threatened advertising revenues, and (2) they carried to local communities signals for which they had paid no copyright fee, claiming that they were merely retransmitting signals.

In the early 1950s, cable was defined by the FCC as an "ancillary service" because of its dependent relationship to broadcasters. It was widely supposed that carrying signals through cables would disappear with the advent of new broadcast technologies like ultrahigh frequency (UHF). However, by the end of the decade, cable operators had begun selling their services in communities with existing broadcast audiences and the local broadcast stations began to complain to the FCC about the unfair competition. In response to broadcast industry pressure, the FCC, in 1962, changed its mind and declared that cable operators using microwave relays to import distant television signals were engaging in activities involving the business of broadcasting and thus threatened to undermine the entire television structure the state had erected by fragmenting local audiences and failing to sustain local program production, the latter being one of the mandates given the FCC under the Communications Act of 1934. In 1966, the commission declared total jurisdiction over cable and called a halt to distant signal importation into the nation's top one hundred markets, thus protecting the three-way monopoly of the major networks. The policy favored the development of a highly structured and centralized agreement between the networks and the sports leagues.

It was during this period of relative stability in the 1960s and early 1970s that the television networks and the sport leagues forged the relationship that would be so profitable for both, each seeking some measure of competitive freedom with respect to the other, neither desiring a completely open marketplace for televised sport. They were able to do so because they were protected by the state: the sport leagues secured immunity from antitrust attack and were thus able to negotiate jointly; and the major networks profited from the benign neglect of the FCC, thus perpetuating the three-network monopoly in most television markets.

This equilibrium was disturbed in the later 1970s as the FCC came under increasing attack from public interest groups for its alleged policy of favoring established broadcast stations (license renewals were rarely refused) and for its neglect of public interest programming. Under pressure from these groups Congress was obliged to instruct the FCC to take a more active role in the regulation of the telecommunications industry. The immediate impact of this new policy on the broadcast networks and cable industry was slight. License renewals did become more difficult for a while, and the commission formulated—and to some degree enforced—obligations on cable operators to give the public access to a number of channels and to initiate locally produced programs. The long-term consequences were to have more impact on sports. The Reagan administration was able to harness this populist sentiment with respect to the telecommunications industry to pursue a completely opposite policy, that of deregulation, a policy designed to bring about more efficiently and assuredly the goal of making the industry more responsive to public needs.

This policy of deregulation clearly favored cable companies in their increasingly cutthroat competition with the networks. For example, in 1979, the FCC removed restrictions on the number of distant signals that cable systems could import, a decision that the broadcasters (and the sport league) challenged in court, without success (*National Football League* v. *Federal Communications Commission*, [1982]). The major networks managed to slow the pace of deregulation with the passage of the Cable Communications Policy Act of 1984, amending the 1934 Communications Act to provide a stronger role for the FCC in the regulation of cable television by shifting the definition of a cable operation to that of a "common carrier" (much like a telephone system), thus subjecting it to federal regulation. However, during the 1980s, the tide certainly ran in favor of the new industry of cable television. The act limited the amount a city could charge a cable operator as a franchise fee and granted the incumbent operator the expectation of renewal when the franchise expired. One year after its passage, the FCC rescinded its "must carry" rule requiring cable systems to carry the signals of local stations after the rule had been found to be a violation of the First Amendment (*Quincy Cable TV* v. *Federal Communications Commission* [1985]).

By the end of the 1980s, the sport owners, who had worked so hard to establish highly structured (and monopolistic) relationships with the three major networks, had seen "the free television marketplace . . . transformed into [a] . . . video marketplace in which over-the-air television is only one of a number of competing technologies delivering programming to what are known as home receiver/monitors" (Ferrall 1989, 28). It is symbolic of the changing structure of the relation between sports and the television industry that the network agreement with baseball that expired in 1989, while it had allowed individual clubs to negotiate cable deals, prohibited the league as a whole from doing so. Under that same contract, Commissioner Kuhn agreed to prohibit local (cable) telecasts from competing with network games. The 1990-93 agreement contained neither provision, and the cable industry had gained a valuable foothold in the baseball market.

The advent of cable television also seriously undermined the owners' property rights in the games they produced. Sport leagues had been fighting the unauthorized retransmission of their broadcasts by cable television since the 1960s (Garrett and Hochberg 1984, 161). The cable industry vigorously denied that it exercised any real, active control over channel selection within the system, simply being an extension of the home viewer's antenna: it was not reperforming a work, simply relaying it. Its position was buttressed by the Supreme Court decision in 1968 that retransmission of broadcast signals was not a violation of copyright. The decision seemed to rob sport clubs of all opportunities to charge cable operators for the retransmission of their games. The question of the property right to telecasted games became even more urgent during the 1970s, with the development of superstations like WGN in Chicago and WOR in New York microwaving up to thirty channels for distances up to three hundred miles and, later, companies specializing in the production of "narrowcast" programming, such as Home Box Office (HBO) and ESPN. Cable was clearly no longer simply a carrier but a seller of entertainment features, and the question of who owned the programs became more controversial.

One reason sport owners lobbied so hard against the cable operator's practice of importing distant signals was that they did not pay for the privilege. They did manage to get the FCC to adopt a rule prohibiting cable systems from carrying events that had been seen regularly on commercial television in a specific market during the previous two years; and they managed to have this increased to five years in 1975. These gains were wiped out, however, by the 1976 Copyright Act granting to cable television a "compulsory license" to carry over-the-air telecasts of sporting events. The National Cable Television Industry convinced Congress that it would be hopelessly impractical for a cable operator to negotiate copyright payments for the hundreds of different shows his system carried, sporting events being an important ingredient of this package. Once a game had been telecast locally, cable systems had the right to carry that game by paying a nominal copyright royalty. Thus, although sports programming made up a sizable proportion of cable's programming, it cost virtually nothing. The cable industry's payments to sport clubs under the terms of the Copyright Act amounted to less than 1 percent of its total revenues in 1983 (Garrett and Hochberg 1984, 16).

While the 1976 Copyright Act awarded cable the right to retransmit sport broadcasts and therefore perpetuated what was, in the owners' opinion, "piracy," it did impose a kind of blackout rule. Under the "same game" rule, a club could require a cable system within 35 miles to delete the distant-signal telecast of that club's home game provided that the home game was not televised locally (i.e., not sold out). Although the NBA owners were willing to settle for this measure of protection, the baseball owners instructed their commissioner to try to overturn the same game rule (Kuhn 1987, 290). Kuhn pointed out that the rule afforded little protection for the typical baseball franchise:

> As an illustration, if the California Angels were playing the Chicago White Sox in Anaheim, the only protection afforded is against the importation by Los Angeles cable systems of the signals from the White Sox television station, WGN–TV. These cable systems can still import the telecasts of games of all the other 24 major league teams, as well as the telecasts of any Angels away games. (U.S. Congress, House, Committee on the Judiciary 1982, 157)

Kuhn was speaking for all sport owners in complaining of the competition from cable sports; but as commissioner of baseball, he was presented with an unusual difficulty because some of his owners also operated cable "superstations." Station WTBS and the Atlanta Braves are owned by the same company, as are WGN and Chicago Cubs. These companies, in seeking to market their product nationwide, threaten both national and locally negotiated agreements. In 1985, Commissioner Ueberroth persuaded these superstations to contribute money to a pool to be evenly distributed across all major league baseball teams (Bellamy 1988, 79). However, they continued to be politically troublesome. In 1991 a federal judge in Chicago ruled that the NBA could not restrict the number of games a franchise might broadcast on a superstation because that would violate antitrust laws. One of the plaintiffs was WGN, owner of the Chicago Bulls, wishing to broadcast the Bulls' games in the Chicago area. The NBA had tried to limit the number of transmissions to twenty, but the judge decided that the league lacked the authority to do so. The NBA discovered that the Sports Broadcasting Act only protected leagues in selling national rights to "sponsored" broadcast entities whose revenues come from advertising. Arrangements such as those between the Bulls and WGN were not covered, so that the NBA's restriction was considered anticompetitive.[2]

Cable television spokesmen replied to Kuhn's complaints with respect to the blackout rule that baseball was only seeking to perpetuate its monopoly over the televising of the game and challenged Kuhn to demonstrate that cable television was hurting live attendance at games. They counterattacked by raising the specter of pay television, a development they were sure congressmen were apprehensive about as a threat to the public's "right" to be able to watch important sporting events. They charged the sport owners with seeking to block the retransmission of games in order to strengthen their hold over the mass mediation of games, with an eye to shifting them all to the much more lucrative medium of pay television in the future. The cable industry thus positioned itself on the side of consumer democracy, a position quite consistent with the Reagan administration's general telecommunications policy, under which the FCC defined its own public interest obligation as seeing that popular tastes were satisfied. Much to the delight of the cable industry lobbyists, David Stern, vice president of the NBA, actually threatened to withdraw from "free" broadcast television entirely and go completely to pay-per-view cable if basketball's rights of exclusivity were not better protected by copyright law or by FCC rules with respect to the importation of distant signals (U.S. Congress, House, Committee on the Judiciary 1982, 1441).

The debate over the same game rule was not actually about sport at all. In this case, the state, in the form of the FCC, was primarily concerned with telecommunications policy, over which it had a clear mandate, rather than sport policy, over which it had no mandate at all. Its goal was not to protect the home gate revenues but to ensure the availability of sport programming on conventional television. Permitting cable systems to broadcast home games might reduce live attendance, which, under the blackout rule, would mean that the game would not be shown on network television (Garrett and Hochberg 1984, 18).

Sports owners initially fought against the spread of cable because it threatened their stable relationship with the major networks and because it threatened to create disunity within their own organization as local cable deals became more attractive. In the end, the owners were to see cable win the congressional battle for access to sport programming not because of any strategic errors on their part but because the drift of government policy in the 1980s toward free-market principles and against monopoly favored the fledgling cable industry and weakened the major networks. The number of households connected to cable rose from 22 percent in 1980 to 53 percent in 1988 (Ferrall 1989, 12). Sport owners learned to enjoy some of the benefits of having more telecommunications outlets competing for their wares. By the end of the 1980s, sport owners were moving to exploit this new opportunity for revenues not just individually but collectively. In 1989, ESPN paid $400 million for four years of major league baseball; Turner Network Television paid $275 million for its own four-year NBA contract. Having begun by opposing cable television, the owners now embraced it, recognizing that sports had become the prize for which cable and network television competed, each seeing sports as essential for its economic survival. They were also reading the Nielsen ratings and were aware that the networks' share of the audience was declining rapidly.

Cable's chalice contained poison, however. Local cable and pay-per-view revenues, unlike network revenues, were not shared among teams in any of the leagues. Teams with aggressive marketing strategies, especially those operating in large metropolitan areas, such as the

Boston Celtics and New York Yankees, were able to increase their local media revenues by several hundred percent during the 1980s, while other franchises experienced no gains. The result was greater inequality in the profitability of franchises, more disagreements between them when it came to planning expansion strategies, and more competition for players. Local variation in television revenues were especially marked in basketball, which might account for the fact that basketball franchises were more prone than teams in other sports to move from city to city and why owners competed intensively for the best free agent players, thus driving up salaries.

The owners' desire to cash in on the cable companies' need to offer sport programming had another undesirable consequence. It allowed the issue of public access to sporting events to surface once more. The 1984 Cable Communications Policy Act had created what some saw as an unregulated monopoly, overcharging customers and strangling competition within communities. Among the most vocal of the industry's critics were those who believed that cable was siphoning off professional sports. By the end of the 1980s, congressmen were beginning to receive complaints from constituents that their local franchise was denying them access to "free" viewing via the networks by signing deals with local cable companies, which charged for hookup and monthly viewing fees. Several Senate and House members hinted that professional baseball and football might lose their immunity from antitrust laws if leagues continued to reduce the number of games available on over-the-air network broadcasts in favor of lucrative contracts with cable companies. In the opinion of some congressmen, the leagues seemed to have lost sight of the fact that "professional football was affected with the public interest"; Senator Arlen Specter reminded Commissioner Rozelle that "there is a quasi-public interest that we talked about back in 1982 when you wanted hearings here because of the problem with the Oakland Raiders" (U.S. Congress, Senate, Committee on the Judiciary 1987, 29). It was also made clear in these 1987 hearings that NFL counsel, Paul Tagliabue, had stated explicitly that the 1961 Sports Broadcasting Act excluded pay-per-view television and cable (p. 55). The FCC concurred that agreements with cable television were not covered by the 1961 act.

Two years later, the chairman of the Senate Antitrust Subcommittee, Howard Meztenbaum, again invoked the implied contract between team and community to warn the leagues against going over to cable, noting that sport fans supported teams as purchasers of tickets, concessions, and team souvenirs, and as local taxpayers subsidizing new stadiums: "Given the level of fan support, team owners ought to take steps to insure that access to sports on TV does not become solely dependent on the individual's ability to pay"; Senator Joseph Lieberman complained, "We're setting up a two-tier system of access to sports, and we're losing something by doing that" (Pytte 1990, 33362). Lieberman was a senator from Connecticut, a bedroom community for New York City; and he was angry at the deals made by New York's professional teams. In the House, similar complaints were voiced by a representative from Long Island, Norman Lent, the ranking Republican member of the Committee on Energy and Commerce. He protested the failure of Cablevision to broadcast Knicks, Rangers, and Yankee games in Long Island: "Cable system operators should—indeed must—acknowledge and respond to their subscribers' desire to see the games of their local professional sports teams" (U.S. Congress, House, Committee on the Judiciary 1989, 428). The sense of injustice aroused by the cable contracts was exacerbated by the fact that only half of all homes at this time were wired for cable, a circumstance over which the ordinary fan had no control.

As if in tacit recognition of the heavy dependence of both cable and network television on sports productions, the policy debate with respect to the regulation of the cable television, where there was now a call to reimpose some government controls, had become entwined with the debate over sport policy. The purported evils of cable monopoly were compounded by their effect on the distribution of opportunities to watch sporting events. Congressman Edward Markey, chairman of the House Subcommittee on Telecommunications and Finance, was concerned that cable not turn America "into a society of sports haves and have nots" (U.S. Congress, House, Committee on Energy 1990, 1). He noted that rural sport fans, without access to cable, would be hurt if a higher proportion of games shifted to cable. Senator Howard Metzenbaum echoed this theme: "The leagues and the owners ought to make sure that access to televised sports does not become solely dependent upon a person's ability to pay" (p. 5).

Congressmen were also concerned that the fragmentation of the telecommunications industry would diminish sport's ability to integrate society. The idea, developed during the 1950s and 1960s, of a national "game of the week" was appealing to state actors because it could be used to conjure up the image of a simultaneous national audience, much like a "huge camp fire." Congressman Richard Neal was worried that "an item that pulls Americans together, now is threatened" (U.S. Congress, House, Committee on Energy and Commerce 1990, 16). Howard Metzenbaum asked, "What is the point of having a national pastime if we can't even have a national game every Saturday afternoon?" (U.S. Congress, Senate, Committee on the Judiciary 1991, 2). It was as if Congress wished to establish televised sporting events (especially such championships as the Superbowl and the World Series) as part of the national heritage that should not be privatized and made the exclusive preserve of a few. Senator Joseph Lieberman referred to access to sporting events as "a basic right" (p. 9).

The sport leagues suffered considerable criticism from Congress during this period because not only were they abetting the growth of a cable telecommunications industry regarded by many congressmen as monopolistic and exploitative, but their greed for more revenues was threatening to remove sporting events from "free" telecasts and make them available only to those with access to, and the ability to pay for, cable television. The implied contract signed in the bills authorizing joint negotiations in the 1960s was regularly invoked to remind league officials that they had a responsibility to the American public when it came to televising sport events. Critics were joined by defenders of network television, such as the National Association of Broadcasters, who liked to describe their package of televised sports as "free." Commissioners Vincent and Tagliabue were forced to respond, citing statistics purporting to show that their agreements with cable companies had actually increased the number of games per season shown on television. Cable had added to, rather than substituted for, network broadcasts. Tagliabue was cunning enough to tie the extra revenues generated from cable television to the prospect of expansion, arguing that the expenses of entering the league could be met by agreements locally negotiated with cable companies (U.S. Congress, House, Committee on Energy and Commerce 1990, 49). The commissioners were supported by more conservative congressmen, such as Senator Oren Hatch, who defined the issue as one of viewers' choice and the maintenance of a healthy market: "As long as all networks and stations are free to compete for sporting products, and as long as fans have access to the games, it seems to me that the sporting leagues should feel free to package their products according to viewer desires" (U.S. Congress, Senate, Committee on the Judiciary 1991, 4). If there was a problem with cable and sports, congressmen like Hatch would be much more sympathetic to breaking the monopoly enjoyed by local cable companies.

COLLEGE SPORTS AND TELEVISION

For professional sports, the policy issues raised by telecasting have to do with the business aspects of this relationship. Does the telecasting of sports violate laws established to govern the use of the airwaves? Does the telecasting of sports restructure the sport industry enough indisputably to create monopoly power? Does the relationship between television and sports undermine the public trust that professional sports have a duty to uphold? Indirectly, but no less importantly, telecasting sport events also raises new questions about labor–management relations and franchise location, both of which are affected by it.

The issue with respect to amateur sports is somewhat different. To many in amateur sports, the relationship with television is clearly a pact with the devil from which more harm than good will result, because television hastens the transformation of college sports into a commercial enterprise. With the growth of television, college sports become, in the words of one president of the NCAA (John Toner), "a money-making tool for college administrators" (U.S. Congress, House, Committee on Energy and Commerce 1984a, 9).

Like the owners of commercial sport enterprises, college administrators were initially very wary about forming a relationship with television. Live attendance at several eastern schools, which had begun to televise almost every game, had declined drastically, while attendance had risen in areas of the country where television had yet to spread (Fizel and Barnett 1989, 981). The NCAA was given authority by its constituent members to develop a television committee in 1952 to coordinate and limit football's television exposure. Colleges began to compete aggressively for television dollars. This competition threatened to create imbalances within the NCAA, another reason to concentrate negotiating powers within a single NCAA committee. While the more attractive football programs such as Notre Dame opposed the plan to permit the NCAA to negotiate on behalf of all constituent members, they were a distinct minority of the three hundred member colleges. Smaller colleges were particularly interested in the plan, because some of the pooled television monies could be used to fund championships in the lower divisions, as well as some postgraduate scholarships for athletes. The networks were also persuaded under the agreement to carry a few division II and III games. Television exposure for smaller colleges was not only important financially, it would also make it easier for them to compete for high school talent. Television was thus set to work very early to help achieve balance and moderation among the member institutions, using the media attractiveness of the larger schools to help pay for amateur athletics in the smaller and using the more popular sports such as football and basketball as the bait to persuade the networks to give coverage to minor sports. Television money was suspect, but its taint was removed by the worthy purpose to which it was devoted. Thus, the 1990 agreement between the NCAA and CBS with respect to the basketball tournament called for the network to broadcast championships in fifteen secondary sports also, including men's lacrosse and women's gymnastics.

The original carrying network of college football was NBC, telecasting twenty games in which thirty different college teams appeared (Lawrence 1987, 80). The rights were actually purchased by Westinghouse Electric Company, which then chose NBC to broadcast the games. In 1952, twelve games were telecast nationally for a fee of $1.14 million. After one year with ABC, the NCAA moved back to NBC for five years. Under this agreement, no team was allowed more than two appearances. In 1960, ABC became the college football network, and annual rights had grown to $3.12 million. With a payment of $5.1 million a year, CBS secured the rights to the 1962 and 1963 seasons. In 1964,

NBC won the rights back with a annual payment of $6.5 million. The dispersion agreement still held: over fifty different institutions were shown by NBC until 1966, when its agreement ran out and ABC regained the contract for a payment of $7.5 million a year. In 1982, ABC began sharing the rights with CBS and with cable television, an agreement providing total rights fees of $263.5 million. The most important legislative action of this period was taken in 1961, when the NCAA managed to have inserted in the Sports Broadcasting Act a clause forbidding the broadcasting of a professional game within seventy-five miles of a college game on a day other than Sunday, thus limiting "pro football competition for the spectator's dollar and assigning the Justice Department to enforce this limit" (p. 95).

As NCAA television revenues rose, support for the principles of distribution and the ideals of amateurism underlying them began to weaken. Abetted by the networks (interested in showing only glamor teams), the larger schools began to voice dissatisfaction with their share of the spoils. They lobbied for an agreement that would provide most money to those who actually appeared on television, with a distribution of the balance to those who made no television appearance. The restructuring of the NCAA in 1973 into three divisions was recognition of this growing disparity of interest. In 1978, the NCAA further reorganized division I into division I-A and division I-AA, the I-A division consisting of the larger schools that maintained nationally competitive football programs and the I-AA division consisting of schools that played major, but not truly "big-time," football—the kind of football television audiences would choose to watch. Unfortunately for the football powers, an amendment proposed by the Ivy League colleges exempting schools that fielded twelve sports from the attendance requirement of an average seventeen thousand paid attendance at home football games was approved by the NCAA assembly. As a result, 137 schools were included in the new division I-A, only five fewer than had been in the original division I; and the goal of making television appearances more exclusive was thwarted.

The fight for television revenues had therefore already begun to fragment the NCAA by 1976, when representatives from fifty-six big-time football schools met to express common complaints about how the NCAA handled their problems. Out of this meeting came the idea of the College Football Association. Sixty-one schools joined this new association. The CFA repeatedly called for the restructuring of division I. However, its members were not pleased with the 1978 reform; for it left far too many schools in division I-A. In 1981, they presented plans to representatives of NBC and ABC for a television contract from which only CFA members would benefit. A new NCAA contract with CBS, ABC, and the Turner Broadcasting System (TBS) to take effect in 1982 and worth nearly $300 million over a three-year period was not enough to keep the CFA in the fold; and its members voted to approve an independent four-year contract with NBC worth $180 million.

The NCAA promptly announced that any member televising its games outside the NCAA agreement would be severely penalized. The CFA sought and obtained an injunction against this threat; and in September 1981, the Universities of Georgia, Oklahoma, and Texas sued the NCAA, charging that its control of television programming of college football was an antitrust violation. Despite the fact that the U.S. Department of Justice filed a friend-of-the-court brief in support of the CFA, the NCAA was confident that it could withstand this challenge. Since the 1975 Supreme Court decision striking down minimum fee schedules in the Virginia bar, the NCAA had been sued a number of times on antitrust grounds. On each occasion, the courts had analyzed the NCAA's practices on a rule-of-reason basis and refused to strike them down. The NCAA maintained that controls on television exposure were essential to keeping a relative balance in college football, as were limits on grants-in-aid, coaching staffs, and numbers of games played. However, to appease the CFA, the NCAA did trim down the size of division I-A by reimposing the attendance requirement, reducing its membership to ninety-two.

Charles Neinas, then executive director of the CFA, saw the basic issue as being that of property rights: "Who owned a school's television rights?" (U.S. Congress, House, Committee on Energy and Commerce 1985a, 106). The position of the smaller colleges was that the political and economic leverage of the CFA had been used to "wrestle political power from the moderate majority of Division I football playing institutions" (p. 110). In deciding the case of *Board of Regents, University of Oklahoma* v. *National Collegiate Athletic Association* (1982), Judge Burciaga held that the right to telecast sporting events was indeed a property right of the institution participating in the game and did not belong to the NCAA. A court of appeals affirmed his decision in 1983. The Supreme Court upheld this verdict in 1984, making clear that the real issue was public access to televised football games, declaring that the NCAA rules with respect to television were a "naked restraint" on price and output, totally unconnected to the goal of enhancing competitiveness and that the NCAA was a "classic cartel" with an almost absolute control over the supply of college football. By curtailing output of football games on television and blunting the ability of member institutions to respond to consumer preferences, the NCAA had diminished, rather than enhanced, the role of intercollegiate athletics in the nation's life. The court dismissed the NCAA argument that its rules were necessary to promote evenness of competition in college athletics. It pointed out that the NCAA made no effort to see that revenues were evenly divided, nor did it regulate how those revenues would be spent so as to ensure equality (Ponsoldt 1986, 1035).

At subsequent congressional hearings on the Supreme Court's decision, the CFA argued that the previous arrangement had been nothing but a system of welfare imposed on the larger colleges. Penn State's coach, Joe Paterno, said:

> At Penn State we have twenty-nine sports. Twenty-eight of them cost money. It all has to be generated by football. If we don't get X number of dollars we have to start thinking about eliminating some of our sports. Our athletic director is hired to handle the Penn State athletic program, not to handle Grambling's. If we deprive 10 girls from playing on the field hockey team at Penn State because we want Grambling to be able to get $50,000 in football, that is a moral problem for me. (U.S. Congress, House, Committee on Energy and Commerce 1985a, 122)

The NCAA was quick to point out that by the action of the Supreme Court, the state had granted to the CFA the very monopoly power for which the NCAA had been condemned. It also predicted that the decision would effectively turn over to the television networks unlimited power to negotiate and obtain college football television rights and dictate the terms of any future plans colleges might develop. Within five years, the FCC had come round to this way of thinking itself and in 1990 formally opened an investigation into the television contracts of the CFA. In September 1990, it voted to charge the CFA, ABC, and ESPN with a violation of antitrust law on grounds that the CFA was primarily a commercial entertainment enterprise. The suit was denied in 1922.

Board of Regents, University of Oklahoma v. *National Collegiate Athletic Association,* and the congressional hearings to which it gave rise illustrate a major difference in state policy with respect to the telecasting of professional, as opposed to amateur, sports. The Sports Broadcasting Act "spares the leagues the uncertainty and expense of litigation over whether their particular pooling arrangements are or can be made consistent with the antitrust laws" (Garrett and Hochberg 1984, 37). The NCAA could draw no such comfort. *Board of Regents, University of Oklahoma* v. *NCAA* undermined the NCAA's organizational solidarity in relation to the telecommunications industry; but it also attracted the attention of Congress, where the issue was not only the monopoly power of the NCAA but the future of amateurism. Both the NCAA and its critics claimed to be upholding the amateur ideal. Those seeking to break down the control of the NCAA and open up the marketplace for college sports on television cited the need to find a source of revenue that would support "minor" sports. Football and basketball were to be sacrificed on the altar of commercialism. The cash cow of television must be milked so that a broad spectrum of truly amateur sports could survive at the collegiate level. Those seeking to preserve the powers of the NCAA by strengthening its hand with respect to the television industry presented this as the only way in which the spirit of amateurism could be sustained. Open competition for television revenues, they argued, would further erode the student–athlete ideal and increase inequalities between rich and poor athletic programs.

CONCLUSION

Emerging from the political debates on the broadcasting of sport events are two themes. The first is that sport is believed to have autonomous values that the state has some responsibility to protect and that, in turn, sports have a civic responsibility to fulfill in order to meet social needs. In other words, there is a substantive rationality to sport that no amount of exposure to the formal rationality of the marketplace should be allowed to erode. The second is a question of democracy. The state has some obligation to ensure public access to major sporting events: they are in the public domain and should not be privatized. Thus, although the politics of televised sport have appeared to revolve around questions of monopoly and copyright, in essence, they have had to do with the nature of the limits democracy must place upon capitalism if sport values are to be preserved.

The responsibility of defending sport values is spelled out most clearly in the debate over the effect of television on the NCAA and its member institutions. There, the issue is framed by consensus that the role of the NCAA is to defend amateur values. The question is whether its relationship to television is making this defense easier or more difficult. But it is also evident in the debate over telecasting professional sports. The political regulation of sports since World War II had assumed a clear separation between the production of a sporting event and its broadcast to the wider public. Had congressmen been paying careful attention, they would have noticed, as early as the 1950s, signs that this distinction could be blurred in the search for profit. The sport of boxing had become so much the creature of television that it reached the point where television producers could determine the number of championship bouts fought and who was to fight in them, all the while reporting the events as news. Boxing had ceased to be an independent sport and become, instead, a programmed event. Those who followed the sport closely noted the possibility of a conflict of interest. Thus, Representative Pat Williams, a tireless campaigner for boxing reform remarked, "The line between broadcaster and business promoter has become blurred—dangerously blurred. Do the networks' exclusive broadcast rights negotiated with fighters affect the way television selects fights for broadcast?" (U.S. Congress, House, Committee on Energy and Commerce 1983, 142).

A further blurring of this line of distinction occurred in the 1960s and 1970s. As both sports and networks began to appreciate the mutual benefits of their relationship, so they came to resemble different stages in a vertically integrated process of production. Sports were expected to fit in with network programming requirements, permitting their playing rules and schedules to be rearranged to suit the marketing convenience of the networks. Tennis promoters agreed to arrange tournaments to guarantee that star players would appear and survive the first few rounds. The networks, in turn, were expected to abstain from criticism of events they reported. During the 1987 football strike,

> the three broadcast networks plus ESPN were, of course, offering coverage and commentary on an event and a league of which they were major financial partners. In fact, since the networks provided over 50 percent of total NFL team revenues, they were the true owners and promoters of the game. Coverage of the strike was, at first, assigned to Sports, which proceeded to guilelessly carry the 'scab' games (thus subsidizing them, and thereby the owners) while simultaneously offering commentary on the 'news' angle of events. As negotiations to settle the strike dragged on, stadium attendance fell off sharply, but the NFLPA was declared the loser, because television ratings declined less sharply, and television, after all, was the most important factor. By the time the strike collapsed and the chastened players returned to work, the victorious league had indicated it would rebate approximately $60 million to its network partners for any damage done to ratings and advertising revenues. (Klatell and Marcus 1988, 220)

Cash inducements were no longer enough to secure the rights to broadcast a league's events. The network was also expected to be "cooperative" in helping to sell the sport to the public by presenting a favorable image of it.

During the 1980s, as the audience for network television shrank in the face of competition from cable, network chiefs decided that rather than making sport programs themselves and selling the advertising, they would hand over responsibility for the entire package to the sponsor or an independent producer, thus displacing the risk of failure. These independent production houses could produce live and taped sporting events of equivalent technical quality at much lower costs than networks tied to union contracts. Many events, such as college basketball, were now sold as complete packages, fully produced, including bartered advertising. One result of this trend was added pressure on the producers to create a sporting event guaranteed to deliver the right kind of sponsor. The sporting event was no longer an independent happening, reported as news, but a packaged offering ready for consumption by the most receptive audience.

As sport ceased to be a news event and became a show, it became more of a commodity, subsumed beneath the formal rationality of the marketplace, substitutable for any other twenty-five-minute entertainment package. Sport was no longer a real event outside television (which the broadcaster merely witnessed), but had become part of television itself. Slowly, congressmen became aware that the relationship between sport and the mass media had changed. Thus, Congressman Edward Markey asked: "What is the role that sports play in American life and the role it has for the children of our country? Are they seeing athletes or are they seeing actors? Have sports commentators turned from being commentators into just being entertainers?" (U.S. Congress, House, Committee on Interstate and Foreign Commerce 1978b, 161). Implied in Markey's complaint was a criticism of the sport industry for not living up to its bargain with the state. Sport had long enjoyed favored economic status. In return, it was expected to produce authentic and honest competitive events open to all with an interest in seeing them. Television also had a responsibility, as payment for the use of the airwaves, to "tell it like it is." The logic of the market, the pursuit of private gain, had benefited from public tolerance and endowments, while at the same time undermining the values for which those endowments were bestowed.

10

SPORT AND
SOCIAL
REFORM

Many commentators have noted the readiness with which political struggles in the United States become tinged with moral overtones. Perhaps this has something to do with the fact that the United States lacks the class organization and sharp class conflict found in many European societies. Not only must politicians submit to moral judgment, but questions of morality (e.g., sobriety, fidelity) must be settled in the public arena. This peculiar feature of American politics is not without significance for the study of sport. In choosing to play certain games in certain ways people express their commitment to a "way of life," a moral community. Games are a coded expression of group identity. They mark the boundary between "us" and "them." Sport thus has a moral dimension and inevitably becomes embroiled in the status politics that makes the United States so distinctive. Public controversy over a particular sport frequently has less to do with the sport itself than with what it says about the type of people who follow it, the kind of morality it implies. This is readily apparent in the unusually heavy burden of moral propriety professional athletes carry. They are "consumed"—much like food and drink—and their consumption symbolizes the consumer's character. Athletes must remain unpolluted in order for the consumer to remain clean. If they become polluted, public morality is endangered.

demnation (Duster 1970, 238). The groups with the most power determine the boundaries of the moral community. They decide what is
"unclean" behavior. This chapter describes various attempts to "clean
up" sports in the name of public decency. They are part of what is called
"status politics" because they arise out of, and seek to preserve, status
hierarchies in society. Mostly, status politics takes place in civil society;
but occasionally, when moral condemnation is not enough, efforts are
made to legislate morality (e.g., "ban boxing"). In this case, state powers
are invoked.

Moral crusades rarely enjoy complete success, as the Prohibition
movement demonstrates. This is partly because groups subordinate in
the status hierarchy and likely to be targeted by moral entrepreneurs
as deviants resist their categorization as outsiders. They might even
question the criteria being used to judge them. The second part of the
chapter will explain why efforts to sanitize sports in the name of public
decency have largely failed.

Assimilative Reform

While sport has never attracted the reforming zeal aimed at
drinking or drug abuse and while it has never ranked with issues like
abortion and sex education as the subject of election campaigns, it has
nevertheless been implicated in many political debates over how Americans should spend their free time. The moral crusades mounted at various times to impose limits on consumption fall into the category of
politics that Gusfield calls "assimilative reform" (1963, 6). The purpose
of these crusades is to incorporate "deviant" groups and practices into
the American mainstream. Their goal is to reform by assimilation, to secure social order by making people more similar. Moral crusaders
identify themselves with the moral center of society, while those whose
life-style differs from their own are on the periphery.

This center–periphery imagery obscures the fact that the definition of "normal" and "mainstream" practices favors those already in
power. Assimilation means not so much becoming more American
as becoming more middle-class American. This is clearly not the politics of production (where sides are taken on the basis of employment
relations), but it is by no means unrelated to class. Class position influences beliefs about both acceptable work and tolerable play. When
middle-class people talk about "improving" play, they mean a sanitized
version of play that replicates middle-class attitudes toward leisure and
consumption in general. They see play as a highly organized activity

separate from, but compensating for, the alienation of work. They believe that the masses would be destructive (even self-destructive) if left unorganized and unsupervised. Boundaries must therefore be placed around the timing and spacing of games. Games should occur only at designated times, they should be moved off the streets and onto the playing field, their physicality or brutality should be controlled lest it spill over into other areas of life, and they should be disassociated from vicious behavior.

The movement of assimilative reform has chiefly consisted of the middle-class's trying to regulate the part played by games in the socialization of youth, paying particular attention to the children of working-class parents. The object of the reform is to "modernize" and "civilize" working-class attitudes toward play and thus improve attitudes toward work. Along the way, reformers have also had to tackle the problem of assimilating largely peasant immigrant groups from many different ethnic backgrounds into the American melting pot. The private, voluntary movements to improve play have been analyzed before (Boyer 1978; Cavallo 1981; Couvares 1984; Goodman 1979; Hardy 1982). The purpose of this chapter is to assess the impact of these movements on the relation between sport and the state. Assimilative reform brought play out of the private sphere and into the public by linking it to national integration and public order. In doing so, however, it promoted a particular view of the nature and benefits of organized play, a view congenial to middle-class individualism, in which self-improvement and hard work come before social development and collective effort. Rather than providing leisure guidance and opportunities, the state was to underwrite individual attempts at constructive leisure.

Assimilative reform met with opposition from two principal sources, both of which I shall describe. The paternalism inherent in moral crusades—their assumption of a coherent moral community to which all belong—reflects a nostalgia for nineteenth-century small-town life that became increasingly difficult to take seriously after the 1920s. A middle-class identified more with consumption as the driving force of the economy began to replace the old, more puritanical middle class. The message of improvement changed from emphasising production values to exalting consumption values. The morality of the marketplace slowly replaced the morality of the workplace and family. Assimilative reform lost out to the forces of capitalization, which demanded a more tolerant attitude toward free time, so long as it did not impede consumption.

The new middle-class morality in which leisure for pleasure was no longer stigmatized but, rather, seen as an important component of an expanding economy is evident in the debate over "Sunday ball," the long-running dispute over whether public gambling on sporting events should be permitted, the effort to achieve some political control over professional boxing, and the changing attitudes toward professional team sports. The new middle-class had a lot to gain from sport as a commodity and tended to ally with working-class customers to legislate its production and sale.

The working-class signaled their opposition to assimilative reform. Not only did they buy tickets in huge numbers to commercial amusements, but they also resisted having their playtime organized for them. This is evident in how working-class youth participated in organized play and in blue-collar workers' guarded response to welfare capitalism. It is also evident in the continued popularity among them of stigmatized sports like boxing and wrestling. For a time in the 1930s, they also had political parties willing to defend their leisure interests. However, they found that left-wing parties could be as paternalistic and as moralistic as middle-class reformers.

Muscles and Morals

The movement to assimilate sport into the middle-class mainstream was guided by two cultural forces. The first was religious, the other a more secular set of beliefs about the role of play in child development. The ideology of leisure time in predominantly Christian cultures contains a vital moral component. Duties are attached to leisure. The Puritans had been so convinced of the evils of idleness that they had condemned the play even of little children. This ascetic attitude toward free time lingered on well into the twentieth century and still shows up in surveys of attitudes toward leisure: leisure has to be earned. Protestant culture also taught that leisure time could be "wasted" just as easily as work time by irrational and purposeless activity. The proper use of leisure was as important as the proper use of work. Leisure was thus defined vocationally, as a means of self-improvement and accomplishment. This idea was supported by the tenets of "muscular Christianity" popularized by Charles Kingsley. Morality was a function of muscularity, as well as piety. Exercise was not only an efficient auxiliary to mental education, it also inculcated habits of order and exactitude. Inspired by these teachings, many Americans took up bodybuilding in the 1890s; and, to meet popular demand, the YMCA transformed itself into a sport-and-fitness organization. Luther Gulick, the man largely responsible for the YMCA's reorientation, believed that exercise would redirect energies otherwise channeled into crime. Exercise was not only an adjunct to right thinking; it could even *substitute* for it as an antidote to delinquency.

In the nineteenth century, vice was commonly associated with too much leisure, rather than too much work. On the job, the employer would be careful to see that time was not wasted; but who would supervise the workers' free time? By calling for the constructive use of free time, reformers could hope to complement the discipline of the factory with the discipline of the playground. They could do more, they could justify the conspicuous idleness of the better-off among them; for it was plain to all that free time was not distributed evenly. Middle-class people enjoyed more leisure than factory operatives or farm laborers; but by preaching reform, they could legitimate their idleness by arguing that free time was not the absence of work but the product of leisure competence.

As free time for all began to increase after the turn of the century and leisure became no longer the choice of a select few but "ours whether we wish it or not" (Cutten 1926, 85), so the problem of leisure for the unfitted and unprepared grew worse: "Obviously, the more leisure there is the more opportunity for the right or wrong use thereof" (Lies 1933, 11). The situation was not improved by the influx of millions of immigrants, few of whom spoke English or were used to industrial discipline and most of whom brought their own ideas of how to fill most pleasantly what little free time they had.

The assimilative reform of sport was spearheaded by the Playground movement. Although the Playground Association of America was formed in 1906, efforts to provide playgrounds for urban youth began in the 1880s. Organized play for adolescents was considered an ideal means of integrating the young into the rhythms and social demands of the new urban industrial order. Team sports would teach ideals of cooperation, group loyalty, and respect for rules. Walter Camp, the most influential football coach of the era and popular advocate of the social benefits of sport participation, saw in football "perfectibility through hard work, hierarchical control and corporate cooperation, an aristocracy of merit based on absolute equality of opportunity" (Oriard 1991, 13). Leaders of the Playground movement looked askance at unsupervised street games (where might so often meant right), for they seemed to epitomize the ruthless competitiveness that could be so ruinous to social order and individual stability. Competition was alright, even desirable; but only under closely controlled conditions. The principle of regulated competition could be taught through team sports. Proper training in play was considered essential to prepare the child for democratic participation: "Some . . . even calculated precisely, and with dense mathematical formulae, how many square feet of play space per child were necessary to prepare children for useful citizenship, which they defined as democratic action that subordinated individual desires to collective needs" (Kirschner 1986, 41). A great deal of time and money was spent persuading city officials that play was too serious to be left to children and parents. Getting permission to use public school buildings for summer vacation schools made it easier to convince the school authorities to build playgrounds on school property for summer use, which, in turn, made it easier to demand playgrounds in vacant spaces within the slums themselves. Between 1899 and 1909, American cities would spend over fifty-five million dollars on play facilities for children (Cavallo 1981, 45).

The principles of the Playground movement guided the founding of the Public Schools Athletic League (PSAL) in 1903 by the City of New York. Designed to conduct athletic contests between New York's schools, the real purpose of the league was to combine the forces of compulsory education and voluntary athletics to bring order and discipline to city teenagers. It was apparent that even at the high school level, "tramp athletes" existed, semitruant boys playing baseball for schools they did not attend. The league's president, Luther Gulick, set out to devise a program that would eliminate the semitruant by linking school attendance and conformity to the opportunity to play sports. The PSAL specifically targeted boys involved in street gangs. Gulick was very active in the YMCA; James Sullivan, secretary of the AAU, was also involved in the league, as was General George Wingate, Civil War veteran, keen advocate of physical training for military preparedness and promoter, within the PSAL, of riflery. Thus were combined the ideals of moral uplift, amateurism, and patriotism. A division for girls was added in 1906, stressing activities with group participation.

Although the New York City Board of Education sanctioned the PSAL and Theodore Roosevelt agreed to serve as honorary vice president (he was especially keen on the rifle shooting), the league remained a private corporation, ineligible for public funding. Money was provided by capitalists such as Rockefeller, Carnegie, Morgan, Vanderbilt, Whitney, Guggenheim, and Dodge (Jable 1979, 9). By 1910, most New York City schools were keeping their playgrounds open under supervision after school hours and during the summer: "The schools offered organized games, folk dancing, theatricals and showers during the summer months" (Spring 1972, 73). The city did eventually incorporate the league under the aegis of the Board of Education in 1914, by which time it had imitators in seventeen other cities, principally in the Northeast.

Although the major target of the Playground movement was the urban working-class, there was a secondary goal. Assimilation meant not only absorbing the native-born working class into American culture but also the largely peasant immigrant groups flooding into the country from Europe. Their different languages and customs were considered an obstacle to economic development and a threat to political stability. Sports were seized upon as a useful tool in the work of assimilation. They cost the state little; they attracted mass audiences; they encountered little serious opposition; and athletic achievement appeared to be independent of language, culture, or national origin. Sports were ideally suited to teaching newcomers the American way.

It is no coincidence that Joseph Lee, one of the leaders of the Playground movement, was also prominent in the effort to restrict immigration. Between 1900 and 1914, immigration averaged one million people a year: "Without industrial skills to offer, often even without literacy in their own language, these newcomers were ill suited to the conditions of urban life or the New World and generally filled the lowest ranks of the labor force" (Kirschner 1986, 29). The Playground movement was intended, among other things, to smooth the process of assimilation. Careful planning and supervision was all the more important in view of the myriad commercial temptations facing these new Americans: dancing, movies, amusement parks, saloons, and commercialized sports, with their attendant gambling. In 1925, the American Legion joined the crusade, voting to inaugurate and conduct junior baseball leagues and tournaments under its Americanization program, which included calls for restrictions on immigration (Seymour 1990, 85).[1]

While the Playground movement targeted amateur sports, professional sports also assumed some responsibility for assimilative reform. The history of baseball had to be rewritten to authorize its American origins. The first president of the National League, Morgan Bulkeley, opined, "There is nothing which will help quicker and better to amalgamate the foreign born, and those born of foreign parents in this country, than to given them a little good bringing up in the good old-fashioned game of Base Ball" (Seymour 1971, 4). Sport could eradicate unwanted immigrant social practices. Asa Spaulding had been instrumental in denying St. Louis and Cincinnati National Association baseball franchises because their largely immigrant population "drank too much and did not behave properly"; the two cities had to be content with American Association baseball, which was dubbed the "beer and whiskey league" (Lowenfish and Lupien 1980, 40).

Sports could be used to assimilate newcomers because the sport creed was also the American creed. The successful athlete was a self-made man, an individual who had "made it" on the basis of natural ability, perseverance, courage, and competitive drive. Sports were a vivid reminder of a lesson occasionally forgot by the masses, namely that the storied American virtues paid off. As for those who do not make it, surely this, too, was part of the system; for not all could make it to the top without rendering that accomplishment meaningless. In sport (or so it seemed) one could still be catapulted to fame and fortune by combining "natural talents" with seriousness of purpose.

In being put to assimilative use, sports underwent a subtle change, the better to articulate distinctively American social values. The sporting tradition imported from England had emphasized sportsmanship—the scrupulous adherence to rules at the possible expense of victory—which a leisure aristocracy assured of its social position could afford to espouse. In the United States, sportsmanship became gamesmanship: "bending the rules or finding loopholes in the rules that would give one side the advantage" was considered smart play (Oriard 1991, 17). Gamesmanship was much more appropriate for a classless, or would-be classless, society, where all was fluidity and flux, the individual had some chance of triumphing over the system, and positions of power and privilege were not assured.

Professional baseball assiduously cultivated its association with American values. It did so by exploiting a peculiarly American idea about the partnership between public and private interests. Sport leagues symbolized the American way of dealing with social challenges—the professional association. They were private bodies "franchised" to provide an essential public service, just like the American Bar Association. They developed specialized knowledge and skills within an organized educational program (the farm system or colleges); they had a real or ostensible commitment to society that purportedly transcended individual self-interest; and they had gatekeepers and disciplinary systems to control (with delegated public governmental authority) admission into the "practice" and impose discipline, and perhaps expulsion, on those who violated their norms. They occupied a special place in the American system, a private corporation with a public mission of "service" to their customers and their community.

The initial reaction to the Chicago Black Sox scandal of 1919 revealed how strongly aligned were the "national game" of baseball and Americanism. Most people, it seemed, were predisposed to think that if the World Series had been fixed, it was the work of foreign powers. When rumours of the fix first began to spread, the editor of the *Sporting News* (a baseball establishment newspaper) could not bring himself to believe any Americans had been involved in the scandal: "Because a lot of dirty, long-nosed, thick-lipped and strong-smelling gamblers butted into the World Series—an American event by the way—and same said gamblers got crossed, stories were peddled that there was something wrong with the games that were played" (Spink 1974, 61). The members of the grand jury appointed to look into the allegations were equally reluctant to believe the worst. Their report read, in part:

> Baseball is more than a national game, it is an American institution, having its place prominently and significantly in the life of the people. In the deplorable absence of military training in this country, baseball and other games having "team play" spirit offer the American youth an agency for development that would be entirely lacking were it relegated to the position to which horse racing and boxing have fallen. The national game promotes respect for proper authority, self-confidence, fair-mindedness, quick judgment and self-control. (p. 63)

The trial jury's acquittal of the players despite convincing evidence of their guilt also symbolized the public's need to believe that the national game was incorruptible.

The link between sport and Americanism, especially baseball, survived the Depression and, more surprisingly, the tremendous commercialization of the game after World War II, when its many business aspects became much more visible. It required some effort to maintain the pristine image of the professional athlete under these circumstances. He had to be protected from being completely profaned by commercialism. He could become professional without "selling out," competitive but not ruthless, ambitious but not greedy, naturally gifted but not lazy. It seemed as if sports could assimilate and inspire only if they were not completely absorbed into "business." Thus, the sportswriter Arthur Daley wrote of Joe Dimaggio in 1949: "Yes, he's a professional, all right, but he's an amateur at heart. The lover of the game comes first. . . . DiMaggio, apparently because of his natural talents, is able to transcend the workaday world in which he operates as a professional" (L. Smith 1975, 93). Baseball stood for democracy, because any player, from any background, could become a hero. The fact that he could do it only on management's terms was not something the public needed to know about.

American youth learn early in life that sports and public morality go together. This gives a youth sport organization like the Little League the air of a moral crusade. Its federal charter, granted in 1964, states its mission:

> To promote . . . and . . . assist the interest of boys who will participate in Little League baseball.
> To help . . . boys in developing qualities of citizenship, sportsmanship and manhood.
> Using the discipline of the native American game of baseball, to teach sport and competitive will to win, physical fitness through individual sacrifice, the values of teamplay and wholesome well-being through healthful association with other youngsters under proper leadership.

The federal charter places Little League on a par with the Boy Scouts of America; and since it is a quasi-governmental agency, its revenues are tax-exempt. Its official rules proclaim that "the movement is dedicated to helping children become good and decent citizens." The Little League Pledge combines religion, patriotism, and sportsmanship:

> I trust in God.
> I love my country and will respect its laws.
> I will play fair and strive to win.
> But win or lose I will always do my best.

Lest any should forget Little League's roots in the effort to assimilate the population into habits of abstemiousness and industry, the organization prohibits playing games on Sunday and "fathers are not expected to alter their work schedules to coach their sons or see them play" (Fine 1987, 17). In the absence of cultural institutions (other than churches),

Boxing: Civilizing Aggression

Secure on its pedestal as "the national pastime," baseball could be used to represent all that was wholesome and admirable in the American character. Assimilative reform tries to "civilize" sports, expunging their more unseemly aspects and sheltering them from the influence of unsavory characters. However, propriety and respectability tend to be defined in middle-class terms; consequently, the whole campaign to civilize play takes on class connotations. Ratting and cockfighting are banned, but fox hunting and coursing are tolerated. Sports like boxing have working-class connotations and thereby seem to pose a greater threat to law and order. Sports like golf, tennis, and baseball are favored because they epitomize middle-class values: "Baseball represented civilized entrepreneurial America and the middle-class; it was supposedly everything boxing was not—clean, wholesome, pastoral, and strategic" (Sammons 1988, 163). Partly as a result of this association, baseball has been left to govern itself, by and large, while individual states and even the federal government have kept a close eye on the sport of boxing. Neither of the main criticisms of boxing—its proclivity to injury and its association with gambling—is unique to the sport. A brief review of the history of public policy toward boxing will reveal that class considerations, while not the only determination of public policy toward boxing, are certainly important.

Sports like wrestling and boxing have a long history. The prearranged fight is a semiritualized means for humans to settle disputes. At first, the element of social control was minimal. Olympic boxing in ancient Greece was as much a test of physical endurance and sheer muscular strength as skill, and serious injuries were frequent. The goal was to win at all costs, by any means. During the eighteenth and nineteenth centuries, with the ascendancy of bourgeois values, boxing became subject to a tighter set of rules designed to protect contestants from serious injury and, not coincidentally (for it made gambling much more exciting), to ensure greater equality of chances (e.g., by introducing weight classes). Further civility was added by hiring other men to do your fighting for you, thus experiencing the dangers of the contest vicariously and confining injuries to the actual combatants:

> Gentlemen promoted contests between lower-class professional fighters, when betting enhanced their excitement as spectators, as in horse-racing and other sports. At the same time, however, boxing also became the "gentlemanly art of self-defence," gradually

used in place of the duel in settling disputes between at least younger males of the gentry class. (Mennell 1989, 149)

Upper-class patronage protected the sport in England but was largely absent in nineteenth-century America, where boxing offended middle-class sensibilities: "The social stigma against prize fighting ran broadly and deeply through American life" (Isenberg 1988, 11). Few Americans outside the working-class wished to acknowledge and have publicly dramatized the message that in the United States, especially in the exploding cities, power, force, and violent behavior could bring money and respect: "The man who could defend himself, physically dominating others and forcing them to yield, was dealing in common and well-understood coin in the workshops, factories, and saloons strewn across urban America" (p. 59). This message did not sit well with a dominant class that praised hard work, sobriety, punctuality, and emotional self-control.

Suitably modulated, boxing did gain some support among the middle-classes. Theodore Roosevelt, a fitness buff and zealous pugilist, regarded boxing as important for military training and encouraged it in the national interest. As police commissioner of New York, he heartily approved of an effort to establish boxing clubs in the city (Isenberg 1988, 67). Law enforcement officers and community leaders became more tolerant of boxing as its regulation improved. Round limits, trained and supervised referees, weight classifications to prevent gross mismatches, gloves for added protection and compulsory rest periods between rounds, eliminated much of the brutality associated with the sport.

Despite these reforms, the commercial variant of boxing was widely disparaged: "Somehow it seemed especially base to pound away at someone *for money*" (Isenberg 1988, 73). While reformers always spoke most loudly about the brutality of the sport, the gambling and rowdiness associated with fights clearly concerned them more. By the early 1900s, most states had laws making professional prizefighting illegal. These laws were ineffectual because there was too much money to be made in professional boxing. In the 1880s, when a good year for a major league baseball player meant about five thousand dollars, John L. Sullivan could earn eighty thousand dollars from boxing (p. 169). As a result—and despite the ban—many fights continued to occur, especially in the South, where they were described as "sparring exhibitions" (Sammons 1988, 16). When arrests were made (and they occured more often during election campaigns), juries were reluctant to convict, despite clear violations.

New York was the first state to legalize boxing, with the Frawley Act of 1911. Boxing was to be supervised by a (highly politicized) state athletic commission. Under Republican control, New York once more banned boxing in 1917, only to see the Democrats relegalize it in 1920. By then, twenty-three other states had followed suit and made boxing legal. Boxing had lost some of its stigma during World War I, because of its association with military training. Typically, a State Athletic Commission would be mandated by the state government to license boxers, authorize exhibitions, and approve contracts signed. Such efforts at control were feeble in the face of the amount of money promoters could make out of the sport. Boxing became so lucrative that states vied with each other to be the site of bouts. Illinois legalized boxing in order to get the Dempsey–Tunney rematch at Chicago's Soldier Field in 1927. Interstate competition led to cutting regulatory corners on the way: "Corrupt promoters and commission officials found ready accomplices in many heavyweight champions whose services meant far more to states and localities in terms of revenues than did scrupulous enforcement of legal codes" (Sammons 1988, 64).

Throughout the 1920s and 1930s, boxing continued to be followed enthusiastically by a largely working-class audience, attracted by major championship contests between such athletes as Gene Tunney, Jack Dempsey, and Joe Louis, all of whom became American folk heroes. During the Depression, however, middle-class reformers found fresh grounds for seeking greater control of the sport in its close association with organized crime, once again linking boxing with immigrant groups and "the criminal element." The association with gambling was not new. Indeed, during the formative years of the sport as a commercial enterprise, "it was a fine question whether the prize fights existed for the gambler or vice versa" (Isenberg 1988, 71). What was new, however, was the organization of gambling on a nationwide scale, which seemed to make the sport that much more threatening to middle-class America.

State action against boxing in the 1940s and 1950s focused largely on the alleged monopolistic practices of the International Boxing Commission (see chapter 4). The ostensible purpose of these actions was to reform the market for boxing, rather than its morals; but there is no doubt that antitrust law was being used also to "clean up" the sport. This is most evident in the series of congressional hearings organized by Senator Estus Kefauver in the early 1960s, Kefauver using his Subcommittee on Anti-trust to carry on "his public crusade against organized crime" (Sammons 1988, 172). Congress heard vivid testimony from former middleweight champion Jacob LaMotta, who confessed to having helped fix several of the fights that had earned him his crown. Kefauver's mission was to establish some federal oversight of boxing without setting up an executive agency specifically for that purpose. By using antitrust law to prohibit conspiracies by organizations like the IBC, Kefauver hoped to make it impossible for organized crime to control the sport. In fact, his attention only served to drive corrupt practices further underground and point up the weaknesses of the sport's own private government and of the athletic commissions appointed by individual states.

It became apparent that ridding boxing of the taint of organized crime was virtually impossible under existing political arrangements. The administration of boxing itself was split between the World Boxing Council and the World Boxing Association. Although most states had their own enforcement mechanisms (not all had state athletic commissions), they were weak and often corrupt. A state known to have an "honest" athletic commission, like Pennsylvania, could find itself blackballed by the powerful IBC (U.S. Congress, Senate, Committee on the Judiciary 1961, 805). To make matters worse, television encouraged states to compete to host title bouts, enabling promoters to televise contests back into those regions of the country that would otherwise have prohibited them. Voluntary efforts at nationwide control, such as the National Boxing Association, had attracted only about 40 percent of the states and, in any case, lacked disciplinary powers.

In light of these obstacles, Kefauver introduced legislation in 1961 to set up a Federal Boxing Commission. He made his purposes clear by proposing to house the federal boxing commissioner in the Department of Justice. Most state boxing commissions supported the idea; but Attorney General Robert Kennedy was lukewarm, and his lack of enthusiasm for the federal regulation of boxing scuttled the bill. Kefauver tried again in 1963 but died before debate on his bill concluded.[3] The next year, another strategem was used to impose some federal control over boxing. The House Committee on Energy and Commerce reported a bill that would have created a Federal Boxing Commission to regulate boxing events televised or broadcast interstate or to other countries. This legislation, using the interstate commerce nature of televised boxing as a means of circumventing the opposition of individual states, passed the House but was defeated in the Senate due to opposition from the administration and the television industry.

State action against boxing subsided during the 1970s but revived in the 1980s. The focus had shifted from organized crime to fair labor standards. The American Medical Association had by this time passed a resolution calling for the government to ban professional boxing altogether, action that had caused some consternation within the industry itself and among its supporters in Congress. Several bills were introduced, whose purpose was to set up a federally chartered, voluntary corporation to provide leadership in the development of uniform health and safety standards. Congressman Pat Williams introduced such a bill every year for ten years but was caught between a "boxing community" that would not "fully and totally embrace" the idea and a Congress very reluctant to become directly involved in the regulation of boxing (U.S. Congress, House, Committee on Energy and Commerce 1985b, 22). Boxing promoters were fearful that if the federal government became responsible for health and safety standards, state powers would gradually extend to the "commercial" aspects of boxing.

Even those most critical of the sport saw little hope of prohibiting boxing. During 1985 congressional hearings, Congressman Bill Richardson had to acknowledge, "The ban on boxing is probably not politically feasible" (U.S. Congress, House, Committee on Energy and Commerce 1985b, 362). Policy recommendations were modified to take into account the arguments of the industry's leading defenders. As against the previous bills, the proposed statutes would not ban boxing altogether; the federal government would not become directly involved in running professional boxing; the central issue was the health and safety of the boxers, not the monopoly power of the promoters and the television networks; and major responsibility for actually regulating boxing would remain with the state athletic commissions, who would heed federal guidelines voluntarily. The last modification was crucial. Without the cooperation of the more powerful state athletic commissions, such as those in Nevada, New York, New Jersey, and California, any bill would be doomed. On the other hand, none of these commissions would agree to the mandatory controls necessary to give a federal agency any clout.

The problems of boxing at this time were twofold. The structure of the sport had not permitted the development of a commissioner system, nor had it lent itself to collective bargaining agreements and players' associations. The former left the door wide open for unscrupulous promoters, and the latter left individual boxers exposed to exploitation. The industry's failure to police itself after the fashion of the team sports was the principal reason given by Pat Williams for the introduction of his bills. Second, the sport was run on a local level and regulated by states and municipalities. These local jurisdictions jealously guarded their powers and competed fiercely with sanctioning bodies in other states. Effective regulation of boxing would have required its federalization and meant robbing these state athletic commissions of their power. Thus, officials from Nevada, one of the more active boxing states, opposed a bill introduced in 1986: "Boxing does not need supervision by a Federal agency with mandatory powers which strip the States of their rightful control of their own boxing industries" (U.S. Congress, House, Committee on Education and Labor 1986, 21).

Realistically, boxing's critics could not hope to get the federal government more closely involved in regulation. The bills introduced in the 1980s all ran afoul of the antiregulation sentiment in Congress. Occasionally, a House committee would favorably report a boxing regulation bill (e.g., in 1983); but it was not until 1985 that a bill to establish a United States Boxing Commission made it to the floor of the House, to be defeated by a two-to-one margin. In 1986, a bill did pass in the House; but despite the fact that the United States Boxing Commission it proposed to set up would rely entirely on voluntary cooperation from state athletic commissions, no further action was taken. Further fruitless efforts were made in 1990, when Congressman Pat Williams introduced the boxing fair labor standards act, which provided for the Secretary of Labor to proceed with an advisory council and draft some minimum health and safety standards.

The sport of boxing has not been outlawed, nor has it become much better regulated. As of 1988, twelve thousand licensed professional boxers in the United States continued to work under the rather lax supervision of the forty-two states and the District of Columbia that have some form of state athletic commission. Nebraska, North Carolina and Oregon regulate at the municipal level; and four states (Colorado, Oklahoma, South Dakota, and Wyoming) do not regulate boxing at all. There is little uniformity in their supervision, and obtaining a license to box or manage a boxer is easy and wide open for corruption. The sport's critics continue to look upon it as merely "a marketing tool for the gambling industry" (Hauser 1986, 60). The failure to sanitize professional boxing can be explained in part by the reluctance of Congress to set up federal authorities to regulate local business. But there are other reasons for this failure, which I shall now address.

LIMITS TO REFORM

As the case of boxing demonstrates, middle-class reformers did not have things all their own way in the world of sport. They met with vigorous opposition from two social forces: a new middle-class morality—a "fun morality" in which leisure was a commodity to be sold, consumed, and enjoyed all in the national interest—and a recalcitrant working-class, intent on finding its own pleasures to fill up its spare time, free of the ministrations of its superiors. Both of these forces thwarted the attempts to "civilize" boxing. The sport has a wide following among working-class people, especially those who like to gamble. It has also become highly commercialized, a multi-million-dollar enterprise, associated with a world of nightclubs, casinos, well-dressed men, and beautiful women, over which several states and municipalities compete vigorously. These forces, in combination, have been sufficient to frustrate all middle-class attempts to eliminate the sport or even dilute its violence.

The Fun Morality

The goal of assimilative reform as far as sport is concerned is to eliminate or curtail those sport practices that might undermine the dominant, middle-class style of life. But the middle-class does not stand still; and as its values change, so will those it seeks to impose on sport. The attitude toward play characteristic of reformers at the turn of the century was typical of the old middle-class of small-town, small-business America, guided by values of self-control, impulse renunciation, discipline, and sobriety. By the end of the 1920s, a new middle class had begun to emerge whose values were those of tolerance and good interpersonal relations, a "fun morality." This new middle class was also responsible for the commercialization of sport. A conflict arose within the middle class itself, between those who desired the complete commercialization of leisure-time activities, (allowing the marketplace to determine which activities survived) and those who saw in play (particularly sports) a two-edged sword—an opportunity to instill essential public morals but also a temptation to dissipation.

The rise of the new middle-class is one reason why the Playground movement declined rapidly in the 1920s. Until the outbreak of World War I, progressives tended to imagine a reconstructed village as the means of maintaining social order and ensuring civilized behavior. Play was of a piece with family, neighborhood, and church. The ideal had lost its appeal by the end of the war; and reformers resigned themselves to the realities of a more anonymous city life, where people could, after all, be free and equal. But this egalitarian, impersonal city favored commercialized entertainments, not supervised play. In accommodating to the city, the progressives seemed to lose their faith in improving play.

In fact, the Playground movement was never able to compete with commercialized amusements. In 1911, at the height of the Progressive Era, a survey of New York City discovered that pool halls, saloons, burlesque houses, and film theaters collectively outnumbered playgrounds by one hundred-to-one (Cavallo 1981, 162). The progressives could not overcome the division within their own ranks, one group arguing for government "intervention" in economic and social life, the other more fearful of "interference" and more convinced of the power of voluntarism to bring about needed reforms. Partly as a result of this division, they failed to get municipal authorities to take responsibility for organizing play and thereby dissipated much of their political potential. Thus, although the Recreation movement became part of the larger moral purpose of the new professional class, this class could not achieve for play what it had achieved for social work, city planning, and health care. The sense of crisis responsible for the rise of public service professionalism passed in the changed economic ethos of the 1920s; and as the claims to expertise and guidance made by professionals underwent new challenges, they tended to draw in their horns and become less ambitious.

Thereafter, reforming groups in society would worry about housing, overcrowding, nutrition, unemployment, poverty, and various "pathologies" (e.g., drug abuse, gambling, and prostitution); but they would never again focus as sharply on the connection between work and play. The reformers of the pre–World War I period had fought to reduce working hours, improve workplace safety, eliminate child labor, and the like; but they had been equally worried about what people would do in their new free time: "Liberation from oppression was necessary, to be sure, but without firm guidance toward desirable modes of conduct and belief it would accomplish little over the long haul" (Kirschner 1986, 37). With its demise, progressivism took with it to the grave this holistic approach to work and play. The Depression and the New Deal that it spawned—the beginnings of the welfare state in America—did not resuscitate it.

Sunday Ball

The new middle-class was also responsible for bringing about some basic changes in the way in which Americans spent their Sundays. By the end of the nineteenth century, most American communities had passed blue laws prohibiting any kind of commercialized entertainment (including sports) on Sunday, the only day of the week free from the demands of paid employment for the working-class. These laws were very controversial and usually difficult to enforce. They aroused considerable resentment among the working-class. Indeed, the politics most visible to the average person during the Populist and Progressive Eras were not constructed around economic controversies like trusts and tariffs but, rather, around issues like temperance and Sunday observance (Hardy and Ingham 1983, 285).

Blue laws were the achievement of the old middle class; for they aimed to curtail and regulate the leisure behavior of the working-class in the interest of public decency, social order, and industrial productivity. But the achievement was relatively short-lived. By the 1920s, blue laws began to collapse:

> At the beginning of the twentieth century, only the five major-league clubs operating in Chicago, St. Louis and Cincinnati could legally play games on Sundays. Before the end of World War One, three more—Detroit, Cleveland, and Washington—were liberated, and thus half the major-league teams could play at home on Sunday. Within fifteen years after World War One the major leagues were completely victorious, the ban having been lifted in their other four cities—New York, Boston, Philadelphia, and Pittsburgh. The relative speed with which the last resistance to Sunday baseball disappeared was in itself a sign of the iconoclastic spirit of the postwar era. (Seymour 1971, 359)

The advent of "Sunday ball" was a victory for the urban, more Catholic population over a more rural, Protestant America. Chicago, St. Louis, and Cincinnati, heavily Catholic, were the first to allow Sunday ball; and New York capitulated when the Catholic Al Smith campaigned for it. It was also a victory for that more liberal form of Protestantism known as "the social gospel," whose advocates believed that industrial man had the right to recreational leisure. The movement was very active in Cleveland, Detroit and Washington (Lucas 1971). Opponents had tried to link baseball to drinking, gambling, and even "Germanization"; but the popularity of baseball in the northern cities was hard to ignore, and full legalization had been prefaced by a long period of evasions (e.g., asking for "donations," rather than charging admission) with law enforcement officials looking the other way or imposing token fines. World War I and the weakening of traditional restraints that it encouraged had in any case hastened the transformation of Sunday into a secular holiday.

Above all, Sunday ball was a victory for the idea that fun could be marketed. Sunday ball became legitimate when its profitability could no longer be ignored. This is well illustrated in the case of Philadelphia, one of the last cities to fall. As late as 1927, the Pennsylvania Supreme Court decided that Sunday commercialized baseball was "unholy"—a blatant form of "worldly employment"—and had forbidden the Philadelphia Athletics from playing on Sunday. By 1932, however, the Depression had decreased tax income; and many politicians began to look to Sunday amusements to generate revenues. Both the mayor of Philadelphia, Harry Mackey, and the governor of Pennsylvania, Gifford Pinchot, became converts to the idea of Sunday baseball. In 1933, a bill permitting local option with regard to Sunday openings passed the state legislature; and by the end of November, most larger cities in the state had voted to permit Sunday baseball (Lucas 1971). The opportunity to watch professional baseball had thus become more widely available to working-class people as one set of middle-class values, in which consumption was highly suspect, was replaced by another, in which consumption was the highest expression of citizenship.

The ascendance of new middle-class values changed the public's attitude toward sport. It was consonant with the fun morality that sport be profaned. People were now more cynical about the world of sport, rather less inclined to see it as sacred ground, and rather more disposed to take the claims of sport authorities with a grain of salt—much as it would any other effort to sell something. In the promotional literature issued by the sport industry during the 1920s and 1930s, sport heroes were used as models for what hard work and dedication could do, even for the lowliest. Thus, Babe Ruth wrote in his autobiography: "The greatest thing about this country is the wonderful fact that it doesn't matter which side of the tracks you were born on, or whether you're homeless or homely or friendless. The chance is still there. I know" (Rader 1983, 12). Most people knew better. Ruth never had to struggle for success in baseball, having natural talents for both pitching and hitting. Indeed, the riotous life he lived seemed designed to destroy what talents he had. Figures like Ruth and Red Grange became more personalities than heroes, objects of fascination for their life-style, rather than objects of emulation for their ideals. The more aggressive marketing of sports did not lessen athletes' power to symbolize an American ideal, it simply changed the ideal. Personality was now more important than character.

Working-Class Resistance

Reformers boasted of the successes of the Playground movement, but statistics on the effect of supervised play on juvenile delinquency could be misleading. After all, constructing playgrounds would almost inevitably lower the arrest rate for delinquency if most arrests were made for violation of street ordinances (Cavallo 1981, 170). Evidence began to accumulate that the use of the schools to promote constructive leisure never did surmount class boundaries. Although the sport programs might have been designed to integrate the working-class into manners and customs of the middle class, the working class were the least likely to participate in them.

It is also debatable how effective sport and recreation programs were in assimilating ethnic groups into the mainstream. Riess points out that providing people with parks to play in did not mean they would be assimilated; for parks tended to be taken over by the nearest ethnic community, so that if they were situated on community borders, they became the site of conflict: "Playgrounds . . . reinforced ethnic biases instead of breaking them down." Riess also points out that sports did not obliterate ethnic differences, at least not at first: there was considerable resistance on the part of first-generation immigrants to abandoning traditional games in favor of American pastimes; and even when recent immigrants did participate, they brought their ethnic identities with them (1989, 146, 108). Urban basketball had a particularly strong ethnic character, with ethnic teams and leagues active in all the major cities. Even the professional level had its Celtics (Irish), Harlem Renaissance Five (African American), Detroit Polaskis, and the South Philadephia Hebrew All-Stars.

There were also problems with trying to use school leagues to teach proper forms of play. Working-class children were frequently truant and the power of school sports to discipline them was perforce feeble. Aware of this problem, reformers targeted the street gangs in which working-class children spent much of their time. In his study of Chicago gang life in the 1920s, Thrasher discovered that of all the attempts to substitute "secondary conflict" for "the primary type," sports and athletics were perhaps the most popular among the boys (1927, 99). Baseball, football, and boxing proved to be most acceptable. Many gangs actually called themselves "athletic associations." Thrasher discovered at least five hundred such associations in Chicago.

There was a natural affinity between gangs and sports. Gangs were geographically based, ethnically distinct, predominantly male and age-stratified. Many gangs had evolved from spontaneously formed play groups. Prowess at sports was a common means of establishing and symbolizing a hierarchy within the gang or gaining admission to it. Yet Thrasher remained skeptical whether sports could be a means of "conventionalizing" the gang or of bringing some semblance of order to the city streets and spaces. He disputed the common assumption that delinquency would be solved by "the multiplication of playgrounds and social centers," because "the physical layout of gangland provides a realm of adventure with which no playground can compete" (1927, 494). More importantly, it is clear that the city boys used sports for their own purposes, rather than allowing sports to use them. Sporting events between gangs, especially football and boxing, frequently ended in fights, which seemed to be more meaningful and memorable than the game itself. Not surprisingly, adults possessed only the most tenuous control over the adolescents' play. Thrasher describes his own attempt to organize a baseball game for one gang:

> The members of the gang played pool for a while. At first the games went smoothly enough, but soon they became characteristically riotous. We adjourned to the adjoining room to organize the team. It was very difficult to get the positions assigned because the boys would not remain in one place long enough to tell "who was who." They were constantly being diverted by all sorts of horseplay and loud noises. . . . I wore out my voice trying to keep them quiet. I finally gave up and asked the captain to give me a list of his players and their positions. (p. 85)

Sports were never imposed on the boys but co-opted by them to suit their own purposes. Gangs would frequently fight—over a place to play, the result of a game, or an incident within it—and fighting itself was a form of play, with excitement, risk, winners, and losers. Nor could Thrasher overlook the fact that funding for these "associations" was often unsavory; for they were frequently subsidized by saloon keepers for advertising purposes or by politicians, who found them useful in promoting interest in machine politics.

Working-class resistance is also evident in the survival of boxing. It had attracted considerable political attention, few sports outside horse racing and dog racing receiving the same amount of scrutiny. It sustained its largely working-class association and did not entirely rid itself of the suspicion of widespread corruption in the promotion of fights. Nevertheless, defenders of the sport asked why boxing had been singled out. If boxing were to be banned, why not football? During congressional hearings in the 1980s, Representative Don Ritter argued that football was favored only because it attracted the "higher- and middle-income inclusive segment of the society" (U.S. Congress, House, Committee on Energy and Commerce 1985b, 357). Boxing's defenders freely acknowledged its association with the lower class, but they saw in this its value to society. To Congressman Florio, boxing was "a means by which various groups have come through our doors as a Nation, have provided for upward mobility" (p. 366). Congressman Joseph Montoya suspected that boxing was the target of government scrutiny only because it was not "an establishment sport": "The truth is that boxing has always been an opportunity for the poorest of the poor, whether they are white, brown or black. . . . So there is a benefit that is hard to measure; it does create an outlet and for some it has created a fantastic opportunity to succeed" (idem, Committee on Education and Labor 1986, 109). For its defenders, the issue with boxing was not one of morality but a question of whether or not a class of workers would be unfairly prevented from earning its livelihood. Defenders of the sport urged critics to remember that the ring was simply a place of work and that boxers had a class allegiance with other manual workers. Some reforms might be needed, but they should not be imposed paternalistically: "Boxers deserve the same protections as all those other workers who are fighting for a living" (idem 1990, 1).

SPORT AS RESISTANCE

In describing the various attempts to reform sport in the interest of middle-class values (not to mention explaining their frequent failure), the actions of the working-class itself, which did not take kindly to having its free time administered, must not be overlooked. Close examination of the struggle over leisure time in particular communities "uncovers the petitions, lobbies, and debates representing the agency of subordinate groups who were as vocal as the elite reformers they sometimes joined and sometimes battled" (Hardy and Ingham 1983, 291). Workers were very interested in spaces for their children to play that were safe and clean, but they did not see why these spaces had to be purchased at the expense of middle-class control over what went on there.

There is an obvious sense in which social reform would provoke resistance, for the tastes of one group are being foisted on another in the name of "decency." But there is a broader sense in which the evolution of sport provokes resistance. Sport is always, to some degree, administered play. Although its intentions might be benign, it creates power differences with respect to play. Democracy is replaced by bureaucracy;

citizens become clients; organizers are separated from the organized, the experts from casual participants. A hierarchy is erected, a vast pyramidal structure, the bottom consisting of organized sports for children (e.g., Little League), the middle layer being the "feeder" system of high schools and colleges, the pinnacle being professional play (even Olympians "turn pro"). People come to accept that they do not have a legitimate interest in controlling leisure time and space—for example, the uses to which school facilities are put, believing instead that they should be more concerned with productive control over their children's athletic labor, that is, making sure that children at each stage are being prepared properly for progression to the next.

Both public and private associations foster the development of this sport hierarchy. For example, amateur athletic programs are geared primarily to producing elite athletes for Olympic competition. An alliance of National Olympic Committees, sport federations, and state agencies forms a bloc "of shared interests in high-performance sport, complete with elaborate centralized facilities, state and commercial sponsorship, and a complex infrastructure of sports scientists, coaches, technical personnel and bureaucrats" (Gruneau 1984, 14). Sport facilities more likely to benefit the working class and sports that are decentralized, community-based, and geared for casual use are neglected. Considerable popular resentment at the expenditure of public revenues to build elaborate facilities for the use of a few elite athletes does not alter this policy.

To the extent that democracy and bureaucracy are antithetical, some opposition from democratic movements and parties to the evolution of modern sport might be expected. The "administration by experts" has a tendency to neglect or rewrite the needs of those being administered. How have social democratic movements in the United States dealt with this problem? Actually, sport has not figured prominently on the agenda of political organizations seeking to promote the interests of the working class. Socialists have rarely taken sport very seriously, for the political tradition of socialism gives physical matters low status: "The body has been seen as a personal, individual concern, somehow apart from society" (Whannel 1983, 14). The Left's failure to mount any opposition to bourgeois sport also has something to do with its commitment to a theory of human behavior that traces everything back to the labor process. Changing the way people play will not change their lives, whereas changing the way they work certainly will.

Socialist politicians are clearly ambivalent about sports. At the height of their influence in the United States, in the first quarter of this century, they were condemning sport for its passive spectatorism, elitism, and chauvinism. Sport was a diversion from the class struggle. The Communist party press (first the *Young Worker*, then the *Daily Worker*) condemned mass sports as too production-oriented (e.g., running for fitness); too passive (e.g., spectatorism); too much like work (hunting); or simply too ephemeral, fleeting, or faddish. Writers argued that the competition in sports simply mirrored the competition in economic life and should be shunned for the same reason. Yet these criticisms did not inspire serious policy debate. Part of the reason must have been the preoccupation of socialists with working conditions and with the distribution of property: play struck them as trivial in comparison. Part of the reason was the obvious appeal of sports to the very working class that they were seeking to mobilize.

Taking their inspiration from Europe, members of the Communist party tried to organize a workers' sport movement in the early 1930s, as an alternative to the commercialism of professional and collegiate sports, the religious overtones of the YMCA, the gentlemanly elitism of the AAU, and the paternalism of company-sponsored leagues. Industrial unions, particularly those in which socialists and communists were active, developed a range of recreational activities for their members. A Labor Sports Union was formed in Detroit as early as 1927 with the specific intention of competing with the AAU. Trade union soccer leagues were organized in New York in 1927 and in Detroit in 1928. The Labor Sports Union organized an International Workers' Olympics in 1932, attracting four hundred athletes (one hundred of them black) and five thousand spectators. Together with the socialists, the Communist party organized a World Labor Athletics Carnival on Randall's Island as a counterpoint to the 1936 Olympics: twenty-five thousand spectators attended.

The socialists' sport effort was far from successful, one reason being cultural. In 1929, only 40 percent of the Communist party spoke English as a first language. Most members did not mix well in their leisure time with other Americans and tended to emphasize sports like soccer and gymnastics, which had little appeal to the native-born. The socialists' failure is underlined by the churches' success: while the Labor Sports Union peaked at around five thousand members, the Catholic Youth League, founded at about the same time and oriented very much toward sports, soon reached a membership in the millions.

After Hitler's rise to power, the Communist party was encouraged by Moscow to break out of its isolation and form limited alliances with trade unions and socialist groups. The party was encouraged to identify with egalitarian trends and popular culture in American, no matter how little they embodied the class struggle theme. The party press began to cover sports in a more orthodox way, giving box scores of baseball games and the like. The party became more tolerant of the working-class sport fan. Strikers were described as passing the time on the picket line by listening to baseball games on the radio. Black workers' solidarity was enhanced by the exploits of Joe Louis: "Communists marched in the spontaneous Harlem parade that followed Louis' victory over German boxer Max Schmeling, shouting antifascist slogans and exulting in the 'joyous fraternization of whites and Negroes' that they observed" (Naison 1983, 214).

In its focus on sport, the Communist party in America associated itself more with the tradition of democratic socialism than with Marxist–feminist teachings. Its most vocal campaign, to break down Jim Crow laws in professional sports (in conjunction with the CIO), took place beneath the banner of democracy, rather than socialism (Naison 1979, 48). The opportunity to participate in sports became the acid test of American democratic values. The *Daily Worker* began to feature articles on the accomplishments of black athletes and interviews with white players advocating the integration of their sport. Naison believes that while the integration of baseball would eventually have come about without communist agitation, the Party did accelerate the process (p. 56).

Some of the socialist uncertainty about how to deal with sport continued to show through, however; for the Party press had surprisingly little to say about the corruption and exploitation of professional sports, said nothing at all about discrimination against women, and made no attempt to reconcile sport competition with socialist values. Indeed, the Party seemed to become more and more reconciled to the structure of capitalist sport, "unable to find a language that could simultaneously express socialist goals and resonate with the values and world view of the mass of American workers" (Naison 1979, 57). Left-wing organizations enjoyed little success in attracting people to sport run on socialist principles. In stripping sport of such intrinsic elements as competition, they robbed it of the very element which accounted for its appeal.

CONCLUSION

Neither middle-class reformers nor socialist political parties have been able to mold sport to suit their political agenda. The earnest middle-class reformers and the crusading working-class agitators alike made the mistake of believing that sport would be taken seriously enough by the masses to become an instrument of social reform. Middle-class reformers were paternalistic and often rather naive. The progressives inveighed against spectator sports on the ground that they were "cheap, enervating and deteriorating," the worst of them leading to "moral and intellectual degeneration"; they threatened work values because they insisted on separating work and play and could be obtained with "comfort and ease"; and they undermined family values because, rather than, for example, making music together, families "now listen passively to radio music" (Cutten 1926, 72, 76).

Middle-class recreational professionals were most disdainful of the leisure preferences of the masses. Thus, a spokesman for the National Recreation Association asked:

> Why do some people spend all their evenings fingering their radio dials, accepting whatever comes along, and others take part in community orchestra and chorus? Why do so many folks indulge in trashy and filthy reading when a work of worthwhile and de-lightful literature is theirs for the asking at the public libraries? Why do some spend hours untold in gambling while others play golf? . . . Why do some prefer the doubtful pleasures of the road-house night club and others the opera? (Lies 1933, 27).

People were being given too much freedom, too many choices, by the marketplace. The unspoken message was that in the workplace, this danger would certainly not be faced, at least by the laboring masses. As one segment of the middle class was increasingly tying leisure to con-sumption, where the pleasure, indeed, lay in the exercise of individual choice, another was worrying about what this "freedom to choose" would do to private and public morals. The moral crusaders had fallen into the "humanist trap" (Rojek 1985). In wanting to conceive of leisure as freely chosen, they had set up a contrast with work (which was pre-sumably not freely chosen), thus betraying an attitude toward work that is either patrician and elitist (as assuming that work must be enslaving for the masses) or patronizing (as assuming that the masses could exer-cise no choice during their work day). They co-opted leisure and used it to label the sphere of freedom, using work as the label for the sphere of obligation. It went almost unnoticed, at the time, that they were also making it virtually impossible for most women to experience leisure; for wives and mothers do not experience the divide between work and free time that this perspective assumes.

Socialist reformers faired little better. This was not because socialism lacked a coherent perspective on leisure. Marx saw the need for free time as an elemental one. The demand for more free time (or a decrease in labor time) runs throughout the first volume of *Capital*. At first, this struggle for free time takes place within capitalism itself; but Marx be-lieved that "from a certain point onwards capitalism is incapable of shortening labor time any further: the need for free time then becomes in principle a radical need, which can only be satisfied with the tran-scendence of capitalism" (Heller 1976, 91). In the third volume of *Capi-tal*, Marx argued that future progress would consist of the gradual reduction of work carried out solely to satisfy elementary needs. The time saved would not be spent in idleness but in free creative activity— the earnest, absorbing toil epitomized in the artist. Marx's model of sat-isfying work was not a technical, orchestrated performance but a composite, with elements of both "work" and "play" in it. He used the composition of music as an example of work that is both play and also serious and draining. The goal of socialism should therefore be to make leisure time and leisure facilities more widely available. Sport must be separated from capitalism (with its emphasis on competition and its method of distributing opportunities on the basis of the ability to pay) and it must also be separated from bureaucracy (its elitism and regimentation transforming play into recreation). Socialist leisure should be noncommercial, participatory, cooperative, associative, and democratic (Whannel 1983, 31). It should provide "sport for all," sport available to everyone in the forms, and at the times, that people could make best use of them; be funded primarily through public monies, perhaps through taxes on gambling; use publicly owned facilities, perhaps schools, which should be democratically controlled; make no special provision for "elite" athletes; and replace intense international competition with less formal contacts between groups and teams from different countries.

Undeniably socialist, these proposals failed to make any impact on the world of sport, a failure only partly accounted for by the weakness of socialist parties in the United States. Socialists have been forced to acknowledge that it is one thing to say that play has the *potential* to liberate and offer resistance to domination and another thing altogether to argue that it will achieve these goals. A million forms of individual "resistance" to institutionalized sport add little politically without organization, and "there has not been much evidence to suggest that oppositional and emergent 'ways of playing' have had much success in fundamentally altering the basic constituting structures and 'official' meanings of sport's dominant moment" (Gruneau 1983, 152).[4] The problem remains the obvious popularity of capitalist sports. In criticizing them, socialists are "seen as spoilsports" (Whitson 1987, 243). They find themselves defending the very (middle-class) amateurism that earlier socialists so bitterly attacked.

The problem with these socialist critiques is twofold. First, they retain much of the puritanism with which Marx's model of work and play is tainted. Marx's utopia of work and leisure combined is simply too serious, too highbrow—at least in the context of the work experience of those at whom socialist appeals are aimed. The second problem is that they exaggerate the power of the dominant ideology. The working-class people whom socialists target have responded to modern sport in a number of ways, none of them amounting to an unreflexive acceptance of what their superiors are telling them. Many went along with the welfare capitalism of the 1920s and 1930s, but not in a naive way. For example, workers were ready to participate in the recreation programs that many employers provided, because they themselves subscribed to a view that participation in sports was beneficial for the individual, inculcating work habits and self-discipline that could just as easily be made to serve the ends of the workers as the capitalists. They did not refuse this largess, then, although they were not particularly taken in by it (Ruck 1987, 36). In any case, industrial recreation programs were always opposed by trade unions, who set up their own recreational leagues in defiance.

There is a more general lesson to be learned in the failure of social reform through sport. Popular culture, of which sport is a prime ingredient, either resists or evades structures of dominance: "Popular culture is always a culture of conflict, it always involves the struggle to make social meanings that are in the interests of the subordinate and that are not those preferred by the dominant ideology" (Fiske 1989, 2). Nowhere is this more likely than in the world of play, which, if it does not contain resources out of which people make their own meanings, will be rejected and will never become popular. Play must be produced for its own sake, it cannot be required: "Human desires for fun, fantasy, and excitement, or for personal mastery, drama and creative expression, are a shaky foundation for hegemony" (Gruneau 1983, 152). Play resists being transformed into recreation: the former is creative, the latter demands submission; the former is excess, the latter is discipline. Even the persuasive medium of television lacks the power to impose meanings where they are not wanted. The television audience comprises a semiotic democracy, in which the production of meanings and pleasures is shared by the viewers. For example, professional wrestling is a "travesty" of sport but also a parody, a subversion, of the ideal of fair play that sport otherwise claims to represent. It is "tasteless" and "vulgar"; but taste is social control—class interest masquerading as a naturally finer sensibility. There is little "fair play" in the life of working-class people.

Sport politics are thus dialectical. They work themselves out in the form of a conflict between the massification produced by the extension of capitalist social relations into play (the creation of vast, homogeneous audiences for sporting events and customers for ancillary products) and the political drive for democratization, the desire for more equal access to power. Capitalization reduces participants in the sport world to a mass, distancing each member of that mass from control over the sport world. It is therefore an antidemocratic tendency. The desire for popular control, however, opposes this tendency, especially at the local level. Two obvious examples of this are the tension involved in franchise location (market vs. local democratic control) and the tension inherent in the athlete's role between the (media) star and the "local hero."

The desire for more local, democratic control over leisure is also evident in the new social movements that have sprung up since World War II. Today, sport is more likely to be part of the agenda of social movements that concern themselves with inequities in "collective consumption," rather than political conflict at the point of production. These movements do not articulate economic demands but are more concerned with cultural issues, such as individual autonomy and communal solidarity. Coalitions in this struggle are not so much determined by production relations as by status—by race, gender, and neighborhood. New social movements are a reaction to the externalities of economic growth and industrial production systems. The Environmental movement, the Anti-nuclear Power movement, neighborhood and tenant associations, and various public interest organizations all mobilize behind consumer issues of one kind or another, many of which crucially involve leisure practices. Many stem from the intersection of capitalist practices and government policy. Many, if not most, are made up of individuals affected by state action and business practices who are not members of solidary communities and who are largely unconnected with each other by production relations. Ironically, this has moved leisure, broadly conceived, closer to the center of the arena of political debate. People demand clean air and water in which to spend their leisure time even if they tolerate something less than that at work; liberty to consume, at will, goods and drugs of their choice but guaranteed free of contaminants; neighborhoods that provide a full range of services, including places to play; and access to sporting events, both live and mediated, which should be freely available consumer goods.

CHAPTER 11

SPORT
IN THE
WORLD SYSTEM

Of all its obligations, the state takes most seriously its task of protecting national security, independence, honor, and greatness. In the case of the United States, this is translated into the defense of freedom, where freedom means free enterprise. Foreign policy for the United States means the defense of capitalism and the version of democracy that will further capitalist values. Sport does not figure large in this effort, but it is by no means insignificant. In all likelihood, informal cultural ties, such as those forged by sporting competition, become more important if formal, political ties weaken (Stoddart 1986, 125). Sport relations are one means of strengthening fragile economic and political ties; conversely, severing sport ties signals disapproval of another nation's actions. Sport competition also enables dominant powers to perpetuate relations of dependency by cultural means. So long as people in newly independent nations judge their progress in all areas against the standard of the former colonial power, they will remain in a dependent condition. International sport relations are thus not simply competition on the field but a fight for supremacy for a particular version of sport itself, a version that symbolizes national values and identity.

This chapter will describe how sport in the United States has been shaped by international politics. The monopoly the state claims over the definition and defence of the national interest means that sport must subordinate itself to that interest. Sport will be a deployable resource when the national interest is threatened. This is particularly evident in times of war, but peacetime processes also make this possible. As indicated in chapter 1, as sport becomes rationalized, it loses its attachment to specific, substantive ends and becomes important in its own right. For example, in the early stages of the Olympics, teams were composed of citizen–athletes—individuals who sought to combine the roles of citizen and athlete as if they naturally belonged together, who were contributing members of their nation, whose life chances were consistent with their contribution, and who had an interest and ability in sport. More recently, Olympic teams have been composed of individuals who are athletes first and citizens second, people whose life chances are contingent on sport and who contribute to society through work opportunities. Under these circumstances, sport becomes a deployable tool, available for use for a variety of different social purposes. Sport becomes a distinct form of cultural capital by means of which nations compete with each other and which they use to complement other forms of capital being traded internationally. Sport is produced and distributed globally as if it were wheat; and, like wheat, it can be used as aid or embargoed if the national interest demands.

The emergence of an international sport order superimposed upon an existing global economic and political order has consequences for the organization of sport at home. The political and economic structure of domestic sport is no more immune from global events than is the political and economic structure of the automobile or textile industry. For example, after many years of playing under quite different rules, Americans changed the rules for women's basketball in 1960 to make the game resemble more closely that of men. This was partly in response to pressure from the feminist movement in the United States; but another impetus was the success of Soviet bloc countries in international sporting competition, particularly in women's sports. Women's basketball in the United States was even less like international basketball than was the men's, and rules were changed in order to make it easier for American women to compete internationally.

Under conditions of globalization, the state encourages the centralization of control over sport and its transition to a quasi-public status. The pressure of international competition forces private governments to restructure and to seek state protection and aid. This tendency can be seen in the search for a single authority for amateur sports and the strategic role played by the state in adjudicating conflicting claims for control and determining athletes' right to participate in the global sport order. But in shifting to a more quasi-public status, sport makes itself more vulnerable to state control. With political globalization, sport becomes a deployable weapon of considerable potential; and the state reaches out to assume more control over it. This process is evident in the development of the sport boycott as a diplomatic weapon. Sport boycotts began as purely private protests within private governments; but they gradually entered the public sphere as sport relations became globalized, for this allowed nation–states to trade in a new diplomatic currency. In order to defend American interests abroad, the state had to acknowledge the link between domestic and international sport politics and take steps to ensure that it served United States interests.

FOCUS ON AMATEUR SPORTS

Why would the process of globalization affect amateur sports in the United States more than the professional version of the game? Sport globalization triggers state action only where a sport is already identified with national values and is seen as representing them, depends to some significant degree on state support, and is already part of the global order. If these three conditions are met, sport is not only deployable as a diplomatic weapon, but it will be subject to much closer state regulation and supervision.

These conditions are much more likely to be met by amateur, than by professional, sports. One reason is that the United States, in the name of liberty, has assumed the mantle of defender of the amateur ideal in the global sport order. Preserving the spirit of amateurism is also preserving "American" ideals of democracy, freedom, and competitiveness. A second reason is that amateur sports receive considerable support from state and local governments, much of it indirectly, through schools and colleges. They are, to a large degree, "state actions." A third reason is that amateur sports in the United States are in practice more international than the professional game. Professional football is uniquely American—as much a cultural marker as are Gaelic sports for Ireland. Not until 1991 did American football clubs begin competing in an international league, when a World League of American Football started. This league still bears the stamp of the NFL, which is trying to become a global company, rather than being merely international. Baseball is also a solidly American game, despite expansion into two Canadian cities. The sport has been exported, for it followed the flag: the sport has been played in Cuba, for instance, since American troops stationed there introduced it in the 1860s (Klein 1991, 16). In countries like the Dominican Republic, baseball is the dominant game, and its players are a source of raw material for the American leagues. But even today there is little competition between the professional clubs of different countries. Professional basketball has diffused more widely. Its rules are relatively simple, its resource requirements are minimal, and (as an indoor sport) it does not have to compete with soccer in Europe and Latin America; but the sport has no international league at the club

level. Only ice hockey spans an international border, but it is possibly 355
the most open in the world.[1]

SPORT IN THE WORLD SYSTEM

The state is obliged to deal with certain minor problems associated with "trade" in professional sports. Importing baseball players from countries like the Dominican Republic is believed by some to take jobs away from American players, or at least depress their wages. The U.S. Department of Labor imposes a quota on the number of foreign players in the minor leagues, each major league club being allowed to recruit a maximum of twenty-four foreign players (Klein 1991, 56). Such quotas are intended, however, to protect American jobs and maintain wage rates, not to protect the "national game" and maintain the nation's competitiveness in international competition. Until recently, when Olympic rules were changed to permit professional basketball players to compete in the games, there was no real American equivalent of ice hockey in Canada, soccer in Brazil, or cricket in the West Indies, where prowess in the professional version of international sporting competition is a foreign policy concern and where international trade in players by private sport firms could seen as a matter of national interest.

KEEPING THE PEACE AT HOME

Most amateur athletes regard representing their country in international athletic competition as the pinnacle of achievement. This is a direct result of the globalization of sport during the last one hundred years. Domestic sport politics determine American's international competitiveness, while events in the international sporting order alter how sports are conducted at home. Domestic disputes over eligiblity can prevent the United States from fielding its best team in the Olympics. Conversely, changes in the international sporting order can force American sport authorities to modify their policies with respect to amateurism and to take a more active role in the cultivation of talent for elite sport competition.

How has the relation between amateur sport and the state has been affected by globalizing trends? As sport ceases to be purely domestic and as different nations become interconnected through more complex and pervasive sport relationships, the tie between sport and the state becomes stronger. When national borders are being crossed, national interests are at stake; and it is the responsibility of the state, rather than the private citizen, to define and protect those interests. Beginning as a private activity, international sport competition becomes increasingly politicized. Organizing and regulating international sport activity becomes almost as complicated as the regulation of trade in manufactured goods—and frequently as controversial. Further problems are caused by the fact that the international sport order possesses its own political hierarchy that does not always coincide perfectly with the hierarchy of power in the political and economic system of nations. Economically powerful states like the United States cannot assume that they carry weight in sport circles. Each country must acknowledge and adapt to its place in the international sporting order.

The major impetus for the globalization of sport was the Olympic movement, revived in 1896. Intended to express autonomous and nonpolitical sport values, the movement represented not so much the transcendence of nation–states as their rearticulation and reaffirmation. The global order of sport was thus born political. The Olympic rules stipulated that only one national Olympic committee could have jurisdiction within a nation–state and that a national Olympic committee could have jurisdiction only within one state. Later, when international athletic federations became important component units of the Olympic movement, their national representatives were given territorial authority limited by the boundaries of nation–states. As the games became more successful, Olympians realized that they could get public support more easily if they could present their accomplishments as evidence of national vitality.

The Amateur Athletic Union Assumes Control

The revival of the Olympic movement in Europe at the end of the nineteenth century caused a restructuring of amateur athletics in the United States. Authority was given to Baron de Coubertin to select the founding members of the International Olympic Committee (IOC); and the American representative he chose was an old friend, Princeton historian William Sloane. Sloane, in turn, helped form the first American Olympic Committee (AOC), in 1896. An informal mixture of college, club, and unaffiliated athletes, the American teams for the 1896 and 1900 games were selected rather casually. The prospect of the games' coming to St. Louis in 1904 (in connection with the Louisiana Purchase Exposition) persuaded the AOC that a more efficient organization was needed to ensure a competitive entry and the Amateur Athletic Union assumed responsibility for the administration not only of the American entry but of the entire games. Throughout the period 1896–1912, all AOC members were also AAU members.

The AAU was a natural choice. For twenty years it had been the governing body of track-and-field in the United States, and track-and-field events were rapidly emerging as the most prestigious of the Olympic categories. Hitherto, the participation of Americans in the Olympic Games had been very much a matter of individual athletes pushing themselves forward or being persuaded to participate. In order to

boost the American medal count, a wider range of events had to be contested on a regular basis, which would require coordination and planning. This, in turn, called for more centralized organization.

The 1904 and 1906 United States Olympic teams were simply not di-
versified enough to win many medals. Critics urged that preparation
for the games become better organized. As a result, the American
Olympic Committee came to rely heavily on the AAU to provide it with
athletes and to manage the team during the games while itself becoming the symbolic focus of the nation's amateur sport. Roosevelt was persuaded to serve as honorary president of the AOC (he had been
instrumental in choosing St. Louis over Chicago for the 1904 games);
and the membership roster included the names of such prominent
businessmen as Morgan, Carnegie, Belmont, Wanamaker, Guggenheim,
and Spalding.

While Americans did somewhat better in the 1908 games in London,
the United States nevertheless failed to compete at all in nineteen
Olympic sport divisions (Flath 1964, 38). Lack of breadth continued to
be a problem for American amateur teams abroad well into the modern
period. To understand why the AAU was unable to solve the problem
on its own, it is necessary to know something about the political position of the AAU in amateur sports during the first quarter of the twentieth century. At least until the end of the nineteenth century, the AAU
worked more or less harmoniously alongside school and college athletic programs. They "responded to the same impulses, and often were
directed by the same personnel" (Violas 1978, 107). Creatures of the
same social forces, they both reflected the "athletic impulse" gripping
the nation during this period. There were many cases in which they
touched each other directly. The physical education profession linked
them, as did many of the athletic leagues formed at this time.

The relationship between scholastic and nonscholastic amateur
sports was also riddled with conflict. From its birth, the AAU was "engaged in a continuous struggle to gain recognition and control over athletic organizations of all kinds" (Betts 1974, 110). Its principal rival was
the NCAA. The seeds of the rivalry were sown in the 1880s, when first
at Princeton and then at Harvard, faculty formed committees to regulate their students' playing schedules, prohibit professionalism, and
control spectatorism. "Conferences" soon followed, to regulate competition between colleges. Conferences provided championships and
thus encouraged competition; they could be used to determine eligibility and enhance the colleges' control over the "market" for college
athletics; and they made it easier for faculty and administrators to
deal with problems common to a number of sports (e.g., scholarships)
and thus ease the transfer of power from students and alumni, who
tended to be interested in only one activity (Hardy and Berryman 1982,
22). Conferences also rearranged the structure of college sports away
from the hierarchical, single-sport arrangement to the horizontal

many-sport arrangement, making it easier for college athletic organizations to claim to represent all amateur athletes.

By far the most important of college sports was football, because it was the major revenue producer. It was also the most controversial, because of its high injury rate and its professionalism. Indeed, the NCAA was formed in 1910 (on the basis of the 1906 thirty-eight-school Interscholastic Athletic Association) chiefly to supervise football competition. In the struggle to control amateur sports, the governance of football became of supreme importance. Football had grown up on the college campus and was seldom played elsewhere: "The game had never caught on with athletic clubs" (Flath 1964, 26). For this reason, the AAU had been forced to relinquish control over football by 1899, although control over basketball and baseball continued to be hotly contested (p. 28). The struggle for control of amateur football meant that by the outbreak of World War I, a schism had occured in the government of amateur sports. On one side were athletic programs administered by colleges, increasingly staffed by professional athletic directors and coaches and dominated by a sport that, while it produced revenues, did not prepare athletes for international competition. On the other side was the AAU, established as a coordinating organization of club-affiliated athletes long before collegiate conferences became an effective political force, with its principal strength in the administration of the track-and-field events that were so important for the Olympic Games but had limited spectator appeal on college campuses.

The growing popularity of the Olympic Games only served to raise the stakes in the struggle for control. As Olympic competition became better organised, pressure on Americans to bring some order to their own athletic government increased. The founding of the International Amateur Athletic Federation in 1912 was especially important, because its purpose was to establish internationally valid and enforceable rules of play and conditions of eligibility. Its constitution provided that in each country, a single organization in each sport should exercise jurisdiction over both international and national aspect of competition. Because of its close relation to the AOC, the AAU was able to secure this job with respect to those sports over which it had jurisdiction. This meant that an American athlete desirous of taking part in an international track meet had to obtain permission from the AAU. The AAU thus secured the "franchise" from international sporting authorities and could rightfully claim to cover more sport territory than did the NCAA. On the other hand, the AAU was a purely voluntary organization run by amateurs on minimal and unpredictable funds, whereas the NCAA was comprised of well-funded and professionally administered bureaucracies.

The NCAA showed little interest in the Olympic Games before 1920 (Lehr 1985, 165). Subsequently, it became more concerned with exercising some influence over the United States' Olympic effort. The rea-

son for this is that the NCAA was becoming more of a national institution: the first national championships in track-and-field were held in
1921. An increasing number of the athletes selected to represent the
United States were college students under the nominal control of the
NCAA; and NCAA officials liked to think of themselves as less elitist and
more professional than their counterparts in the AAU. The NCAA lobbied hard for the founding of a National Amateur Athletic Association
of America, which would be an umbrella organization for all amateur
sports in the United States and a natural springboard for the Olympic
effort. In this organization, the NCAA would be on a more equal footing
with the AAU.

The AAU had long been criticized for its elitism, and the NCAA was
not alone in being dissatisfied with the AAU on grounds of its gentlemanly aura. The Progressive Era spawned innumerable social reform
organizations. Because they included the proper management of
leisure time in their purview, many became the rivals of the AAU for
control over organized play. School athletic league organizers like
Luther Gulick espoused an educational and holistic view of athletics:
play must both teach values and be woven seamlessly into the rest of the
child's life. They criticized the AAU for being too specialized, having little to offer organizations "which conduct athletics as one of many other
activities" and doing "little or nothing in the way of promoting the educational view of athletics" (Kallenberg 1912, 504). The AAU preferred to
cater to "expert performers," to "corral all the 'star' athletes in order to
beat some other club, win a meet and furnish a spectacle."[2]

An alternative to the AAU would eventually be formed, although its
life would be short. The National Amateur Athletic Federation (NAAF),
founded in 1922, had as member organizations not only the NCAA but
also all four arms of the military, the National Federation of State High
School Athletic Associations, the Playground and Recreation Association, the YMCA, the American Legion, the Boy Scouts, the United States
Lawn Tennis Association, the Boys' Club Federation, the American
Turnerbund, the National Rifle Association, the Order of Demolay, and
the Catholic Boys' Brigade.[3] The AAU thus found itself embattled on two
fronts. From the NCAA it attracted increasingly powerful resistance to
its control over international competition and the determination of eligibility of athletes, even in nonrevenue sports. From the constituent
members of organizations like the NAAF it had to fight off charges that
it was elitist and overspecialized and had spurned the social reform
goals of the Playground movement.

Between 1920 and 1923, the NCAA maneuvered adroitly to weaken
the influence of the AAU over the United States Olympic organization. The AAU's handling of the 1920 Olympic Games in Antwerp confirmed the worst fears of its critics. The games proved to be a logistical
nightmare for the American team, provoking bitter complaints from
athletes about inadequate accommodations, poor food, and crowded

transportation. Many believed the fault lay in the AAU's reliance on part-time and inexperienced administrators. A period of organizational upheaval and political squabbling followed the games as various interest groups fought to determine the direction of future Olympic campaigns. The AAU tried to fend off efforts to weaken its position. When, just prior to the Antwerp games, a new organization, the American Olympic Commission, was formed the AAU managed to secure control of most of the votes. After the Antwerp debacle and under pressure not only from the NCAA but also the navy and the army, an American Olympic Association with broader representation and more democratic electoral procedures was organized. The NCAA was still not satisfied with its representation, however; for it was given only three votes compared to the AAU's thirty-three. The NCAA refused to join until the disparity in voting strength was reduced (Flath 1964, 55). In any case, the new association did not prove to be a very effective coordinating body. The army and the navy withdrew in 1926, as did the NAAF and, most damagingly, the NCAA. The NCAA charged that the AAU was using its control over the Olympic movement (bestowed upon it by a "foreign" body, the International Amateur Athletic Federation) as a means of gaining control over the sports under its jurisdiction; for to determine "eligibility" for Olympic participation was fast becoming the most important instrument of control over individual athletes.

Despite these increasingly well coordinated attacks, the AAU held on to its position of power in amateur athletics. The reasons are not hard to find. The NCAA was rather isolationist during the 1920s, insensitive to the realities of international sporting competition. It underestimated the importance of working within international rules and assumed that it could impose an American structure on international "trade." But the sport world was becoming increasingly globalized, with sports organized into international bodies exercising tremendous power with respect to playing rules, eligibility, and the structure of competition. The NCAA, in refusing to acknowledge the ascendance of these international bodies, cut itself off from the Olympic movement.

Another result of the NCAA's isolationism was its failure to appreciate the scorn with which officials from other countries regarded its claim to be defending the amateur ideal. Many Europeans had difficulty distinguishing the American college student from the state-supported athlete in the Soviet Union:

> The American type of university, and especially its control of amateur athletics and of its athletes, is practically, if not altogether, unknown on the Continent and quite generally unappreciated in England. . . . No distinction in principle can be made between athletes representing colleges in the United States and the athletes of Russia, because of the complications that always result from payment for "broken time." (Savage 1929, 219)

The NCAA had never fully adopted the British-inspired definition of amateurism by which the international federations and International Olympic Committee operated. In the United States, professionalism did not suffer quite the same level of condemnation as in Europe. American colleges wanted it both ways: they wanted to have the elite status and aura of the British public school but at the same time to use many professional practices and personnel in order to win. Eventually, the NCAA was able to establish domestic credibility for its version of amateurism, despite many abuses public and private. Many were all too willing to look upon the NCAA as their guardian of the amateur ideal. The International Olympic Committee, however, saw things differently; for its charter at this time declared that "individuals subsidized by governments, educational institutions, or business concerns because of their athletic ability are not amateurs." Only when communist countries, with their "state athletes," were admitted to the Olympic movement after World War II was this criticism of college athletics muted. Olympic officials, cognizant of the fact that the NCAA was itself intended to "clean up" college sports, felt it had made little headway during the 1920s. College sports were associated with "demoralization of college and academic work, dishonesty, betting and gambling, professionalism, recruiting and subsidizing, the employment and payment of the wrong kind of men as coaches, . . . evil effects of college athletics on school athletics, the roughness and brutality of football, extravagant expenditures of money, and the general corruption of youth" (p. 25).

The need to prepare for the 1928 games brought the NAAF and the NCAA back into the Olympic fold in 1927, and they promptly resumed lobbying for better representation. In 1930, an important constitutional change was made to the American Olympic Association giving the AAU ninety votes and the NCAA eighty. The association's members also changed the voting rules to require a two-thirds, rather than a simple, majority of votes to approve motions, a reform that protected the less well represented bodies: "That was an important point in the movement toward parity between the AAU and the NCAA" (Lehr 1985, 185).

The NCAA had more clout at the end of the decade than at the beginning, because it was much better organized. Ironically, this had resulted, in part, from its rivalry with the AAU. Until the 1930s,

the NCAA had no specific power base, partially because it had no place where the principals of that body could meet and plan. It was a nomadic organization, normally having its meetings in different parts of the country each year. Its communications network was inferior to the AAU's; hence, its reaction to situations often had to wait until its yearly meetings. . . . The AAU, on the other hand, was essentially an Eastern organization with a very strong power base in New York City. The majority of the key members of the AOA [American Olympic Association] and the AOC were AAU members and most of them were members of the huge Metropolitan AAU. Many of them were also members of the New York Athletic Club. (Lehr 1985, 272).

The power of the NCAA was also enhanced by the fact that during the "golden age of sports" in the 1920s, it enjoyed its most rapid growth in membership (Stern 1979, 248). Subsequently, especially during the Depression, the NCAA was able to counterbalance the tie between the AAU and the Olympic movement with its superior financial and manpower resources. The various rules committees established between 1903 and 1931 helped the NCAA reap "the external benefits" of a visible commitment to the sport in question and formed "a power base from which to influence sport federations, which were often dominated by the AAU" (p. 257).

A sign of the shifting balance of power in amateur athletics as the 1920s ended was the agreement that athletes could be "certified" as being amateur if they were in full-time attendance at an NCAA-affiliated institution. This represented a victory for the NCAA perspective on amateurism. The AAU tended to focus more upon the individual athlete, while the NCAA's concern was more institutional. The AAU adhered to rather old-fashioned notions of the sport role, more appropriate for an age of individualism and elite participation, where the decision to engage in competitive athletics on an amateur basis could plausibly be seen as an individual one. The approach of the NCAA, however, was more typical of the organizational age. The concept of amateur athletics was seen as an organizational phenomenon, created and maintained by the right kind of organizational practices, rather than the right kind of individual commitment and scrupulousness—hence the difference between the "license" the AAU sought to grant and the membership of a "certified" organization the NCAA favored. The first placed the onus on the individual, the second on the organization; the first saw amateurism as a matter of personal commitment and integrity, the second as a matter of organizational efficiency and exactitude. The AAU stood for tradition, the NCAA for modernity. Thus, the president of the NCAA, speaking in 1926, said: "It is my belief that the AAU cannot succeed in its efforts to perpetuate its system of control upon amateur sports. It is un-American and out-of-date. It places responsibility for amateurism on the individual instead of on the organization he may represent" (Flath 1964, 83).

The 1930s were a much more harmonious time for amateur athletics than had been the 1920s: "Eventually the NCAA and the AAU. . . . agreed to joint control of track and field, swimming, boxing, wrestling, men's gymnastics, basketball, ice hockey, and handball" (Lehr 1985, 191). The NCAA was granted the right to qualify athletes for Olympic trials through its own competitions and the right to have college coaches ap-

The Dispute Becomes Public

Throughout the 1920–50 period, the struggle for control over amateur sports took place almost entirely in the private sphere. While each side found it expedient to invoke the national interest in making its claim, neither sought to harness the power of the state to settle the dispute. Nor did state officials seem disposed to become embroiled. This changed after World War II and the dispute over the control of amateur sports spilled out of the private sphere onto the public stage, the state becoming a reluctant actor in the play.

Two trends were responsible for the change in the relation between sport and the state at this time. The most important was the Cold War. The Soviets were admitted to the international Olympic movement in 1951. The Cold War had become a sport war. In the 1952 Summer Games, the USSR was awarded 553.5 points, compared to 614 for the United States. Four years later, the Soviets' total was 622, compared to 497 for the United States. The Soviet Union participated in the Winter Olympics for the first time in 1956 and promptly took first place in the medal count. By the end of the 1950s, Soviet-bloc countries were outperforming the United States with some predictability. These developments aroused deep concern among sport administrators in the United States.

The second trend had to do with the increasing commercialization of the NCAA as competition for student–athletes heated up after the end of the war. The NCAA began to permit college athletes to receive scholarships without demonstrating financial need, confirming the worst suspicions of the AAU and its Olympic allies. Avery Brundage declared that "college athletes who receive scholarships because of their ability in sports become, in fact, professionals" (Flath 1964, 119). Brundage's charge was politically motivated, intended to discredit any claim on the part of the NCAA to be the guardian of United States amateur athletics. He must have known that the Soviets used the example of the American college student to justify their own practice of "broken time" payments, and the International Olympic Committee could hardly deny the Soviets what they were already tacitly allowing the Americans. The admission of the Soviets tarnished the amateurism image of the International Olympic Committee and threatened to weaken its American ally, the AAU.

The politics of sport at home thus became embroiled in a complex and multilayered international struggle for supremacy, in which the distinction between amateur and professional became a political "football." The Soviets cleverly exploited an interpretation of amateurism that had emerged in the United States to legitimate college athletics. The *motive for playing* defined amateurism, not the source or amount of support. The Soviets took the line that an athlete could remain an amateur as long as he was not participating in a program called "professional sport," of which none existed in the Soviet Union. They emphasized the subtle but accepted distinction between those who receive money (or other forms of support) while they improved their skills and those whose motive for playing was money.

Brundage realized that the Soviet model threatened to legitimate the NCAA practice of funding athletes and discredit the amateurism promoted by the AAU. More importantly, he had his own distinction to preserve, in which amateurism stood for freedom and autonomy and professionalism stood for servitude and subservience—a hired hand. In the Cold War atmosphere, the Olympic movement could benefit politically by exposing the professionalism of the Soviet athletes. This, in turn, demanded redoubled efforts to deny the existence of any engagement of the state in U.S. Olympic sports, however indirect (MacAloon 1991, 267). This meant separating the Olympic movement from the NCAA model.

Once more, the AAU and the NCAA seemed to be growing further apart, at the very time when a better-coordinated international effort seemed called for by pressure from abroad. The first sign of concern from state officials that the private Olympic effort needed more public clout was the congressional decision in 1950 to grant a charter to the American Olympic Association, renamed the United States Olympic Committee (USOC). The charter incorporated the committee, meaning that in return for preparing a United States team for the Olympic Games and general oversight of amateur sports, the USOC would be granted exclusive rights to market products in the United States under the Olympic logo. The charter, although a very weak political instrument (it bestowed no statutory powers upon the USOC), proved to be an important source of revenue for the committee. The incorporation of the USOC was not sufficient, however, to bring the AAU and the NCAA closer together. The NCAA felt itself underrepresented in the USOC and the AAU was hamstrung by its difficulties in securing a supply of athletic talent without the support of the colleges. In the late 1950s, the NCAA was still complaining bitterly about the poor management of athletic meets by the AAU, its neglect of sport medicine research, its "dictatorial attitude," its reluctance to investigate complaints, and its failure to maintain international sporting ties (Flath 1964, 129). The AAU, through its control over the U.S. Olympic campaign, was assigned the blame for "unworthy and unpatriotic" efforts. The NCAA called for yet another umbrella organization—similar to the NAAF—that would embrace all forms of amateur sports in the United States and thus dilute the impact of the AAU.

The ascendance of Soviet-bloc countries continued through the 1960 Summer Games, and the federal government began to exert more pressure for reconciliation between the AAU and the NCAA. Lacking an "official spokesman" or agency for sport, the government mobilized its symbolic resources. Robert Kennedy, then attorney general, told reporters, "They know how we feel about this situation. We hope that the two groups will get together and iron out their differences so that the United States will be well represented in the Olympics in 1964" (Flath 1964, 157). Flath speculates that "the federal government" was probably instrumental in engineering a truce (the "Washington Alliance") between the parties in the fall of 1962. It is quite certain that Kennedy visited Olympic House in New York on November 12, 1962, to mediate a truce between the NCAA and the AAU at a meeting called by the president of the United States Olympic Committee.[4]

From the NCAA standpoint, the issue was chiefly the refusal by the AAU to share authority over amateur sports. The athletic director of the University of Chicago told the delegates assembled at the NCAA Convention in 1963, "The problem is that the upper echelon of the AAU feels it has the sole right to determine policy affecting amateur athletics in this country and will do anything to retain this power" (Flath 1964, 170). The executive director of the AAU saw things differently. For him, it was all a matter of greed: "I think they want to take the college kids out of any events they can't make money on. They have seen how much they can make with a football monopoly" (Flath 1964, 169).

It is necessary at this point to recapitulate the reasons for the powers of survival possessed by the AAU, which had much more to do with its international connections than its domestic resources. While the United States Olympic Committee was officially neutral in this dispute, it had always favored the AAU and thus helped bolster its position in relation to the much more powerful NCAA. This was, in part, because of its continued opposition to the professionalism of the NCAA. Avery Brundage, former president of the AAU and now president of the International Olympic Committee, reminded the NCAA not to overlook the important IOC rule that "makes ineligible for Olympic competition any athlete awarded a scholarship mainly for his athletic ability" (Flath 1964, 175).

There was another reason for the United States Olympic Committee's tilt toward the AAU. A conflict had arisen within the international sport order between the International Olympic Committee and its various constituent sport federations, a conflict in which the United States Olympic Committee needed the support of the AAU. International Olympic Committee rules provided for the formation of national Olympic committees and authorized them to join with the national sport federations of their respective countries to organize and control the representatives of their country at the Olympic Games. Only national Olympic committees recognized and approved by the International Olympic Committee could enter competitors into the Olympic Games. The national federations were members of the national Olympic committee and also held membership in their various respective international federations. Only one organization per country could hold membership in any one international federation. In most cases, this would mean a separate national member for each sport. The United States was highly unusual in having the AAU act as the national member for eleven different sports, including swimming and track-and-field.

The individual sport federations were becoming increasingly powerful in relation to the International Olympic Committee, in part because of sponsorship money provided by sporting goods manufacturers like Addidas.[5] The NCAA, an active member of most of these federations, abetted their drive toward independence not only from the IOC and national Olympic committees but also from the AAU, which had always attempted to serve as an umbrella organization for them all. The AAU resisted this drive toward autonomy by refusing to permit athletic meets to have "dual sanctioning" from both itself and an individual sport federation. During the 1960s, the NCAA sought to undermine the power of the AAU by fostering federation growth—where necessary, setting up federations to rival the AAU subcommittees in charge of a sport. Thus, in 1962, it helped form the United States Track and Field Federation (USTFF) and the Basketball Federation of the United States; a year later, it helped form the United States Gymnastic Federation. In each instance, a struggle for control over the sport ensued.

The schism between the NCAA and AAU meant that the international franchise for the major Olympic sports (held by the AAU) was divorced from the domestic program providing the means of supplying athletic talent for those sports. The NCAA continued to maintain that it must have jurisdiction over amateur sports because it supplied the resources. The USTFF joined in the attack, accusing the AAU of being an old-fashioned "umbrella organization" claiming jurisdiction over a wide variety of different sports when the trend worldwide was to give more power to the individual sport federations. The USTFF (a creature of the NCAA) could therefore attack the AAU for being inefficient and monopolistic, a charge the cartel-like NCAA itself would find hard to make. *Track and Field News*, the USTFF house organ, accused the AAU of failing to provide athletes with channels to air grievances; arbitrarily issuing invitations to participate in international meets; failing to consult or employ the best coaches; dropping behind the Soviets in training, techniques, and equipment; putting on poorly staffed and poorly organized track meets; and cheating on amateurism rules (U.S. Congress, Senate, Committee on Commerce 1965b, 379). The AAU resisted the encroachments of the federations and justified its role as an umbrella organization by arguing that this permitted weak sports to be

supported by stronger sports, such as track-and-field and swimming.
Colonel David Hall, executive director of the AAU, described the basketball and track-and-field federations as "a group of schemers after power and money" (p. 370). However, his arguments were futile in the face of the increasing division of labor in sport administration. The gymnasts united in one body in 1970, the basketball war ended in 1976, and the track-and-field dispute was settled in 1978—victory in each case going to the federation and the NCAA.

The State as Arbiter

This was the state of affairs faced by state officials concerned to improve the United States' performance in the Olympic Games but at the same time to leave the whole enterprise in private hands. The USOC could not be relied upon to be a neutral "private government" for amateur sports in the United States and arbitrate the conflict between the AAU and the NCAA, because its own survival was more closely tied to the fortunes of the AAU than the NCAA. No wonder that state efforts up to this time to engineer the more efficient coordination of amateur sports had not been conspicuously successful. Robert Kennedy had asked General Douglas MacArthur to arbitrate the track-and-field dispute in 1962. MacArthur did eventually reach a settlement (announced in January 1963), in which he granted an amnesty to all athletes hitherto declared ineligible and proposed the establishment of an Olympic Eligibility Board composed of three members from the AAU and three members from the United States Track and Field Federation ("as the duly constituted agent of the NCAA"). The general himself would act as arbitrator in the event of failure to reach agreement by the board. There is little question that the approaching 1964 games contributed to the parties' willingness to follow MacArthur's recommendations, and President Kennedy was able to set his seal on the agreement.[6]

MacArthur's services as arbitrator were soon in demand again as a dispute arose over the sanctioning of a track meet in Los Angeles. MacArthur decided, in this case, that the USTFF had the right to sanction *athletes*, while the AAU had the right to sanction *meets*. Typically, the AAU declared this a victory for its policy of no "dual sanctions," while the NCAA saw his judgment as backing up the right of the USTFF to determine eligibility.

Time was to show that MacArthur exercised no real power over two warring private organizations. In 1965, the United States lost its first dual track meet with the Soviets since the series began in 1958. Many experts blamed the loss on the NCAA–AAU dispute over the Los Angeles meet, which had been intended to serve as a qualifier, and from which the NCAA had withdrawn its athletes ("The Government of

Amateur Athletics" 1968, 464). Losses to the Soviets were very costly in terms of cultural capital at a time of considerable tension between the two superpowers, when there were virtually no economic linkages to cement the relationship and the allegiance of Third World countries was the victor's prize. Defeat at the hands of the Soviets caused a public furor and sparked two weeks of hearings in Congress on the state of amateur sports in the United States. This marked a qualitative leap in state involvement in a hitherto private sphere, a step beyond the highly personalized and mainly symbolic intervention of Robert Kennedy and General MacArthur. The congressional hearings culminated in a joint resolution calling for the establishment of a Sports Arbitration Board under the chairmanship of Theodore Kheel, a professional arbitrator. The board's brief was confined to track-and-field. Both the AAU and the NCAA agreed to abide by the ruling of the board, whose members were appointed by Vice President Hubert Humphrey. Robert Kennedy described his brother President Kennedy as being "deeply concerned about the effect which factional disputes would have on all of our athletic endeavours and particularly on our participation in the Olympics" (U.S. Congress, Senate, Committee on Commerce 1965b, 430). However, each side staked out its territory in advance: the AAU declared its "responsibility" to the International Amateur Athletic Federation (IAAF), the NCAA, its duty to protect the educational welfare of its students, as non negotiable.

The recommendations of the Sport Arbitration Board, finally made in 1968, were intended to secure to each of the combatants its principal objectives. To the AAU, most anxious about its control over international competition, it recommended that eligibility for participation in international competition continue to be the jurisdiction of the AAU and its member organizations. To the NCAA, with its central concern being the ability to control the athletic activities of its students, it granted the exclusive right to sanction "closed" meets and athletic activities between semesters and during vacations, when the activity was based on a college facility or used college coaches. However, the board noted in its final report:

> The basic contest is one for power, and "jurisdiction" and "sanctioning" are the boundaries and tools of power. Each side claims with evident sincerity that it would use the power more wisely than the other, but the protestations cannot be allowed to obscure the essential character of the contest. It is—we repeat—a struggle for power in which the athletes are being used by both sides as pawns as long as the contest continues. (U.S. Congress, Senate, Committee on Commerce 1968, 18)

The board's recommendations did little to diminish the power of the AAU because the pinnacle of amateur athletic achievement remained international competition, principally the Olympic Games. The reward structure of amateur athletics was focused on the prospect of Olympic medals, awarded every four years by a private, international body over which the state had little control. The IAAF rules called for the disbarment of an athlete from international competition who had been disqualified by the AAU. The Sports Arbitration Board publicly worried whether the AAU would continue to "use its international competition in order to boost its control over purely domestic aspects of competition" (U.S. Congress, Senate, Committee on Commerce 1968, 26). The board was also aware, however, of the potentially exploitative power vested in the NCAA by virtue of its control over the coaching staff and capital resources for athletics. The NCAA had shown its clout in 1965, after the 1964 Olympics, when it recommended that its members withdraw from AAU committees and no longer make their facilities available to the AAU.

To improve the United States' preparation for the 1968 Olympic Games, the board recommended the establishment of a "coordinating committee" made up of representatives from the AAU and NCAA and chaired by a neutral third party. The committee was never formed, each side blaming the other for the failure. As Kheel had predicted, "You cannot create an organization in the field of private endeavor by an order" (U.S. Congress, Senate, Committee on Commerce 1968, 3). The NCAA refused to work with the committee because the USTFF was not given complete control over track-and-field. The USTFF continued to run "open" meetings without seeking AAU sanction.[7]

Exasperated congressmen, watching the continual squabbling of the two sides, had sought to strengthen the Sports Arbitration Board's arm by threatening legislation. Senator James Pearson introduced a bill in 1967 aimed at resolving the conflict by subordinating both parties to a regulatory commission for amateur athletics. Pearson and his supporters were clearly reluctant to create a public agency for the regulation of sport but despaired of otherwise controlling the work of a private agency.

The prospect of legislation only exacerbated the conflict, as each party staked out its position in advance of congressional hearings, during which the two associations continued to fling charges at each other. The president of the NCAA dismissed the claims of the AAU to represent American track-and-field athletes: "All that the AAU has is a piece of paper from an international body, the IAAF" (U.S. Congress, Senate, Committee on Commerce 1967, 73). The NCAA indicated its readiness to support federal legislation creating a single governing body for each sport but only so long as there was "representation according to contribution," a voting structure that would privilege the NCAA. The NCAA, with some irony, accused the AAU of violating the Sherman Act by seeking to monopolize amateur sports. A spokesman for the USTFF was even more critical of the AAU, which he described as "the exclusive preserve of affluent gentlemen who have the time and money to regard amateur sports administration as a hobby" (p. 96). Pearson's bill did not make it out of committee.

Interorganizational squabbles were once again blamed for the poor showing of the United States in the 1972 Olympic Games in Munich. As usual, track-and-field generated most controversy (the coach responsible for two sprinters, misreading the schedule, failed to get them to the starting line punctually), but the favored United States basketball team also lost in the final to the Soviets, in a hotly disputed game. The Americans complained that the Soviets won unfairly because their final points came one second after the buzzer should have sounded. However, the fact that the Soviets were even given the chance to win the game was enough to convince NCAA-affiliated coaches that the AAU simply could not provide the best coaches or the best teams for the United States Olympic Basketball Committee.

Legislating Peace

The NCAA was able to change the governing structure of amateur basketball in 1973 as a result of the problems in Munich, but the new Amateur Basketball Association of the United States (ABAUS) did not give college coaches the control they sought. The NCAA was strongly tempted to deny coaches and athletes to the ABAUS altogether, but it could not undermine the AAU without appearing unpatriotic. This was made clear in 1973 when the NCAA at first refused to permit college students to play against a touring Soviet basketball team, thus preventing the United States from fielding its best team. Coming on the heels of the loss of the basketball gold medal to the Russians the year before, this struck many congressmen as positively un-American. To make matters worse, the United States lost a track meet to the Russians in Richmond, Virginia, in March 1973, in large part because student athletes had not been allowed to participate. The news media had questioned the NCAA's patriotism when two of the students had gone to court seeking a temporary restraining order to forestall the ban.

The result was a flurry of bills, all with more or less the same purpose. Two bills, virtually identical, would have set up a Federal Scholastic and Amateur Sports Commission and amended the Higher Education Act of 1965 to protect the freedom of student–athletes and their coaches to participate as representatives of the United States in amateur international athletic events. Three other bills proposed an amateur sport authority to which both the AAU and the NCAA would be answerable (S1018, to create a National Commission on Olympic Sports; S1192, to create a Federal American Sports Commission; S1580, to create a United States Amateur Sports Association Board; S1690, to create a National Amateur Sports Development Foundation). James

> In recent years the bureaucracies which control national and in-
> ternational amateur athletic competition have repeatedly demon-
> strated their inability to meet the needs of today's athletes. They
> have failed to fulfill their obligations to develop teams for interna-
> tional competition which represent the best our Nation has to of-
> fer. Instead, I think they have demonstrated an inordinate capacity
> to engage in petty disputes coupled with a fierce determination to
> perpetuate their own rule over amateur sports. (U.S. Congress,
> Senate, Committee on Commerce 1973, 3)

The bill's supporters believed that only direct federal intervention
would solve the problem. They noted that the United States had no organization, public or private, concerned with policy, planning, conduct, and development of amateur sports as a whole. As a result, sports
had developed unevenly, opportunities to participate were unequal,
and the science of sport medicine was underdeveloped. Coaches in "minor" sports like speed skating worked unpaid. In many sports, athletes
had no chance to compete at all: the United States did not even field a
men's volleyball team at this time and would not do so until 1984. To
those who argued that sports should be immune from political control,
the bills' supporters pointed out that most colleges relied heavily on
federal support and yet felt free, through the NCAA, to pursue their
own interests when it came to international competition.

Hearings on these bills, important for their display of concern as
much as for their legislative intent, showed congressmen's sentiments
in this case to be against the NCAA, which was accused of treating students as "pawns" and "hostages" in a power struggle and of causing the
United States to face the Soviets with less than the best. It did not help
the NCAA that it resigned from the United States Olympic Committee after the 1972 Olympics, not rejoining until 1978. Amateur sport thus
faced its biggest crisis, with the NCAA monopolizing resources and athletes and the AAU holding onto the authority to sanction international
meets and select the vast majority of coaches and athletes for the
Olympic Games. Nor did it help the NCAA that the National Association
of Intercollegiate Athletics (NAIA) testified on behalf of the AAU, touting
its own simon-pure principle of making an athlete an integral part of the
total education program "rather than a commercial and a promotional
adjunct" (U.S. Congress, House, Committee on Education and Labor
1973, 20). But the weakness of the NCAA did not translate into support
for a quasi-public agency responsible for amateur sport.

Only one of the 1973 bills made it to the floor of the Senate, where it
died. Nevertheless, the congressional hearings, together with a letter
signed by fifty-eight senators protesting the NCAA basketball ban, were

sufficient to change the mind of the NCAA; and it rescinded its ban on the games against the Soviets. And one of the 1973 bills was reintroduced in the next Congress, as the amateur athletics act of 1974. This bill proposed to establish an Amateur Sports Board as an independent agency of the executive branch of the federal government with the power to charter sport organizations, make rules, and enforce them. The Commerce Committee again recommended passage and on this occasion Senator Pearson's bill was approved by the Senate by a two-thirds vote. No action was taken in the House.

The policy question at issue in the 1973 congressional hearings was not merely who should run amateur sports. The Civil Rights movement had focused attention on the undemocratic structure of the governance of Olympic sports in the United States. Athletes complained that their rights to participate were trampled upon in the warfare between the AAU and the NCAA, in which they frequently served as pawns; that the governing committees in amateur sports, with powers to select athletes and coaches and distribute resources, rarely included currently active athletes; and that the interests of minorities, especially women, were frequently overlooked.[8] The Kheel board had paid only cursory attention to the issue of athletes' civil rights.

Presidential Commission on Olympic Sports

Under the threat of legislation that would force it to operate more democratically, the United States Olympic Committee amended its constitution in 1973 to include seven Olympic athletes on its board of directors, and a forty-two-member Athletes' Advisory Council was formed to broaden communication between the United States Olympic Committee and currently active athletes. These reforms were not sufficient to stifle demands for a more successful Olympic organization, however; and in 1975, President Ford appointed a Commission on Olympic Sports to try once and for all to resolve the question of who should govern amateur athletics. The commission undertook to include within its purview the question of athletes' rights.

In its 1977 report, the presidential commission described the United States Olympic Committee as "a maddening complex of organizations" (U.S. President's Commission on Olympic Sports 1977, 17). Nevertheless, it noted, the United States Olympic Committee had been drawn into a vacuum created by the unmet needs of United States amateur sports, and recommended that a federally chartered Central Sports Organization be set up to relieve the United States Olympic Committee of its heavy burden. It also decided that "massive new funding for amateur sports is absolutely essential for the long-term improvement of the

American sports effort" (p. 24) and proposed $215 million as an initial sum, with subsequent annual appopriations of $80 million.[9]

The commission made some significant recommendations with regard to the structure of amateur sports. It bowed to both domestic and international pressure to abstain from direct government control. President Killanin of the International Olympic Committee had urged congressmen to reject the Amateur Athletic Act of 1974 precisely because it contemplated a presidentially appointed five-man amateur sport board to oversee the work of the United States Olympic Committee. Killanin saw this as a violation of the Olympic Charter. During the presidential commission's hearings, "International Olympic Committee officials repeatedly expressed the concern that if ever the United States, symbol of free enterprise, were to opt for government control of sports, any influence the International Olympic Committee had been able to exert to keep sports free from politics would be completely undermined" (U.S. President's Commission on Olympic Sports 1977, 18). While avoiding direct state control, the commission did recommend some major changes in the structure of the United States Olympic Committee and its relation to other governing bodies in amateur sport. The United States Olympic Committee would acquire the power to "recognize" just one governing body in an Olympic sport. Significantly, no "multi-sport organization" could qualify as a national governing body, thus barring the AAU from performing this role. The NCAA did not escape censure either; for the commission also proposed that the United States Olympic Committee charter be amended to give individual athletes the right to submit to arbitration disputed claims to participate, a direct attack on the NCAA's control over college athletes. The commission also criticised the narrow focus of the NCAA: "While our school/college sports system is the envy of the world, other countries have found ways to finance their amateur sports more adequately *throughout* the athlete's competitive life" (p. 70). Basketball was a notorious case. Commission members concluded that the lack of an effective postgraduate basketball program was wasting valuable resources: players were no sooner brought to the peak of their performance by the colleges than they graduated and turned professional. The commission predicted, quite accurately, that the United States would soon be competing less successfully against increasingly proficient and mature teams from foreign countries. The commission also blamed the NCAA for the United States' poor performance in minor sports, which were neglected because the colleges did not support them.

The recommendations of the commission were received with guarded enthusiasm by the affected parties, and there is some reason to believe that the commission would have suffered the fate of so many others had not evidence of the continued fragmentation of the amateur sports effort continued to accumulate. On the heels of the commission's report, the United States Wrestling Federation (USWF), prodded by the NCAA, filed a request with the American Arbitration Association to determine whether it or the wrestling division of the AAU was better qualified to be the national governing body for amateur wrestling. To the consternation of the AAU and its supporters on the commission, the arbitrator decided in favor of the USWF.

The Amateur Sports Act

Lacking any sign that congressional exhortation would bring a halt to this private warfare, the recommendations of the commission were written into a bill, sponsored by Senators Stevens, Culver, and Stone (all of whom had served on the commission), entitled the amateur sports act. The most important change proposed by the bill concerned the United States Olympic Committee. The charter for the corporation would be amended to make clear that its purpose was to coordinate and develop amateur athletic activity in the United States directly relating to international amateur athletic competition so as to foster working relationships among sports-related organizations; exercise exclusive jurisdiction over all matters pertaining to the participation of the United States in the Olympic and Pan-American games; provide for the swift resolution of conflicts involving amateur athletes, national governing bodies, and sport organizations; protect the opportunity for amateur athletes, coaches, and trainers to participate in amateur athletic competition; and provide assistance for amateur athletic activities for women and for racial and ethnic minorities. For any sport included in the program of the Olympic or Pan-American games, the corporation was authorized to recognize as a national governing body an amateur sport organization filing an application and eligible for such recognition. To be eligible for recognition, the national governing body would have to demonstrate autonomy from any other sport organization and show that it provided equal opportunity for participation on its board of directors for athletes currently active in the sport for which recognition was sought. Without doubt, the most important of these criteria was that stipulating "autonomy" from any "outside organization." The acknowledged target was the AAU, whose officials accused the bill's sponsors of an "overwhelming desire to destroy the AAU" (U.S. Congress, Senate, Committee on Commerce, Science, and Transportation 1978, 193).

In public debate on the bill, the issues were framed in predictably different ways. For the AAU and its allies, the chief issue was the right of the individual athlete to participate, a right that should be protected by the organization having the "franchise" for international competition, which was, of course, the AAU itself. For the NCAA, the issue was that of organizational integrity, the task of ensuring that college athletes were properly supervised and athletic programs honestly administered, a job that could only be done by the NCAA. While the NCAA opposed the sections on athletes' rights and favored those on restructuring, the AAU opposed the sections on restructuring and favored the guarantees of athletes' rights. The proposal intended to protect the rights of individual athletes to participate met "with strong resistance by the high school and college communities"; the bill would have required that "no governing body, educational institution, or sports organization may deny or threaten to deny any eligible amateur athlete the opportunity to participate in any sanctioned international amateur athletic competition" (U.S. Congress, House, Committee on the Judiciary 1978). Walter Byers, executive director of the NCAA, warned congressmen that the member institutions of the NCAA were "already . . . chafing under far too many governmental dictates"; he opposed the clause in the bill giving an athlete the right to submit to arbitration a disputed claim to participate, on the grounds that this would constitute government interference in the affairs of a private organization (p. 62). The NCAA asked Congress to leave student's eligibility up to the member institutions and apply a "reasonableness" test to specific cases. Speaking for the other side, Edward Williams, chairman of the United States Olympic Committee's Athletes' Advisory Council, insisted on the importance of statutorily guaranteeing athletes' rights:

> Thus, under the NCAA's proposal, an educational institution would be permitted, at its discretion, to preclude an athlete from competing in an international competition simply by making a determination that, for whatever reason, such participation would not be "reasonable." No mention was made of the fact that the test the NCAA would apply is not whether it would be reasonable from the athlete's point of view. (U.S. Congress, Senate, Committee on Commerce, Science, and Transportation 1978, 225)

President of the AAU, Joel Ferrell, accused the NCAA of elitism—of dealing with, and profiting from, only the cream of the athletic crop: "Too often we look at the fruit developed and neglect to see who has been watering the tree" (p. 191).

The NCAA eventually gave its support to the bill but only after the United States Olympic Committee agreed to a change intended to further weaken the AAU's authority. The clause on athletes' rights was expunged before the bill reached the floor of the senate. A compromise was reached that certain substantive provisions on athletes' rights would be included in the United States Olympic Committee constitution, not in the bill (U.S. Congress, Senate, Committee on Commerce, Science, and Transportation 1978, 5). The athlete was given the right to appeal to the United States Olympic Committee if denied the opportunity to participate. The AAU thus lost its fight for athletes' rights, which it hoped would weaken the control of the NCAA, and partially lost its fight to avoid restructuring. The NCAA not only won the battle over restructuring but also beat back the move to strengthen athletes' rights. The NCAA, in its lobbying on the bill, could shelter beneath the protection of numerous court decisions in which the absolute right of an athlete to participate in amateur athletics had been consistently denied.

The terms of the Amateur Sports Act of 1978 made the United States Olympic Committee the coordinating body for amateur sports in the United States, instructed national governing bodies to diversify sport participation to take into consideration all levels and abilities, designated two new training centers (at Colorado Springs and Lake Placid), set up a sport medicine program, planned a National Sports Festival for every year except that of the Olympics; and designed job opportunities programs for prospective Olympic athletes in conjunction with business corporations. The act settled many of the administrative problems faced by the United States when preparing for international sport competition. It did much to strengthen the powers of the individual sport federations. One year after passage of the bill, the Athletics Congress was established as the national governing body of track-and-field in the United States. In this body, the NCAA and the National Federation of State High School Associations were the dominant actors.

Funding for Amateur Sports

The act did little to solve the problem of how amateur sports should be funded. The United States Olympic Committee had always prided itself on being the only national Olympic association receiving no government support. Some funds had been appropriated for the 1960 Winter Olympics in Squaw Valley, California; the 1979 Pan-American games in San Juan, Puerto Rico; and the 1980 Lake Placid Winter Olympics—but these had always comprised a tiny fraction of the budget. The government occasionally gave larger amounts to defray the costs of hosting games but was always careful to justify the expenditure on more appropriate grounds. In 1976, it gave forty-nine million dollars for the Lake Placid games, principally for housing that would eventually become a youth detention facility. In any case, these were funds intended to help communities host the games, rather than to defray the expenses of athletes preparing for them. The United States Olympic Committee rarely lobbied the state directly and specifically for money.[10]

Despite the reforms mandated by the Amateur Sports Act, the United States Olympic effort remained feeble in comparison to what the coun-

try could have achieved. It had a vast "capital stock" of sport amenities
(tracks, fields, pools, gymnasiums, courts); but they were underused,
because they were tied up in educational institutions. The coaching talent available to United States was excellent but decentralized and disorganized. The United States did not appoint its first full-time national
coach in track-and-field until 1982, by which time the Federal Republic
of Germany, with a population a quarter the size, had thirteen full-time
track-and-field coaches, plus one for each of the states (Riordan 1986,
84). A one-time payment of sixteen million dollars to help fund three
new Olympic training centers was authorized in 1981; but only after
considerable wrangling between the legislative and executive branches
of government and by the use of a parliamentary stratagem to attach the
provision to a fiscal authorization bill did the measure get by Congress.

While many congressmen found it convenient to remind the public
that International Olympic Committee rules prohibit direct government control of a National Olympic Committee, they omitted to point
out that Olympic rules say nothing about either the proper source of
funds for amateur athletics or how individual athletes should be
trained and supported. As a policy option, more efficient use of educational facilities rarely received a hearing. Congressmen never mentioned the possibility of state-funded colleges' making athletic facilities
available to nonstudents. Instead, they sought to give state sanction and
symbolic weight to the private, voluntary efforts of the U.S. Olympic
movement.

Typical of this strategy was the Olympic Coin Act of 1988, enabling
the United States Olympic Committee to sell silver and gold commemo-
rative coins minted by the U.S. Treasury. Since Herbert Hoover's presidency, coin programs had been frowned upon on the grounds that
they would open the floodgates to all kinds of worthwhile causes and
thus debase the currency. The decision to upset precedent and permit
Olympic coinage did not mark a victory for government intervention,
however; for the state was merely making it easier for the USOC to market itself by trading on a vague association with the national interest.

For a while, the United States Olympic Committee basked in the eu-
phoria created by the performance of the United States team in the
1984 games, which even the Soviet boycott had not dampened. But as
preparations for the Seoul games in 1988 got underway, criticisms
of the committee's functioning were renewed. The committee was
accused of being a top-heavy bureaucracy. Some blamed the poor
showing at the 1988 Winter Olympic Games in Calgary (the United
States' total of six medals was fewer than in any Winter Olympic Games
since 1936) on the misallocation of funds to administrative work (Voy
1991, 139). The president of the United States Olympic Committee,
Robert Helmick, assembled a task force, headed by New York Yankees
owner and USOC vice president George Steinbrenner, to consider

improvements. In 1989, the Olympic Overview commission reported a series of recommendations to the United States Olympic Committee, including proposals to (1) provide more money to U.S. athletes through expanded tuition assistance, job programs, and direct financial payments, to be paid for by raising licensing fees for the use of Olympic logos and a larger share of the television revenues from the International Olympic Committee (in 1989, the International Olympic Committee agreed to give the United States Olympic Committee 10 percent of the International Olympic Committee's American television revenues); (2) create an organization to identify and develop promising young athletes; (3) streamline United States Olympic Committee decision making by eliminating sixteen of the twenty-nine committees and reducing the executive board from eighty-nine to forty-six members; (4) relocate the United States Olympic Committee's licensing and media operations and model them after professional sports; and (5) hire a public relations firm to lobby Congress. The changes proposed were relatively modest, and did little to redistribute amateur sport opportunities. This is hardly surprising, given that all members of the commission came from the USOC's executive board (Voy 1991, 159). They did little to alter the fact that a tiny proportion of USOC revenues went directly to athletes; and they emphasized more than ever before the development of elite athletes for international competition, at the expense of a sport-for-all policy that would have provided funds for a wider range of noncollege and postgraduate athletes. Above all, the reforms reaffirmed the understanding that the organization and funding of the United States Olympic effort (and, more generally, amateur sport) should be private, rather than public.

The Collapse of Amateurism

Ironically, just at a time when the United States was finding imaginative new ways of increasing its aid to amateur athletes, Olympic rules were being relaxed to permit payments to athletes and thus professionalize them. In 1982, the IOC agreed to permit amateur athletes to accept sponsorship money as long as it was deposited in a trust fund administered by the athletes' national sport federation. This meant that some "professional" athletes could not compete in the Olympics, while their better-paid "amateur" counterparts could. It also raised the public policy question of whether it was appropriate for the state to subsidize the training of an athlete who was actually earning a six-figure salary from endorsements. Nevertheless, the global tendency was for the wall between amateur and professional to crumble. Sports such as soccer, tennis, basketball, and ice hockey began to allow professional athletes to compete in the Olympics, improving the chances of Western athletes to boost their medal count, while Eastern-bloc athletes demanded to keep the winnings they had earned on the various sport circuits, helping legitimate the professional athlete in their countries. These developments promised to reverse a trend underway since World War II, whereby East and West had grown further apart in the international sport order: the communist nations dominated Olympic sports; and the capitalist countries dominated professional sports, such as football, baseball, soccer, rugby, basketball, tennis, golf, and motor racing.

The power of domestic organizations to defend amateurism declined the more the line between amateur and professional on the international level became blurred. When, in 1986, the IOC gave individual sport federations the power to decide for themselves who was eligible to participate in their sport, most relaxed their definition of amateur to permit more freedom of payment and to tolerate amateurs competing against or with professionals. This created a possible conflict of interest between sport federations and the NCAA—former staunch allies—further fragmenting the government of amateur sports. For example, a student–athlete could now compete on the same team as professionals and retain eligibility in the eyes of the International Hockey Federation but at the same time lose his NCAA eligibility. The trust fund set up by the Athletic Congress, from which Olympic track-and-field athletes in training were entitled to receive payments, also undermined NCAA eligibility.

The overall result of the global movement to abolish the distinction between amateur and professional has been further to decentralize power in the Amateur Athletics movement, shifting power to the individual sport federations. This means a further loss of power for the AAU, guardian of the old amateur ideal. While the NCAA has in the past been the dominant actor in sport federations because of its ability to supply athletes, coaches, and facilities, the decline of amateurism has also diminished its power to govern amateur sports because one of its chief sources of legitimation has been the defense of (its own version of) the amateur ideal. The United States has thus moved further away from, rather than closer to, state-administered amateur sports.

SPORT AS DIPLOMACY

An unintended consequence of the centralization of amateur sport authority that occured in the 1970s was that sport became more deployable as a diplomatic weapon by the state. The Amateur

Sports Act legitimated the United States Olympic Committee, but the price was the U.S. boycott of the Moscow Olympic Games in 1980 and the Soviet's retaliatory abstention in 1984.

In peacetime, sport takes it place alongside a number of other cultural practices as a resource to be contested and deployed for national advantage. Compared to many other countries, the United States government has rarely involved itself in the global circulation of sport capital. The United States gives little direct sport aid to developing nations, whereas the export of coaches and sport medicine, as well as the use of sporting contests to build bridges, was for many years a staple of foreign policy for communist states. Far from using sport as an export item or as a diplomatic tool, the United States has been a net importer of sport services, luring promising athletes away from their homeland and using them in the United States. A study undertaken for the State Department in 1971 observed that sports had been almost totally ignored in American diplomacy, in stark contrast to the communist states, and recommended that the department become much more active in the "export" of American sports abroad (Nafziger 1988a, 54). The study fell on deaf ears, however, and successive American administrations have steered well clear of programming or sponsoring international sporting events.

Only when the state decides that modifying the flow of sport capital will serve foreign policy ends does it intervene in domestic sport politics. It might place a "trade embargo" on sport or, more ambitiously, endeavor to pressure competitors in the global economy by means of a sport boycott. Boycotting international athletic events, particularly the Olympic Games, is now an established weapon in international politics; but the earliest campaigns were private—part of civil society—and it is only recently that the boycott has been adopted as a diplomatic weapon. The reason for this is that the competing amateur sports authorities were unable to settle their differences without state intervention. Having gained quasi-public authority, the American Olympic movement had to obey the dictates of the state.

Private Boycotts

Boycotts are a form of collective action intended to pressure the target group to change. They are part of civil society. The first boycott campaign was mounted from the political Left. A series of Workers' Olympiads, sponsored by the Socialist Workers' Sports International in the 1920s and 1930s, were intended to bolster international working-class solidarity. They were "a response to the exclusion of workers on class grounds from the 'bourgeois' sports clubs of late 19th-century Europe" and were designed as an alternative to the Olympic games

They were also a declaration of support for the 381
principle that the welfare of the athlete is more important than the cal-
iber of his performance.

The Berlin Olympics in 1936 also sparked a boycott campaign. A
Workers' Olympics in Barcelona was timed to compete with Hitler's
games, as was a World Labor Athletic Carnival, held on Randall's Island,
where New York mayor Fiorello LaGuardia acted as honorary chairman. Calls for the United States to boycott the Berlin games were issued
the moment the AOC received the invitation to attend, in January 1934.
Members of the AOC could not agree whether to accept the invitation,
given the restrictions Hitler had imposed on the participation of Jews
on the German Olympic team. Avery Brundage was dispatched to make
an on-the-spot investigation of German preparations for the games. Personally opposed to the boycott scheme, he needed little convincing that
the Germans would respect the Olympic spirit. On his return, and at his
recommendation, the American Olympic Committee voted to urge the
full membership to accept the invitation. Meanwhile, many groups outside amateur sports were pressuring the association not to participate
in the games. Most vocal in their opposition were left-wing alliances
such as the Friends of Democracy and the Anti-Nazi League; but more
mainstream groups, including Methodist, Catholic, and Jewish organizations, as well as the American Federation of Labor and National Association for the Advancement of Colored People, also opposed
participation in the games. The campaign was coordinated by the Fair
Play in Sports Committee. Notwithstanding Brundage's plea that "American athletes should not become needlessly involved in the present
Jew–Nazi altercation," in December 1934, the AAU voted to postpone acceptance of the invitation until German intentions became clearer
(Guttmann 1984, 71). A Gallup poll conducted in March 1935 showed
nearly half the American public in favor of a boycott.

Despite widespread press coverage of the boycott campaign, the issue of American participation in the games received no state support.
Representative Emmanuel Celler, who had joined the boycott campaign
at its inception, did introduce a bill to prohibit the use of government
money for United States Olympic athletes; but the gesture was purely
symbolic. Celler knew full well that Congress had shown little inclina-
tion to fund amateur athletics in the past, but he saw in the opportunity
to debate his bill a chance to publicize the boycott campaign. His stratagem failed, for the bill died without being taken up for discussion. To
his chagrin, he was then forced to watch Congress pass a bill authorizing the secretary of war to pay expenses incident to the training, attendance, and participation of athletes (chiefly military officers) involved
in Olympic equestrian events. Nor did the boycott movement win over
many of the organizations responsible for running amateur sports. By
1935, the AAU, the NCAA, and even the YMCA had voted to support the
American Olympic Committee in its decision to attend the games. The

boycott movement did force the Olympic Association to search more diligently than usual for voluntary contributions; but despite the public opposition, it managed to return from Germany with a small surplus.

Boycotts and the Cold War

After World War II, boycotts became a weapon in the ideological struggle between East and West and in the efforts by Third World nations to gain political recognition on the world stage. Olympic boycotts occurred in 1956 over the Soviet invasion of Hungary and the British invasion of Egypt and again in 1976 over the inclusion of New Zealand in the Montreal Games (stigmatized for its refusal to boycott South African sports). American Olympians neither participated in, nor expressed support for, these boycotts.

There is little evidence before the 1980s that the United States Olympic Committee was moving in the direction of endorsing the boycott as a means of bringing about change, either in the international sport order itself or in the political system as a whole. The USOC maintained the position that boycotts were always politically motivated and that politics should play no part in the organization of the Olympic games. It also steadfastly maintained its independence from the state. As a private organization, it was free to pursue its own policy with respect to participation in international athletics.

During the 1970s and partly as a result of the Cold War, much of this independence had been undermined, as the USOC became a quasi-public agency. It had become available as a tool of international diplomacy. The idea of mounting a boycott of the Moscow Olympics in retaliation against the Soviet's invasion of Afghanistan was first broached by the West Germans at a NATO meeting in Brussels on January 1, 1980. The invasion had sparked immediate speculation in Olympic circles that the Moscow games were now at risk, given the state of relations between the Soviets and the Americans—enough speculation to induce NBC (the network granted broadcast rights to the games) to take out boycott insurance (Hoberman 1986, 65).

The idea was soon picked up in the United States by Vice President Walter Mondale's staff and introduced by him into cabinet thinking.[11] Carter's call for the United States to decline the invitation to participate in the games received swift and bipartisan support from Congress. On January 24, 1980, the House of Representatives backed Carter's boycott idea by a vote of 386 to 12. The Senate, by a vote of 88 to 4, followed suit five days later. The issue was deemed so important that in the House, the full Foreign Affairs Committee held hearings on the issue, rather than delegate the work to its Subcommittee on International Organizations. Congressmen sought to tie the boycott to an expression of disapproval of the Soviet's violation of the amateurism rule to which they believed Americans (even college student–athletes) were faithful adherents. Many congressmen, harking back to the 1936 Olympics in Germany and clearly disturbed by the original decision to hold the games in Moscow, were not at all disappointed to see the Soviets frustrated.

The United States Olympic Committee's president, Robert Kane, and executive director, Don Miller, initially rejected Carter's proposal. In the early stages of the debate, most committee members also disapproved of the idea. Perhaps they felt protected by the law, which technically made it very difficult for Carter to back up his call. The Amateur Sports Act of 1978 had vested exclusive jurisdiction in the United States Olympic Committee over all matters pertaining to the participation of the United States in the Olympic Games. While Carter frequently spoke as if he had the authority to prevent Olympic participation, his legal powers were limited (Nafziger 1988b, 232). However, the United States Olympic Committee's argument that the best way to fight Soviet aggression was to beat them on the playing fields "fell on deaf ears" (Kanin 1981, 118). The White House threatened to use its influence to cut off federal support for Olympic sports. It also threatened to use the Internal Revenue Service to tax the United States Olympic Committee on its other sources of income. The State Department issued vague warnings that an American Olympic presence would threaten national security (p. 121). Publicity was given to a meeting between Carter and congressional leaders to assess the feasibility of amending the Amateur Sports Act to make it more difficult for voluntary agencies to circumvent government policy (Hulme 1990, 35). A public opinion poll conducted on February 7, 1980 showing 73 percent in favor of the boycott suggested that these threats would be backed up by the general public, which almost certainly overestimated the state's legal power over the USOC: "Newspaper editors and letters admonished the athletes to stop being selfish and to accept the fact that governments often, especially in times of war and international crisis, demand more of some citizens than others" (p. 28). In the face of this pressure, President Kane hastened to assure congressmen that he could not conceive of the United States Olympic Committee's ignoring the boycott call if the president insisted. Despite being in the private sector, he explained, "we are still Americans and we still represent the United States"; the national interest would have to come before the interests of the United States Olympic Committee and its athletes (U.S. Congress, House, Committee on Foreign 1980, 23). Throughout these hearings, no dissenting voices were heard; and no one questioned the president's powers to enforce the boycott. Few were surprised when, after hearing from Vice President Mondale that "history holds its breath," the USOC House of Delegates voted to endorse its executive committee's recommendation not to participate in the games.

The Carter administration, while denying that it was engaged in a boycott of the games (it "declined to participate"), tried to induce other countries to stay away from Moscow. The campaign was mismanaged and insensitive: "The West Europeans did not feel that the U.S. had consulted with them adequately before embarking on the sanctions route, and specifically found the Olympic boycott not to their liking" (Kanin 1981, 124). The British Olympic Association voted to attend despite the opposition of the Thatcher government. The West German Olympians, more financially dependent on government support, eventually joined the boycott, while the French, with the support of their government, opposed it. In the end, the only European nations to side with the United States were West Germany, Turkey, Liechtenstein, and Monaco— a severe embarrassment to Washington (p. 139).

The United States did little better in the Third World. In Africa, in particular, the campaign was poorly managed. The United States, having opposed the 1964–76 boycott campaigns against South Africa and Rhodesia, was not in a good position to argue the merits of the strategy. To make matters worse, the United States sent Muhammad Ali to Africa to drum up support. "It was a poor move because Ali, for all his stature, was not a political leader capable of impressing Africans with how seriously the United States took African support. In addition, Ali seemed not have been well briefed, either on the politics of international sport nor on the positions of the countries he was to visit" (Kanin 1981, 143). Of the 146 nations in the Olympic movement at that time, 81 eventually participated in the Moscow games. Kanin estimates that about 55 nations did not participate because of the boycott (p. 145).

Carter and his aids failed to understand the structure and politics of the International Olympic Committee, treating it as if it were a representative assembly, oblivious of the fact that it was "a fiercely independent, nongovernmental, transnational actor that utilizes the state unit not because it is subservient to it, but rather because such a structure provides an expedient means of organizing and conducting the Olympic Games" (Hulme 1990, 106). Carter insisted on working through governments, rather than through the IOC itself and never gained anything close to a majority support for his position. American congressmen shared this ignorance and were incensed by the failure of many Third World countries to fall into line. In 1980, they passed an amendment to the foreign aid bill directing the president to take into account whether a country had boycotted the 1980 Summer Olympics when deciding aid amounts.

Even those most sympathetic to the boycott and its aims could not claim that it had done much to remove the Soviets from Afghanistan: "Boycotts of sports competition seldom accomplish their purposes and are typically counterproductive" (Nafziger 1988a, 122). As is customary when they fail, the boycott was reinterpreted to be less a material act than a symbolic expression, an eloquent cry of protest, "a medium for appropriate public expression of the deterioration of superpower relations" (Kanin 1981, 145). And perhaps there is some truth to the argument that the removal of Soviet troops as a result of the boycott was never realistically expected. There is every evidence that Carter intended from the outset to wield the boycott in a punitive fashion, rather than in hope of prying the Soviets out of Afghanistan. The deadline for withdrawal was set unrealistically close and was issued in the form of an ultimatum that the Soviets could not have met without losing face (Hulme 1990, 18). The boycott was symbolic of sacrifice and resolve and thus was especially appealing to the ascetic Carter. However, it meant that the primary injury would always be to the United States itself and that it was intended as much for internal, as for external, consumption. Touting the *symbolism* of America's absence could not, however, conceal the failure of the United States to marshal support for its policy on Afghanistan in general: "The 1980 boycott was a low point in foreign sports policy" (Nafziger 1988a, 120).

Effect of the 1980 Boycott on the United States Olympic Committee

Ironically, while the boycott made little impression on Soviet foreign policy, it sullied the image many Americans had of their own role in the Olympic movement. The USOC had refused to join in the 1956 and 1976 boycotts because they were political. In its dealings with the state, it thought of itself as a nonpolitical organization. In 1977, when the President's commission on Olympic Sport issued its final report, Executive Director Michael Harrington tried to get the House Subcommittee on International Organizations to support a U.S. bid for the 1984 games by declaring, "Only the United States can turn the clock back to a games that is free of politics" (U.S. Congress, House, Committee on Foreign Affairs 1977, 7). Until the 1980 boycott, it was always other countries who injected politics into the Olympics.

Harrington's disingenuous position was designed to placate congressmen reluctant to see the state become involved in sport, but it flew in the face of the realities of international athletics. In the Olympic movement in particular, broader political problems would inevitably crop up. Many states dismissed the possibility of separating politics and sport. Countries also had a habit of dividing along political lines into two nations (e.g., China, Korea, Germany, Vietnam), giving the IOC the job of deciding which was legitimate, a necessarily political position. Other countries would deny rights of athletic participation to certain groups (e.g., Jews, African-Americans), violating human rights principles and prompting calls for their expulsion from the movement. And all countries imposed restrictions on sport exchange in the interest of national security. After 1980, the United States could no longer claim that politics played no part in the Olympic movement, nor could they pretend to be the guardian of the founding Olympic principles.

The Soviets Boycott the Los Angeles Games

To nobody's surprise, the 1984 Olympic Games were boycotted by the Soviets and most of their allies. Potentially a severe blow to the Olympic movement in the United States and the host city of Los Angeles, there is little indication that the Soviet threat to boycott the games ever became an important policy issue for the Reagan administration. While its hard line toward the Soviets furnished the pretext for the boycott, its practices only provided the excuse for which the Soviets searched. For example, although IOC rules state that identity cards should be issued by host countries to the individuals listed by each national Olympic committee and that no visas should be required, the State Department had forced the United States Olympic Committee to agree that a visa could be denied to anyone suspected of being a terrorist. At the last moment, it refused to issue a visa to Oleg Yermishkin. There is little doubt that Yermishkin was an intelligence agent and not simply the attaché he claimed to be, but the State Department had been assuming with equanimity for some years that a considerable influx of spies would occur when the games were held. Its refusal to go along with the pretense necessary in this kind of diplomatic exchange provided a useful pretext for the Soviet's absence from the games.

The Soviet boycott did not occasion a defensive drawing together of sport and the state in the United States. Instead, it drove them further apart, as the USOC determined to demonstrate that it could put on an "American" free enterprise games, quite independently of government assistance or supervision. The games were, of course, heavily politicized but in the sense of being an expression of national pride and national identity (with subsidies from local state governments), which, in their very commercialism and enterpreneurialism, did as much to broadcast abroad the supremacy of American values as any state administration could have achieved.

CONCLUSION

The state's role in amateur sports changes under conditions of globalization. The mass media help make sports (a universal language) an important part of global culture. This, in turn, centralizes and bureaucratizes sport administration within nation–states. Globalization thus increases state control over domestic sport politics. The state deploys not only its legal, but also its moral, authority to ensure that domestic sport politics serve national interests abroad. Authority passes to quasi-government agencies, especially during periods when international performance could be crippled by domestic disputes. Recent boycotts indicate that even the most liberal democratic states—those in which the wall between sport and politics is thought to be highest—now see sport as a public resource.

Yet the United States has not developed a state apparatus either to administer its sport effort abroad or to prepare at home for international sport competition. Seemingly on the brink of doing this in the 1970s, it has withdrawn from intervention and permitted market forces to build and fuel the United States' international sport effort. Sport policy has favored a market solution to the problem of international competitiveness, in part because of long-standing prejudices against government "interference" in an activity that is only a little less private because it means crossing national borders; in part because of the end of the Cold War and the resumption of more normal economic and political relations between First and Second World countries, diminishing the strategic significance of sport; and in part because of the commercialization of the global sport order, which has broken down the distinction between amateur and professional that the United States had formerly defended.

POLICY BY
DEFAULT

It has been the guiding thesis of this book that public policy domains are defined by culture. There is nothing inherent in sport that would propel it onto the public stage, nor is there necessarily a set of organizational actors in society who claim responsibility for such matters. Indeed, there is considerable opposition to the idea that sport belongs on the public stage at all. It is considered too trivial, too private, too ephemeral for serious public debate. Yet it is clear from the material presented that for many people, sport is not mere diversion. Those who care about sport are guided by higher aspirations than simply to provide entertainment. Sport, they believe, adds quality to people's lives, enriches communities, strengthens bonds, affirms nationality. To this extent, there is a public good at stake about which public officials should care.

The way that sport policy has evolved in the United States is a reminder that the most fundamental level on which political struggle is waged is over the legitimacy of concepts and ideologies. Contestants must first establish that sport belongs in the political arena at all. If they succeed, they must fight over the meaning of terms like professional, amateur, contact sport, and eligibility and debate the broader significance of a player's commitment to his team, a city's hold over a franchise, the true significance of the Superbowl, and what a low medal count in the Olympic Games says about a nation's standing in the global

bates do not always speak the same political language. They do not talk about gender in the same way, and they think differently about the purposes of education. They are divided on the proper role of unions in society, more or less inclined to let the market determine economic fortunes, and more or less chauvinistic when it comes to America's competitiveness abroad.

Because American culture discourages public goals for sport, policy is usually justified as a necessary response to specific problems requiring intervention and control. Policy consists of a loose bundle of "issues" to which the state responds reactively and negatively. Positive statements of policy are rare (e.g., that sport can help sustain and build communities). This is not only because of public antipathy to the idea of sport policy but also because of opposition from private interests who feel threatened by sport planning (e.g., limiting franchise movement shackles capital mobility, and providing public amenities unfairly competes with private entertainment). What little positive policy there is works indirectly. For example, a more balanced distribution of sport franchises is achieved by an implicit contract with private capital: in return for self-regulation that has the appearance of monopoly, the industry must meet public goals of equal access, both in telecommunications and in franchise location.

What is remarkable about the relation between sport and the state in America is not this or that policy, but the fact that there is a policy at all—although, to fully appreciate this argument, it is necessary to remember that when governments abstain from taking action, they are making policy as much as when they do. This is especially important to remember because, since World War II, and particularly since the 1970s, the impulse to plan or administer sport has been muted in the face of calls for greater freedom of economic opportunity. The market model for sports has become increasingly popular both at home and abroad. At home, professional sports have become firmly established as the model for junior amateur sports, the collegiate game, and (most recently) the Olympic movement. The state has done little to slow this trend, having no alternative sport policy. Athletic resources have thus been allowed to flow into those sports for which paying spectators can be found, rather than a wide range of sports where participation is the chief reward. The professional leagues are allowed to create farm teams out of college campuses, siphoning off and stockpiling talent that would otherwise go to a wider range of amateur sports. Quasi-public but privately controlled and profit-oriented educational institutions have usurped the power of voluntary organizations like the AAU. The state, by its manipulation of the law to suit professional sports, and its subsidy to colleges and universities, therefore plays as active a role in shaping opportunities for international athletic success as did the communist states of old, albeit indirectly.

With respect to the governance of amateur sports, as with all the other issues covered in this book, it is plain that Americans, firm believers in the autonomy of civil society, prefer to think of sport as being located there, rather than being part of, or even seriously affected by, the state. The goal of public policy should be to free all elements of civil society from political interference. The state's chief purpose is the protection of individual rights—to function as umpire or referee while individuals pursue in civil society, according to rules of economic competition and free exchange, their own interests. Sport should be the outcome of free contracts in civil society, not a public issue or a matter for the state. These views have prevailed in such widely differing areas as athletes' rights to participate in international track meets and the rights of franchise owners to move their clubs from one town to another.

These views presume the formally equal capacity of citizens to protect their own interests, an assumption belied by basic inequalities caused by gender, race, and class. Sport opportunities thus continue to be determined in large part by criteria of social qualification that have little to do with athletic ability. It also presumes that formal political equality guarantees real freedoms in civil society, for example, in the workplace. Professional athletes have thus struggled for many years to obtain a measure of economic democracy to complement the right to representation they possess in the public sphere. It also presumes that the state can function as a neutral arbiter among all interests, an assumption belied by the influence that business corporations wield over the state and therefore over the nature of democratic outcomes. Sport capitalists have succeeded in securing and, for the most part preserving, highly favorable treatment by the state, all the while protesting the need to free civil society from political interference and, particularly, to keep politics out of sport.

Alternate voices have not been entirely silenced. Citizens now expect their local governments "to provide certain types of facilities, opportunities, and services where people can meet and play" (Sessoms 1984, 120), although they do not attach so much importance to leisure facilities as to fire and police protection. At the state and federal level, social democrats have pointed out that to enjoy liberty means not only to enjoy equality before the law but also to have the capacities to be able to pursue different courses of action and that the state must provide these capacities if the market denies them. But the idea that sport should be subject to planning is a distinctly minority view. It is likely to remain so as long as the world of sport is confused with the world of play, so long as people continue to look upon their opportunities for sport participation and enjoyment as properly free of political influence and control.

The democratic impulse has also been muted in the global order of sports. The Olympic reforms of the 1980s, instituted in the face of an increasingly professional sport world and under pressure from the mass media to supply the best talent for their sport programs, helped abolish the distinction between amateur and professional. The result was not to make sport participation more widely available or sport administration more democratic but to create a new elitism and to restructure the administration of international amateur competition along the lines of a business corporation. The state's ability to control the Olympics was diminished by the IOC's own determination to market itself as a product. The Olympic ideal, especially since the 1988 games, is packaged and then sold as a concept to corporate sponsors across the world, such as Coca-Cola, Eastman-Kodak, and Phillips, themselves multinational corporations engaged in global marketing.

As chapter 11 showed, there is no guarantee that a country will develop a coherent sport policy once it has become clear that sport performance is in the national interest. During the period when the new international sporting order was emerging, the United States government engaged in no continuous sport activity: sport never became the day-to-day responsibility of any particular government agency. For the most part the production of athletes and athletic events for international purposes has been left to private, voluntary organizations. This, in turn, has inhibited the development of a coherent sport policy. Another obstacle to the development of sport policy is the intermittent nature of events in the international sporting calendar. The global sport order is dominated by the quadrennial Olympic Games: the flow of "trade" or "exchange" is sporadic. The United States amateur sport effort lurches from one games to the next and sport policy becomes a matter of periodic crisis management. Each games focuses attention on amateur sport for a while, as preparations are made, the events occur, and lessons are learned. During these crises, latent conflicts become manifest, problems swept under the rug during the hiatus between games reappear, and different interest groups seize the opportunity to make their case before the public. For a while, amateur sports become overtly politicized. Once the crisis is passed, the myth of a politics-free sport is revived and sport returns once more to the private sphere, where many people believe it belongs.

NOTES

1 | PLAYING BY THE RULES

1. Usually, the impact of the state on sport is more subtle and indirect. Sport is predominantly male in part because the personal politics of the household give more free time for men and because government policies with regard to employment and child care do little to disturb these arrangements.

2. This loose definition excludes much outdoor recreation, "activities of a recreational nature that normally take place in a natural environment and depend primarily upon that environment for satisfaction," such as hiking (Sessoms, 1984:237). Many sports take place in outdoor settings, of course; by they are background for the competition, which is the main event. This distinction is important, for state and federal governments have had much more to do with outdoor recreation than with sport: "For the most part, federal and state involvements have been limited to the management and operation of park and recreation lands and to the activities of its regulatory agencies" (p. 133).

3. Media attention does not, of course, determine whether or not an activity is a sport. The sport world is comprised of thousands of sport subcultures. For example, rodeos are a familiar item in the popular culture of the American West; but there has also been a sport associated with them for over one hundred years. Today, the National Finals Rodeo lacks nothing in comparison with an event like the U.S. Open Tennis Tournament except perhaps that the crowds are somewhat smaller and the prize money is more modest. Originating in the play of working cowboys, rodeo became a spectator sport as early as 1888, when admission was first charged at a rodeo in Prescott, Arizona. Rodeos soon be-

came regular events; and by the end of the 1920s, "world championships" were being staged in Madison Square Garden in New York. By 1940, over one hundred "sanctioned" rodeos were being held annually (Fredriksson 1985). The National Finals Rodeo, which began in 1959, is a nine-day tournament in which the season's top fifteen money winners compete in a number of events to determine the champion in each. Most contestants will belong to the Professional Rodeo Cowboys' Association, which boasts over five thousand paid-up members. The leading professional rodeo cowboys (one of whom is a cowgirl) earn over one-hundred thousand dollars a year and might well compete in over one hundred rodeos annually. The finals are held in Las Vegas, drawing 150,000 spectators, who pump $70 million into the local economy. Prize money in 1989 totaled $2.2 million. The event has a major commercial sponsor, Bluebell (Wrangler Jeans), as well as support from tobacco and beer companies.

4. Politics are evident in the meanings given to leisure. Power is concealed by an abstract definition of leisure as "time free from the constraints imposed by employers, family dependents and the need for one's own survival," because it says nothing about what kinds of activities should occupy this free time. Middle-class people might feel sorry for a working class that enjoys less leisure, but only because they enjoy less *middle-class* leisure; they might well have plenty of their own. Men might think that women have "leisure deficits," simply because they have less of the kind of leisure recognizable, and acceptable, to men. Even the definition of leisure as free time is political. Middle-class males are disposed to accept the view that work and leisure, or work and family, are related but separate; but it makes little sense to working-class women, who routinely must find "leisure in work" (Hollands 1988, 30) in the form of games and pranks and who must fit their leisure into the interstices of both wage work and household responsibilities.

2 | CAN I PLAY?

1. Women are virtually invisible in the major sport policy debates of the twentieth century. Thus, much of this book deals with a male world, where class and race differences among men are the issue. Women are altogether absent from the debate over employment practices, market imperfections, and collective bargaining. In debates over other issues, such as how sports are to be governed, how freely franchises should locate, and how access to mass-mediated sports is to be guaranteed, the unspoken assumption is that women have no distinct interests that need to be represented: their interests are either marginal and can be ignored or are the same as men's. In broader discussions of the "contribution" of sport to national solidarity and societal integration, the idea that only men—or women on men's terms—benefit from this contribution rarely surfaces. As I shall show, women have by no means been totally excluded from the sport world (see Howell 1982 for a general historical account of women's sports in the United States and Mitchell 1977 for women's exclusion from the Olympic movement); but gender has not been an issue in the relation between sport and the state.

2. This discussion of the pursuit of equality of opportunity will focus entirely on amateur sports, because only in amateur sports were state powers invoked to achieve the goal. Apart from a brief experiment with women's baseball during World War II, women were entirely excluded from the professional sport labor market until the 1970s. A women's basketball league failed, but gender barriers have been broken down in noncontact sports, such as tennis and golf, particularly those that promise advertising revenues for the television networks. In 1970, Billy Jean King helped organize the Virginia Slims Circuit to rival the United States Lawn Tennis Championships, which offered women champions a fraction of the prize money earned by men. In 1973, she helped form the Women's Tennis Association. In that same year, the USLTA revised its policy and declared a goal of equal prize money for men and women champions.

3. Griffiths' bill (never passed) would have applied only to Little League. Youth football, without the burden of the public charter, was not so vulnerable to congressional pressure or civil suits. A Texas court refused to uphold the claim of a girl to play Pee Wee football because it was considered private conduct (Wong and Ensor 1986, 375). Nevertheless, the drift of legal opinion during the 1970s and 1980s was to make it easier for girls to play on predominantly boys' teams. More liberal states moved to equalize eligibility rules.

4. The decision in *Grove City College* v. *Bell* (1984) caused some women to despair of a federal solution to the problem of gender discrimination; and they sought protection, instead, in the equal rights amendments passed by individual states. They were to find that equal rights were not always desirable. In *Blair* v. *Washington State University* (1987) the state's superior court found that Washington State University had violated the state equal rights amendment and the state law against discrimination. The university was required to award sport scholarships to women in proportion to the number of female undergraduates. However, the court excluded from the requirement of equal funding distribution the revenue generated by any specific sport or program. The court ruled that the college was prohibited from discriminating in the allocation of funds awarded by the state legislature but could do so in the case of revenues generated by the sport itself. The supreme court's affirmation of this exclusion for football diminished "any thrill of victory accorded [Washington State University's] sports in *Blair*" (Richardson 1988, 533). The victory in *Blair* therefore signaled danger. State's equal rights amendments make the enforcement of Title IX no easier, because under this constitutional reform males would have to be allowed to try out for females' teams. A rule that permitted women to try out for men's sports but did not allow men to try out for women's would deny equal protection to men. It matters little that the equal rights amendments thus ignore the fact that equal protection, given existing differences in strength and speed, would mean that teams would end up being male once more.

5. Guttmann points out that most American women did not attend college during the period of "play days" and were thus unaffected by them (1991, 143). Many more women would have participated in the industrial recreation leagues popular between 1920 and 1950, where softball and bowling were the most popular pastimes. Mildred "Babe" Didrikson, perhaps the most famous woman athlete of the interwar years, did not attend college but worked for the Employers Casualty Insurance Company as a stenographer and starred on the company's "Golden Cyclones" basketball team, which won the AAU national basketball championship in 1931.

6. The AIAW grew from 278 founding member institutions to 973 in 1980 (Acosta and Carpenter 1985, 316).

7. The collapse of AIAW resulted in a loss of coaching and managerial jobs for women as men took over the administration of women's teams. Title IX was used as the justification for merging mens' and womens' physical education departments, usually resulting in a male's assuming control of both (Acosta and Carpenter 1985, 318). As more money was channeled to women's programs, coaches were offered higher salaries and more money for recruiting. More men became interested in jobs that had previously relied heavily on volunteer or part-time labor. Female coaches of womens' teams were replaced by male coaches and mens' sports became even more a male preserve (Holmes and Parkhouse 1981). It also meant that women would be vastly underrepresented on the NCAA Council, its various subcommittees, and in the assembly at large.

8. Women had made little progress in high school coaching. One study—of high school coaches in Ohio—reported that the proportion of female high school head coaches rose from .5 percent in 1974 to 2 percent in 1989. There was only one female head coach of a boys' team sport in the entire state (Kane and Stangl 1991).

9. Where public facilities are concerned, such as playgrounds and swimming pools, the logic of the market does not operate, and competitive resources are not useful. Here, the subordinate group must rely entirely on pressure resources to achieve desegregation. On the other hand, the goods are indivisible; and members of the majority group

feel less threatened than when private, divisible goods are contested. This is why public leisure facilities were desegregated earlier than private.

10. As president of the National League, Ford Frick would echo this theme fifty years later, refusing to accept that baseball had any responsibility to end racial segregation in the sport: the absence of blacks from the National League was a social problem, not a baseball problem, and thus lay beyond his jurisdiction (J. Moore 1988, 22). Today, by contrast, the NFL refused to allow Arizona to host the Superbowl because the state did not legislate a holiday to honor Martin Luther King.

11. The NBA was the result of the merger of three leagues: the National Basketball League (1937), the American Basketball League (1945) and the Basketball Association of America (BAA—1946). Today's NBA traces its roots to the BAA (i.e., to 1946, rather than to 1937 or 1949) because most of its founders came from that league.

12. The NFL obtained its first black coach with the appointment of Art Shell by the Los Angeles Raiders in 1989; the Minnesota Vikings appointed the second, Dennis Green, in 1992. In the NBA, eighteen blacks have served as coach on twenty-five occasions since Bill Russell was appointed by the Boston Celtics in 1966. In 1992, 11 percent of the NBA head coaches were black (72 percent of the players were black at this time). Frank Robinson became the first black manager in baseball in 1974 when he was appointed by the Cleveland Indians. His later appointment by the Baltimore Orioles brought the number of black management tenures to four. In 1992, when 18 percent of all players are black, 8 percent of major league baseball managers are black.

13. There is sociological evidence to support both sides of the argument about whether it is harmful for black youth to focus their energies and aspirations on athletic achievement. The odds of becoming a professional athlete are very slim for black youth (Leonard and Reyman 1988). As for the more general benefits, although blacks are more likely than whites to think that mobility can be achieved through athletics (Oliver 1980), the evidence is not definitive enough to be used as a basis for making rational decisions about the investment of large amounts of time in organized athletics. While Braddock (1980) concludes that on balance, the evidence suggests that athletics enhances social mobility, Eitzen and Purdy (1986) see little evidence that the many blacks who do not become professional athletes gather academic credits as a side benefit.

14. Today, class differences in hours worked are less important than income in determining attendance at sporting events. An increasing proportion of seats are being sold in the form of season tickets, luxury boxes, box seats, and reserved seats that only business corporations and wealthy individuals can afford to buy (Scully 1989, 103).

15. "It is a common belief that America is a relatively classless society. You will see relatively less visible evidence of class conflict than in most European countries. But there is a mistake lodged in that perception. We do not see evidence of class conflict, I suggest, because the dominant classes in the United States have been more effective than their counterpart classes in European societies in teaching . . . other elements in the society to accept their styles of life, their values, their political preferences" (Lindblom 1988, 85).

16. Vamplew cites the case of Jack Kelly (father of Grace Kelly), who, as late as the 1920s, was banned from rowing at Henley because he had once been a bricklayer (1988, 186). In 1936, an Australian eight-oared shell was disqualified because one of the team members was a policeman (Nafziger 1988a, 35).

17. Working-class rowers who wished to compete without turning professional were left to found their own organization, the National Amateur Rowing Association, in 1890.

18. There is a parallel here with a similar distinction that began to be drawn at about the same time and for many of the same reasons. This is the distinction between "art for art's sake" and art produced for commercial reasons. The idea that art carried its own justification, its own measure of worth only became part of public culture when the middle class began to consume art and reproductions of art on a large scale, threatening the elite's control over aesthetic taste. Just like amateurism, the "art for art's sake"

movement did not precede the modern era but arose simultaneously with it, as commerce and culture moved closer together, making commerce into a maker of beautiful images and culture into a matter of trade.

19. In a gesture of symbolic importance, the one-house legislature of Nebraska passed a bill in 1988 decreeing that football players at the University of Nebraska be paid a stipend for their athletic services. Under the terms of the bill, the law would not go into effect unless four other states with Big Eight schools passed similar bills. In any case, Governor Kay Orr vetoed it. Nebraska's football program generated revenues of nine million dollars in 1987 while paying out six hundred thousand in scholarships.

20. The commercialization of sport imposes its own version of democracy. Athletes are rewarded if they win, regardless of their social background, comportment, or demeanor on the court. One spectator's dollar is as good as another's. The infusion of professionalism into a formerly amateur sport thus not only introduces the cash nexus and an "impurity" of motives, but it also means a loss of control by the ruling sport elite. This is nowhere better illustrated than in the case of lawn tennis. As tennis developed a high media profile during the 1960s, corporations began to invest money in the sport for promotional purposes. As tournaments became more dependent on corporate sponsorship, sponsors began to demand more control over events. The governing body of tennis, the International Lawn Tennis Federation, however, relied heavily on gate receipts to finance its operations: "The one weak link in the ILTF power and control chain was money. Once tennis accepted professionalism and the financial freedom and independence it would bring to the players, the essential relationship would break down between them and their national associations" (Brasher 1986, 203). In the process of commercialization, tennis lost a great deal of its exclusivity. This is not to say that tennis became available to all: only the more affluent could afford the club memberships, equipment, and tournament tickets necessary to play and watch the game. But the sport lost its honorific status—its capacity to "improve" and instruct—and therefore some of its power to encode class differences.

3 | FROM PEONS TO PROFESSIONALS

1. Incursions into the college ranks were particularly likely during interleague competition. Interleague wars were the cause of changes in eligibility rules in hockey. Rivalry between the National Hockey League and World Hockey Association encouraged raiding of college ranks and, in the 1977 case, *Linesman* v. *World Hockey Association*, hockey's eligibility rule was declared illegal, causing the WHA and NHL to reduce the minimum age to eighteen. (The NHL and WHA merged in 1979.)

2. In 1992, baseball also modified its eligibility rules, further lowering the boundary between college and professional players. The owners voted that beginning that year, a team that drafted a high school senior who decided to go to college would retain the right to sign that player for up to five years. Another rule change permitted a team to draft a player after any year in college, rather than waiting until after his third or fourth year.

3. Option contracts are common today in boxing. A promoter agrees to let another boxer fight his client but only on condition that the challenger agree to let the promoter handle the challenger's next three (or more) fights should he win. Option contracts are legal but considered by many to be exploitative.

4. Only the stars could resist. Ty Cobb did not report for spring training in 1912 because he had received no increase on his $9,000 salary since 1909, despite having won his fifth straight American League batting title. Cobb's subsequent suspension caused a public furor. Senator Hoke Smith and Representative Thomas Hardwick (both of Ty Cobb's home state of Georgia) called for a congressional investigation of the reserve system. A settlement was swiftly reached granting Cobb $11,332 a year. His salary was to rise rapidly thereafter. Cobb's treatment nevertheless left a bad taste in the mouth; and in

1912 and 1913, Illinois congressman Thomas Gallagher tried to get Congress to appoint a seven-man commission to investigate baseball as "the most predacious trust in the country" on account of its reserve clause. His bills died in committee (Seymour 1971, 177).

397

NOTES TO CHAPTER 3

5. Farming of players had become a serious problem. As early as the 1890s, several National League clubs had obtained minor league affiliates. In 1913, the National Commission forbade joint ownership between major and minor league clubs, although it restored the right in 1921, perhaps in response to the threat of an antitrust decision from the Supreme Court. Once immunized by the Supreme Court in 1922 (see chapter 4), Branch Rickey was able to proceed with a more ambitious assembly of teams at various levels and classifications. (By 1936, the St. Louis Cardinals had twenty-eight teams in twenty-six leagues.) This system of vertical integration proved practicable only during the Depression, when there was an oversupply of labor and attendances remained high.

6. The immunity had been granted in 1922 by the Supreme Court, which ruled that baseball was exempt from antitrust prosecution because it did not fit the description of interstate commerce (see chapter 4).

7. After sitting out a year, Flood eventually signed with the Washington Senators, in 1971.

8. Final-offer arbitration was introduced as part of the 1973 basic agreement between owners and the players' union. It was limited to players with more than two years' playing experience in the major leagues.

9. There is little doubt, however, that arbitration has been a boon to the players. Using time-series data from the 1987–89 seasons, Burgess and Marburger show that qualifying for final-offer arbitration increased the salaries of hitters, starting pitchers, and relief pitchers by 86 percent, 89 percent, and 58 percent, respectively (1992, 58). Even negotiated settlements are affected by arbitration, for the procedures generate a contract zone within which negotiations tend to take place.

10. Before 1972, free agency had not been allowed in hockey. With the formation of the rival World Hockey Association, NHL players challenged the reserve clause in their contract by jumping to the new league. Because limited free agency was sanctioned in the courts, the NHL owners decided in 1973 to replace the perpetual reservation system with a one-year option clause in standard player contracts. This meant that teams could hold players for only one year after their contracts had expired. Compensatory players were to be awarded to the selling club, with disagreements over the amount of compensation to be settled by arbitration.

11. Professional ice hockey had its version of the Rozelle Rule. It, too, required the buying team to compensate the selling team, usually in the form of draft picks. Disputed compensation could be submitted to an arbitrator for final determination. Hockey players considered the compensation rule a signficant brake on the market for players.

12. The war between the NBA and the ABA had been a boon to the players, and many jumped from the NBA to the ABA in order to earn more money. NBA owners fought to keep star players, like Rick Barry and Zelmo Beatty, who were ordered to sit out a year before joining the ABA because they were held by the courts to have violated their NBA contract.

13. The basketball players had by this time agreed to a cap on salaries for each club. Beginning in 1983, the amount each club could spend on player salaries was fixed at 55 percent of gross league revenues divided by the number of teams in the league. Designed to equalize franchise labor costs, the cap no doubt reduced competition for players and therefore functioned in part as a substitute for the reserve clause: "The salary cap's anticompetitive effects on player mobility and player salaries are severe" (Foraker 1985, 180).

14. With the inauguration of Plan B, two kinds of player movement became possible. For the conditional kind of movement, a player's contract must expire, and he must receive an offer sheet from another club. His current team had the right to match the offer and retain the player or allow him to move. If he did not move, his new team must give his former team two first-round slots in the following NFL drafts. The unconditional kind of movement was that offered under Plan B for players other than the protected thirty-

seven. They were free to accept the offer of the highest bidder for their services, and the selling team suffered no penalty.

15. In 1991, 139 of the 518 eligible players had signed with new teams. In 1992, there was more movement under the plan: of 541 players eligible, 166 moved. Players who moved earned an average of 60 percent more.

16. At the beginning of the 1990 basic agreement negotiations, the owners proposed that a salary cap be introduced at 48 percent of ticket and broadcast revenues. The union rejected the idea. This is probably what Commissioner Fay Vincent was referring to when, in 1992, he began to talk publicly about the need for "partnership" between owners and players, which he thought might come in the form of "revenue participation."

4 | NATURAL MONOPOLIES

1. This suspicion of syndication notwithstanding, it is common knowledge in the sport business that economically fragile leagues often tacitly cooperate to sustain weaker franchises. The American Basketball Association, competing with a much stronger NBA without a television contract or much media exposure, routinely "allocated" players on the basis of need, sending star players like Julius Erving from Virginia to New York, where they would attract more publicity and helping struggling franchises purchase the contracts of players who could bolster their fortunes (Pluto 1990).

2. Judge Landis had eight years earlier fined Standard Oil over twenty-nine million dollars for violation of the Sherman Act (a verdict later overturned) and was considered a trust-buster. However, he delayed calling the case in the hope that an out-of-court settlement could be reached. It transpired that he was a keener baseball fan than he was trust-buster. "Both sides," he warned, "must understand that any blows at the thing called baseball would be regarded by this court as a blow to a national institution" (Lowenfish and Lupien 1980, 90). In the cooling-off period, the owners were at liberty to contemplate that only the players were benefiting from the protracted litigation between them; and in December 1915, they reached an agreement out of court. The only real gain made by the Federal League was the admission of two federal franchises, the Chicago Cubs and the St. Louis Browns, into organized baseball. The Federal League withdrew its suit and disbanded. However, the Baltimore franchise, disappointed at not being awarded a place in either the National or the American League, refused to throw in the sponge and in March 1916 filed suit in federal district court in Philadelphia, charging organized baseball with conspiracy in restraint of trade under the recently enacted Clayton Anti-trust Act.

Continuing negotiations to admit the Baltimore franchise or pay compensation prompted the club's owners to withdraw their suit. However, negotiations eventually broke down once more; and in April 1919, Baltimore filed suit again, this time in federal district court in Washington. The court decided in their favor, although they were awarded only $240,000 of the $900,000 damages they demanded. Organized baseball appealed; and in December 1920, the circuit court overturned the lower court. Organized baseball's chief lawyer, George Wharton Pepper, swayed the court by arguing that baseball was essentially a local enterprise. He drew a parallel between a baseball game and a Chautauqua lecture. Both baseball players and professional speakers crossed state boundaries to reach their destinations, but both lecture and game were local activities (Lowenfish and Lupien 1980, 106). Not only did the appeals court agree that baseball was not "interstate," but it also concluded that any profits were incidental and that baseball was "still sport, not trade." It was now Baltimore's turn to appeal, and it carried the case to the United States Supreme Court.

3. Thompson ruled that the AFL could not claim damages if the NFL was only seeking to exclude the AFL from some cities, rather than from all cities. He based this decision on the calculation that there were thirty-one cities capable of supporting a professional team. He also pointed out that the AFL had access to hundreds of competent players and that it was the AFL, not the NFL, that had by then negotiated a network television contract.

4. The first clause of amendment 4 of this tax bill actually did speak to the tax treatment of professional sport enterprises; but the most important part of amendment 4, as far as the owners were concerned, was clause 3, stipulating that "the anti-trust laws are not to apply to a joint agreement by which members of clubs of two or more professional leagues combine their operations in an expanded single league." The amendment was introduced on the Senate floor after the Senate Finance Committee had reported the bill.

5. The owners had worked hard for it. The Commissioner's office had helped the staff of the Senate Judiciary Committee write the original merger bill (U.S. Congress, House, Committee on the Judiciary 1966, 77). Furthermore, there were suspicions among some House members that a suit brought against the NFL by an AFL franchise (Denver) was little but a pretext for the legislation to immunize the merger. Under the terms of the proposed merger, the Denver Broncos franchise had been denied the Chicago location it sought and had refused to go along. The NFL came to Congress predicting a plague of such lawsuits if the merger were not statutorily approved.

6. Baseball still permits considerable independence for individual franchises to negotiate individual media rights; but this is not enough for businessmen like New York Mets owner, Nelson Doubleday, who complained in the 1980s that Commissioner Kuhn's efforts to enforce revenue sharing were a form of "socialism" (Kuhn 1987, 375).

7. *Deesen* v. *Professional Golfers Association of America* (1966) saw the court approve the PGA's right to monitor the playing quality of its players, and expel those who fell below acceptable standards, thus excluding them from the tournment circuit. The state also backed up the Ladies' Professional Golf Association in a 1973 case in which Barbara Jane Blalock protested her disqualification and placement on probation for the rest of the season as a result of having illegally moved her ball during the course of tournament play. The state (as in *Gunter Harz Sports* v. *United States Tennis Association*[1981]) also recognized the need for governing associations to regulate equipment used in the interests of fair competition.

Regulations standardizing the rules of the game serve to give a sport a more distinct identity and promote spectator interest, result in greater rewards for promoters and players, and are usually considered reasonable business practices. However, as with sport leagues, there is a fine line to be drawn between rules intrinsic to the game and rules that, whether on purpose or not, have the effect of stifling economic competition. Although the courts rejected the argument by the sporting goods manufacturer Gunter Hartz that its tennis racket should not have been banned by the USTA, sport's governing bodies must nevertheless tread very carefully in this area lest antitrust laws be invoked. In 1989, Karsten Manufacturing Corporation filed suit against the United States Golf Association (USGA) in response to a USGA ban on its "PING EYE2" golf club, on the grounds that it did not conform to USGA equipment rules, specifically the rule regulating the grooves on the club face. The PING EYE2 was thought to provide an unfair advantage by imparting additional spin on the ball and was the best selling club in the United States at the time. Karsten challenged the USGA with violation of the Sherman Act and questioned its rule-making authority. In an out-of-court settlement in January 1990, the USGA agreed to treat clubs made before March 1990 as conforming; but Karsten undertook to change the club face.

8. At the same time as the MTC was sueing IMG, ProServ was engaged in a legal battle with Ivan Lendl. Lendl brought suit in Washington District Federal Court against ProServ (*Taconic Enterprises* v. *Proserv* (1987) for breach of contract and fraud. ProServ was accused by Lendl of acting in a dual role as the operator or paid representative of an exhibition or event in which it also negotiated with the event's sponsors to supply the services of their client, Lendl. ProServ acted simultaneously as a paid representative of Volvo and an agent for Lendl in his negotiations with Volvo. The case was eventually settled out of court.

9. The NCAA also strengthened its grip over college athletics by moving to control "after-season competition," particularly football bowl games. After World War II, these events (not all of them chiefly charitable) had mushroomed. In 1949, there were fifty bowl games played. The NCAA exercised no control over revenues from these games, and the opportunity to play in a bowl game was a powerful incentive for many colleges to fund

and organize football teams. With the proliferation of bowls threatening to diminish the value of the product, the NCAA declared that colleges could participate in bowl games only with its permission. The next year, 1952, the number of bowl games dropped to nine (Lawrence 1987, 91). Bowl games would soon become popular television events, for which networks and advertisers were willing to pay considerable sums of money.

10. When he became baseball commissioner, Bowie Kuhn adopted the same strategy. He rarely missed an opportunity to outline the "contribution" of baseball to the community, always in glowing terms. The owners had kept ticket prices low and stable, been content to simply operate their businesses on a break-even basis, (rather than seeking to amass profits), "allowed" the televising of games "to make these great events available to everybody," developed "extensive mechanisms for resolving disputes in the player relations area through independent third party arbitration," stifled corruption and gambling, and sustained a minor league syssystem to "provide wholesome and popular sports entertainment" (U.S. Congress, House, Select Committee on Professional Sports 1976, 351–55). Almost all of these claims to public service were disputable. Baseball ticket pricing has been "consistent with revenue maximization" (Scully 1989, 115). A number of owners did consistently make profits, especially in the larger cities; and many of those who did not used their franchise as a tax shelter. Owners had only begun to permit televising of games once their fears of net loss of revenues were assuaged; and the arbitration system had been forced on the owners by the players' association.

11. The owners also benefited from the distinction drawn between horizontal and vertical restraints on the market. The Chicago school of economists so influential on the Reagan administration did not spurn all government regulation of business. Horizontal restraints, such as price fixing, were anathema. However, vertical restraints were tolerated. Vertical restraints, in the form of agreements backward and forward in the chain of production (e.g., between companies and suppliers) were likely to form where the market failed to allow for the efficient supply of inputs, in which case "nonmarket" contracting arrangements were efficient and legal. Players, of course, were considered "inputs."

5 | MANAGEMENT AND LABOR

1. Marvin Miller believes that Kuhn saw unionism as a direct attack on the position of the commissioner: "All the Players Association's victories. . . . involved the removal of the commissioner as the so-called impartial arbitrator. . . . And Kuhn took the loss of power and prestige as a personal insult" (1991, 293–94).

2. The rule then in force stipulated that a team signing a free agent might be asked by an arbitrator to compensate the losing team, either in players or draft choices. Two compensation awards made during the summer of 1991 were considered by players to have been harsh and punitive.

3. James Miller reports that between 1960 and 1968 the Baltimore Orioles had nine player representatives in nine seasons: the club "traded them, released them, or left them available for restocking drafts" (1990, 145).

6 | PRIVATE GOVERNMENTS

1. The NCAA was established to supervise safety and determine eligibility in student athletics. Its professed concern has always been the welfare of student–athletes. But these student–athletes neither participate directly in the group's rule making nor have an opportunity to select representatives to act on their behalf. The association's member institutions would claim that they should be free to act as they please, without government interference, because their interests are also the student's inter-

ests; but this is patently not the case in many instances: "An administrator's desire for stability in his or her athletic programs may lead to a different view of restrictions on transfers than is taken by an athlete who must bear the corrosive effects of having to endure an unpleasant relationship with his coach" (Weistart 1984, 170). Private governments can be held to have violated due process rights if their control becomes total. If the opportunity to participate in intercollegiate competition is regarded as a property right and if that property right is thought to carry with it due process protection, on grounds that such participation is a prerequisite to lucrative professional careers (a notion that the NCAA has done nothing to discredit), then denial of this entitlement becomes a matter of legal action.

2. Because of its command over the flow of college sports across the airwaves, the NCAA has become subject to the same government scrutiny as that given to professional associations, whose exclusions or sanctions may have severe effects on individual practitioners and on customers. Remarkably late, the courts decided, in *Buckton v. National Collegiate Athletic Association* (1973), that the NCAA did indeed now perform "a public function, sovereign in nature, that subjects it to constitutional scrutiny" (Martin 1976, 397). College athletic programs that rely, however indirectly, on federal scholarship aid or that use an infrastructure (e.g., a stadium) paid for by taxpayers will be subject to more intense scrutiny than privately funded institutions. Likewise, to the extent that sport programs seek to legitimate themselves by pointing to their educational role as part of the extracurricular activities of a school, they must share regulatory power with public governments. When prowess in athletics becomes a de facto entrance requirement for college, then the NCAA has assumed a governmental role and is subject to executive, judicial, and legislative oversight.

3. With this trend, the distinction between private and public organization shifted again. A business corporation, despite the fact that it was privately owned, might be regarded as public, while a public agency might operate, to all intents and purposes, in a private manner so far as public access and input were concerned. As a result, people began to think of the line between public and private as distinguishing nonprofit and for-profit organizations. Profit-oriented entities are more exposed to public regulation and inspection because of their intricate involvement in the welfare of the economy and their effect on the national interest, while nonprofit associations are assigned to the voluntary, private sphere and are largely unregulated: antitrust law, for example, was not applied to nonprofit entities.

4. "Public" politics often affect "private" politics. For example, the politics of allowing sport leagues to operate as virtual monopolies gives them much greater "policing power" over member teams and players. This is also true at the collegiate level, where power is exercised by athletic conferences. As long as the NCAA could monopolize the "sale" of college sports, its power was supreme. However, once this monopoly power was challenged in court, in 1984, when the right of the NCAA to bargain exclusively with the television networks was successfully challenged, the association lost its power to prohibit a college from appearing on live television and thus much of its ability to influence and constrain its constituent members.

5. In 1888, alarmed at the increasing brutality of football, the inroads of athletics into academic work time, widespread practices of payments to athletes, and the professionalization of coaching, Harvard University set up an athletic committee comprised of three students, three faculty, and three alumni that became a model for other institutions of higher learning. The committee at Harvard soon acquired considerable power, derived from its mandate from Harvard's controlling body, the Corporation, to oversee athletics. Twice in the 1890s, it turned back attempts to abolish football at Harvard (R. Smith 1988, 130). Committees at other institutions developed similar powers.

6. Professional coaching began with the Yale crew of 1864, but it was not until the early 1900s that coaches could be said to be in command. By this time, they had instituted year-round training, carefully chosen schedules, and "scientifically" based strategies for winning. Just as the emphasis on winning encouraged the hiring of coaches, so

the hiring of coaches intensified the need to win, because an individual's job was on the line. Professional coaches wrested control from the very students who had hired them.

7. Coaches exhorted the less talented that the success of the team depended on the contribution of each individual, no matter how lowly his position. In this way, winning and character building were viewed as compatible pursuits. Each athlete would be taught to put aside selfish interests, to deal with adversity, to accept the unequal consequences of competition without complaining. Through sports he would come to realize that the burden rested on his shoulders to demonstrate his usefulness to the organization. The emergence of the coach was thus also the creation of a new kind of "worker" role for the athlete, a subordinate status that left him with little opportunity for "voice" or "exit."

8. As it turned out, the mechanisms for regulation were much too crude. Many colleges balked at being prohibited from covering a student's living expenses, and the punishment—exclusion—was too harsh. An effort, in 1950, to expel seven colleges found in violation of the Sanity Code failed to get a two-thirds vote. In 1951, the NCAA Convention voted to end the restriction on financial aid, which effectively "killed the sanity code" (Lawrence 1987, 49). The larger colleges thus agreed to live with the new sanctioning system, but under conditions much more favorable to them than to smaller colleges.

9. Athletes have no representation of any kind, do not appear at NCAA conventions, propose no new legislation, and make only token appearances on university athletic councils. The result is the feeling that government powers are being used to exploit student–athletes: "The NCAA's insistence on defining athletes as amateurs allows universities to stage mass athletic spectacles for commercial gain while compensating athletes with salaries below the minimum wage" (Sack 1982, 85). Only in the 1990s did the NCAA begin to consider enlarging the role of the student in its governance; and even then, that role was limited to advice. Thus, the 1992 NCAA Convention approved an increase in the number of students of the Student–Athlete Advisory Committee from sixteen to twenty-eight.

10. The six adopted were (1) the development of a statute of limitations, (2) the establishment of evidentiary standards closer to those of a court of law, (3) the elimination of an alleged "gag" rule, (4) direct access by student-athletes to enforcement proceedings, (5) an enforcement policy that prohibits *ex parte* contacts with the Committee on Infractions, and (6) elimination of the Committee on Infractions' close supervision of the enforcement staff (to separate prosecution and judgeship). The NCAA partially implemented a proposal to provide advice on self-incrimination and right to counsel to those accused of infractions. However, the NCAA rejected demands that written transcripts be made available (on grounds that confidentiality might be endangered); that investigations be conducted jointly between the NCAA and the accused institution; and that the NCAA, rather than the institution, make the declaration of student ineligibility (U.S. Congress, House, Committee on Interstate and Foreign Commerce 1978a, 30).

11. In 1991, the NCAA sued the governor of Nevada in federal court, challenging the constitutionality of a state law regulating sport investigations, claiming that the law had made proceeding with the inquiry into possible abuses in the University of Nevada, Las Vegas (UNLV) men's basketball program virtually impossible. The NCAA's case was that the Nevada statute violates the interstate commerce clause of the U.S. Constitution by making it impossible for the NCAA to enforce regulations that would apply to its members in all fifty states.

12. There were at this time no laws against throwing games in professional sports, although the scandal did move various state legislatures to provide for fines and imprisonment for throwing games and bribing ball players in the future (by 1960, at least thirty-two states had such laws) (Seymour 1971, 388). The prosecutors in the Black Sox trial had to jerry-rig an elaborate indictment alleging conspiracy to defraud the public and to carry on a confidence game (Rosenberg 1987, 138).

13. There was another model for baseball's private government in the juvenile justice system. The juvenile courts had only recently emerged in recognition of the special "rights" and "protections" flowing to children by virtue of their special status in society.

did not always work to the best interests of the weak, in this case juveniles. Many believed that baseball, too, suffered when overexposed to market forces: "Landis treated players not as adults, able to make intelligent decisions on their own, but as PINS, persons in need of supervision and fatherly guidance" (Rosenberg 1987, 142).

14. Ironically, private law was again more strict than public; for outgoing President Reagan pardoned Steinbrenner for this offence in 1988.

15. Marvin Miller, former executive director of the MLBPA, pointed out that had Rose been a player at the time of his suspension, his case would have been referred to an impartial arbitrator by the players' association; but by 1989, he was part of management and thus "deprived of recourse to the grievance and arbitration procedures and due process provided by the basic agreement" (1991, 396).

16. In 1988, the National Hockey League, reacting to a case involving the New Jersey Devils, who had obtained a temporary restraining order in May 1988 against the commissioner's suspension of coach Jim Schoenfeld, enacted a new bylaw imposing a one-million-dollar fine on any club leapfrogging the league's internal justice system and going straight to the courts.

17. The presence of unions in professional sports makes a difference to their government. It legitimates the idea that each sport has a government, with two parties that vie for control of policy. For private drug-testing programs to win public approval, they must seem to reflect consensus between these parties. Drug testing must be integrated into a collective bargaining agreement, rather than unilaterally imposed. In return, players agree to limit their individual rights by consenting to be represented by unions who negotiate collective agreements on their behalf. Unions argue that even individually negotiated drug-testing clauses in contracts violate the basic agreements reached in collective bargaining. Drug-testing clauses must be collectively bargained by representatives of the players and the teams, although such agreements will generally accede to the commissioner's right to take action to preserve the integrity of, or maintain public confidence in, the game.

7 | BIG LEAGUE CITIES

1. Another reason for having a franchise in as many major cities as possible is that the television networks are more interested in national, than in regional, sports. This is one important reason why professional ice hockey has not been able to sign a contract with a major television network since the late 1970s.

2. This new view of the city as a "growth machine" encouraged major corporations to reevaluate their powers of mobility. Using new communications and production technologies, corporations could be more flexible with respect to location. They could now regard cities as bundles of physical and social assets suitable for exploitation. The rise of the power of finance capital—even less bound by location—accelerated this trend. Host cities could no longer be so sure that corporations were bluffing about moving, and aspirant cities could realistically hope to attract them.

3. The competition for college football games is not entirely free-wheeling; the NCAA's Extra Events Committee must approve and sanction a bowl. Furthermore, in the past some bowls have entered into agreement with conferences within the NCAA to give preference to the team which finishes at the top of the conference. However, competition for attractive teams is intense. Hosting a bowl game can generate revenues for a city and attract favorable publicity.

4. The Fiesta Bowl has a year-round staff of eighteen and recruits dozens of other workers during the month leading up to the game. The event is estimated to generate one hundred million dollars for the local economy. Local teams like Arizona and Arizona State, which would not attract visitors, are rarely invited to participate.

5. Besides the professional leagues and college bowl games, cities also compete for amateur sports. For example, the city of Indianapolis has set out to become the "amateur sport capital" of the United States. Boosted by contributions from the Lilly Endowment of between $50 million and $60 million, the city combined federal, state, and local government funds to build an array of sport facilities, including a downtown arena for basketball and the Hoosier Dome that was eventually to lure the NFL Colts from Baltimore. In 1987, the city hosted the Pan-American Games, a fifteen-day event that pumped $1.75 million into the local economy. The purpose of all this was to create a positive image for the city. A study commissioned by city fathers had discovered that Indianapolis had neither a positive nor a negative image. Worse, it had no image at all.

6. In 1987, the city of New York granted NBC $135 million in tax breaks to prevent it from moving to New Jersey. In that same year, the mayor began negotiations with the Chase Manhattan Bank to head off a move to Jersey City—negotiations that would eventually see the city giving away $235 million in tax breaks and energy subsidies.

7. As the national economy turned sour toward the end of the 1970s, municipal competition for franchises became even more fierce. More and more cities were forced to "move from a position of maximizing profit or insuring that the marginal costs equal the marginal revenue, to a defensive position of reducing losses" (Wong 1985, 43). Leasing agreements became increasingly complex, involving greater concessions and further inducements to the franchise owners, with minimal reciprocation on their part. The issue was no longer one of obtaining a boost to an already growing economy but of preventing further losses of tax base and jobs.

8. The Federal League collapsed because it could not afford to build the bigger stadia fans were demanding. Between 1905 and 1915, major league baseball built or reconstructed thirteen new ballparks. Pittsburgh's new Forbes Field stadium became a major tourist spectacle, attracting thousands even on a Sunday, when no games were permitted (Bluthardt 1987, 50). The mayor of Philadelphia, in his speech on the day Shibe Park opened, cited the swift growth of homes and businesses in the park's neighborhood as one of its contributions to the community. Realtors touted the proximity of Ebbets Field as a reason to buy homes in Flatbush.

9. Some state actors were in sympathy with the idea that the owners owed as much to their community as the community owed them. Thus, a judge in *Reynolds* v. *National Football League* (1978) declared, "Professional sports are set up for the enjoyment of paying customers and not solely for the benefit of the owners or the benefit of the players" (Freedman 1987, 3). It is hardly conceivable that this kind of sympathy would be accorded to customers of filling stations or beauty parlors. A sport franchise is a public institution.

10. Judicial authority was not entirely lacking for rules of ownership in the other major team sports. Various court decisions upheld league authority to deny transfers of club ownership (*Levin* v. *National Basketball Association* [1974]) and to decline to add a new club (*Mid-South Grizzlies* v. *National Football League* [1983]). In *San Francisco Seals* v. *National Hockey League* (1983), the court rejected an owner's suit under the Sherman Act challenging the NHL's denial of his request to move his team from San Francisco to Vancouver, a city without a National Hockey League franchise. The court reasoned that the Seals franchise did not compete economically with other National Hockey League teams but was a member of a single entity competing with other professional sport leagues. It was quite appropriate for the management committee of this single entity to decide where its respective "branches" should be located. The court here seemed to feel that the "market" in which competition must be maintained was that of sport entertainment in general, not just hockey, and that the NHL was but a single firm, competing with other sport firms, in this marketplace. This determination is important. The market is the entity whose health is being preserved in antitrust law, not particular firms in that market.

11. Al Davis, the Raiders owner, had always chafed at the commissioner's attempts to exercise authority over his business affairs. He was ready to find a pretext to undermine the commissioner's authority. On the other hand, the decision by the NFL to oppose the move to Los Angeles is difficult to understand unless some consideration is

doubt that a city the size of Los Angeles could easily support two football teams, especially after the move of the Rams out to Anaheim. The Bay Area had supported two
teams for over a decade, although it is true that the Bay Area had two teams in the
first place only because the Raiders were an old American Football League franchise. (When the NFL and AFL merged, the Oakland Raiders were accepted into the
united league, although they were obliged to pay other teams an "indemnity.") The
Bay Area could well have supported a replacement for the Raiders. However, the
NFL opposed this solution. Many congressmen and union representatives concluded
from this that the principal issue at stake was not so much the precise location of a
franchise as the artificial scarcity of such franchises. The Raiders took the position
that they should be able to move to Los Angeles and, if need be, have an additional
franchise move into their vacated slot in Oakland. The NFL opposed the idea of
expansion.

12. In a subsequent trial on the damages issue, the jury awarded the Raiders $11.55
million and the Coliseum Commission $4.86 million. After statutory trebling, damages
amounting to a total in excess of $49 million were assessed against the league. The NFL
had also by this time incurred legal fees of $10 million (Harris 1986, 555). In June 1986,
the federal appeals court returned the damages judgment to the lower court, ruling it
excessive in light of the financial windfall provided to the franchise by its move from
Oakland to Los Angeles. In 1989, the Los Angeles Raiders and the NFL finally reached
settlement, the NFL agreeing to pay the Raiders $20 million.

13. To make matters worse, one important plank supporting the owners' attempt to
control franchise moves was being removed by judgments in another area. The
Supreme Court, in *Northwest Wholesale Stationers* v. *Pacific Stationary and Printing* (1985),
seemed to indicate that "due process" questions were not relevant to the determination
of antitrust liability; that is, giving a frustrated owner a fair hearing within the league's
councils would not immunize the league from antitrust action if the result of its actions
was to inhibit economic competition (Tagliabue 1987). The news for the leagues was not
all bad, however. In neither case did the judicial branch dispute a league's right to prohibit franchise movements. In both cases, the justices affirmed that the freedoms of individual owners could be curtailed, as long as the rules for so doing were quite specific
and had been agreed upon by all owners in the league.

14. Commissioner Kuhn was highly sensitive to the fact that many congressmen, regarding Washington as their second home, and looking upon baseball as "the national
pastime," resented the fact that Washington had no baseball franchise. When, in 1976,
the American League expanded into Toronto (thus imparting at least some legitimacy to
the title "World Series"), many congressmen felt that an opportunity to return baseball to
the nation's capital had been missed. Kuhn later wrote that for this unpatriotic act baseball probably paid "a costly price when an unhappy Congress got around to tax reform
and deleted the tax shelter advantages of owning a professional sports club in the Tax
Reform Act of 1976" (1987, 194).

15. The class politics of franchise movement are clearly illustrated in the case of the
Brooklyn Dodgers' move to Los Angeles. The mayor who orchestrated Los Angeles' effort to lure the Dodgers was Norris Poulson. In his 1953 election campaign, he attacked
the city's holding of 183 acres of land at Chavez Ravine for the purposes of constructing
public housing. Poulson associated public housing with socialism. However, he was not
averse to using socialism to attract professional sports. Public spending was much more
attractive if it aided the accumulation of private capital rather than substituted for it or
competed with it. The Los Angeles real estate industry and Home Builders' Association
led the opposition to using the land for public housing and lobbied in favor of its use as a
stadium (Sullivan 1987, 85).

16. Johnson notes, however, that local officials have also been adroit at "exploiting
federal programs, especially Industrial Revenue Bonds and Economic Development Administration programs (e.g. Buffalo, Hartford), spreading the burden among their state's

tax-paying population (e.g. Louisiana, New York, New Jersey), or imposing special taxes on others, such as hotel–motel guests (e.g. Houston, Indianapolis)" (1986, 433).

8 | SPORT AND CITIZENSHIP

1. The recreation division was only one of many arms of the WPA (and its staff of eighteen was one of the smallest), but it was much more clearly oriented to the perceived needs of the unemployed than was, say, the arts project. The latter came to define its mission as giving employment to professional musicians, artists, actors, and writers—hardly members of the masses. Administrators in the recreation division accused arts project people of elitism, while the latter accused recreation workers of having no standards, no professional heritage. In this sense, the recreation division was much more democratic than the arts project. The professional artists in the employ of the arts project for the most part thought of themselves as performers; their primary responsibility was not to the people but to certain artistic standards. Their products were just as much "luxury goods" as were those of artists working in the private sphere (Cline 1939, 17). Recreation division workers, on the other hand, showed a greater willingness to provide what the public seemed to want. Thus was established early in this New Deal experiment a tension or contradiction in the idea of leisure as entitlement. Should the government give the public what it needs or what it wants?

2. The Housing Act of 1961 is an example of leisure policy riding on the back of other programs considered more important. It "provided for open space and outdoor recreation provisions in areas being built or redeveloped with federal support" (Kelly 1982, 384). The Economic Opportunity Act of 1964, intended to attack the causes of poverty, is another example. The residential training of the job corps had a recreation component, and Volunteers in Service to America volunteers made summer recreation programs possible for city youth.

3. The superior appeal of interscholastic sports lay not only in their excitement in contrast to the dull pedagogy of physical education. They also benefited by being contrasted with professional sports. For many years, Americans remained highly ambivalent about the professional game—especially football, which had blue-collar associations. Professional sports, after all, had no other purpose than to make money, while the college version was more "wholesome": players were performing not for themselves but for their school, and spectators were watching not an entertainment but a school activity. Commenting in 1928 on the huge crowds at college football games, Charles Kennedy asked, "How many of these thousands would attend were the very same men playing, with the very same skill, but representing no one but themselves?" (quoted in Ryan 1929, 35). Well into the 1920s, college sports were far more popular as entertainment than their professional version. Reports from 135 colleges and universities revealed that the seating facilities for football spectators increased from 929,523 in 1920 to 2,307,850 in 1930: "These institutions reported 74 concrete stadia, 55 of which had been erected between 1920 and 1930" (Steiner 1933, 91). College players became media stars. Savage complained, "The quest of the sensational leads to the publication in Sunday supplements of half-tones or rotogravure pictures of football captains and players who may be entirely respectable young men, but who in these sheets resemble cannibals or criminals" (1929, 276). College football continued to outsell professional football well into the 1950s. Today, the story is rather different. Ironically, college football managed to retain its highly favorable public image long after it began to imitate the professional game. Amos Alonzo Stagg, together with Walter Camp, the most famous of early college coaches, believed that the college game was becoming "a nursery for professional gladiators" and questioned whether football was any longer a "moral asset to the school" (Ryan 1929, 75).

4. As early as 1885, the historian E. H. Hartwell was writing, in a government report, "When college men are willing to travel with professional ballplayers, and especially un-

der assumed names, it is time for college authorities to recognize and regulate college athletics" (Ryan 1929, xxi). Harvard's President Eliot believed that "strict organization" and the "tendency toward commercialism" were beginning to take "the joy out of the game": "In football, for example, great numbers of boys do not play football, as in English schools and colleges, for the fun of it. A few play intensely. The great body of students are onlookers" (Savage 1929, xv). In the 1930s, the University of Chicago's President Robert Hutchins used the freedom from dependence on tuition money granted by a thirty-million-dollar donation from Rockefeller to drop interscholastic athletics altogether.

5. Despite these much-publicized reports, the pressure of competition continued to erode the amateur ideal: after years of debate, the NCAA finally adopted, in 1972, a motion making freshmen eligible for football and basketball; the member institutions repeatedly turned back proposals during the 1970s to award athletic grants-in-aid solely on the basis of need.

6. A 1977 NCAA-financed survey revealed that the operating expenses (e.g., travel, equipment, supplies, administrative personnel) of athletic programs were increasing at a rate much faster than either the rate of inflation or the rate of increase in grants-in-aid. A 1982 report revealed that the expenditures allocated to uses other than grants-in-aid had reached 33 percent of all money spent (Lawrence 1987, 125).

7. If there is any doubt that presidents can lose control over their athletic programs, the case of Auburn University is to hand. College football is very popular in Alabama, where there are no professional sport franchises. The most important event on the football calendar is the game between the University of Alabama and Auburn University. During the 1960s and 1970s, under the leadership of coach Paul Bryant, Alabama won thirteen of the eighteen games between these two teams. In 1981, Auburn initiated a search for a new coach, who might restore balance to the rivalry. The most influential member of the search committee was Bobby Lowder, president of Auburn's alumni association. A powerful banker, Lowder "is credited almost single-handedly with bringing Mr. [Pat] Dye to Auburn" (Lederman 1991, A41). In a private arrangement that had no official connection to the university, Dye's salary was supplemented by a personal services contract with Lowder's bank, Dye serving as "consultant." Four months after his arrival at Auburn, Dye asked for, and received, the additional role of athletics director. Dye and Lowder instituted a regime that virtually excluded both faculty and president from the governance of the athletic program. For example, in October 1985, the faculty proposed to toughen the requirements by which Auburn students would remain in good academic standing, a matter that would normally be sent to the trustees' academic affairs subcommittee. Lowder asked the president in writing to transfer the proposal to the board's planning and priorities committee, to which Lowder belonged. The president agreed; and in 1988, that committee proposed a much weaker set of standards, which the full board approved. In December 1989, the trustees voted to assume officially the authority to hire and fire the athletics director and the football and basketball coaches, thus circumventing the president and faculty entirely.

9 | SPORT IN THE WIRED CITY

1. Both the American Basketball Association (1967–76) and the United States Football League (1983–86) collapsed because they could not generate television revenues. The ABA never secured a regular season contract, and the USFL failed when it decided to compete with the NFL in the fall and found itself locked out of television time by the monopoly exercised by the NFL.

2. The case was appealed; but in April 1992, the United States Court of Appeals for the Seventh Circuit affirmed the lower-court decision that the NBA had violated the Sherman Antitrust Act. The ruling created further doubt about a league's ability to impose limitations on superstations.

1. Where a sport was ill suited to the task of assimilation, it would be modified to serve the purpose better. When Americans imported gymnastics from Prussia, they certainly intended to use them for military training, as had Fredrich Jahn; but they also saw them as a way for all classes of society to mingle and find a common, democratic ground and thus be reminded that America was a nation where social background counted for little. By the end of the nineteenth century, gymnasiums had "became one urban gathering place where, like the church, groups of like-minded people might both get to know their neighbours and learn ways to combat the health and moral hazards of the big city" (Green 1986, 182).

2. The major sport policy decisions of the 1960–90 era were made on the assumption that sport was an essential component of the sacred community called the nation. When Justice Henry Blackmun wrote the majority opinion denying Curt Flood's suit against the baseball commissioner, he invoked a pantheon of former players to sacralize the Supreme Court's decision, prefacing his statement with a list of eighty-seven names of players who had "sparked the diamond and its environs." There is irony in the fact that the Court's decision upheld baseball's antitrust immunity and reaffirmed the owners' right to treat those players and their descendants as peons.

3. In June 1964, the Congress did pass, and President Johnson signed into law, an amendment to Title XVIII of the United States Code "to prohibit schemes in interstate or foreign commerce to influence by bribing the outcome of sporting contests" (Sammons 1988, 177).

4. "Play power" was to become a slogan of the Yippies during the 1960s, in another attempt to disturb hegemonic ideas about the salience of *work* and play's subservience to it. The Yippies incorporated playful elements into their political protests, advocating radical freedom through play. But for all the disruptions it caused, "the politics of play proved more culturally than politically liberating" (Oriard 1991, 460); and it was eventually absorbed and conventionalized as the cultural narcissism of the "me decade" and the quest for self-realization of the New Age movement.

11 | SPORT IN THE WORLD SYSTEM

1. The insularity of American professional sports occasions commentary from European observers:

> Few aspects of American culture seem more peculiar, incomprehensible and irritating to European sports fans than calling the contest between two domestic teams for what essentially is the United States championship "the world series" as in baseball, and—following that sport—"world championship" in both professional football and basketball. What better reflects America's self-contained, parochial yet at the same time self-assured, even smug, culture than equating itself with the world, at least as far as sports are concerned? (Markovits 1988, 150)

2. School athletics organizers disputed the AAU's claim to be the only *national* organization for amateur sports: AAU officials boasted a national membership of 538 clubs in 1912; but since there were between 400 and 500 clubs in "Chicago, Philadelphia and North Eastern Pennsylvania alone" at this time, they could hardly claim to be representative (Kallenberg 1912, 504).

3. The aim of the NAAF was

> to create and maintain in the United States a permanent organization representative of amateur athletics and of organizations devoted thereto; to establish and

maintain the highest ideals of amateur sport in the United States; to promote the 409 development of physical education; to encourage the standardization of rules of all amateur athletic games and competitions, and the participation of this country in the international Olympic Games. (Ryan 1929, 147)

4. "The meeting dragged on through thirteen hours of haggling in its first day's attempt at solving the differences among the sport bodies with no progress in the negotiations despite efforts of Attorney General Kennedy, who joined the group at 9 p.m. and spent over three hours trying to bring about a truce" (Flath 1964, 160).

5. In 1991, the IOC was to break precedent by voting to give its president the power to name two members to the organization without regard to nationality or current residence. No secret was made of the fact that this would enable the powerful International Amateur Athletic Federation, the world governing body of track-and-field, to maintain a member on the IOC.

6. Kennedy is reported to have said: "Settlement of the dispute which had threatened to unjustly penalize hundreds of athletes and weaken American participation in the 1964 Olympic Games is most welcome. The real winners are the athletes" (quoted in Flath 1964, 177).

7. The AAU did bend a little, acceding to a request that dual sanctioning of "open" (i.e., both student and nonstudent) domestic track-and-field events be permitted.

8. Harry Edwards and his 1968 Olympic Project for Human Rights had been the first to stir interest in the question of athletes' rights. Harold Connolly, hammer-throw Olympian, testified at hearings on the 1973 sport bills that the dismissive treatment of OPHR by the Olympic authorities caused many athletes to lose faith in the United States Olympic Committee (U.S. Congress, Senate, Committee on Commerce 1973, 4).

9. The money to pay for these improvements would come from the sale of coins and stamps, an excise tax on professional sporting events, a modified state lottery system, broken-time payments for athletes in full-time employment, and tax credits for parents supporting Olympic athletes.

10. The question of funding athletes must be separated from the question of subsidizing the games themselves. The United States government has been slightly more inclined to provide funds for the latter, on the grounds that infrastuctural support is being provided for an essentially private enterprise that will, however, boost the local economy. This kind of public–private partnership was exemplified in the 1984 Summer Games, held in Los Angeles. Having been awarded the games, the city of Los Angeles was allowed to turn them over to an independent organizing committee, which accepted joint responsibility with the United States Olympic Committee for running the games, despite rule 4 of the Olympic Charter, which stipulates that the games are awarded to a city, which is entrusted with the honor and financial responsibility of hosting the games. For the first time, the games were to be run by a private corporation.

The International Olympic Committee could do little to prevent privatization. Los Angeles was the only serious bidder after Tehran withdrew. More important, the International Olympic Committee had to take into account the realities of American city politics, of which it had every right to be wary. After awarding the 1976 Winter Games to Denver, its offer had to be rescinded when voters refused to fund the event on environmental grounds. Environmentalists had also threatened the campaign to secure the 1980 Winter Olympics for Lake Placid, New York. On this occasion, they had been defeated by an alliance of forces arguing that the area's high unemployment could be reduced if the games were held there. In the end, the House of Representatives passed a nonbinding resolution supporting Lake Placid's bid for the games (which was to prove successful); but it must have been all too clear to the International Olympic Committee that American political support for public expenditures on the Olympics was rather fragile. When the 1984 games were awarded to Los Angeles, opposition to public funding seemed to be even stronger. The city council placed a charter amendment on the municipal ballot to prohibit the expenditure of any city funds on the games, excepting funds raised by a 6 percent Olympic ticket tax and a .5 percent surcharge on the hotel occupancy tax. The ballot measure was approved by 72 percent of the voters in the November 1978 election.

The 1984 games were eventually held with a minimum of state participation or funding, except for security expenditures. The games made a profit of $227 million, $89 million going to the United States Olympic Committee, $89 million to a Southern California–based Amateur Athletic Foundundation, and the rest to the national sport governing bodies. In light of the history of private sponsorship of the Olympics, it is not too cynical to argue that the Los Angeles games became famous as the "free-enterprise" games not because they relied on the private sector for much of their funding but because they made a profit, a feat that could be achieved only by getting security free and being provided the use of existing facilities at bargain rates.

Nevertheless, for many Americans, the lesson of the 1984 games was that public funding of amateur sports was unnecessary and that the best policy was to rely on a mixture of volunteer labor and the Olympic movement's ability to sell itself to sponsors, advertisers, and the media. Government policy thus shifted away from the interventionism of the 1970s.

11. The possibility of a sport boycott had been in the air since the trial of dissident Anatoly Shcharansky in 1978, but President Carter had expressed no interest in this strategy at the time (Kanin 1981, 116).

REFERENCES

Acosta, R. Vivian, and Linda Jean Carpenter. 1985. "Women in Sport." In *Sport and Higher Education*, ed. Donald Chu, Jeffrey Segrave, and Beverly Becker. Champaign, Ill.: Human Kinetics.

———1990. "Women in Intercollegiate Sport, 1977–1990." Typescript.

Allison, Lincoln. 1986. "Sport and Politics." In *Politics and Sport*, ed. Lincoln Allison. Manchester: Manchester University Press.

Anderson, Dave. 1985. *The Story of Football.* New York: William Morrow.

Anderson, Mark. 1968. "The Sherman Act and Professional Sports Association Use of Eligibility." *Nebraska Law Review* 47:82–90.

Aris, Stephen. 1990. *Sportsbiz: Inside the Sports Business* London: Hutchinson.

Atkinson, Mark. 1984. "Workers' Compensation and College Athletics." *Journal of College and University Law* 10:197–208.

Baade, Robert, and Richard Dye. 1988. "An Analysis of the Economic Rationale for Public Subsidization of Sports Stadiums." *Annals of Regional Science* 22:37–47.

Baxter, Vern, and Charles Lambert. 1990. "The NCAA and the Governance of Higher Education." *Sociological Quarterly* 31:403–21.

Bellamy, Robert. 1988. "The Impact of the Television Marketplace on the Structure of Major League Baseball." *Journal of Broadcasting and Electronic Media* 32:73–87.

Bennett, Roberta, K. Gail Whitaker, Nina Jo Woolley Smith, and Ann Sablove. 1987. "Changing the Rules of the Game." *Women's Studies International Forum* 10:360–79.

Berry, Robert, William Gould and Paul Staudohar. 1986. *Labor Relations in Professional Sports.* Dover, Mass.: Auburn House.

Berry, Robert, and Glenn Wong. 1986. *Law and Business of the Sports Industry.* Dover, Mass.: Auburn House.

Betts, John. 1974. *America's Sporting Heritage:1850–1950.* Reading, Mass.: Addison-Wesley.

———1984. "The Technological Revolution and the Rise of Sports, 1850–1900." In *The American Sports Experience*, ed. Steven Riess. West Point: Leisure.

411

412   Birrell, Susan. 1988. "Discourses in the Gender/Sport Relationship: From Women in Sport to Gender Relations." *Exercises and Sport Sciences Review*, 16:459–502.

Birrell, Susan, and Diana Richter. 1987. "Is a Diamond Forever? Feminist Transformations of Sport." *Woman Studies International Forum* 10:395–409.

Blalock, Hubert. 1970. *Toward a Theory of Minority Group Relations*. New York: Capricorn Books.

Bluthardt, Robert. 1987. "Fenway Park and the Golden Age of the Baseball Park, 1909–1915." *Journal of Popular Culture* 21:43–52.

Bourdieu, Pierre. 1978. "Sport and Social Class." *Social Science Information* 17:819–40.

Boyer, Paul. 1978. *Urban Masses and Moral Order in America, 1820–1920*. Cambridge: Harvard University Press.

Braddock, Jomills. 1980. "Race, Sports, and Social Mobility." *Sociological Symposium* 30:18–28.

———.1989. "Sport and Race Relations in American Society." *Sociological Spectrum* 9:53–76.

Brammell, Roy P. 1933. *Intramural and Interscholastic Athletics*. Washington.

Brasher, Kate. 1986. "Traditional Versus Commercial Values in Sport." In *The Politics of Sport*, ed. Lincoln Allison. Manchester, UK: Manchester University Press.

Bright, Charles. 1984. "The State in the United States During the Nineteenth Century." In *State Making and Social Movements*, ed. Charles Bright and Susan Harding. Ann Arbor: Michigan University Press.

Brown, Bill. 1991. "The Meaning of Baseball." *Public Culture* 4:43–70.

Bryson, Lois. 1987. "Sport and the Maintenance of Masculine Hegemony." *Women's Studies International Forum* 10:349–60.

Burdge, Rabel. 1969. "Levels of Occupational Prestige and Leisure Activity." *Journal of Leisure Research* 1:262–74.

Burgess, Paul, and Daniel Marburger. 1992. "Bargaining Power and Major League Baseball." In *Diamonds Are Forever*, ed. Paul Sommers. Washington: Brookings Institution.

Burstein, Paul. 1991. "Policy Domains: Organization, Culture, and Policy Outcomes." *Annual Review of Sociology* 17:327–50.

Campbell, John and Leon Lindberg. 1990. "Property Rights and the Organization of Economic Activity by the State." *American Sociological Review* 55:634–47.

Canes, Michael. 1974. "The Local Benefits of Restrictions on Team Quality." In *Government and the Sports Business*, ed. Roger Noll. Washington: Brookings Institution.

Carpenter, Linda. 1985. "The Impact of Title IX on Women's Intercollegate Sport." In *Government and Sport*, ed. Arthur Johnson and James Frey. Totawa, N.J.: Rowman & Allanheld.

Carpenter, Linda, and R. Vivian Acosta. 1991. "Back to the Future: Reform with a Woman's Voice." *Academe* 77:232–327.

Cavallo, Dominick. 1981. *Muscles and Morals: Organized Playgrounds and Urban Reform, 1880–1920*. Philadelphia: University of Pennsylvania Press.

Chandler, Joan. 1985. "The Association for Intercollegiate Athletics for Women: The End of Amateurism in United States Intercollegiate Sport." *Studies in the Social Sciences* 24:5–18.

Chass, Murray. 1989. "Rose is Said to be Banned for Life," *New York Times* (August 24, Sec A, p.1, Col.5).

Chu, Donald. 1979. "Origins of the Connection of Physical Education and Athletics at American Universities, 1890–1930." In *Sport in American Education*, ed. Wayne Ladd and Angela Lumpkin. Washington: American Alliance for Health, Physical Education, Recreation, and Dance.

———.1989. *The Character of American Higher Education and Intercollegiate Sport*. Albany: State University of New York Press.

Cline, Dorothy. 1939. *Training for Recreation Under the WPA*. Chicago: University of Chicago Press.

Coalter, Fred, John Long, and Brian Duffield. 1988. *Recreational Welfare*. Brookfield, Vt.: Avebury.

"The Government of Amateur Athletics: The NCAA–AAU Dispute." 1968. *Southern California Law Review* 41:404–90.

Cornfield, Dan. 1986. "Declining Union Membership in the Post–World War II Era." *American Journal of Sociology* 91:1112–53.

Connell, R. W. 1990. "An Iron Man: The Body and Some Contradictions of Hegemonic Masculinity." In *Sport, Men and the Gender Order*, ed. Michael Messner and Don Sabo. Champaign, Ill.: Human Kinetics.

Couvares, Frances. 1984. *The Remaking of Pittsburgh: Class and Culture in an Industrializing City 1877–1919*. Albany: State University of New York Press.

Crandall, Jeffrey. 1981. "The Agent–Athlete Relationship in Professional and Amateur Sports." *Buffalo Law Review*. 30:815–49.

Crepeau, Richard. 1980. *Baseball, America's Diamond Mind: 1919–1941*. Orlando: University of Central Florida Press.

Cross, Gary. 1990. *A Social History of Leisure*. State College, Pa.: Venture.

Cutten, George. 1926. *The Theory of Leisure*. New Haven: Yale University Press.

Daly, George, and William Moore. 1981. "Externalities, Property Rights, and the Allocation of Resources in Major League Baseball." *Economic Inquiry* 19:77–95.

Davenport, David. 1969. "Collusive Competition in Major League Baseball." *American Economist* 13:6–30.

Deem, Rosemary. 1986. *All Work and No Play? The Sociology of Women and Leisure*. Philadelphia: Open University Press.

Demak, Richard. 1991. "Corporately Yours." *Sports Illustrated*, June 12, p. 15.

DiMaggio, Paul, and Walter Powell. 1983. "Institutional Isomorphism." *American Sociological Review* 48:147–60.

DiNicola, Ronald, and Scott Mendeloff. 1983. "Controlling Violence in Professional Sports." *Duquesne Law Review* 21:843–916.

Dollard, John. 1957. *Caste and Class in a Southern Town*. New York: Doubleday.

Donnelly, Peter, and Kevin Young. 1988. "The Construction and Confirmation of Identity in Sport Subcultures." *Sociology of Sport Journal* 5:223–40.

Duster, Troy. 1970. *The Legislation of Morality*. New York: Free Press.

Dworkin, James. 1981. *Owners Versus Players: Baseball and Collective Bargaining*. Boston: Auburn House.

——.1986. "Salary Arbitration in Baseball: An Impartial Assessment After Ten Years." *Arbitration Journal* 41:63–69.

Edelman, Lauren. 1990. "Legal Environments and Organizational Governance." *American Journal of Sociology* 95:1401–40.

Edwards, Harry. 1980. *The Struggle That Must Be*. New York: Macmillan.

——.1984. "Sport Politics: Los Angeles, 1984–'The Olympic Tradition Continues'." *Sociology of Sport Journal* 1:172–83.

Eisner, Marc. 1991. *Antitrust and the Triumph of Economics*. Chapel Hill: University of North Carolina Press.

Eitzen, D. Stanley, and D. A. Purdy. 1986. "The Academic Preparation and Achievement of Black and White Collegiate Athletes." *Journal of Sport and Social Issues* 10:15–27.

Eitzen, D. Stanley, and George Sage. 1986. *Sociology of North American Sport*. Dubuque, Iowa: Brown.

Eitzen, D. Stanley, and Norman Yetman. 1979. "Immune from Racism?" In *Sport in Contemporary Society*, ed. D. Stanley Eitzen. New York: St Martin's.

Elias, Norbert, and Eric Dunning. 1986. *The Quest for Excitement*. Oxford: Basil Blackwell.

Ferrall, Victor. 1989. "The Impact of Television Regulation on Private and Public Interests." *Journal of Communications* 39:8–38.

Fine, Gary. 1987. *With the Boys: Little League Baseball and Preadolescent Culture*. Chicago: University of Chicago Press.

Finegold, Kenneth, and Theda Skocpol. 1984. "State, Party, and Industry." In *State Making and Social Movements*, ed. Charles Bright and Susan Harding. Ann Arbor: University of Michigan Press.

Fiske, John. 1989. *Reading the Popular*. Boston: Allen Unwin.

Fizel, John, and Randall Barnett. 1989. "The Impact of Football Telecasts on College Football Attendance." *Social Science Quarterly* 70:980–93.

Flath, Arnold. 1964. *A History of Relations Between the National Collegiate Athletic Association and the Amateur Athletics Union of the United States, 1905–1906*. Champaign, Ill.: Stipes.

Flint, W. C., and D. Stanley Eitzen. 1987. "Professional Sports Team Ownership and Entrepreneurial Capitalism." *Sociology of Sport Journal* 4:17–27.

Flood, Curt. 1971. *The Way It Is*. New York: Trident.

Foraker, Scott. 1985. "The National Basketball Association Salary Cap: An Antitrust Violation?" *Southern California Law Review* 59:157–81.

Fredricksson, Kristine. 1985. *American Rodeos*. College Station: Texas A&M University Press.

Freedman, Warren. 1987. *Professional Sports and Anti-trust*. New York: Quorum Books.

Freeman, William. 1987. *Physical Education and Sport in a Changing Society*. New York: Macmillan.

Friedman, Lawrence. 1985. *A History of American Law*. New York: Simon & Schuster.

Galanter, Marc. 1986. "Adjudication, Litigation and Related Phenomena." In *Law and Social Sciences*, ed. Leon Lipson and Stanton Wheeler. New York: Russell Sage.

Gaona, David. 1981. "The National Collegiate Athletic Association: Fundamental Fairness and the Enforcement Program." *Arizona Law Review* 23:1065–1102.

Garrett, Robert, and Paul Hochberg. 1984. "Sports Broadcasting and the Law." *Indiana Law Journal* 59:156–93.

Gelber, Steven. 1984. "'Their Hands Are All Out Playing': Business and American Baseball." *Journal of Sport History* 11:5–27.

Giamatti, Bartlett. 1989. *Take Time for Paradise: Americans and Their Games*. New York: Summit Books.

Goldstein, Warren. 1989. *Playing for Keeps: A History of Early Baseball*. Ithaca: Cornell University Press.

Goodman, Cary. 1979. *Choosing Sides: Playground and Street Life on the Lower East Side*. New York: Schocken Books.

Gordon, David, Richard Edwards, and Michael Reich. 1982. *Segmented Work, Divided Workers*. Cambridge: Cambridge University Press.

Gorton, Slade. 1985. "Professional Sports Franchise Relocation: Introductory Views from the Hill." *Seton Hall Legislative Journal* 9:1–6.

Green, Harvey. 1986. *Fit for America: Health, Fitness and Sport in American Society*. New York: Pantheon Books.

Gregory, Paul. 1956. *The Baseball Player*. Washington: Public Affairs.

Grundman, Adolf. 1986. "The Image of Intercollegiate Sports and the Civil Rights Movement." In *Fractured Focus*, ed. Richard Lapchick. Lexington, Mass.: Lexington Books.

Gruneau, Richard. 1983. *Class, Sports, and Social Development*. Amherst: University of Massachusetts Press.

——.1984. "Commercialism and the Modern Olympics." In *Five-Ring Circus: Money, Power and Politics in the Olympic Games*, ed. Alan Tomlinson and Garry Whannel. London: Pluto.

——.1988. "Modernization and Hegemony: Two Views of Sport and Social Development." In *Not Just a Game*, ed. Jean Harvey and Hart Cantelon. Ottawa: University of Ottawa Press.

Gusfield, Joseph. 1963. *Symbolic Crusade*. Urbana: University of Illinois Press.

Guttmann, Allen. 1982. "The Tiger Devours the Literary Magazine: On Intercollegiate Athletics in America." In *The Government of Intercollegiate Athletics*, ed. James Frey. West Point: Leisure.

——.1984. *The Games Must Go On: Avery Brundage and the Olympic Movement*. New York: Columbia University Press.

———.1991. *Women's Sports* New York: Columbia University Press.

Hall, Richard. 1991. *Organizations: Structures, Processes, Outcomes*. Englewood Cliffs, N.J.: Prentice Hall.

Hanford, George. 1974. *An Inquiry into the Need for and Feasibility of a National Study of Intercollegiate Athletics*. Washington: American Council on Education.

Hantrais, Linda. 1989. "Central Government Policy in France Under the Socialist Administration, 1981–1986." In *Leisure and Urban Processes*, ed. Peter Bramham, et al. London: Routledge.

Hardy, Stephen. 1982. *How Boston Played*. Boston: Northeastern University Press.

Hardy, Stephen, and Jack Berryman. 1982. "A Historical View of the Governance Issue." In *The Government of Intercollegiate Athletics*, ed. James Frey. West Point: Leisure.

Hardy, Stephen, and Alan Ingham. 1983. "Games, Structure and Agency–Historians on the American Play Movement." *Journal of Social History* 17:285–301.

Hargreaves, Jennifer. 1984. "Women and the Olympic Phenomenon." In *Five-Ring Circus*, ed. Alan Tomlinson and Garry Whannel. London: Pluto.

Hargreaves, John. 1986. *Sport, Power, and Culture*. New York: St Martin's.

Harris, David. 1986. *The League: The Rise and Decline of the NFL*. New York: Bantam Books.

Hauser, Thomas. 1986. *The Black Lights: Inside the World of Professional Boxing*. New York: McGraw-Hill.

Heidt, Robert. 1985. "Don't Talk Fairness: The Chicago School's Approach Toward Disciplining Professional Athletes." *Indiana Law Journal* 61:53–64.

Heller, Agnes. 1976. *The Theory of Need in Marx*. New York: St. Martin's.

Herberg, Will. 1960. *Protestant, Catholic, Jew*. New York: Anchor Books.

Hetzel, James. 1987. "Gender Based Discrimination in High School Athletics." *Seton Hall Legislative Journal* 10:275–95.

Hoberman, John. 1986. *The Olympic Crisis: Sport Politics and the Moral Order*. New Rochelle: Caratzas.

Hoffman, Robert. 1969. "Is the NLRB Going to Play the Ballgame?" *Labor Law Journal* 20:239–46.

Hofstadter, Richard. 1965. *The Paranoid Style in American Politics*. New York: Alfred Knopf.

Hollands, Robert. 1988. "Leisure, Work, and Working-Class Cultures." In *Leisure, Sport, and Working-Class Cultures*, ed. Hart Cantelon, et al. Toronto: Garamond.

Holmes, M., and B. L. Parkhouse. 1981. "Trends in the Selection of Coaches for Female Athletes." *Research Quarterly in Exercise and Sport* 52:9–18.

Holway, John. 1988. *Blackball Stars: Negro League Pioneers*. Westport: Meckler Books.

Horowitz, Donald. 1977. *The Courts and Social Policy* Washington: Brookings Institute.

Horowitz, Helen. 1987. *Campus Life*. New York: Alfred Knopf.

Howard, James. 1987. "Incentives Are Needed To Investigate Graduation Rates of Scholarship Athletes." *Seton Hall Legislative Journal* 10:210–12.

Howell, Reet. 1982. *Her Story in Sport*. West Point: Leisure.

Hulme, Derick. 1990. *The Political Olympics*. New York: Praeger.

Hunnicut, Benjamin. 1988. *Work Without End: Abandoning Shorter Hours for the Right to Work*. Philadelphia: Temple University Press.

Isenberg, Michael. 1988. *John L. Sullivan and His America*. Urbana: University of Illinois Press.

Jable, J. Thomas. 1979. "The Public Schools Athletic League of New York City." In *Sport in American Higher Education*, ed. Wayne Ladd and Angela Lumpkin. Washington: American Alliance for Health, Physical Education, Recreation, and Dance.

Jennings, Kenneth. 1990. *Balls and Strikes: The Money Game in Professional Baseball*. New York: Praeger.

Jennings, Susan. 1981. "As American as Hot Dogs, Apple Pie, and Chevrolet: The Desegregation of Little League Baseball." *Journal of American Culture* 4:81–91.

Jensen, Judy. 1986. "Women's Collegiate Athletics: Incidents in the Struggle for Influence and Control." In *Fractured Focus*, ed. Richard Lapchick. Lexington, Mass.: Lexington Books.

Johnson, Arthur. 1979. "Congress and Professional Sports: 1951-1978." *Annals of American Association of Political and Social Science* 45:102-15.

———.1982. "The Uneasy Partnership of Cities and Professional Sport: Public Policy Considerations." In *Sport and the Sociological Imagination*, ed. Nancy Theberge and Peter Donnelly. Fort Worth: Texas Christian University Press.

———.1983. "Managerial Administration and the Sports Franchise Relocation Issue." *Public Administration Review* 43:519-27.

———.1986. "Economic and Policy Implications of Hosting Sports Franchises: Lessons from Baltimore." *Urban Affairs Quarterly* 21:411-33.

Kallenberg, Henry. 1912. "The Present Situation in the Administration of Athletics and What to Do." *American Physical Education Review* 17:500-510.

Kane, Mary Jo, and Jane Stangl. 1991. "Employment Patterns of Female Coaches in Men's Athletics." *Journal of Sport and Social Issues* 15:21-41.

Kanin, David. 1981. *A Political History of the Olympic Games* Boulder: Westview.

Kelly, John. 1982. *Leisure.* Englewood Cliffs, N.J.: Prentice-Hall.

Kidd, Benjamin. 1987. "Sport and Masculinity." In *Beyond Patriarchy*, ed. M. Kaufman. Toronto: Oxford University Press.

Kirschner, Don. 1986. *The Paradox of Professionalism: Reform and Public Service in Urban America, 1900-1940.* Westport, Conn.: Greenwood.

Klare, Karl. 1979. "Law Making as Praxis." *Telos* 40:123-43.

Klatell, David, and Norman Marcus. 1988. *Sports for Sale.* New York: Oxford University Press.

Klein, Alan. 1991. *Sugarball: The American Game, the Dominican Dream.* New Haven: Yale University Press.

Koch, James. 1983. "Intercollegiate Athletics: An Economic Explanation." *Social Science Quarterly* 64:360-74.

———.1985. "The Economic Realities of Amateur Sport Organization." *Indiana Law Journal* 61:9-29.

Kolback, Kimberly. 1985. "Property Rights: Athletes Await the Call from the Referee of the Courtroom." *Entertainment and Sports Law Journal* 2:214-42.

Krasnow, Erwin, and Herman Levy. 1963. "Unionization and Professional Sports." *Georgetown Law Journal* 51:749-82.

Kuhn, Bowie. 1987. *Hardball: the Education of a Baseball Commissioner.* New York: McGraw-Hill.

Kutner, Joan. 1976. "Sex Discrimination in Athletes." *Villanova Law Review* 21:876-903.

Lapchick, Richard. 1984. *Broken Promises.* New York: St. Martin's.

———.1986. "The Promised Land." In *Fractured Focus*, ed. Richard Lapchick. Lexington, Mass.: Lexington Books.

Lawrence, Paul. 1987. *Unsportsmanlike Conduct: The NCAA and the Business of College Football.* New York: Praeger.

Lederman, Douglas. 1988. "Supreme Court Agrees to Review Case of Nevada Coach." *Chronicle of Higher Education* 34:A31-32.

———.1991. "An Explosive Football Scandall Raises a Tough Question: Who Runs Auburn?" *Chronicle of Higher Education.* November 20, p. A41.

Lehr, Robert. 1985. "The American Olympic Committee, 1896-1940: From Chaos to Order." Ph.D. diss. Pennsylvania State University.

Lenskyj, Helen. 1986. *Out of Bounds: Women, Sport, and Sexuality.* Toronto: Women's.

Leonard, Wilbur, and Jonathan Reyman. 1988. "The Odds of Attaining Professional Athlete Status." *Sociology of Sport Journal* 5:162-69.

Leuchtenberg, William. 1958. *The Perils of Prosperity, 1914-1942.* Chicago: University of Chicago Press.

Levine, Rhonda. 1988. *Class Struggle and the New Deal.* Lawrence: University of Kansas Press.

Lies, Eugene. 1933. *The New Leisure Challenge for the Schools: Shall Recreation Enrich or Impoverish?* New York: National Recreation Association.

Lindblom, Charles. 1988. *Democracy and the Market System*. Oslo: Norwegian University Press.

———.1977. *Politics and Markets*. New York: Basic Books.

Lipset, Seymour Martin. 1986. "Labor Unions in the Public Mind." In *Unions in Transition*, ed. Seymour Martin Lipset. San Francisco: Institute for Contemporary Studies Press.

Lowenfish, Lee, and Tony Lupien. 1980. *The Imperfect Diamond*. New York: Stein & Day.

Loy, John, Barry McPherson, and Gerald Kenyon. 1978. *Sport and Social Systems*. Reading, Mass.: Addison–Wesley.

Lucas, John. 1971. "The Unholy Experiment–Professional Baseball's Struggle Against Pennsylvania Sunday Blue Laws, 1926–1936." *Pennsylvania History* 38:163–75.

MacAloon, John. 1991. "Are Olympic Athletes Professionals?" In *The Business of Professional Sports*, ed. Paul Staudohar and James Mangan. Urbana: University of Illinois Press.

Macaulay, Stewart. 1986. "Private Government." In *Law and the Social Sciences*, ed. Leon Lipson and Stanton Wheeler. New York: Russell–Sage.

MacPhail, Lee. 1989. *My Nine Innings*. Westport: Meckler Books.

Marcuse, Herbert. 1964. *One Dimensional Man*. New York: Beacon.

Markham, Jesse, and Paul Teplitz. 1981. *Baseball Economics and Public Policy*. Lexington, Mass.: Lexington Books.

Markovits, Andrei. 1988. "The Other American Exceptionalism—Why is There No Soccer in the United States?" *Praxis International* 8:125–50.

Martin, Gordon. 1976. "The NCAA and the Fourteenth Amendment." *New England Law Review* 11:383–404.

McBride, Deborah. 1989. "The NCAA Drug-Testing Program and the California Constitution." *University of San Francisco Law Review* 23:253–90.

McCormick, Robert. 1982. "Baseball's Third Strike: The Triumph of Collective Bargaining in Baseball." *Vanderbilt Law Review* 35:1131–69.

McCormick, Robert, and Matthew McKinnon. 1984. "Professional Football's Draft Eligibility Rule: The Labor Exemption and the Antitrust Laws." *Emory Law Journal* 33:375–440.

McCormick, Robert. 1989. "Labor Relations in Professional Sports." *Employee Relations Law Journal* 14:501–12.

Medoff, Marshall. 1975. "A Reappraisal of Racial Discrimination Against Blacks in Professional Baseball." *Review of Black Political Economy* 5:259–68.

Meisel, John. 1978. "Leisure, Politics and Political Science." *Social Science Information* 17:185–209.

Mennell, Stephen. 1989. *Norbert Elias: Civilization and the Self–Image*. Oxford: Basil Blackwell.

Miller, James. 1990. *The Baseball Business*. Chapel Hill: University of North Carolina Press.

Miller, Marvin. 1991. *A Whole Different Ball Game*. Secaucus, N.J.: Carol.

Mitchell, Susan. 1977. "Women's Participation in the Olympic Games, 1901–1926." *Journal of Sport History* 4:208–28.

Mitnick, Eric. 1984. "Public Recreation Is a Legitimate Basis for Using Eminent Domain." *University of California, Davis Law Review* 17:963–1007.

Mollenkopf, John. 1983. *The Contested City*. Princeton: Princeton University Press.

Monaghan, Peter. 1988. "Federal Court Rules NCAA's Drug Testing Program Does Not Violate Athlete's Privacy Rights." *Chronicle of Higher Education* 34:37–39.

Moore, Joseph. 1988. *Pride Against Prejudice*. Westport Conn.: Greenwood.

Moore, Wilbert. 1963. *Man, Time, and Society*. New York: Wiley.

Murdock, Eugene. 1982. *Ben Johnson: Czar of Baseball*. Westport: Greenwood.

Nafziger, James. 1988a. *International Sports Law*. Dobbs Ferry: Transnational.

———.1988b. "Diplomatic Fun and Games: A Commentary on the United States' Boycott of the 1980 Summer Olympics." In *The Olympic Games in Transition*, ed. Jeffrey Segrave and Donald Chu. Champaign, Ill.: Human Kinetics.

418 Naison, Mark. 1979. "Lefties and Righties: The Communist Party and Sports During the Great Depression." *Radical America* 13:47–59.

——.1983. *Communists in Harlem During the Depression*. Urbana, Ill.: University of Illinois Press.

Noll, Roger. 1982. "Major League Sports." In *The Structure of American Industry*, ed. Walter Adams. New York: MacMillan.

——.1991. "Professional Basketball: Economic and Business Perspectives." In *The Business of Professional Sports*, ed. Paul Staudohar and James Mangan. Urbana, Ill.: University of Illinois Press.

Novak, Michael. 1976. *The Joy of Sports*. New York: Basic Books.

Okner, Benjamin. 1974. "Subsidies of Stadiums and Arenas." In *Government and the Sports Business*, ed. Roger Noll. Washington: Brookings Institute.

Oliver, Melvin. 1980. "Race, Class and the Family's Orientation to Mobility Through Sport." *Sociological Symposium* 3:62–86.

Oriard, Michael. 1991. *Sporting with the Gods*. Cambridge: Cambridge University Press.

Pachman, Matthew. 1990. "Limits on the Discretionary Powers of Professional Sports Commissioners." *Virginia Law Review* 76:1409–39.

Parkhouse, Bonnie and Jackie Lapin. 1980. *Women Who Win: Exercising Your Rights in Sports*. Englewood Cliffs, N.J.: Prentice-Hall.

Parsons, Talcott. 1971. *The System of Modern Societies*. Englewood Cliffs, N.J.: Prentice-Hall.

Pelissero, John, Beth Henschen, and Edward Sidlow. 1991. "Urban Regimes, Sports Stadiums, and the Politics of Economic Development." *Policy Studies Review* 10:117–29.

Perrone, Luca. 1984. "Positional Power, Strikes and Wages." *American Sociological Review* 49:412–21.

Peterson, Robert. 1990. *Cages to Jump Shots: Pro Basketball's Early Years*. New York: Oxford University Press.

Pluto, Terry. 1990. *Loose Balls: The Short, Wild Life of the American Basketball Association*. New York: Simon & Schuster.

Polsky, Ned. 1969. *Hustlers, Beats and Others*. New York: Anchor.

Ponsoldt, James. 1986. "The Unreasonableness of Coerced Cooperation: A Comment Upon the NCAA Decision Rejection of the Chicago School." *Antitrust Bulletin* 31:1003–44.

Powell, Michael. 1985. "Regulation of Lawyers." *Social Forces* 64:281–305.

Pytte, Alyson. 1990. "Joe Sixpack: This One's for You." *Congressional Quarterly* 47:33362.

Quirk, James, and Mohamed El-Hodiri. 1974. "The Economic Theory of a Professional Sports League." In *Government and the Sports Business*, ed. Roger Noll. Washington: Brookings Institute.

Rable, George. 1989. "Patriotism, Platitudes, and Politics: Baseball and the American Presidency." *Presidential Studies Quarterly* 19:363–72.

Rader, Benjamin. 1983. "Compensatory Sport Heroes: Ruth, Grange and Dempsey." *Journal of Popular Culture* 16:11–22.

——.1989. "The Recapitulation Theory of Play: Motor Behavior, Moral Reflexes and Manly Attitudes in Urban America, 1880-1920." In *Manliness and Morality: Middle Class Masculinity in Britain and America, 1800-1940*, ed. J. A. Mangan and James Walvin. New York: St. Martin's.

Rafferty, Robert. 1983. "The Status of the College Scholarship Athlete—Employee or Student?" *Capital University Law Review* 13:87–103.

Raimondo, Henry. 1983. "Free Agents' Impact on the Labor Market for Basketball Players." *Journal of Labor Research* 4:183–93.

Raskin. A. H. 1986. "Labor: A Movement in Search of a Mission". In *Unions in Transition*, ed. Seymour Martin Lipset. San Francisco: Institute for Contemporary Studies Press.

Reiger, John. 1986. *American Sportsmen and the Origins of Conservation*. Norman: University of Oklahoma Press.

Richardson, Kristin. 1988. "Touchdown, but a Flag on the Play." *Willamette Law Review* 24:525–38.

Riess, Stephen. 1980. *Touching Base: Professional Baseball and American Culture in the Progressive Era*. Westport, Conn.: Greenwood.

——.1989. *City Games: The Evolution of American Urban Society and the Rise of Sports*. Urbana: University of Illinois Press.

——.1990. "Professional Sports as an Arena of Social Mobility in America: Some Myths and Realities." In *Sport History and Sport Mythology*, ed. Donald Kyle and Gary Stark. University of Texas A&M Press.

——.1991. "A Social Profile of the Professional Football Player, 1920–1982." In *The Business of Professional Sports*, ed. Paul Staudohar and James Mangan. Urbana: University of Illinois Press.

Riordan, Jim. 1986. "Elite Sport Policy in East and West." In *Politics of Sport*, ed. Lincoln Allison. Manchester: Manchester University Press.

Roberts, Gary. 1984. "Sports Leagues and the Sherman Act." *University of California, Los Angeles Law Review* 32:219–301.

——.1986. "Sports League Restraints on the Labor Market: the Failure of Stare Decisis." *University of Pittsburg Law Review* 47:337–406.

Roediger, David. 1988. "The Limits of Corporate Reform: Fordism, Taylorism, and the Working Week in the United States, 1914–1929." In *Worktime and Industrialization*, ed. Gary Cross. Philadelphia: Temple University Press.

Rojek, Chris. 1985. *Capitalism and Leisure Theory*. New York: Tavistock.

Rose, Laurence, and Timothy Girard. 1988. "Drug Testing in Professional and College Sports." *University of Kansas Law Review* 36:787–821.

Rosenbaum, Thane. 1987. "Antitrust Implications of Professional Sports Leagues." *University of Miami Law Review* 41:729–822.

Rosenberg, Norman. 1987. "Here Comes the Judge: The Origin of Baseball's Commissioner System and American Legal Culture." *Journal of Popular Culture* 20:129–46.

Rosentraub, Mark. 1988. "Public Investment in Private Business: the Professional Sports Mania." In *Business Elites and Urban Development*, ed. Scott Cummings. Albany: State University of New York Press.

Ross, Stephen. 1989. "Monopoly Sports Leagues." *Minnesota Law Review* 73:643–761.

Roth, Guenther. 1985. "Marx and Weber in the United States—Today." In *A Marx-Weber Dialogue*, ed. Robert Antonio and Ronald Glassman. Lawrence: University of Kansas Press.

Rowe, Karol. 1985. "NCAA vs. Board of Regents." *Journal of College and University Law* 11:377–97.

Ruck, Rob. 1987. *Sandlot Seasons: Sport in Black Pittsburgh*. Urbana: University of Illinois Press.

Rudy, Willis. 1965. *Schools in An Age of Mass Culture*. Englewood Cliffs: Prentice-Hall.

Ryan, W. Carson. 1929. A Study of the Literature of American Schools and College Athletics. *Bulletin No. 24*. New York: Carnegie Foundation for the Advancement of Teaching.

Sack, Allen. 1982. "Cui Bono? Contradictions in College Sports and Athlete's Rights." In *The Governance of Intercollegiate Athletics*, ed. James Frey. West Point: Leisure.

Sage, George. 1982. "The Intercollegiate Sport Cartel and Its Consequences for Athletes." In *The Governance of Intercollegiate Athletics*, ed. James Frey. West Point: Leisure.

——.1990. *Power and Ideology in American Sport*. Champaign, Ill.: Human Kinetics.

Sammons, Jeffrey. 1988. *Beyond the Ring: The Role of Boxing in American Society*. Urbana: University of Illinois Press.

Sartori, Giovanni. 1987. *The Theory of Democracy Revisited*. Chatham, N.J.: Chatham House.

Savage, Howard. 1929. American College Athletics. *Bulletin No. 23*. New York: Carnegie Foundation for the Advancement of Teaching.

Schor, Juliet. 1991. *The Overworked American*. New York: Basic Books.

420 Scott, Frank, James Cong, and Ken Somppi. 1983. "Free Agents, Owner Incentives, and the NFL Players' Association." *Journal of Labor Research* 4:257–64.

Scully, Gerald. 1974. "Discrimination: The Case of Baseball." In *Government and the Sports Business*, ed. Roger Noll. Washington: Brookings Institute.

———.1989. *The Business of Major League Baseball*. Chicago: University of Chicago Press.

Seha, Ann. 1984. "Administrative Enforcement of Title IX in Intercollegiate Athletics." *Law and Inequality* 2:121–326.

Selznick, Philip. 1969. *Law, Society, and Industrial Justice*. New York: Russell Sage Foundation.

Sessoms, H. Douglas. 1984. *Leisure Services*. Englewood Cliffs, N.J.: Prentice–Hall.

Seymour, Harold. 1971. *Baseball: The Golden Age*. New York: Oxford University Press.

———.1990. *Baseball: The People's Game*. New York: Oxford University Press.

Shivers, Jay. 1986. "Institutional Roles and Relationships." In *The President's Commission on the American Outdoors: A Literature Review*. Washington.

Shropshire, Kenneth. 1990. *Agents of Opportunity: Sports Agents and Corruption in Collegiate Sports*. Philadelphia: University of Pennsylvania Press.

Shuck, Donald. 1979. "Administration of Amateur Athletics." *Fordham Law Review* 48:53–82.

Shulman, Leonard. 1985. "Compensation for Collegiate Athletes: A Run for More Than the Roses." *San Diego Law Review* 22:701–23.

Simmel, Georg. 1950. *The Sociology of Georg Simmel*. New York: Free Press.

Sklar, Kathryn. 1988. "The Greater Part of the Petitioners Are Female: The Reduction Women's Working Hours in the Paid Labor Force, 1840–1917." In *Worktime and Industrialization*, ed. Gary Cross. Philadelphia: Temple University Press.

Sklar, Martin. 1988. *The Corporate Reconstruction of American Capitalism, 1890–1916*. New York: Cambridge University Press.

Slatton, Bonnie. 1982. "AIAW: The Greening of American Athletics." In *The Governance of Intercollegiate Athletics*, ed. James Frey. West Point: Leisure.

Smith, Leverett. 1975. *The American Dream and the National Game*. Bowling Green: Bowling Green University Popular Press.

Smith, Ronald. 1983. "Preludes to the NCAA: Early Failures of Faculty Intercollegiate Control." *Research Quarterly for Exercise and Sport* 54:372–82.

———.1988. *Sports and Freedom: The Rise of Big Time College Athletics*. New York: Oxford University Press.

Smith, Thomas. 1987. "Civil Rights and the Gridiron: the Kennedy Administration and the Desegregation of the Washington Redskins." *Journal of Sports History* 14:189–208.

———.1988. "Outside the Pale: The Exclusion of Blacks from the National Football League, 1934–1946." *Journal of Sports History* 15:255–81.

Spink, J. G. Taylor. 1974. *Judge Landis and Twenty Five Years of Baseball*. St. Louis: Sporting News.

Spring, Joel. 1972. *Education and the Rise of the Corporate State*. Boston: Beacon.

Staples, Louise. 1943. A Study of the Functions of Physical Education in Higher Education. *Contributions to Education* No. 876. New York: Teachers College Bureau of Publications.

Staudohar, Paul. 1986. *The Sports Industry and Collective Bargaining*. Ithaca: Industrial and Labor Relations.

Steiner, Jesse. 1933. *Americans at Play: Recent Trends in Recreation and Leisure Time Activities*. New York: McGraw–Hill.

———.1937. *Research Memorandum on Recreation and the Depression*. New York: Social Science Research Council.

Stern, Robert. 1979. "Development of an Interorganizational Control Network: The Case of Intercollegiate Athletics." *Administrative Science Quarterly* 24:242–66.

Stoddart, Brian. 1986. "Sport, Culture and Postcolonial Relations" In *Sport and Politics*, ed. Gerald Redmond. Champaign, Ill.: Human Kinetics.

Stotlar, David. 1985. "The College Participant: Student Athlete or Paid Professional?" In *Sport and Law: Contemporary Issues*, ed. Herb Appenzeller. Charlottesville: Mickie.

Sullivan, Michael. 1984. "Remedying Athlete–Agent Abuse: A Securities Law Approach." *Entertainment and Sports Law Journal* 2:53–77.

Sullivan, Neil. 1987. *The Dodgers Move West*. New York: Oxford University Press.

Tagliabue, Paul. 1987. "Antitrust Development in Sports and Entertainment." *Antitrust Law Journal* 56:341–59.

Talbot, Margaret. 1988. "Understanding the Relationships Between Women and Sport." *International Review of Sociology of Sport* 23:31–42.

Taylor, Frederick. 1906. "A Comparison of University and Industrial Discipline Methods." *Science* 24:577–83.

Theberge, Nancy. 1987. "Sport and Women's Empowerment," *Women's Studies International Forum* 10:387–93.

Thrasher, Frederick. 1927. *The Gang*. Chicago: University of Chicago Press.

Truxall, A. O. 1929. *Outdoor Recreation Legislation and Its Effectiveness*. New York: Columbia University Press.

Turner, Bryan. 1986. *Citizenship and Capitalism*. London: Allen & Unwin.

Tygiel, Jules. 1983. *Baseball's Great Experiment: Jackie Robinson and His Legacy*. New York: Oxford University Press.

U.S. Congress, House, Committee on Education and Labor. 1972. *Labor Relations in Professional Sports*. Washington.

——.1973. *Protection of College Athletes*.

——.1982. *Hearings on Equal Employment Opportunities in National League Football: Before the Subcommittee on Employment Opportunities*.

——.1986. *Hearings on H.R. 1689, To Create an American Boxing Corporation: Hearings Before the Subcommittee Labor Standards*.

——.1989. *Hearings on the Role of Athletics in College Life: Before the Subcommittee on Secondary Education*.

——.1990. *Hearings on the Boxing Fair Labor Standards Act: Before the Subcommittee on Labor Standards*.

U.S. Congress House, Committee on Energy and Commerce. 1983. *Boxing Reform: Hearings Before the Subcommittee on Commerce, Transportation, and Tourism*. Washington.

——.1984. *Televised College Football: Hearings Before the Subcommittee on Oversight and Investigations*.

——.1985a. *Professional Sports: Hearings Before the Subcommittee on Commerce, Transportation and Tourism*.

——.1985b. *United States Boxing Commission*.

——.1990. *Cable Television Regulation (Part 2): Hearings Before the Subcommittee on Telecommunications and Finance*.

U.S. Congress, House, Committee on Foreign Affairs. 1977. *Hearings on the 1984 Summer Olympic Games: Before the Subcommittee on International Organizations*. Washington.

——.1980. *United States Participation in the 1980 Summer Olympic Games*.

U.S. Congress, House, Committee on Interstate and Foreign Commerce. 1973. *Evaluation of the Necessity for Television Blackouts of Professional Sporting Events: Report by the Special Subcommittee on Investigations*. Washington.

——.1978a. *Hearings on the Enforcement Program of the National Collegiate Athletic Association: Before the Subcommittee on Oversight and Investigations*.

——.1978b. *Network Sport Practices: Hearings before the Subcommittee on Communications*.

——.1978c. *Hearings on Sports Anti–Blackout Legislation: Before the Subcommittee on Communications*.

——.1979a. *Hearings on Sports Anti–Blackout Legislation: Before the Subcommittee on Communications and Power*.

——.1979b. *The National Collegiate Athletic Association: Hearings Before the Subcommittee on Oversight and Investigations*.

U. S. Congress, House, Committee on the Judiciary. 1957. *Hearings on Organized Professional Team Sports: Before the Subcommittee on Antitrust.* Washington.

——.1966. *Hearings on the Professional Football League Merger: Before the Subcommittee on Antitrust.*

——.1972. *Hearings on the Antitrust Laws and Organized Professional Team Sports, Including Consideration of the Proposed Merger of the American and National Basketball Associations: Before the Subcommittee on Antitrust.*

—— 1977. *Hearings on the Rights of Professional Athletes: Before the Subcommittee on Monopolies and Commercial Law.*

—— 1978. *Hearings on the Amateur Athletic Act: Before the Subcommittee on Administrative Law and Governmental Relations.*

—— 1982. *Hearings on Copyright/Cable Television: Before the Subcommittee on Courts, Civil Liberties and the Administration of Justice.*

—— 1984. *Hearings on Antitrust Policy and Professional Sports: Before the Subcommittee on Monopolies and Commercial Law.*

—— 1989. *Competitive Problems in the Cable TV Industry: Hearings Before the Subcommittee on Antitrust, Monopolies and Business Rights.*

—— 1990. *Abuse of Steroids in Amateur and Professional Athletics: Hearings Before the Subcommittee on Crime.*

U.S. Congress, House. 1976. *Inquiry into Professional Sports.* Washington, D.C.: U.S. Government Printing Office.

—— 1977. *Final Report: Inquiry into Professional Sports.*

U.S. Congress Senate Committee on Commerce. 1965a. *Professional Sports Anti-Trust Bill: Hearings Before the Subcommittee on Antitrust and Monopolies.* Washington.

—— 1965b. *The NCAA–AAU Dispute.*

—— 1967. *Track and Field Dispute.*

—— 1968. *Sports Arbitration Board Report.*

—— 1972. *Hearings on the Blackout of Sporting Events on TV: Before the Subcommittee on Communications.*

U.S. Congress, Senate, Committee on Commerce, Science, and Transportation. 1973. *Amateur Sports.* Washington.

—— 1975. *Hearings on TV Blackout of Sporting Events: Before the Subcommittee on Communications.*

—— 1978. *Amateur Sports Act of 1978, A Report.*

—— 1984. *Professional Sports Team Community Protection Act of 1984.*

—— 1985. *Professional Sports Community Protection Act of 1985.*

U. S. Congress Senate Committee on the Judiciary. 1961. *Hearings on Professional Boxing: Before the Subcommittee on Antitrust and Monopoly.* Washington.

—— 1972. *Hearings on Professional Basketball: Before the Subcommittee on Antitrust and Monopoly.*

—— 1983. *Professional Sports Antitrust Immunity.*

—— 1986. *Professional Sports Antitrust Immunity.*

—— 1987. *Antitrust Implications of the Recent NFL Television Contract: Hearings before the Subcommittee on Antitrust, Monopolies and Business Rights.*

—— 1990. *Steroids in Amateur and Professional Sports.*

—— 1991. *Sports Programming and Cable Television: Hearings before the Subcommittee on Antitrust, Monopolies, and Business Rights.*

U.S. Congress, Senate, Committee on Labor and Human Resources. 1989. *The Student–Athlete Right-to-Know Act.* Report 101–209. Washington.

U.S. President's Commission on Olympic Sports. 1977. *Final Report of the President's Commission on Olympic Sports.* Washington.

Vamplew, Wray. 1988. *Pay Up and Play the Game: Professional Sport in Britain 1875–1914.* Cambridge: Cambridge University Press.

Violas, Paul. 1978. *The Training of the Urban Working Class.* Chicago: Rand–McNally.

Voigt, David. 1970. *American Baseball: From the Commissioners to Continental Expansion.* Norman: University of Oklahoma Press.

—— 1983. *American Baseball: From Postwar Expansion to the Electronic Age.* University Park, Pennsylvania: Penn State University Press.

Voy, Robert. 1991. *Drugs, Sport and Politics.* Champaign, Illinois: Leisure Press.

Walker, Louis. 1931. *Distributed Leisure: Approaches to the Problem of Overproduction and Underemployment.* New York: Century.

Wallace, Michael, Larry Griffin, and Beth Rubin. 1989. "The Positional Power of American Labor, 1963-1977." *American Sociological Review* 54:197-215.

Warren, Mary Anne. 1983. "Justice and Gender in School Sports." In *Women, Philosophy and Sport*, ed. Betsy Postow. Metuchen, N.J.: Scarecrow.

Weber, Max. 1978. *Economy and Society.* Berkeley: University of California Press.

Weistart, John. 1984. "Legal Accountability and the NCAA." *Journal of College and University Law* 10:167-80.

Weistart, John, and Cym Lowell. 1979. *The Law of Sports.* Charlotte: Bobbs-Merril.

Whannel, Garry. 1983. *Blowing the Whistle.* London: Pluto.

Whitson, Dave. 1987. "Leisure, the State and Collective Consumption." In *Sport, Leisure, and Social Relations*, ed. John Horne, David Jary, and Alan Tomlinson. London: Routledge & Kegan Paul.

—— 1990. "Sport in the Social Construction of Masculinity." *Sport, Men and the Gender Order Champaign.* In ed. Michael Messner and Donald Sabo. Champaign, Ill.: Human Kinetics.

Wiggins, David. 1989. " 'Great Speed but Little Stamina': The Historical Debate over Black Athletic Superiority." *Journal of Sport History* 2:158-85.

Williamson, Oliver. 1986. *Economic Organization.* New York: New York University Press.

Wirtz, Willard. 1952. "Government by Private Groups." *Lousiana Law Review* 13:440-75.

Wolfe, Alan. 1977. *The Limits of Legitimacy.* New York: Free Press.

Wong, Glenn. 1985. "Of Franchise Relocation: Expansion and Competition in Professional Team Sports." *Seton Hall Legislative Journal* 9:7-79.

—— 1986a. "A Survey of Grievance Arbitration Cases in Major League Baseball." *Arbitration Journal* 41:42-62.

—— 1986b. "Major League Baseball's Grievance Arbitration System: A Comparison with Nonsports Industry." *Employee Law Relations Journal* 12:464-90.

Wong, Glenn, and Richard Ensor. 1986. "Sex Discrimination in Athletics." *Gonzaga Law Review* 21:345-94.

Wrong, Dennis. 1984. "Marx, Weber and Contemporary Sociology," In *Max Weber's Political Sociology*, ed. Ronald Glassman and Vatro Murvar. Westport, Conn.: Greenwood.

Wuthnow, Robert. 1991. "The Voluntary Sector," In *Between States and Markets.* Princeton: Princeton University Press.

Yergin, M. 1986. "Who Goes to the Game?" *American Demographics* 8:42-43.

Zimbalist, Andrew. 1992. "Salaries and Performances." In *Diamonds Are Forever*, ed. Paul Sommers. Washington: Brookings Institution.

INDEX

425